W9-DET-647

U.S. Regulation of Hedge Funds

SHARTSIS FRIESE LLP

Douglas L. Hammer
Carolyn S. Reiser
Geoffrey W. Haynes
Neil J. Koren
Anthony J. Caldwell
James J. Frolik
Christina E. Mickelson
Barry H. Sacks
John F. Milani
Hannah E. Dunn

Defending Liberty
Pursuing Justice

The materials contained herein represent the opinions of the authors and editors and should not be construed to be the action of either the American Bar Association or the Section of Business Law unless adopted pursuant to the bylaws of the Association.

Nothing contained in this book is to be considered as the rendering of legal advice for specific cases, and readers are responsible for obtaining such advice from their own legal counsel. This book and any forms and agreements herein are intended for educational and informational purposes only.

© 2005 by the American Bar Association.
All rights reserved.
Printed in the United States of America.

No part of the publication may be reproduced, stored in a retrieval system, or transmitted in any form or by any means, electronic, mechanical, photocopying, recording, or otherwise, without the prior written permission of the publisher. Permission requests should be sent to the American Bar Association Copyrights & Contracts Department via e-mail at copyright@abanet.org or via fax at (312) 988-6030.

Library of Congress Cataloging-in-Publication Data
ISBN 1-59031-297-X

U.S. regulation of hedge funds / Shartsis Friese LLP, Douglas L. Hammer ... [et al.].
    p. cm.
  Includes index.
  ISBN 1-59031-297-X
  1. Hedge funds--Law and legislation—United States. I. Title: United States regulation of hedge funds.
II. Shartsis Friese LLP. III. Hammer, Douglas L.

  KF1078.U14 2005
  346.73'0922--dc22   2005006581

Discounts are available for books ordered in bulk. Special consideration is given to state and local bars, CLE programs, and other bar-related organizations. Inquire at ABA Publishing, American Bar Association, 321 North Clark Street, Chicago, Illinois 60610.

09 08 07 06   5 4 3 2

Summary of Contents

Contents

CHAPTER **1**

Introduction

§ 1.1 The Nature of Hedge Funds

"Hedge fund" has no uniformly accepted meaning, but commonly refers to a professionally managed pool of assets used to invest and trade in equity securities, fixed-income securities, derivatives, futures and other financial instruments. Participation in a hedge fund typically is restricted to relatively wealthy individual and institutional investors that satisfy private offering standards.[1] Inclusion of "hedge" in the term is useful for distinguishing a hedge fund from another type of investment pool (such as a mutual fund, a venture capital fund, a private equity fund or a commodity pool), but has little descriptive value—a hedge fund may or may not hedge against risks.

Indeed, some hedge funds invest only in securities and only for the long term. Some hedge funds never invest at all, but only trade to profit from market or security depreciation (this subspecies of hedge funds is sometimes called "short funds"). Some long-short hedge funds sell securities short to guard against risks in their long investments; some sell securities short opportunistically to profit from expected declines in the prices of the securities; and some do both. Some hedge funds trade in put and call options or futures contracts to hedge; others do so hoping to profit from directional security or market bets. Some hedge funds are fundamental investors, while others rely on technical analysis. Some hedge funds invest and trade only distressed debt instruments. Some hedge funds attempt to take advantage of pricing discrepancies between different markets in the same instruments through any of an array of arbitrage strategies. Some hedge funds specialize in the exotica of currency trading, while some refuse even to consider a security that is not denominated in U.S. dollars. Some hedge funds eschew any kind of borrowing, while others margin their portfolios to the maximum extent allowed by law.[2] At least one hedge fund based trading decisions on its interpretation of astrological charts.

---

1. *See* Chapter 5, *infra.*
2. *See* Implications of the Growth of Hedge Funds, Staff Report to the SEC, § IV.A, at 33–43 (Sep. 2003), (hereinafter "Staff Report"), *available at* www.sec.gov/news/studies/hedgefunds0903.pdf (last visited Oct. 25, 2004).

Almost all hedge funds compensate their portfolio managers by periodic (usually quarterly) fees calculated as a percentage of assets managed and by performance or incentive fees or allocations. The asset-based fee typically is calculated at an annual rate of one to two percent of assets. The performance or incentive fee or allocation most often is calculated as twenty percent of profits above a high-water mark.[3] The asset-based fee is generally viewed as needed to cover the manager's operating overhead. The performance or incentive fee or allocation is intended to compensate the manager as long as the investors enjoy positive overall returns, and aligns the manager's interests with those of the investors.[4] The paternalistic regulatory concern that performance compensation could create incentive for the manager to make trades that are overly speculative[5] was largely abandoned[6] in 1998, perhaps partly in recognition that both hedge fund managers and hedge fund investors ordinarily have enough experience and sophistication to take a longer view of portfolio management.

Hedge funds thus do not represent an asset class or any particular style of portfolio management. The investment philosophies of hedge funds are as diverse as their portfolio managers. Hedge funds' investment techniques and methods represent their managers' individual experiences, backgrounds and biases. If any common thread runs through the hedge fund community, it is that hedge fund managers retain flexibility to manage their portfolios as they consider best calculated to achieve returns for their investors and concomitantly for themselves. They are subject only to their fiduciary obligations and such investment restrictions as they impose on themselves. Hedge funds are excepted from regulation as mutual funds under the Company Act[7] and as a result are not constrained by the Company Act's rigid and often obtuse rules about such matters as hedging, leverage and diversification, leading some unknowing pundits to suggest that hedge funds are unregulated or lightly regulated.[8] Hedge fund managers are, however, subject to requirements and constraints of a panoply of federal and state laws, such as the Adviser's Act,[9] the Securities Act,[10] state securities laws,[11] the Exchange Act,[12] ERISA,[13] the Tax Code[14] and (depending on investment choices) the Commodity Exchange Act.[15]

---

3. *See* Chapter 15, *infra.*

4. By contrast, the investment adviser to a mutual fund expects to be paid regardless of the mutual fund's performance.

5. *See* Adviser's Act Rule 205-3, 17 C.F.R. § 275.205-3, prior to its amendment in 1998 by Adviser's Act Release No. 1731 (July 15, 1998), 63 F.R. 39,022 (July 21, 1998).

6. The risk should, however, be disclosed. *See* Chapter 6, *infra.*

7. *See* Chapter 3, *infra.* This book does not address a recent trend, if it is one, of offering hedge funds or funds of hedge funds to the public in offerings registered under the Securities Act; such offerings typically are promoted by large brokerage firms for small investors. This book also does not generally address funds of hedge funds, or the special considerations that may arise for them.

8. *See, e.g.,* William Safire, *Watch the Hedgehogs,* N.Y. Times, Apr. 12, 2004, at A19.

9. *See* Chapters 2, 12, 14 and 17, *infra.*

10. *See* Chapters 5, 6, 8 and 9, *infra.*

11. *See* Chapters 2 and 7, *infra.*

12. *See* Chapters 10, 13 and 14, *infra.*

13. *See* Chapter 11, *infra.*

14. *See* Chapters 11 and 16, *infra.*

15. *See* § 2.9, *infra.*

§ 1.2 Organization

Hedge funds in the United States are most commonly organized as limited partnerships, although in recent years a few have been organized as limited liability companies. Offshore hedge funds usually are organized as corporations (or an equivalent form in the jurisdiction of organization). If an investment adviser manages the portfolios of both U.S. and offshore hedge funds, they may be organized in a master-feeder structure, in which the U.S. and offshore hedge funds are the limited partners (feeders) of a master limited partnership, allowing the investment adviser to trade a single portfolio.[16] If a hedge fund is organized as a limited partnership, the investment adviser typically is its general partner. Occasionally, however, for tax or other reasons, the general partner is a separate entity without portfolio management responsibility and the portfolio manager is the investment adviser under an investment management agreement between the hedge fund and the portfolio manager. If the hedge fund is an offshore corporation, it also enters into an investment management agreement with the investment adviser. In the master-feeder structure, the investment adviser typically is the general partner of and investment adviser to the master fund, the general partner of the domestic feeder and the investment adviser to the offshore feeder.[17] Whatever the structure, the portfolio manager is an investment adviser, subject to federal or state registration as such, unless an exemption from registration is available.[18]

A hedge fund typically continues as long as its manager or management team wants to continue it and its investors continue to believe in its management. Most hedge funds permit investors to withdraw quarterly or at some other periodic interval. Sometimes withdrawals are permitted only after a lock-up period, which may be a few months or one or two years from the initial investment, if the manager's services are in sufficient demand or the investment strategy cannot tolerate earlier withdrawals. If a hedge fund's returns are wanting, new investors may not be interested in investing, earlier investors may be expected to withdraw, and, in the absence of performance-based compensation, the manager may want to look for a more consistently lucrative position.

Interests in hedge funds can be offered to U.S. persons only in private offerings under Securities Act section 4(2).[19] A hedge fund typically conducts a continuous offering, at least until its assets approach the maximum amount that its manager believes it can effectively invest. Most domestic hedge funds accept investments only from "accredited investors,"[20] each of whom has sufficient net worth to comply with the performance fee rule,[21] or in the case of a section 3(c)(7) fund, only

---

16. *See* Chapter 4, *infra.*
17. *Id.*
18. *See* § 2.2, *infra.*
19. 15 U.S.C. § 77(d)2. Regulation D, Rule 506, 17 C.F.R. § 230.506, also provides for private offerings under § 4(2). *See* Chapters 3, 5 and 6, *infra. See also* note 7, supra.
20. *See* §§ 5.3.2.ii and 5.3.2.iii, *infra.*
21. Advisers Act Rule 205-3, 17 C.F.R. § 275.205-3. *See* § 15.2.3, *infra.*

from "qualified purchasers."[22] Notwithstanding a published SEC staff comment that hedge funds "generally are not required to meet prescribed disclosure requirements,"[23] a hedge fund is obligated to make comprehensive disclosures to potential investors, both to satisfy fiduciary obligations under the Advisers Act[24] and state law and to comply with the anti-fraud provisions of the securities laws and the requirements of the private offering exemptions.[25]

§ 1.3 Regulatory Prospects

Alfred Winslow Jones organized the first hedge fund in 1949.[26] When we began our practice representing hedge fund managers in the early 1980s, U.S. hedge funds numbered fewer than 100 and managed only a few billion dollars of assets,[27] but the hedge fund business generally escaped (or avoided) public notice and its magnitude was largely unexamined.[28] After the stock market crash in October 1987, the government briefly shined a low-wattage spot light on hedge funds,[29] but did not implement major regulatory initiatives directed at them. The Staff Report estimated in 2003 that 6,000 to 7,000 hedge funds were operating in the United States, managing assets of $600,000,000,000 to $650,000,000,000.[30]

Inspired by this growth and notorious financial scandals since 2001, especially those involving managers of large mutual fund complexes, the SEC and other regulatory agencies became highly motivated (whether for political or other reasons) at least to appear to be pursuing with vigor remedies to publicly perceived regulatory and institutional weaknesses. In an avowed effort to learn more about the theretofore-veiled hedge fund business, the SEC in 2002 directed its staff to examine the hedge fund business and, in May 2003, convened a "Roundtable" to provide a public forum for discussion and debate about the implications of hedge fund growth.[31]

The resulting Staff Report recommended that the SEC consider several regulatory initiatives,[32] including:

---

22.   *See* § 3.3.2, *infra. See* §§ 5.4, 5.5 and 8.3, *infra,* regarding securities offering requirements applicable to offshore hedge funds.

23.   Staff Report, §I.B, at ix.

24.   *See* §§ 2.6, 2.7, 6.5, 8.2 and 8.4, *infra.*

25.   *See* §§ 5.3.1, 5.3.2.vii, 6.2, 6.3, 6.4 and 8.2, *infra.*

26.   Staff Report § II.A, at 3.

27.   Hennessee Group LLC, *10th Annual Manager Survey – 2004.*

28.   *See* Ralph S. Janvey, *Hedge Funds,* Rev. of Sec. & Commodities Reg., Vol. 21, No. 11, at 91 (June 8, 1988), and authorities cited there.

29.   *Id.*

30.   Staff Report at vii. Hennessee Group LLC, *10th Annual Manager Survey – 2004,* reported that managed assets have since grown to $795,000,000,000.

31.   Staff Report § I, at 2. *See generally* Sec. Reg. & L. Rep. (BNA), Vol. 35, No. 20, at 851-856 (May 19, 2003).

32.   Staff Report §VII, at 88-103.

- Requiring hedge fund advisers to register as investment advisers under the Advisers Act,
- Addressing valuation, suitability and fee disclosure issues relating to funds of hedge funds,
- Permitting general solicitation[33] in hedge fund offerings limited to qualified purchasers,[34]
- Monitoring closely capital introduction services provided by brokers,
- Encouraging hedge funds to embrace and further develop best practices, and
- Continuing efforts to improve investor education regarding hedge funds.

In recent testimony about the mutual fund industry before a Senate committee, SEC Chair William H. Donaldson expressed personal concerns regarding hedge funds' valuation practices, access to and use of inside information, trading practices (including front-running mutual funds and other large investors), and participation in initial public offerings.[35] These concerns differ from, and are in some respects narrower than, the topics recommended for consideration in the Staff Report. Mr. Donaldson also said, however, that additional regulation of hedge funds could be implemented by requiring hedge fund managers to register with the SEC as investment advisers and developing SEC oversight programs for the hedge fund business.[36] Registration and oversight could be implemented to address not only Mr. Donaldson's expressed concerns but also the recommendations in the Staff Report, as well as the SEC inspection staff's usual checklist of compliance issues.

In July 2004, the SEC voted three to two to propose new rules that would prevent most hedge fund managers whose assets under management are $25,000,000 or more from relying on the Private Adviser Exemption.[37] The SEC's reasons for proposing the new rules include:[38]

- collecting necessary data regarding hedge funds and their advisers;
- deterring and detecting fraud early;
- preventing unfit persons from managing hedge funds;
- protecting investors by adopting compliance controls; and
- discouraging "retailization" of hedge funds by requiring each investor in a hedge fund to be a qualified client for purposes of the performance fee rule.[39]

---

33. *See* §§ 5.3.1, 5.3.2.vi and 8.2, *infra*.

34. *See* § 3.3.2, *infra*.

35. Christopher Faille, *Donaldson Has 'Personal' Concerns Re Hedge Funds,* HedgeWorld Daily News, Apr. 12, 2004; Deborah Brewster, *SEC Head Adamant on Hedge Fund Managers,* Financial Times (London, England), USA Edition 2, Apr. 10, 2004.

36. *Id.*

37. *See* §§ 2.1.2.iii, 2.1.2.iv and 2.2.1–2.2.4, *infra. See generally* S&P's The Rev. of Sec. & Commodities Reg., Vol. 37, No. 15 (Sep. 15, 2004).

38. Advisers Act Release No. 2266 (July 20, 2004), 69 F.R. 45,172 (July 28, 2004).

39. *See* § 15.2.3.i, *infra*.

This rule proposal was met with vociferous opposition, both from the two dissenting Commissioners and other public officials (Alan Greenspan among them) and from numerous representatives of the hedge fund business. Favorable comments were mostly confined to Mr. Donaldson and his two allies on the SEC, a few institutional investors and representatives of the mutual fund industry (perhaps demonstrating concern about hedge funds' incursion onto their proprietary turf).[40] Objections to the proposed rules, included, among others:

- that the proposed rule will not elicit useful information;
- that evidence does not show disproportionate fraudulent activity by hedge fund managers;
- that SEC registration is unlikely to detect or deter fraudulent activity, given the infrequency of SEC examinations;
- that the cost of additional SEC resources and expertise to regulate the additional 700 to 1,200 private fund advisers that the SEC staff estimated would be required to register is outweighed by the unproven benefit of regulation, especially given the relative sophistication of the investors in those private funds;
- that registration does not determine whether an investment adviser is unfit;
- that the evidence of significant "retailization" is at best sparse; and
- that the proposed rules exceed the SEC's statutory authority.

After a brief comment period (the SEC having refused several requests to extend it), at a meeting on October 26, 2004, as we were finishing this book, Mr. Donaldson had his way,[41] and the SEC, again by a three to two vote, adopted the proposed rules to become effective on February 1, 2006.[42] We cannot foretell whether the new rules will achieve their stated purposes (depending in part perhaps on which of the purposes were sincerely stated).

We also cannot predict what other law or rule changes may ensue. Registration will subject heretofore unregistered hedge fund managers to the same sort of oversight as the SEC now exercises over investment advisers managing mutual funds, institutional portfolios and individual accounts. We would expect (and hope) that further fundamental rule-making initiatives would be deferred until the SEC develops understanding and experience about the hedge fund business.[43]

---

40.   *But see* Ron Orol, *Regulation? Bring It on,* Daily Deal/The Deal (Oct. 11, 2004), citing a California hedge fund manager's support of the new rules as a barrier to entry into the hedge fund business for start-up managers (such as his employees).

41.   *See, e.g.,* Jenny Anderson, *Hedge Funds to SEC: Who Made You Boss?,* The New York Post, at 39 (Sep. 17, 2004) ("Donaldson has expressed keen support for the proposal, and many inside the commission sense it is a key 'legacy' issue for him as he approaches the likely end of his term").

42.   Advisers Act Release No. 2333 (Dec. 2, 2004), 69 F.R. 72,054 (Dec. 10, 2004), which includes the dissent of the two Commissioners who opposed the new rules. *See* §§ 2.1.2.iii and 2.1.2.iv, *infra.*

43.   *See generally* Steven Drachman, The SEC's *Company Act and Advisers Act Agenda,* Rev. of Sec. & Commodities Reg., Vol. 36, No. 13 (July 2003); and Charles E. Dropkin, *The SEC Stakes Out Hedge Fund Regulation,* Wall Street Lawyer, Vol. 7, No. 5, at 1 (Oct. 2003).

§ 1.4 A Note on Conventions

Depending on the context, we use "limited partnership," "limited liability company" and "corporation" interchangeably in referring to hedge funds, and use "investment adviser," "manager" and "general partner" interchangeably in referring to the person that manages a hedge fund. For convenience, we also use the following abbreviations:

Advisers Act	Investment Advisers Act of 1940[44]
CEA	Commodity Exchange Act[45]
CFTC	Commodity Futures Trading Commission
Company Act	Investment Company Act of 1940[46]
CPO	commodity pool operator
CTA	commodity trading adviser
DOL	Department of Labor
ERISA	Employee Retirement Income Security Act of 1974[47]
Exchange Act	Securities Exchange Act of 1934[48]
FinCEN	Financial Crimes Enforcement Network of the Treasury Department
FTC	Federal Trade Commission
GLBA	Gramm-Leach-Bliley Act (Financial Services Modernization Act of 1999)[49]
IARD	Investment Adviser Registration Depository of the NASD
IRS	Internal Revenue Service
NASD	National Association of Securities Dealers, Inc.
NASDR	National Association of Securities Dealers Regulation, Inc.
NFA	National Futures Association
NYSE	New York Stock Exchange, Inc.
SEC	Securities and Exchange Commission
SEC-Exempt Adviser	An investment adviser exempt from registration with the SEC[50]
Securities Act	Securities Act of 1933[51]
Tax Code	Internal Revenue Code of 1986[52]

---

44. 15 U.S.C. §§ 80b-20 *et. seq.*
45. 7 U.S.C. §§ 1 *et. seq.*
46. 15 U.S.C. §§ 80a-51 *et. seq.*
47. 29 U.S.C. §§ 1001 *et. seq.*
48. 15 U.S.C. §§ 78a *et. seq.*
49. Pub. L. No. 106-102, 114 stat. 3928 (codified as amended in scattered sections of 12 U.S.C. and 15 U.S.C.).
50. *See* § 2.1.2, *infra.*
51. 15 U.S.C. §§ 77a *et. seq.*
52. 26 U.S.C. § 1 *et. seq.*

CHAPTER **2**

Investment Adviser Registration and Regulation

§ 2.1 Federal Definition of "Investment Adviser"

The Advisers Act defines "investment adviser" as any person (including a natural person or an entity) who for compensation is engaged in the business of advising others or issuing reports or analyses regarding securities.[1] Many financial planners, pension consultants and agents (for example, of athletes or entertainers) are investment advisers.[2]

Whether a person is "in the business" depends on the frequency and regularity with which that person gives advice about securities or engages in other advisory activities. A person giving advice about securities will be deemed "in the business" unless the advice is solely incidental to a non-advisory business, the advice does not specify particular securities and the person does not receive special compensation for the advice.[3] Investment advice need not be a person's primary or even a major activity for that person to be "in the business" of providing investment advice.[4]

"Compensation" includes any economic benefit that a person receives, whether advisory fees, commissions on the sale of financial products, or indirect economic or other benefits, including fees or benefits received from sources other than the recipient of the advice. If an adviser receives compensation for providing several types of services to clients, it will be deemed to receive compensation for investment advisory services if the services it provides include investment advisory services.[5]

"Securities" include any note, stock, treasury stock, security future, bond, debenture, evidence of indebtedness, certificate of interest or participation in any profit-sharing agreement, collateral trust certificate, preorganization certificate or subscription, transferable share, investment contract, or put, call, straddle, option or privilege on any security or group or index of securities.[6] Advice about securities need not relate to specific securities. The advice can be as general as recommending

---

1. Advisers Act § 202(a)(11), 15 U.S.C. § 80b-2(a)(11).
2. *Id.*
3. Advisers Act Release No. 1092, 52 F.R. 38,400 (Oct. 16, 1987).
4. *Id.*
5. *Id.*
6. Advisers Act § 202(a)(18), 15 U.S.C. § 80b-2(a)(18).

investing in securities rather than other types of investments,[7] market timing[8] or selecting or evaluating investment advisers.[9]

1. Exclusions from the Investment Adviser Definition

The following persons are excluded from the federal definition of "investment adviser":[10]

- Banks and bank holding companies that are not investment companies, except for banks and bank holding companies, or separately identifiable departments or divisions of banks or bank holding companies, that act as investment advisers to registered investment companies;[11]
- Lawyers, accountants, engineers and teachers who give investment advice that is solely incidental to the practice of their respective professions;
- Brokers who give investment advice that is solely incidental to their brokerage business and who receive no "special compensation" for giving investment advice;
- Publishers of bona fide newspapers, magazines or business or financial publications of general and regular circulation that are not primarily vehicles for distributing investment advice;[12] and
- Investment advisers whose advice relates solely to U.S. government securities (including securities issued by government-sponsored enterprises or federal agencies).

The SEC has not specifically defined when investment advice is "solely incidental" to another business. The staff has noted, however, that if a broker establishes a limited partnership and provides investment advice as its general partner, those activities may

---

7. *New Directions Group, Inc.*, SEC No-Action Letter (Mar. 6, 1985, reconsidered and reaffirmed May 2, 1985).

8. *Maratta Advisory, Inc.*, SEC No-Action Letter (July 16, 1981).

9. *Greater Cleveland Hospital Ass'n*, SEC No-Action Letter (May 11, 1995); Advisers Act Release No. 1092, 52 F.R. 38,400 (Oct. 8, 1987).

10. Advisers Act § 202(a)(11), 15 U.S.C. § 80b-2(a)(11).

11. Advisers Act § 202(a)(11)(A), 15 U.S.C. § 80b-2(a)(11)(A), effective May 12, 2001. A "separately identifiable department or division" of a bank is a unit (a) that is under the direct supervision of an officer designated by the bank's board of directors to be responsible for the day-to-day conduct of the bank's investment adviser activities for one or more investment companies, including the supervision of all bank employees performing such activities, and (b) for which all records relating to its investment adviser activities are separately maintained or extractable from the unit's own facilities or the facilities of the bank, and for which the records are so maintained or otherwise accessible to permit independent examination and enforcement by the SEC of the Advisers Act or the Company Act and the rules and regulations thereunder. Advisers Act § 202(a)(26), 15 U.S.C. § 80b-2(a)(26).

12. *See Lowe v. SEC*, 472 U.S. 181 (1985). The exemption for publishers also extends to the publisher of a website, if the website is "bona fide" and of "general and regular" circulation. A website is "bona fide" if it contains disinterested commentary and analysis (that is, the publisher is not encouraging readers to invest in securities in which the publisher has invested or intends to invest) and does not promote a security in which the publisher has an interest or for which the publisher is compensated. A website may not be considered "bona fide" when the publisher emails advice to its subscribers or answers questions in a chatroom. A website may not be of "general and regular" circulation where updates to it are triggered by specific market activity or events affecting or having the ability to affect the securities industry. *See SEC v. Park (a/k/a "Tokyo Joe")*, 99 F. Supp. 2d 889 (N.D. Ill. 2000).

not be solely incidental to the broker's conduct of a brokerage business.[13] In addition, such a broker may receive "special compensation" in the form of reimbursement for expenses incurred in offering the limited partnership's securities.[14]

2. Investment Advisers Exempt from Registration

Some persons that are included within the definition of "investment adviser" are nevertheless exempt from registration as such under the Advisers Act by virtue of specific exemptions in the Advisers Act and the rules under it (each, an "SEC-Exempt Adviser"). An SEC-Exempt Adviser is not subject to the Advisers Act provisions relating to registration, recordkeeping or performance fees, but is subject to the anti-fraud provisions of Advisers Act section 206.[15] Persons excluded from the definition of investment adviser are not, however, subject to Advisers Act section 206.[16] The activities of both SEC-Exempt Advisers and persons excluded from the definition of "investment adviser" are subject to other federal securities laws and regulations, such as Rule 10b-5[17] under the Exchange Act. The categories of SEC-Exempt Adviser are described below.

i. Intrastate Investment Advisers

An investment adviser is an SEC-Exempt Adviser if all of its clients are residents of the state in which it maintains its principal office and place of business and it does not advise about securities listed or admitted to unlisted trading privileges on any national securities exchange.[18]

ii. Investment Advisers with Only Insurance Company Clients

An investment adviser whose only clients are insurance companies is an SEC-Exempt Adviser.[19]

iii. Private Investment Advisers

An investment adviser is an SEC-Exempt Adviser if it has had fewer than fifteen clients during the preceding twelve months, does not advise any registered investment companies or business development companies and does not hold itself out generally to the public as an investment adviser (the "Private Adviser Exemption").[20] In October 2004, however, the SEC adopted rule amendments[21]

---

13. *Terwilliger*, SEC No-Action Letter (June 27, 1977).
14. *Id.*
15. *See* §§ 2.7.1, 8.4, 9.3.2 and 9.4, *infra*.
16. *See* § 2.1.1, *supra*.
17. 17 C.F.R. § 240.10b-5. *See* Chapter 6, *infra*.
18. Advisers Act § 203(b)(1), 15 U.S.C. § 80b-3(b)(1).
19. Advisers Act § 203(b)(2), 15 U.S.C. § 80b-3(b)(2).
20. Advisers Act § 203(b)(3), 15 U.S.C. § 80b-3(b)(3).
21. Advisers Act Release No. 2333 (Dec. 2, 2004), 69 F.R. 72,054 (Dec. 10, 2004). *See also* the proposing release, Advisers Act Release No. 2266 (July 20, 2004), 69 F.R. 45,172 (July 28, 2004).

that will, when they become obligatory in February 2006, severely curtail the Private Adviser Exemption, rendering it generally unavailable to an investment adviser that manages a hedge fund and has $25,000,000 or more under management.[22] Under the current rule, each of the following is a single "client" for purposes of the Private Adviser Exemption:[23]

- A natural person, any minor child of the natural person, any relative or spouse, or relative of the spouse, of the natural person who has the same principal residence as the natural person, and all accounts and trusts of which the natural person and the above persons are the only primary beneficiaries; and
- A corporation, general or limited partnership, limited liability company, trust or other entity that receives investment advice based on its investment objectives rather than the individual investment objectives of its owners (this includes most hedge funds), and any two or more of such entities that have identical owners.

In addition, for the purpose of the Private Adviser Exemption:

- An owner of an entity is counted as a client if the investment adviser provides investment advisory services to the owner separate and apart from the investment advisory services provided to the entity. An owner is not counted as a client solely because the investment adviser, on behalf of the entity, reports periodically to or offers or sells interests in the entity to the owner.
- A limited partnership or limited liability company is a client of any general partner, manager or other person that acts as an investment adviser to the entity and provides advice based on the investment objectives of the entity and not those of the investors in the entity.[24]
- Any person to whom an investment adviser provides services without compensation is not counted as a client. Compensation includes any economic benefit, whether or not in the form of an advisory fee, and may be provided by a third party.[25] Nevertheless, an investment adviser has the same fiduciary obligations to a client who receives advisory services free of charge as it has to paying clients.
- An investment adviser that has its principal office and place of business outside the United States counts only its U.S. clients, but an investment adviser in the United States counts all clients, U.S. and non-U.S.[26]

In general, under the rules in effect until the amendments become obligatory in February 2006, a hedge fund is deemed to be a single client for the purpose of determining whether its investment adviser qualifies for the Private Adviser Exemption. Hedge fund limited partners, however, who are allowed to transfer

---

22.   *See* § 2.1.2.iv, *infra*.
23.   Advisers Act Rule 203(b)(3)-1(a), 17 C.F.R. § 275.203(b)(3)-1(a).
24.   Advisers Act Rule 203(b)(3)-1(a), 17 C.F.R. § 275.203(b)(3)-1(a).
25.   *See* § 2.1, *supra*.
26.   Advisers Act Rule 203(b)(3)-1(b), 17 C.F.R. § 275.203(b)(3)-1(b).

assets between hedge funds managed by the same investment adviser, or who can elect whether to participate in each investment that their hedge fund makes, may be treated as separate clients of that investment adviser for purposes of the Private Adviser Exemption.[27] On the other hand, offering limited partners the option of receiving partnership distributions in cash or in kind will not, by itself, result in the limited partners, rather than the hedge fund, being considered separate clients of the investment adviser for purposes of the Private Adviser Exemption.[28]

Like all SEC-Exempt Advisers, a general partner of a hedge fund that relies on the Private Adviser Exemption is subject to the fiduciary duty rules under the Advisers Act,[29] even if the general partner is not registered as an investment adviser with the SEC or under any state laws. Such a general partner must also comply with the fiduciary duty laws of the state in which its business is located.

The SEC staff broadly interprets a person's holding itself out generally to the public as an investment adviser to include, among other things:

- Advertising its investment advisory activities;
- Maintaining a listing as an adviser in a telephone or building directory;[30]
- Letting it be known by word of mouth or otherwise that the investment adviser will accept new investment advisory clients[31] (including entering into wrap fee arrangements with broker-dealers who refer clients to the investment adviser);[32]
- Engaging a solicitor to attract clients;[33]
- Using letterhead or business cards that use the term "investment adviser" or a similar term or that refer to investment advisory activities;[34]
- Using a publicly available electronic medium, such as a website, to provide information about advisory services;[35] or
- Allowing the person's name to be included in a database of investment advisers available on the Internet without complying with specified restrictions.[36]

An investment adviser to a hedge fund should not be deemed to be holding itself out to the public as such solely because it participates in a private offering of the hedge fund's interests under the Securities Act.[37]

---

27. *Burr, Egan, Deleage & Co., Inc.*, SEC No Action Letter (Apr. 27, 1987).

28. *Latham & Watkins*, SEC No Action Letter (Aug. 24, 1998).

29. Advisers Act § 206, 15 U.S.C. § 80b-6; *SEC v. Capital Gains Research Bureau, Inc.*, 375 U.S. 180 (1963).

30. *See Peter H. Jacobs*, SEC No Action Letter (Feb. 7, 1979).

31. *See id.*

32. *See* Chapter 14, *infra*.

33. Advisers Act Release No. 688 (July 12, 1979), 44 F.R. 42,126 (July 18, 1979); *see* Chapter 8, *infra*.

34. *See Resource Bank and Trust*, SEC No Action Letter (Mar. 29, 1991).

35. Advisers Act Release No. 1562, 61 F.R. 2,644 (May 9, 1996).

36. *Lamp Technologies, Inc.*, SEC No Action Letter (May 29, 1997); *Lamp Technologies, Inc.*, SEC No Action Letter (May 29, 1998). Additional restrictions apply to non–U.S. advisers. Advisers Act Release No. 1710, 63 F.R. 14,806 (Mar. 23, 1998). *See* Chapter 9, *infra*.

37. Advisers Act Rule 203(b)(3)-1(c), 17 C.F.R. § 275.203(b)(3)-1(c). *See* § 8.4.3, *infra*.

iv. Curtailment of Private Adviser Exemption

In October 2004, over the dissent of two Commissioners, the SEC adopted rule amendments to eliminate the Private Adviser Exemption for almost any investment adviser that manages one or more hedge funds, which, together with other securities portfolios that the investment adviser manages, have an aggregate value of $25,000,000 or more.[38] In general, as discussed below,[39] an investment adviser that has aggregate assets under management of less than $25,000,000 is not permitted to register with the SEC, but instead must comply with applicable state investment adviser registration laws. The rule amendments adopted by Release 2333 are aimed principally at forcing hedge fund managers, many of which have relied on the Private Adviser Exemption, to register with the SEC as investment advisers under the Advisers Act.

New Advisers Act Rules 203(b)(3)-1 and 203(b)(3)-2[40] will generally require hedge fund managers to count as "clients," for purposes of the Private Adviser Exemption, all of the shareholders, limited partners, members and other security holders or beneficiaries (called "owners" in the new rules) of their hedge funds. The new rules use the term "private fund" to refer to a hedge fund, defining that term as a company:

- that would be an investment company under Company Act section 3(a)[41] but for the exception provided by Company Act section 3(c)(1) or 3(c)(7); [42]
- that permits its owners to redeem any of their ownership interests within two years of purchasing those interests, except on account of events that the investment adviser finds after reasonable inquiry to be extraordinary; and
- interests in which are or have been offered based on the investment advisory skills, ability or expertise of the investment adviser.

New Rule 203(b)(3)-1 excepts from the "private fund" definition any company whose principal office and place of business are outside the United States, that publicly offers its securities publicly in a country outside the United States and that is regulated as a public investment company under the laws of that country.

Release 2333 also amended the books and records rule[43] to permit investment advisers that manage hedge funds and had relied on the Private Adviser Exemption before February 10, 2005, to continue to advertise their performance for any period ended before that date, even after registering with the SEC and even if they did not keep all of the records needed to substantiate the performance advertising under that rule.[44] The books and records rule was also amended to require the records of a hedge fund to be kept as records of the investment adviser if the investment adviser

---

38.   Advisers Act Release No. 2333 (Dec. 2, 2004), 69 F.R. 72,054 (Dec. 10, 2004) (hereinafter "Release 2333"); *see also* Advisers Act Release No. 2266 (July 20, 2004), 69 F.R. 45,172 (July 28, 2004).

39.   *See* § 2.2, *infra.*

40.   17 C.F.R. §§ 275.203(b)(3)-1 and 275.203(b)(3)-2.

41.   15 U.S.C. § 80a-3(a).

42.   15 U.S.C. § 80a-3(c)(1) or 80a-3(c)(7); *see* Chapter 3, *infra.*

43.   Advisers Act Rule 204-2, 17 C.F.R. § 275.204-2.

44.   *See* § 2.8, *infra.*

or any related person is the hedge fund's general partner, managing member or the like.

Release 2333 also amended the performance fee rule[45] to allow an investment adviser that manages a hedge fund and is required to register with the SEC as a result of the amendments to continue to charge a performance fee or allocation to investors that invested in the hedge fund before February 10, 2005, even if it would be prohibited from doing so were those investors to invest in the hedge fund after the investment adviser becomes SEC-registered. Release 2333 also amended Form ADV[46] to elicit information about whether the investment adviser manages one or more hedge funds and, if so, limited information about each such hedge fund, although Release 2333 did not remedy numerous ambiguities in Form ADV in the context of a hedge fund manager, including ambiguities in the questions it added.

v. Other Organizations

Charitable and religions organizations and some non-U.S. advisers that conduct no activities in the United States are SEC-Exempt Advisers.[47]

---

§ 2.2 Federal and State Registration of Advisers

---

1. Mandatory SEC Registration

The Investment Advisers Supervision Coordination Act, a part of the National Securities Markets Improvement Act of 1996,[48] allocates regulatory responsibilities for investment advisers between the SEC and the states.[49] A state may not require registration of an investment adviser that is registered or required to be registered with the SEC.[50] Unless an exemption from SEC registration is available, an investment adviser must register with the SEC if it:

- Has one or more investment company clients;[51]
- Has $30,000,000 or more in "assets under management";[52]
- Maintains its principal place of business in a state that does not require registration of advisers (currently, only Wyoming);

---

45. Adviser Act Rule 205-3, 17 C.F.R. § 275.205-3; *see* § 15.2, *infra*.

46. *See* § 2.4, *infra*.

47. Advisers Act § 203(b)(4), 203(b)(5), 203(a), 15 U.S.C. §§ 80b-3(b)(4), 80b-3(b)(5), § 80b-3(a); Advisers Act Release No. 1710, 63 F.R. 14,806 (Mar. 23, 1998); Edward F. Greene, et al., *U.S. Regulation of the International Securities and Derivatives Markets*, Third Ed., Vol. 1, § 10.03.

48. Pub. L. No. 104-290, 110 Stat. 3416 (1996) (codified in various sections of the U.S. Code) (hereinafter, the "1996 Act").

49. 15 U.S.C. § 80b-3A.

50. Advisers Act § 203A(b), 15 U.S.C. § 80b-3A(b).

51. Advisers Act § 203A(a), 15 U.S.C. § 80b-3A(a).

52. *See* § 2.2.3, *infra*; Advisers Act Rule 203A-1, 17 C.F.R. § 275.203A-1.

- Maintains its principal place of business outside the United States, but has U.S. clients;
- Is a nationally-recognized statistical rating organization (rating agency);[53]
- Is a pension consultant with respect to assets of plans (employee benefit plans, governmental plans and church plans under certain sections of ERISA) with an aggregate value of at least $50,000,000 as of the end of the investment adviser's last fiscal year;[54] or
- Is affiliated (in a control relationship) with an SEC-registered investment adviser, if the two investment advisers share a principal office and place of business.[55]

"Control" is the power to direct or cause the direction of the management or policies of the investment adviser, whether through ownership of securities, by contract or otherwise. Direct or indirect ownership of twenty-five percent or more of the voting securities or entitlement to twenty-five percent or more of the profits of the other investment adviser creates a presumption of control. "Principal office and place of business" is the executive office of the investment adviser from which the officers, partners or managers of the investment adviser direct, control and coordinate its activities.[56]

An investment adviser to one or more hedge funds with aggregate assets greater than $30,000,000 is required to register as such with the SEC, unless (as will be unlikely after February 1, 2006) it is eligible for an exemption from SEC registration.[57]

2. Optional SEC Registration

An investment adviser that is not otherwise required to register with the SEC and that has assets under management between $25,000,000 and $30,000,000 may, but is not required to, register with the SEC.[58] If an SEC-registered investment adviser's assets under management drop below $25,000,000, and it is not otherwise eligible to register with the SEC, the investment adviser must withdraw from SEC registration within 180 days after the end of that fiscal year.[59]

An investment adviser may elect to register with the SEC if it would otherwise be required to register as an investment adviser with at least thirty states at the time of its initial application to the SEC and would be required to register with at least twenty-five states at the time of filing its annual updating amendment. Such an investment adviser must maintain a record of the states in which it would be

---

53. Advisers Act Rule 203A-2(a), 17 C.F.R. § 275.203A-2(a).

54. Advisers Act Rule 203A-2(b), 17 C.F.R. § 275.203A-2(b). In determining the aggregate value of plan assets, the adviser may include only that portion of the plan's assets for which the adviser provides investment advice, including any advice with respect to the selection of an investment adviser to manage the assets. *Id.* As used in Rule 203A-2(b), "assets of plans" is not limited to securities portfolios.

55. Advisers Act Rule 203A-2(c), 17 C.F.R. § 275.203A-2(c).

56. Advisers Act Rule 203A-3(c), 17 C.F.R. § 275.203A-3(c)

57. *See* § 2.1.2, *supra.*

58. Advisers Act Rule 203A-1(a)(2), 17 C.F.R. § 275.203A-1(a)(2).

59. Advisers Act Rule 203A-1(b), 17 C.F.R. § 275.203A-1(b)

required to register for at least five years from the date on which the application or amendment is filed.[60]

A newly formed investment adviser that reasonably expects to be eligible for SEC registration within 120 days of the effective date of its registration may elect to register with the SEC.[61] If the investment adviser fails to attain assets under management of at least $25,000,000 within 120 days after its registration with the SEC becomes effective, the investment adviser must withdraw its SEC registration.[62]

Any investment adviser that does not register with the SEC may instead be required to register under applicable state law. An investment adviser that is eligible but not required to register with the SEC may desire to avoid SEC registration to reduce its exposure to the SEC's inspections and regulations. Alternatively, some investment advisers choose to register with the SEC to gain whatever marketing cachet SEC registration might afford or to avoid potentially more burdensome or less predictable state regulation. Under no circumstances, however, may an investment adviser ever claim that it has been sponsored, recommended or approved, or that the investment adviser's abilities or qualifications have in any respect been passed on, by the United States, the SEC, any other federal agency or any of their officers.[63]

3.   "Assets under Management"

For the purpose of determining whether an investment adviser must register with the SEC or under state law, the investment adviser's "assets under management" is defined to include any "securities portfolios" with respect to which the investment adviser provides "continuous and regular supervisory or management services."[64] A "securities portfolio" is an account or accounts of which securities represent at least fifty percent of the total value.[65] Cash and cash equivalents may be treated as securities for this purpose.[66] The entire value of the account or accounts, and not only the value of the securities portion, is included in determining the amount of the investment adviser's assets under management.[67]

Accounts over which an investment adviser has discretionary authority and for which it provides ongoing supervisory or management services qualify as accounts

---

60.   Advisers Act Rule 203A-2(e), 17 C.F.R. § 275.203A-2(e). In its application or amendment, the adviser must undertake to withdraw from SEC registration if it is required to register in fewer than twenty-five states at the time of filing its next annual updating amendment.

61.   Advisers Act Rule 203A-2(d), 17 C.F.R. § 275.203A-2(d). In its initial application, the adviser must undertake to withdraw from SEC registration if it is not eligible for SEC registration on the 120th day after its SEC registration becomes effective. Such an adviser may choose to register under applicable state law during the 120-day period if it is not certain whether it will be eligible to be SEC-registered at the end of the 120-day period, because no grace period for state law registration is provided at the end of that period.

62.   *Id.*

63.   15 U.S.C. § 80b-8.

64.   Advisers Act § 203A(a)(2), 15 U.S.C. § 80b-3A(a)(2).

65.   Form ADV, Instructions for Part 1A, Item 5.F, 17 C.F.R. § 279.1.

66.   *Id.*

67.   *Id.*

that receive continuous and regular supervisory or management services.[68] Nondiscretionary advisory arrangements may also qualify under specified circumstances as receiving continuous and regular supervisory or management services.[69] If an investment adviser provides continuous and regular supervisory or management services for only part of a securities portfolio (as in the case of a hedge fund portfolio managed by more than one investment adviser), the investment adviser should include as assets under management only the portion of the securities portfolio with respect to which it provides such services.[70] No deduction should be made for securities purchased on margin.[71] Generally, accounts should be valued for determining assets under management in the same way as they are valued for purposes of client reporting and determining fees for investment advisory services.[72]

"Assets under management" includes accounts of clients that do not pay fees to the investment adviser.[73] For example, a hedge fund may include capital provided by the investment adviser, its affiliates, family members and other investors for whom fees are waived.

4. Transition Between State and SEC Registration

Form ADV requires an investment adviser registering with the SEC to specify the amount of assets it manages.[74] As discussed below,[75] an SEC-registered investment adviser must amend and update its Form ADV within ninety days after the end of each fiscal year.[76] If an SEC-registered investment adviser files an annual updating amendment showing that its assets under management have fallen below $25,000,000, so that it is no longer eligible for SEC registration, that investment adviser must file Form ADV-W[77] to withdraw from SEC registration within 180 days of that investment adviser's fiscal year end, and the investment adviser must register with the applicable state authority, if required by state law.[78] If the investment adviser's assets under management again increase to more than $25,000,000 during this 180 day period, it may remain SEC-registered.[79]

An investment adviser that is not otherwise subject to mandatory SEC registration becomes eligible to register with the SEC if its assets under management increase to $25,000,000.[80] An investment adviser that is not an SEC-Exempt Adviser must register with the SEC within ninety days if it is registered under a state law that requires an annual filing as to the amount of assets under management (such as Part

---

68. *Id.*
69. *Id.*
70. *Id.*
71. *Id.*
72. *Id.*
73. *Id.*
74. *See* § 2.4.1, *infra.*
75. *Id.*
76. Advisers Act Rule 204-1(a)(1), 17 C.F.R. § 275.204-1(a)(1).
77. 17 C.F.R. § 279.2.
78. Advisers Act Rule 203A-1(b)(2), 17 C.F.R. § 275.203A-1(b)(2).
79. *Id.*
80. Advisers Act Rule 203A-1(a)(2), 17 C.F.R. § 275.203A-1(a)(2).

1A of Form ADV) and it makes such a filing reporting assets under management of $30,000,000 or more.[81] If the investment adviser's assets under management decrease to less than $25,000,000 within that ninety-day period, the investment adviser is prohibited from registering with the SEC. If the investment adviser is not required to make such state filings, it must register with the SEC promptly when its assets under management reach $30,000,000 unless it is an SEC-Exempt Adviser.

5. State Regulation of "Investment Adviser Representatives"

The 1996 Act established that state laws requiring the registration, licensing or qualification of an investment adviser or supervised person of an investment adviser may not be applied to an SEC-registered investment adviser or its supervised persons, except that a state may license, register or otherwise qualify any "investment adviser representative" who has a place of business in that state.[82] The Advisers Act defines an "investment adviser representative" of an investment adviser as a "supervised person" of that investment adviser (a) who has more than five clients who are natural persons (other than "excepted persons") and (b) more than ten percent of whose clients are natural persons (other than "excepted persons").[83] An investment adviser who only manages one hedge fund would not have any investment adviser representatives, since the hedge fund counts as a single client and thus fewer than ten percent of the investment adviser's clients are natural persons. An investment adviser who also, however, manages numerous separate accounts may have investment adviser representatives. A "supervised person" is a partner, officer, director or employee of an investment adviser, or other person who provides investment advice on behalf of the investment adviser and is subject to the supervision and control of the investment adviser.[84] A supervised person is not an investment adviser representative of an investment adviser if the supervised person (a) does not on a regular basis solicit, meet with or communicate with clients of the investment adviser, or (b) provides only impersonal investment advice (advice that does not purport to meet the objectives or needs of specific individuals or accounts).[85] A "place of business" is an office at which the investment adviser representative regularly provides or is held out to the public as providing investment advisory services, or solicits, meets with or otherwise communicates with clients.[86] An "excepted person" is a client who is a natural person and (a) has at least $750,000 under the investment adviser's management, (b) has a net worth (together with his or her spouse) of more than $1,500,000, (c) is an executive officer, director, trustee or general partner of the investment adviser, (d) is an employee of the investment adviser who participates in the investment activities of the investment adviser as

---

81. Advisers Act Rule 203A-1(b)(1), 17 C.F.R. § 275.203A-1(b)(1).
82. Advisers Act § 203A(b)(1), 15 U.S.C. § 80b-3A(b)(1).
83. Advisers Act Rule 203A-3(a)(1), 17 C.F.R. § 275.203A-3(a)(1).
84. Advisers Act § 202(a)(25), 15 U.S.C. § 80b-2(a)(25).
85. Advisers Act Rule 203A-3(a)(2), 17 C.F.R. § 275.203A-3(a)(2).
86. Advisers Act Rule 203A-3(b), 17 C.F.R. § 275.203A-1-3(b).

part of his or her regular functions or duties and has been performing such duties or functions for the investment adviser or another investment adviser for at least twelve months, or (e) has (together with his or her spouse) at least $5,000,000 in investments.[87] Persons soliciting clients for investment advisers are also governed by these definitions. Rules of various states define "investment adviser representative" differently, sometimes mirroring the Advisers Act definition, and sometimes not.

6. National *de Minimis* Exemption

Even if an investment adviser is exempt from SEC registration, a state may require that investment adviser to register only if it has a place of business (as defined above) in that state or has more than five clients that are residents of that state during any twelve-month period.[88] For purposes of counting clients for this national *de minimis* exemption, the SEC has adopted the same rules used in connection with the Private Adviser Exemption, without regard to the new rules about counting each owner of a hedge fund as a client for purposes of the Private Adviser Exemption.[89] An SEC-Exempt Adviser that advises only five or fewer hedge funds would qualify for the *de minimis* exemption whether or not more than five persons have invested in the hedge funds.

This exemption is not relevant for SEC-registered investment advisers, because a state may not require registration of any investment adviser that is registered or required to be registered with the SEC.[90] It may be useful, however, to an investment adviser that has clients, either limited partnerships or separate accounts, in several states but is not SEC-registered in reliance on the Private Adviser Exemption or because it has less than $25,000,000 in assets under management.

7. State Notice Filings

Notwithstanding the *de minimis* exemption and the federal preemption of state registration of any investment adviser that is registered or required to be registered with the SEC, a state may require an investment adviser with one or more clients in that state to make notice filings and pay related fees. State notice filing requirements vary from state to state. Some states accept notice filings through the IARD system, while others require notice filings to be made on paper directly with the state regulatory authorities. In addition, although the SEC no longer requires investment advisers to file Part II of Form ADV with the SEC, some states continue to require the investment adviser to file Part II of its Form ADV with their regulatory authorities.

---

87. Advisers Act Rules 203A-3(a)(3)(i) and 205-3(d)(1), 17 C.F.R. §§ 275.203A-3(a)(3)(i) and 275.205-3(d)(1). The definition of "investments" for this purpose is complex. *See* § 3.3.2.i.f, *infra*.

88. Advisers Act § 222(d), 15 U.S.C. § 80b-22(d).

89. *See* §§ 2.1.2.iii and 2.1.2.iv, *supra*.

90. Advisers Act § 203A(b), 15 U.S.C. § 80b-3(b).

§ 2.3 State Requirements

1. Registration

i. Filings

All states (except Wyoming), the District of Columbia and Puerto Rico have a registration or licensing requirement for investment advisers.[91] These requirements may include:

- Registration or licensing of the investment adviser (unless the investment adviser is SEC-registered);
- Notice filings by SEC-registered investment advisers;[92]
- Exam requirements for each individual acting as an investment adviser or investment adviser representative; many states require investment adviser representatives to pass either the NASD Series 65 or Series 66 examination, although many states exempt individuals with certain industry certifications (such as certified financial planners, chartered financial analysts and chartered financial consultants);[93]
- Payment of fees for processing the applications;
- Certain disclosures to the securities agency or the public;
- Registration of branch offices; and
- Bonding or minimum net capital.

ii. Licensing Period

An investment adviser and its investment adviser representatives ordinarily must renew their registration and licenses annually. In many states, the term is from January 1 through December 31, although some states have different renewal periods.

2. Recordkeeping

States may impose recordkeeping requirements.[94] The Advisers Act, however, prohibits a state from imposing requirements related to books, records, net capital or bonding that are beyond the requirements imposed by the state in which an investment adviser is registered and has its principal place of business (as long as the investment adviser complies with its home state's requirements).[95] An investment

---

91.   NASAA Investment Adviser Guide, www.nasaa.org/nasaa/invadvisor/IA%20Guide%20Final3.doc, May 30, 2003.

92.   *See* § 2.2.7, *supra.*

93.   *See, e.g.,* California Code of Reg., § 260.236; New York GBL § 359-e.

94.   Advisers Act § 222(c) and (d), 15 U.S.C. §§ 80b–18a(c) and (d).

95.   Advisers Act § 222(c), 15 U.S.C. § 80b–18a(c).

adviser's principal place of business is the office at which it regularly provides investment advisory services and solicits, meets with or otherwise communicates with clients.[96]

3. Custody

If an investment adviser has direct or indirect access to client funds or securities, it is considered to have custody[97] of client assets and may be subject to additional state regulatory requirements. For example, the state in which it is registered may require it to maintain specified net capital.[98]

4. Fiduciary Duty

The Advisers Act anti-fraud provisions[99] and most state laws[100] impose on state-registered investment advisers fiduciary duties to their clients.

5. Inspections

State-registered investment advisers are subject to periodic, sometimes un-announced, inspections by state regulatory authorities, to determine compliance with the applicable licensing, books and records, and anti-fraud requirements.

---

§ 2.4 SEC and State Registration Processes

---

1. Federal

Effective on January 1, 2001, the SEC adopted a new Part 1 of Form ADV for investment adviser applications. An applicant registering as an investment adviser with the SEC must file an application on Part 1A of the new Form ADV electronically through the IARD, operated by NASDR,[101] unless the applicant

---

96. Advisers Act Release No. 1633 (May 15, 1987), 62 F.R. 28,112 (May 22, 1997); 17 C.F.R. § 275.222-1.

97. *See* Chapter 12, *infra.*

98. *See, e.g.,* California Code of Reg., § 260.237.2.

99. Advisers Act § 206, 15 U.S.C. § 80b-6; *see also SEC v. Capital Gains Research Bureau, Inc.,* 375 U.S. 180 (1963).

100. *See, e.g.,* California Code of Reg., § 260.238.

101. Advisers Act Rule 203-1, 17 C.F.R. § 275.203-1. Additional information about filing on the IARD can be obtained at the IARD website, www.iard.com, and at the SEC website, www.sec.gov/iard.

receives a temporary or continuing hardship exemption.[102] The SEC recently further amended Part 1A and Schedule D of Form ADV.[103]

The SEC purportedly has also been considering, since April 2000, a proposal to amend Part II of Form ADV.[104] Although an SEC–registered investment adviser is not yet required to file Part II with the SEC, the investment adviser must complete Part II when it files its application on Part 1A of the new Form ADV and must maintain a current copy of Part II (and any brochure the investment adviser delivers to clients) in its files, which is deemed to be filed with the SEC.[105] The investment adviser must deliver a copy of Part II (or the brochure) to each of its clients at least forty-eight hours before entering into any advisory contract, or at the time of entering into the contract if the client has the right to terminate the contract without penalty within five business days after entering into the contract.[106] An investment adviser should also furnish a copy of Part II (or the brochure) to each prospective investor in a hedge fund that the investment adviser manages.[107]

Form ADV includes substantial disclosure, such as disciplinary information, background information about portfolio managers and controlling persons, fees charged, brokerage allocation practices and other aspects of an investment adviser's business. The Advisers Act does not require an investment adviser or its associated persons to pass any exam or otherwise demonstrate competence to become SEC registered. It does, however, disqualify individuals from registering with the SEC as investment advisers or serving as associated persons of investment advisers if they have been convicted of crimes, violated federal or state securities laws or filed false or misleading statements with the SEC.[108]

---

102. Advisers Act Rule 203-1(b), 17 C.F.R. § 275.203-1(b). An applicant may request a temporary hardship exemption when it experiences unanticipated technical difficulties that prevent it from filing on the IARD system, but the applicant nevertheless must file Part 1 of Form ADV electronically within seven business days after the filing is due. Advisers Act Rule 203-3(a), 17 C.F.R. § 203-3(a). A continuing hardship exemption permits the applicant to submit its Form ADV to NASDR on paper. Advisers Act Rule 203-3(b), 17 C.F.R. § 275.203(3)(b). The continuing hardship exemption is available only to small businesses that are able to demonstrate that the electronic filing requirements are prohibitively burdensome or expensive. *Id.* A "small business" for purposes of this exemption is a business that (a) had total assets of less than $5,000,000 on the last day of its most recent fiscal year, (b) is not in control of, controlled by or under common control with another person (other than a natural person) that had total assets of $5,000,000 or more on the last day of that person's most recent fiscal year and (c) is not in control of, controlled by or under common control with another adviser that had assets under management of $25,000,000 or more on the last day of that adviser's most recent fiscal year. Advisers Act Rule 203-3(b)(5), 17 C.F.R. § 275.203-3(b)(5); Form ADV, Item 12, 17 C.F.R. § 279.1.

103. Release 2333; *see* § 2.1.2.iv, *supra.*

104. Advisers Act Release No. 1862 (Apr. 5, 2000), 65 F.R. 20,524 (Apr. 17, 2000).

105. Advisers Act Rule 203-1(b), 17 C.F.R. § 275.203-1(b).

106. Advisers Act Rule 204-3, 17 C.F.R. § 275.204-3.

107. Electronic Filing by Investment Advisers; Proposed Amendments to Form ADV, Exchange Act Release No. 42620 (Apr. 15, 2000), 65 F.R. 20,524 (Apr. 5, 2000). Although Rule 203(b)(3)-1(a)(2) permits an adviser to treat a partnership as a single client under certain conditions, the adviser cannot do so with respect to its brochure delivery requirements. The SEC has noted that such an interpretation would mean that an adviser need only deliver the brochure to the general partner, that is, itself. This position results, for all practical purposes, in the delivery of no brochure and is inconsistent with the remedial purposes of the rule. *Id.* The SEC has proposed amendments to the instructions to Form ADV, clarifying that an investment adviser acting as the general partner for a limited partnership must provide a brochure to each limited partner. *Id.* at n. 117.

108. Advisers Act § 203, 15 U.S.C. § 80b-3.

2. State Laws

State-registered investment advisers filing through the IARD ordinarily complete the same forms as SEC-registered investment advisers. Some states, however, require an investment adviser to file Part II of its Form ADV, whereas the SEC requires an investment adviser merely to keep a copy of Part II in its files and to make it available to prospective investors and the SEC. Application for state registration or licensing typically includes, in addition to filing Form ADV:

- Providing required state-specific forms and evidence of compliance with any examination requirements for investment adviser representatives;
- Filing a Form U-4 application for each investment adviser representative who will provide services on behalf of the investment adviser; and
- Paying registration fees for the investment adviser and its investment adviser representatives.

Some states allow or require an investment adviser registering with them to file Form ADV and Forms U-4 electronically via the IARD. An SEC-registered investment adviser generally makes a state notice filing by:

- Filing a complete copy of its Form ADV as filed with the SEC;
- Filing a Form U-4 application for each investment adviser representative who will provide services on behalf of the investment adviser; and
- Paying filing fees.

An SEC-registered investment adviser must make any required state notice filings electronically via the IARD, rather than on paper.

§ 2.5 Reporting Requirements and Annual Fees

An investment adviser must update its Form ADV when certain changes occur and at least annually.

1. Federal

An SEC-registered investment adviser must:

- Offer to provide Part II of the investment adviser's Form ADV or a brochure containing equivalent information at least annually to each advisory client.[109] The offer should also be made to each investor in a hedge fund that the investment adviser manages. The offer can conveniently be made

---

109. Advisers Act Rule 204-3, 17 C.F.R. § 275.204-3.

by including a sentence to that effect in an individual account client's first quarter bill or in a letter to hedge fund investors reporting the preceding year's results.

- Promptly amend its Form ADV if any information provided in response to Item 1, 3, 9 or 11 of Part 1A of its Form ADV or Item 1, 2.A through 2.F or 2.I of Part 1B of its Form ADV becomes inaccurate in any way, or any information provided in response to Item 4, 8 or 10 of Part 1A of its Form ADV or Item 2.G of Part 1B of its Form ADV becomes materially inaccurate.[110]
- Amend its Form ADV within ninety days of the end of the investment adviser's fiscal year.[111]
- Promptly amend Part II of its Form ADV if any information in Part II becomes materially inaccurate.[112]

The investment adviser must make amendments to Part 1A or Part 1B of Form ADV electronically using the IARD system. Amendments to Part II must be maintained in the investment adviser's files.

2. States

States may also require annual renewals, amendments and fee payments. For example, California and New York require an investment adviser to pay an annual fee, amend its Form ADV within ninety days of the investment adviser's fiscal year end and file an amendment within thirty days after a change occurs.[113]

3. Surprise Inspection by Accountant

If an investment adviser has custody of any of its clients' funds or securities,[114] federal and some states' rules may require the investment adviser's independent accountant to conduct annually a surprise inspection of the investment adviser to verify the funds and securities held by the investment adviser in accounts within its custody. The accountant must file a report of such inspection on Form ADV-E[115] with the SEC or the appropriate state regulatory authority.[116]

4. Filings Required under the Exchange Act

If an investment adviser, its control persons or its discretionary clients acquire security positions of a certain size, they may be required to report such positions to the SEC, and possibly also to the issuer and the exchange on which the securities are listed.[117]

---

110. Advisers Act Rule 204-1(a), 17 C.F.R. § 275.204-1(a). *See also* Instructions to Form ADV, 17 C.F.R. § 279.1.
111. Advisers Act Rule 204-1(a), 17 C.F.R. § 275.204-1(a).
112. Instructions to Form ADV, 17 C.F.R. § 279.1.
113. California Code of Reg., § 260.231(b); 13 New York CRR 11.4(f).
114. *See* Chapter 12, *infra*.
115. 17 C.F.R. § 279.8.
116. Advisers Act Rule 206(4)-2, 17 C.F.R. § 275.206(4)-2; Title 10, California Code of Reg., § 260.237.
117. *See,* § 13.1, *infra*.

§ 2.6 Disclosure of Financial and Disciplinary Information

Federal and State anti-fraud laws apply to hedge fund managers and other investment advisers whether or not registered with the SEC or in any state.[118] Anti-fraud provisions of the Advisers Act and some state laws obligate an investment adviser to disclose facts relating to legal or disciplinary events that occurred within the preceding ten years and that are material to an evaluation of the investment adviser's integrity or its ability to meet its contractual commitments.[119] If an investment adviser has discretionary authority over client accounts, has custody or control of clients' funds or securities, or requires payment of fees of more than $500 six months or more in advance, it must also disclose to any client or prospective client all material facts about its financial condition that are likely to impair its ability to meet its contractual commitments to its clients.[120] These matters must be disclosed to existing clients promptly and to potential clients at least forty-eight hours before entering into an advisory contract. The investment adviser may delay disclosure to a prospective client until the contract is signed if the client has a right to terminate the contract, without penalty, within five business days after entering into the contract.[121]

§ 2.7 Fiduciary Duties; Policies and Procedures

1. General Duty

The federal fiduciary duty requirements apply to all investment advisers, whether or not registered with the SEC or in any state. An investment adviser has a fiduciary duty to act in the best interests of its clients, to put its clients' interests before its own interests and to deal fairly with its clients in all respects. An investment adviser's fiduciary duties under federal law include, among other things:

- Having a reasonable, independent basis for its investment advice;[122]

---

118.   *See, e.g.,* Advisers Act Release No. 2203, 2003 SEC LEXIS 2958 (Dec. 15, 2003).
119.   Advisers Act Rule 206(4)-4, 17 C.F.R. § 275.206(4)-4(c); *see, e.g.,* Title 10, California Code of Reg., § 260.235.4.
120.   *Id.*
121.   Advisers Act Rule 206(4)-4(c), 17 C.F.R. § 275.206(4)-4(c); *see, e.g.,* Title 10, California Code of Reg., § 260.235.4(c).
122.   Advisers Act Release No. 897, 1984 SEC LEXIS 2429 (Jan. 11, 1984); Advisers Act Release No. 1689 1997 SEC LEXIS 2628 (Dec. 23, 1997).

- Obtaining best execution for client securities transactions if the investment adviser determines or recommends the broker used;[123] and
- Being loyal to clients.[124]

An investment adviser has a duty to provide advice that is suitable for the client based on the investment adviser's knowledge of the client, and the investment adviser is obligated to inquire about the client's investment objectives, financial situation and needs.[125] An investment adviser may not exceed the authority the client grants it.[126] An investment adviser should not cause trading in a client's account that is excessive in magnitude and frequency in view of the financial resources, investment objectives and other characteristics of the client.[127]

States may impose additional duties on investment advisers registered under state laws.[128] For example, a California-registered investment adviser may not (a) borrow money or securities from a client unless the client is a broker-dealer, an affiliate of the investment adviser or a financial institution engaged in the business of lending funds or securities,[129] (b) lend money to a client unless the investment adviser is a financial institution engaged in a lending business or the client is an affiliate of the investment adviser,[130] or (c) provide a report or recommendation to any client prepared by someone other than the investment adviser without disclosing this fact (although this prohibition does not apply if the investment adviser uses published research reports or statistical analyses to render advice or if the investment adviser orders such reports in the normal course of providing service).[131]

The SEC has proposed Advisers Act Rule 206(4)-5 that would make express the fiduciary obligation of an investment adviser to make only suitable recommendations to its client, after a reasonable inquiry into the client's financial situation, investment experience and investment objectives.[132] The SEC has also proposed Advisers Act Rule 206(4)-6, which would prohibit an SEC-registered investment adviser from exercising investment discretion with respect to client accounts, unless the investment adviser has a reasonable belief that the custodians of those accounts send account statements to the clients at least quarterly.[133] Neither of these proposed rules has yet been adopted.[134]

Investment advisers to investment companies are subject to additional fiduciary duties under the Company Act, but those duties are not addressed in this book.

---

123. *See* § 14.1, *infra*.

124. Advisers Act Release No. 40, 11 F.R. 10,997 (Feb. 5, 1945); Advisers Act Release No. 232, 43 S.E.C. 911 (Oct. 16, 1968).

125. *In re John G. Kinnard & Co., Inc.*, SEC No Action Letter (Nov. 30, 1973); *see, e.g.*, Title 10, California Code of Reg., § 260.238(a).

126. *See, e.g.*, Title 10, California Code of Reg., §§ 260.238(b), (c) and (d).

127. *See, e.g.*, Title 10, California Code of Reg., § 260.238(e).

128. *See, e.g.*, California Corporations Code § 25235; New York General Business Law § 352-c.

129. *See, e.g.*, Title 10, California Code of Reg., § 260.238(f).

130. *See, e.g.*, Title 10, California Code of Reg., § 260.238(g).

131. *See, e.g.*, Title 10, California Code of Reg., § 260.238(i).

132. Advisers Act Release No. 1406, 59 F.R. 13,464 (Mar. 16, 1994).

133. *Id.*

134. On May 3, 2001, the Office of Chief Counsel for the Division of Investment Management stated that although proposed Rule 206(4)-5 has not been adopted, the SEC's position on suitability is consistent with proposed Rule 206(4)-5. The Office of Chief Counsel also confirmed that proposed Rule 206(4)-6 had neither been adopted nor withdrawn. *See also, MLC Limited*, SEC No Action Letter (July 21, 1997).

2. ERISA

Investment advisers to ERISA Plans and to hedge funds whose assets constitute "plan assets" owe fiduciary duties to such plans and hedge funds.[135]

3. Compliance Programs for SEC-Registered Investment Advisers

Since October 2004, every SEC-registered investment adviser has been required to (a) adopt and implement written policies and procedures reasonably designed to prevent violations of the federal securities laws, (b) review those policies and procedures annually, and (c) designate a chief compliance officer to administer the policies and procedures.[136] Failure to adopt and implement adequate compliance policies and procedures is by itself unlawful, independent of any other securities law violation.[137]

Under this rule, an SEC-registered investment adviser must adopt and implement written policies and procedures reasonably designed to prevent violation of the Advisers Act by the investment adviser or any of its supervised persons. In preparing these policies and procedures, an investment adviser should identify conflicts and other compliance factors that create risk exposure for the investment adviser and its clients in light of its operations and design the policies and procedures to address those risks. At a minimum, the policies and procedures should address the following issues, to the extent applicable to the investment adviser:

- Portfolio management processes, including allocation of investment opportunities among clients and consistency of portfolios with clients' investment objectives, disclosures by the investment adviser and applicable regulatory restrictions;
- Trading practices, including procedures by which the investment adviser satisfies its best execution obligation, uses client brokerage to obtain research and other services (so-called "soft dollar arrangements"), and allocates aggregated trades among clients;
- Proprietary trading by the investment adviser and personal trading activities of its supervised persons;
- The accuracy of disclosures made to investors, clients and regulatory authorities, including account statements, advertisements and published prior performance;
- Safeguarding of client assets from conversion or inappropriate use by investment advisory personnel;
- The accurate creation of required records and their maintenance in a manner that secures them from unauthorized alteration or use and protects them from untimely destruction;

---

135. *See* Chapter 11, *infra*.
136. Advisers Act Rule 206(4)-7, 17 C.F.R. § 275.206(4)-7.
137. *Id.*

- Marketing practices, including the use of solicitors;
- Procedures to value client holdings and assess fees based on those valuations;
- Safeguards to protect the privacy of client records and information; and
- Business continuity plans to protect client interests if the investment adviser becomes unable to provide advisory services (for example, after a natural disaster).

This list is not exhaustive and does not include matters required by other laws and rules to be addressed in written policies and procedures, such as insider trading, privacy, anti-money laundering and proxy voting.[138]

Each investment adviser is required to review its policies and procedures annually to determine their adequacy and effectiveness. The review should consider any compliance matters that arose during the previous year, any changes in the business activities of the investment adviser or its affiliates and any changes in the Advisers Act or applicable regulations. Investment advisers also should consider interim reviews in response to significant compliance events, changes in business arrangements and regulatory developments.

Each investment adviser is required to designate a chief compliance officer to administer its policies and procedures. The chief compliance officer should be competent and knowledgeable regarding the Advisers Act and should have full responsibility and authority to develop and enforce appropriate policies and procedures.

Investment advisers are required to maintain copies of all policies and procedures in effect during the previous five years. Investment advisers also are required to keep records documenting the annual review. Investment advisers may maintain these records electronically.

4. Code of Ethics

The SEC recently adopted new Advisers Act Rule 204A-1[139] and related amendments to Advisers Act Rule 204-2[140] and Form ADV that require SEC-registered investment advisers to adopt and enforce codes of ethics applicable to their supervised persons.[141] These new rules are intended to prevent fraud by reinforcing the fiduciary principles that govern the conduct of investment advisory firms and their personnel. An investment adviser's code of ethics must, at a minimum:

- Establish standards of conduct that are expected of the investment adviser's supervised persons and that reflect the investment adviser's fiduciary duties. Supervised persons are required to acknowledge, in writing, receipt of a copy of the code of ethics and any amendments.
- Require the investment adviser's supervised persons to comply with applicable federal securities laws.

---

138. Advisers Act Release No. 2204, 68 F.R. 74,214 (Dec. 13, 2003). *See* §§ 2.7.4–2.7.8, *infra*.

139. 17 C.F.R. § 275.204A-1.

140. 17 C.F.R. § 275.204-2.

141. Advisers Act Release No. 2256, 69 F.R. 41,696 (July 9, 2004). Compliance with the new rules was required as of January 7, 2005.

- Require certain supervised persons, called "access persons," to report their personal securities holdings and transactions, including transactions in mutual funds advised by the investment adviser or an affiliate.
- Require access persons to pre-clear any personal investments in initial public offerings and limited offerings.
- Require supervised persons to report, promptly, any violations of the investment adviser's code of ethics to the investment adviser's chief compliance officer or to other designated persons.

5. Insider Trading

An SEC-registered investment adviser must (and every investment adviser should) establish, maintain and enforce written policies and procedures that are reasonably designed, taking into consideration the nature of the investment adviser's business, to prevent insider trading and the misuse of material, nonpublic information by the investment adviser or any person associated with the investment adviser.[142]

6. Privacy

The Gramm-Leach-Bliley Act (the "GLBA")[143] requires the SEC and the FTC to enact rules establishing appropriate standards for investment advisers and investment limited partnerships to (a) insure the security and confidentiality of their customer records and information, (b) protect against any anticipated threats or hazards to the security or integrity of such records, and (c) protect against unauthorized access to or use of such records or information that could result in substantial harm or inconvenience to any customer.[144] The SEC's rules apply only to SEC-registered investment advisers; the FTC's rules apply to state-registered and unregistered investment advisers.

Under both sets of rules, investment advisers are required to adopt policies and procedures to protect the privacy of the personal information about their "customers" and to provide their customers with initial and annual privacy notices describing their policies and procedures for collecting and disclosing nonpublic personal information.[145] "Customer" generally includes any individual who obtains financial services for personal, family or household purposes.

Under Regulation S-P adopted by the SEC, SEC-registered investment advisers must adopt policies and procedures that address administrative, technical, and physical safeguards for the protection of customer records and information. These policies and procedures must be reasonably designed to:

---

142.   Advisers Act § 204A, 15 U.S.C. § 80b-4A; Advisers Act Rule 204A-1, 17 C.F.R. § 275.204A-1. *See* § 13.7, *infra.*

143.   15 U.S.C. §§ 6801-6831.

144.   15 U.S.C. § 6801(b).

145.   17 C.F.R. §§ 248.4, 248.5; 16 C.F.R. § 313.6(a)(8).

- Insure the security and confidentiality of customer records and information;
- Protect against any anticipated threats or hazards to the security or integrity of customer records and information; and
- Protect against unauthorized access to or use of customer records or information that could result in substantial harm or inconvenience to any customer.[146]

Under the FTC's rules, state registered and unregistered investment advisers must "develop, implement and maintain a comprehensive information security program that is written in one or more readily accessible parts." Such investment advisers must:

- Designate an employee or employees to coordinate the program;
- Identify reasonably foreseeable internal and external risks to the security, confidentiality and integrity of customer information and assess the sufficiency of any safeguards in place to control these risks;
- Design and implement information safeguards to control the risks and regularly test or otherwise monitor the effectiveness of the safeguards;
- Oversee service providers; and
- Evaluate and adjust their information security program in light of the results of testing and monitoring.

A CTA or CPO[147] that is registered with the SEC as an investment adviser or securities broker may comply with the privacy regulations by complying with Regulation S-P promulgated by the SEC.[148] Similarly, a CTA or CPO that is registered or required to be registered with the state in which it maintains its principal office and place of business may comply with the privacy regulations by complying with similar regulations adopted by the FTC.[149] Otherwise, CTAs and CPOs must comply with the CFTC's privacy rules. The CFTC's privacy regulations require every CTA and CPO to:

- Provide an initial notice to each of its customers disclosing the types of non-public personal information the CTA or CPO collects and the extent to which such information may be disclosed;[150]
- Provide an annual notice to its existing customers;[151]
- Amend (if necessary) any existing agreements with non-affiliated parties under which the CTA or CPO discloses non-public personal information about customers, to require the non-affiliated parties to protect the confidentiality of customers' non-public personal information, and include the same protections in new agreements;[152]

---

146. 17 C.F.R. § 248.30.
147. *See* § 2.9, *infra.*
148. SEC Privacy of Consumer Financial Information Rule 248, 17 C.F.R. § 248.
149. FTC Privacy of Consumer Financial Information Rule 313, 16 C.F.R. § 313.
150. 17 C.F.R. §§ 160.4 and 160.6.
151. 17 C.F.R. § 160.5.
152. 17 C.F.R. §§ 160.13(a)(ii), 160.18(c).

- Establish policies and procedures to protect the confidentiality of customer records;[153] and
- On an ongoing basis, determine whether disclosure to non-affiliated third parties of non-public personal information about customers or individuals who have applied to be customers triggers other requirements of the privacy regulations.

7. Anti-Money Laundering

The Financial Crimes Enforcement Network (FinCEN) of the U.S. Treasury Department released proposed rules on April 29, 2003, that would require registered and certain unregistered investment advisers to establish anti-money laundering programs pursuant to section 352 of the ironically named Uniting and Strengthening America by Providing Appropriate Tools Required to Intercept and Obstruct Terrorism Act (the USA PATRIOT Act). The proposed rules would require investment advisers to:

- Establish and implement policies, procedures and internal controls reasonably designed to detect and prevent money laundering and terrorist financing;
- Provide for independent testing for compliance;
- Designate a person or persons responsible for implementing and monitoring the investment adviser's anti-money laundering program; and
- Provide for ongoing employee training.[154]

8. Proxy Voting

i. SEC Registered Investment Advisers

An SEC-registered investment adviser with voting authority over its clients' securities must:

- Establish a written policy reasonably designed to ensure that the investment adviser votes client securities in the best interests of clients. The policy must describe how the investment adviser addresses material conflicts that may arise between its interests and its clients' interests. An investment adviser's policy should be tailored to suit its particular situation. An investment adviser may include its policy in Schedule F of its Form ADV, or maintain it in a separate document.
- Disclose to clients (for example, in Schedule F of Form ADV) how they may obtain information about how the investment adviser voted proxies.
- Describe its policy to clients (again, in Schedule F) and furnish the policy to any client on request.

---

153.   17 C.F.R. § 160.30
154.   68 F.R. 23,649-51 (May 5, 2003); *see* § 2.10, *infra.*

- Keep records of votes the investment adviser casts on behalf of its clients and copies of (a) its policy, (b) each proxy statement it receives regarding its clients' securities, (c) any document that is material to the investment adviser's decision on how to vote a proxy or that describes the basis for that decision and (d) each written client request for information about how the investment adviser voted proxies and each written response by the investment adviser to such a client request (written or oral). An investment adviser may rely on a third party (such as a broker) to keep voting records and copies of proxy statements, or may rely on obtaining those copies through the SEC's EDGAR system.

An investment adviser with no voting authority over any of its clients' securities is not required to comply with these rules. An investment adviser that desires not to have voting authority should expressly provide in its investment management agreements that the clients reserve all voting rights with respect to their securities, and should forward all proxy statements to the clients. An investment adviser that is the general partner of a hedge fund cannot avoid proxy voting authority, because the investment adviser, as general partner, controls the "client."

ii. State-Registered Investment Advisers

Although the foregoing proxy voting policy rules apply only to SEC-registered investment advisers, some states may require investment advisers registered or doing business there to comply with record-keeping and other rules that are the same as or similar to those for SEC-registered investment advisers, including rules relating to proxy voting policies. An investment adviser in any such state must adopt such a policy and maintain the required records, even if the investment adviser is not registered with the SEC.

iii. NASD and Stock Exchange Requirements

A broker that is an NASD member is required to forward proxy solicitation and certain other materials to the beneficial owner of securities held in the broker's name, if that owner requests and gives the broker satisfactory assurance that it will reimburse the broker for the cost of forwarding.[155] The broker must include a letter with proxy solicitation materials noting the time limit for completing and returning the proxy. An NASD member may vote proxies where it holds the stock as executor, administrator, guardian, trustee or in a representative or fiduciary capacity with authority to vote. An NASD member designated by a named ERISA plan fiduciary as the investment manager of stock held as assets of the ERISA plan may vote the proxies in accordance with the ERISA plan fiduciary responsibilities if the ERISA plan expressly grants discretion to the investment manager to manage, acquire or dispose of any plan asset, and has not

---

155. NASD Conduct Rule 2260, "Forwarding of Proxy and Other Materials."

expressly reserved the proxy voting right for the named ERISA plan fiduciary.[156] Any designated investment adviser may also vote such proxies.

A broker that is a member of the NYSE may not give or authorize giving a proxy to vote securities registered in its name or the name of its nominee, unless the broker beneficially owns the securities.[157] Such a broker, however, that has been designated by a named fiduciary as the investment manager of securities held as assets of an ERISA Plan that expressly grants discretion to the investment manager to manage, acquire or dispose of any plan asset and that has not expressly reserved the proxy voting right for the named fiduciary, may vote the proxies in accordance with its ERISA Plan fiduciary responsibilities.[158] Similarly, an NYSE member that is also an SEC-registered investment adviser, that exercises investment discretion pursuant to an advisory contract for the beneficial owner, and that has been designated in writing by the beneficial owner to vote proxies for securities in the member's possession or control, may vote such proxies.[159]

If a person soliciting proxies furnishes the NYSE member with copies of soliciting material and satisfactory assurance that he will reimburse the member for out-of-pocket expenses, the member must forward the soliciting material to the beneficial owner or the beneficial owner's "designated investment adviser,"[160] along with (a) a request for voting instructions (and, for matters that may be voted without instructions, an explanation of what happens if instructions are not received)[161] or (b) a signed proxy indicating the number of shares held for such beneficial owner and bearing a symbol identifying the proxy records of the member, and a letter explaining the necessity for completing the proxy form and forwarding it to the person soliciting proxies so the shares may be represented at the meeting.[162] A member may not vote with respect to equity compensation plans unless the beneficial owner has given voting instructions.[163]

The relevant American Stock Exchange rules are similar to those of the NYSE.[164]

---

156. *See also* Chapter 11, *infra.*
157. NYSE Rules 450-460.
158. NYSE Rule 450(1); *see also* Chapter 11, *infra.*
159. NYSE Rule 450(2).
160. A designated investment adviser is an SEC-registered investment adviser that exercises investment discretion pursuant to an advisory contract for the beneficial owner and has been designated in writing by the beneficial owner. NYSE Rule 451(a).
161. NYSE Rule 451(b)(1). Specifically, as to matters that may be voted without instructions under NYSE Rule 452, the member must state that, if instructions are not received ten days before the meeting, the member may vote the proxy. Such a statement may only be made, however, if the material has been forwarded at least fifteen days before the meeting.
162. NYSE Rule 451(b)(2).
163. NYSE Rule 452.
164. American Stock Exchange Rules 575-577.

§ 2.8 Books and Records Requirements under the Advisers Act

1. General Rule

Under Advisers Act Rule 204-2,[165] an SEC-registered investment adviser is required to keep the following records in an easily accessible place for five years from the end of the fiscal year in which the last entry in such record was made or, in the case of communications and notices, for five years after dissemination of the materials (for the first two of the five years, these records must be kept in the investment adviser's office):

- Copies of all written agreements entered into with any client or otherwise relating to the investment adviser's business;
- Investment management agreements, powers of attorney and other grants of discretionary authority by a client to the investment adviser;
- A list of all accounts over which the investment adviser has any discretionary authority with respect to any client;
- General and auxiliary ledgers or comparable records reflecting the investment adviser's assets, liabilities, reserves, capital, income and expense accounts;
- A journal or journals, including cash receipts and disbursement records and any other records of original entry, forming the basis for entries in any ledger of the investment adviser;
- The investment adviser's check books, bank statements, cancelled checks and cash reconciliations;
- Copies of bills and statements (paid and unpaid) relating to the business of the investment adviser;
- The investment adviser's trial balances, financial statements and internal audit working papers;
- Copies of all written communications sent by the investment adviser and originals of written communications received by the investment adviser concerning: recommendations made or proposed to be made by the investment adviser and advice given or proposed to be given; receipt, disbursement or delivery of funds or securities; and placing or execution of buy/sell orders;
- Records of every transaction in a security in which the investment adviser or an "advisory representative"[166] has or acquires direct or indirect beneficial ownership (such records must state titles and amounts of securities, dates

---

165. 17 C.F.R. § 275.204-2.

166. An advisory representative is any officer or director of the investment adviser, any employee of the investment adviser who makes investment recommendations, participates in determining recommendations or obtains information about the investment adviser's recommendations before they are disseminated, and any control person of the investment adviser and that person's affiliates who obtain information about the investment adviser's recommendations before they are disseminated. 17 C.F.R. § 275.204-2(a)(12)(iii)(A).

and nature of transactions, and prices and names of brokers, and copies of account statements or brokers' confirmations containing this data will suffice; excluded from this requirement, however, are transactions in shares of open-end mutual funds, cash equivalents and direct obligations of the United States and transactions for accounts over which the investment adviser and its advisory representatives have no direct or indirect influence or control);[167]

- Copies of Part II of the investment adviser's Form ADV provided to clients and prospective clients in accordance with Advisers Act Rule 204-3,[168] and records of the dates such document was given or offered to each client, or any prospective client that subsequently became a client;

- Written acknowledgements of receipt by clients of disclosure statements delivered to clients by solicitors engaged by the investment adviser (as required under the Advisers Act),[169] and copies of such disclosure statements;

- Current records with respect to each client account showing the securities purchased and sold for that client and the date, amount and price of each purchase or sale;

- Memoranda of each purchase and sale order by the investment adviser and of any instructions from a client concerning the purchase, sale, receipt or delivery of a particular security, and of any modification or cancellation of such order or instruction (such memoranda should show the terms and conditions of the order, identify the person connected with the investment adviser who recommended the transaction and placed the order, and show the account for which the order was placed, the date and the broker that executed the order; orders entered pursuant to the exercise of discretionary power should be so designated);

- The articles of incorporation and bylaws, minute books, stock certificate records and other corporate filings of the investment adviser, and all amendments to them (until at least three years after the investment adviser's business terminates);

- Each notice, circular, advertisement, newspaper article, bulletin, investment letter or other communication the investment adviser distributes to ten or more persons (if such communication recommends the purchase or sale of a security without stating the reasons for it, the investment adviser must also keep a memorandum stating the reasons for the recommendation); and

- Performance data or rate of return of all managed accounts or securities recommendations shown in any communication distributed to ten or more persons (with respect to managed accounts, account statements reflecting all debits, credits and other transactions in the accounts and worksheets calculating performance are sufficient);[170]

- A copy of the investment adviser's code of ethics adopted pursuant to Advisers Act Rule 204A-1,[171] records of violations of the code of ethics and resulting

---

167. *LNC Equity Sales Corp.,* SEC No-Action Letter (Aug. 8, 1997).
168. 17 C.F.R. § 275.204-3.
169. *See* Advisers Act Rule 206(4)-3, 17 C.F.R. § 275.206(4)-3, and §§ 8.4.5 and 10.1.3, *infra.*
170. *See* § 2.1.2.iv, *supra,* and § 8.4 and Chapter 17, *infra.*
171. 17 C.F.R. § 275.204A-1. *See* § 2.7.4, *supra.*

action taken, copies of acknowledgements of receipt of the code of ethics by supervised persons and related records; and

- Records of access person reports, the names of access persons and decisions regarding their trading.[172]

At all times, the investment adviser also must maintain current information with respect to each security in which any client has a current position, from which the investment adviser can promptly furnish the name of each such client and the current amount or interest of such client.

The documents used to organize a hedge fund and solicit investments in the hedge fund are within the scope of Advisers Act Rule 204-2. The hedge fund's offering circular, agreement of limited partnership or other charter documents, subscription agreements, offering questionnaires and other documents (discussed in Chapters 4, 5 and 6) constitute records subject to the rule.[173]

2. Custody

An investment adviser that has custody of any client funds or securities must retain additional records.[174]

3. Past Performance Records

If the investment adviser furnishes past performance data to its clients, it must retain the records listed above in section 2.8.1 with respect to that performance data. As noted above, for managed account performance data, it is sufficient if the investment adviser retains copies of account statements (reflecting all debits, credits and other transactions in the accounts) and worksheets calculating the performance.[175]

4. Storage Media; Electronic Records

All of the foregoing records may be maintained on paper, micrographic or electronic media. Advisors Act Rule 204-2(g)[176] governs electronic recordkeeping. If the investment adviser keeps the required records in electronic format, it must:

- Arrange and index the records in a way that permits easy location, access and retrieval of any particular record;
- Provide promptly at the SEC's request (a) a copy of the records in the medium and format in which they are stored, (b) a printout of the records, and (c) means to access, view and print the records; and
- Separately store a duplicate copy of the records in an electronic, micrographic or paper medium.

---

172. *See* § 2.7.4, *supra.*
173. *See* § 8.4.7, *infra.*
174. *See* Advisers Act Rule 206(4)-2, 17 C.F.R. § 275.206(4)-2, and Chapter 12, *infra.*
175. *See* Chapter 17, *infra.*
176. 17 C.F.R. § 275.204-2(g).

The investment adviser must also establish and maintain procedures to (a) maintain and preserve the electronic records to reasonably safeguard them from loss, alteration or destruction, (b) limit access to the records to properly authorized personnel and the SEC, and (c) reasonably ensure that any reproduction of a non-electronic original record on an electronic storage medium is complete, true and legible when retrieved.

§ 2.9 Commodity Trading Activities

1. General

Securities markets and futures and commodity option markets are regulated under separate statutory schemes. The Commodity Exchange Act (the "CEA")[177] and the regulations promulgated thereunder (the "CEA Regulations")[178] govern the trading of futures and commodity option contracts and are administered by the Commodity Futures Trading Commission (the "CFTC").[179] The CFTC has delegated[180] significant authority and responsibilities to the National Futures Association (the "NFA"), the self-regulatory organization for the commodity futures trading business.

The CEA and the CEA Regulations regulate an investment adviser who trades futures contracts (including securities futures, such as single stock futures, and financial futures, such as S&P Index futures) or commodity options (including options on futures and options on certain commodities). The CEA and the CEA Regulations require any person that manages an investment portfolio for others and that trades or invests in any futures contracts or commodity options to register with the CFTC as a commodity trading adviser (a "CTA") or a commodity pool operator (a "CPO"), unless an exemption is available.[181] Historically, because only very limited exemptions were available, most advisers that engaged in even very limited futures or commodities trading were required to register with the CFTC. Exemptions from CFTC registration adopted in 2003, however, are now available for many investment advisers. The discussion below is based in part on formal and informal interpretations of the CEA and CEA Regulations by the CFTC and the NFA. These interpretations are not necessarily binding and might be modified by the CFTC, the NFA or their respective staffs.

---

177. 7 U.S.C. §§ 1, *et seq.*
178. 17 C.F.R. Ch. 1.
179. CEA § 2, 7 U.S.C. § 2.
180. *See, e.g.*, 62 F.R. 36,050 (July 3, 1997).
181. CEA §§ 6m and 6n, 7 U.S.C. §§ 6m and 6n.

2. Jurisdiction of the CFTC

Under the CEA, the CFTC has jurisdiction over trading of:

- Contracts for future delivery of commodities, securities and securities indices (collectively, "futures");
- Options to acquire futures and certain options to acquire commodities (collectively, "commodity options");
- Foreign currency futures and currency options traded on an organized exchange (except for currency options traded on a national securities exchange, which are not subject to CFTC jurisdiction); and[182]
- Foreign currency futures and currency options traded off-exchange (over-the-counter) between members of the retail public and unregulated entities.

The CFTC shares jurisdiction with the SEC over trading of contracts for the sale for future delivery of a single security or a narrow-based security index (collectively, "securities futures").[183] Futures and commodity options within the CFTC's jurisdiction are collectively called "commodity interests." Investment advisers and general partners of investment funds are generally subject to regulation under the CEA even if they trade only foreign commodity interests, if they do so on behalf of clients in the United States or its territories and possessions.[184]

The CEA and CFTC do not have jurisdiction over:

- Trading of options on securities and securities indices, over which the SEC has jurisdiction;[185]
- Off-exchange trading of foreign currency futures, foreign currency options and other "excluded commodities" (which include interest rates, exchange rates, security indices and other financial products and instruments) by "eligible contract participants" (which include certain regulated entities, such as registered brokers and futures commission merchants, and other persons and entities that meet certain net worth standards, such as commodity pools with more than $5,000,000 in assets);[186]
- The purchase of commodities for current delivery, in cash forward or spot transactions;
- Non-agricultural swap transactions between "eligible contract participants" that are subject to individual negotiation by the parties and are not executed on a trading facility;[187]
- Hybrid investments that are predominantly securities; or[188]

---

182. CEA §§ 2(a)(1)(A), 2(a)(1)(C)(ii) and 2(c), 7 U.S.C. §§ 2(a)(1)(A), 2(a)(1)(C)(ii) and 2(c).

183. CEA §§ 2(a)(1)(D)(i) and 1(a)(31), 7 U.S.C. §§ 2(a)(1)(D)(i) and 1(a)(31). The term "narrow-based security index" is defined in CEA § 1a(25), 7 U.S.C. § 1a(25).

184. CEA Reg. § 30.4, 17 C.F.R. § 30.4.

185. CEA §§ 2(a)(1)(C)(i) and 2(a)(1)(D)(i), 7 U.S.C. §§ 2(a)(1)(C)(i) and 2(a)(1)(D)(i).

186. CEA § 2(d), 7 U.S.C. § 2(d). The term "eligible contract participant" is defined at CEA § 1a12, 7 U.S.C. § 1a12. The term "excluded commodity" is defined at CEA § 1a13, 7 U.S.C. § 1a13.

187. CEA § 2(g), 7 U.S.C. § 2(g).

188. CEA § 2(f), 7 U.S.C. § 2(f).

- Off-exchange trading of "exempt commodities" (defined as commodities other than agricultural commodities and financial instruments, which leaves commodities such as metals and energy) between "eligible contract participants" (although various anti-fraud provisions of the CEA do apply to such transactions).[189]

3. Commodity Pool Operators

i. Definition

The CEA defines a CPO as:

> any person engaged in a business that is of the nature of an investment trust, syndicate, or similar form of enterprise, and who, in connection therewith, solicits, accepts, or receives from others, funds, securities, or property, either directly or through capital contributions, the sale of stock or other forms of securities, or otherwise, for the purpose of trading in any commodity for future delivery on or subject to the rules of any contract market or derivatives transaction execution facility, except that the term does not include such persons not within the intent of the definition of the term as the [CFTC] may specify by rule, regulation or order.[190]

The CFTC generally regards any pooled investment vehicle (whether organized as a trust, partnership, limited liability company, corporation or otherwise) as a commodity pool if it invests any assets in commodity interests.[191] Generally, CPOs include the trustees of a pool organized as a trust, the officers and directors of a pool organized as a corporation, the managers of a pool organized as a limited liability company, and the general partners of a pool organized as a partnership, if those persons make decisions about the pool's trading in commodity interests or solicit investors for the pool.

An investment adviser that acts as the portfolio manager of a hedge fund that invests in commodity interests is a CPO. The investment adviser of an offshore hedge fund usually is not within the above definition of a CPO because it generally has a more limited relationship with the offshore hedge fund, providing only investment management services pursuant to an investment management contract. The offshore hedge fund's directors and administrator generally operate the offshore hedge fund, including soliciting, accepting and receiving contributions from investors. Typically, however, neither the directors nor the administrator of an offshore hedge fund are willing or licensed to serve as the CPO. Because the CFTC takes the position that each pool must have at

---

189. CEA § 2(h)(1), 7 U.S.C. § 2(h)(1). The term "exempt commodity" is defined at CEA § 1a14, 7 U.S.C. § 1a14.

190. CEA § 1a(5), 7 U.S.C. § 1a(5).

191. CEA Reg. § 4.10(d), 17 C.F.R. § 4.10(d).

least one CPO, this generally leaves the investment adviser to serve as the CPO of an offshore hedge fund, unless a "sponsor" or some other entity managing the offshore hedge fund's operations is willing to be designated as its CPO.

A CPO is generally required to register with the CFTC,[192] unless it qualifies for an exemption from registration.

ii. Exclusions from CPO Definition

CEA Rule 4.5 excludes the following entities and their principals and employees (collectively, "Section 4.5 Accounts") from the definition of a CPO: investment companies registered under the Company Act; insurance companies, with respect to separate accounts they establish or maintain; banks, with respect to the assets of trusts, custodial accounts or other separate units for which they act as fiduciaries and are vested with investment authority; and trustees or named fiduciaries of plans subject to Title I of ERISA, with respect to such plans. A person or entity claiming this exclusion must file a notice of eligibility with the NFA before trading Commodity Interests for Section 4.5 Accounts, must furnish prospective participants in each Section 4.5 Account with written disclosure about the exclusion from the CPO definition, and must submit to any special calls for information that the CFTC requires to determine compliance with section 4.5.[193]

A CPO that relies on the section 4.5 exclusion with respect to some of its accounts may also qualify for an exemption from CPO registration (for example, under CEA Rule 4.13, as discussed below) with respect to pools or accounts that are not covered by section 4.5.[194]

iii. Exemptions from CPO Registration

a. Non-Compensated and Small Pool Operators

A CPO is exempt from CFTC registration if (a) it receives no direct or indirect compensation for operating a pool (other than reimbursement of ordinary administrative operating expenses), (b) it operates only one commodity pool at a time, (c) it is not otherwise required to register with the CFTC and is not affiliated with any person or entity required to register with the CFTC, and (d) no advertising occurs in connection with the pool.[195] For this purpose, "advertising" includes the systematic solicitation of prospective participants by telephone or seminar presentation.[196]

A person or entity is also exempt from CPO registration if the aggregate capital contributions to all of its pools do not exceed $400,000, and none of its pools has more than fifteen participants at any time (excluding each pool's CPO and CTA

---

192. CEA § 4m(1), 7 U.S.C. § 4m(1).
193. CEA Reg. § 4.5, 17 C.F.R. § 4.5.
194. CEA Reg. § 4.5(g), 17 C.F.R. § 4.5(g).
195. CEA Reg. § 4.13(a)(1), 17 C.F.R. § 4.13(a)(i).
196. CEA Reg. § 4.13(a)(1)(iv), 17 C.F.R. § 4.13(a)(1)(iv).

and their principals, any of those persons' children, siblings, parents and spouses, and those persons' spouses and relatives who live in the same residence).[197]

A CPO relying on either of the above exemptions must furnish participants in each of the pools with copies of the pool's monthly statements from the futures commission merchant that executes transactions in Commodity Interests for the pool, showing net profits and losses from transactions in Commodity Interests.[198]

b. Limited Trading Exemption

A 2003 amendment to the CEA Regulations exempts a CPO from CFTC registration (the "Limited Trading Exemption") with respect to any pool:[199]

- whose interests are exempt from registration under the Securities Act and are offered and sold without marketing to the public in the United States;
- that satisfies one of the following tests: either (1) the aggregate initial margin and premiums required to establish positions in Commodity Interests, measured when the most recent position was established, do not exceed five percent (excluding the in-the-money amounts of options that are in-the-money at the time of purchase) of the liquidation value of such pool (after taking into account unrealized profits and losses on such positions) or (2) the aggregate net notional value of the pool's Commodity Interest positions, measured when the most recent position was established, does not exceed the liquidation value of the pool's portfolio (after taking into account unrealized profits and losses on such positions);
- that is not marketed to the public as a commodity pool or as a vehicle for trading in commodity futures or commodity options markets; and
- in which participation is limited to (1) accredited investors, as defined in Securities Act Rule 501,[200] (2) trusts formed by accredited investors for the benefit of family members, (3) "knowledgeable employees" as defined in Company Act Rule 3c-5,[201] and (4) certain "qualified eligible persons" ("QEPs") as defined in CEA Rule 4.7(a)(2)(viii)(A)[202] (which includes only the pool's CPO, CTA, investment adviser, and certain of their employees, principals and family members).

The CFTC has promulgated special guidance regarding the application of the Limited Trading Exemption to funds-of-funds, describing alternative methods for imposing and calculating the trading limits at the investee fund level.[203]

---

197. CEA Reg. § 4.13(a)(2), 17 C.F.R. § 4.13(a)(2).
198. CEA Reg. § 4.13(c)(3), 17 C.F.R. § 4.13(c)(3).
199. CEA Reg. § 4.13(a)(3), 17 C.F.R. § 4.13(a)(3).
200. *See* § 5.3.2.ii, *infra.*
201. *See* §§ 3.2.2.iv and 3.3.2.xiii, *infra.*
202. 17 C.F.R. § 4.7(a)(2)(viii)(A).
203. CEA Reg., Appendix A. *See* § 2.9.3.iii.e, *infra.*

c. Sophisticated Participant Exemption

Another 2003 amendment to the CEA Regulations exempts a CPO from CFTC registration (the "Sophisticated Participant Exemption") with respect to any pool:[204]

- whose interests are exempt from registration under the Securities Act and are offered and sold without marketing to the public in the United States; and
- in which all investors that are individuals or self-directed employee benefit plans for individuals are Non-Portfolio Requirement QEPs,[205] and all investors that are entities are QEPs or accredited investors.[206]

d. Additional Conditions of Exemptions

A CPO that relies on any of the exemptions from CPO registration described in the preceding sections a, b and c must also file a notice of eligibility with the NFA prior to the date it delivers a subscription document for the pool to any prospective investor. The notice must include, among other things, representations that each eligible pool will be operated in accordance with the requirements of the applicable exemption.[207] The CPO must also provide specified disclosure to each prospective participant in a pool with respect to which the CPO is exempt from registration, describing the criteria of the exemption and noting that, unlike a registered CPO, it is not required to deliver a disclosure document or certified annual report, to pool participants.[208] The CPO must also retain specified records and submit to special calls by the CFTC.[209]

If a CPO operates pools that are eligible for the Limited Trading Exemption or the Sophisticated Participant Exemption, and also operates pools with respect to which it must register as a CPO, the CPO is required to register as a CPO, but is exempt from all other requirements imposed on a CPO under the CEA with respect to the eligible pools, except the anti-fraud and anti-manipulation provisions. Such a CPO must, however, furnish certain additional disclosures to participants in the exempt pools. If an existing pool operated by a CPO would qualify as an eligible pool but for the fact that the CPO has not filed the required notice, the CPO may convert the pool into an eligible pool by providing notice to all participants in the pool of the CPO's intention to convert the pool into an eligible pool and giving them the right to withdraw prior to such conversion. The CPO may then file a notice of eligibility with the CFTC.[210]

---

204.   CEA Reg. § 4.13(a)(4), 17 C.F.R. § 4.13(a)(4).
205.   *See* § 2.9.10.iii, *infra.*
206.   *See* § 5.3.2.ii, *infra.*
207.   CEA Reg. § 4.13(b), 17 C.F.R. § 4.13(b).
208.   CEA Reg. § 4.13(a)(5), 17 C.F.R. § 4.13(a)(5).
209.   CEA Reg. § 4.13(c), 17 C.F.R. § 4.13(c).
210.   CEA Reg. § 4.13(e)(2), 17 C.F.R. § 4.13(e)(2).

A CPO may claim one of the exemptions from CPO registration in CEA Rule 4.13(a)[211] and may also qualify for an exclusion from the CPO definition under CEA Rule 4.5 with respect to a different account.[212]

e. Funds-of-Funds

The CFTC recently added Appendix A to Part 4 of the CEA Regulations to clarify application of the Limited Trading Exemption in the fund-of-funds context. The Appendix lists six scenarios:

- If an investor fund CPO allocates its assets to one or more investee funds, none of which meets the trading limits of the Limited Trading Exemption and each of which is operated by a registered CPO, and does not allocate any of the investor fund's assets directly to commodity interest trading, the investor fund may claim relief under the Limited Trading Exemption if the investor fund itself meets the trading limits of that exemption.
- If an investor fund CPO allocates its assets to investee funds whose CPOs are either themselves claiming the Limited Trading Exemption or are registered CPOs complying with the trading restrictions of the Limited Trading Exemption, and if the investor fund CPO does not allocate any assets directly to commodity interest trading, the investor fund CPO may rely on the investee fund CPOs' representations that they comply with trading limits of the Limited Trading Exemption.
- If an investor fund CPO allocates its assets to investee funds, each of which operates under a percentage restriction on the amount of margin or option premiums that may be used to establish commodity interest positions (by contract, for example), and does not allocate any of the investor fund's assets directly to commodity interest trading, the investor fund CPO may multiply the percentage restriction applicable to each investee fund by the percentage of the investor fund's allocation of assets to that investee fund to determine whether the investor fund CPO complies with the trading restrictions of the Limited Trading Exemption.
- If an investor fund CPO allocates its assets to one or more investee funds and has actual knowledge of the investee funds' trading limits and commodity interest positions, and does not allocate assets directly to commodity interest trading, the investor fund CPO may aggregate commodity interest positions across investee funds to determine whether it complies with the trading restrictions of the Limited Trading Exemption.
- If an investor fund CPO allocates no more than fifty percent of its assets to investee funds that trade commodity interests (without regard to the level of commodity interest trading that those investee funds engage in) and does not allocate any of its assets directly to commodity interest trading, the investor fund CPO may claim relief under the Limited Trading Exemption.

---

211.   *See* §§ 2.9.3.iii.a–2.9.3.iii.c, *supra.*
212.   CEA Reg. § 4.13(f), 17 C.F.R. § 4.13(f). *See* § 2.9.3.ii, *supra.*

If an investor fund CPO allocates its assets both to investee funds and to direct trading of commodity interests, the investor fund CPO must treat the amount of investor fund assets committed to such direct trading as a separate pool for purposes of determining compliance with the Limited Trading Exemption, and the commodity interest trading of that pool must meet the criteria of the Limited Trading Exemption independently of the portion of investor fund assets allocated to investee funds.

4. Commodity Trading Advisers

i. Definition

In general, a CTA is any person or entity that engages for compensation in the business of giving advice about trading in commodity interests.[213] An investment adviser that desires to cause any of its clients to invest in any commodity interests should comply with the regulations applicable to CTAs. CTAs must comply with CEA rules on registration, disclosure, reporting, recordkeeping and fraudulent practices. A CTA generally must register with the CFTC, unless it qualifies for an exemption from registration.[214]

ii. Exclusions from CTA Definition

Any person or entity excluded from the definition of a CPO by section 4.5 of the CEA Regulations,[215] and any of its principals or employees, is also excluded from the definition of a CTA if its advice about commodity interests is solely incidental to its management of Section 4.5 Accounts, it files a notice of eligibility with the NFA to claim relief under section 4.5 with respect to its Section 4.5 Accounts before providing trading advice about commodity interests to its Section 4.5 Accounts, and it submits to the CFTC's special calls to demonstrate compliance with this exclusion.[216]

iii. Exemptions from CTA Registration

a. Private CTA Exemption

A CTA is exempt from CTA registration if during the preceding twelve months it has not furnished commodity trading advice to more than fifteen persons and it does not "hold [itself] out generally to the public" as a CTA.[217] For this purpose, a pool counts as a single person. In addition, a natural person, that person's minor children, spouse, relatives living in the same residence, and accounts and trusts

---

213.   CEA § 1a(6), 7 U.S.C. § 1a(6).
214.   CEA § 4m(1), 7 U.S.C. § 4m(1).
215.   *See* § 2.9.3, *supra.*
216.   CEA Reg. § 4.6(a)(2), 17 C.F.R. § 4.6(a)(2).
217.   CEA § 4m(1), 7 U.S.C. § 4m(1).

of which such persons are the only primary beneficiaries, collectively count as a single person.[218]

b. Registered Investment Adviser Exemption

Another exemption from CTA registration is available for a CTA that is registered as an investment adviser under the Advisers Act, whose business does not consist primarily of acting as a CTA, and that does not act as a CTA to any investment trust, syndicate or similar form of enterprise that is engaged primarily in trading Commodity Interests.[219] The CFTC has not offered guidance on how much a pool may invest in Commodity Interests before it is deemed to be "engaged primarily" in trading Commodity Interests.

Similarly, a CTA registered as such is exempt from registration as an investment adviser if its business does not consist primarily of acting as an investment adviser and it does not act as an investment adviser to an investment company registered under the Company Act or a business development company under the Company Act.[220]

c. Registered CPO Exemption

A person or entity that is registered as a CPO or exempt from CPO registration, and whose commodity trading advice is directed solely to the pools it operates, is exempt from registration as a CTA.[221] Thus, an investment adviser that registers as a CPO and confines its trading advice regarding Commodity Interests to U.S. and offshore hedge funds that it manages would not also be required to register as a CTA.

d. Section 4.14(a)(8) Exemption

A CTA that is registered as an investment adviser under the Advisers Act or state law, or that is exempt from registration as an investment adviser, or that is excluded from the definition of "investment adviser" under Advisers Act section 202(a)(2) or 202(a)(11)[222] (such as a securities broker or publisher), is exempt from registration as a CTA,[223] if:

- The adviser's trading advice regarding Commodity Interests is directly solely to: (1) Section 4.5 Accounts with respect to which a notice of eligibility has been filed; (2) certain ERISA plans defined in CEA Rule 4.5(a)(4);[224] (3) pools organized and operated offshore that were not so organized to enable their CPO to avoid registration, that are not marketed from within the United States or to U.S. persons, and that limit participation by U.S. persons to the pools' CPO, CTA and their principals, who may own in the aggregate

---

218.   CEA Reg. § 4.14(a)(10), 17 C.F.R. § 4.14(a)(10).
219.   CEA § 4m(3), 7 U.S.C. § 4m(3).
220.   Advisers Act § 203(b)(6), 15 U.S.C. § 80b-3(b)(6).
221.   CEA Reg. §§ 4.14(a)(4) and 4.14(a)(5), 17 C.F.R. §§ 4.14(a)(4) and 4.14(a)(5).
222.   15 U.S.C. 80b-2(a)(2) or 80b-2(a)(11).
223.   CEA Reg. § 4.14(a)(8), 17 C.F.R. § 4.14(a)(8).
224.   17 C.F.R. § 4.5(a)(4).

no more than ten percent of each such pool; and (4) pools whose CPO is relying on or is eligible to rely on the Limited Trading Exemption or the Sophisticated Participant Exemption from CPO registration;[225]

- The adviser's trading advice regarding Commodity Interests is solely incidental to its business of providing securities investment advice;
- The adviser does not otherwise hold itself out as a CTA;[226] and
- The adviser files a notice of exemption with the NFA.[227]

The adviser must also retain certain records and submit to special calls by the CFTC.[228]

e. Non-U.S. Accounts

In certain circumstances, a U.S. investment adviser that advises only non-U.S. clients (including offshore hedge funds) that are not directly or indirectly owned by any U.S. citizens or residents may obtain from the CFTC a special exemption from CTA registration. The CFTC issues such relief on a case-by-case basis. Advisers that have received such exemptions have generally satisfied some or all of the following conditions: are registered with the SEC as investment advisers, provide Commodity Interest trading advice to non-U.S. clients in a manner solely incidental to their securities advice to those clients, invest in Commodity Interests solely for bona fide hedging purposes, and invest no more than five percent of each client's assets under their management in initial margin and option premiums on positions in Commodity Interests.

5. CTA and CPO Registration

i. Registration Requirements for CTAs and CPOs

The CFTC has delegated the review of CTA and CPO registration applications to the NFA.[229] An applicant for registration as a CTA or CPO or both must complete NFA Form 7-R and file it with the NFA,[230] with a Form 8-R and fingerprint card for each principal of the CPO or CTA. Registered CPOs and CTAs must also join the NFA. Form 7-R includes an application for NFA membership. The application fee is $200. NFA membership dues are $1,000 per year.

Registration forms must be filed electronically with the NFA using its Online Registration System ("ORS").[231] An applicant may not act as a CPO or CTA until the registration is granted.[232] The NFA may deny or revoke the registration of any

---

225. CEA Reg. § 4.14(a)(8)(i), 17 C.F.R. § 4.14(a)(8)(i).
226. CEA Reg. § 4.14(a)(8)(ii), 17 C.F.R. § 4.14(a)(8)(ii).
227. CEA Reg. § 4.14(a)(8)(iii), 17 C.F.R. § 4.14(a)(8)(iii).
228. CEA Reg. § 4.14(a)(8)(iv), 17 C.F.R. § 4.14(a)(8)(iv).
229. CEA § 17(b), 7 U.S.C. § 17(b); CEA Reg. § 3.2, 17 C.F.R. § 3.2.
230. CEA Reg. § 3.1(a)(1), 17 C.F.R. § 3.1(a)(1).
231. NFA Registration Rule 801.
232. NFA Registration Rule 802.

CTA or CPO if it determines that the applicant or registrant is not fit to be a CTA or CPO or for good cause.[233]

ii. Registration Requirements for APs and Principals

An associated person (an "AP") of a CPO or CTA is any person who solicits, or supervises anyone else who solicits, clients or client funds, securities or property on behalf of the CPO or CTA or who is in the supervisory chain of command (such as the CPO's or CTA's president, chief executive officer, managing director or managing partner).[234] An individual who does not solicit clients or supervise anyone else who solicits clients is not an AP, even if he or she makes investment decisions regarding commodity interests. "Principal" is a broader category that includes any owner of at least ten percent of the CPO or CTA and any contributor of at least ten percent of the CPO's or CTA's capital (measured on an ongoing basis), any officer whose duties relate to commodity interests activities, any director or general partner of the CPO or CTA, and any person who has the ability, directly or indirectly, to exert a controlling influence over the activities of the CPO or CTA.[235] A person may be both an AP and a principal. The NFA may deny or revoke the registration of any AP if it determines that the applicant is not fit to be an AP or for good cause.

Each principal and AP of a CPO or CTA must file a Form 8-R with the NFA using the ORS,[236] as well as a fingerprint card. Each AP must generally pass the Series 3 examination administered by the NASD or obtain an exemption from this requirement.[237]

Recent amendments to the Exchange Act require the NFA to adopt minimum competence and training standards for its members concerning trading securities futures.[238] The NFA is updating the Series 3 examination to cover securities futures. Current APs and APs who register with the NFA while the Series 3 examination is being updated and who want to trade securities futures can meet these new requirements by taking courses that comply with NFA guidelines.[239] Such APs must be able to demonstrate to the NFA during an NFA audit that they have completed the required course. APs permitted to qualify by taking a course must do so by December 31, 2006; thereafter, they will be required to take the revised Series 3 examination or its successor before being able to trade securities futures.[240]

---

233.   CEA § 8a(2), 7 U.S.C. § 8a(2).
234.   CEA Reg. § 1.3(aa), 17 C.F.R. § 1.3(aa).
235.   CEA Reg. § 3.1(a), 17 C.F.R. § 3.1(a); NFA Registration Rule 101(a).
236.   NFA Registration Rule 801.
237.   NFA Registration Rule 401.
238.   Exchange Act § 15A(k)(2)(D), 15 U.S.C. § 78o-3(k)(2)(D).
239.   NFA Notice to Members No. I-02-15 (Aug. 29, 2002).
240.   *Id.*

iii. Exemptions from Registration as an AP

a. Certain Principals

CEA Rule 3.12(h)[241] exempts a person in the supervisory chain of command of a CPO or CTA (such as the general partner, manager or chief operating officer) who would otherwise be an AP from registration as an AP and from the NASD Series 3 examination requirement if:

- That person is registered as a principal of the CPO or CTA;
- The CPO or CTA has not been found to have committed fraud or failed to supervise an employee under the CEA or the CEA Regulations and is not subject to any pending proceeding alleging such fraud or failure;
- That person is not authorized to solicit or accept client funds, solicit funds for a pool, solicit clients or supervise persons engaged in such activities;
- That person has no authority with respect to hiring, firing or other personnel matters involving employees of the CPO or CTA who are engaged in activities related to commodity interests;
- At least one other person is registered as an AP of the CPO or CTA and exercises full and final supervisory authority over client activities of the CPO or CTA relating to commodity interests and over hiring and firing personnel of the CPO or CTA who engage in such activities (if such person ceases to have such authority, the CPO or CTA must notify the NFA within twenty days of such occurrence and the identity of such person's successor); and
- Commodity interest activities account for no more than ten percent of the CPO's or CTA's annual revenues.[242]

This exemption requires the CPO or CTA to file appropriate resolutions with the NFA indicating compliance with the foregoing requirements.[243]

b. APs of Certain CTAs

A person who is exempt from registering as a CTA or is associated with a person who is exempt from registering as a CTA under the exemptions described above in section 2.9.4.iii is not required to register as an AP of that CTA.[244] This exemption is not available for any person who solicits or supervises persons who solicit discretionary client accounts for a CTA that does not qualify for the exemptions described above in section 2.9.4.iii or that does qualify for an exemption but is registered as a CTA.[245]

---

241.   17 C.F.R. § 3.12(h).
242.   CEA Reg. § 3.12(h)(1)(iii), 17 C.F.R. § 3.12(h)(1)(iii).
243.   *Id.*
244.   CEA Reg. § 3.12(h)(2), 17 C.F.R. § 3.12(h)(2).
245.   *Id.*

c. Registered Representatives and Principals of NASD Members

An individual who is a registered representative, registered principal, limited representative or limited principal of a member of the NASD is exempt from registration as an AP of a CPO if he or she only solicits pool participants or supervises any person who does so for that member and does not engage in any other activity regulated by the CFTC.[246]

d. Non-U.S. APs

A non-U.S. individual who solicits for a CTA or a CPO only potential clients or investors who are not U.S. persons and conducts such solicitations entirely outside the United States is exempt from registration as an AP of that CTA or CPO.[247] Such an individual cannot undertake any marketing activity that could reasonably be expected to have the effect of soliciting U.S. persons.[248]

iv. Exemption from Examination Requirement

The NFA may waive the NASD Series 3 examination requirement for APs of a CPO, if (a) the CPO or its pools are regulated by a federal or state regulatory authority or the pools are privately offered pursuant to an exemption from registration under the Securities Act and (b) the CPO limits its commodity interests activities to operating pools that (1) engage principally in securities transactions, (2) commit no more than ten percent of their assets (measured on an ongoing basis) as initial margin and premiums for commodity interests, and (3) use commodity interests only for hedging or risk management purposes. A similar waiver is available to APs of a CTA if a federal or state regulatory authority regulates the CTA, and the CTA's advice to each client regarding commodity interests is incidental to the securities advice it provides and is for hedging or risk management purposes.[249]

v. Amendments to Forms 7-R and 8-R

Registration as a CPO or CTA remains effective for only one year.[250] Accordingly, each registered CPO or CTA must file a Form 7-R with the NFA annually on a

---

246.   CEA Reg. § 3.12(h)(1)(ii), 17 C.F.R. § 3.12(h)(1)(ii).

247.   CFTC Interpretive Letters No. 88-8 (Apr. 8, 1988) (concerning APs of CTAs); Nos. 90-4 (Jan. 31, 1990) and 93-106 (Oct. 12, 1993) (concerning APs of CPOs).

248.   CFTC Interpretive Letter No. 93-106 (Oct. 12, 1993). The term "U.S. person" includes
   •   a natural person who is a resident of the United States;
   •   a partnership, corporation or other entity organized under the laws of the United States or which has its principal place of business in the United States;
      •   any estate or trust, the income of which is subject to U.S. income tax regardless of source; or
   •   any entity organized principally for passive investment such as a commodity pool, investment company or other similar entity (other than a pension plan for the employees, officers or principals of an entity organized and with its principal place of business outside the United States) in which U.S. persons hold units of participation representing in the aggregate ten percent or more of the beneficial interest in the entity, or which has as a principal purpose the facilitating of investment by a U.S. person in a commodity pool with respect to which the operator is exempt from certain requirements of Part 4 of the CEA Regulations by virtue of its participants being non-U.S. persons. CFTC Interpretive Letter No. 92-3 (Feb. 4, 1992).

249.   NFA Interpretive Notice 9018 (Aug. 1, 1992); NFA Interpretive Notice 9022 (Sep. 21, 1993).

250.   CEA § 4n(2), 7 U.S.C. § 4n(2).

date specified by the NFA. If the CPO or CTA does not make this filing on time, the NFA will regard the failure as a request to withdraw from registration.

CPOs, CTAs and APs of a CPO or CTA must report promptly, on Form 3-R, any changes in the information on their respective Forms 7-R or Forms 8-R.[251] If the change is the addition of a new principal who is a natural person, the CPO or CTA must file a Form 8-R and fingerprint card concerning the new principal.[252] The CPO or CTA must report an additional non-natural person on Form 3-R.[253] If an AP or principal of a CPO or CTA terminates its relationship with the CPO or CTA, the CPO or CTA must file a notice of that termination on Form 8-T with the NFA within twenty days of the termination.[254] Forms 3-R and 8-T must be filed using the ORS.[255]

If a registered CPO or CTA changes its form of organization from one entity to another (such as from a partnership to a corporation), the CPO or CTA must report such change on a Form 3-R but generally is not required to file a new registration application for the reorganized entity. If a CPO or CTA changes from a sole proprietorship to a business entity, or from a business entity to a sole proprietorship, however, the CPO or CTA must file a Form 7-W to withdraw the registration of the original entity or sole proprietorship and file a Form 7-R to register the successor entity or sole proprietorship.[256] The reorganized entity will be liable for the obligations of the pre-existing entity under the CEA and CEA Regulations.[257]

6. Disclosure Requirements

Disclosure requirements for registered CPOs and CTAs are discussed below in section 6.6.

7. Required Reports to Clients and Pool Participants

A CTA is not required to send periodic reports to its clients. A futures commission merchant, which conducts business as a broker in commodity interests, is required to send confirmations and month-end account statements directly to the clients of a CTA and to the CTA that controls these accounts.[258]

In contrast, a futures commission merchant sends confirmations directly to CPOs, not to pool participants.[259] Accordingly, a CPO must provide pool participants with a monthly account statement that includes financial statements prepared in accordance with generally accepted accounting principles and any previously undisclosed material business dealings between the pool and its CPO, CTA, futures commission merchant or any of their respective principals.[260] In addition, the CPO

---

251. CEA Reg. § 3.31, 17 C.F.R. § 3.31.
252. CEA Reg. § 3.31(a)(3), 17 C.F.R. § 3.31(a)(3).
253. *Id.*
254. CEA Reg. § 3.31(c), 17 C.F.R. § 3.31(c).
255. www.nfa.futures.org/member/newsLetterArticle.asp?Article ID=580 (Apr. 13, 2004).
256. CEA Reg. § 3.31(a)(1), 17 C.F.R. § 3.31(a)(1).
257. CEA Reg. § 3.31(a)(2), 17 C.F.R. § 3.31(a)(2).
258. CEA Reg. § 1.33, 17 C.F.R. § 1.33.
259. CEA Reg. § 1.33(b)(4), 17 C.F.R. § 1.33(b)(4).
260. CEA Reg. § 4.22, 17 C.F.R. § 4.22.

must provide pool participants with an annual report, within ninety days after the end of the fiscal year, which includes performance data and financial statements prepared in accordance with generally accepted accounting principles and audited by an independent public accountant.[261] CEA Rule 4.22[262] identifies the information that must be disclosed in the account statement and annual report.

If the annual report is sent to pool participants within forty-five days of the end of the pool's fiscal year, the CPO is not required to deliver an account statement for the final month of that fiscal year.[263] A copy of the annual report must be filed with the NFA.[264] If a CPO cannot distribute the report within ninety days from the end of the pool's fiscal year, the CPO may request an extension from the NFA.

8. Reports of Substantial Market Positions

CTAs and CPOs are required to report to the CFTC their positions in commodity interests that exceed thresholds set forth in CEA Regulations and must maintain books and records detailing the CTA's or CPO's positions and transaction in such commodity interests.[265] CEA Regulations also limit a CTA's or CPO's speculative trading and the size of the position that any person may hold.[266] Generally, all accounts controlled by a CTA or a CPO are aggregated for reporting and position limit purposes.[267]

9. Recordkeeping Requirements

A CTA or CPO must maintain the following records:

- Acknowledgments from clients of receipt of the CTA's or CPO's disclosure document;
- Copies of each confirmation of a commodity interest transaction, each purchase and sale statement and each monthly statement received from a futures commission merchant concerning each client account, the CTA's or CPO's own account and the accounts of its principals;
- Copies of all materials sent to clients and prospective clients, including the text of oral presentations, showing the date of first distribution;
- Itemized daily records of all transactions in commodity interests by the CTA or CPO; and
- Books and records of other transactions and business dealings by the CTA or CPO and its principals relating to trading commodity interests or engaging in cash market transactions.[268]

---

261.   CEA Reg. § 4.22(c), 17 C.F.R. § 4.22(c). The SEC has no similar audit requirement. Thus, investment advisers that do not trade commodity interests would not for this reason be required to provide their hedge fund investors with audited financial statements. *But see* Chapter 12, *infra*.

262.   17 C.F.R. § 4.22.

263.   CEA Reg. § 4.22(b), 17 C.F.R. § 4.22(b).

264.   CEA Reg. § 4.22(c), 17 C.F.R. § 4.22(c); NFA Compliance Rule 2-13.

265.   CEA Reg. §§ 15 and 18, 17 C.F.R. §§ 15 and 18.

266.   CEA Reg. § 150, 17 C.F.R. § 150.

267.   CEA Reg. §§ 18.01, 150.4 and 150.5, 17 C.F.R. §§ 18.01, 150.4 and 150.5(g).

268.   CEA Reg. §§ 4.23 and 4.33, 17 C.F.R. §§ 4.23 and 4.33.

A CTA must also maintain all powers of attorney and other documents authorizing the CTA to trade commodity interests on behalf of clients; copies of all written agreements between the CTA and its clients; and a list or other record of all commodity interest accounts directed by the CTA and of all transactions effected for those accounts.[269] A CPO must maintain additional records, including, journals, ledgers, periodic income statements and balance sheets of each pool operated by the CPO and all other records, data and memoranda prepared or received by the CPO in the operation of the pool.[270] CTAs and CPOs must maintain the required records for five years.[271]

10. Exemptions from Certain Disclosure, Recordkeeping and Reporting Requirements

CEA Regulations[272] offer registered CPOs and CTAs relief from some of the disclosure, recordkeeping and reporting requirements with respect to certain commodity pools and separate accounts that they manage. Such relief applies only to qualifying pools and accounts, rather than to the CPO or CTA generally, and the CPO or CTA must file a notice with the NFA to claim such relief.

i. Section 4.12(b) Pools

Under CEA Rule 4.12(b),[273] qualifying commodity pools ("4.12(b) Pools") are exempt from some disclosure, reporting and recordkeeping requirements that generally apply to CPOs. To qualify as a 4.12(b) Pool, a pool must:

- Be offered and sold in accordance with the registration provisions of the Securities Act or an exemption therefrom;
- Generally and routinely engage in buying and selling securities and securities derivative instruments;
- Not enter into commodity interest contracts for which the aggregate initial margin and premiums exceed ten percent (excluding the in-the-money amount of options that are in-the-money at the time of purchase) of the fair market value of the pool's assets (measured on an ongoing basis), after taking into account unrealized profits and unrealized losses on such contracts to which the pool is already a party;
- Trade commodity interests in a manner solely incidental to its securities trading activities; and
- Disclose to pool participants and prospective participants the restrictions in the third and fourth points above.

To claim this exemption, a 4.12(b) Pool's CPO must file a notice with the NFA before the 4.12(b) Pool enters into its first transaction in commodity interests and include certain additional legends in the 4.12(b) Pool's disclosure document.[274]

---

269. CEA Reg. § 4.33, 17 C.F.R. § 4.33.
270. CEA Reg. § 4.23, 17 C.F.R. § 4.23.
271. CEA Reg. § 1.31, 17 C.F.R. § 1.31.
272. CEA Reg. §§ 4.22, 4.33 and 4.34, 17 C.F.R. §§ 4.22, 4.33 and 4.34.
273. 17 C.F.R. § 4.12(b).
274. CEA Reg. § 4.12(b)(3), 17 C.F.R. § 4.12(b)(3).

The disclosure document for a 4.12(b) Pool is not required to include some of the cautionary legends or any of the past performance disclosure required in disclosure documents of other pools.[275] If, however, the CPO of a 4.12(b) Pool chooses to provide performance data to prospective participants, that performance disclosure must comply with the applicable CEA Regulations.[276]

The CPO of a 4.12(b) Pool may solicit, accept and receive funds and other property from prospective participants (even investors that are not accredited investors[277] under Regulation D under the Securities Act) immediately after filing the pool's disclosure document with the NFA and providing that document to such participants.[278] The utility of this exemption from the twenty-one day advance filing requirement is limited, however, because if the NFA requires changes to the disclosure document, the CPO may be required to provide the revised document to all prospective investors who would have received the original version.

The NFA generally does not review even the initial disclosure document of a fund-of-funds that is a 4.12(b) Pool and that invests in commodity interests only through other 4.12(b) Pools.[279]

CPOs of 4.12(b) Pools also are relieved from some of the reporting and recordkeeping requirements. For example, CPOs are required to send reports only quarterly, rather than monthly, to participants in their 4.12(b) Pools, and the reports are not required to be as detailed as reports to participants in other pools.[280]

ii. Offshore Pools

A registered CPO that operates an offshore pool is exempt[281] from all disclosure and reporting and some recordkeeping requirements of the CEA Regulations with respect to that pool, if:

- The pool is organized and operated outside the United States;
- The pool does not hold pool owner meetings or conduct administrative activities within the United States;
- No pool owner is a resident or citizen of the United States, an entity organized or having its principal place of business in the United States, or an investment entity ten percent or more of which is owned by any such U.S. persons;
- The pool does not contain any capital directly or indirectly contributed from sources within the United States; and
- The CPO, the pool and persons affiliated with them will not solicit participation in the offshore hedge fund by U.S. persons.

To claim this exemption with respect to an offshore pool, a CPO must file a notice with the NFA before beginning to operate the pool.[282]

---

275. CEA Reg. § 4.12(a)(2), 17 C.F.R. § 4.12(a)(2).
276. CEA Reg. § 4.41, 17 C.F.R. § 4.41.
277. *See* § 5.3.2.ii, *infra.*
278. CEA Reg. § 4.8, 17 C.F.R. § 4.8.
279. CFTC Advisory 95-44 (Apr. 20, 1995).
280. CEA Reg. § 4.12(b)(2), 17 C.F.R. § 4.12(b)(2).
281. CFTC Advisory 18-96 (Apr. 11, 1996).
282. *Id.*

iii. QEP Pools and Accounts

Under CEA Rule 4.7(a),[283] a CPO is not required to provide any disclosure document and is granted significant relief from periodic reporting and record-keeping requirements with respect to a pool (a "QEP Pool"), the interests of which are offered and sold only to "qualified eligible persons" ("QEPs") in an offering that is exempt from registration under the Securities Act pursuant to section 4(2) or Regulation S.[284] A registered CTA is granted similar relief under CEA Rule 4.7(b) with respect to the account of any client that is a QEP and has agreed to be treated as a QEP (a "QEP Account").[285]

A QEP is any person that a CPO or CTA reasonably believes, at the time the person purchases a pool participation or opens an account, is:[286]

- A registered futures commissions merchant;
- A securities broker or dealer registered under the Exchange Act;
- A registered CPO, CTA or investment adviser that has been registered and active as such for two years or advises pools or accounts, as the case may be, that have aggregate assets in excess of $5,000,000;
- A qualified purchaser, as defined in Company Act section 2(a)(51);[287]
- A knowledgeable employee, as defined in Rule 3c-5 under the Company Act;[288]
- With respect to a QEP Pool, the CPO, CTA or investment adviser of the pool, any of their affiliates, any principal of any of the foregoing, certain employees of any of the foregoing, certain family members of any such principal or employee (provided the investment is made at the direction of such principal or employee), certain persons acquiring an interest in the pool through gift, bequest or divorce and any company established by any of the foregoing;
- With respect to a QEP Account, any affiliate or principal of the CTA, certain employees of the CTA, certain family members of any such affiliate, principal or employee (provided the account is established at the direction of such affiliate, principal or employee), certain persons acquiring an interest in the account through gift, bequest or divorce, and a company established by any of the foregoing;
- A trust not formed for the specific purpose of investing in a QEP Pool or opening a QEP Account if the trustee or other person authorized to make the investment decisions for the trust and each settlor of the trust is a QEP;
- Certain charitable organizations if the trustee or other person authorized to make the investment decisions for the trust and each settlor of the trust is a QEP;
- Any Non-U.S. Person (as defined below); and

---

283. 17 C.F.R. § 4.7(a).
284. *See* Chapters 5 and 8, *infra*.
285. CEA Reg. § 4.7(c), 17 C.F.R. § 4.7(c).
286. CEA Reg. § 4.7(a)(2), 17 C.F.R. § 4.7(a)(2).
287. 15 U.S.C. § 80a-2(a)(1).
288. 17 C.F.R. § 270.3c-5.

- Any entity in which all of the owners or participants are QEPs, QEP Pools or Section 4.5 Accounts in which all owners or participants are QEPs.

"Non-U.S. Person" is a person who is not a resident of the United States, an entity (other than an entity organized principally for passive investment) that is organized under the laws of a non-U.S. jurisdiction and has its principal place of business in a non-U.S. jurisdiction, an estate or trust whose income is not subject to U.S. taxation, and an entity organized principally for passive investment (such as an investment pool) if fewer than ten percent of the beneficial interests in such entity are owned by persons who are not QEPs or Non-U.S. Persons and the entity was not formed principally to facilitate investment by persons who do not qualify as Non-U.S. Persons.[289]

In addition to the categories of QEP listed above ("Non-Portfolio Requirement QEPs"), certain other persons and entities are QEPs if they satisfy a specified portfolio requirement. Those persons and entities include certain government entities and most persons that meet the definition of an accredited investor, as well as pools, trusts, insurance company separate accounts and bank collective trusts with assets in excess of $5,000,000 that were not formed for the purpose of opening a QEP Account or investing in a QEP Pool. Any such person or entity is a QEP if the CPO reasonably believes that such person or entity:[290]

- Owns securities of issuers not affiliated with such person and other investments (including real estate held for investment purposes) with an aggregate market value of at least $2,000,000; or
- Has had on deposit with a futures commission merchant, for such person's own account at any time during the six-month period preceding either the date of sale to the QEP of a participation in a QEP Pool or the date of opening a QEP Account, at least $200,000 in commodity exchange-specified initial margin and option premiums for commodity interest transactions; or
- Owns a portfolio comprising a combination of the funds or properties described in the preceding two points in which the sum of the funds or property includable under the first point, expressed as percentage of the minimum amount required thereunder, and the amount of commodity interests margin and option premiums includable under the second point, expressed as a percentage of the minimum amount required thereunder, equals at least 100 percent (for example, a composite portfolio consisting of $1,000,000 in securities and other investments and $100,000 in exchange-specified initial margin and option premiums on commodity interests would satisfy this requirement.)

To claim the relief available to a QEP Pool or QEP Account, the CPO or CTA must file a notice with the NFA.[291] Although the CEA and CEA Regulations do not require the CPO of a QEP Pool to provide a disclosure document to

---

289. CEA Reg. § 4.7(a)(1)(iv), 17 C.F.R. § 4.7(a)(1)(iv).
290. CEA Reg. §§ 4.7(a)(1)(v) and 4.7(a)(3), 17 C.F.R. §§ 4.7(a)(1)(v) and 4.7(a)(3).
291. CEA Reg. § 4.7(d), 17 C.F.R. § 4.7(d).

prospective investors, compliance with the requirements of the Securities Act and SEC rules under the Securities Act necessitates complete and adequate disclosure.[292] The disclosure document is not subject to review by the CFTC or the NFA and need not include any CFTC-mandated disclosure, except for a legend required by the CEA Regulations.[293]

11. Anti-Fraud Provisions

CTAs and CPOs are subject to broad anti-fraud provisions under the CEA. It is unlawful for any CTA or CPO:

> to employ any device, scheme, or artifice to defraud any client or participant or prospective client or participant or to engage in any transaction, practice, or course of business which operates as a fraud or deceit upon any client or participant or prospective client or participant.[294]

Examples of fraudulent practices include false and deceptive advertising, un-authorized trading, churning, taking the other side of a client's order without prior consent, crossing orders between clients in lieu of competitive market execution and misrepresentations and omissions in disclosure documents (including, among other things, concealment of commission kickbacks and non-disclosure of certain risks of trading in commodity interests).

12. Other Considerations

A pool must operate as a separate entity from its CPO. All funds received by the CPO for use in pool activities must be received in the pool's (not the CPO's) name. The CPO may not commingle funds of the pool with funds of another person.[295] CTAs and CPOs, as such, are not subject to net capital requirements. CTAs and CPOs are subject to periodic surprise inspections by the CFTC and the NFA.[296] CTAs and CPOs may be subject to additional requirements under state law.[297]

In October 2001, the CFTC issued a Statement of Acceptable Practices for ethics training that replaced its Rule 3.34.[298] This Statement is a safe harbor, outlining acceptable procedures for ethics training programs and topics that ethics training programs should address. Because the Statement is general, the NFA adopted Compliance Rule 2-9, "Ethics Training Requirements."[299] The NFA's rule requires firms to have written procedures that outline their ethics training

---

292. *See* Chapters 6, 8 and 9, *infra*.
293. CEA Reg. §§ 4.7(b) and 4.7(c), 17 C.F.R. §§ 4.7(b) and 4.7(c).
294. CEA Reg. § 4o, 17 C.F.R. § 4o.
295. CEA Reg. § 4.20, 17 C.F.R. § 4.20.
296. CEA § 4n(3)(A), 7 U.S.C. § 4n(3)(A); CEA Reg. § 1.31, 17 C.F.R. § 1.31.
297. *See, e.g.,* California Corporations Code § 29500, *et seq;* NY GBL § 359-e.
298. 17 C.F.R. Ch. 1, Pt. 3, App. B, 66 F.R. 53,510 (Oct. 23, 2001).
299. NFA Compliance Rule 2-9: Ethics Training Requirements.

programs. NFA members may obtain ethics training from third party providers, although members are still responsible for ensuring that the provider is qualified. Training format and frequency depends the member's specific business operations and work force. Members must document compliance with their procedures.

§ 2.10 Anti-Money Laundering

In an effort to curtail money-laundering activities, the USA PATRIOT Act amended the Bank Secrecy Act of 1970[300] to cover a broader range of financial institutions and activities and to increase the reporting and record-keeping obligations thereunder. The U.S. Department of Treasury has proposed a new anti-money-laundering rule that will require SEC-registered investment advisers who manage client assets to establish anti-money-laundering programs. Certain unregistered investment advisers also are covered by the proposed rule.

1. Registered and Unregistered Investment Advisers

Investment advisers registered with the SEC and SEC-Exempt Advisers that have more than $30,000,000 under management will be required to comply with the FinCEN's proposed rules, if adopted. An investment adviser might be excluded from the proposed rules, however, if it were otherwise required to have an anti-money-laundering program (for example, if the investment adviser is also a CPO or CTA). If the investment adviser sponsors and manages a hedge fund that is also required to implement an anti-money-laundering program, the investment adviser does not need to adopt a separate program for that hedge fund.[301]

Under the proposed rules, if adopted, an investment adviser will be required to (a) establish and implement policies, procedures and internal controls reasonably designed to detect and prevent money laundering and terrorist financing; (b) provide for independent testing for compliance; (c) designate a person or persons responsible for implementing and monitoring the anti-money-laundering program; and (d) provide for ongoing employee training.[302]

i. Policies, Procedures and Control

The investment adviser's anti-money laundering program will be required to be in writing and tailored to the investment adviser's business operations. The investment adviser will be required to take into account the risks presented by the nature

---

300. Uniting and Strengthening America by Providing Appropriate Tools Required to Intercept and Obstruct Terrorism (USA PATRIOT Act) Act of 2001, Pub. L. 10756, 115 Stat. 1402 (codified as amended in scattered sections of the U.S. code).

301.   68 F.R. 23,648 (May 5, 2003).

302.   68 F.R. 23,649-51 (May 5, 2003).

of its services and clients and to identify its vulnerabilities to money laundering and terrorist financing. Factors to consider include the types of clients and their country of origin, and whether the client is a pooled investment vehicle sponsored by someone other than the investment adviser and, if so, whether that investment vehicle is subject to the Bank Security Act rules. The program itself should:

- Identify unusual transactions;
- Identify unusual withdrawals;
- Have procedures in place to scrutinize further potential clients who seek to remain anonymous; and
- Provide for currency transaction reports to be filed with the FinCEN for transactions over $10,000.

The investment adviser may delegate responsibility for conducting the program to a third party, but the investment adviser remains responsible for its effectiveness. The program must be approved in writing by the investment adviser's board of directors, general partner, managing member or person with similar authority.

ii. Designated Compliance Officer

The investment adviser must appoint someone to serve as the anti-money-laundering compliance officer. The compliance officer must be competent and knowledgeable on the subject of anti-money laundering and Bank Security Act requirements and empowered to develop and enforce appropriate policies and procedures.

iii. Employee Training

Personnel whose responsibilities could expose them to money laundering or terrorist financing risks would be required to undergo anti-money-laundering training on a periodic basis. This training may be provided internally or by a third party. The program should provide general awareness of Bank Security Act requirements and job-specific guidance. The FinCEN also suggests periodic updates and refreshers regarding the program.

iv. Independent Testing

An investment adviser will be required to test its program periodically. The audit could be conducted by an independent third party or internally by an employee of the investment adviser other than the compliance officer or someone directly supervised by the compliance officer.

2. Notice Provision for Unregistered Investment Advisers

An unregistered investment adviser will be required to file a notice annually with the FinCEN. This notice will contain the name of the investment adviser and its contact information, name and contact information for the investment adviser's compliance officer, the total number clients and the investment adviser's total assets under management.

3. Commodity Trading Advisers

The rules for CTAs will be essentially the same as those for SEC-registered and SEC-Exempt Advisers.[303] The proposed rules apply to CTAs that "direct" commodity futures or option accounts. "Direct" means agreements whereby a person is authorized to cause transactions to be effected for a client's commodity interest account without the client's specific authorization. The rules would not apply to CTAs that limit their services to providing trading advice but do not direct accounts for clients and investment advisers that are exempt from CTA registration pursuant to CFTC Rule 4.14(a).[304]

303.   68 F.R. 23,640 (May 5, 2003).
304.   C.F.R. § 4.14(a).

CHAPTER 3

Exclusions from Investment Company Act Requirements

The Company Act defines an investment company as, among other things, an issuer that "is or holds itself out as being engaged primarily…in the business of investing, reinvesting, or trading in securities."[1] Hedge funds engage in that business, but avoid most of the regulations applicable to investment companies under the Company Act by relying on the exclusions from the definition of "investment company" in Company Act sections 3(c)(1) and 3(c)(7).[2]

§ 3.1 Summary of Registration Requirements

1. Key Limitations on Registered Investment Companies

An investment company that does not qualify for an exclusion from the definition of "investment company" may not offer or sell a security in the United States,[3] unless the company is registered under Company Act section 8.[4] A registered investment company is subject to technical, complex and extensive substantive regulation of its activities. For example, a registered investment company must have a board of directors or similar body, at least forty percent (to be increased to seventy-five percent beginning in January 2006) of the members of which must be independent of the company.[5] A registered investment company must disclose to

---

1. Company Act § 3(a)(1), 15 U.S.C. § 80a-3(a)(1).
2. 15 U.S.C. §§ 80a-3(c)(1) and 80a-3(c)(7).
3. Company Act § 7(a), 15 U.S.C. § 80a-7(a).
4. 15 U.S.C. § 80a-8.
5. Company Act § 10(a), 15 U.S.C. § 80a-10(a). Over the dissent of two Commissioners, the SEC has amended its rules to require that, by January 16, 2006, most investment company boards of directors be composed of at least seventy-five percent independent directors. Company Act Release No. 26520 (July 27, 2004), 69 F.R. 46,378 (Aug. 2, 2004). *See also* the proposing release, Company Act Release No. 26323, 69 F.R. 3,472 (Jan. 23, 2004). The U.S. Chamber of Commerce has sued the SEC to enjoin application of this amendment, as (among other things) exceeding the SEC's statutory authority; *U.S. Chamber of Commerce v. SEC*, D.D.C., Case No. 1:04CV01522 (Sep. 2, 2004).

its investors those of its investment policies that it believes are fundamental,[6] and those policies can only be changed by a shareholder vote. The Company Act also limits a registered investment company's ability to employ leverage, sell securities short and engage in transactions with affiliates.[7]

2. Consequences of Failure to Register and to Comply with Limitations

If a fund is required by the Company Act to register as an investment company and does not do so, the fund and the fund's general partner, manager or promoter would be subject to criminal or civil penalties, administrative actions, injunctive relief that would prohibit the fund from continuing to do business until it registers under the Company Act, or private actions to require refunds of market losses or advisory fees.[8]

§ 3.2 Section 3(c)(1) Exclusion

1. General Statement of Rule

Company Act section 3(c)(1)[9] excludes any pooled investment vehicle from the definition of an investment company if it does not have more than 100 beneficial owners of its outstanding securities (the "100-Owner Limit") and does not make or propose to make a public offering of its securities. A hedge fund that relies on this exclusion is commonly called a "3(c)(1) Fund."

2. Determination of Beneficial Ownership

i. Partnerships, Corporations, Trusts and Other Entities

The Company Act and SEC rules promulgated under it prevent in certain circumstances the use of multi-tiered pooled investment vehicles to avoid the 100-Owner Limit, by looking through an entity (an "Investing Entity") that invests

---

6. Company Act § 8(b), 15 U.S.C. § 80a-8(b).

7. Company Act § 18(f), 15 U.S.C. § 80a-18(f); Company Act Release No. 10666 (Apr. 18, 1979), 44 F.R. 25,128 (Apr. 27, 1979).

8. Company Act § 42(d), 15 U.S.C. § 80a-42(d) ("… a court of equity may, to the extent it deems necessary or appropriate, take exclusive jurisdiction and possession of the investment company or companies involved and the books, records and assets thereof, wherever located; and the court shall have jurisdiction to appoint a trustee, who with the approval of the court shall have power to dispose of any or all such assets …"). Company Act section 42(d) also authorizes the SEC to transmit evidence of any violation of the Company Act to the U.S. Attorney General for institution of criminal proceedings. Company Act § 42(e), 15 U.S.C. § 80a-42(e), authorizes the SEC to impose monetary penalties for violations of the Company Act.

9. 15 U.S.C. § 80a-3(c)(1).

in a 3(c)(1) Fund and counting the beneficial owners of the Investing Entity's outstanding securities as if they were direct beneficial owners of outstanding securities of the 3(c)(1) Fund. The SEC and its staff have established standards for determining whether to look through an Investing Entity. Those statutory provisions, rules and other standards and their applications are described below.

a. The Ten Percent Look-Through Test

Under Company Act section 3(c)(1)(A),[10] each beneficial owner of outstanding securities of an Investing Entity is counted as a beneficial owner of outstanding securities of a 3(c)(1) Fund for the purpose of the 100-Owner Limit, if both of the following conditions (the "3(c)(1)(A) Tests") exist:

- The Investing Entity is an investment company, as defined in the Company Act (such as a mutual fund), or is a 3(c)(1) Fund or a fund that relies on Company Act section 3(c)(7) (a "3(c)(7) Fund") (each, a "Covered Company"); and
- The Investing Entity owns ten percent or more of the 3(c)(1) Fund's outstanding voting securities (the "10% Test").[11]

If only one of the 3(c)(1)(A) Tests is met, no look-through is required. In addition, the analysis described above is necessary only when an Investing Entity acquires a voting security of the 3(c)(1) Fund, and no look-through is necessary if the interest of an Investing Entity that is a Covered Company increases to ten percent of a 3(c)(1) Fund's outstanding voting securities solely because of the redemption of other voting securities of the 3(c)(1) Fund.[12] If an Investing Entity is a fund of funds (that is, its business is to invest a pool of investor funds in 3(c)(1) Funds and other professionally managed accounts), the Investing Entity may be expected in most cases to meet the first 3(c)(1)(A) Test. In such case, a 3(c)(1) Fund in which it invests should either limit the Investing Entity's investment to less than ten percent of the 3(c)(1) Fund's investor assets or assume that each of the Investing Entity's direct and indirect owners will be deemed to be a beneficial owner of the 3(c)(1) Fund.

Section 3(c)(1)(A) does not require a look-through unless the Investing Entity is an investment company, as defined in the Company Act, or a private investment company. Before accepting an investment from any Investing Entity that is not a natural person, a 3(c)(1) Fund should require that Investing Entity to disclose whether or not it is a Covered Company. If the Investing Entity is a Covered Company, the 3(c)(1) Fund should determine whether the Investing Entity exceeds the 10% Test.

---

10. 15 U.S.C. § 80a-3(c)(1)(A).

11. Company Act Rule 3c-1, 17 C.F.R. § 270.3c-1, provides, however, that a Covered Company that owns ten percent or more of a 3(c)(1) Fund's outstanding voting securities is considered to be only one beneficial owner of the 3(c)(1) Fund (that is, the Covered Company is not subject to a look-through), if (a) the Covered Company owned ten percent or more of the 3(c)(1) Fund's outstanding voting securities on April 1, 1997, and (b) on each date that the Covered Company invests in the 3(c)(1) Fund, no more than ten percent of the Covered Company's total assets are invested in the 3(c)(1) Fund and other Covered Companies.

12. Company Act Release No. 22597 (Apr. 3, 1997), 62 F.R. 17,512 (Apr. 9, 1997) (hereinafter, "1997 Release"), at § III.A.2.

The 10% Test refers to ownership of ten percent or more of the 3(c)(1) Fund's "voting securities." Most 3(c)(1) Funds are organized as limited partnerships. The SEC generally considers limited partner interests to be voting securities.[13] In certain instances, however, limited partner interests may not be voting securities, so that no investor owns outstanding voting securities of the 3(c)(1) Fund and the 10% Test is not met. The SEC staff has stated that a limited partner interest generally is not considered to be a voting security if: (1) the Investing Entity is not formed for the purpose of investing in the (3)(c)(1) Fund and does not contribute the majority of the 3(c)(1) Fund's capital; (2) no limited partner takes part in the conduct or control of the business of the (3)(c)(1) Fund or has the right to vote on the election, replacement or removal of the general partner or investment manager (even if the general partner or investment manager withdraws from the 3(c)(1) Fund); and (3) no limited partner itself relies on section 3(c)(1) to avoid registration under the Company Act.[14] Even if these conditions are met, the SEC may consider a limited partner interest to be a voting security if a limited partner can seek to amend or renew the partnership agreement at regular intervals or if a limited partner exercises sufficient control through economic power that the limited partner interests are the functional equivalent of voting securities.[15] A general partner's interest ordinarily is excluded in determining the total amount of voting securities of a 3(c)(1) Fund.[16]

If both 3(c)(1)(A) Tests are met, all of the beneficial owners of the Investing Entity are deemed to be beneficial owners of the 3(c)(1) Fund. If a beneficial owner of the Investing Entity is another entity, the SEC may determine whether that other entity by itself meets both 3(c)(1)(A) Tests, and, if it does, the SEC may look through to that entity's beneficial owners.[17] The SEC has not specified the manner in which such a second look-through might be calculated.

b. Investing Entity's Owners That Can Vary the Size of Their Indirect Investments in a 3(c)(1) Fund

If the investors in an Investing Entity have the right or authority to specify the amount of their participation in particular investments made by that Investing Entity, each participating owner of that Investing Entity is considered, for purposes of the 100-Owner Limit, a beneficial owner of a 3(c)(1) Fund in which the Investing Entity has an interest.[18]

---

13.   *Horsley Keogh Venture Fund*, SEC No-Action Letter (Apr. 27, 1988).

14.   *Rogers, Casey & Associates, Inc.*, SEC No-Action Letter (June 16, 1989); *Weiss, Peck & Greer Venture Associates II, L.P.*, SEC No-Action Letter (Apr. 10, 1990); *Clemente Global Growth Fund, Inc. v. Pickens*, 705 F. Supp. 958, 967 (S.D.N.Y. 1989); *Kohlberg Kravis Roberts & Co.*, SEC No-Action Letter (Sep. 9, 1985); *MMC Fund, L.P.*, SEC No-Action Letter (Mar. 31, 1989); *Laifer Inc.*, SEC No-Action Letter (Jan. 5, 1993); *Standish Equity Investments, Inc.*, SEC No-Action Letter (Dec. 15, 1993).

15.   *Rogers, Casey & Associates, Inc.*, SEC No-Action Letter (June 16, 1989). *Devonshire Capital Corporation*, SEC No-Action Letter (Feb. 15, 1976); *Pierce, Lewis & Dolan*, SEC No-Action Letter (Apr. 21, 1972).

16.   *See* § 3.2.2.vi, *infra*

17.   *Clemente Global Growth Fund, Inc. v. Pickens, et al.*, 705 F.Supp. 958, 965 (S.D.N.Y. 1989).

18.   *Tyler Capital Fund, L.P./South Market Capital*, SEC No-Action Letter (Sep. 28, 1987); *Six Pack*, SEC No-Action Letter (Nov. 13, 1989).

Some Investing Entities, such as funds of funds and family partnerships, treat their limited partners differently based on their different investment objectives. A limited partnership whose general partner consults with its limited partners to determine their investment objectives and apportions each limited partner's participation in the partnership's investments in accordance with those investment objectives will not be considered a single beneficial owner of a 3(c)(1) Fund, even if the general partner (and not the limited partners) makes the ultimate investment allocation decisions.[19] Such an Investing Entity probably would be ignored for purposes of section 3(c)(1) and each of its participating beneficial owners probably would be deemed a beneficial owner of a 3(c)(1) Fund in which the Investing Entity invests. It is unclear, however, whether a 3(c)(1) Fund should count a beneficial owner of such an Investing Entity that directs the Investing Entity not to invest any of the owner's capital in the 3(c)(1) Fund.

The SEC staff has indicated that an employee benefit plan that permits participants to direct their investments will be disregarded and all of its participants will be counted as beneficial owners of any 3(c)(1) Fund in which the plan invests.[20] On the other hand, the SEC staff has allowed a 3(c)(1) Fund to count as a single beneficial owner a participant-directed defined contribution plan whose participants could allocate their capital to generic investment options, but had no role in deciding whether assets allocated to a particular option would be invested in the 3(c)(1) Fund.[21] In the case of a participant-directed plan sponsored by the investment adviser and general partner of a 3(c)(1) Fund, the SEC staff allowed the 3(c)(1) Fund to count the employee benefit plan as a single beneficial owner of the 3(c)(1) Fund's securities.[22] The SEC staff's decision depended particularly on the employee plan's participants' high level of access to information about the 3(c)(1) Fund's operations and investments.

c. Entity Formed for the Purpose of Investing in a 3(c)(1) Fund— Forty Percent Test

The SEC staff has indicated that a 3(c)(1) Fund must count toward the 100-Owner Limit each of the investors in any Investing Entity that was formed for the purpose of investing in the 3(c)(1) Fund. The SEC staff has also indicated that an Investing Entity usually will be deemed to have been formed for the purpose of investing in a 3(c)(1) Fund if forty percent or more of its committed capital is invested in the 3(c)(1) Fund.[23] Except in unusual circumstances, an Investing Entity should

---

19. *WR Investment Partners Diversified Strategies Fund, L.P.*, SEC No-Action Letter (Apr. 15, 1992).

20. *The PanAgora Group Trust*, SEC No-Action Letter (Apr. 29, 1994).

21. *The Standish, Ayer & Wood, Inc. Stable Value Group Trust*, SEC No-Action Letter (Dec. 28, 1995).

22. *Caxton Corporation*, SEC No-Action Letter (Dec. 28, 1994).

23. *Merrill Lynch & Co., Inc.*, SEC No-Action Letter (Apr. 23, 1992); *CMS Communications Fund, L.P.*, SEC No-Action Letter (Apr. 17, 1987). *But see Cornish & Carey Commercial, Inc.*, SEC No-Action Letter (June 21, 1996) (allowing an Investing Entity that invests more than forty percent of its capital in a 3(c)(1) Fund to be counted as one beneficial owner of the 3(c)(1) Fund, provided that, among other things, the Investing Entity is not structured or operated to circumvent section 3(c)(1)). *See also American Bar Association Section of Business Law*, SEC No-Action Letter (Apr. 22, 1999) (hereinafter "*American Bar Association*"), Answer D (noting that, in determining whether an Investing Entity is formed for the purpose of investing in a 3(c)(7) Fund, the percentage of the Investing Entity's assets invested in the 3(c)(7) Fund is relevant, but not determinative).

not be regarded as having been formed for the purpose of investing in a 3(c)(1) Fund, and should not be looked through on that basis, if less than forty percent of its committed capital is invested in the 3(c)(1) Fund, even if one of its express purposes is to invest in the 3(c)(1) Fund.[24] The SEC staff has not addressed whether the forty percent test would be applied to an Investing Entity formed a significant time before making a forty percent or greater investment in a 3(c)(1) Fund.

d. Trusts

In other contexts, the SEC has indicated that the main factor in determining whether a trust can be considered one investor is whether one or more of the beneficiaries or trustees can revoke the trust.[25] If the SEC applies a similar analysis in deciding how to count revocable trusts toward the 100-Owner Limit, the SEC would count only the persons possessing that power, and not all of the trust's beneficial owners, against the 100-Owner Limit. An irrevocable trust that is not a Covered Company and does not have more than forty percent of its assets invested in a 3(c)(1) Fund is usually counted as one beneficial owner of the 3(c)(1) Fund for the purposes of section 3(c)(1).[26]

If a trust invests more than forty percent of its assets in a 3(c)(1) Fund, a beneficiary who does not contribute to the trust and does not elect to be a beneficiary of the trust probably would not be considered a beneficial owner of the trust.[27] Accordingly, even if such a trust were to be looked through, involuntary noncontributory beneficiaries probably would not be counted against the 100-Owner Limit.

Investing Entities that are trusts can create complicated issues. For example, because it is not always clear who, if anyone, is the "beneficial owner" of a trust, it may be impossible to look through a trust to its beneficial owners.

ii. Spouses and Other Family Members

The SEC considers securities of a 3(c)(1) Fund owned jointly by both spouses (directly or through an entity) to be owned by only one beneficial owner,[28] but spouses with separate interests count as two beneficial owners.[29] In addition,

---

24.   In *Clayton and Dubilier Associates IV Limited Partnership*, SEC No-Action Letter (Nov. 2, 1992), the SEC staff stated that it would consider a family partnership created to invest in a particular 3(c)(1) Fund, and other funds, for estate planning purposes, to be only one beneficial owner, when the family partnership's capital invested in the 3(c)(1) Fund represented less than forty percent of the family partnership's assets and less than ten percent of the 3(c)(1) Fund's capital. *See also Cornish & Carey Commercial, Inc.*, SEC No-Action Letter (June 21, 1996).

25.   The SEC has determined that certain revocable trusts, which (due to powers retained by the grantors) would be deemed not to exist as a legal entity, will be disregarded for purposes of Advisers Act Rule 205-3, 17 C.F.R. § 275.205-3 (the so-called "Performance Fee Rule"). *See* § 15.2.3.i, *infra*, and Securities Act Rule 501(a)(8), 17 C.F.R. § 230.501(a)(8) (an entity is an "accredited investor" if all of its equity owners are accredited investors). The SEC will look instead to the grantors of the trust to determine if they meet the net worth requirements of those sections. Securities Act Release No. 6455 (Mar. 3, 1983), 48 F.R. 10,045 (May 10, 1983); and *Capital Technology Fund*, SEC No-Action Letter (Mar. 10, 1989). The SEC might apply a similar analysis to the 100-Owner Limit under section 3(c)(1).

26.   *Nemo Capital Partners, L.P.*, SEC No-Action Letter (July 28, 1992); *Handy Place Investment Partnership*, SEC No-Action Letter (July 19, 1989); *OSIRIS Management, Inc.*, SEC No-Action Letter (Feb. 17, 1984).

27.   *Long-Term Capital Management, L.P.*, SEC No-Action Letter (Apr. 28, 1994).

28.   1997 Release, note 69; *American Bar Association*, Answer I.2.

29.   *American Bar Association*, Answer I.1.

investors who are related other than by marriage, such as a parent and children, count as separate beneficial owners.[30] Therefore, to minimize the number of beneficial owners, investments by parents and minor children could be made through the parents or a single entity, such as an appropriate trust or partnership that qualifies as a single investor.[31]

iii. Multiple Ownership Interests of an Investor

If an investor has a direct interest in a 3(c)(1) Fund and also has an indirect interest in the same 3(c)(1) Fund through a wholly-owned subsidiary or an affiliate or as the sole beneficiary of a trust or individual retirement account (an "IRA"), such multiple interests should be considered to be owned by only one investor. Similarly, if several Investing Entities all have the same beneficial owner, they should be counted as only one investor. Generally, if the owners of a subsidiary or affiliate or the beneficiaries of a trust are not identical to the individual investors, then each record holder of an interest in a 3(c)(1) Fund is counted separately. This is the result even for trusts having the same trustee, if their beneficiaries differ in any respect.[32] If a group of investors owns interests in a 3(c)(1) Fund through various Investing Entities and no one else has an interest in those Investing Entities, the 3(c)(1) Fund may count only the individual investors, and not the separate Investing Entities, even if their ownership proportions in the Investing Entities are not identical.[33]

iv. Knowledgeable Employees

For purposes of the 100-Owner Limit, the following owners of the 3(c)(1) Fund's securities are excluded:

- a person who at the time he or she acquired such securities was, or who subsequently becomes,[34] a Knowledgeable Employee;
- a company owned exclusively by Knowledgeable Employees; and
- a person who, by one or more transfers permitted under the Company Act,[35] acquired securities originally acquired by a Knowledgeable Employee.[36]

In addition, the following owners of securities of a 3(c)(1) Fund do not count against the 100-Owner Limit: (1) a Knowledgeable Employee and his or her spouse who hold the securities as a joint interest; (2) an entity jointly owned by a Knowledgeable Employee and his or her spouse; (3) a family company trust or similar estate planning vehicle for which a Knowledgeable Employee makes the investment decisions and contributes the invested assets (individually or jointly

---

30. *American Bar Association*, Answer A.4(i).

31. *But see* § 3.2.2.i.c, *supra.*

32. *OSIRIS Management, Inc.*, SEC No-Action Letter (Feb. 17, 1984); *Railbox Co.*, SEC No-Action Letter (Sep. 10, 1984); *Nemo Capital Partners, L.P.*, SEC No-Action Letter (July 28, 1992).

33. *Nemo Capital Partners, L.P.*, SEC No-Action Letter (July 28, 1992); *Wm. S. Barnickle & Company*, SEC No-Action Letter (Nov. 1, 1994).

34. *American Bar Association*, Answers A.6 and A.7.

35. *See* § 3.2.2.v, *infra.*

36. Company Act Rule 3c–5, 17 C.F.R. § 270.3c–5.

with his or her spouse); or (4) an alter ego entity of a Knowledgeable Employee (such as an IRA or self-directed retirement plan account) that is owned only by the Knowledgeable Employee (individually or jointly with his or her spouse) and for which the Knowledgeable Employee makes all investment decisions (an "Alter Ego Entity").[37]

"Knowledgeable Employee" is defined as an executive officer, director, trustee, general partner or board member of, or person serving in a similar capacity with, the 3(c)(1) Fund or 3(c)(7) Fund. It also includes persons serving in such capacities for an affiliate of the 3(c)(1) Fund or 3(c)(7) Fund that manages the investment activities of the 3(c)(1) Fund or 3(c)(7) Fund. It also includes an employee (other than an employee performing solely clerical, secretarial or administrative functions) of the 3(c)(1) Fund or 3(c)(7) Fund, its affiliates or, in certain cases, affiliates of the investment adviser to the 3(c)(1) Fund or 3(c)(7) Fund, who, in connection with his or her regular duties, participates in the investment activities[38] of the 3(c)(1) Fund or 3(c)(7) Fund or the investment activities of other Covered Companies,[39] offshore funds, banks, insurance companies or savings and loan associations, or who participates in the investment activities of such affiliates that manage assets of certain pension or profit-sharing plans, underwriters, brokers or market intermediaries, provided in each case that the employee has performed those duties, or substantially similar duties on behalf of another company, for at least twelve months.[40] "Knowledgeable Employees" do not generally include marketing and investor relations professionals, attorneys, analysts, traders or financial, compliance, operations or accounting officers, unless they are executives of the 3(c)(1) Fund or 3(c)(7) Fund or an investment management affiliate.[41]

v. Transfers of Interests in 3(c)(1) Funds

Except in the limited circumstances discussed below, each transferee who receives an interest in a 3(c)(1) Fund is counted as a beneficial owner of the 3(c)(1) Fund.

a. Permitted Transfers

Under Company Act Rule 3c-6,[42] beneficial ownership by a transferee is deemed to be beneficial ownership by the transferor, if the transferee is:

- the estate of the transferor;
- a donee (defined as a person who acquires the security or interest as a gift or bequest or pursuant to an agreement relating to a legal separation or divorce); or

---

37. *American Bar Association*, Answers A.4 and A.8.

38. Knowledge of an appropriate entity's investment activities is insufficient unless accompanied by actual participation in those activities. *American Bar Association*, Answer A.1.

39. *See* § 3.2.2.i.a, *supra*.

40. Company Act Rule 3c-5, 17 C.F.R. § 270.3c-5; *PPM America Special Investments CBO II, L.P.*, SEC No-Action Letter (Apr. 16, 1998); *American Bar Association*, Answer A.2.

41. *American Bar Association*, Answer A.1.

42. 17 C.F.R. § 270.3c-6.

- a company established by the transferor exclusively for the benefit of (or owned exclusively by) the transferor and the persons specified in the preceding clauses.

This exception applies only to the specific transfers described in Rule 3c-6, and does not cover additional securities that such a transferee acquires from the 3(c)(1) Fund.[43] In addition, the SEC has not addressed many issues related to transfers of interests in 3(c)(1) Funds, including whether securities transferred under Rule 3c-6 can be transferred again and continue to be covered by the rule.

In addition, the SEC staff has issued several no-action letters when it has considered transfers to be involuntary and outside the 3(c)(1) Fund's control. For example, if an Investing Entity is a limited partnership and the general partner dies, causing the dissolution of the partnership and distribution of the interests of the 3(c)(1) Fund to the limited partners of that Investing Entity, the former limited partners of the Investing Entity will not be counted against the 100-Owner Limit and the former Investing Entity will continue to be considered to be the sole owner of the distributed interests.[44] On the other hand, the SEC staff refused to grant no-action relief for an investment in a 3(c)(1) Fund by an employee benefit plan that was terminated and that distributed the plan's interest in the 3(c)(1) Fund to the plan participants, because the SEC staff viewed that termination as voluntary.[45]

b. Public Charities

If an investor in a 3(c)(1) Fund donates an interest in the 3(c)(1) Fund to one or more public charities, the SEC staff will count the charities and the donor as a single beneficial owner of the 3(c)(1) Fund. This position reflects the public policy of supporting charitable organizations.[46]

vi. General Partner's Interest

A general partner's interest in a 3(c)(1) Fund usually should not be considered to be a security, with the possible exception of a general partner that is a passive investor and that does not actively participate in managing the 3(c)(1) Fund. As long as the general partner participates in management and does not own an interest as a limited partner, the general partner is not counted as a beneficial owner for purposes of the 100-Owner Limit.[47]

vii. Non-U.S. Investors

A non-U.S. individual or entity is counted against the 100-Owner Limit if the 3(c)(1) Fund is organized in the United States.[48]

---

43. 1997 Release, § III.C.

44. *Boston Ventures Limited Partnership*, SEC No-Action Letter (Aug. 5, 1992).

45. *Trivest Special Situations Fund 1985, L.P.*, SEC No-Action Letter (July 13, 1989).

46. *Id.*; *Commodities Corporation*, SEC No-Action Letter (June 7, 1991); *Wm. S. Barnickel & Company*, SEC No-Action Letter (Nov. 1, 1994).

47. *Colony Realty Partners 1986 L.P.*, SEC No-Action Letter (Apr. 27, 1988); *Shoreline Fund, L.P. and Condor Fund International, Inc.*, SEC No-Action Letter (Nov. 14, 1994).

48. *See* § 3.2.4, *infra.*

3. Integration

i. Integration of 3(c)(1) Funds

In some circumstances, two or more 3(c)(1) Funds with the same or related general partners, sponsors, promoters or investment advisers may be treated as a single 3(c)(1) Fund ("integrated") for purposes of determining whether the 100-Owner Limit is exceeded.[49]

a. The "Reasonable Investor" Test

The factors that the SEC staff considers in determining whether integration is appropriate under the Company Act include: (1) whether a reasonable investor would consider the interests in two or more 3(c)(1) Funds to be materially different; (2) whether the 3(c)(1) Funds share the same investment objectives, portfolio securities and portfolio risk/return characteristics; and (3) whether one or more of the following five factors (relevant to the question of integration under Securities Act section 4(2)) exist: (a) the different offerings are part of a single plan of financing; (b) they involve the issuance of the same class of securities; (c) the offerings are made at or about the same time; (d) the same type of consideration is received; and (e) the offerings are made for same general purpose.[50]

The first two of these factors are both difficult to distinguish from each other and subjective, affording the SEC ample latitude to challenge any arrangement that its staff disfavors. They also seem to be the most influential. In *Equitable Capital Management Corporation*,[51] for example, the SEC staff noted that three 3(c)(1) Funds trading in collateralized bond obligations had similar investment objectives, portfolio securities and risk/return characteristics. The SEC staff determined, however, that the 3(c)(1) Funds need not be integrated, because a reasonable investor would consider them materially different. The investors or underwriters had extensively negotiated the structure of each 3(c)(1) Fund, resulting in differences in the basic terms, including (1) different capital structures (different classes and relative proportions of various debt securities), (2) different projected yields and anticipated average lives of the securities, (3) different degrees of portfolio management discretion and (4) different management fees.

In *Oppenheimer Arbitrage Partners, L.P.*,[52] the SEC staff said it would not integrate two 3(c)(1) Funds that shared a general partner. One 3(c)(1) Fund was offered to tax-exempt investors, would not engage in short sales or financial futures transactions or write uncovered options and generally expected a low risk of loss;

---

49. *Monument Capital Management, Inc.*, SEC No-Action Letter (July 12, 1990) (common investment advisers); *Madison Park Investment Management, Inc.*, SEC No-Action Letter (Apr. 4, 1986) (common sponsor); *Joseph H. Moss*, SEC No-Action Letter (Feb. 27, 1983) (common promoter).

50. *Monument Capital Management, Inc.*, SEC No-Action Letter (July 12, 1990); *Equitable Capital Management Corporation*, SEC No-Action Letter (Jan. 6, 1992).

51. *Equitable Capital Management Corporation*, SEC No-Action Letter (Jan. 6, 1992).

52. *Oppenheimer Arbitrage Partners, L.P./Oppenheimer Institutional Arbitrage Investors, L.P.*, SEC No-Action Letter (Dec. 26, 1985).

the other was offered to taxable investors, engaged in short sales, leveraged its assets to the maximum extent permitted and expected a high rate of return and risk.

Two 3(c)(1) Funds also shared a general partner in *Meadow Lane Associates, L.P.*,[53] in which the SEC staff conditioned its decision not to integrate the 3(c)(1) Funds on the understanding that one invested in a wide range of growth securities while the other sought capital appreciation through arbitrage opportunities. The SEC staff noted that the risk/return characteristics of the two 3(c)(1) Funds were different, that they would be separately administered, and that no limited partner of either would, as an investor in that 3(c)(1) Fund, have the right to participate in the assets of the other.

In *Welsh, Carson, Anderson & Stowe*,[54] the SEC staff said it would not integrate three 3(c)(1) Funds that had affiliated general partners. One of the 3(c)(1) Funds was offered only to institutional clients, principally tax-exempt investors, and could not use leverage, purchase put options or sell securities short. The other two were offered solely to individuals and were allowed to use leverage, sell securities short and purchase put options. Nevertheless, these two funds were not integrated because one invested only in the health care industry and the other only in the information services industry, and only individuals familiar with the respective industry were allowed to invest in it.

The SEC staff has also indicated that it would not integrate an offshore hedge fund with a U.S. 3(c)(1) Fund even when the offshore hedge fund was formed to invest in the 3(c)(1) Fund, since the different tax laws and regulations of different countries would make them materially different to an investor.[55] The SEC staff similarly said it would not recommend integrating an offshore hedge fund with a U.S. 3(c)(1) Fund, even though they were to be managed virtually identically, because the different tax treatment of investments in those vehicles created materially different investments.[56] As a consequence, some investment pool managers create offshore hedge funds for non-U.S. investors and U.S. investors that are exempt from U.S. taxes and do not permit such investors to invest in the U.S. 3(c)(1) Funds that they manage.[57]

In other circumstances, the SEC staff declined to provide comfort regarding integration. In *Frontier Capital Management Company, Inc.*,[58] the SEC staff considered three separate limited partnerships with the same general partner: the "Capital Fund" would invest in a diverse portfolio consisting primarily of equity securities issued by companies with significant capital; the "Small Cap Fund" would purchase primarily corporate and equity securities of companies thought to have high growth potential; and the "Balanced Fund" would invest in a mix of common stocks and high grade fixed-income securities to balance growth, income and stability. Refusing to take a no-action position, the SEC staff stated that it did not find the three hedge funds to be materially different to a reasonable investor qualified to

---

53. *Meadow Lane Associates, L.P.*, SEC No-Action Letter (May 24, 1989).
54. *Welsh, Carson, Anderson & Stowe*, SEC No-Action Letter (June 18, 1993).
55. *Pasadena Investment Trust*, SEC No-Action Letter (Jan. 22, 1993).
56. *Shoreline Fund, L.P.*, SEC No-Action Letter (Apr. 11, 1994).
57. *See* § 4.4.1, *infra*.
58. *Frontier Capital Management Company, Inc.*, SEC No-Action Letter (July 13, 1988).

purchase any of them. The SEC staff cited the similar investment objectives of the first two hedge funds and the potentially overlapping portfolios of all three hedge funds, and noted that all three hedge funds were designed, in essence, for one group of investors with similar investment profiles.

Similarly, in *Monument Capital Management, Inc.*,[59] the SEC staff took the position that a reasonable investor would not view two limited partnerships as being materially different. The two partnerships had unaffiliated general partners, but were advised by closely affiliated investment advisers and shared a common investment objective with respect to all of one partnership's capital and up to eighty percent of the other partnership's capital. The staff did not agree that simply because the two partnerships had unaffiliated general partners they should not be integrated.

In *Madison Park Investment Management*,[60] the SEC staff denied a no-action request with respect to integration for a series of trusts formed to provide high rates of return by writing covered options. The proposed trusts would have differed only with respect to option strategy as a result of the timing of the formation of each trust.

Accordingly, to avoid integration, at least in the SEC staff's view, 3(c)(1) Funds need to be distinguished by more than different general partners, different portfolios or different expected rates of return. To support an argument that integration is not warranted, the manager should consider tailoring different 3(c)(1) Funds for distinctly different groups of investors (such as tax–exempt versus taxable investors) and avoiding overlap in the specific portfolios of the 3(c)(1) Funds or even their categories of investments.

b. Consequences of Integration

If two or more 3(c)(1) Funds are integrated, the beneficial owners are counted as if the different 3(c)(1) Funds were a single 3(c)(1) Fund. Accordingly, logic would seem to dictate that an investor in both 3(c)(1) Funds should be counted only once. The 10% Test should be calculated with respect to the assets and liabilities of the 3(c)(1) Funds on a combined basis.

In the only no-action letter specifically addressing how to calculate the number of beneficial owners when funds are integrated, however, the SEC staff stated that an entity cannot use the integration doctrine to avoid the Company Act's registration requirement.[61] In that instance, the sponsor of two 3(c)(1) Funds, each with a small number of limited partners, argued that the two 3(c)(1) Funds should be integrated for purposes of determining whether a single Investing Entity held more than ten percent of the integrated 3(c)(1) Fund's voting securities. Without addressing the factual basis for integrating the two 3(c)(1) Funds, the staff declined to assure the sponsor that the voting securities of the two 3(c)(1) Funds would be aggregated for purposes of applying the 10% Test.

---

59.   *Monument Capital Management, Inc.*, SEC No–Action Letter (July 12, 1990).
60.   *Madison Park Investment*, SEC No–Action Letter (Mar. 4, 1986).
61.   *Weiss, Peck & Greer Venture Associates II, L.P.*, SEC No–Action Letter (Apr. 10, 1990).

ii. No Integration of 3(c)(1) and 3(c)(7) Funds

A 3(c)(1) Fund and a 3(c)(7) Fund are not integrated for purposes of determining whether the 3(c)(1) Fund's 100-Owner Limit is exceeded.[62]

iii. Integration of Hedge Funds and Separately Managed Accounts

The manager of a 3(c)(1) Fund may also manage separate client accounts outside the 3(c)(1) Fund. The SEC staff could attempt to integrate a 3(c)(1) Fund and separate accounts managed by the same investment adviser. Even if an investment adviser does not manage a 3(c)(1) Fund, in some situations the SEC may attempt to integrate the investment adviser's managed accounts and view them as forming an investment company.[63] This may occur, for example, if the investment adviser manages multiple brokerage accounts through a so-called "wrap fee" program. In a typical wrap fee program an investment adviser employs the same investment strategy for all participants in that wrap fee program. The program participants participate through their brokerage accounts, and not by purchasing an interest in a partnership or other company (which would be subject to the 100-Owner Limit). The SEC could argue that the investment adviser effectively created an investment company for the brokerage accounts participating in the wrap fee program and apply the 100-Owner Limit.

If necessary to avoid reaching the 100-Owner Limit, an investment adviser may avoid integration of separately managed accounts with each other or with a 3(c)(1) Fund by following Company Act Rule 3a-4.[64] Rule 3a-4 provides that an investment adviser is not deemed to have created an investment company if the following conditions are satisfied:

- each client's account is managed on the basis of the client's individual needs and restrictions;
- each client can instruct the investment adviser to sell, or not to buy, particular securities that otherwise might be held or purchased;
- on opening the account and at least annually thereafter, the investment adviser determines each client's financial situation and objectives and gives the client the opportunity to impose or modify restrictions on the account;
- at least quarterly, the investment adviser gives each client an account statement and the opportunity to communicate to the investment adviser any change in the client's financial situation and to impose or modify restrictions on the account;
- appropriate employees of the investment adviser are reasonably available to each client for consultation; and
- each client maintains all indicia of ownership of the account's securities and funds, such as the right to withdraw and vote securities, and receives notification of each transaction.

---

62. Company Act § 3(c)(7)(E), 15 U.S.C. § 80a-3(c)(7)(E).
63. *See Clarke Lanzen Skalla Investment Firm, Inc.*, SEC administrative proceeding (June 16, 1995).
64. 17 C.F.R. § 270.3a-4.

4. Non-U.S. Funds

Company Act section 7(d)[65] prohibits a fund organized outside the United States from using the mails or any means or instrumentality of interstate commerce (such as the telephone) to offer for sale, sell or deliver after sale, in connection with a public offering, any security that it has issued. The SEC staff interprets Company Act section 3(c)(1)[66] in conjunction with section 7(d); a non-U.S. fund may conduct a private offering of its securities in the United States in reliance on section 3(c)(1) and at the same time conduct a public offering of its securities outside the United States if it never has more than 100 beneficial holders of its securities residing in the United States and does not conduct a public offering within the United States.[67] Accordingly, a non-U.S. fund should appropriately restrict transfers of its securities to ensure that it does not exceed the 100–Owner Limit with respect to its U.S. beneficial owners.

5. Public Offering Prohibition

A 3(c)(1) Fund may not make or propose to make a public offering of its securities.[68] The SEC interprets the non-public offering condition consistently with Securities Act section 4(2).[69] Section 4(2) provides that the registration provisions of Securities Act section 5[70] do not apply to an issuer transaction that does not involve any public offering. To avoid engaging in a public offering, most hedge funds rely on the safe harbor provided by Rule 506[71] promulgated by the SEC under Securities Act section 4(2).[72]

---

§ 3.3 Section 3(c)(7) Exclusion

---

1. General Statement of the Rule

Company Act section 3(c)(7)[73] excludes any pooled investment vehicle from the definition of an investment company if all of the beneficial owners of its

---

65.   15 U.S.C. § 80a-7(d).
66.   15 U.S.C. § 80a-3(c)(1).
67.   *Touche Remnant & Co.*, SEC No-Action Letter (Aug. 27, 1984).
68.   Company Act § 3(c)(1), 15 U.S.C. § 80a-3(c)(1).
69.   15 U.S.C. § 77(d)(2). See *Arthur E. Fox*, SEC No-Action Letter (Dec. 12, 1974); *Underwood Neuhaus & Co., Inc.*, SEC No-Action Letter (Feb. 13, 1975); *Glenwood Investment Corp.*, SEC No-Action Letter (Aug. 10, 1994). While offerings made in conformity with Rule 506 of Regulation D under the Securities Act are deemed not to involve a public offering under section 3(c)(1), offerings made in compliance with Rule 147, 504 or 505 under, or section 3(a)(11) of, the Securities Act are not necessarily nonpublic within the meaning of this section. *J.Y. Barry Arbitrage Management Inc.*, SEC No-Action Letter (Oct. 18, 1989); *C. Evans Patterson*, SEC No-Action Letter (Mar. 9, 1988); *San Jose Capital Corp.*, SEC No-Action Letter (Feb. 14, 1983).
70.   15 U.S.C. § 77e.
71.   17 C.F.R. § 230.506.
72.   *See* § 5.3, *infra*.
73.   15 U.S.C. § 80a-3(c)(7).

outstanding securities are "qualified purchasers," as defined under the Company Act ("Qualified Purchasers"),[74] and it does not make or propose to make a public offering of its securities.[75]

2. Permitted Owners of 3(c)(7) Funds

Securities of 3(c)(7) Funds may be held only by Qualified Purchasers and other persons described below in this section.

i. Qualified Purchasers

A Qualified Purchaser is defined as:

- an individual (including any person who holds a joint, community property or other similar shared ownership interest with that person's spouse) who holds at least $5,000,000 in Investments (as defined below);[76]
- a Family Company (defined as a legal entity or other organized group of persons that is wholly[77] owned directly or indirectly by or for two or more individuals who are related as siblings or spouses (including former spouses), or direct lineal descendants by birth or adoption, spouses (including former spouses)[78] of such persons, the estates of such persons, or foundations, charitable organizations or trusts established by or for the benefit of such persons), that owns at least $5,000,000 in Investments;[79]
- a trust that is not a Family Company as described above and that is not formed for the specific purpose of investing in the 3(c)(7) Fund and of which each trustee who makes investment decisions on behalf of the trust[80] and each contributor is a Qualified Purchaser;[81]
- a person, acting for such person's own account or the accounts of other Qualified Purchasers, who owns and invests on a discretionary basis at least $25,000,000 in Investments;[82] or

---

74. Company Act § 2(a)(51), 15 U.S.C. § 80a-2(a)(51).

75. *See* § 3.2.5, *supra*. The SEC has not considered the non-public offering condition with respect to a 3(c)(7) Fund, but almost certainly would apply the same standards as apply to a 3(c)(1) Fund, although the SEC staff may be considering relieving 3(c)(7) Funds from the prohibition on general solicitation and advertising.

76. Company Act § 2(a)(51)(A)(i), 15 U.S.C. § 80a-2(a)(51)(A)(i); Company Act Rule 2a51-1(g)(2), 17 C.F.R. § 270.2a51-1(g)(2).

77. *American Bar Association*, Answer C.4.

78. *Redwood Investment Fund, LLC*, SEC No-Action Letter (Oct. 14, 1997).

79. Company Act § 2(a)(51)(A)(ii), 15 U.S.C. § 80a-2(a)(51)(A)(ii). The family relationship requirement is also satisfied if all beneficiaries of a family trust are lineal descendants of the trust's settlor and are related as aunts, uncles, nieces and nephews. *Meadowbrook Real Estate Fund*, SEC No-Action Letter (Aug. 26, 1998).

80. *American Bar Association*, Answer C.2.

81. Company Act § 2(a)(51)(A)(iii), 15 U.S.C. § 80a-2(a)(51)(A)(iii). A trust can be a Qualified Purchaser, notwithstanding that its settlor was not a Qualified Purchaser when he or she contributed assets to the trust, if the settlor (a) is alive, (b) is a Qualified Purchaser when the trust invests in a 3(c)(7) Fund and (c) has authority to approve the investment. *Meadowbrook Real Estate Fund*, SEC No-Action Letter (Aug. 26, 1998). The Qualified Purchaser status of all of a trust's beneficiaries, however, is generally insufficient to make the trust a Qualified Purchaser. *American Bar Association*, Answer C.3.

82. Company Act § 2(a)(51)(A)(iv), 15 U.S.C. § 80a-2(a)(51)(A)(iv).

- a company (regardless of the amount of such company's Investments) beneficially owned exclusively by Qualified Purchasers[83] or by the company's Knowledgeable Employees.[84]

For purposes of the second and fifth categories, a company will not be a Qualified Purchaser if it is formed for the specific purpose of investing in the 3(c)(7) Fund, unless each beneficial owner of the company's securities is a Qualified Purchaser.[85] The SEC staff has indicated that an employee benefit plan that permits participants to direct their investments will be disregarded and all of its participants must be Qualified Purchasers.[86] On the other hand, the SEC staff has stated that a 3(c)(7) Fund may look to the Qualified Purchaser status of an employee benefit plan, and not the plan's participants, if the plan is a participant-directed, defined-contribution plan whose participants could allocate their capital to generic investment options, but have no role in deciding whether assets allocated to a particular investment option will be invested in the 3(c)(7) Fund.[87]

An individual Qualified Purchaser's Alter Ego Entity, such as an individual retirement account or self-directed retirement account, is also considered to be a Qualified Purchaser.[88]

ii. Investments

"Investments"[89] is defined to include:

- Securities of an issuer that does not have a control relationship with the prospective Qualified Purchaser that owns the securities, unless the issuer is (1) a company that files reports pursuant to Exchange Act section 13 or 15(d),[90] or that has a class of securities that are listed on a "designated offshore securities market," as defined by Regulation S[91] under the Securities Act, (2) an investment company, as defined by the Company Act, a company exempt from the definition of investment company under certain sections of the Company Act, or a commodity pool, or (3) a company with shareholders' equity of at least $50,000,000.[92]
- Real estate held for investment, not used for personal purposes, and not used as a place of business or in connection with the conduct of a trade or business

---

83.   Company Act Rule 2a51-3(b), 17 C.F.R. § 270.2a51-3(b). For purposes of this rule "company" does not include a trust. *American Bar Association*, Answer C.3.

84.   *Paragon Advisers, Inc.*, SEC No-Action Letter (Oct. 1, 1998).

85.   Company Act Rule 2a51-3(a), 17 C.F.R. § 270.2a51-3(a).

86.   *H.E. Blatt Grocery Company*, SEC No-Action Letter (May 18, 2001).

87.   *Id.*

88.   *American Bar Association*, Answer B.2.

89.   Company Act Rule 2a51-1, 17 C.F.R. § 270.2a51-1.

90.   15 U.S.C. § 78n or 78o.

91.   17 C.F.R. §§ 230.901 *et seq.*

92.   Company Act Rules 2a51-1(a)(3), 2a51-1(a)(7) and 2a51-1(b)(1), 17 C.F.R. §§ 270.2a51-1(a)(3), 270.2a51-1(a)(7) and 270.2a51-1(b)(1). An equity interest in a securities-related business (such as a hedge fund) is deemed a "security" for purposes of Company Act Rule 2a51-1(b)(1), regardless of whether it would be deemed a "security" for purposes of the Securities Act. *Sullivan & Cromwell*, SEC No-Action Letter (Dec. 29, 1997).

by a prospective Qualified Purchaser or a family member. Real estate owned by a prospective Qualified Purchaser that is engaged primarily in the business of investing, trading or developing real estate may be deemed to be held for investment. Residential real estate will be deemed held for investment if deductions with respect to the property are not disallowed by Tax Code section 280A.[93]

- Commodity interests held for investment, including commodity futures contracts, options on commodity futures contracts, and options on physical commodities traded on or subject to the rules of a contract market designated for trading such instruments under the CEA or a board of trade or exchange outside the United States as contemplated by certain provisions of the CEA rules ("Commodity Interests").[94]

- Physical commodities held for investment, including any commodity held in physical form with respect to which a Commodity Interest is traded on a market described in the preceding clause.[95]

- Certain financial contracts[96] entered into for investment purposes, such as swaps and repurchase agreements.[97]

- Certain unfunded capital commitments[98] from investors in a prospective Qualified Purchaser that is a Covered Company or a commodity pool.[99]

- Cash and cash equivalents (including non-U.S. currencies) held for investment, including bank deposits, certificates of deposit, bankers acceptances and similar bank instruments, and the net cash surrender value of insurance policies.[100]

- Commodity Interests, physical commodities and financial contracts will be deemed held for investment if held by a prospective Qualified Purchaser primarily engaged in investing or trading in such Investments.[101]

---

93. Company Act Rules 2a51-1(b)(2) and 2a51-1(c)(1), 17 C.F.R. §§ 270.2a51-1(b)(2) and 270.2a51-1(c)(1).

94. Company Act Rules 2a51-1(a)(1) and 2a51-1(b)(3), 17 C.F.R. §§ 270.2a51-1(a)(1) and 270.2a51-1(b)(3).

95. Company Act Rules 2a51-1(a)(5) and 2a51-1(b)(4), 17 C.F.R. §§ 270.2a51-1(a)(5) and 2a51-1(b)(4).

96. A financial contract is any arrangement that "(a) takes the form of an individually negotiated contract, agreement, or option to buy, sell, lend, swap, or repurchase, or other similar individually negotiated transaction commonly entered into by participants in the financial markets; (b) is in respect of securities, commodities, currencies, interest or other rates, other measures of value, or any other financial or economic interest similar in purpose or function to any of the foregoing; and (c) is entered into in response to a request from a counter party for a quotation, or is otherwise entered into and structured to accommodate the objectives of the counter party to such arrangement." Company Act § 3(c)(2)(B)(ii), 15 U.S.C. § 80a-3(c)(2)(B)(ii).

97. Company Act Rule 2a51-1(b)(5), 17 C.F.R. § 270.2a51-1(b)(5).

98. A capital commitment is a firm agreement or similar binding commitment pursuant to which a person agrees to acquire an interest in, or make a capital contribution to, a prospective Qualified Purchaser. Company Act Rule 2a51-1(b)(6), 17 C.F.R. § 2a51-1(b)(6).

99. *Id.* The SEC staff also permitted a company exempted from certain provisions of the Company Act under section 6(b) to avail itself of 17 C.F.R. § 270.2a51-1(b)(6). *The BSC Employee Fund, L.P.,* SEC No-Action Letter (Oct. 14, 1997).

100. Company Act Rule 2a51-1(b)(7), 17 C.F.R. § 270.2a51-1(b)(7).

101. Company Act Rule 2a51-1(c)(2), 17 C.F.R. § 270.2a51-1(c)(2).

iii. Valuation

The value of an Investment may be, at the option of the 3(c)(7) Fund, either the Investment's cost or its "fair market value" on the most recent practicable date. In the absence of recent market trading, fair market value may be determined by an appraisal by an independent third party.[102] Commodity Interests are valued by the initial margin or portion of the premium deposited.[103]

iv. Deductions for Acquisition Debt

Any outstanding debt incurred to acquire the Investment is deducted from the value of the Investment.[104] If a prospective Qualified Purchaser is a Family Company, any outstanding debt incurred by an owner of the Family Company to acquire the Investments held by the Family Company is deducted.[105]

v. Jointly Held Investments

A natural person may include in the amount of the person's Investments any Investments held jointly with the person's spouse, and Investments in which the person shares with the spouse a community property or similar shared ownership interest. If spouses make a joint investment as Qualified Purchasers, each spouse may include in the amount of that spouse's Investments any Investments owned by the other spouse, whether or not such Investments are held jointly. In determining the amount of a joint Investment, the outstanding amount of any debt incurred by either spouse to acquire the Investment is deducted.[106]

vi. Pension and Retirement Plans

An individual may include in the amount of his or her Investments any Investments held in his or her individual retirement account or similar account, such as a 401(k) plan, if he or she makes all of the investment decisions for the account.[107] This is true even if the plan's trustee or sponsor selects the range of investment options from which the individual can choose.[108]

A participant-directed, defined-contribution plan cannot be a Qualified Purchaser unless all participants are Qualified Purchasers. A defined-benefit or other retirement plan that owns $25,000,000 of Investments and does not permit participants to decide whether or how much to invest in particular investment alternatives may be a Qualified Purchaser.[109]

---

102.   Company Act Rule 2a51-1(d), 17 C.F.R. § 270.2a51-1(d); 1997 Release, § II.A.3.a.
103.   Company Act Rule 2a51-1(d)(1), 17 C.F.R. § 270.2a51-1(d)(1).
104.   Company Act Rule 2a51-1(e), 17 C.F.R. § 270.2a51-1(e).
105.   Company Act Rule 2a51-1(f), 17 C.F.R. § 270.2a51-1(f).
106.   Company Act Rule 2a51-1(g)(2), 17 C.F.R. § 270.2a51-1(g)(2).
107.   Company Act Rule 2a51-1(g)(4), 17 C.F.R. § 270.2a51-1(g)(4).
108.   1997 Release, note 77.
109.   1997 Release, § II.A.8.

vii. Other Forms of Holding Investments

Investments held by a prospective Qualified Purchaser's Alter Ego Entity may be attributed to the prospective Qualified Purchaser.[110] For example, investments held in a prospective Qualified Purchaser's individual retirement account are attributable to that prospective Qualified Purchaser.[111]

viii. Investments Held by Affiliated Entities

In determining the amount of Investments owned by an entity, there may be included Investments owned by (a) majority-owned subsidiaries of the entity, (b) investments owned by a parent company (a "Parent Company") of which such entity is a majority-owned subsidiary, and (c) a majority-owned subsidiary of the Parent Company and other majority-owned subsidiaries of the Parent Company.[112]

ix. Qualified Institutional Buyers

An investor in a 3(c)(7) Fund that is a "qualified institutional buyer," as defined in Securities Act Rule 144A[113] (a "QIB"), is a Qualified Purchaser, if (a) it is (1) an institution that owns and invests on a discretionary basis $100,000,000 of securities of unaffiliated issuers ("QIB Securities"), (2) a bank that meets such $100,000,000 test and that has an audited net worth of at least $25,000,000 or (3) a registered dealer that owns and invests on a discretionary basis at least $25,000,000 of QIB Securities, and (b) it is acting for its own account, the account of another QIB or the account of a Qualified Purchaser.[114] A QIB that is a self-directed employee benefit plan, such as a 401(k) plan, "will not be deemed to be acting for its own account if investment decisions with respect to the plan are made by the beneficiaries of the plan, except with respect to investment decisions made solely by the fiduciary, trustee or sponsor of the plan."[115] That is, such investment decisions must be made by a Qualified Purchaser.

x. Funds of Funds

A Covered Company[116] that desires to become a Qualified Purchaser (a "Purchasing Fund") must obtain the consent of its Beneficial Owners (defined below) that acquired interests in the Purchasing Fund before May 1, 1996.[117] "Beneficial Owners" in most cases means the investors in the Purchasing Fund. A Family Company or trust, however, need only obtain unanimous consent of all trustees,

---

110. 1997 Release, § II.A.7.

111. *See* § 3.2.2.xiv, *infra*

112. Company Act Rule 2a51-1(g)(3), 17 C.F.R. § 270.2a51-1(g)(3).

113. 17 C.F.R. § 230.144A.

114. Company Act Rule 2a51-1(g)(1), 17 C.F.R. § 270.2a51-1(g)(1).

115. Company Act Rule 2a51-1(g)(1)(ii), 17 C.F.R. § 270.2a51-1(g)(1)(ii).

116. *See* § 3.2.2.i.a, *supra*.

117. Company Act § 2(a)(51)(C), 15 U.S.C. § 80a-2(a)(51)(C).

directors or general partners.[118] Persons that were, before May 1, 1996, Beneficial Owners of any Covered Company that directly or indirectly owns any of the securities of the Purchasing Fund (an "Owning Fund") must also consent to the treatment of the Purchasing Fund as a Qualified Purchaser if:

- the Owning Fund is an investment company or a Covered Company;
- on April 30, 1996, the Owning Fund owned ten percent or more of the Purchasing Fund's limited partner, member or other interests;
- on April 30, 1996, the Owning Fund had more than ten percent of its total assets invested in 3(c)(1) Funds, including the Purchasing Fund; and
- the Owning Fund controls,[119] is controlled by, or is under common control with, either the Purchasing Fund or the 3(c)(7) Fund in which the Purchasing Fund desires to invest (the "Target Fund").[120]

An Owning Fund is not deemed to own indirectly the securities of the Purchasing Fund unless there is a control relationship between the Owning Fund and either the Purchasing Fund or the Target Fund.[121] The beneficial owners of any Covered Company that owns the securities of the Owning Fund need not consent, and are deemed beneficial owners of the Purchasing Fund, unless a control relationship exists between the Owning Fund and either the Purchasing Fund or the Target Fund.[122] A Purchasing Fund can obtain a general consent with respect to most transactions in which it will be a Qualified Purchaser. A specific consent may be required in situations where a control relationship exists between the Purchasing Fund or certain of its beneficial owners and the Target Fund.[123]

xi. Reasonable Belief

Any person that a 3(c)(7) Fund or its representative "reasonably believes" is a Qualified Purchaser may be treated as such.[124] Neither the Company Act nor the Company Act rules prescribe the documentation required to support a reasonable belief that an investor is a Qualified Purchaser. The SEC expressly declined to prescribe such a list when promulgating the rules interpreting Company Act section 3(c)(7).[125] Nevertheless, it should be reasonable to rely on a properly completed and signed subscription agreement, at least in the absence of notice of facts that would cast doubt on the representations in the subscription agreement.

---

118.   *Id.*

119.   For this purpose, "control" means the power to control the management or policies of a company (unless such power is solely the result of an official position in the company), or the ownership, either directly or through one or more intermediaries, of more than twenty-five percent of the voting securities of a company. 1997 Release, note 38.

120.   Company Act § 2(a)(51)(C), 15 U.S.C. § 80a-2(a)(51)(C); Company Act Rule 2a51-1(g)(1)(ii), 17 C.F.R. 270.2a51-1(g)(1)(ii).

121.   Company Act Rule 2a51-2(d), 17 C.F.R. § 270.2a51-2(d).

122.   Company Act Rule 2a51-2(e), 17 C.F.R. § 270.2a51-2(e).

123.   1997 Release, § II.B.2.b.

124.   Company Act Rule 2a51-1(h), 17 C.F.R. § 270.2a51-1(h).

125.   *See* 1997 Release, § II.A.6.

xii. When Qualified Purchaser Status is Determined

An investor in a 3(c)(7) Fund must be determined to be a Qualified Purchaser each time the investor makes an investment in the 3(c)(7) Fund, except for an additional investment pursuant to the investor's pre-existing binding commitment.[126]

xiii. Knowledgeable Employees

A Knowledgeable Employee[127] is deemed not to be a beneficial owner of a 3(c)(7) Fund's securities. Accordingly, for the purpose of determining whether all of the owners of the outstanding securities of a 3(c)(7) Fund are Qualified Purchasers, Knowledgeable Employees are excluded.[128] A 3(c)(7) Fund may rely on Company Act section 3(c)(7) if Knowledgeable Employees that are not Qualified Purchasers invest in that Fund and if the Fund otherwise complies with the requirements of Company Act section 3(c)(7).

xiv. Holders of Transferred Interests in 3(c)(7) Funds

Except in the limited circumstances discussed below, each transferee who receives an interest in a 3(c)(7) Fund is counted as a beneficial owner of the 3(c)(7) Fund and, therefore, must be a Qualified Purchaser.

a. Permitted Transfers

Recipients of 3(c)(7) Fund securities from Qualified Purchasers or Grandfathered Investors (defined below)[129] by gift or bequest or under circumstances such as death, divorce, legal separation or other involuntary event are treated as Qualified Purchasers with respect to that 3(c)(7) Fund.[130] In addition, beneficial ownership by a company established by a Qualified Purchaser or Grandfathered Investor transferor exclusively for the benefit of (or owned exclusively by) the transferor and the transferees described in the preceding sentence is deemed to be beneficial ownership by the transferor.[131] These exceptions apply only to these specific transfers, however, and do not cover additional securities acquired by a transferee from the 3(c)(7) Fund.[132] In addition, the SEC has not addressed many issues related to transfers of interests in 3(c)(7) Funds, including whether securities transferred under these exceptions can be transferred again within these exceptions.

b. Public Charities

The SEC has not indicated whether, if a Qualified Purchaser or other permitted investor in a 3(c)(7) Fund donates an interest in the 3(c)(7) Fund to one or more

126. 1997 Release, § II.A.9.
127. *See* § 3.2.2.iv, *supra*.
128. Company Act Rule 3c-5(b), 17 C.F.R. § 270.3c-5(b).
129. *American Bar Association*, Answer C.5(i).
130. Company Act § 3(c)(7)(A), 15 U.S.C. § 80a-3(c)(7)(A); Company Act Rule 3c-6, 17 C.F.R. § 270.3c-6.
131. Company Act Rule 3c-6(b)(3), 17 C.F.R. § 270.3c-6(b)(3).
132. 1997 Release, § III.C.

public charities, each charity would be considered a Qualified Purchaser with respect to the 3(c)(7) Fund. An affirmative position on this issue would, however, be consistent with SEC no-action letters regarding 3(c)(1) Funds, which reflect the public policy of supporting charitable organizations.[133]

xv. General Partner's Interest

A general partner's interest in a 3(c)(7) Fund usually should not be considered a security if the general partner actively participates in managing the 3(c)(7) Fund and does not own an interest as a limited partner. Such a general partner is deemed not to be a beneficial owner of securities of the 3(c)(7) Fund and does not need to be a Qualified Purchaser.[134]

xvi. Non-U.S. Investors

A non-U.S. individual or entity that invests in a 3(c)(7) Fund must be a Qualified Purchaser (or other permitted person) if the 3(c)(7) Fund is organized in the United States.[135]

3. Integration of Separately Managed Accounts

Many 3(c)(7) Fund managers separately manage client accounts in addition to their 3(c)(7) Funds. The SEC staff could attempt to integrate a 3(c)(7) Fund and separate accounts managed by the same investment adviser. If the SEC staff were to succeed in doing so, the 3(c)(7) Fund would not be able to rely on the exclusion provided by Company Act section 3(c)(7), unless, perhaps, the account holders were Qualified Purchasers whom the investment adviser did not publicly solicit. Company Act Rule 3a-4 also applies to 3(c)(7) Funds.[136]

4. Non-U.S. Funds

A fund organized outside of the United States may not sell its securities to U.S. persons in connection with a public offering.[137] A non-U.S. fund may conduct a private offering to U.S. persons who are Qualified Purchasers in reliance on Company Act section 3(c)(7).[138]

---

133. *Trivest Special Situations Fund 1985, L.P.*, SEC No-Action Letter (July 13, 1989); *Commodities Corporation*, SEC No-Action Letter (June 7, 1991); *Wm. S. Barnickel & Company*, SEC No-Action Letter (Nov. 1, 1994) (each allowing a 3(c)(1) Fund to count various charities to which an investor had donated securities of the 3(c)(1) Fund as a single investor for the purposes of the 100-Owner Limit).

134. Cf. *Colony Realty Partners 1986 L.P.*, SEC No-Action Letter (Apr. 27, 1988); *Shoreline Fund, L.P. and Condor Fund International, Inc.*, SEC No-Action Letter (Nov. 14, 1994) (a 3(c)(1) Fund's general partner is not counted as a beneficial owner for purposes of the 100-Owner Limit).

135. *See* § 3.3.4, *infra.*, regarding offshore hedge funds.

136. *See* § 3.2.3.iii, *supra.*

137. *See* § 3.2.4, *supra.*

138. *Goodwin, Proctor & Hoar*, SEC No-Action Letter (Feb. 28, 1997); *Goodwin, Proctor & Hoar*, SEC No-Action Letter (Oct. 5, 1998). *See* § 3.2.4, *supra.*

5. Corporate Taxation

Under the Tax Code, some risk exists that a 3(c)(7) Fund with more than 100 investors could be taxed as a corporation for federal income tax purposes.[139]

6. Exchange Act Reporting Obligations

If a 3(c)(7) Fund has more than 500 investors, it may be required to register[140] under the Exchange Act and file reports under Exchange Act section 13,[141] such as annual reports on Form 10-K, quarterly reports on Form 10-Q, occasional reports on Form 8-K, proxy statements under Exchange Act section 14 and other reports and statements. In that case, certain of its investors and its directors and officers would be subject to reporting requirements and restrictions with respect to their interests in the 3(c)(7) Fund.

---

§ 3.4 Converting 3(c)(1) Fund to 3(c)(7) Fund

---

1. Procedure

A 3(c)(1) Fund may be converted to a 3(c)(7) Fund if each investor in the converting hedge fund (the "Converting Fund") that first invested in the Converting Fund after September 1, 1996, is a Qualified Purchaser.[142] Before the conversion, the Converting Fund must give each Beneficial Owner (defined below), including Beneficial Owners that are Qualified Purchasers,[143] (a) notice that future investors must be Qualified Purchasers and will no longer be limited to 100 and (b) a reasonable opportunity to redeem the Beneficial Owner's interest in the Converting Fund for a proportionate share of the Converting Fund's net assets, even if the Converting Fund's governing documents normally would not allow such a redemption at that time.[144]

In most cases, the investors in the Converting Fund are deemed to be its "Beneficial Owners" and notice need not be provided to the constituent owners of investors that are entities (such as a fund of funds). The notice and redemption opportunity must, however, be provided to each of the security holders of any investor in the Converting Fund, if all of the following apply to the investor:

---

139. *See* § 16.1.2, *infra.*
140. Exchange Act § 12, 15 U.S.C. § 78(l).
141. 15 U.S.C. § 78(n).
142. Company Act § 3(c)(7)(B)(i), 15 U.S.C. § 80a-3(c)(7)(B)(i).
143. 1997 Release, § II.B.1.c.i.
144. Company Act § 3(c)(7)(B)(ii), 15 U.S.C. § 80a-3(c)(7)(B)(ii).

- the investor is an investment company or a Covered Company;[145]
- on October 11, 1996, the investor owned at least ten percent of the Converting Fund's limited partner interests;
- on October 11, 1996, more than ten percent of the investor's total assets were invested in 3(c)(1) Funds, including the Converting Fund; and
- the investor controls, is controlled by, or is under common control with, the Converting Fund.[146]

The Beneficial Owner's proportionate share of the Converting Fund's net assets is determined according to the Converting Fund's governing documents.[147] In many cases, the governing documents provide for a hold-back of five or ten percent of the amount to be paid to a redeeming limited partner until the Converting Fund's books are audited at the end of the Converting Fund's fiscal year. The SEC has stated that such hold-backs may be permissible in the context of a redemption in connection with a 3(c)(7) conversion if they do not act as a penalty for exercising the redemption right.[148]

The redemption payment must be made in cash unless the Converting Fund elects to provide the investor with the option of receiving, and the investor agrees to receive, assets in kind. If this option is provided, disclosure concerning this opportunity must be included in the notice of conversion.[149]

The conversion rules do not override any provisions in the Converting Fund's governing documents or other agreements or applicable law that could prevent a conversion. For example, if a 3(c)(1) Fund's partnership agreement prohibits the 3(c)(1) Fund from having more than 100 investors, that agreement would need to be amended before the 3(c)(1) Fund could sell its securities to more than 100 investors, even if the 3(c)(7) conversion rules are followed.[150] The conversion rules also do not override the fiduciary duties that a 3(c)(1) Fund manager may have to its investors. For example, a manager may need to consider whether the conversion, and the concomitant increase in the Converting Fund's assets and number of investors, is in the best interests of the Converting Fund's security holders.[151]

2. Additional Investments by Grandfathered Investors

An investor that invested in a Converting Fund before September 2, 1996 (a "Grandfathered Investor"), and has not thereafter withdrawn from the Converting Fund, may continue to acquire securities of the Converting Fund (directly or through an Alter Ego Entity)[152] or may transfer securities of the 3(c)(7) Fund to an Alter Ego Entity,[153] whether or not the Grandfathered Investor is a Qualified Purchaser.

---

145. *See* § 3.2.2.i.a, *supra*.
146. Company Act Rule 2a51-2(b), 17 C.F.R. § 270.2a51-2(b).
147. 1997 Release, § II.B.1.c.ii.
148. *Id.*
149. Company Act § 3(c)(7)(C), 15 U.S.C. § 80a-3(c)(7)(C).
150. 1997 Release, § II.B.1.c.ii.
151. *Id.*
152. *American Bar Association*, Answers B.1 and C.5(ii).
153. *American Bar Association*, Answer C.5(i).

3. Integration with New 3(c)(1) Fund

If an investment adviser manages a 3(c)(1) Fund and a 3(c)(7) Fund, even with identical investment strategies, the two hedge funds are not integrated in calculating the number of investors in the 3(c)(1) Fund.[154] An investment adviser that converts its existing 3(c)(1) Fund into a 3(c)(7) Fund and then begins a new 3(c)(1) Fund (thereby creating 100 new openings for non-Qualified Purchasers) must, however, undertake the conversion in good faith, based on the bona fide purpose of selling securities in the Converting Fund to Qualified Purchasers.[155] Whether the Converting Fund has such a bona fide purpose will be determined by the relevant facts and circumstances, including whether the Converting Fund does in fact sell its securities to Qualified Purchasers.[156]

§ 3.5 Limitations on Investments by Registered Investment Companies in Hedge Funds

If an investment company registered under the Company Act acquires or holds five percent or more of the outstanding interests in a 3(c)(1) Fund or a 3(c)(7) Fund, that hedge fund would be deemed to be a "portfolio affiliate"[157] of that investment company. Company Act Rule 17(d)-1[158] prohibits a registered investment company from engaging in a joint enterprise or profit-sharing plan with a portfolio affiliate. This may, among other things, prohibit payment of the management fee to the general partner and allocation of the special profit allocation to the general partner. Exempted[159] from this prohibition, however, is a joint enterprise or profit-sharing plan between a registered investment company and a portfolio affiliate, if certain affiliates of the registered investment company, such as the company's investment adviser, persons controlling the company, and persons under common control with the company, are not parties to the transaction and do not have a financial interest[160] in a party to the transaction.

---

154. Company Act § 3(c)(7)(E), 15 U.S.C. § 80a-3(c)(7)(E).
155. 1997 Release, § II.D.
156. *Id.*
157. Company Act Rule 17a-6(a), 17 C.F.R.§ 270.17a-6(a).
158. 17 C.F.R. § 270.17d-1.
159. Company Act Rule 17d-1(d)(5), 17 C.F.R. § 270.17d-1(d)(5).
160. Company At Rule 17d-1(d)(5)(ii), 17 C.F.R. § 270.17d-1(d)(5)(ii).

CHAPTER 4

Fund Structures

§ 4.1 Introduction

"Hedge fund" is not a term of art, but typically refers to a pooled investment vehicle that is not offered to the public and invests and trades in securities and other instruments. A hedge fund may be distinguished from other types of pooled investment vehicles, such as leverage buyout funds and venture capital funds, by some of its characteristics, such as relatively frequent capital contributions and withdrawals. A hedge fund is distinguishable from a mutual fund because, as a result of being excepted from application of most provisions of the Company Act, the former may use aggressive investment strategies that mutual funds may use only to a limited extent or not at all, including use of options, futures and derivatives, short selling, margin trading and investing in restricted securities. An investment adviser organizing a hedge fund must bear in mind two overriding concerns:

- First, the hedge fund's structure must comply with many laws and regulations, perhaps ironically for the primary purpose of minimizing the scope of regulation to which the hedge fund would otherwise be subject. For example, a hedge fund for U.S. investors must comply with Company Act section 3(c)(1) or 3(c)(7)[1] to avoid being subject to the regulatory framework applicable to registered investment companies (mutual funds) and with the private offering exemption under the Securities Act[2] to avoid registering the offering of the hedge fund's securities as a public offering.[3]
- Second, the hedge fund's structure must appeal to investors. While failure to comply with regulatory requirements may discourage investors, compliance by itself will not attract investors. An investment adviser is usually well-advised to avoid inventing new ways of structuring its hedge fund in an effort to distinguish it from other hedge funds, unless the modified structure provides pronounced and easily explained benefits. Added complexity may add documentation, accounting and other costs. From an investor's perspective, the most important distinguishing factor between one hedge fund and another

---

1. *See* Chapter 3, *supra.*
2. *See* § 5.3, *infra.*
3. An offshore hedge fund should comply with Regulation S in selling shares to offshore investors. *See* § 5.4, *infra.*

is likely to be the investment adviser's skill and character and, over time, each fund's performance.

§ 4.2 Pooled Investment Vehicle—Limited Partnership, Limited Liability Company or Corporation

Hedge funds typically have many common characteristics: investors have limited liability, the structure is tax efficient, and the investment adviser has nearly complete flexibility and authority to manage the hedge fund. A U.S. hedge fund organized as a limited partnership or limited liability company can have these characteristics. An offshore hedge fund may exhibit these characteristics as a partnership, limited liability company or corporation.

Most U.S. hedge funds are organized as limited partnerships, instead of limited liability companies, mainly because the statutes enabling organization as limited liability companies are relatively recent (all having been adopted since the 1980s) and the limited liability company form does not afford significant advantages over the limited partnership form.[4] Accordingly, except in those few instances where we want to point out a distinctive characteristic of the limited liability company form, we refer below only to the limited partnership form, but our comments apply as well to limited liability companies. Similarly, where we refer to partners of a limited partnership, we are also referring to members of a limited liability company.

1. Limited Liability

Whether a hedge fund is organized as a limited partnership or a corporation, its investors have limited liability. Thus, an investor can lose its investment in the hedge fund and undistributed profits, but is not liable beyond that for the hedge fund's debts.[5]

2. Tax Efficiency

For a U.S. hedge fund, tax efficiency is one of the most significant advantages of the limited partnership structure. Unlike a corporation subject to tax under Subchap-

---

4. The only possible advantage of a limited liability company is that it may afford its manager a shield from personal liability for the hedge fund's debts, and no similar shield is available to the general partner of a limited partnership. If, however, the general partner of a hedge fund is organized as a corporation or limited liability company, its owners should be shielded from its liabilities, including its liabilities for debts of the hedge fund.

5. *See, e.g.*, the Delaware General Corporation Law § 102(b)(6), the Delaware Revised Uniform Limited Partnership Act § 17-303 and the Delaware Limited Liability Company Act § 18-303.

ter C of the Tax Code,[6] a limited partnership does not itself pay U.S. income taxes and its distributions to partners are ordinarily not subject to income tax. Taxable income or loss is instead allocated to the partners, who pay the income tax on it, whether or not they receive any distributions.[7] Thus, a U.S. hedge fund structured as a limited partnership passes through to its partners all income, gains, losses and deductions, and the partners report those items directly on their own income tax returns.

Investors thus incur income tax liability for their allocable shares of the hedge fund's taxable income for each year in which hedge fund income is realized. Because hedge funds typically do not distribute any assets to their investors, the investors must either use other assets or make withdrawals from their hedge funds to pay their tax liabilities on the taxable income allocated to them. Because taxable income arises only from gains that are realized, an investor may have taxable income even in periods when the overall value of its investment in the hedge fund declines (because net unrealized losses exceed net realized gains).

When an investor makes an initial contribution to the capital of a hedge fund organized as a limited partnership, a capital account is established for that investor. An investor's capital account is increased by the investor's additional capital contributions and hedge fund profits allocated to the investor and is reduced by withdrawals by and distributions to the investor and hedge fund losses allocated to the investor. An investor's capital account represents its pro rata interest in the hedge fund at any time based on the capital accounts of the hedge fund's investors and its general partner or manager.[8] The general partner of the hedge fund values the hedge fund's assets and determines its liabilities whenever an investor makes a capital contribution or a withdrawal, the hedge fund makes a distribution or the hedge fund allocates profits and losses. At the end of each such measurement period, the hedge fund's profits and losses are allocated to the hedge fund's investors and general partner, based on their respective capital account balances at the beginning of that measurement period.[9]

The limited partnership structure allows the hedge fund to pass through the tax characteristics of the hedge fund's income and loss (for example, long-term capital gain treatment) to the hedge fund's investors. The general partner of a hedge fund ordinarily receives a special incentive or performance allocation from each investor in the hedge fund based on the realized and unrealized profits of the hedge fund allocated to that investor in excess of that investor's high water mark. That special incentive or performance allocation for tax purposes comprises the same proportions of short-term and long-term capital gains and ordinary income as the profits on which it is based.[10]

---

6. *See* Chapter 16, *infra*. A United States hedge fund could be organized as a corporation and elect to be taxed as an S Corporation to achieve a single level of tax, but the limitations of Subchapter S, particularly the limits on the number and types of shareholders and the requirement that an S corporation have only one class of stock, generally render it unavailable for a hedge fund.

7. *See* Chapter 16, *infra*.

8. A "manager" of a limited liability company performs the same functions as a general partner of a limited partnership. Unless the context otherwise requires, all references to a "general partner" of a limited partnership in this Chapter 4 refer also to a "manager" of a limited liability company.

9. Some profits and losses are not, however, always allocated in proportion to capital accounts, including profits from new issues and special incentive or performance allocations to the general partner. *See* §§ 13.3 and 15.2, respectively, *infra*.

10. *See* §§ 15.2.1 and 16.3, *infra*.

The accounting for an offshore hedge fund organized as a corporation, and the consequent income tax treatment, differs markedly from a limited partnership. A corporation does not generally pass through to its owners any income tax consequences of its business, but itself pays income tax on its income. A corporation that is organized under the laws of an appropriate non-U.S. "tax haven" jurisdiction and whose sole activity is trading in securities for its own account generally is not, however, subject to U.S. income tax and its income is not taxed by the jurisdiction of organization, which enhances its appeal to non-U.S. investors. Non-U.S. investors also are potentially subject to U.S. estate tax when they invest in U.S. hedge funds.[11] Tax-exempt U.S. investors, such as ERISA plans and charitable organizations, also often prefer an offshore hedge fund to a U.S. hedge fund, particularly if the hedge fund trades on margin.[12]

3. Flexibility of Governance: The General Partner Makes the Rules

Limited partnership laws do not impose significant restrictions on how a limited partnership is managed or governed. Subject to principles of fiduciary duty[13] and specific limitations in the agreement of limited partnership, the general partner completely controls the activities of a hedge fund organized as a limited partnership. Although U.S. state corporation laws typically require that shareholders be given certain protections and rights, limited partnership laws generally mandate few protections and powers for limited partners. The limited partners are free to agree to provisions that would vest control in the hedge fund's general partner. Similar flexibility is generally available in the structuring of the charter documents of an offshore hedge fund.

This flexibility of governance extends beyond the general partner's power to manage the business and affairs of the hedge fund. The flexibility may also extend to the economic arrangements within the hedge fund. As discussed above in section 4.2.2, the investors in a limited partnership typically share profits and losses of the hedge fund based on capital account balances. Because the general partner's special incentive or performance allocation is calculated on an investor-by-investor basis, the general partner may negotiate special incentive or performance allocation provisions that vary among the investors, subject to the general partner's fiduciary duty and disclosure obligations.[14]

---

11. *See* § 16.7.1, *infra.*
12. *See* §§ 4.3 and 16.7.6, *infra.*
13. *See, e.g.,* Advisers Act § 206, 15 U.S.C. § 80b-6; Delaware Revised Uniform Limited Partnership Act § 17-403, and § 2.7, *supra*, and Chapter 11, *infra.*
14. *See* § 2.7, *supra*, and Chapter 6, *infra.*

§ 4.3 Basic Structure of a U.S. Hedge Fund— Limited Partnership

Most U.S. hedge funds are structured as limited partnerships. The diagram below depicts the most common limited partnership hedge fund structure.

Diagram 1

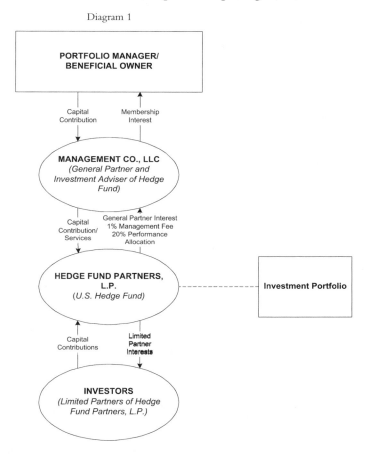

1. Parties

A hedge fund structured as a limited partnership has three main types of parties: the general partner, the investment adviser and the limited partners.

i. The General Partner

The general partner is either a natural person or, more commonly, a separate legal entity, such as a limited liability company or corporation. The general partner ordinarily has exclusive responsibility and authority in the management of the business and affairs of the limited partnership, including portfolio management.[15]

---

15.   If the general partner and the investment adviser of a limited partnership are not the same entity, the investment adviser manages the limited partnership's portfolio and the general partner oversees the investment adviser. *See* § 4.3.1.ii, *infra*.

The general partner also has unlimited liability for any of the limited partnership's debts and obligations that the limited partnership cannot satisfy. The general partner typically owes to the hedge fund's limited partners a fiduciary duty[16] and other duties provided in the hedge fund's agreement of limited partnership or similar charter documents. The general partner or its owners often invest their own money in the hedge fund, but typically have no legal or contractual duty to do so. If the general partner's owners invest directly in the hedge fund as limited partners, they are not subject to the general partner's unlimited liability with respect to their limited partner interests.[17]

Tax efficiency and limited liability are as relevant to the organization of the general partner as they are to the organization of a hedge fund. Like investors in a hedge fund, the owners of the general partner typically want pass-through tax treatment of the income and losses allocated to the general partner, both to avoid double taxation and to preserve the tax characteristics (for example, long-term capital gain) of the income or loss allocated to the general partner. The general partner's owners also want to limit their liability with respect to the management of the hedge fund to their investment in the general partner. Provisions in the federal securities laws, however, impose liability for acts of controlled persons directly on their controlling persons, which owners who actively manage the general partner may not be able to avoid.[18]

Because of these concerns, the general partner is typically organized as a limited liability company, although the general partners of hedge funds organized before widespread enactment of state limited liability company statutes often were organized as corporations or limited partnerships. As discussed above, the limited liability company form provides the flexibility of a limited partnership in both governance and the economic arrangements among its owners, and enjoys the same tax efficiency. It also provides greater liability protection for the owners. Because the general partner of a limited partnership has unlimited liability, the general partner of a hedge fund is rarely organized as a limited partnership, unless its ultimate owners are shielded by other entities.

The hedge fund general partner may also be organized as a corporation and elect to be taxed under Subchapter S of the Tax Code.[19] The S corporation form can provide tax efficiency in appropriate circumstances that is similar to that of a limited partnership. The S Corporation is, however, less flexible with respect to governance and economic arrangements among the shareholders. For example, an S corporation can have only one class of stock and the shareholders must share the S corporation's income in proportion to their share ownership.[20] Pro rata sharing may be desirable in some instances, but it can be an impediment to other desired economic arrangements. For example, if a general partner has four shareholders and manages two hedge funds, but three shareholders primarily manage one

---

16.   *See, e.g.*, the Delaware Revised Uniform Limited Partnership Act § 17-403.

17.   *See* §§ 3.2.2.iv and 3.3.2.xiii, *supra*, for a discussion about how "knowledgeable employees" of the general partner are treated for purposes of Company Act § 3(c)(1) or 3(c)(7).

18.   *See* Securities Act § 15, 15 U.S.C. § 770; and Chapter 6, *infra*.

19.   Tax Code § 1361, 26 U.S.C. § 1361.

20.   Tax Code § 1361(b), 26 U.S.C. § 1361(b). The S corporation can pay salaries and bonuses to the owners/principals that are not based on pro rata share ownership.

hedge fund and the fourth primarily manages the second hedge fund, the four principals may want to share the income and losses relating to the two hedge funds disproportionately to their ownership interests. It may be difficult or impossible to achieve that result through the S corporation. The S corporation must also observe corporate formalities and may be subject to state income tax. As a result, the general partner is rarely organized as a corporation, especially if it may have more than one or two shareholders.

The general partner may also be a natural person who manages the hedge fund as a sole proprietorship. The sole proprietorship form is simple and tax-efficient, but provides no shield from liabilities of the general partner's business or the hedge fund (although a hedge fund organized as a limited liability company may shield its manager from its liabilities). In addition, unlike a limited liability company, limited partnership or S corporation, each of which can have more than one owner and add or remove owners, a sole proprietorship is limited to one owner.

If two or more persons own the general partner, they should consider many issues relating to the day-to-day operation and management of the general partner and the relationships among themselves, including:

a. Allocation of Profits and Losses

The owners must determine how to allocate the general partner's profits and losses among themselves. The limited liability company form allows the owners to agree on profit and loss sharing arrangements that differ from their relative capital contributions or capital account balances. For example, a limited liability company may allocate in varying agreed proportions among its members its profits and losses from different sources, such as different hedge funds, different forms of compensation from a hedge fund or proceeds from a sale of the limited liability company.

b. Capital Contributions

The owners must determine how much capital, if any, each of them will contribute to the general partner. They must also determine the consequences of a default on an obligation to contribute capital.

c. Management

The owners must determine how the general partner will be managed and who makes the decisions. They must determine whether one owner can act alone on behalf of the general partner without the consent of the other owners, or the consent of a majority of the owners is required or unanimous consent of the owners is required. They may also allocate responsibility and authority for various management functions to designated owners.

d. Expulsion of One or More Owners

The owners must decide whether an owner may be expelled by other owners from the general partner and if so, under what circumstances and on what terms and conditions.

e. Withdrawal of an Owner

The owners must decide on the consequences of the withdrawal by an owner, whether withdrawal would breach their agreement and the terms and conditions of withdrawal under various foreseeable circumstances.

f. Dispute Resolution

The owners should agree on reasonable ways to resolve disputes among them short of arbitration or litigation, whether through buy-out options, an auction procedure or otherwise.

The general partner of a hedge fund and the general partner's management personnel have fiduciary duties to the hedge fund and its investors that arise under limited partnership laws.[21] For example, the general partner and its managers must put the investors' interests ahead of their own and conduct the business in the interests of the hedge fund and its limited partners generally. All registered and unregistered investment advisers also have fiduciary duties under investment adviser laws to the hedge funds they manage and their investors.[22] To some extent, the nature and extent of fiduciary duties to the hedge fund and its investors can be established and limited by contract (such as the hedge fund's agreement of limited partnership). A hedge fund's agreement of limited partnership and offering circular should clearly and specifically disclose any matter that, but for an express agreement to the contrary, could constitute a breach of fiduciary duty. Such matters include, for example, (a) the general partner's and its owners' devotion of time to the hedge fund and ability to conduct other related and unrelated activities, (b) the general partner's and its owners' ability to invest outside of the hedge fund and the related obligation to present those investment opportunities to the hedge fund, and (c) potential conflicts of interest, such as might arise from use of "soft" or commission dollars generated by brokerage commissions that the hedge fund generates.[23] Regulatory authorities, however, may determine that some types of conduct constitute breach of fiduciary duty even if permitted by the contract and fully and accurately disclosed to potential investors.[24]

ii. The Investment Adviser

Typically, the general partner and the investment adviser to the hedge fund are the same entity.[25] Under some circumstances, however, it may be desirable to separate the general partner's rights and obligations in one company and the investment adviser's rights and obligations in another.

A hedge fund usually compensates the management company in two ways: (a) management fees, based on total net assets of the hedge fund from time to time, and (b) performance or incentive allocations (sometimes called a "special profit

---

21. *See, e.g.*, Delaware Revised Uniform Limited Partnership Act § 17–403.

22. *See* Advisers Act § 206, 15 U.S.C. § 80b-6; and *see* § 2.7, *supra*.

23. *See* Chapter 14, *infra*.

24. *See, e.g.*, §§ 14.2.5 and 15.5, *infra*.

25. For purposes of this discussion, an entity that serves as both the general partner and the investment adviser of a hedge fund is called a "management company."

allocation"), which are a specified percentage of each limited partner's periodic hedge fund profits (typically allocated quarterly or annually).[26] The tax consequences may occasionally be preferable if the general partner and the investment adviser are separate entities, the former entitled to the special profit allocation and the latter entitled to the asset-based management fees. For example, in some jurisdictions this two-entity structure may be used to shield the special profit allocation from state or local taxes, which then apply only to the management fees.

iii. The Limited Partners/Investors

The hedge fund investor base is rapidly changing. In the past, hedge fund investors typically were wealthy individuals or families. The success and increased publicity relating to hedge funds have prompted other types of investors to consider these investment opportunities. Institutional investors, funds of hedge funds, endowments, private foundations and pension plans (governmental and private) have increasingly become interested in hedge funds. The organizer of a hedge fund business must consider not only the regulatory framework, but also its potential investor base. Among other things, the management company must determine:

- whether the hedge fund will rely on the exemption from regulation as an investment company pursuant to Company Act section 3(c)(1) or section 3(c)(7);[27]
- the extent, if any, to which the hedge fund will invest in futures contracts or commodity interests and the need for registration as a commodity pool operator or commodity trader;[28]
- the need for registration as an investment adviser with the SEC or with a state regulatory authority;[29]
- whether the hedge fund's investment strategy will generate unrelated business taxable income ("UBTI") that would have adverse tax consequences for some tax-exempt prospective investors;[30]
- whether the investor base will include employee benefit plans, pension plans or other investors that are subject to ERISA;[31] and
- whether any non-U.S. investors will invest in the hedge fund.[32]

Because hedge funds rely on the private offering exemption in offering their limited partner interests, the investors should all be "accredited investors," as defined in Rule 501 of Regulation D under the Securities Act.[33]

---

26. *See* Chapter 15, *infra.*
27. *See* Chapter 3, *supra.*
28. *See* § 2.9, *supra.*
29. *See* §§ 2.1-2.4, *supra.*
30. UBTI is defined as the gross income from any trade or business unrelated to the tax-exempt business of a tax-exempt entity. *See* §§ 4.4.1.ii and 16.3.13, *infra.*
31. *See* Chapter 11, *infra.*
32. *See also* §§ 3.2.3.i.a and 3.3.2.v, *supra,* and § 16.7, *infra.*
33. *See* § 5.3, *infra.* Although the hedge fund may permit up to thirty-five non-accredited investors to purchase securities in the hedge fund's private offering, it is inadvisable for the hedge fund to admit any non-accredited investors. *See* §§ 5.3.2.iii and 15.2.3, *infra.*

Some investors or types of investors may expect or demand that the hedge fund have particular terms and features. In considering investment in a hedge fund, an investor may consider a variety of issues, such as:

- What is the hedge fund's investment strategy? Does the hedge fund focus on the technology sector, "blue chip" securities, micro-cap securities, bonds, futures or other investment products? How risky is the hedge fund's investment strategy? Does the hedge fund trade on margin? Does it in fact hedge its investments (such as through short selling or option trading)? Most investors will consider such factors in connection with their overall investment strategies, diversification and asset allocation.
- Does the hedge fund's investment strategy generate UBTI? If a hedge fund generates UBTI, it may be inappropriate for tax-exempt investors.
- What is the portfolio manager's background and performance history?
- Is the investor subject to ERISA? Are twenty-five percent or more of the hedge fund's assets contributed by "plan investors"? If so, an ERISA investor may want certain controls in place to ensure that the hedge fund and management company comply with requirements of ERISA, such as the prohibited transaction rules and the investment adviser's bonding requirements. Similarly, the management company must be counseled about the additional responsibilities that apply to it, such as the additional fiduciary responsibilities and co-fiduciary liability.[34]

2. Basic Documents

To attract prospective investors to a hedge fund, the general partner must prepare an offering circular, an agreement of limited partnership and forms of a subscription agreement and an investor questionnaire.

i. The Offering Circular

The offering circular serves two primary functions. First, it is a marketing document for the hedge fund. Second, it should satisfy the general partner's obligation to disclose to potential investors all facts material to a decision whether to invest in the hedge fund.[35] To fulfill both of these objectives, the offering circular describes (a) the hedge fund's investment strategy, objectives and restrictions, (b) the general partner and portfolio manager, (c) investor suitability requirements, (d) the hedge fund's material terms (which are formally provided in the agreement of limited partnership and include matters such as limited partner withdrawal rights, compensation of the general partner and profit and loss allocations), (e) risk factors associated with investing in the hedge fund, (f) applicable regulatory and compliance requirements, (g) conflicts of interest that the general partner may face and (h) U.S. federal income tax considerations for an investor in the hedge fund.

---

34.   *See* Chapter 11, *infra.*
35.   *See* §§ 5.3.1.iii and 5.3.2.vii and Chapter 6, *infra.*

If the hedge fund trades in futures or other commodity interests, the offering circular may also need to include detailed disclosure required by the CFTC.[36]

ii. The Agreement of Limited Partnership

The agreement of limited partnership is the main contract between the general partner and the investors. The agreement of limited partnership ordinarily (a) grants plenary authority to the general partner to manage the hedge fund and its portfolio (although the general partner sometimes agrees to circumscribe its authority if it considers doing so necessary or desirable to attract investors), (b) establishes the allocation rules for the hedge fund (including the special profit allocation for the management company[37]); (c) provides for the management fee and its payment terms; (d) establishes the investors' withdrawal (redemption) rights and the general partner's right to expel investors; (e) specifies which expenses relating to the hedge fund will be borne by the hedge fund, (f) provides a mechanism for complying with the NASD new issue rule,[38] and (g) establishes voting and amendment rights. As a corollary to the general partner's comprehensive management authority, the investors usually have minimal or no rights to vote or to amend the agreement in most respects, except on matters that materially affect their economic deal with the general partner. Except for economic terms, the general partner normally has unilateral management authority, including authority to amend the agreement in many respects. An investor's primary remedy if it disagrees with an action by the general partner is to withdraw from the hedge fund.

iii. The Subscription Agreement

The subscription agreement (a) provides the terms on which a prospective investor may purchase a limited partner interest in the hedge fund, (b) includes representations and warranties that are necessary for the hedge fund and the general partner to comply, or evidence of their compliance, with applicable securities, anti-money-laundering and other laws and regulations, and (c) appoints the general partner as attorney-in-fact for the investor to sign the agreement of limited partnership and other instruments.

iv. The Offering Questionnaire

The offering questionnaire elicits information about the investor, including biographical and background information, needed to establish a reasonable basis for the general partner to conclude that the investor is sufficiently sophisticated to understand the investment and has sufficient means to bear the risk of the investment. The offering questionnaire also elicits information to support the investor's representations and warranties in the investor's subscription agreement and information to aid the general partner in complying with applicable laws and

---

36. *See* § 2.9, *supra*, and § 6.6, *infra*.
37. *See* § 15.2, *infra*.
38. *See* § 13.3.1, *infra*.

regulations (such as the NASD's new issue rule, if the hedge fund may invest in new issues).

§ 4.4 Offshore Hedge Funds

1. Why Organize an Offshore Hedge Fund?

Before 1997, Tax Code section 864[39] provided that a non–U.S. corporation would not be treated as engaged in a U.S. trade or business, and would thus not be subject to U.S. tax on all of its income, if it: (a) traded solely for its own account; (b) was not a "dealer;"[40] and (c) did not have its principal office in the United States. U.S. Treasury Regulations[41] listed ten activities, which were called the "ten commandments,"[42] all or substantially all of which were required to be performed by the non–U.S. corporation outside of the United States to avoid a determination by the IRS that the non–U.S. corporation maintained a principal office in the United States. The Regulations and IRS rulings offered little guidance about how many of these activities needed to be conducted outside of the United States to comply with Tax Code section 864. Therefore, an investment adviser would organize an offshore hedge fund as a non–U.S. corporation and retain an offshore administrator to conduct the offshore corporation's activities, other than portfolio management, in accordance with the ten commandments. If the non–U.S. corporation complied with the ten commandments, it would not itself be subject to U.S. taxation, other than withholding taxes on certain U.S. source dividends and interest, and the offshore hedge fund's non–U.S. shareholders would not be subject to U.S. tax on dividends received from the hedge fund, or on gain from a sale of the hedge fund's stock.

In 1997, however, the euphemistically named Taxpayer Relief Act of 1997 repealed the ten commandments and thereby eliminated a principal rationale (avoiding U.S. taxation of non–U.S. investors on their capital gains) for organizing an offshore hedge fund. The Taxpayer Relief Act also abolished the requirement that the principal office of a non–U.S. entity that trades for its own account must be outside the United States for that entity to avoid being treated as engaged in a U.S.

---

39.   26 U.S.C. § 864.

40.   For this purpose, a "dealer" is a merchant in securities with an established place of business, which is regularly engaged in purchasing securities and selling them to customers with a view to the gains and profits to be derived therefrom. Treas. Reg. § 1.864-2(c)(2)(C)(iv), 26 C.F.R. § 1.864-2(c)(2)(C)(iv).

41.   Treas. Reg. § 1.864-2(c)(2)(C)(iii), 26 C.F.R. § 1.864-2(c)(2)(C)(iii).

42.   The "ten commandments" involved: (a) communicating with shareholders; (b) communicating with the general public; (c) soliciting sales of stock; (d) accepting subscriptions from prospective shareholders; (e) maintaining its principal corporate records and books of account; (f) auditing books of account; (g) disbursing payments of dividends, legal fees, accounting fees, and officers' and directors' salaries; (h) publishing or furnishing the offering and redemption price of shares of stock issued; (i) conducting meetings of shareholders and board of directors; and (j) redeeming stock.

trade or business. Thus, although an offshore hedge fund must still be organized in a non-U.S. jurisdiction to avoid U.S. taxation, most, if not all, of the record keeping, communications and shareholder service activities now may be conducted in the United States. Assuming that an offshore hedge fund is not engaged in a U.S. trade or business and does not invest in U.S. real property interests, non-U.S. investors in the offshore hedge fund generally will not be subject to U.S. tax on dividends they receive from the offshore hedge fund, or on gains from sales of their interests in the offshore hedge fund.[43]

Although one of the tax reasons for establishing an offshore hedge fund no longer applies and the costs of organizing and operating an offshore hedge fund generally exceed the costs of organizing and operating a U.S. hedge fund,[44] offshore hedge funds have remained popular, primarily for marketing reasons. Non-U.S. investors are generally much more amenable to investing in an offshore hedge fund than in a U.S. hedge fund. Although this preference may arise partly out of habit and convention, investing in a U.S. hedge fund structured as a partnership can result in disclosure of the investor's identity to the IRS, and can cause the investor, if an individual, to be subject to U.S. estate tax. Offshore hedge funds are also beneficial for U.S. tax-exempt investors who want to avoid unrelated business taxable income.

A second effect of the Taxpayer Relief Act was to enable non-U.S. investors to invest in a U.S. investment partnership that trades securities solely for its own account, without being taxed on capital gains of the hedge fund, even if the hedge fund buys and sells frequently enough to be deemed to be a "trader." The U.S. hedge fund must, however, withhold tax from the non-U.S. investor's allocable share of certain U.S. source dividend and interest income of the hedge fund. If a significant number of potential offshore investors do not demonstrate interest in a hedge fund, it may be preferable to allow those few who do to invest directly in a U.S. hedge fund rather than incurring the expense of establishing an offshore hedge fund. An investment adviser that selects this alternative must comply with the tax withholding requirements to avoid liability for amounts that are not properly withheld. Also, state and local tax treatment of non-U.S. partners in a partnership may vary, so the investment adviser should determine whether non-U.S. investors will be subject to state or local taxes by investing directly in the U.S. hedge fund.

i. Investor Confidentiality

Many non-U.S. investors are concerned about protecting their confidentiality, particularly by avoiding disclosure to U.S. tax and regulatory authorities, and prefer to deal with an offshore administrator rather than a U.S.-based investment adviser. An offshore hedge fund's administrator should be responsible for maintaining the shareholder registry and communicating with the offshore hedge fund's investors

---

43. *See* § 16.7.3, *infra.*

44. Offshore hedge funds typically cost more to organize and to operate because of the additional service providers that the investment adviser and the offshore hedge fund must engage, such as the offshore attorneys and the administrator, and because of the added cost of complying with the laws and regulations of the jurisdiction in which the offshore hedge fund is organized.

and prospective investors. Although a U.S. partnership files income tax information returns with the IRS that identify all of the hedge fund's investors (including non-U.S. investors), the identities of non-U.S. investors in an offshore hedge fund are not ordinarily reported to the IRS or other U.S. governmental agencies for tax or other purposes. The offshore hedge fund, on its own behalf and on behalf of its investment adviser and administrator, should, however, reserve its rights to disclose each investor's identity and information about the investor to cognizant U.S. or non-U.S. governmental authorities to the extent required under anti-money-laundering laws.[45]

ii. Taxation

Non-U.S. investors are not subject to U.S. income tax on their ownership interests in an offshore hedge fund. Depending on the investment adviser's investment strategy, some U.S. tax-exempt investors, such as pension plans and charitable organizations, have tax reasons to prefer to invest in the investment adviser's offshore hedge fund. Because an offshore hedge fund is typically organized as a corporation instead of a partnership, which is a pass-through vehicle for U.S. tax purposes, if the investment adviser to both a U.S. and an offshore hedge fund trades on margin, a U.S. tax-exempt investor would receive debt-financed income from the U.S. hedge fund but not from the offshore hedge fund. Debt-financed income is "unrelated business taxable income" under Tax Code section 514, which is taxable to a tax-exempt investor.[46]

The investment adviser to an offshore hedge fund should pay attention to where the offshore hedge fund's administrative activities[47] are conducted for two primary reasons. First, the jurisdiction where the administrator is located may have its own laws and regulations that apply to hedge funds administered there. The offshore hedge fund and its investment adviser should understand those laws and regulations and how they affect the hedge fund. For example, if a hedge fund organized in the British Virgin Islands has an administrator in Ireland, the Irish anti-money-laundering laws and regulations that apply to the administrator may not be the same as the anti-money-laundering laws and regulations of the British Virgin Islands. Second, if the administrator performs all or part of its services in a jurisdiction (including the United States) other than the jurisdiction in which the offshore hedge fund is organized, those activities may cause the hedge fund to be subject to taxes imposed by the administrator's jurisdiction. For example, if the administrator performs services in the United States, the offshore hedge fund could be subject to U.S. state and local taxes. Some states have adopted the U.S. federal rules for determining whether a non-U.S. entity is subject to state tax, but some have not and may regard a local office of the administrator as an office of the offshore hedge fund.

---

45.   *See* § 2.10, *supra.*
46.   *See* § 16.7.6, *infra.*
47.   It is not uncommon for an offshore hedge fund organized in one non-U.S. jurisdiction to have an administrator located in another jurisdiction, which may be a U.S. or non-U.S. jurisdiction, or an administrator that subcontracts some of its administrative duties to another entity located in another jurisdiction.

Except in the case of an offshore hedge fund that is organized as a partnership, the offshore hedge fund is not a pass-through vehicle for U.S. income tax purposes and the tax characteristics (as long-term or short-term capital gain or ordinary income) of an offshore hedge fund's taxable income are not passed through to its investors. As a result, the investment adviser may desire to trade and invest the offshore hedge fund's portfolio differently from the investment adviser's U.S. hedge fund's portfolio. For example, an offshore hedge fund's investment adviser may cause the offshore hedge fund to sell a security that the offshore hedge fund has held for less than one year; although this will result in short-term capital gain for the offshore hedge fund on the profits of that sale, that characteristic will not pass through to the investors in the offshore hedge fund. At the same time, that investment adviser might cause its U.S. hedge fund to hold the same security until the gain on the sale can be characterized as long-term capital gain, which will pass through to the investors in the U.S. hedge fund—any benefit to the investors in the U.S. hedge fund of selling the security simultaneously with the offshore fund's sale may be outweighed by the higher tax liability on short-term than on long-term capital gain.

iii. Additional 3(c)(1) "Slots"

As discussed above,[48] many U.S. hedge funds comply with the 100 beneficial owner limit of Company Act section 3(c)(1) to be excluded from the definition of "investment company" under the Company Act. Non-U.S. investors that are admitted to a U.S. hedge fund count toward that 100 beneficial owner limit.[49] Additionally, if a U.S. hedge fund is managed with a similar investment strategy as an offshore hedge fund, if each fund relies on Company Act section 3(c)(1), and if the offshore hedge fund admits U.S. taxable investors or the U.S. hedge fund admits non-U.S. investors, then, for purposes of section 3(c)(1), both the U.S. and the non-U.S. investors in the offshore hedge fund will be integrated with the investors in the U.S. hedge fund, and all will be counted toward each fund's 100 beneficial owner limit.[50] If, however, the offshore hedge fund is available only to U.S. tax-exempt investors and non-U.S. investors, and the U.S. hedge fund is available only to U.S. taxable investors, the SEC staff has indicated that, for purposes of section 3(c)(1), U.S. investors in the offshore hedge fund will not necessarily be integrated with the investors in the side-by-side U.S. hedge fund.[51]

iv. Securities Regulation Issues

If the administrator of an offshore hedge fund performs some or all of its services in the United States, the requirements for avoiding registration of the hedge fund's offering under the Securities Act may differ from the requirements that would

---

48. *See* § 3.2, *supra*.

49. *See* § 3.2.2.vii, *supra*.

50. Investors admitted to an offshore hedge fund that properly relies on Company Act § 3(c)(7) will not be integrated with the U.S. hedge fund, even if U.S. taxable investors are admitted to the offshore hedge fund. *See* § 3.2.3.i, *supra*.

51. *See* § 3.2.3.i.a, *supra*.

otherwise apply.[52] In addition to U.S. securities laws, such an offshore hedge fund must comply with the securities laws of each jurisdiction in which it offers its securities.[53]

v. Familiarity

Although some of the tax advantages of organizing a hedge fund offshore have been eliminated, investment advisers continue to organize offshore hedge funds and engage offshore administrators for them, because non–U.S. investors may be more familiar and comfortable with offshore hedge funds and may have concerns about confidentiality. Investment advisers organizing offshore hedge funds typically continue to rely on offshore administrators to maintain the offshore hedge funds' registered offices, share registries and other books and records, and to communicate with the investors, including disseminating offering documents and processing subscriptions and redemptions.

2. Typical Offshore Hedge Fund Structure (Side-by-Side Structure)

Unlike a U.S. hedge fund, which is typically organized as a limited partnership, an offshore hedge fund is typically organized in the applicable offshore jurisdiction as a corporation that issues shares to its investors.[54] The diagram below depicts the most common offshore hedge fund structure.

Diagram 2

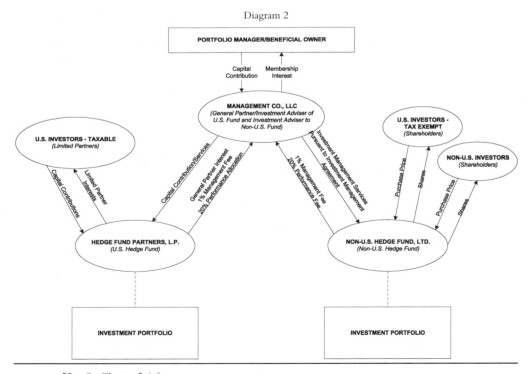

---

52. *See* Chapter 5, *infra.*
53. Non-U.S. securities laws are not addressed in this book.
54. *See* § 4.2, *supra.*

The offshore hedge fund's directors typically control the management of the offshore hedge fund. The directors usually delegate routine administrative duties (such as calculation of the offshore hedge fund's net asset value ("NAV")) to an offshore administrator[55] pursuant to an administration agreement and delegate portfolio management duties to a U.S. investment adviser pursuant to an investment adviser agreement.

3. Basic Documents

i. Charter Documents

An offshore hedge fund's charter documents include most of the material terms and conditions of the relationship of management to the investors and the economic consequences of the investment, analogous to a U.S. hedge fund's agreement of limited partnership.[56] The charter documents establish, for example, withdrawal (redemption) rights, which expenses the offshore hedge fund must bear, and voting and amendment rights. The charter documents set forth the equity structure of the offshore hedge fund, including, for example, the different classes and series of shares and the manner of calculating the incentive fees and the high water mark.[57]

ii. Private Placement Memorandum

The private placement memorandum for an offshore hedge fund serves the same purposes as the offering circular for a U.S. hedge fund. It should disclose all material terms and risks of the offering, the terms of the shares to be issued, the offshore hedge fund's directors, regulatory matters, tax aspects, information about the administrator and the fees it charges and information about the investment adviser and the investment adviser agreement.[58] The preparation of this disclosure document is complicated by the involvement of several parties, including lawyers, administrators and accountants (generally all in non-U.S. jurisdictions) whose expertise is required.

iii. Subscription Agreement and Offering Questionnaire

The subscription agreement and offering questionnaire serve essentially the same purposes for an offshore hedge fund as they do for a U.S. hedge fund,[59] but are drafted to reflect differences in applicable laws and regulations and the different hedge fund structures. If an offshore hedge fund will sell shares to U.S. persons, as well as non-U.S. persons, it will need a different form of each of the subscription agreement and the offering questionnaire for U.S. persons and non-U.S. persons, because of the different regulations that apply with respect to each group.[60]

---

55. *See* § 4.4.1.ii, *supra.*
56. *See* § 4.3.2.ii, *supra.*
57. *See* § 15.3, *infra.*
58. *See* § 4.3.2.i, *supra.*
59. *See* §§ 4.3.2.iii and 4.3.2.iv, *supra.*
60. *See* Chapter 5, *infra.*

iv. Investment Adviser Agreement

The investment adviser agreement is a contract between the offshore hedge fund and the U.S. investment adviser, pursuant to which the offshore hedge fund's directors delegate to the investment adviser the authority to manage the offshore hedge fund's securities portfolio. The portfolio management powers delegated to the investment adviser are typically substantially similar to the portfolio management powers granted to the general partner of a U.S. hedge fund.[61]

The investment adviser agreement also provides for the investment adviser's compensation by the offshore hedge fund. The investment adviser typically receives a management fee, which is based on the periodic net asset value of the offshore hedge fund, and a performance-based fee, which is based on increases in the net asset value, including realized and unrealized gains and losses. Unlike a U.S. hedge fund, however, the performance-based compensation is a fee, not a special profit allocation.[62]

4. Different Capital Structures to Accommodate Performance Fees

Performance fees with respect to offshore hedge funds are typically based on the performance of the offshore hedge fund as a whole, rather than an individual investor's capital account, as usually is the case with a U.S. hedge fund. As a result, calculating the investment adviser's performance fee can create accounting complexity for offshore hedge funds in the following circumstances:

- If an investor invests in the offshore hedge fund at the then-current NAV when the offshore hedge fund has sustained earlier losses that have created a high water mark, the investor may enjoy a windfall because it will enjoy appreciation in the offshore hedge fund without paying a performance fee until the prior losses related to the high water mark are recovered.
- If an investor invests in the middle of a performance fee measurement period at the then-current NAV when the offshore hedge fund has had positive performance for that measurement period, the investor may be burdened with a portion of the performance fee that is charged at the end of the measurement period on appreciation that occurred before that investor invested in the offshore hedge fund.

These issues are typically addressed by one of several types of adjustments, some of which impose quasi-partnership accounting methods on the corporate structure.[63]

---

61.   *See* § 4.3.2.ii, *supra.*
62.   *See* § 15.2, *infra.*
63.   *See* § 15.3, *infra.*

5. Other Service Providers

i. U.S. and Offshore Attorneys

U.S. counsel may draft the offshore hedge fund's charter documents and offering documents, but parts of those documents must be drafted, or reviewed and approved, by counsel that is licensed in the jurisdiction of the offshore hedge fund's organization. The offshore counsel also usually files all of the offshore hedge fund's organizational documents with the appropriate officials in that jurisdiction and advises on compliance with the laws of that jurisdiction on an ongoing basis.

ii. The Administrator

Notwithstanding the repeal of the ten commandments, many of the typical offshore hedge fund's administrative functions continue to be administered offshore by a third-party administrator. Among other things, the administrator typically calculates the NAV, maintains investor lists, accepts subscriptions, processes sales and redemptions of shares, transmits communications from the offshore hedge fund or the investment adviser to current and prospective investors, pays the offshore hedge fund's bills and administers corporate housekeeping requirements.[64]

iii. Offshore Accountant/Auditor

Before the repeal of the ten commandments, accounting functions, like administrative functions, were performed outside the United States. Although those functions may now be performed in the United States, some offshore jurisdictions, such as the Cayman Islands, require a local audit firm to issue the audit report with respect to an offshore hedge fund organized in that jurisdiction. Many U.S. accounting firms that provide services to hedge funds have offices in the Cayman Islands and other offshore jurisdictions where offshore hedge funds are frequently organized to facilitate compliance with these local requirements.

6. Jurisdiction of Organization

When selecting a jurisdiction in which to organize an offshore hedge fund, investment advisers should focus on the following issues:

- Is the target group of prospective investors familiar and comfortable with the proposed jurisdiction?
- Does the proposed jurisdiction impose local taxes or other regulatory burdens? Most preferred offshore jurisdictions do not impose substantial local taxes on hedge funds organized there.
- Are adequate professional service firms, such as administrators, accountants and attorneys, available to provide services to offshore hedge funds in the proposed jurisdiction?
- Is the proposed jurisdiction politically stable?

---

64. *See* § 4.4.1, *supra.*

- Are regulatory and service-provider costs associated with an offshore hedge fund in the proposed jurisdiction reasonable? Such costs can vary substantially.

7. Master-Feeder Structure

A management company faces certain inherent inefficiencies when it manages a U.S. hedge fund and an offshore hedge fund side-by-side using the same investment strategy. For example, the management company must allocate trades ("split" tickets) among its U.S. and offshore hedge funds and try to maintain similar performance among its hedge funds. A management company may try to overcome these inefficiencies and reduce certain costs and administration burdens by organizing a "master-feeder" structure.

A typical master-feeder structure comprises one "master" fund and two "feeder" funds. The feeder funds are typically a U.S. limited partnership for taxable U.S. investors[65] and a non-U.S. corporation for non-U.S. investors and tax-exempt U.S. investors.[66] Both feeder funds invest all of their capital in the master fund. The master fund is typically a non-U.S. entity and all of the portfolio investment activities are conducted at the master fund level. The diagram below depicts this common master-feeder structure.

Diagram 3

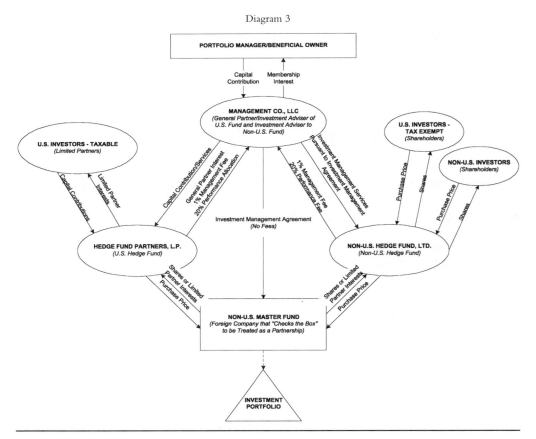

---

65.   See § 4.2, *supra.*
66.   See § 4.4.2, *supra.*

The non-U.S. master fund, whether organized as a partnership or corporation, generally can elect to be taxed as a partnership for U.S. tax purposes by making the appropriate check-the-box election on Form 8832 within seventy-five days of the master fund's organization. If the master fund is taxed as a partnership, the partners in the U.S. feeder fund will receive pass-through treatment for their shares of the U.S. feeder fund's income.[67]

The investment adviser for the master fund typically also serves as the investment adviser for the feeder funds. The investment adviser can receive its management fees and performance fees or performance allocations from either the master fund or the feeder funds. It may be preferable for the investment adviser to receive the management fees and performance fees or allocations from the feeder funds for the following reasons:

- The performance allocation from the U.S. feeder fund, which is typically a partnership, will be made in the form of an allocation and will give the investment adviser the tax benefits of the pass-through treatment of capital gains;
- If the investment adviser's investment strategy generates a significant amount of short-term capital gains, it may be beneficial for the investment adviser to defer receipt of the performance fee from the non-U.S. feeder fund and its corresponding tax liability;[68] and
- Charging fees at the feeder fund level gives the investment adviser flexibility to charge different fees with respect to the different feeder funds.

If, however, the investment adviser's investment strategy generates a significant amount of long-term capital gains, the investment adviser may prefer to receive its performance-based compensation with respect to both feeder funds at the master fund level (and receive pass-through treatment of capital gains). Such a fee structure may afford preferable tax treatment to the investment adviser because if it receives its performance-based compensation with respect to the non-U.S. feeder fund directly from that feeder fund as a performance fee, that fee would be taxed at ordinary income tax rates.

An alternative master-feeder structure uses the U.S. hedge fund as the master fund, organized as a U.S. limited partnership with U.S. taxable investors and an offshore feeder fund. The diagram below depicts this structure.

---

67. *See* § 16.7.7, *infra.*
68. *See* § 16.8.6, *infra.*

Diagram 4

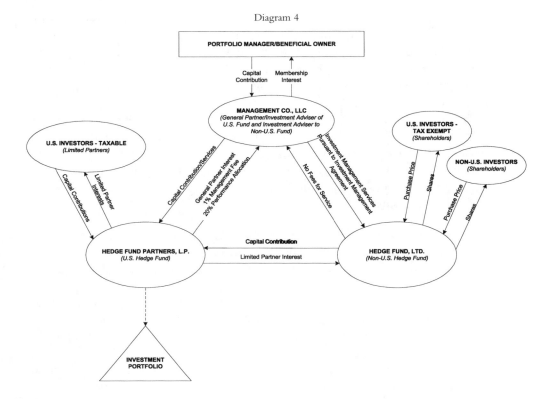

This structure allows the investment adviser to receive a performance allocation and take advantage of the tax benefits of the pass-through of capital gains. This structure is limited, however, by the constraints under the Company Act because both the U.S. and non–U.S. investors will be counted toward the 100 beneficial owner limit under Company Act section 3(c)(1), if the master fund relies on that section, or must be "qualified purchasers," if the master fund relies on Company Act section 3(c)(7).[69]

i. Advantages

a. Portfolio Management

Traditionally, the primary reason for organizing a master-feeder structure has been the ease of portfolio management. Managing one securities portfolio rather than several has some advantages. For example, the investment adviser does not need to allocate trades among its side-by-side U.S. and offshore hedge funds. It also is easier for the investment adviser to maintain uniformity of performance results. If the feeder funds are managed separately, substantial withdrawals or redemptions in one feeder fund could disproportionately affect that feeder fund; the investment adviser may be required to sell a substantial portion of the affected feeder fund's securities at a time or price when it is not advantageous to do so, which may result in the two feeder funds no longer having similar portfolios; or it may be difficult or

---

69.   *See* Chapter 3, *supra*, and § 4.4.7.iii.b, *infra*.

impractical for the investment adviser to rebalance the two feeder funds' portfolios. Any of these circumstances may reduce one feeder fund's performance relative to the other feeder fund.

b. Tax Efficiency for the Investment Adviser

If the master fund is organized as a pass-through vehicle for tax purposes and recognizes substantial long-term capital gains, the investment adviser may enjoy the tax benefits of taking a performance allocation rather than a performance fee.[70]

c. Additional Feeders/No Start-Up Risk

If a master-feeder structure is in place, another feeder fund, such as a "private label" fund for an institution, can simply be added as a new investor in the master fund, assuming the investment adviser continues to comply with the various applicable rules and regulations.[71] That is, the new feeder fund can feed into the master fund. The new feeder can avoid much of the start-up risk, because it will immediately have a diversified and invested portfolio. The new feeder fund can also have a fee structure that differs from the other feeder funds (assuming fees are charged at the feeder fund level rather than by the master fund).

ii. Disadvantages

a. More Entities, More Administration and More Cost

Creating and administering additional entities require additional effort and cost. Organizing and maintaining a master-feeder structure entail additional legal, accounting and administrative fees, in addition to the fees typically incurred at the feeder fund level.

b. Portfolio Management

While the master-feeder structure can simplify portfolio management, it also creates complexities and portfolio management challenges. For example, allocating the master fund's costs, profits and losses among the feeder funds may be complex and cumbersome, because of issues such as special allocations of profits and losses from "new issues"[72] and accounting adjustments relating to subscriptions and redemptions

---

70. Alternatively, an investment adviser may achieve similar tax benefits by organizing its offshore hedge fund as a limited partnership in which non-U.S. investors invest directly. The principal disadvantage of this structure is that some non-U.S. investors are wary of investing in partnerships. To avoid this problem, the investment adviser can organize another version of a master-feeder structure, in which the non-U.S. investors invest directly in an offshore hedge fund organized as a corporation (the so-called "feeder" fund), which is the sole limited partner of a limited partnership (the so-called "master" fund). The U.S.-based investment adviser may be a co-general partner with an offshore entity that is responsible for the administration of the master fund and may receive an incentive allocation based on the master fund's appreciation. The distinction between this master-feeder structure and the other master-feeder structures is that no U.S. hedge fund "feeds" into this master fund. *See* §§ 15.2.1 and 16.7.7, *infra*.

71. Such as, for example, Company Act § 3(c)(1) or 3(c)(7), 15 U.S.C. § 80c-3(c)(1) or 80c-3(c)(7).

72. *See* § 13.3.1, *infra*.

in the feeder funds (that is, for each subscription or redemption there must be a corresponding transaction between the master fund and applicable feeder fund). In addition, tax considerations may affect how the master fund's portfolio is managed. As noted above in section 4.4.1.ii, an investment adviser may not desire to trade securities of side-by-side U.S. and offshore hedge funds in a manner that is exactly parallel, because of tax considerations. For example, the investment adviser may cause the offshore hedge fund to sell a security that the offshore hedge fund has held for less than one year while at the same time causing the U.S. hedge fund to hold the same security until the gain on the sale can be characterized as long-term capital gain. In a master-feeder structure, the investment adviser of the master fund must consider the net results of its trades on all investors in the feeder funds and does not have the luxury of being able to trade the portfolios of the feeder funds differently to accommodate disparate tax or investment considerations of the investors in those funds.

iii. Regulatory Issues

a. Regulations D and S under the Securities Act

Sales of limited partner interests in the U.S. feeder funds and sales of shares of the non-U.S. feeder funds to U.S. investors must comply with the private placement exemption under the Securities Act (which may include compliance with Regulation D thereunder).[73] Sales of shares in the non-U.S. feeder funds to non-U.S. investors must comply with Regulation S under the Securities Act, which applies to offers and sales of securities made outside of the United States.[74]

b. Investment Company Act of 1940

In a master-feeder structure, not only must the feeder funds each comply with the Company Act, as they would otherwise do if they were side-by-side hedge funds, but the master fund must also comply with the Company Act. Thus, if the master fund relies on Company Act section 3(c)(1),[75] which limits the master fund to not more than 100 beneficial owners, the master fund must count all of the underlying beneficial owners of the feeder funds toward its 100 beneficial owner limit.[76] Alternatively, if the master fund relies on Company Act section 3(c)(7), which is not limited in the number of its beneficial owners but requires all of the beneficial owners to be qualified purchasers, all of the underlying owners of the feeder funds must be qualified purchasers.[77] In both cases, the investor base is more limited than it would be if the hedge funds were traded side-by-side rather than in a master-feeder structure.

---

73.   *See* § 5.3, *infra.*

74.   *See* § 5.4, *infra.*

75.   *See* § 3.2, *supra.*

76.   The underlying beneficial owners of a feeder fund must be counted because (a) the feeder fund has been formed for the purpose of investing in the master fund, (b) the feeder fund constitutes more than ten percent of the master fund's outstanding voting securities or (c) more than forty percent of the assets of the feeder fund is invested in the master fund. *See* § 3.2.2, *supra.*

77.   *See* § 3.3.2, *supra.*

CHAPTER **5**

Private Offerings[1]

§ 5.1 Application of Securities Act to Hedge Funds

The Securities Act regulates the offer and sale of securities. "Security" is broadly defined in the Securities Act, and includes instruments such as stock and notes.[2] Interests in limited partnerships and limited liability companies are not specifically identified in the definition, but are comprehended by the catch-all category of "investment contracts."[3] An "investment contract" is an arrangement where individuals are "led to invest money in a common enterprise with the expectation that they would earn a profit solely through the efforts of the promoter or of some one other than themselves."[4] Investment contracts include limited partner interests and limited liability company member interests when the limited partners or members do not have significant management authority.[5]

Most offshore hedge funds are organized as corporations that issue shares to their investors. Most U.S. hedge funds are organized as limited partnerships or

---

1. This chapter is intended as an overview of the registration requirements of the Securities Act and the exemptions therefrom, as they relate to the operation and marketing of a hedge fund. This chapter does not analyze the Securities Act registration requirements, the registration process or the exemptions from registration. For an in-depth discussion of those topics, see J. William Hicks, *Exempted Transactions Under the Securities Act of 1933*, 2nd Ed. (West Group, 2003), and Harold S. Bloomenthal, *Securities Law Handbook*, 2003 Ed. (West Group, 2002).

2. Securities Act § 2(a)(1), 15 U.S.C. § 77b(a)(1), defines a security as "any note, stock, treasury stock, security future, bond, debenture, evidence of indebtedness, certificate of interest or participation in any profit-sharing agreement, collateral-trust certificate, preorganization certificate or subscription, transferable share, investment contract, voting-trust certificate, certificate of deposit for a security, fractional undivided interest in oil, gas or other mineral rights, any put, call, straddle, option or privilege on any security, certificate of deposit, or group or index of securities (including any interest therein or based on the value thereof), or any put, call, straddle, option, or privilege entered into on a national securities exchange relating to foreign currency, or, in general, any interest or instrument commonly known as a 'security,' or any certificate of interest or participation in, temporary or interim certificate for, receipt for, guarantee of, or warrant or right to subscribe to purchase, any of the foregoing."

3. *Id.*

4. *Securities & Exchange Commission v. W.J. Howey Co.*, 328 U.S. 293, 66 S. Ct. 1100 (1945).

5. *See, e.g., Mayer v. Oil Filed Systems Corp, et al.*, 721 F.2d 59 (2d Cir., 1983) (limited partner interests); *McGreghar Land Company*, 521 F.2d 822 (9th Cir., 1975) (limited partner interests); *KFC Ventures, L.L.C. v. Metairie Medical Equipment Leasing Corp., et al.*, 2000 U.S. Dist. LEXIS 8294 (E.D. La., 2000) (limited liability company interests); *Cogniplex, Inc., et al. v. Hubbard Ross, L.L.C., et al.*, 2001 U.S. Dist. LEXIS 11113 (N.D. Ill., 2001) (limited liability company interests).

limited liability companies. The investors in both offshore and U.S. hedge funds typically have few managerial powers, and as a result, interests in hedge funds are generally securities.[6] Offers and sales of interests in offshore and U.S. hedge funds must therefore comply with the requirements of the Securities Act.

§ 5.2 Registration Requirements under the Securities Act

The Securities Act prohibits the public offering or sale of securities, unless a registration statement has been filed with respect to such securities or an exemption from the registration requirement is available.[7] The Securities Act registration requirement applies to any transaction in securities that involves interstate commerce or use of the U.S. mail.[8] "Interstate commerce" includes:

> trade or commerce in securities or any transportation or com- munication relating thereto among the several States or between the District of Columbia or any Territory of the United States and any State or other Territory, or between any foreign country and any State, Territory or the District of Columbia.[9]

As a result, the Securities Act registration requirements apply to offers and sales of securities by U.S. or non-U.S. issuers within the United States. The registration requirement also applies to an offer or sale of securities issued by a U.S. or non-U.S. issuer to a non-U.S. investor if a jurisdictional nexus to the United States is established, such as a call being placed to or from the United States in connection with the transaction. If a jurisdictional nexus exists, a U.S. or offshore hedge fund offering interests or shares must comply with the registration requirement, or rely on an exemption from registration.

§ 5.3 Exemptions from Registration

The Securities Act includes several exemptions from its registration requirements, and the SEC has promulgated rules providing additional exemptions. Most hedge funds rely on the exemption provided by Securities Act section 4(2), which exempts

---

6. *See* Chapter 4, *supra*, for a discussion of typical hedge fund structures.
7. Securities Act § 5(c), 15 U.S.C. § 77e(c).
8. Securities Act § 5, 15 U.S.C. § 77e.
9. Securities Act § 2(a)(7), 15 U.S.C. § 77b(a)(7).

from the registration requirements of the Securities Act any securities issued in "transactions by an issuer not involving any public offering."[10] This is commonly called the "private offering" exemption. As discussed below,[11] the Securities Act does not define "public offering," and the courts typically have examined the facts and circumstances to determine what constitutes a "public offering." These tests involve a number of factors, with different courts giving varying weight to different factors, and the factors often require subjective judgment.[12] In addition, courts construe the private offering exemption narrowly to further the purposes of the Securities Act.[13] As a result, in many instances, reliance on the exemption provided by section 4(2) involves risks that are unquantifiable and to some extent unpredictable.

The SEC promulgated Regulation D[14] to provide greater certainty for an issuer seeking to rely on the private offering exemption. Regulation D Rule 506[15] establishes a safe harbor under Securities Act section 4(2).[16] An issuer that complies with all of the requirements of Rule 506 is deemed not to be engaged in a transaction involving a public offering.[17] An issuer that fails to comply with the requirements of this safe harbor may nevertheless be able to rely on another exemption from registration (such as the section 4(2) private offering exemption) if the issuer can establish all of the elements of that exemption. Given the subjectivity of the interpretation of the private offering exemption under the Securities Act, an issuer typically is well-advised to attempt to comply fully with the conditions of both the traditional private offering exemption under section 4(2) and the Regulation D safe harbor. In addition, each U.S. or offshore hedge fund that relies on Company Act section 3(c)(1) or 3(c)(7) for an exclusion from the definition of "investment company" under the Company Act[18] may not make a public offering of its securities and thus must comply with one or both of the Securities Act section 4(2) and Regulation D exemptions.

For offshore offers and sales of securities, whether by a U.S. or an offshore issuer, the SEC promulgated Regulation S to clarify when the Securities Act registration requirements apply. Regulation S also establishes safe harbors for the issuance and re-sales of securities to non-U.S. investors.[19]

1. Private Offering Exemption under Securities Act Section 4(2)

Securities Act section 4(2)[20] exempts from the registration requirements of Securities Act section 5[21] securities sold in a "transaction by an issuer not

---

10. Securities Act § 4(2), 15 U.S.C. § 77d(2).
11. *See* § 5.3.1, *infra.*
12. *Id.*
13. *Securities & Exchange Commission v. Murphy*, 626 F. 2d 633, 641 (9th Cir., 1980).
14. 17 C.F.R. §§ 230.501 *et seq.*
15. 17 C.F.R. § 230.506.
16. *See* § 5.3.2, *infra.*
17. Regulation D Rule 506(a), 17 C.F.R. § 230.506(a).
18. *See* Chapter 3, *supra*, for a description of the exclusions from the definition of "investment company."
19. *See* § 5.4, *infra.*
20. 15 U.S.C. § 77d(2).
21. 15 U.S.C. § 77e.

involving any public offering."[22] The Securities Act does not, however, define what constitutes a "public offering," leaving the courts, the SEC and issuers of securities to determine whether an issuer is or is not engaged in a transaction not involving a public offering.

In *Securities & Exchange Commission v. Ralston Purina Co.*, the U.S. Supreme Court held that a critical factor is whether the particular class of persons to whom the offering is made need the protection of the Securities Act or are "able to fend for themselves."[23] The purpose of the Securities Act "is to protect investors by promoting full disclosure of information thought necessary to informed investment decisions."[24] In determining whether a transaction constitutes a public offering, the focus of the courts should be on whether the offerees had access to "the same kind of information that the [Securities] Act would make available in the form of a registration statement."[25]

Following *Ralston Purina*, courts have looked to a variety of factors to determine if a transaction constitutes a public offering. These factors have varied from circuit to circuit and from case to case. For example, the First Circuit has identified a private offering as one in which "the purchasers (a) are limited in number, (b) are sophisticated, and (c) have a relationship with the issuer enabling them to command access to information that would otherwise be contained in a registration statement."[26] The Second Circuit considers (a) the number of offerees, (b) the sophistication and experience of the offerees, or the ability of the offerees to evaluate the merits of the issue or the size of the offering, (c) the nature and kind of information provided, or to which the offerees have ready access, and (d) the size of the offering and the precautions taken to prevent the offerees from reselling their securities.[27] The Fifth and Sixth Circuits have considered (a) the number of offerees and their relationship to each other and the issuer, (b) the number of units offered, (c) the size of the offering, and (d) the manner of offering.[28] The Ninth Circuit has considered (a) the number of offerees, (b) the sophistication of the offerees, (c) the size and manner of the offering, and (d) the relationship of the offerees to the issuer.[29] The Tenth Circuit has considered (a) the number of offerees, (b) the sophistication of the offerees, including their access to the type of information that would be contained in a registration statement, and (c) the manner of the offering.[30]

---

22.   Securities Act § 4(2), 15 U.S.C. § 77d(2).

23.   *Securities & Exchange Commission v. Ralston Purina Co.*, 346 U.S. 119, 125, 73 S. Ct. 981, 984 (1953).

24.   *Id.* at 124, *Hill York Corp., et al. v. American International Franchises, Inc., et al.*, 448 F. 2d 680, 689 fn. 8 (5th Cir., 1971) ("the need for the protection of the [Securities] Act is greater when speculative securities in new ventures … are offered than when a new offering of the securities of an already established firm with an available operating record is involved.")

25.   *Securities & Exchange Commission v. Ralston Purina Co.*, 346 U.S. 119, 125-126, 73 S. Ct. 981, 985 (1953).

26.   *Cook, et al., v. Pritchard, et. al.*, 573 F. 2d 685, 691 (1st Cir., 1978) (citing *Doran Petroleum Mgmt. Corp.* and *Hill York Corp.*).

27.   *Barrett, et al. v. Triangle Mining Corp., et al.*, Fed. Sec. L. Rep. (CCH) ¶ 95,438, 1976 U.S. Dist. LEXIS 16883 (S.D.N.Y., 1976); *Securities & Exchange Commission v. Manus, et al.*, Fed. Sec. L. Rep. (CCH) ¶ 98,307, 1981 U.S. Dist. LEXIS 15317 (S.D.N.Y., 1981).

28.   *Hill York Corp., et al. v. American International Franchises, Inc., et al.*, 448 F. 2d 680, 687-689 (5th Cir., 1971); *Mark v. FSC Securities Corporation*, 870 F. 2d 331, 333 (6th Cir., 1989).

29.   *Securities & Exchange Commission v. Murphy*, 626 F. 2d 633, 644-645 (9th Cir., 1980).

30.   *U.S. v. Arutunoff, et al.*, 1 F. 3d 1112, 1118 (10th Cir., 1993).

Courts thus typically consider (a) the sophistication of the offerees, (b) the offerees' ability to assume financial risk, (c) the offerees' relationship with the issuer, (d) the offerees' access to information, (e) the size and manner of the offering, (f) the number of offerees and (g) the relationship of the offerees to each other.[31] These factors are interrelated, and courts accord them varying weight, depending on the circumstances. That one of these factors weighs heavily in favor of a private offering is not sufficient to ensure the availability of the exemption.[32] In addition, these factors are not exhaustive, but "serve as guideposts to the court in attempting to determine whether subjecting the offering to registration requirements would further the purposes of the [Securities] Act."[33]

In assessing the availability of the section 4(2) exemption, courts examine the qualifications of all of the offerees; the judicial inquiry is not confined to offerees that accept an offer and in fact invest.[34] The issuer must be prepared to offer evidence of the offerees' qualifications. This characteristic of the judicial gloss on section 4(2) provided impetus for the SEC's adoption of Regulation D,[35] which confines the inquiry to investors and has substantially reduced the issuer's burden in ascertaining and documenting the qualifications of offerees even before making offers to them. Nevertheless, a manager of a hedge fund is well advised to maintain records establishing the qualifications of each person to whom an interest in the hedge fund is offered to permit reliance on section 4(2).

An issuer claiming the section 4(2) exemption has the burden of proving that the offering meets the requirements of the exemption.[36] A court may insist that the issuer bear this burden even if an investor misrepresents to the broker selling the securities the facts on which the issuer relies to establish the private offering exemption.[37]

An issuer that relies on the private offering exemption is nevertheless subject to the anti-fraud provisions of the Securities Act.[38]

---

31. *Mark v FSC Securities Corporation*, 870 F. 2d 331, 333 (6th Cir., 1989); *Kunz v. Securities & Exchange Commission*, 2003 U.S. App. LEXIS 6011 (10th Cir., 2003); *Sorrell v. Securities & Exchange Commission*, 679 F.2d 1323 (9th Cir., 1982); *Securities & Exchange Commission v. Ralston Purina Co.*, 346 U.S. 119, 73 S. Ct. 981 (1953); *Barrett, et al. v. Triangle Mining Corp., et al.*, Fed. Sec. L. Rep. (CCH) ¶ 95,438, 1976 U.S. Dist. LEXIS 16883 (S.D.N.Y., 1976); *Securities & Exchange Commission v. Manus, et al.*, Fed. Sec. L. Rep. (CCH) ¶ 98,307, 1981 U.S. Dist. LEXIS 15317 (S.D.N.Y., 1981).

32. *Doran v. Petroleum Mgmt. Corp., et al.*, 545 F. 2d 893, 900 (5th Cir. 1977).

33. *Id.*

34. *Barrett, et al. v. Triangle Mining Corp., et al.*, Fed. Sec. L. Rep. (CCH) ¶ 95,438, 1976 U.S. Dist. LEXIS 16883 (S.D.N.Y., 1976) (finding that, although the defendant had demonstrated that it had met the requirements of the section 4(2) exemption with respect to the plaintiff investors, the exemption was unavailable to the defendant because the defendant had not offered evidence concerning the sophistication or access to information of other offerees); *Securities & Exchange Commission v. Continental Tobacco Co. of South Carolina*, 463 F. 2d 137, 160 (5th Cir., 1972).

35. Securities Act Release No. 6389, 46 F.R. 41,791 (Aug. 18, 1981). *See also* § 5.3.2. *infra*.

36. *Securities & Exchange Commission v. Ralston Purina Co.*, 346 U.S. 119, 126-127, 73 S. Ct. 981, 985 (1953).

37. *Woolf, et al., v. S.D. Cohn & Co., et al.*, 515 F. 2d 591, 605 (5th Cir., 1975).

38. Securities Act § 4, 15 U.S.C. §77d; *see* § 6.4, *infra*.

i. Sophistication of Offerees

The sophistication of the offerees is generally an important factor in determining whether an offering constitutes a private offering,[39] although some courts have held that the offerees do not need to be sophisticated for the offering to be private.[40] Courts consider both the offeree's expertise in the business in which the issuer will engage and the offeree's investment sophistication.[41] For an offeree to make an informed decision whether to invest, the offeree must be able to analyze, understand and evaluate the merits and risks of the investment. An offeree may be sufficiently sophisticated to analyze, understand and evaluate an offered investment in an operating company, by virtue, for example, of long-term executive experience in the industry where that company operates. If, however, an offeree is offered an investment in a hedge fund, executive experience in an operating company may not offer significant relevant sophistication. Offers to invest in a hedge fund should be confined, then, for purposes of the section 4(2) exemption, to investors that are experienced and knowledgeable in financial and investment matters. An offeree's relationship to the issuer may also be relevant, as in the case, for example, of a knowledgeable employee of the investment adviser that manages the hedge fund.[42]

ii. Ability to Take Risk

Courts sometimes include in the section 4(2) mix consideration of whether each offeree had sufficient financial means to absorb the possible loss of the investment without undue hardship.[43] This factor, too, is addressed in context. If the amount invested is small relative to the net worth or earning capacity of the offeree or if the risk of loss is slight, this factor may not be given significant consideration. Conversely, a relatively large investment in a risky venture ordinarily warrants more scrutiny, not only of the offeree's ability to take risk, but also of the offeree's sophistication and access to material information.

iii. Relationship of Offerees to the Issuer and Access to Information

A critical factor in determining the availability of the section 4(2) exemption is whether the offerees have access to information similar to what would be provided by a registration statement.[44] Even if all offerees have a high degree of investment

---

39. *See, e.g., Securities & Exchange Commission v. Manus, et al.,* Fed. Sec. L. Rep. (CCH) ¶ 98,307, 1981 U.S. Dist. LEXIS 15317 (S.D.N.Y., 1981); *Securities & Exchange Commission v. Murphy,* 626 F.2d 633, 646 (9th Cir., 1980).

40. *Doran v. Petroleum Mgmt. Corp., et al.,* 545 F. 2d 893, 902 (5th Cir. 1977).

41. *Id.; Barrett, et al. v. Triangle Mining Corp., et al.* Fed. Sec. L. Rep. (CCH) ¶ 95,438, 1976 U.S. Dist. LEXIS 16883 (S.D.N.Y., 1976).

42. *See* § 5.3.1.iii, *infra.*

43. *Securities & Exchange Commission v. Manus, et al.,* Fed. Sec. L. Rep. (CCH) ¶ 98,307, 1981 U. S. Dist. LEXIS 15317 (S.D.N.Y., 1981).

44. *Id.;* Securities & *Exchange Commission v. Ralston Purina,* 346 U.S. 119, 124–126, 73 S.Ct. 981, 984–985 (1953); *Doran v. Petroleum Mgmt. Corp., et al.,* 545 F. 2d 893 (5th Cir. 1977); *Sorrel v. Securities & Exchange Commission,* 679 F.2d 1323, 1326–1327 (9th Cir., 1982).

sophistication, the exemption will not be available if the offerees are not provided with or given access to all of the information that would be material to a decision whether to invest.[45] An offeree's sophistication avails little if the issuer does not make available adequate and accurate information about the investment so that the offeree can exercise his or her skills.[46] For example, in *Doran v. Petroleum Mgmt. Corp.*, the plaintiff sued an oil drilling limited partnership in which he had invested. The plaintiff held a degree in petroleum engineering, had a net worth in excess of $1,000,000 and held interests in approximately twenty-six oil and gas properties valued at $850,000. The court noted that all other offerees were similarly sophisticated. The court held that this alone was insufficient to establish that the offering was a private offering, absent evidence that the offerees had available the information that registration would provide. The court remanded the case for determination of whether such information was available.[47]

In *Lawler v. Gilliam*, a sophisticated businessman invested in an investment fund that later turned out to be fraudulent. The court noted that if the investor had been provided with the type of information required in a registration statement, including copies of contracts, financial statements, the identity of the other partners and the specific purpose for which the funds were to be used, the investor would have been able to detect the fraud. The court ruled that the businessman's sophistication and desire to participate in the program "do not supplant his lack of access to the information that a registration statement would show."[48]

An offeree may have access to information through a relationship with the issuer, such as employment or family relationships, or through contract or economic bargaining power that enables the offeree to obtain such information.[49] For example, in *Barrett, et al. v. Triangle Mining Corp., et al.*, the investors, sophisticated businessmen who were close friends of the organizer of the issuer, were encouraged to visit the issuer's mining operation before investing, were provided with "considerable information" concerning the enterprise and were invited to audit the issuer's books and help set up proper accounts. Although the investors did not avail themselves of these opportunities, the court found that the issuer had provided them with access to substantially the same information as would have been disclosed in a registration statement.[50]

---

45.   *Lawler v. Gilliam*, 569 F.2d 1283, 1290 (4th Cir., 1978), *Doran v. Petroleum Mgmt. Corp., et al.*, 545 F. 2d 893 (5th Cir. 1977).

46.   *Hill York Corp., et al. v. American International Franchises, Inc.*, 448 F. 2d 680, 690 (5th Cir., 1971); *Lawler v. Gilliam, et al.*, 569 F. 2d 1283, 1290 (4th Cir., 1978). *See also Doran v. Petroleum Mgmt. Corp., et al.*, 545 F. 2d 893 (5th Cir. 1977) (although the offering involved a "small number of units offered, relatively modest financial stakes, and an offering characterized by personal contact between the issuer and offerees free of public advertising or intermediaries," the court remanded the case for a determination concerning whether the offerees received or were provided access to information a registration statement would have provided to a prospective investor in a public offering).

47.   *Doran v. Petroleum Management Corp., et al.*, 545 F.2d 893 (5th Cir. 1977).

48.   *Lawler v. Gilliam, et al.*, 569 F. 2d 1283, 1290 (4th Cir., 1978).

49.   *See Securities & Exchange Commission v. Ralston Purina Co.*, 346 U.S. 119, 125-126, 73 S. Ct. 981, 985 (1953) (stating that an offering to "executive personnel who because of their position have access to the same kind of information that the [Securities] Act would make available in the form of a registration statement" may be exempt under section 4(2)); *Barrett, et al. v. Triangle Mining Corp., et al.*, Fed. Sec. L. Rep. (CCH) ¶ 95,438, 1976 U.S. Dist. LEXIS 16,883 (S.D.N.Y., 1976); *Doran v. Petroleum Mgmt. Corp., et al.*, 545 F. 2d 893, 902 (5th Cir. 1977).

50.   *Barrett, et al. v. Triangle Mining Corp., et al.*, Fed. Sec. L. Rep. (CCH) ¶ 95,438, 1976 U.S. Dist. LEXIS 16,883 (S.D.N.Y., 1976). The court went on to find against the defendant, however, because the defendant failed to offer evidence concerning the sophistication and access to information of investors other than the plaintiffs.

When an issuer relies on access without disclosing all material information, the issuer must demonstrate that "the offerees occupied a privileged position relative to the issuer that afforded them an opportunity for effective access to the information registration would otherwise provide."[51] "If the offerees know the issuer and have special knowledge as to its business affairs, such as high executive officers of the issuer would possess, then the offering is apt to be private."[52] The relationship must be sufficient to permit the offeree to have effective and complete access to all information that registration would require.[53]

Instead of merely providing access to information, the issuer may furnish directly the information that would be provided by a registration statement, as in a private offering memorandum that fully discloses such information.[54] A hedge fund's private offering memorandum should contain all of the information required in a registration statement filed on Form S-1 under the Securities Act and Form N-1A under the Company Act.[55] The hedge fund should obtain a written representation from each offeree that the offeree has received and read the private offering memorandum (although such a representation by the offeree may not be sufficient by itself to establish the availability of the private offering exemption[56]).

The provision of information required by section 4(2) is, of course, subject to the anti-fraud provisions of the Securities Act and the Exchange Act.[57]

iv. Size and Manner of the Offering

Courts also consider the manner in which an issuer offers and sells its securities in determining whether the transaction constitutes a private offering. "A private offering is more likely to arise when the offer is made directly to the offerees rather than through the facilities of a public distribution such as investment bankers or the securities exchanges. In addition, public advertising is incompatible with the claim of private offering."[58] On the other hand, the absence of contact between an offeree and the issuer or the issuer's agents tends to indicate a public offering rather than a private offering.[59]

The fewer the number of units to be sold and the smaller the offering, the more likely the sale is private.[60] One court indicated in 1980 that a $7,500,000 offering was sufficiently large to be considered public absent a significant showing that the investors did not need the protection of the Securities Act.[61]

---

51.   *Id.*

52.   *Hill York Corp., et al. v. American International Franchises, Inc.*, 448 F. 2d 680, 688 (5th Cir., 1971).

53.   *Doran v. Petroleum Mgmt. Corp., et al.*, 545 F. 2d 893, 906, fn. 18 (5th Cir. 1977).

54.   *Id.*, at 902 and 906.

55.   *See* § 6.2.1.i, *infra*.

56.   *Woolf et al. v. S. D. Cohn & Co., et al.*, 515 F. 2d 591, 610 (5th Cir., 1975), citing *Securities & Exchange Commission v. Continental Tobacco Co.*, 463 F. 2d 137, 160 (5th Cir., 1972).

57.   *Woolf* at 608. *See* Chapter 6, *infra*.

58.   *Hill York Corp., et al. v. American International Franchises, Inc., et al.*, 448 F. 2d 680, 689 (5th Cir., 1971); *Securities & Exchange Commission v. Murphy*, 626 F. 2d 633, 644-645 (9th Cir., 1980).

59.   *Woolf, et al., v. S.D. Cohn & Co., et al.*, 515 F. 2d 591, 614 (5th Cir., 1975); *Securities & Exchange Commission v. Murphy*, 626 F. 2d 633, 644-645 (9th Cir., 1980).

60.   *Hill York Corp., et al. v. American International Franchises, Inc., et al.*, 448 F. 2d 680, 689 (5th Cir., 1971); *Securities & Exchange Commission v. Murphy*, 626 F. 2d 633, 644-645 (9th Cir., 1980).

61.   *Securities & Exchange Commission v. Murphy*, 626 F. 2d 633, 644-645 (9th Cir., 1980).

v. Number of Offerees

There is no maximum limitation on the number of offerees an issuer may solicit without engaging in a public offering. The Supreme Court has indicated, however, that "it may well be that offerings to a substantial number of persons would rarely be exempt" under section 4(2).[62] Subsequent court decisions have held that a large number of offerees indicates that the offering is a public offering.[63] In addition, courts typically consider the number of offerees "in order to ascertain the magnitude of the offering and in order to determine the characteristics and knowledge of the persons thus identified."[64] The greater the number of offerees, the more difficult it may be for the issuer to establish that each offeree was of a class of investors that does not require the protection of the Securities Act. Again, the courts consider the number of offerees, not the number of purchasers, for this purpose.[65] On the other hand, an offering to only one offeree could be regarded as public, depending on the qualifications of the offeree, the availability of information and the manner of conducting the offering.[66]

As noted,[67] the burden of proving the availability of the private offering exemption is on the person claiming it. An issuer that fails to keep records of the number of offerees in an offering may not be able to rely on the private offering exemption, because it will be unable to prove that all offerees had the necessary qualifications and had access to all of the information that would be in a registration statement.[68] One court has stated that an issuer's failure to number its private offering memoranda and keep records of the persons to whom they were delivered is evidence that the issuer failed to monitor the number of offerees.[69]

Accordingly, a hedge fund manager should maintain records of each person to whom the hedge fund offers its interests. All offers of interests in a hedge fund should be made only through a private offering memorandum.[70] The hedge fund should consecutively number each copy of the memorandum[71] and maintain a list identifying each offeree and the number of the memorandum provided to that offeree.

---

62. *Securities & Exchange Commission v. Ralston Purina Co.*, 346 U.S. 119, 125 (1953). *See also Lawler v. Gilliam, et al.*, 569 F. 2d 1283, 1290 (4th Cir. 1978).

63. *See, Securities & Exchange Commission v. The Infinity Group Co.*, 993 F. Supp. 324, 327 (E.D. Penn., 1998) (finding a public offering where over 10,000 investors in the U.S. and overseas were solicited by facsimile, mailings and a website); *Doran v. Petroleum Mgmt. Corp. et al.*, 545 F. 2d 893, 900 (5th Cir., 1977); *Hill York Corp., et al. v. American International Franchises, Inc., et al.*, 448 F. 2d 680, 688 (5th Cir., 1971); *Securities & Exchange Commission v. Murphy*, 626 F. 2d 633, 645 (9th Cir., 1980).

64. *Doran v. Petroleum Mgmt. Corp., et al.*, 545 F. 2d 893, 900 (5th Cir. 1977).

65. *Id.*

66. *See Swenson v. Engelstad*, 626 F.2d 421, 427 (5th Cir., 1980).

67. *Securities and Exchange Commission v. Ralston Purina Co.*, 346 U.S. 119, 73 S. Ct. 981 (1953); *see* notes 36–38 and accompanying text, *supra*.

68. *Doran v. Petroleum Mgmt. Corp. et al.*, 545 F. 2d 893, 900 (5th Cir., 1977); *Woolf, et al., v. S.D. Cohn & Co., et al.*, 515 F. 2d 591, 610 (5th Cir., 1975); *Hill York Corp., et al. v. American International Franchises, Inc., et al.*, 448 F. 2d 680, 691 (5th Cir., 1971); *Mark, et al. V. FSC Securities Corp., et al.*, 870 F. 2d 331, 334 (6th Cir., 1989).

69. *Securities & Exchange Commission v. Murphy*, 626 F. 2d 633, 645 (9th Cir., 1980).

70. *See* Chapter 6, *infra*.

71. *Securities & Exchange Commission v. Murphy*, 626 F. 2d 633 (9th Cir. 1989) (issuer's failure to number its offering memoranda indicates that issuer failed to monitor volume of offers it made).

vi. Relationship of the Offerees to Each Other

Courts may also consider the relationship among the offerees in determining whether an offering is a public offering. If an offering is made to a diverse and unrelated group, the offering is more likely to be considered public, but if the offering is made to a select group of offerees who know each other and have similar interests and knowledge of the offering, the offering is more likely to be considered private.[72]

2. Regulation D

SEC Regulation D[73] provides three non-exclusive safe harbor exemptions from registration under Securities Act sections 4(2)[74] and 3(b).[75] Hedge funds typically rely on the safe harbor of Regulation D Rule 506[76] under Securities Act section 4(2), in addition to relying on the statutory section 4(2) exemption, in offering and selling their interests.[77] The Rule 506 safe harbor provides an exemption from the registration requirements of the Securities Act, but not from the anti-fraud, civil liability or other provisions of the Securities Act.[78] The Rule 506 safe harbor also adapts some of the conditions of the section 4(2) exemption, but with more specificity and objectivity, as discussed below. Regulation D is not available, however, for any issuer that, although complying with the technical requirements of Regulation D, is engaged in a plan or scheme to evade the registration requirements of the Securities Act.[79]

i. General

An issuer seeking to rely on the Regulation D Rule 506 safe harbor must:

- comply with the information delivery requirements of Regulation D Rule 502(b);[80]
- not employ any advertising or general solicitation in offering or selling its securities;[81]

---

72. *Hill York Corp., et al. v. American International Franchises, Inc., et al.*, 448 F. 2d 680, 688 (5th Cir. 1971).

73. 17 C.F.R. §§ 230.501 to 230.508. For a more detailed analysis of the Regulation D exemption, see J. William Hicks, *Limited Offering Exemptions: Regulation D*, 2002-2003 Ed. (West Group, 2002).

74. 15 U.S.C. § 77d(2).

75. Securities Act § 3(b), 15 U.S.C. § 77c(b), grants the SEC the authority to adopt rules and regulations exempting securities from the registration requirements of the Securities Act if the aggregate amount at which such securities are offered to the public does not exceed $5,000,000.

76. 17 C.F.R. § 230.506.

77. Regulation D Rules 504 and 505, 17 C.F.R. §§ 230.504 and 230.505, permit an issuer to issue securities in an offering pursuant to Securities Act § 3(b), 15 U.S.C. § 77c(b), having an aggregate offering price of no more than $1,000,000 or $5,000,000, respectively, in any twelve month period. Because an offering pursuant to § 3(b) may be made to the public (*see* Chapter 3, *supra*) and because of the limits on the aggregate dollar value of such an offering, the Rule 504 and 505 safe harbors are unsuitable for a hedge fund and are not discussed in this book. For a detailed discussion of the requirements and applicability of the Rule 504 and 505 safe harbors, see J. William Hicks, *Limited Offering Exemptions: Regulation D*, 2002-2003 ed. (West Group, 2002).

78. Regulation D Preliminary Note 1, 17 C.F.R. § 230.501. *See* § 6.4, *infra*.

79. Regulation D Preliminary Note 6, 17 C.F.R. § 230.501.

80. 17 C.F.R. § 230.502(b).

81. Regulation D Rule 502(c), 17 C.F.R. § 230.502(c).

- limit sales of its securities in an offering to not more than thirty-five nonaccredited investors, although the number of accredited investors is not limited in an offering under Rule 506;[82]
- take steps to restrict resales of any of its securities sold in reliance on the Rule 506 safe harbor;[83] and
- file a notice on Form D[84] with the SEC within fifteen days of the first sale of its securities pursuant to Regulation D.[85]

Regulation D Rule 507 prohibits reliance on Rule 506 if the issuer or any of its predecessors or affiliates have been enjoined for failing to comply with Regulation D Rule 503,[86] unless the SEC determines otherwise on a showing of good cause.

ii. Accredited Investors

Regulation D Rule 501 defines an "accredited investor"[87] as any person that is within, or that an issuer reasonably believes is within, one of the following categories:

- a bank as defined in Securities Act section 3(a)(2)[88] or a savings and loan association or other institution as defined in Securities Act section 3(a)(5)(A),[89] whether acting in its individual or fiduciary capacity;
- a broker or dealer registered pursuant to Exchange Act section 15;[90]
- an insurance company as defined in Securities Act section 2(13);[91]
- an investment company registered under the Company Act or a business development company as defined in Company Act section 2(a)(48);[92]
- a small business investment company licensed by the U.S. Small Business Administration under section 301(c) or (d) of the Small Business Investment Act of 1958;[93]
- a plan established and maintained by a state, its political subdivisions, or any agency or instrumentality of a state or its political subdivisions, for the benefit of its employees, if such plan has total assets in excess of $5,000,000;
- an employee benefit plan within the meaning of ERISA (a) if the investment decision is made by a plan fiduciary, as defined in ERISA section 3(21),[94]

---

82.   Regulation D Rule 506(b)(2), 17 C.F.R. § 230.506(b)(2).
83.   Regulation D Rule 502(d), 17 C.F.R. § 230.502(d).
84.   17 C.F.R. § 239-500.
85.   Regulation D Rule 503(a), 17 C.F.R. § 230.503(a). If an issuer fails to comply with the notice filing requirements of Regulation D, the issuer may be subject to an order enjoining such issuer from relying on any of the safe harbors provided by Regulation D in the future, unless the SEC determines on a showing of good cause that it is not necessary to deny the exemption. *See also* Regulation D Rule 507, 17 C.F.R. § 230.507.
86.   17 C.F.R. § 230.503.
87.   Regulation D Rule 501(a), 17 C.F.R. § 230.501(a).
88.   15 U.S.C. § 77c(a)(2)(c)(iii).
89.   15 U.S.C. § 77c(a)(5)(A).
90.   15 U.S.C. § 78o.
91.   15 U.S.C. § 77b(a)(13).
92.   15 U.S.C. § 80a-2(a)(48).
93.   15 U.S.C. § 681.
94.   29 U.S.C. § 1002(21).

which is a bank, a savings and loan association, an insurance company, or a registered investment adviser, or (b) if the employee benefit plan has total assets in excess of $5,000,000, or (c) if the employee benefit plan is a self-directed plan, with investment decisions made solely by persons that are accredited investors;

- a private business development company as defined in Advisers Act section 202(a)(22);[95]
- an organization described in Tax Code section 501(c),[96] a corporation, Massachusetts or similar business trust, or a partnership, if such entity was not formed for the specific purpose of acquiring the securities offered and has total assets in excess of $5,000,000;
- a director, executive officer, or general partner of the issuer selling the securities being offered or sold, or any director, executive officer or general partner of a general partner of the issuer;
- any natural person whose individual net worth, or joint net worth with that person's spouse, at the time of purchase exceeds $1,000,000;
- any natural person who had an individual income in excess of $200,000 in each of the two most recent years or joint income with that person's spouse in excess of $300,000 in each of those years and has a reasonable expectation of reaching the same income level in the current year (due to the $1,500,000 minimum net worth requirement for an investment adviser charging a performance fee to a client or a limited partner in a hedge fund,[97] these annual income tests for accredited investors ordinarily are irrelevant for a hedge fund);
- a trust, with total assets in excess of $5,000,000, not formed for the specific purpose of acquiring the securities offered, whose purchase is directed by a person who has such knowledge and experience in financial and business matters that such person is capable of evaluating the merits and risks of such investment; and
- an entity in which all of the equity owners are accredited investors.

Whether or not an investor is an accredited investor is determined at the time of investment.[98] Changes in the investor's status after investment will not result in a loss of the Rule 506 exemption, unless the investor's investment was part of a plan or scheme to evade the Securities Act registration requirements.[99]

Even if an investor is not within one of the foregoing categories, that investor may nevertheless be considered an accredited investor if the issuer reasonably believed at the time of investment that the investor was within one of those categories.[100] Accordingly, before accepting investments, a hedge fund should take reasonable steps to establish that each investor is within one of the foregoing categories, by,

---

95.   15 U.S.C. § 80b-2(a)(22).
96.   26 U.S.C. § 501(c).
97.   *See* § 15.2.3, *infra.*
98.   Regulation D Rule 501(a), 17 C.F.R. § 230.501(a); Securities Act Release No. 6455, question 1, 48 F.R. 10,045 (Mar. 10, 1983).
99.   Securities Act Release No. 6455, question 1, fn. 3, 48 F.R. 10,045 (Mar. 10, 1983).
100.   Regulation D Rule 501(a), § 17 C.F.R. § 230.501(a).

for example, requiring each investor to represent in writing that the investor is an accredited investor and to complete an offering questionnaire that requires the investor to identify which of the categories applies. The hedge fund should retain these documents in its records, because they may be needed to prove that the hedge fund validly relied on the Rule 506 safe harbor[101] and because the Advisers Act requires the hedge fund's investment adviser (if SEC-registered) to retain them.[102]

a. Trusts

As described above, a trust is an accredited investor if it has total assets in excess of $5,000,000, it is not formed for the specific purpose of acquiring the securities offered and its decision to invest is directed by a person who has enough knowledge and experience in financial and business matters to be able to evaluate the merits and risks of such investment.[103] A trust also qualifies as an accredited investor if its trustee is a bank and the bank makes the investment decision on behalf of the trust, because a bank acting in a fiduciary capacity is an accredited investor.[104] In addition, a revocable trust or an individual retirement account also qualifies as an accredited investor if all of the grantors are accredited investors and the grantors may amend or revoke the trust at any time.[105] On the other hand, an irrevocable trust that does not have assets in excess of $5,000,000 and whose trustee is not a bank does not qualify as an accredited investor, even if all of its beneficiaries are accredited investors.[106]

b. Limited Liability Companies

Although limited liability companies are not expressly included in the definition of "accredited investor," the SEC staff has opined that a limited liability company is an accredited investor if it was not formed for the specific purpose of acquiring the securities offered and has total assets in excess of $5,000,000.[107]

c. Directors and Executive Officers

As described above, a director, executive officer or general partner of a hedge fund or a director, executive officer or general partner of a general partner of a hedge fund is an accredited investor.[108] An executive officer is the "president, any vice president in charge of a principal business unit, division or function (such as

---

101. *Mark v. FTC Securities Corp.*, 870 F. 2d 331, 336-337 (6th Cir., 1989) (holding that the burden of proving the qualification of the purchasers of an issuer's securities "could have been met by offering each of the twenty-eight purchasers' executed subscription documents into evidence …").

102. *See* § 2.8, *supra.*

103. Regulation D Rule 501(a)(7), 17 C.F.R. § 230.507(a)(7).

104. Securities Act Release No. 6455, question 26, 48 F.R. 10,045 (Mar. 10, 1983); Regulation D Rule 501(a)(1), 17 C.F.R. § 230.501(a)(1).

105. Securities Act Release No. 6455, question 30, 48 F.R. 10,045 (Mar. 10, 1983).

106. *Id.*

107. *Wolf, Block, Schorr and Solis-Cohen*, SEC No-Action Letter (Dec. 11, 1996), 1996 SEC No-Act. LEXIS 913.

108. Regulation D Rule 501(a)(4), 17 C.F.R. § 230.501(a)(4).

sales, administration or finance), any other officer who performs a policy making function or any other person who performs similar policy making functions for the issuer."[109] If a person is a director or executive officer of a parent entity of the general partner of the hedge fund, such person is only an accredited investor if that person is also a director or executive officer of the general partner.[110] An executive officer of a parent entity of the general partner will be considered an executive officer of the general partner if he or she performs policy-making functions for the general partner.[111]

iii. Non-Accredited Investors

A hedge fund relying on Rule 506 may also sell interests to up to thirty-five non-accredited investors.[112] An investor that is not an accredited investor must have sufficient knowledge and experience in financial and business matters to be capable of evaluating the merits and risks of the prospective investment, or the issuer must reasonably believe immediately prior to making a sale to such an investor that the investor meets this requirement.[113] To permit it to meet the burden of proving that each of its investors meets the requirements of Rule 506, a hedge fund should obtain written representations from each investor, by, for example, requiring each investor to sign a subscription agreement containing representations concerning the investor's sophistication and knowledge and to complete an offering questionnaire that elicits sufficient information concerning the investor's background and experience.[114]

Determining investment sophistication is a matter of subjective judgment, and determining whether a non-accredited investor qualifies to participate in a Rule 506 offering is invariably uncertain. In addition, a hedge fund is required to disclose substantial information to each non-accredited investor in the hedge fund.[115] Because the net worth requirement in the performance fee rule under the Advisers Act is higher than the net worth test for individual accredited investors, a hedge fund will ordinarily be prohibited from charging a performance fee or allocation to a natural person who is a nonaccredited investor and is a U.S. person.[116] For these reasons, hedge funds ordinarily do not accept investments from non-accredited investors.

iv. Purchaser Representatives

A non-accredited investor may employ a purchaser representative to meet the sophistication requirement of Rule 506.[117] A purchaser representative is a person

---

109.   Regulation D Rule 501(f), 17 C.F.R. § 230.501(f).

110.   Securities Act Release No. 6455, question 6, 48 F.R. 10,045 (Mar. 10, 1983).

111.   Securities Act Release No. 6455, question 33, 48 F.R. 10,045 (Mar. 10, 1983).

112.   Regulation D Rule 506(b)(2)(i), 17 C.F.R. § 230.506(b)(2)(i).

113.   Regulation D Rule 506(b)(2)(ii), 17 C.F.R. § 230.506(b)(2)(ii). *See also* § 5.3.1.i, *supra*, discussing investment sophistication for purposes of Securities Act section 4(2), 15 U.S.C. § 77d(2), which is similarly used for purposes of Regulation D.

114.   *Mark v. FTC Securities Corp.*, 870 F. 2d 331, 335-337 (6th Cir., 1989).

115.   *See* § 5.3.2.vii, *infra*.

116.   *See* § 15.2.3.i, *infra*.

117.   Regulation D Rule 506(b)(2)(ii), 17 C.F.R. § 230.506(b)(2)(ii).

who assists an investor in evaluating the investment and who has, or who the issuer reasonably believes has, enough knowledge and experience in financial and business matters to be able to evaluate the merits and risks of the investment, whether alone, with the purchaser or with the purchaser's other purchaser representatives.[118] An issuer must obtain sufficient information from a purchaser representative to form a reasonable belief about the purchaser representative's qualifications; if the issuer fails to do so, it ordinarily may not rely on the purchaser representative to establish that an investor is sufficiently sophisticated under Rule 506.[119] A hedge fund should obtain sufficient written information from the purchaser representative, through the use of a questionnaire, to enable it to determine that the purchaser representative is qualified to act as such.

An affiliate, director, officer or other employee of the issuer, or a beneficial owner of ten percent or more of any class of the issuer's equity securities or of ten percent or more of the equity interests in the issuer cannot act as a purchaser representative for an investor.[120] The "issuer" is the "person who issues or proposes to issue any security."[121] An "affiliate" is "a person that directly, or indirectly, through one or more intermediaries, controls or is controlled by, or is under common control with, the person specified."[122] This prohibition extends to officers and directors of a corporate general partner of an issuer.[123] Accordingly, none of the hedge fund, its general partner or their respective owners, directors, officers or employees can serve as a purchaser representative for an investor. If a hedge fund has a separate investment adviser, the investment adviser may not act as a purchaser representative if the investment adviser controls, is controlled by or is under common control with the hedge fund or its general partner. These prohibitions do not apply, however, in certain cases when the investor and the purchaser representative are closely related or affiliated, including when the investor is:

- a relative of the purchaser representative by blood, marriage or adoption not more remote than first cousin;
- a trust or estate in which the purchaser representative and any persons related to the purchaser representative as specified in the preceding item or the following item collectively have more than fifty percent of the beneficial interest (excluding contingent interests) or of which the purchaser representative serves as trustee, executor or in any similar capacity; or
- a corporation or other organization of which the purchaser representative and any persons related to the purchaser representative specified in the preceding two items collectively are the beneficial owners of more than fifty percent of the equity securities (excluding directors' qualifying shares) or equity interests.[124]

---

118. Regulation D Rule 501(h)(2), 17 C.F.R. § 230.501(h)(2).

119. *See, e.g., Western-Realco Limited Partnership, et al. v. Harrison*, 791 P. 2d 1139, 1146 (Col. App. Ct., 1989).

120. Regulation D Rule 501(h)(1), 17 C.F.R. § 230.501(h)(1).

121. Securities Act § 2(a)(4), 15 U.S.C. § 77b(a)(4); Regulation D Rule 501(g), 17 C.F.R. § 230.501(g).

122. Regulation D Rule 501(b), 17 C.F.R. § 230.501(b).

123. Securities Act Release No. 6455, question 38, 48 F.R. 10,045 (Mar. 10, 1983).

124. Regulation D Rule 501(h)(1), 17 C.F.R. § 230.501(h)(1).

An investor employing a purchaser representative must acknowledge in writing to the issuer during the transaction that the purchaser representative is acting as the investor's purchaser representative with respect to the investment.[125] The purchaser representative must disclose to the investor in writing a reasonable time prior to the investment any material relationship between the purchaser representative or the representative's affiliates and the issuer or its affiliates that exists at the time, that is mutually understood to be contemplated or that has existed at any time during the preceding two years.[126] Such disclosure must include the compensation received or to be received by the purchaser representative as a result of the relationship.[127] The purchaser representative may be compensated by the issuer for acting as a purchaser representative, but only if such compensation is disclosed to the investor.[128]

v. Limitations on Number of Investors

Rule 506 permits sales of an unlimited amount of securities to up to thirty-five investors,[129] excluding:

- any relative, spouse or relative of the spouse of an investor who has the same principal residence as the investor;
- any trust or estate in which an investor or any of the persons described in the preceding item or any entity described in the following item collectively hold more than fifty percent of the beneficial interest (excluding contingent interests);
- any corporation or other organization of which any of the persons described in the two preceding items collectively are beneficial owners of more than fifty percent of the equity securities (excluding directors' qualifying shares) or equity interests; and
- any accredited investor.[130]

Rule 506 thus permits investment by an unlimited number of accredited investors, and up to thirty-five non-accredited investors.

vi. Manner of Sale—No Advertising or General Solicitation

No form of general solicitation or advertising may be used in offering or selling securities under Regulation D.[131] This prohibition includes any mass mailing, any advertisement, article, notice or other communication published in any magazine, newspaper or newsletter or broadcast over television or radio, and any seminar or meeting where the attendees have been invited by any mass mailing, general

---

125. Regulation D Rule 501(h)(3), 17 C.F.R. § 230.501(h)(3).
126. Regulation D Rule 501(h)(4), 17 C.F.R. § 230.501(h)(4).
127. *Id.*
128. Securities Act Release No. 6455, question 39, 48 F.R. 10,045 (Mar. 10, 1983).
129. Regulation D Rule 506(b)(2), 17 C.F.R. § 230.506(b)(2).
130. Regulation D Rule 501(e), 17 C.F.R. § 230.501(e).
131. Regulation D Rule 502(c), 17 C.F.R. § 230.502(c).

solicitation or general advertising.[132] This prohibition is derived from cases interpreting the Securities Act section 4(2) exemption.[133]

vii. Information Delivery Requirements

A hedge fund relying on the Rule 506 safe harbor must provide to any purchaser that is not an accredited investor, a reasonable time before the sale,[134] the same kind of information required to be delivered in Part I of a registration statement filed under the Securities Act on the form that the issuer would be entitled to use. Regulation D does not require an issuer to deliver this information to an accredited investor, but in observance of the anti-fraud provisions of the securities laws, the issuer should provide accredited investors with the same information as it would be required to provide to non-accredited investors.[135] In addition, the anti-fraud provisions of the Securities Act prohibit misstatements or omissions of material fact in connection with any offer or sale of securities and may require an issuer to deliver information to accredited investors, even if it makes no offers to non-accredited investors.[136]

In addition, a reasonable time before the sale of interests to a non-accredited investor, a hedge fund must advise the investor of the limitations on resale,[137] and must give the investor a brief written description of any material written information about the offering that has been provided by the issuer to any accredited investor but not previously provided to the non-accredited investor and, on request by the non-accredited investor, copies of that written information. The hedge fund also must give each investor, at a reasonable time before the investor invests, an opportunity to ask questions and receive answers about the terms and conditions of the offering and to obtain any additional information that the hedge fund has or can acquire without unreasonable effort or expense that is necessary to verify the accuracy of the information furnished to the investor.[138]

viii. Restrictions on Resale

Regulation D Rule 502(d) provides that securities acquired pursuant to the Rule 506 safe harbor have the status of securities acquired in a private offering under Securities Act section 4(2), and cannot be resold unless they are registered or exempt from registration under the Securities Act.[139] The registration requirements of Securities Act section 5 apply to sales of securities by any person, not only an issuer.[140] As a result, an investor that purchases an interest in a hedge fund may not resell that interest, unless either the interest is registered under the Securities Act or the investor establishes that an exemption from registration applies. Securities

---

132. *Id.*
133. *See* § 5.3.1, *supra*, and § 8.2, *infra*.
134. Regulation D Rule 502(b), 17 C.F.R. § 230.502(b).
135. *Id.*
136. *See* § 6.4, *infra*.
137. *See* § 5.3.2.viii, *infra*.
138. Regulation D Rules 502(b)(2)(iv), (v) and (vii), 17 C.F.R. §§ 502(b)(2)(iv), (v) and (vii).
139. Regulation D Rule 502(d), 17 C.F.R. § 230.502(d).
140. Securities Act § 5, 15 U.S.C. § 77e.

acquired in a Rule 506 offering are "restricted securities" under Rule 144 under the Securities Act.[141] Accordingly, such securities can be resold in accordance with Rule 144 without registration under the Securities Act.[142]

Regulation D Rule 502(d) also requires issuers of securities under the Rule 506 safe harbor to exercise reasonable care to assure that the purchasers of the securities are not underwriters.[143] An "underwriter" is "any person who has purchased from an issuer with a view to, or offers or sells for an issuer in connection with, the distribution of any security, or participates or has a participation in the direct or indirect underwriting of any such undertaking."[144] An issuer can demonstrate that it has taken reasonable care not to sell to an underwriter by:

- making a reasonable inquiry to determine if the purchaser is acquiring the securities for the purchaser's own account or for other persons;
- providing written disclosure to each purchaser prior to sale that the securities have not been registered under the Securities Act and cannot be resold unless they are so registered or unless an exemption from registration is available; and
- placing a legend on the certificate or other document that evidences the securities stating that the securities have not been registered under the Securities Act and setting forth or referring to the restrictions on transferability and sale of the securities.[145]

This is not the only method by which an issuer can establish that it exercised reasonable care in assuring that a purchaser is not an underwriter.[146] A hedge fund should attempt, however, to comply with these steps. The disclosures and legends identified in Rule 502(d) should be included in the subscription agreement by which an investor acquires interests in the hedge fund.

c. Failure to Comply with Requirements of Regulation D

As discussed above, if an issuer does not comply with the requirements of Regulation D Rule 506, the issuer may nevertheless rely on the section 4(2) private offering exemption, if its requirements are met. In addition, even if the issuer fails to comply with a term, condition or requirement of the Regulation D Rule 506 safe harbor, it may still rely on the safe harbor for an offer or sale to a particular person, if it can show that (1) the failure to comply did not pertain to a term, condition or requirement directly intended to protect that particular person, (2) the failure to comply was insignificant with respect to the offering as a whole, and (3) the issuer

---

141.   Securities Act Rule 144(a)(3), 17 C.F.R. § 230.144(a)(3), provides that "restricted securities means: (i) securities acquired directly or indirectly from the issuer, or from an affiliate of the issuer, in a transaction or chain of transactions not involving any public offering; (ii) securities acquired from the issuer that are subject to the resale limitations of section 230.502(d) under Regulation D...." 17 C.F.R. §§ 230.144(a)(3)(i) and (ii).

142.   For a discussion of the requirements of Rule 144, see J. William Hicks, *Resales of Restricted Securities*, ch. 4, 2003 ed. (West Group, 2003).

143.   Regulation D Rule 502(d), 17 C.F.R. § 230.502(d).

144.   Securities Act § 2(a)(11); 15 U.S.C. § 77b(a)(11).

145.   Regulation D Rule 502(d), 17 C.F.R. § 230.502(d).

146.   *Id.*

made a good faith and reasonable attempt to comply with all applicable terms, conditions and requirements of the Rule 506 safe harbor.[147] Failing to comply with the limitations on the number of purchasers or the amount of securities to be sold or with the limitations on advertising and general solicitation is considered significant to the offering as a whole.[148] The foregoing good faith compliance rule does not, however, preclude the SEC from bringing an action against an issuer that fails to comply with any requirement of Regulation D.[149]

§ 5.4 Regulation S

The Securities Act registration requirements apply to any transaction in securities that involves interstate commerce or use of the U.S. mail.[150] "Interstate commerce" includes "trade or commerce in securities or any transportation or communication relating thereto … between any foreign country and any State, Territory or the District of Columbia."[151] This broad scope could encompass any transaction in securities issued by a non-U.S. company to a non-U.S. investor if a jurisdictional nexus is established, such as a call being placed to or from the United States in connection with such transaction. As a result, the Securities Act registration requirements could, and often do, apply to the offer and sale of shares in an offshore hedge fund. To clarify the application of the registration requirements to offshore transactions, the SEC adopted Regulation S.[152]

Regulation S provides that, for purposes of Securities Act section 5,[153] the terms "offer," "offer to sell," "sell," "sale," and "offer to buy" include offers and sales that occur within the United States but do not include offers and sales that occur outside the United States.[154] For purposes of Regulation S, the United States "means the United States of America, its territories and possessions, any State of the United States, and the District of Columbia."[155] Whether a transaction occurs outside the United States depends on the facts and circumstances of each case.[156]

Regulation S establishes safe harbor exemptions from the registration requirements for offers and sales of securities by issuers and distributors in offshore

---

147. Regulation D Rule 508(a), 17 C.F.R. § 230.508(a).
148. Regulation D Rule 508(a)(2), 17 C.F.R. § 230.508(a)(2).
149. Regulation D Rule 508(b), 17 C.F.R. § 230.508(b).
150. Securities Act § 5, 15 U.S.C. § 77e.
151. Securities Act § 2(a)(7), 15 U.S.C. § 77b(a)(7).
152. Securities Act Release No. 6863 (Apr. 24, 1990), 55 F.R. 18,306 (May 2, 1990) ("Release 6863"). Before the SEC adopted Regulation S, Securities Act Release No. 4708 (July 9, 1964), 29 F.R. 9,828 (July 9, 1964), which was superseded by Regulation S, provided guidance on application of Securities Act § 5 to offshore transactions.
153. 15 U.S.C. § 77e.
154. Regulation S Rule 901, 17 C.F.R. § 230.901.
155. Regulation S Rule 902(l), 17 C.F.R. § 230.902(l).
156. Release 6863.

transactions and for resales of securities in offshore transactions.[157] A distributor is any "underwriter, dealer or other person who participates, pursuant to a contractual arrangement, in the distribution of the securities offered or sold in reliance on Regulation S."[158] This section focuses on the safe harbor for offers and sales of securities by issuers and distributors and does not address offshore resales.

A transaction that complies with Regulation S is deemed to be outside the United States and, therefore, is not subject to the registration requirements of Securities Act section 5. Regulation S exempts offshore transactions only from the requirements of section 5 of the Securities Act; it does not affect the anti-fraud and other provisions of the Securities Act, compliance with the requirements of the Exchange Act or any applicable state securities laws.[159]

The Regulation S safe harbor for offers of securities by issuers and distributors requires that:

- the offer be made in an offshore transaction; and
- no directed selling efforts be made in the United States by the issuer, a distributor, any affiliate of the issuer or a distributor or any person acting on behalf of any of them.[160]

Additional requirements may apply depending the nature of the issuer and the securities being offered and sold.

1. Offshore Transaction

For purposes of the issuer and distributor safe harbor provided by Regulation S Rule 903,[161] an offer or sale of securities is made in an "offshore transaction" if the offer is not made to a person in the United States and either of the following requirements is met:

- at the time the buy order is originated, the buyer is outside the United States or the seller and any person acting on its behalf reasonably believes that the buyer is outside the United States or
- the transaction is executed in, on or through a physical trading floor of an established foreign securities exchange that is located outside the United States.[162]

Offers and sales of securities specifically targeted at identifiable groups of U.S. citizens abroad, such as members of the U.S. armed forces serving overseas, are not considered to be made in "offshore transactions."[163] An offer or sale to a dealer or other professional fiduciary organized, incorporated or (if an individual) resident in the United States that holds a discretionary account or similar account (other

---

157.   Regulation S Rules 903 and 904, 17 C.F.R. §§ 230.903 and 230.904.
158.   Regulation S Rule 902(d), 17 C.F.R. § 230.902(d).
159.   Regulation S Preliminary Notes 1, 2 and 3, 17 C.F.R. § 230.901.
160.   Regulation S Rule 903(a), 17 C.F.R. § 230.903(a).
161.   17 C.F.R. § 230.903.
162.   Regulation S Rule 902(h)(1), 17 C.F.R. § 230.902(h)(1).
163.   Regulation S Rule 902(h)(2), 17 C.F.R. § 230.902(h)(2).

than an estate or trust) for the benefit or account of a non–U.S. person or to a non–governmental organization of a specified type is considered to be made in an "offshore transaction."[164]

2. No Directed Selling Efforts to United States

i. General

An issuer or distributor relying on the Regulation S safe harbor may not engage in any directed selling efforts to the United States. "Directed selling efforts" means any activity undertaken for the purpose of, or that could reasonably be expected to have the effect of, conditioning the market in the United States for any of the securities being offered in reliance on Regulation S.[165] The SEC identifies as directed selling efforts mailing printed material to U.S. investors, conducting promotional seminars in the United States or placing advertisements with radio or television stations in the United States that "discuss the offering or are otherwise intended to condition, or could reasonably be expected to condition, the market for the securities purportedly being offered abroad."[166] Directed selling efforts also include placing an advertisement that refers to the offering of securities in reliance on Regulation S in a publication with a general circulation in the United States. A publication has a general circulation in the United States if it is printed primarily for distribution in the United States or has had an average circulation in the United States of 15,000 or more copies per issue during the preceding twelve months.[167] If a publication has both U.S. and non–U.S. editions that would not constitute publications with general circulation in the United States, advertising only in the non–U.S. editions would not constitute directed selling efforts to the United States.[168]

ii. Excluded Activities

Legitimate selling activities carried out in the United States in connection with an offering of securities registered under the Securities Act or exempt from registration, such as a private offering under Securities Act section 4(2) or a sale under Regulation D Rule 506,[169] do not constitute directed selling efforts with respect to offers and sales under Regulation S.[170] As a result, an offshore hedge fund may sell shares to investors in the United States pursuant to Regulation D while also selling shares to investors outside the United States under Regulation S.[171] In

---

164. Regulation S Rule 902(h)(3), 17 C.F.R. § 230.902(h)(3). Specifically, the non-governmental organizations are the International Monetary Fund, the International Bank for Reconstruction and Development, the Inter-American Development Bank, the Asian Development Bank, the African Development Bank, the United Nations and their agencies, affiliates and pension plans, and any other similar international organizations, their agencies, affiliates and pension plans. Regulation S Rule 902(k)(2)(vi), 17 C.F.R. § 230.902(k)(2)(vi).

165. Regulation S Rule 902(c)(1), 17 C.F.R. § 230.902(c)(1).

166. Release 6863.

167. *Id.*

168. *Id.*

169. *See* § 5.3, *supra.*

170. Release 6863.

171. *See* § 5.5, *infra.*

addition, the following activities do not constitute "directed selling efforts" under Regulation S:[172]

- Placement of an advertisement required to be published under U.S. or non-U.S. law, rules or regulations, as long as the advertisement contains no more information than legally required and includes a statement to the effect that the securities have not been registered under the Securities Act and may not be offered or sold in the United States (or, in some instances, to a U.S. person) absent registration or an applicable exemption from the registration requirements;
- Contact with a dealer or other professional fiduciary organized, incorporated or (if an individual) resident in the United States that holds a discretionary account or similar account (other than an estate or trust) for the benefit or account of a non-U.S. person or with a non-governmental organization of a specified type;
- Tombstone advertisements in publications with a general circulation in the United States, if specified requirements are met;
- Bona fide visits to and tours of real estate, plants or other facilities located in the United States and for a prospective investor by an issuer, a distributor, any affiliate of an issuer or distributor, or any person acting on behalf of an issuer or distributor;
- Distribution in the United States of a non-U.S. broker's quotations by a third party system that distributes such quotations primarily in other countries, if (a) securities transactions cannot be executed between non-U.S. brokers and persons in the United States through the system, and (b) the issuer, distributors, affiliates of the issuer and distributors, persons acting on behalf of any of the issuer, distributors or such affiliates, non-U.S. brokers and other participants in the system do not initiate contacts with any U.S. person in the United States, beyond those contacts exempted under Exchange Act Rule 15a-6;[173]
- Publication of notices of an issuance of securities in accordance with Securities Act Rules 135 and 135c;[174] and
- Providing journalists with access to press conferences held outside the United States, to meetings with the issuer conducted outside the United States or to written press-related materials released outside the United States, at or in which the proposed offering of securities is discussed, in compliance with the requirements of Securities Act Rule 135e.[175]

One area of concern with respect to directed selling efforts is the use of the Internet to market securities being sold under Regulation S. According to the SEC, whether the Securities Act registration requirements apply to offers made over the Internet depends on whether Internet offers, solicitations or other communications are targeted to the United States.[176] The SEC will not "view

---

172. Regulation S Rule 902(c)(3), 17 C.F.R. § 230.902(c)(3).
173. 17 C.F.R. § 240.15a-6.
174. 17 C.F.R. §§ 230.135 and 230.135c.
175. 17 C.F.R. § 230.135e.
176. Securities Act Release No. 7516, 63 F.R. 14,806 (Mar. 27, 1998).

issuers, broker-dealers, exchanges, and investment advisers that implement measures that are reasonably designed to guard against sales ... to U.S. persons to have targeted persons in the United States with their internet offers."[177]

Whether measures are adequate to prevent U.S. persons from participating in an offshore internet offering depends on all of the facts and circumstances, although the SEC will typically not consider an offshore internet offering made by a non-U.S. offeror as targeted at the United States, if:

- the website includes a prominent disclaimer making clear that the offering is directed only to countries other than the United States (for example, stating that the securities are not being offered in the United States or identifying the non-U.S. jurisdictions in which the securities are being offered); and
- the website offeror implements procedures reasonably designed to guard against sales to U.S. persons in the offshore offering (for example, ascertaining the investor's residence by obtaining his or her mailing address or telephone number).

The disclaimer included on a website must be specific and meaningful. For example, a disclaimer that "the offer is not being made in any jurisdiction in which the offer would or could be illegal" is not sufficient, because it is not meaningful, whereas a disclaimer that "this offering is intended only to be available to residents of the countries within the European Union" would be meaningful. If a U.S. person invests in the securities being offered on the Internet, notwithstanding adequate procedures reasonably designed to prevent the investment, the SEC will not for that reason alone view the offering as targeted at the United States, unless the issuer should have been on notice that the investor was a U.S. person, by virtue of such circumstances as receipt of payment drawn on a U.S. bank, provision of a U.S. taxpayer identification number, or statements by the investor indicating that he or she is a U.S. resident.[178]

The SEC's guidelines apply to the use of Internet websites, not to the use of targeted communications, such as e-mail.[179] Targeted messages are more akin to use of the mails, and an issuer using such communications must ensure that it complies with the requirements of the Securities Act.[180]

3. Additional Requirements

Regulation S may impose additional restrictions on issuers depending on the nature of the issuer and the securities being issued. To determine whether additional requirements will be imposed, Regulation S divides securities into three categories.

An issuer or distributor may rely on the Regulation S safe harbor for offers and sales of category 1 securities without additional requirements.[181] Securities

---

177. *Id.*
178. *Id.*
179. *Id.*
180. *Id.*
181. Regulation S Rule 903(b)(1), 17 C.F.R. § 230.903(b)(1).

are eligible for this category, if, among other things, they are issued by a non–U.S. issuer that reasonably believes at the commencement of the offering that no substantial U.S. market interest[182] exists in the class of securities to be offered or sold; no substantial U.S. market interest[183] exists in the issuer's debt securities;[184] and the securities are offered and sold in an overseas directed offering.[185] Shares issued by an offshore hedge fund may thus qualify as category 1 securities if the offshore hedge fund is a non–U.S. issuer and there is no substantial U.S. market interest in that class of shares.

A "foreign issuer" is any issuer that is a foreign government, a national of any foreign country or a corporation or other organization incorporated or organized under the laws of any foreign country.[186] A "foreign private issuer" is any foreign issuer other than a foreign government, except an issuer meeting the following conditions:

---

182.   *See* § 5.4.4, *infra.*

183.   *Id.*

184.   Regulation S Rule 902(a) defines "debt securities" as "any security other than an equity security as defined in section 230.405, as well as:

(1) Non-participatory preferred stock, which is defined as non-convertible capital stock, the holders of which are entitled to a preference in payment of dividends and in distribution of assets on liquidation, dissolution, or winding up of the issuer, but are not entitled to participate in residual earnings or assets of the issuer; and

(2) Asset–backed securities, which are securities of a type that either:

(i) Represent an ownership interest in a pool of discrete assets, or certificates of interest or participation in such assets (including any rights designed to assure servicing, or the receipt or timeliness of receipt by holders of such assets, or certificates of interest or participation in such assets, of amounts payable thereunder), provided that the assets are not generated or originated between the issuer of the security and its affiliates; or

(ii) Are secured by one or more assets or certificates of interest or participation in such assets, and the securities, by their terms, provide for payments of principal and interest (if any) in relation to payments or reasonable projections of payments on assets meeting the requirements of paragraph (a)(2)(i) of this section, or certificates of interest or participations in assets meeting such requirements.

(iii) For purposes of paragraph (a)(2) of this section, the term 'assets' means securities, installment sales, accounts receivable, notes, leases or other contracts, or other assets that by their terms convert into cash over a finite period of time." Regulation S Rule 902(a), 17 C.F.R. § 230.902(a).

Regulation C Rule 405 defines "equity security" as "any stock or similar security, certificate of interest or participation in any profit sharing agreement, preorganization certificate or subscription, transferable share, voting trust certificate or certificate of deposit for an equity security, limited partnership interest, interest in a joint venture, or certificate of interest in a business trust; any security future on any such security; or any security convertible, with or without consideration into such a security, or carrying any warrant or right to subscribe to or purchase such a security; or any such warrant or right; or any put, call, straddle, or other option or privilege of buying such a security form or selling a security to another without being bound to do so." 17 C.F.R. § 230.405.

185.   An "overseas directed offering" is, in relevant part:

(a) An offering of securities of a foreign issuer that is directed into a single country other than the United States to the residents thereof and that is made in accordance with the local laws and customary practices and documentation of such country; or

(b) An offering of non-convertible debt securities of a domestic issuer that is directed into a single country other than the United States to the residents thereof and that is made in accordance with the local laws and customary practices and documentation of such country, provided that the principal and interest of the securities (or par value, as applicable) are denominated in a currency other than U.S. dollars and such securities are neither convertible into U.S. dollar-denominated securities nor linked to U.S. dollars (other than through related currency or interest rate swap transactions that are commercial in nature) in a manner that in effect converts the securities to U.S. dollar-denominated securities. Regulation S Rule 903(b), 17 C.F.R. § 230.903(b).

186.   Regulation C Rule 405, 17 C.F.R. § 230.405. Regulation S Rule 902(e), 17 C.F.R. § 230.902(e), provides that "'Domestic Issuer' means any issuer other than a 'foreign government' or 'foreign private issuer' (both as defined in section 230.405). 'Foreign Issuer' means any issuer other than a 'domestic issuer.'"

(1) More than fifty percent of the outstanding voting securities of such issuer are directly or indirectly owned of record by residents of the United States; and

(2) Any of the following:

(i) The majority of the executive officers or directors are United States citizens or residents;

(ii) More than fifty percent of the assets of the issuer are located in the United States; or

(iii) The business of the issuer is administered principally in the United States.[187]

An offshore hedge fund may thus qualify as a foreign private issuer if less than fifty percent of its outstanding voting securities are held by U.S. residents.[188] "Voting securities" are securities whose holders are entitled to vote for the election of directors.[189] The shares of some offshore hedge funds are divided into separate classes, with only one class of shares entitled to vote for the election of directors. Investors in such an offshore hedge fund receive non-voting shares. In such an offshore hedge fund, the residence of the investors therefore is irrelevant to the determination whether the offshore hedge fund is a foreign private issuer.

If the investors in an offshore hedge fund receive shares that entitle them to vote for directors, then whether the offshore hedge fund is a foreign private issuer will depend on the residence of its investors. If the offshore hedge fund is unable to obtain information about the amount of shares represented by accounts of customers resident in the United States after reasonable inquiry, the offshore hedge fund may assume that the customers are residents of the jurisdictions in which the investors' nominees have their principal places of business.[190] Record ownership should be calculated in accordance with Exchange Act Rule 12g3-2(a),[191] except that the offshore hedge fund may limit its inquiry as to the amount of shares represented by accounts of customers resident in the United States to brokers, dealers, banks and other nominees in the United States, the offshore hedge fund's jurisdiction of incorporation and the jurisdiction that is the primary trading market for the offshore hedge fund's voting securities.[192]

4. Substantial U.S. Market Interest

Securities issued by an offshore hedge fund are typically equity securities.[193] "Substantial U.S. market interest" in a class of an issuer's equity securities means:

---

187. Regulation C Rule 405, 17 C.F.R. § 230.405.

188. *Id.*

189. *Id.*

190. *Id.*

191. 17 C.F.R. § 240.12g3-2(a), referring to Exchange Act Rule 12g5-1, 17 C.F.R. § 240.12g5-1, which in general summary prescribes the manner of keeping the share register and rules for counting owners separately or as single owners.

192. Regulation C Rule 405, 17 C.F.R. § 230.405.

193. *See* § 4.4, *supra.* Although "equity securities" is not defined in Regulation S, the SEC has indicated that the definition of equity securities under Regulation C Rule 405 applies to Regulation S. Securities Act Release No. 7505, 63 F.R. 9,632 (Feb. 25, 1998).

- the securities exchanges and inter-dealer quotation systems in the United States in the aggregate constituted the single largest market for such class of securities in the shorter of the issuer's prior fiscal year or the period since the issuer's incorporation, or
- twenty percent or more of all trading in such class of securities took place in, on or through the facilities of securities exchanges and inter-dealer quotation systems in the United States and less than fifty-five percent of such trading took place in, on or through the facilities of securities markets of a single non-U.S. country in the shorter of the issuer's prior fiscal year or the period since the issuer's incorporation.[194]

Shares of offshore hedge funds typically are not traded on securities exchanges or inter-dealer quotation systems in the United States. Accordingly, shares of an offshore hedge fund ordinarily are not subject to substantial U.S. market interest.

5. Category 2

Category 2 securities are securities that are not eligible for category 1[195] and that are equity securities of a reporting foreign issuer or debt securities of a reporting issuer or of a non-reporting foreign issuer.[196] A "reporting issuer" is an issuer, other than an investment company registered or required to be registered under the Company Act, that has a class of securities registered pursuant to Exchange Act section 12(b) or 12(g) or is required to file reports pursuant to Exchange Act section 15(d) and has filed all the material required to be filed pursuant to Exchange Act section 13(a) or 15(d) for a period of at least twelve months preceding the offer or sale of securities pursuant to Regulation S or for such shorter period that the issuer was required to file such material.[197] This category typically will not apply to securities of an offshore hedge fund, because offshore hedge funds typically are not reporting issuers and do not issue debt securities.[198]

6. Category 3

Category 3 securities are any securities that are not eligible for category 1 or 2.[199] In addition to complying with the requirements that its securities be issued in an offshore transaction and that it not engage in any directed selling efforts to the United States, an offshore hedge fund issuing category 3 securities and any distributor offering or selling such securities must impose offering restrictions and transactional restrictions.[200] In addition, any distributor that sells securities to a distributor, dealer or person receiving a selling concession, fee or other remuneration, before the distribution compliance period[201] expires, must send a

---

194.   Regulation S Rule 902(j)(1), 17 C.F.R. § 230.902(j)(1).

195.   *See* § 5.4.3, *supra*.

196.   Regulation S Rule 903(b)(2), 17 C.F.R. § 230.903(b)(2).

197.   Regulation S Rule 902(i), 17 C.F.R. § 230.902(i).

198.   *See* note 184, *supra*, for the definition of "debt security."

199.   Regulation S Rule 903(b)(3), 17 C.F.R. § 230.903(b)(3).

200.   *Id.*

201.   *See* § 5.4.6.i, *infra*.

confirmation or other notice to the purchaser stating that the purchaser is subject to the same restrictions on offers and sales that apply to a distributor.[202]

i. Offering Restrictions

An offshore hedge fund issuing category 3 securities, any distributor, their affiliates and any person acting on their behalf must implement the following offering restrictions. Each distributor must agree in writing with the offshore hedge fund that all offers and sales of the securities before the "distribution compliance period" expires will be made only in accordance with Regulation S Rules 903 and 904, pursuant to registration of the securities under the Securities Act or pursuant to an available exemption from such registration requirements.[203] With respect to offers and sales of equity securities of U.S. issuers, each distributor must also agree in writing not to engage in hedging transactions with respect to such securities before the distribution compliance period expires, unless in compliance with the Securities Act.[204]

The distribution compliance period begins when the securities are first offered to persons other than distributors in reliance on Regulation D or the date of closing of the offering, whichever is later. It continues with respect to equity securities for a period of one year.[205] In the case of a continuous offering, which is typical of an offshore hedge fund, the distribution compliance period does not begin until the managing underwriter or person performing similar functions determines and certifies that the distribution is complete.[206] Accordingly, the offshore hedge fund's distribution compliance period will continue throughout its offering and for a year after the offering ends.

---

202. Regulation S Rule 903(b)(3)(iv), 17 C.F.R. § 230.903(b)(3)(iv).

203. Regulation S Rule 902(g)(1)(i), 17 C.F.R. § 230.902(g)(1)(i).

204. Regulation S Rule 902(g)(1)(ii), 17 C.F.R. § 230.902(g)(1)(ii). This restriction would not ordinarily be relevant to an offshore hedge fund, which is not a U.S. issuer and does not issue shares that are traded in public securities markets.

205. Regulation S Rule 902(f), 17 C.F.R. § 230.902(f), provides that "'Distribution compliance period' means a period that begins when the securities were first offered to persons other than distributors in reliance upon this Regulation S (section 230.901 through 230.905, and Preliminary Notes) or the date of closing of the offering, whichever is later and continues until the end of the period of time specified in the relevant provision of section 230.903, except that:

(1) All offers and sales by a distributor of an unsold allotment or subscription shall be deemed to be made during the distribution compliance period;

(2) In a continuous offering, the distribution compliance period shall commence upon completion of the distribution, as determined and certified by the managing underwriter or person performing similar functions;

(3) In a continuous offering of non-convertible debt securities offered and sold in identifiable tranches, the distribution compliance period for securities in a tranche shall commence upon completion of the distribution of such tranche, as determined and certified by the managing underwriter or person performing similar functions; and

(4) That [sic] in a continuous offering of securities to be acquired upon the exercise of warrants, the distribution compliance period shall commence upon completion of the distribution of the warrants, as determined and certified by the managing underwriter or person performing similar functions, if requirements of section 230.903(b)(5) are satisfied."

Regulation S Rule 903(b)(3)(iii), 17 C.F.R. § 230.903(B)(3)(iii), provides that the distribution compliance period for equity securities is one year.

206. Regulation S Rule 902(f)(2), 17 C.F.R. § 230.902(f)(2).

ii. Transaction Restrictions

An offshore hedge fund issuing category 3 securities, its distributors, their affiliates and any person acting on the offshore hedge fund's or distributors' behalf, must also comply with transaction restrictions. The transaction restrictions vary depending on whether the securities are equity securities or debt securities. Offshore hedge funds typically issue only equity securities, so the restrictions on equity securities typically apply. Each of these restrictions applies with respect to any offer or sale made before the one-year distribution compliance period expires.[207]

The offer or sale of equity securities, if made before the distribution compliance period expires, cannot be made to a U.S. person or for the account or benefit of a U.S. person (other than a distributor).[208] A "U.S. person" is:

- any natural person resident in the United States;
- any partnership or corporation organized or incorporated under the laws of the United States;
- any estate of which any executor or administrator is a U.S. person;
- any trust of which any trustee is a U.S. person;
- any agency or branch of a non-U.S. entity located in the United States;
- any non-discretionary account or similar account (other than an estate or trust) held by a dealer or other fiduciary for the benefit or account of a U.S. person;
- any discretionary account or similar account (other than an estate or trust) held by a dealer or other fiduciary organized, incorporated or (if an individual) resident in the United States; or
- any partnership or corporation organized or incorporated under the laws of any non-U.S. jurisdiction that is formed by a U.S. person principally for the purpose of investing in securities not registered under the Securities Act, unless it is organized or incorporated, and owned, by accredited investors who are not natural persons, estates or trusts.[209]

A person's residence, not citizenship, determines U.S. person status. Accordingly, a non-U.S. citizen residing in the United States is a U.S. person for purposes of Regulation S.

Regulation S also excludes from the definition of U.S. person the following:

- any discretionary account or similar account (other than an estate or trust) held for the benefit or account of a non-U.S. person by a dealer or other professional fiduciary organized, incorporated, or (if an individual) resident in the United States;
- any estate of which any professional fiduciary acting as executor or administrator is a U.S. person if an executor or administrator of the estate who is not a U.S.

---

207.   Regulation S Rule 903(b)(3)(iii), 17 C.F.R. § 230. 903(b)(3)(iii).
208.   Regulation S Rule 903(b)(3)(iii)(A), 17 C.F.R. § 230.903(b)(3)(iii)(A).
209.   Regulation S Rule 902(k)(1), 17 C.F.R. § 230.902(k)(1).

person has sole or shared investment discretion with respect to the assets of the estate and the estate is governed by non-U.S. law;

- any trust of which any professional fiduciary acting as trustee is a U.S. person, if a trustee who is not a U.S. person has sole or shared investment discretion with respect to the trust assets, and no beneficiary of the trust (and no settlor if the trust is revocable) is a U.S. person;

- an employee benefit plan established and administered in accordance with the law of a country other than the United States and customary practices and documentation of such country;

- any agency or branch of a U.S. person located outside the United States if the agency or branch operates for valid business reasons and the agency or branch is engaged in the business of insurance or banking and is subject to substantive insurance or banking regulation, respectively, in the jurisdiction where it is located; and

- certain non-governmental organizations.[210]

The purchaser of the securities (other than a distributor) must certify either that it is not a U.S. person and is not acquiring the securities for the account or benefit of any U.S. person or that it is a U.S. person who purchased securities in a transaction that did not require registration under the Securities Act.[211] The purchaser also must agree (a) to resell such securities only in accordance with Regulation S, pursuant to registration under the Securities Act, or pursuant to an available exemption from registration,[212] and (b) not to conduct hedging transactions involving the securities except in compliance with the Securities Act.[213] An offshore hedge fund should include these representations in the subscription documents that it requires investors to execute.

The issuer must, either by contract or a provision of its bylaws, articles, charter or comparable document, refuse to register any transfer of the securities not made in accordance with Regulation S, pursuant to registration under the Securities Act, or pursuant to an available exemption from registration.[214] If the securities are in bearer form or non-U.S. law prevents the issuer of the securities from refusing to register securities transfers, however, other reasonable procedures (such as placing a legend on the securities) may be implemented to prevent any transfer of the securities not made in accordance with Regulation S.[215] To comply with these requirements, an offshore hedge fund should include appropriate language in its memorandum and articles of organization or similar charter document.[216]

---

210. Regulation S Rule 902(k)(2), 17 C.F.R. § 230.902(k)(2). Specifically, the non-governmental organizations are the International Monetary Fund, the International Bank for Reconstruction and Development, the Inter-American Development Bank, the Asian Development Bank, the African Development Bank, the United Nations and their agencies, affiliates and pension plans, and any other similar international organizations, their agencies, affiliates and pension plans.

211. Regulation S Rule 903(b)(3)(iii)(B)(*1*), 17 C.F.R. § 230.903(b)(3)(iii)(B)(*1*).

212. Regulation S Rule 903(b)(3)(iii)(B)(*2*), 17 C.F.R. § 230.903(b)(3)(iii)(B)(*2*).

213. *Id.*

214. Regulation S Rule 903(b)(3)(iii)(B)(*4*), 17 C.F.R. § 230.903(b)(3)(iii)(B)(*4*).

215. *Id.*

216. If an issuer is a U.S. issuer, the securities must bear a legend to the effect that their transfer is prohibited except in accordance with Regulation S, pursuant to registration under the Securities Act or pursuant to an

§ 5.5 Concurrent Regulation D and Regulation S Offerings

A hedge fund may make offers and sales of securities to investors in the United States in accordance with Regulation D Rule 506 and concurrently to investors outside the United States in accordance with Regulation S. The SEC has stated that legitimate sales activities in the United States in connection with an offering of securities exempt from registration under the Securities Act do not constitute directed selling efforts under Regulation S.[217] Similarly, Regulation D allows an issuer to rely on Regulation S for sales outside of the United States at the same time that it offers and sells its securities in the United States under Regulation D.[218] Purchasers of securities pursuant to Regulation S and the proceeds of such sales are not included in determining the number of purchasers or the aggregate offering price for purposes of Regulation D.[219] Resales of securities pursuant to the safe harbor provided by Regulation S Rule 904, being exempt from registration by that rule, would not be subject to the resale limitations applicable to shares sold under Regulation D.

§ 5.6 Consequences of Failure to Register

An investor may bring a claim against an issuer of securities sold in violation of the registration requirement of section 5 to recover the consideration paid for such security with interest (but less any income received on the security) or for damages if the investor no longer owns the security.[220] Liability may be imposed on any person who actively solicits an order, participates in the negotiations or arranges the sale.[221] The investor may recover from the direct seller and any controlling person.[222] The test is whether "the injury to the plaintiff flows directly and proximately from the actions of this particular defendant."[223]

The availability of this private right of action is intended as a "means of detecting and deterring wrongdoing on the part of issuers and their agents or underwriters

---

available exemption from registration and that hedging transactions involving the securities may not be conducted except in compliance with the Securities Act. Regulation S Rule 903(b)(3)(iii)(B)(3), 17 C.F.R. § 230.903(b)(3)(iii)(B)(3). Offshore hedge funds ordinarily are not U.S. issuers.

217.   Release 6863.

218.   Regulation D Preliminary Note 7, 17 C.F.R. § 230.501.

219.   *Id.*

220.   Securities Act § 12(a), 15 U.S.C. § 77l(a).

221.   *Lawler v. Gilliam, et al.*, 569 F. 2d 1283, 1288 (4th Cir. 1978); *Hill York Corp., et al. v American International Franchises, Inc., et al.*, 448 F. 2d 680, 693 (5th Cir., 1971).

222.   *Hill York,* 448 F. 2d at 693; Securities Act § 15, 15 U.S.C. § 77o.

223.   *Hill York,* 448 F. 2d at 693.

who have not registered the securities being offered for sale," because no filings are required to be made with the SEC and the SEC has limited ability to review such sales.[224] As a result, a plaintiff may bring an action against the hedge fund, its general partner, the employees of the general partner that are engaged in selling efforts, and any other person engaged in selling interests in the hedge fund.

In addition, the SEC can bring an action against the issuer for monetary penalties of up to $100,000 per violation for a natural person or $500,000 per violation for other persons.[225] The SEC may also issue cease and desist orders with respect to violations or potential violations of the Securities Act.[226]

---

224. *Woolf, et al. v. S.D. Cohn & Co., et al.*, 515 F. 2d 591, 605 (5th Cir., 1975).
225. Securities Act § 20(d), 15 U.S.C. § 77t(d).
226. Securities Act § 8A, 15 U.S.C. § 77h-1.

CHAPTER **6**

Disclosure Obligations

§ 6.1 Introduction

The Securities Act requires issuers offering or selling securities in registered offerings to make extensive disclosure. The Company Act imposes similar disclosure obligations on registered investment companies. Although private hedge funds are not registered under the Company Act as discussed in Chapter 3 and issue securities that are not registered under the Securities Act in reliance on the exemptions described in Chapter 5, those exemptions generally require disclosure of or access to the information that would be required to be disclosed in a registration statement under the Securities Act. In addition, the anti–fraud rules of the Securities Act and the Exchange Act, among other things, prohibit an issuer of securities from making any untrue statement of material fact or omitting to state a material fact necessary to make the statements made, in light of the circumstances under which they were made, not misleading.[1]

In addition to the disclosure requirements of the Securities Act, the Exchange Act and the Company Act, other federal and state laws require disclosures by hedge funds and their general partners and investment advisers. The Advisers Act and the SEC rules under it, and similar state laws and rules, impose disclosure obligations on investment advisers to hedge funds. Some hedge funds that trade commodity futures and options are subject to disclosure requirements under the CEA rules and regulations.[2] Finally, rules adopted by the SEC and the FTC under the GLBA[3] impose disclosure obligations on investment advisers and hedge funds with respect to their use and disclosure of non–public personal information of clients and investors.

---

1.   *See, e.g.*, Securities Act § 17(a), 15 U.S.C. § 77q(a); Exchange Act § 10(b), 15 U.S.C. § 78j(b); and Exchange Act Rule 10b-5, 17 C.F.R. § 240.10b-5.
2.   CEA Rules 4.21 and 4.31, 17 C.F.R. §§ 4.21 and 4.31.
3.   GLBA, 15 U.S.C. § 6781 *et seq.*; Regulation S-P, 17 C.F.R. pt. 248; FTC Privacy Rule, 16 C.F.R. pt. 313.

§ 6.2 Public Offering and Mutual Fund Disclosure Obligations

1. Securities Act

i. Disclosure Obligations in Public Offerings

As discussed in Chapter 5, an issuer may not offer or sell securities unless a registration statement is in effect with respect to those securities, or the securities or the transactions in which they are offered are exempt from registration.[4] The SEC has adopted several forms of registration statement on which an issuer may register securities. The registration statement on Form N-1A, adopted by the SEC under the Company Act, may be used by certain investment companies to register their securities under the Securities Act.[5] In addition, an issuer that does not qualify to use any other form may use Form S-1 for its registration statement.[6] If a hedge fund were to register the securities it issues under the Securities Act, it would be required to use either Form N-1A or Form S-1. The requirements of those forms are discussed in sections 6.2.1.ii and 6.2.1.iii below.

Forms N-1A and S-1 were not, however, designed with hedge funds in mind, and some of their requirements are inappropriate to a greater or lesser degree in the hedge fund context. Securities Act section 4(2)[7] and Regulation D[8] under the Securities Act generally contemplate that the issuer in a private offering will furnish or make available to investors the information that would be included in a registration statement on the appropriate form, to the extent that such information is material to a decision whether to invest.[9] Because no single registration form is entirely appropriate for a hedge fund, a hedge fund disclosure document should contain all of the information that would be required by either Form N-1A or Form S-1, to the extent it is material to a prospective investor.[10]

ii. Form N-1A

Form N-1A may be used by open-end management investment companies, other than separate accounts of insurance companies or companies that issue periodic payment plan certificates or that are sponsors or depositors of companies issuing such certificates.[11] An "open-end management investment company" is "a management company which is offering for sale or has outstanding any redeemable security

---

4.   Securities Act § 5(a), 15 U.S.C. § 77e(a).
5.   Form N-1A General Instruction B.1(a). The text of Form N-1A does not appear in the code of Federal Regulations, but may be obtained from the SEC. *See* 17 C.F.R. §§ 274.0-1 and 274.11A.
6.   Form S-1 General Instruction I. The text of Form S-1 does not appear in the Code of Federal Regulations, but may be obtained from the SEC. *See* 17 C.F.R. §§ 239.0-1 and 239.11.
7.   15 U.S.C. § 77d(2).
8.   17 C.F.R. §§ 501–508.
9.   *See* §§ 5.3.1.iii and 5.3.2.vii, *supra*, and § 6.3, *infra*.
10.   *But see* § 6.3.2, *infra*.
11.   Company Act Rule 11A, 17 C.F.R. § 274.11A.

of which it is the issuer."[12] A "redeemable security" is any security, other than short-term paper, under the terms of which the holder, upon its presentation to the issuer or a person designated by the issuer, is entitled (whether absolutely or only out of surplus) to receive approximately his proportionate share of the issuer's current net assets, or the cash equivalent thereof.[13]

Most hedge funds are organized as limited partnerships or limited liability companies from which an investor may withdraw capital or redeem interests periodically on request. Accordingly, hedge funds ordinarily are similar to open-end management investment companies.

Form N-1A comprises three parts: the prospectus, the statement of additional information, and other information that must be filed with the SEC. The issuer must deliver the prospectus before or concurrently with the delivery of any security for sale or for delivery after sale.[14] The issuer is not required to deliver the statement of additional information but must offer to do so, on written or oral request and without charge, when the prospectus is delivered to the prospective investor.[15]

a. Prospectus

The prospectus is intended "to provide essential information about a fund in a way that will help investors make informed decisions about whether to purchase the fund's shares."[16] The prospectus "should clearly disclose the fundamental characteristics and investment risks of the fund, using concise, straightforward, and easy to understand language" and "should emphasize the fund's overall investment approach and strategy."[17] The principal information that a fund's prospectus must disclose under Form N-1A is summarized below.

(1) Front and Back Cover Pages

The front cover page of the prospectus must include the fund's name, the date of the prospectus and a legend to the effect that the SEC has not approved or

---

12.   Company Act § 5(a)(1), 15 U.S.C. § 80a-5(a)(1). A "management company" is an investment company that is not a face-amount certificate company or a unit investment trust. Company Act § 4(3), 15 U.S.C. § 80a-4(3). A face-amount certificate company is an investment company "which is engaged or proposes to engage in the business of issuing face-amount certificates of the installment type, or which has been engaged in such business and has any such certificate outstanding." Company Act § 4(1), 15 U.S.C. § 80a-4(1). A "face-amount certificate of the installment type" is a "certificate, investment contract, or other security which represents an obligation on the part of its issuer to pay a stated or determinable sum or sums at a fixed or determinable date or dates more than twenty-four months after the date of issuance, in consideration of the payment of periodic installments of a stated or determinable amount." Company Act § 2(a)(15), 15 U.S.C. § 80a-2(a)(15). A "unit investment trust" is "an investment company which (A) is organized under a trust indenture, contract of custodianship or agency, or similar instrument, (B) does not have a board of directors, and (C) issues only redeemable securities, each of which represents an undivided interest in a unit of specified securities, but does not include a voting trust." Company Act § 4(2), 15 U.S.C. § 80a-4(2). As discussed in Chapter 4, *supra*, hedge funds typically are not organized as either of the latter two types of entities and therefore typically are management companies.

13.   Company Act § 2(a)(32), 15 U.S.C. § 80a-2(a)(32).

14.   Securities Act § 5(b), 15 U.S.C. § 77e(b); Securities Act Rule 430(b), 17 C.F.R. § 230.430(b).

15.   Securities Act Rule 430(b), 17 C.F.R. § 230.430(b).

16.   Form N-1A General Instruction C.2(a).

17.   Form N-1A General Instruction C.1(a); Company Act Rule 11A, 17 C.F.R. § 274.11A.

disapproved the securities being offered or passed on the accuracy or adequacy of the disclosure in the prospectus and that any contrary representation is a criminal offense.[18] The front cover page may also state the fund's investment objectives, briefly describe its operations and include other information, as long as the other information "is not incomplete, inaccurate or misleading and does not, because of its nature, quantity or manner of presentation, obscure or impede understanding of the information that is required to be included" on the front cover page.[19]

The outside back cover page of the prospectus must include disclosure about other documents available from the fund, such as the fund's statement of additional information and its annual and semi-annual reports, a toll-free telephone number that investors can use to obtain information about the fund and statements about whether information is incorporated by reference.[20]

(2) Risk/Return Summary

Following the front cover page and the table of contents, the prospectus must include a summary of the following information in the following order:

- a description of the fund's investment objectives or goals;[21]
- a summary of how the fund intends to achieve its investment objectives, which identifies the fund's principal investment strategies (including the types of securities in which the fund principally invests or will invest) and any policy to concentrate in securities of issuers in a particular industry or group of industries;[22]
- a summary of the principal risks of investing in the fund, including the risks to which the fund's portfolio as a whole is subject, the circumstances reasonably likely to affect adversely the fund's net asset value, yield and total return, and, if the fund is non-diversified, a statement to that effect, a description of the effect of non-diversification (for example, that compared with other funds, the fund may invest a greater percentage of its assets in a particular issuer) and a summary of the risks of investing in a non-diversified fund;[23]
- a bar chart showing the fund's annual total returns for each of the preceding ten years (or for the life of the fund, if shorter) and for the current year to date through the end of the most recent quarter, as well as the fund's highest and lowest returns for any quarter during that period;[24]
- a table showing the fund's average annual total return, average annual total return after taxes on distributions and average annual total return after taxes on distributions and redemptions, and returns of an appropriate broad-based securities market index, for the one-year, five-year and ten-year periods

---

18.   Form N-1A Item 1(a); Securities Act Rule 481(b)(1), 17 C.F.R. § 230.481(b)(1).
19.   Form N-1A Instruction to Item 1(a) and General Instruction C.3(b).
20.   Form N-1A Item 1(b).
21.   Form N-1A Item 2(a).
22.   Form N-1A Item 2(b).
23.   Form N-1A Item 2(c)(1).
24.   Form N-1A Item 2(c)(2).

ending with the most recently completed calendar year (or for the life of the fund, if shorter);[25] and

- a table showing the fees that may be paid by the fund's shareholders, including sales charges, redemption and exchange fees, account fees and management fees, and examples of the costs that would have been incurred by an investor on a $10,000 investment in the fund over the one-year, three-year, five-year and ten-year periods ending on the date of the most recently completed calendar year.[26]

(3) Investment Objectives, Strategies and Related Risks

The prospectus must disclose the fund's investment objectives and whether those objectives may be changed without shareholder approval.[27] In addition, the prospectus must describe how the fund intends to achieve its investment objectives, including a description of the fund's principal investment strategies (including the particular types of securities in which the fund principally invests or will invest) and an explanation, in general terms, of how the fund's investment adviser decides which securities to buy and sell.[28] The instructions to Form N-1A provide that:

> Whether a particular strategy, including a strategy to invest in a particular type of security, is a principal investment strategy depends on the strategy's anticipated importance in achieving the Fund's investment objectives, and how the strategy affects the Fund's potential risks and returns. In determining what is a principal investment strategy, consider, among other things, the amount of the Fund's assets expected to be committed to the strategy, the amount of the Fund's assets expected to be placed at risk by the strategy, and the likelihood of the Fund's losing some or all of those assets from implementing the strategy.[29]

The prospectus also should disclose "any policy to concentrate in securities of issuers in a particular industry or group of industries (*i.e.*, investing more than 25% of a Fund's net assets in a particular industry or group of industries)."[30] The fund also should disclose whether it "may engage in active and frequent trading of portfolio securities to achieve its principal investment strategies."[31] If so, the prospectus should "explain the tax consequences to shareholders of increased portfolio turnover, and how the tax consequences of, or trading costs associated with, a Fund's portfolio turnover may affect the Fund's performance."[32] If applicable, the fund should disclose "that the Fund may, from time to time, take

---

25.   *Id.*
26.   Form N-1A Item 3.
27.   Form N-1A Item 4(a).
28.   Form N-1A Item 4(b).
29.   Form N-1A Item 4(b)(1), Instruction 2.
30.   Form N-1A Item 4(b)(1), Instruction 4.
31.   Form N-1A Item 4(b)(1), Instruction 7.
32.   *Id.*

temporary defensive positions that are inconsistent with the Fund's principal investment strategies in attempting to respond to adverse market, economic, political or other conditions" and "the effect of taking such a temporary defensive position (*e.g.*, that the Fund may not achieve its investment objective)."[33]

The fund also must "disclose the principal risks of investing in the fund, including the risks to which the fund's particular portfolio as a whole is expected to be subject and the circumstances reasonably likely to affect adversely the fund's net asset value, yield or total return."[34] The risk disclosure should describe not only generic risks, but also the specific risks applicable to the fund and their potential consequences. Failure to disclose a specific risk of which the fund is or should be aware can result in liability for the fund under the anti-fraud provisions of the securities laws.[35] Adequate disclosure of risks, however, can provide the fund with a defense from liability.[36]

Failure to comply with the fund's investment objectives or to follow the fund's investment strategy, as disclosed in the fund's prospectus, can give rise to a securities fraud claim against the fund and its investment advisers.[37] In *In the Matter of Fundamental Portfolio Advisors, Inc., et al.,* an investment company's investment adviser committed securities fraud by disclosing in the fund's prospectus that the fund would seek high returns with maximum safety and that the fund would limit the duration of its investments to three years or less, when in fact the investment adviser invested up to thirty percent of the fund's net assets in highly volatile "inverse floaters" that had durations significantly longer than three years.[38]

In *In re TCW/DW North American Government Income Trust Securities Litigation,* the court held that the plaintiff class of investors in an investment company could state a claim for securities fraud under the securities laws based on the fund's failure to disclose the consequences of prepayment of mortgage-backed securities.[39] On the other hand, the court in *Olkey v. Hyperion 1999 Term Trust, Inc.* dismissed fraud claims made by a class of investors in an investment company on the ground that the fund's prospectus described the effect of interest rate changes on the fund's net asset value.[40]

(4) Management, Organization and Capital Structure

The prospectus must disclose the name and address of each investment adviser to the fund. The fund must describe each investment adviser's experience as an investment adviser and the advisory services it provides to the fund.[41] In addition,

---

33.   Form N-1A Item 4(b)(1), Instruction 6.

34.   Form N-1A Item 4(c).

35.   *See In re TCW/DW North American Government Income Trust Sec. Lit.*, 941 F. Supp. 326 (S.D.N.Y., 1996).

36.   *See Olkey, et al. v. Hyperion 1999 Term Trust, Inc., et al.*, 98 F.3d 2 (2nd Cir., 1996); *Sheppard v. TCW/DW Term Trust 2000, et al.*, 938 F. Supp. 171 (S.D.N.Y., 1996).

37.   *See, e.g., In the matter of Fundamental Portfolio Advisors, Inc., et al.*, SEC Initial Decisions Release No. 180, 2001 SEC Lexis 156 (Jan. 29, 2001).

38.   *Id.*

39.   *In re TCW/DW North American Government Income Trust Sec. Lit.*, 941 F. Supp. 326, 331 (S.D.N.Y., 1996).

40.   *Olkey, et al. v. Hyperion 1999 Term Trust, Inc., et al.*, 98 F.3d 2 (2nd Cir., 1996).

41.   Form N-1A Item 5(a)(1).

the prospectus must state the name, title and length of service of each person employed by or associated with an investment adviser who is primarily responsible for the day-to-day management of the fund's portfolio and each such person's business experience for the preceding five years.[42]

The fund also must describe the compensation of each investment adviser. If the fund has operated for a full fiscal year, it must state the aggregate fees paid to the investment adviser for the most recent fiscal year as a percentage of the fund's average net assets. If the fund has not operated for a full fiscal year, the fund must describe the investment adviser's fee as a percentage of average net assets, including any break points. If the investment adviser charges a fee, such as a performance fee, that is not based on a percentage of the fund's average net assets, the fund must describe the basis of the investment adviser's compensation.[43]

The prospectus must describe any material pending legal proceedings to which the fund or the fund's investment adviser is a party, other than ordinary routine litigation incidental to its business.[44] The fund also must include information about legal proceedings instituted, or known to be contemplated, by a governmental authority against any of these parties.[45] The description should include the name of the court in which the proceedings are pending, the date instituted, the principal parties involved, a description of the factual basis alleged to underlie the proceedings and the relief sought.[46] Legal proceedings are material if they are likely to have a material adverse effect on the fund or on the investment adviser's ability to perform its contract with the fund.[47]

(5) Shareholder Information

The prospectus must describe the procedures for pricing the fund's shares, including an explanation that the price of the shares is based on the fund's net asset value, the method used to value fund shares, and when net asset value is calculated.[48] The prospectus also must identify any holidays on which shares will not be priced. The fund may use any means that effectively communicates such holidays, such as an explanation that shares will not be priced on days on which the NYSE is closed for trading.[49]

The prospectus must describe the procedures for purchasing the fund's shares, including any minimum investment requirements.[50] In addition, the fund must state the procedures for redeeming shares, including any restrictions on redemptions, any redemption charges (including how they will be collected and under what circumstances they will be waived), whether the fund has the right to redeem its shares in kind, the circumstances (if any) under which the fund may redeem shares automatically without action by shareholders who hold less than a certain

---

42. Form N-1A Item 5(a)(2).
43. Form N-1A Item 5(a)(1).
44. Form N-1A Item 5(a)(3).
45. *Id.*
46. *Id.*
47. Form N-1A Instruction to Item 5(a)(3).
48. Form N-1A Item 6(a).
49. Form N-1A Item 6(a) and Instruction 1 thereto.
50. Form N-1A Item 6(b).

number or value of shares, and the circumstances (if any) under which the fund may delay honoring a redemption request for a certain time after a shareholder's investment.[51] The fund must also describe its policies with respect to dividends and distributions.[52] The risks of frequent purchases and sales of fund shares and the fund's policies with respect to such purchases and sales also must be disclosed.[53] Finally, the fund must describe the tax consequences to shareholders of buying, holding, exchanging and selling the fund's shares.[54]

(6) Distribution Arrangements

The fund must describe any sales commissions ("loads"), including deferred sales loads, that apply to purchases of its shares.[55] The fund also must disclose whether sales loads are imposed on shares purchased with reinvested dividends or distributions.[56] If deferred sales loads are charged, the prospectus must describe how they are imposed and calculated.[57] The prospectus also must describe any arrangements that eliminate or reduce sales loads.[58]

If the fund is part of a master-feeder fund, the main features of the structure of the fund must be described.[59] If the feeder fund can change the master fund in which it invests, the prospectus must describe the circumstances under which it can do so.[60]

(7) Financial Highlights

The prospectus also must include the information in the following table (with the heading "Financial Highlights") for the fund, or for the fund and its subsidiaries, audited for at least the last five years and consolidated as required by Regulation S-X under the Securities Act:[61]

> The financial highlights table is intended to help you understand the fund's financial performance for the past 5 years [or, if shorter, the period of the fund's operations]. Certain information reflects financial results for a single fund share. The total returns in the table represent the rate that an investor would have earned [or lost] on an investment in the fund (assuming reinvestment of all dividends and distributions). This information has been audited by _____, whose report, along with the fund's financial statements, are included in [the statement of additional information or annual report], which is available on request.[62]

---

51. Form N–1A Item 6(c).
52. Form N–1A Item 6(d).
53. Form N–1A Item 6(e).
54. Form N–1A Item 6(f).
55. Form N–1A Item 7(a)(1).
56. Form N–1A Item 7(a)(1), Instruction 2.
57. Form N–1A Item 7(a)(1), Instruction 3.
58. Form N–1A Item 7(a)(2).
59. Form N–1A Item 7(c). *See* § 4.4.7, *supra,* for a description of the master-feeder fund structure.
60. Form N–1A Item 7(c).
61. Form N–1A Item 8(a); Regulation S-X, 17 C.F.R. pt. 210.
62. Form N–1A Item 8(a).

	Year 1	Year 2	Year 3	Year 4	Year 5
Net Asset Value, Beginning of Period	$_____	$_____	$_____	$_____	$_____
Income from Investment Operations					
Net Investment Income	$_____	$_____	$_____	$_____	$_____
Net Gains or Losses on Securities (both realized and unrealized)	$_____	$_____	$_____	$_____	$_____
Total from Investment Operations	$_____	$_____	$_____	$_____	$_____
Less Distributions					
Dividends (from net investment income)	$_____	$_____	$_____	$_____	$_____
Distributions (from capital gains)	$_____	$_____	$_____	$_____	$_____
Returns of Capital	$_____	$_____	$_____	$_____	$_____
Total Distributions	$_____	$_____	$_____	$_____	$_____
Net Asset Value, End of Period	$_____	$_____	$_____	$_____	$_____
Total Return					
Ratios/Supplemental Data					
Net Assets, End of Period	$_____	$_____	$_____	$_____	$_____
Ratio of Expenses to Average Net Assets	__%	__%	__%	__%	__%
Ratio of Net Income to Average Net Assets	__%	__%	__%	__%	__%
Portfolio Turnover Rate	__%	__%	__%	__%	__%

The financial highlights table should include information for the period between the end of the last fiscal year and the date of the fund's latest balance sheet or statement of assets and liabilities.[63] With respect to information for less than a year, a note should be included stating that the total return is not annualized.[64] The narrative explanation must appear before the table, although it may be modified if it contains information comparable to that shown.[65] Form N-1A imposes specific requirements on how the information in the financial highlights table is calculated.[66]

b. Statement of Additional Information

The purpose of a statement of additional information is to provide additional information about a fund that the SEC has concluded is not necessary or appropriate to be in the prospectus, but that some investors may find useful.[67] In a statement of additional information, the fund may "expand discussions of the matters described in the prospectus by including additional information that the Fund believes may be of interest to some investors."[68] A statement of additional information should not duplicate information that is provided in the prospectus unless it is necessary

---

63. Form N-1A Item 8(a), Instruction 1(a).
64. Form N-1A Item 8(a), Instruction 3(e).
65. Form N-1A Item 8(a), Instruction 1(c).
66. Form N-1A Instructions to Item 8(a).
67. Form N-1A General Instruction C(2)(b).
68. *Id.*

to do so to make the statement of additional information comprehensible as a document independent of the prospectus.[69]

(1) Fund History

The statement of additional information should provide the fund's date, form and jurisdiction of organization, any other names used by the fund during the preceding five years and the approximate date of any name change. If the fund has engaged in business other than that of an investment company during the preceding five years, the statement of additional information should describe the nature of the other business and give the approximate date on which the fund commenced business as an investment company.[70]

(2) *Expanded Disclosure of Investments and Risks*

The statement of additional information should describe any investment strategies that an investment adviser uses in managing the fund that are not principal strategies and the risks of those strategies.[71] The fund must describe its policies with respect to issuing senior securities, borrowing money (including the purposes for which the proceeds will be used), underwriting securities of other issuers, concentrating investments in a particular industry or group of industries, purchasing or selling real estate or commodities, making loans and any other policy that the fund deems fundamental or that may not be changed without shareholder approval.[72]

If applicable, the fund must disclose the types of investments that it may make while assuming a temporary defensive position, as described in the prospectus.[73] The fund must also explain any significant variation in its portfolio turnover rates over the preceding two fiscal years and any anticipated variation in the future portfolio turnover rate from that reported for the last fiscal year in the financial highlights table.[74] The fund also must disclose its policies and procedures for disclosing its portfolio securities to any person and any ongoing arrangements to make information about its portfolio securities available to any person.[75]

(3) Management and Principal Shareholders

The fund must provide extensive disclosure about its board of directors and officers, including information regarding positions and responsibilities with the fund, other occupations and directorships, potential conflicts of interest and compensation.[76] The fund also must disclose the name and address of each person who controls the fund and describe the effect of such control on the voting rights of other shareholders, including the percentage of the fund's voting securities owned by

---

69.   *Id.*
70.   Form N-1A Item 10.
71.   Form N-1A Item 11(b).
72.   Form N-1A Item 11(c).
73.   Form N-1A Item 11(d).
74.   Form N-1A Item 11(e).
75.   Form N-1A Item 11(f).
76.   Form N-1A Item 12.

the control person or any other basis for such control.[77] In addition, the fund must disclose the name, address and percentage ownership of each person who owns of record or is known by the fund to own beneficially five percent or more of any class of the fund's outstanding voting securities.[78]

(4) Proxy Voting Policy

The fund must also disclose the policies and procedures that it uses to determine how to vote proxies relating to portfolio securities. This description must address the procedures the fund uses when a vote presents a conflict between the interests of fund shareholders and the interests of the fund's investment adviser, principal underwriter or any affiliated person of the fund or that affiliate's investment adviser or principal underwriter. The description should include the procedures that the fund's investment adviser or any other third party uses to vote proxies on the fund's behalf.[79] Including copies of the policies and procedures themselves may satisfy these requirements.[80]

(5) Investment Advisory and Other Services

The statement of additional information must identify any person who controls the fund's investment adviser and the basis for such person's control.[81] The fund also must identify any person who is an affiliated person of both the fund and the investment adviser and list all capacities in which that person is affiliated with each entity.[82] In addition, the fund must disclose the method of calculating the investment advisory fee payable by the fund and the total dollar amounts that the fund paid to the investment adviser under the investment advisory contract for the last three fiscal years.[83]

The statement of additional information must describe all services performed for or on behalf of the fund that its investment adviser supplied or paid for wholly or in substantial part,[84] as well as all fees, expenses and costs of the fund that are to be paid by persons other than an investment adviser or the fund and identify such persons.[85]

If any person, other than a director, officer, member of an advisory board, employee or investment adviser, regularly advises the fund or its investment adviser about investing in, purchasing or selling securities or other property or has the authority to determine what securities or other property the fund should purchase or sell and receives remuneration through any formal or informal understanding, the fund must disclose that person's name, the nature of the arrangement, the advice or information provided, the remuneration paid and how and by whom the

---

77. Form N-1A Item 13(a).
78. Form N-1A Item 13(b).
79. Form N-1A Item 12(f).
80. Form N-1A Item 12(f), Instruction 1; *see* § 2.7.8, *supra*.
81. Form N-1A Item 14(a)(1).
82. Form N-1A Item 14(a)(2).
83. Form N-1A Item 14(a)(3).
84. Form N-1A Item 14(c)(1).
85. Form N-1A Item 14(c)(2).

remuneration was paid.[86] This requirement does not apply to persons who provide only statistical and other factual information, advice about economic factors and trends, or advice on occasional transactions in specific securities without generally advising on the fund's purchase or sale of securities, or to persons who advise the investment adviser or the fund solely through uniform publications distributed to subscribers.[87]

The fund must disclose the name and principal business address of its principal underwriter (if any), custodian and independent public accountant,[88] and describe generally the services provided by its custodian and independent public accountant.[89]

The statement of additional information must summarize the substantive provisions of any other management-related service contract that may be of interest to a purchaser of the fund's shares, indicating the parties to the contract, the nature of the services provided, the basis of the compensation paid, the total compensation paid for the past three years and who paid it.[90] The summary should include any direct or indirect relationships of the service provider with the fund, the investment adviser or the principal underwriter.[91] This requirement includes "any contract with the fund to keep, prepare or file accounts, books, records or other documents required under federal or state law or to provide any similar services with respect to the daily administration of the fund."[92] It does not include investment advisory agreements, agreements for custodial, transfer agent or dividend-paying services, or contracts for personal employment or outside legal or accounting services.[93]

(6) Portfolio Managers

The statement of additional information must include additional information about each person, or portfolio manager, who is identified in the fund's prospectus as being primarily responsible for the day-to-day management of the fund's portfolio.[94] For each such portfolio manager, the fund must disclose the total number of registered investment companies, other pooled investment vehicles and other accounts managed by him or her and the aggregate assets under his or her management in each such category. The statement of additional information also must disclose the number of those accounts with respect to which the portfolio manager earns a performance-based advisory fee, and the total assets in those accounts.[95] The fund must disclose any material conflicts of interest that may arise in connection with the portfolio manager's management of the fund's portfolio and these other accounts, including conflicts among investment strategies of

---

86. Form N-1A Item 14(e).
87. Form N-1A Item 14(e), Instructions (a) and (b).
88. Form N-1A Items 14(b) and 14(h)(3).
89. Form N-1A Item 14(h)(3).
90. Form N-1A Item 14(d).
91. Form N-1A Item 14(d), Instruction 3.
92. Form N-1A Item 14(d), Instruction 1.
93. *Id.*
94. Form N-1A Item 15(a). *See* § 6.2.1.ii.a(4), *supra.*
95. Form N-1A Item 15(a)(2) and (3).

the accounts and in allocating investment opportunities among the accounts.[96] If the portfolio manager is part of a committee, team or group that is jointly and primarily responsible for the day-to-day management of another account, information concerning that account must be included.[97] Information must be disclosed as of the end of the fund's most recently completed fiscal year, unless the statement of additional information is part of the fund's initial registration or is being updated to reflect the addition of a new portfolio manager, in which case information must be provided as of the most recent practicable date.[98]

The structure and method of determining the compensation to be received by each portfolio manager, including salary, bonuses, deferred compensation and pension and retirement plans, must be disclosed in the statement of additional information.[99] The criteria on which compensation is based must be described with specificity, but the value of the compensation is not required to be disclosed.[100] For example, the statement of aditional information should disclose whether compensation is fixed, is based on the fund's pre- or post-tax performance and, if so, how it is determined, or is based on the value of the fund's assets and, if so, how it is determined.[101] Information must be disclosed as of the end of the fund's most recently completed fiscal year, unless the statement of additional information is part of the fund's initial registration or is being updated to reflect the addition of a new portfolio manager, in which case information must be provided as of the most recent practicable date.[102] The fund also must disclose the dollar range of the fund's equity securities that the portfolio manager owns.[103]

(7) Brokerage Allocation and Practices[104]

The statement of additional information must disclose how "transactions in portfolio securities are effected, including a general statement about brokerage commissions, markups, and markdowns on principal transactions and the aggregate amount of any brokerage commissions paid by it during its three most recent fiscal years."[105] The fund should explain the reasons for any material differences between the aggregate dollar amount of brokerage commissions it paid during its most recent fiscal year and either of the two preceding years.[106] The fund must disclose more detailed information about commissions it paid to any broker that is an affiliated person of the fund or that has an affiliated person who is also an affiliated person of the fund, the investment adviser or the principal underwriter.[107]

---

96. Form N-1A Item 15(a)(4).

97. Form N-1A Item 15(a), Instruction 2.

98. Form N-1A Item 15(a), Instruction 1.

99. Form N-1A Item 15(b).

100. Form N-1A Item 15(b) and Instruction 2 thereto.

101. *Id.*

102. Form N-1A Item 15(b), Instruction 1.

103. Form N-1A Item 15(c). The dollar ranges to be identified are: "none, $1-$10,000, $10,001-$50,000, $50,001-$100,000, $100,001-$500,000, $500,001-$1,000,000, or over $1,000,000." *Id.*

104. *See also* Chapter 14, *infra.*

105. Form N-1A Item 16(a).

106. *Id.*

107. Form N-1A Item 16(b).

In addition, the statement of additional information must describe how the fund selects brokers to effect its securities transactions and how it evaluates the overall reasonableness of brokerage commissions paid, including the factors that it considers in making these determinations.[108] If the fund considers the receipt of research services or products or services other than brokerage or research services, it must identify the nature of such research services and specify any such other products and services.[109] The fund must state "whether persons acting on the fund's behalf are authorized to pay a broker a higher brokerage commission than another broker might have charged for the same transaction in recognition of the value of brokerage or research services provided by the broker."[110] The fund must explain if any research services provided by brokers through which it effects securities transactions may be used by the fund's investment adviser in servicing all of its accounts and whether or not all of these services may be used by the investment adviser in connection with the fund.[111] The fund also must explain any other policies or practices relating to the allocation of research services provided by brokers.[112] If the fund or its investment adviser directed the fund's brokerage transactions during the last fiscal year to a broker, whether through an agreement or understanding with the broker or through an internal allocation procedure, because of research services provided by the broker, the fund must state the amount of the transactions and the related commissions.[113]

(8) Taxation of the Fund

The statement of additional information must disclose any special or unusual tax aspects of the fund, such as taxation resulting from non–U.S. investments.[114]

(9) Underwriters

For each principal underwriter distributing the fund's securities, the statement of additional information must describe the nature of the obligation to distribute such securities, whether the offering is continuous and the aggregate dollar amount of underwriting commissions and the amount retained by the principal underwriter for each of the fund's last three fiscal years.[115] The fund also must provide information about the commissions and other compensation that each principal underwriter who is an affiliated person of the fund or an affiliated person of that affiliated person received, directly or indirectly, from the fund during the fund's most recent fiscal year.[116] In addition, the fund must disclose the name and address of any

---

108. Form N-1A Item 16(c).
109. Form N-1A Item 16(c), Instructions 1 and 2.
110. Form N-1A Item 16(c), Instruction 3.
111. Form N-1A Item 16(c), Instruction 4.
112. *Id.*
113. Form N-1A Item 16(d).
114. Form N-1A Item 19; *see also* Chapter 16, *infra.* The fund also must disclose whether it is or intends to qualify under SubChapter M of the Tax Code, 26 U.S.C. § 851, *et seq.*, and the consequences to the fund if it does not so qualify. Hedge funds do not qualify under SubChapter M of the Tax Code.
115. Form N-1A Item 20(a).
116. Form N-1A Item 20(b).

underwriter or dealer in the fund's shares who received any payments from the fund during the fund's last fiscal year, the amount paid and basis for determining that amount, the circumstances surrounding the payments and the consideration received by the fund.[117] This last requirement does not apply to payments made through deduction from the offering price at the time of sale or payments of the purchase price or commissions on the purchase and sale of portfolio securities.[118]

iii. Form S-1

If a hedge fund were to register its securities under the Securities Act and Form N-1A were unavailable, the hedge fund would be required to use Form S-1. As described above, Form S-1 is used by an issuer that is not eligible to use any other form.[119] No other registration statement form would be available for most hedge funds.[120]

Form S-1 comprises cover pages and two parts. Part I specifies the information that must be included in a prospectus that the issuer must deliver to prospective investors.[121] Delivery of this prospectus must precede or accompany the delivery of any security for sale or delivery after sale.[122] Part II specifies the information and exhibits that must be filed with the SEC but delivered to investors only on request.[123]

Part I of Form S-1 requires that the following information, among other things, be included in the prospectus:

- a brief summary of the information contained in the prospectus where the length and complexity of the prospectus makes a summary useful;[124]
- under the heading "Risk Factors," a logically organized and concise discussion of the most significant factors that make the offering speculative or risky and that explains how the risks affect the issuer or its securities;[125]
- a statement of the principal purposes for which the net proceeds of the securities offering are intended to be used and the approximate amount intended to be used for each such purpose;[126]
- a description of the factors considered in determining the offering price of the securities;[127]
- a description of the plan of distribution, including the identities of any principal underwriters, material relationships between such principal underwriters and

---

117.   Form N-1A Item 20(c).

118.   Form N-1A Item 20(c)(1), (2) and (3).

119.   Form S-1 General Instruction I.

120.   Form S-2 General Instruction I.B; Form S-3 General Instruction I.A.2, 17 C.F.R. § 239.13; Form S-4 General Instruction A.1; Form S-6 General Instruction 1; Form S-11 General Instruction A; Form S-8 General Instruction A.1; Form SB-1 General Instruction A.1; Form SB-2 General Instruction A.1; Regulation S-B Rule 10(a)(1), 17 C.F.R. § 228.10(a)(1); and Regulation C Rule 405, 17 C.F.R. § 230.405.

121.   Form S-1 Part I.

122.   Securities Act § 5(b), 15 U.S.C. § 77e(b).

123.   Form S-1 Part II.

124.   Form S-1 Item 1; Regulation S-K Item 503(a), 17 C.F.R. § 229.503(a).

125.   Form S-1 Item 1; Regulation S-K Item 503(c), 17 C.F.R. § 229.503(c).

126.   Form S-1 Item 4; Regulation S-K Item 504, 17 C.F.R. § 229.504.

127.   Form S-1 Item 5; Regulation S-K Item 505, 17 C.F.R. § 229.505.

the issuer, the terms of any agreements, arrangements or understandings with any brokers or dealers that will sell the securities, a description of the basis on which any securities will be offered (other than cash), and a description of underwriters' compensation and the amount of discounts and commissions to be paid for each security and in total;[128]

- a description of the securities being offered;[129]
- a description of the issuer's business;[130]
- a description of the issuer's materially important physical properties;[131]
- a description of any material pending legal proceedings, other than ordinary routine litigation incidental to the issuer's business, to which the issuer is a party or its property is subject;[132]
- a description of the principal U.S. market in which each class of the issuer's common equity is traded (or a statement that there is no public trading market for a class of common equity), the approximate number of holders of each class of common equity as of the latest practicable date, information concerning the frequency and amount of cash dividends paid during the past two fiscal years, and information concerning compensation plans of the issuer under which equity securities of the issuer are authorized for issuance;[133]
- financial statements for the issuer for the preceding three years;[134]
- selected financial information of the issuer for each of the past five fiscal years and any additional fiscal years necessary to keep the information from being misleading;[135]
- management's discussion and analysis of the issuer's financial condition and results of operations;[136]
- information about changes in and disagreements with accountants during the two most recent fiscal years;[137]
- information about the issuer's directors and executive officers, executive compensation and security ownership of certain beneficial owners and management; [138]
- information about any transaction or series of similar transactions since the beginning of the issuer's last fiscal year, or any currently proposed transaction or series of similar transactions, involving more than $60,000 and in which any director or executive officer of the issuer, any nominee for election as a director of the issuer, any person who directly or indirectly beneficially owns more than five percent of any class of the issuer's voting securities, or any

---

128.   Form S-1 Item 8; Regulation S-K Item 508, 17 C.F.R. § 229.508.
129.   Form S-1 Item 9; Regulation S-K Item 202, 17 C.F.R. § 229.202.
130.   Form S-1 Item 11(a); Regulation S-K Item 101, 17 C.F.R. § 229.101.
131.   Form S-1 Item 11(b); Regulation S-K Item 102, 17 C.F.R. § 229.102.
132.   Form S-1 Item 11(c); Regulation S-K Item 103, 17 C.F.R. § 229.103.
133.   Form S-1 Item 11(d); Regulation S-K Item 201, 17 C.F.R. § 229.201.
134.   Form S-1 Item 11(e). The requirements for financial statements are set forth in Regulation S-X, 17 C.F.R. pt. 210, and are not addressed in this book.
135.   Form S-1 Item 11(f); Regulation S-K Item 301, 17 C.F.R. § 229.301.
136.   Form S-1 Item 11(h); Regulation S-K Item 303, 17 C.F.R. § 229.303.
137.   Form S-1 Item 11(i); Regulation S-K Item 304, 17 C.F.R. § 229.304.
138.   Form S-1 Items 11(k), (l) and (m); Regulation S-K Items 401, 402 and 403, 17 C.F.R. §§ 229.401, 229.402 and 229.403.

immediate family member of any of the foregoing persons, has a direct or indirect material interest;[139] and

- a description of the indemnification provisions relating to directors, officers and controlling persons of the issuer against liability arising under the Securities Act.[140]

The description of the indemnification provision must include a statement in substantially the following form:

> Insofar as indemnification for liabilities arising under the Securities Act of 1933 may be permitted to directors, officers or persons controlling the registrant pursuant to the foregoing provisions, the registrant has been informed that in the opinion of the Securities and Exchange Commission such indemnification is against public policy as expressed in the Act and is therefore unenforceable.[141]

2. Company Act

As discussed in Chapter 3, an investment company typically must register as such under the Company Act before offering its securities to investors.[142] As under the Securities Act, the SEC has adopted several different forms that investment companies may use to register under the Company Act. The registration form that most hedge funds would use to register with the SEC, if required to register under the Company Act, is Form N-1A, which is summarized above in section 6.2.1.ii.

3. Plain English Requirements

In 1998, the SEC adopted Securities Act Rule 421,[143] which requires issuers to use the SEC's version of plain English principles in drafting specified parts of a prospectus. Rule 421 applies to prospectuses under the Securities Act and the Company Act.[144] Under Rule 421, information "in a prospectus must be presented in a clear, concise and understandable manner."[145] The issuer should:

- present information in clear, concise sections, paragraphs and sentences and, whenever possible, use short, explanatory sentences and bullet lists;
- use descriptive headings and subheadings;
- avoid frequent reliance on glossaries or defined terms as the primary means of explaining information in the prospectus and define terms in a glossary

---

139. Form S-1 Item 11(n); Regulation S-K Item 404, 17 C.F.R. § 229.404.
140. Form S-1 Item 12; Regulation S-K Item 510, 17 C.F.R. § 229.510.
141. *Id.*
142. Company Act § 7(a), 15 U.S.C. § 80a-7(a).
143. 17 C.F.R. § 230.421.
144. *See* Form N-1A General Instruction B.4(c).
145. Securities Act Rule 421(b), 17 C.F.R. § 230.421(b).

or other section of the document only if the meaning is unclear from the context and it facilitates understanding of the disclosure; and

- avoid legal and highly technical business terminology.[146]

In addition, "to enhance the readability of the prospectus, [the issuer] must use plain English principles in the organization, language, and design of the front and back cover pages, the summary, and the risk factors section."[147] Each of these sections should be drafted so that, at a minimum, it substantially complies with the SEC's plain English writing principles by using:

- short sentences;
- definite, concrete, everyday words;
- active voice;
- tabular presentation or bullet lists for complex material, wherever possible;
- no legal jargon or highly technical business terms; and
- no multiple negatives.[148]

An issuer may include pictures, logos, charts, graphs or other design elements, as long as the design is not misleading and the required information is clear. The rule encourages the use of tables, schedules, charts and graphic illustrations of the results of operations, balance sheet and other financial data that present the information in an understandable way. Any presentation must be consistent with the financial statements and non-financial information in the prospectus. Graphs and charts must be drawn to scale. Any information provided must not be misleading.[149] Although the SEC's plain English rules apply only to prospectuses used in public offerings or by mutual funds, the general partner of a hedge fund should comply with Rule 421 when feasible.

§ 6.3 Disclosure Obligations in Connection with Private Offerings and Regulation D

1. Private Offerings under Securities Act Section 4(2)

An issuer seeking to rely on the private offering exemption from registration provided by Securities Act section 4(2)[150] must give offerees access to "the same kind of information that the [Securities] Act would make available in the form of

---

146. *Id.*
147. Securities Act Rule 421(d)(1), 17 C.F.R. § 230.421(d)(1).
148. Securities Act Rule 421(d)(2), 17 C.F.R. § 230.421(d)(2).
149. Securities Act Rule 421(d)(3), 17 C.F.R. § 230.421(d)(3).
150. *See* Chapter 5 and § 6.2.1.i, *supra,* and § 8.2, *infra.*

a registration statement."[151] Hedge funds ordinarily should satisfy this requirement by providing each offeree with a private offering memorandum that discloses the required information.[152] The private offering memorandum should be prepared on the basis of Company Act Form N-1A and Securities Act Form S-1, as discussed above in section 6.2.

2. Regulation D Offerings

Regulation D specifies information that must be delivered to nonaccredited investors in a Rule 506 offering.[153] This information must be provided a "reasonable time before the sale" of the securities to a nonaccredited investor.[154] Although Regulation D does not require that the specified information be furnished to purchasers if a hedge fund sells its interests only to accredited investors, the SEC has noted that "nothing in Regulation D states that an issuer need not give disclosure to an investor."[155] In light of the potential liability under the Securities Act and Exchange Act anti-fraud provisions (discussed below in section 6.4), a hedge fund should fully disclose all facts material to a decision whether to invest.

With respect to nonaccredited investors, an issuer that is not subject to the reporting requirements of Exchange Act section 13 or 15(d) (such as a hedge fund) is required to deliver the same kind of information as would be required in Part I of a registration statement filed under the Securities Act on the form that the issuer would be entitled to use.[156] A 1988 SEC staff no-action letter directed a hedge fund to use Form N-1A to determine the information that it is required to deliver under Regulation D.[157] The hedge fund is only required to deliver that information "to the extent material to an understanding of the issuer, its business and the securities being offered."[158]

The issuer must also deliver to nonaccredited investors the financial statements that would be required in a registration statement filed with the SEC on the form that the issuer would be entitled to use.[159] Again, the SEC staff has stated that Form N-1A is the appropriate form for guidance concerning the appropriate financial statements to include in a disclosure document for a hedge fund.[160]

Regulation D also requires the issuer to identify the contents of material exhibits required to be filed with the SEC as part of the registration statement and make them available or provide them to the purchaser on the purchaser's written request

---

151. *SEC v. Ralston Purina Co.*, 346 U.S. 119, 125-126, 73 S. Ct. 981 (1953).

152. *Doran v. Petroleum Mgmt. Corp., et al.*, 545 F. 2d 893, 902 (5th Cir. 1977).

153. Regulation D Rule 502(b)(1), 17 C.F.R. § 230.502(b)(1). *See* § 5.3.2.vii, *supra*.

154. *Id.*

155. Regulation D Rule 502(b)(1), 17 C.F.R. § 230.502(b)(1); Securities Act Release No. 33-6455, 48 F.R. 10,045 (Mar. 3, 1983).

156. Regulation D Rule 502(b)(2)(i)(A), 17 C.F.R. § 230.502(b)(2)(i)(A). An issuer that is eligible to use Regulation A may deliver the information required by that Regulation, but few hedge funds are eligible to use Regulation A because it is limited to offerings of securities with an aggregate offering price of $5,000,000 or less. *See* Regulation A Rule 251(b), 17 C.F.R. § 230.251(b).

157. *Robert T. Willis, Jr., P.C.*, SEC No-Action Letter (Jan. 18, 1988).

158. *Id.*; Regulation D Rule 502(b)(2)(i), 17 C.F.R. § 230.502(b)(2)(i).

159. Regulation D Rule 502(b)(2)(i)(B)(*3*), 17 C.F.R. § 230.502(b)(2)(i)(B)(*3*).

160. *Robert T. Willis, Jr., P.C.*, SEC No-Action Letter (Jan. 18, 1988).

a reasonable time before the purchase.[161] Among the exhibits required to be filed with a Form N-1A registration statement are the fund's articles or certificate of incorporation and bylaws, investment adviser agreements, custodial agreements, other material agreements, and legal opinions concerning whether the securities to be issued, when sold, will be legally issued, fully paid and nonassessable and concerning the tax consequences that are material to investors, if the filing makes representations about tax consequences.[162] The SEC has stated that a hedge fund's disclosure documents should describe the contents of these legal opinions and the hedge fund should make the legal opinions available to purchasers.[163] In addition, if the hedge fund is organized as a limited partnership or limited liability company, its agreement of limited partnership or limited liability company agreement should be described and made available to investors.

§ 6.4 Anti-Fraud Provisions

The Exchange Act and Securities Act anti-fraud provisions apply to sales of securities pursuant to the exemptions provided by Securities Act section 4(2) and Regulation D.[164] An investor in a hedge fund may bring an action for fraud under Exchange Act section 10(b)[165] and Rule 10b-5 thereunder.[166] The SEC also may bring an action against a hedge fund under these provisions and under Securities Act section 17(a).[167]

1. Exchange Act Provisions

Exchange Act Section 10(b) provides that:

> It shall be unlawful for any person, directly or indirectly, by the use of any means or instrumentality of interstate commerce or of the mails, or of any facility of any national securities exchange… (b) to use or employ, in connection with the purchase or sale of any security registered on a national securities exchange or any security not so registered, or any securities-based swap agreement (as defined in section 206B of the Gramm-Leach-Bliley Act), any manipulative or deceptive device or contrivance in contravention of such rules and regulations as the commission may prescribe as

---

161.   Regulation D Rule 502(b)(2)(iii), 17 C.F.R. § 230.502(b)(2)(iii).
162.   Form N-1A Items 23(i) and (j); Regulation S-K Item 601(b)(8), 17 C.F.R. § 229.601(b)(8).
163.   Securities Act Release No. 33-6455, Question 52, 48 F.R. 10,045 (Mar. 3, 1983).
164.   *Landreth Timber Co. v. Landreth, et al.*, 471 U.S. 681, 692, 105 S. Ct. 2297, 2305 (1985).
165.   15 U.S.C. § 78j(b).
166.   17 C.F.R. § 240.10b-5.
167.   15 U.S.C. § 77q(a).

necessary or appropriate in the public interest or for the protection of investors.[168]

Pursuant to Exchange Act section 10(b), the SEC adopted Rule 10b-5 on May 21, 1942.[169] Rule 10b-5 provides that:

> It shall be unlawful for any person, directly or indirectly, by the use of any means or instrumentality of interstate commerce, or of the mails, or of any facility of any national securities exchange,
>
> (a) to employ any device, scheme, or artifice to defraud,
> (b) to make any untrue statement of a material fact or to omit to state a material fact necessary in order to make the statements made, in light of the circumstances under which they were made, not misleading, or
> (c) to engage in any act, practice, or course of business which operates or would operate as a fraud or deceit upon any person,
>
> in connection with the purchase or sale of any security.[170]

The provisions of Exchange Act section 10(b) and Rule 10b-5 "are broad and, by repeated use of the word 'any,' are obviously meant to be inclusive."[171]

The SEC may enforce Rule 10b-5 by, among other things, imposing a monetary penalty on the offender or seeking an injunction against the offender.[172] In addition, the Supreme Court has recognized an implied private right of action under Exchange Act section 10(b) and Rule 10b-5, pursuant to which a purchaser or seller of securities may bring an action for fraud in connection with the purchase or sale.[173] Only a person that actually buys or sells a security, or that has contracted to buy or sell a security, may bring an action under Rule 10b-5.[174] A person that decides not to buy or sell a security based on an omission or misrepresentation does not have standing to sue under Rule 10b-5.[175] Rule 10b-5 applies to both oral and written contracts to buy or sell a security.[176]

i. Omissions

Rule 10b-5 prohibits any omission of a material fact that is necessary to make statements made, in light of the circumstances under which they were made, not

---

168.   15 U.S.C. § 78j(b).

169.   Exchange Act Release No. 34-3230, 13 F.R. 8,177 (May 21, 1942).

170.   17 C.F.R. § 240.10b-5.

171.   *Affiliated Ute Citizens of Utah, et al. v. United States, et al.*, 406 U.S. 128, 151, 92 S. Ct. 1456, 1471 (1972).

172.   Exchange Act § 21(d), 15 U.S.C. § 78u(d).

173.   *See, e.g., Ernst & Ernst v. Hochfelder, et al.*, 425 U.S. 185, 196, 96 S. Ct. 1375, 1382 (1976); *Blue Chip Stamps v. Manor Drug Stores*, 421 U.S. 723, 730, 95 S. Ct. 1917, 1922-1923 (1975); *Affiliated Ute Citizens v. United States*, 406 U.S. 128, 150-154, 92 S. Ct. 1456, 1471-1472 (1972); *Superintendent of Ins. of New York v. Bankers Life & Casualty Co., et al.*, 404 U.S. 6, 13 n. 9, 92 S. Ct. 165, 169 n. 9 (1971).

174.   *Blue Chip Stamps v. Manor Drug Stores*, 421 U.S. 723, 749, 95 S. Ct. 1917, 1932 (1975).

175.   *Id.*

176.   *The Wharf (Holdings) Limited, et al. v. United International Holdings, Inc.*, 532 U.S. 588, 594-595, 121 S. Ct. 1776, 1781 (2001).

misleading,[177] even if the statement giving rise to such duty is not required to be made. In other words, "a duty to speak the full truth arises when a defendant undertakes a duty to say anything."[178] In addition, liability under Rule 10b-5 may arise from an omission, even absent any affirmative representation by the party that omitted the information, if that party has a duty to disclose information, such as a fiduciary duty or other relation of trust and confidence.[179]

ii. Materiality

Rule 10b-5 only applies to omissions or misrepresentations that are material. The Supreme Court has determined that, in connection with Rule 10b-5, "an omitted fact is material if there is a substantial likelihood that a reasonable shareholder would consider it important" in deciding whether to buy or sell.[180] "There must be a substantial likelihood that the disclosure of the omitted fact would have been viewed by the reasonable investor as having significantly altered the 'total mix' of information made available."[181]

A plaintiff may bring an action under Rule 10b-5 based on opinions and forward-looking statements included in an offering document.[182] "[S]uch statements of 'soft information' may be actionable misrepresentations if the speaker does not genuinely and reasonably believe them."[183] An issuer will not be liable for such statements, even if they prove to be incorrect, if "1) the speaker genuinely believes the statement is accurate; 2) there is a reasonable basis for that belief; and 3) the speaker is unaware of any undisclosed facts that would tend seriously to undermine the accuracy of the statement."[184]

The materiality of statements of opinion or forward-looking statements may be diminished by cautionary statements in the offering document.[185] As the court in *In re Trump Casinos Securities Litigation* stated,

> ... when an offering document's forecasts, opinions or projections are accompanied by meaningful cautionary statements, the forward-looking statements will not form the basis for a securities fraud claim if those statements did not affect the "total mix" of information the document provided investors. In other words, cautionary language,

---

177.   Exchange Act Rule 10b-5, 17 C.F.R. § 240.10b-5.

178.   *Rubinstein v. Collins*, 20 F.3d 160, 170 (5th Cir. 1994) (quoting *First Virginia Bankshares v. Benson*, 559 F.2d 1307, 1317 (5th Cir. 1977)).

179.   *Chiarella v. U.S.*, 445 U.S. 222, 228, 100 S. Ct. 1108, 1114 (1980). *See also, Affiliated Ute Citizens v. United States*, 406 U.S. 128, 92 S. Ct. 1456 (1972).

180.   *Basic Inc., et al. v. Levinson, et al.*, 485 U.S. 224, 231, 108 S. Ct. 978, 983 (1988) (quoting *TSC Industries, Inc. v. Northway, Inc.*, 426 U.S. 438, 449, 96 S. Ct. 2126, 2132 (1976)).

181.   *Basic Inc., et al. v. Levinson, et al.*, 485 U.S. 224, 231-232, 108 S. Ct. 978, 983 (1988) (quoting *TSC Industries, Inc. v. Northway, Inc.*, 426 U.S. 438, 449, 96 S. Ct. 2126, 2132 (1976)).

182.   *See In re Donald J. Trump Casino Sec. Lit.*, 7 F.3d 357, 368 (3rd Cir., 1993), cert. denied, *Gollomp v. Trump*, 510 U.S. 1178, 114. S. Ct. 1219 (1994).

183.   *Id.* (citations omitted).

184.   *Rubinstein v. Collins*, 20 F.3d 160, 166 (5th Cir. 1994) (citations omitted).

185.   *See, e.g., Olkey v. Hyperion 1999 Term Trust, Inc.*, 98 F.3d 2 (2nd Cir. 1996); *In re Donald J. Trump Casino Sec. Lit.*, 7 F.3d 357, 371-72 (3rd Cir., 1993), cert. denied, *Gollomp v. Trump*, 510 U.S. 1178, 114 S. Ct. 1219 (1994); *In re Worlds of Wonder Securities Litigation*, 35 F.3d 1407 (9th Cir. 1994).

if sufficient, renders the alleged omissions or misrepresentations immaterial as a matter of law.[186]

Boilerplate disclaimers do not, however, affect the materiality of statements in an offering document. Instead, "the cautionary statements must be substantive and tailored to the specific future projections, estimates or opinions in the prospectus which the plaintiffs challenge."[187] In addition, "the inclusion of general cautionary language regarding a prediction would not excuse the alleged failure to reveal known material, adverse facts."[188]

iii. Reliance

To succeed in a claim under Rule 10b-5, a plaintiff must prove that it relied on an omission or misrepresentation.[189] The injured party can demonstrate reliance in the case of an omission, if the facts withheld are "material in the sense that a reasonable investor might have considered them important in the making of this decision."[190] Under the "bespeaks caution" doctrine discussed above in section 6.4.1.ii, a plaintiff may not be able to prove reliance where the potential risks have been adequately disclosed.[191]

iv. Scienter

A private plaintiff seeking damages under Rule 10b-5 must demonstrate that the defendants acted with scienter.[192] Scienter also is a required element in an action for injunctive relief under section 10(b) and Rule 10b-5,[193] and in any action brought by the SEC under section 10(b) or Rule 10b-5.[194] "Scienter" is a "mental state embracing intent to deceive, manipulate or defraud."[195] In determining what rises to the level of scienter, however, the courts have reached varying conclusions. Scienter has been variously held to require actual knowledge, constructive knowledge, intent to defraud or recklessness.[196]

2. Securities Act Provisions

Securities Act sections 11 and 12(a)(2) provide express private rights of actions to purchasers of securities.[197] Securities Act section 11 applies, however, only to

---

186. *In re Donald J. Trump Casino Sec. Lit.*, 7 F.3d 357, 371-72 (3rd Cir., 1993), cert. denied, *Gollomp v. Trump*, 510 U.S. 1178, 114 S. Ct. 1219 (1994).

187. *Id.* at 368.

188. *Rubinstein v. Collins*, 20 F.3d 160, 171 (5th Cir. 1994).

189. *Basic Inc., et al. v. Levinson, et al.*, 485 U.S. 224, 243, 108 S. Ct. 978, 989 (1988).

190. *Affiliated Ute Citizens of Utah, et al. v. U.S., et al.*, 406 U.S. 128, 151, 92 S. Ct. 1456, 1471 (1972) (citations omitted).

191. *Rubinstein v. Collins*, 20 F.3d 160, 167 (1994).

192. *Ernst & Ernst v. Hochfelder, et al.*, 425 U.S. 185, 193, 96 S. Ct. 1375, 1381 (1976).

193. *Aaron v. SEC*, 446 U.S. 680, 691, 100 S. Ct. 1945, 1952-1953 (1980).

194. *Id.*

195. *Ernst & Ernst v. Hochfelder*, et al., 425 U.S. 185, 193 n. 12, 96 S. Ct. 1375, 1381 n. 12 (1976).

196. *See* 4 Alan R. Bromberg & Lewis D. Lowenfels, Bromberg and Lowenfels on Securities Fraud & Commodities Fraud, § 7:125, *et seq.*, and cases cited therein.

197. Securities Act §§ 11(a) and 12(a)(2), 15 U.S.C. §§ 77k(a) and 77l(a)(2).

statements in registration statements filed with the SEC.[198] Similarly, the Supreme Court has held that Securities Act section 12(a)(2) applies only to statements in prospectuses and oral communications relating to public offerings of securities.[199] Accordingly, neither of these provisions applies to the sale of securities in a hedge fund pursuant to the exemptions from registration provided by Securities Act section 4(2) and Regulation D.

On the other hand, Securities Act section 17(a) applies to any "offer or sale of any securities." It provides that:

> It shall be unlawful for any person in the offer or sale of any securities or any security-based swap agreement (as defined in section 206B of the Graham-Leach-Bliley Act) by the use of any means or instruments of transportation or communication in interstate commerce or by use of the mails, directly or indirectly—
>
> (1) to employ any device, scheme or artifice to defraud, or
> (2) to obtain money or property by means of any untrue statement of material fact or any omission to state a material fact necessary in order to make the statements made, in light of the circumstances under which they were made, not misleading; or
> (3) to engage in any transaction, practice, or course of business which operates or would operate as a fraud or deceit upon the purchaser.[200]

Although this statute is similar to Exchange Act Rule 10b-5, discussed above in section 6.4.1, the two provisions have been interpreted differently. Most courts that have considered the issue have held that no private right of action can be implied under Securities Act section 17(a).[201] The Supreme Court has identified the issue in several cases, but has refused to address whether an implied cause of action exists under section 17(a).[202] Although the SEC must prove scienter under Rule 10b-5, it must only prove scienter with respect to subsection 1 of section 17(a).[203] Subsections 17(a)(2) and 17(a)(3) require a showing of only negligence by the defendant.[204] Section 17(a) applies only to fraud by a seller of securities, while Rule 10b-5 applies to fraud by either a buyer or a seller.[205]

---

198. Securities Act § 11(a), 15 U.S.C. § 77k(a).

199. *Gustafson, et al. v. Alloyd Co., Inc., et al.*, 513 U.S. 561, 584, 115 S. Ct. 1061, 1073-74 (1995).

200. 15 U.S.C. § 77q(a).

201. *See, Finkel, et al., v. Stratton Corp., et al.*, 962 F.2d 169, 172 (2nd Cir., 1992); *Newcome v. Esrey, et al.*, 862 F.2d 1099, 1101 (4th Cir., 1988); *Schlifke v. Seafirst Corp.*, 866 F.2d 935, 942-943 (7th Cir., 1989); *Deviries v. Prudential-Bache Securities, Inc.*, 805 F.2d 326, 328 (8th Cir., 1986); *In re Washington Public Power Supply System Sec. Lit.*, 823 F.2d 1349, 1358 (9th Cir., 1987); *Bath, et al., v. Buchkin, Gaims, Gaines and Jonas, et al.*, 913 F.2d 817, 819 (10th Cir., 1990), overruled on other grounds by *Rotella v. Wood, et al.*, 528 U.S. 549, 120 S.Ct. 1075 (2000); *Currie v. Cayman Resources Corp., et al.*, 835 F.2d 780, 784-785 (11th Cir., 1988). The Sixth Circuit recognized, however, a private cause of action under § 17(a) in *Kellman v. ICS, Inc.*, 447 F.2d 1305, 1308-09 (6th Cir., 1971), and *Craighead, et al., v. E.F. Hutton & Co., Inc., et al.*, 899 F. 2d 485, 492 (6th Cir., 1990).

202. *See, e.g., Aaron v. SEC*, 446 U.S. 680, 689, 100 S. Ct. 1945, 1951-1952 (1980).

203. *See Aaron v. SEC*, 446 U.S. 680, 701-702, 100 S. Ct. 1945, 1958 (1980).

204. *Id.*

205. Securities Act § 17(a), 15 U.S.C. § 77q(a); Exchange Act Rule 10b-5, 17 C.F.R. § 240.10b-5.

§ 6.5 Disclosure Obligations under the Advisers Act

1. Part II of Form ADV

An investment adviser registered with the SEC is required to furnish a written disclosure document (a "brochure") to clients and prospective clients. The brochure may be either Part II of the investment adviser's Form ADV or a separate written document containing at least the information required by Part II of Form ADV.[206] For purposes of this requirement, the SEC considers each limited partner of a hedge fund to be a "client."[207] The investment adviser is initially required to deliver this document at least forty-eight hours before entering into an advisory agreement with the client, or at the time of entering into the contract if the client can terminate the contract without penalty within five business days after entering into it.[208] An investment adviser must also annually deliver or offer in writing to deliver, without charge, a copy of the disclosure document on written request from a client.[209] An investment adviser must mail its brochure to a client within seven days of the client's request.[210] Accordingly, an investment adviser to a hedge fund should include its brochure with its private offering memorandum and offer at least annually to deliver a current brochure to the limited partners.

Some states have adopted rules similar to the SEC's brochure rule, requiring that any investment adviser registered there deliver Part II of its Form ADV, or a brochure containing similar information, to clients and prospective clients.[211] General principles of fiduciary duty suggest that an investment adviser should comply with the Advisers Act brochure rule as if it were SEC-registered, even if it is not registered with the SEC or in a state that has a similar rule. The brochure rule does not, however, relieve an investment adviser of any obligation to disclose information to its advisory clients under any other provision of the Advisers Act, the rules and regulations thereunder or any other federal or state law.[212]

2. Disclosure of Material Facts about Financial Condition

The SEC requires an investment adviser that is registered or required to be registered under the Advisers Act to disclose to any client or prospective client any material fact about the financial condition of the investment adviser "that is reasonably likely to impair the ability of the adviser to meet contractual commitments to

---

206. Advisers Act Rule 204-3(a), 17 C.F.R. § 275.204-3(a). *See* § 8.4.4, *infra*.

207. SEC Release No. IA-1862, 34-42620, 65 F.R. 20,524, 20,533 n. 117 (Apr. 17, 2000). *See also, Abrahamson v. Fleschner, et al.*, 568 F. 2d 862 (2nd Cir., 1977) (holding that duties of an investment adviser under the Advisers Act anti-fraud provisions applied to limited partners in an investment limited partnership).

208. Advisers Act Rule 204-3(c)(4), 17 C.F.R. § 204-3(c)(4).

209. Advisers Act Rule 204-3(c), 17 C.F.R. § 204-3(c).

210. Advisers Act Rule 204-3(c)(4), 17 C.F.R. § 204-3(c)(4).

211. *See, e.g.*, Unif. Sec. Act Rule 203(b)-1 (1987). See § 7.2, *infra*.

212. Advisers Act Rule 204-3(e), 17 C.F.R. § 275.204-3(e).

clients."[213] This requirement only applies if the investment adviser has express or implied discretionary authority over the client's funds or securities or custody of the client's funds or securities, as typically is the case for investment advisers to hedge funds, or if the investment adviser requires the client to prepay advisory fees of more than $500 more than six months in advance.[214] The investment adviser must disclose this information during the same period in which it must provide Part II of its Form ADV.[215] Some states impose similar disclosure requirements on investment advisers registered or located there.[216]

3. Disclosure of Legal and Disciplinary Proceedings

The SEC requires an investment adviser that is registered or required to be registered under the Advisers Act to disclose to any client or prospective client all material facts about any "legal or disciplinary event that is material to an evaluation of the adviser's integrity or ability to meet contractual commitments to clients."[217] Unlike the disclosure requirements for financial information, however, the investment adviser must make this disclosure to all clients, regardless of the investment adviser's authority or fee arrangements.[218]

The SEC has established a rebuttable presumption that each of the following events involving an investment adviser or one of its management persons that is not resolved in such person's favor or subsequently reversed, suspended or vacated is material for ten years after the date of the event:

- a criminal or civil action in a court of competent jurisdiction in which the person (a) was convicted of or pleaded guilty or no contest to a felony or a misdemeanor, or is the named subject of a pending criminal proceeding that involved an investment-related business, fraud, false statements or omissions, wrongful taking of property, bribery, forgery, counterfeiting or extortion, (b) was found to have been involved in a violation of an investment-related statute or regulations, or (c) was the subject of any order, judgment or decree permanently or temporarily enjoining the person from, or otherwise limiting the person from, engaging in any investment-related activity;
- administrative proceedings before the SEC, any other federal regulatory agency or any state agency in which the person (a) was found to have caused an investment-related business to lose its authorization to do business or (b) was found to have been involved in a violation of any investment-related statute or regulation and was the subject of an order by such agency denying, suspending or revoking the authorization of the person to act in, or barring or suspending the person's association with, an investment-related business, or otherwise significantly limiting the person's investment-related activities; or

---

213.   Advisers Act Rule 206(4)-4(a)(1), 17 C.F.R. § 275.206(4)-4(a)(1).
214.   *Id. See* § 2.6, *supra*, and Chapter 12, *infra*.
215.   Advisers Act Rule 206(4)-4(c), 17 C.F.R. § 275.206(4)-4(c); *see* § 6.5.1, *supra*.
216.   *See, e.g.*, 10 Cal. Code Reg. § 260.235.4.
217.   Advisers Act Rule 206(4)-4(a)(2), 17 C.F.R. § 275.206(4)-4(a)(2).
218.   *Id.*

- self-regulatory organization proceedings in which the person (a) was found to have caused an investment-related business to lose its authorization to do business or (b) was found to have been involved in a violation of such organization's rules and was subject of an order by such organization barring or suspending the person from membership or from association with other members or expelling the person from membership, fining the person more than $2,500 or otherwise significantly limiting the person's investment-related activities.[219]

The date of any of these events is the date on which the final order, judgment or decree is entered, or the date on which all rights of appeal from a preliminary order, judgment or decree lapse.[220]

A "management person" is a person "with power to exercise, directly or indirectly, a controlling influence over the management or policies of an adviser which is a company or to determine the general investment advice given to clients."[221] "Investment-related" means "pertaining to securities, commodities, banking, insurance, or real estate (including, but not limited to, acting as or being associated with a broker-dealer, investment company, investment adviser, government securities broker or dealer, municipal securities dealer, bank, savings and loan association, entity or person required to be registered under the [CEA] or fiduciary)."[222] A "self regulatory organization" is "any securities or commodities exchange, registered association, or registered clearing agency."[223] "Found" means "determined or ascertained by adjudication or consent in a final [self-regulatory organization] proceeding, administrative proceeding or court action."[224] "Involved" means "acting or aiding, abetting, causing, counseling, commanding, inducing, conspiring with or failing reasonably to supervise another in doing an act."[225]

4. Proxy Voting Regulations

An investment adviser registered with the SEC under the Advisers Act is required to establish proxy voting policies and procedures.[226] Such an investment adviser also must describe these policies and procedures to its clients, furnish a copy of the policies and procedures to any client that requests them, and disclose to its clients how they may obtain information about how the investment adviser voted securities on the client's behalf.[227]

---

219. Advisers Act Rule 206(4)-4(b), 17 C.F.R. § 275.206(4)-4(b).
220. Advisers Act Rule 206(4)-4(e), 17 C.F.R. § 275.206(4)-4(e).
221. Advisers Act Rule 206(4)-4(d)(1), 17 C.F.R. § 275.206(4)-4(d)(1).
222. Advisers Act Rule 206(4)-4(d)(3), 17 C.F.R. § 275.206(4)-4(d)(3).
223. Advisers Act Rule 206(4)-4(d)(5), 17 C.F.R. § 275.206(4)-4(d)(5).
224. Advisers Act Rule 206(4)-4(d)(2), 17 C.F.R. § 275.206(4)-4(d)(2).
225. Advisers Act Rule 206(4)-4(d)(5), 17 C.F.R. § 275.206(4)-4(d)(5).
226. *See* § 2.7.8, *supra*.
227. Advisers Act Rules 206(4)-6(b) and 206(4)-6(c), 17 C.F.R. §§ 275.206(4)-6(b) and 275.206(4)-6(c).

5. Finders and Solicitors

The "solicitor's rule" under the Advisers Act generally prohibits an investment adviser from paying a cash fee to an independent contractor who solicits clients, unless certain conditions are met.[228] To pay such a cash fee, the investment adviser must enter into a written contract with the solicitor requiring, among other things, that the solicitor give each potential client written disclosure about the relationship between the investment adviser and the solicitor (including the compensation), that the potential client acknowledge in writing receipt of the written disclosure, and that the solicitor deliver each such acknowledgement to the investment adviser, which must retain the disclosure and acknowledgements.[229] A partner, officer, director or employee of an investment adviser is subject to the solicitors rule and must disclose his or her affiliation with the investment adviser, but is not required to disclose his or her compensation for solicitation activities or to receive an acknowledgment from the client.[230]

§ 6.6 Disclosure Obligations under the CEA

The general partner or investment adviser of a hedge fund that trades in commodity interests may be required to register as a commoditiy pool operator (a "CPO") or a commodity trading advisor (a "CTA") under the CEA.[231] An investment entity, such as a hedge fund, that invests in commodity futures and other commodity interests is called in the CEA a "commodity pool." The CEA imposes disclosure and reporting obligations on CPOs and CTAs.

Many general partners and investment advisers of hedge funds are exempt from registration as CPOs and CTAs. Rules under the CEA that were adopted in 2003 create two exemptions from registration that are widely used by hedge fund general partners and investment advisers, one based on the fund's limited trading of commodity interests, and the other based on the sophistication of the fund's participants.[232] If the general partner or investment adviser of a hedge fund relies on either of these exemptions to avoid registering as a CPO or CTA, the CEA rules require that the reliance on the exemption and certain other related facts be disclosed to investors in the funds. This disclosure is typically included in the hedge fund's disclosure document. The various CEA disclosure requirements that apply to registered CPOs and CTAs are described below.

---

228.   Advisers Act Rule 206(4)-3, 17 C.F.R. § 275.206(4)-3. *See* §§ 8.4.5 and 10.1.3, *infra*.
229.   Advisers Act Rule 206(4)-3(b), 17 C.F.R. § 275.206(4)-3(b).
230.   Advisers Act Rule 206(4)-3(a)(2)(ii), 17 C.F.R. § 275.206(4)-3(a)(2)(ii). *See also* Chapter 10, *infra*.
231.   *See* § 2.9, *supra*.
232.   *See* §2.9.3, *supra*.

1. Disclosure Requirements

A CPO that is registered or required to register under the CEA and that does not qualify for relief from the CEA's disclosure requirements discussed below for certain offshore pools and QEP Pools must deliver a disclosure document to each prospective investor in a commodity pool of which it is the CPO no later than the time that it delivers a subscription agreement to the prospective investor.[233] A CTA that is registered or required to be registered under the CEA and that does not qualify for relief from the CEA's disclosure requirements may not enter into an agreement with a prospective client until the CTA delivers a disclosure document to that prospective client.[234] An investment adviser that is registered as both a CTA and a CPO is required to furnish only its CPO disclosure document, and not its CTA disclosure document, to persons who are clients solely by virtue of their participation in a pool operated by the CPO. Before a CPO that is required to provide a disclosure document may accept funds from a prospective investor, the prospective investor must sign an acknowledgment of receipt of the disclosure document and deliver it to the CPO.[235] CEA regulations specify many types of disclosure that must be included in a CPO disclosure document, including detailed disclosure of the past performance of the CPO's pool and, in some cases, the past performance of the CPO's principals.[236] The entire CPO disclosure document, rather than only certain sections specified in Securities Act Rule 421, must comply with the plain English rule.[237]

The CEA regulations generally require that a disclosure document be submitted to the NFA for review prior to its use.[238] A CPO must generally file all CEA-required disclosure documents with the NFA at least twenty-one days before sending them to any prospective investor.[239] A CPO that continually solicits investors must update any CEA-mandated disclosure document at least every nine months, because no CPO may use such a disclosure document dated more than nine months preceding its use.[240]

If interests in a pool are offered and sold solely to accredited investors in an offering exempt from the registration requirements of the Securities Act pursuant to Rule 505 or 506 of Regulation D,[241] the twenty-one-day advance filing requirement does not apply, and a registered CPO may solicit, accept and receive funds and other property from prospective participants on filing the disclosure document with the NFA and providing it to such participants.[242] A CPO may decide, however, not to take advantage of this relief, because the NFA may require changes to the CPO's disclosure document and require the CPO to redistribute

---

233.   CEA Rule 4.21(a), 17 C.F.R. § 4.21(a).

234.   CEA Rules 4.21 and 4.31, 17 C.F.R. §§ 4.21 and 4.31.

235.   CEA Rules 4.21(b) and 4.31(b), 17 C.F.R. §§ 4.21(b) and 4.31(b).

236.   The required content of a CPO's disclosure document is set forth in CEA Rules 4.24 and 4.25. *See* 17 C.F.R. §§ 4.24 and 4.25.

237.   NFA Compliance Rule 2-35(a)(1). *See* § 6.2.3, *supra*, regarding the plain English rule.

238.   CEA Rule 4.26(d); 17 C.F.R. § 4.26(d).

239.   *Id.*

240.   CEA Rule 4.26(a)(2); 17 C.F.R. § 4.26(a)(2).

241.   *See* § 5.3.2, *supra*.

242.   CEA Rule 4.8, 17 C.F.R. § 4.8.

the revised document to all prospective investors who received the original version and to offer rescission of any investment made on the basis of the original version. CEA Rule 4.12(b),[243] described below, provides similar relief from the twenty-one day requirement for certain commodity pools.

If the disclosure document becomes inaccurate or incomplete, the CPO must furnish a corrected document to existing clients and file it with the NFA within twenty-one-days after the CPO has reason to know of the deficiency.[244] The CPO may not accept funds from a prospective investor until the prospective investor has received the corrected disclosure document.[245]

2. Required Reports to Clients and Pool Participants

A CPO receives confirmations and month-end account statements for a hedge fund from the hedge fund's futures commission merchant, which conducts business as a commodity interest broker.[246] The futures commission merchant is required to send the confirmations only to the CPO, not to investors in the CPO's pool.[247] A CPO registered or required to be registered under the CEA that does not qualify for any of various exemptions from the CEA's reporting requirements described below must provide investors with account statements that include financial statements prepared in accordance with generally accepted accounting principles and any previously undisclosed material business dealings between the pool and its CPO, CTA, futures commission merchant or any of their respective principals.[248] These statements must be provided within thirty days of the end of each month, although in some cases such statements are required only quarterly, and may be less detailed.[249] In addition, the CPO must provide investors with annual reports, within ninety days after the end of each fiscal year of the pool, which include performance data and financial statements prepared in accordance with generally accepted accounting principles and audited by an independent public accountant.[250] CEA Rule 4.22 identifies the information that must be disclosed in the account statements and annual reports.[251]

If the annual report is sent to pool participants within forty-five days of the end of the pool's fiscal year, the CPO is not required to deliver an account statement for the final month of that fiscal year.[252] A copy of each annual report must be filed with the NFA.[253] If a CPO cannot distribute the report within ninety days from the end of the pool's fiscal year, the CPO may request an extension from the NFA.[254]

---

243.   *See* § 6.6.4.i, *infra.*
244.   CEA Rules 4.26(c) and 4.26(d)(2), 17 C.F.R. §§ 4.26(c) and 4.26(d)(2).
245.   CEA Rule 4.26(c); 17 C.F.R. § 4.26(c).
246.   CEA Rule 1.33, 17 C.F.R. § 1.33.
247.   CEA Rule 1.33(b)(4), 17 C.F.R. § 1.33(b)(4).
248.   CEA Rule 4.22(a), 17 C.F.R. § 4.22(a).
249.   *Id. See* § 6.6.4, *infra.*
250.   CEA Rule 4.22(c), 17 C.F.R. § 4.22(c).
251.   17 C.F.R. § 4.22.
252.   CEA Rule 4.22(b), 17 C.F.R. § 4.22(b)
253.   CEA Rule 4.22(c), 17 C.F.R. § 4.22(c); NFA Compliance Rule 2-13(c).
254.   NFA Compliance Rule 2-13(c).

3. Reports of Substantial Market Positions

CPOs must report to the CFTC positions in commodity interests that exceed thresholds set forth in the CEA regulations and must maintain books and records detailing the CPO's positions and transactions in such commodity interests.[255] CEA regulations also limit a CPO's speculative trading and the size of the positions that any CPO may hold.[256] Generally, all accounts controlled by a CPO are aggregated for reporting and position limit purposes.[257]

4. Exemptions from Certain Disclosure and Reporting Requirements

CEA regulations offer registered CPOs relief from some of the disclosure, recordkeeping and reporting requirements with respect to certain commodity pools that they manage. This relief applies only to qualifying pools, not to the CPO generally, and the CPO must file a notice with the NFA to claim the relief.

i. Rule 4.12(b) Pools

Under CEA Rule 4.12(b), a CPO to a qualifying commodity pool (a "4.12(b) Pool") is exempt from some disclosure, reporting and recordkeeping requirements that generally apply to CPOs.[258] To qualify as a 4.12(b) Pool, a pool must:

- be offered and sold in accordance with the registration provisions of the Securities Act or an exemption therefrom;
- generally and routinely engage in buying and selling securities and securities derived instruments;
- not enter into commodity future and commodity options contracts for which the aggregate initial margin and premiums exceed ten percent of the fair market value of the pool's assets (measured on an ongoing basis), after taking into account unrealized profits and unrealized losses on such contracts to which the pool is already a party, but excluding the in-the-money amount of options that are in-the-money at the time of purchase;[259]
- trade commodity interests in a manner solely incidental to its securities trading activities; and
- disclose to investors and prospective investors the foregoing restrictions before the pool starts trading commodity interests.[260]

---

255.   CEA Rules 15.00(b) and 15.03 and part 18, 17 C.F.R. §§ 15.00(b) and 15.03 and pt. 18.

256.   CEA Rules part 150, 17 C.F.R. pt. 150.

257.   CEA Rules 18.01, 150.4 and 150.5(g), 17 C.F.R. §§ 18.01, 150.4 and 150.5(g).

258.   17 C.F.R. § 4.12.

259.   CEA Rule 4.12(b)(1)(i)(c), 17 C.F.R. § 4.12(b)(i)(c). The "in-the-money amount" of an option is defined as "(1) with respect to a call option, the amount by which the value of the physical commodity or the contract for sale of a commodity for future delivery which is the subject of the option exceeds the strike price of the option; and (2) with respect to a put option, the amount by which the value of the physical commodity or the contract for sale of a commodity for future delivery which is the subject of the option is exceeded by the strike price of the option." CEA Rule 190.01(x), 17 C.F.R. § 190.01(x).

260.   CEA Rule 4.12, 17 C.F.R. § 4.12.

To claim this exemption, a CPO must file a notice with the NFA before the 4.12(b) Pool enters into its first transaction in commodity interests and include specified additional legends in the 4.12(b) Pool's disclosure document.[261]

The disclosure document for a 4.12(b) Pool is not required to include some of the cautionary legends or any of the past performance disclosure that is required in disclosure documents of other commodity pools.[262] This rule, however, does not relieve a CPO from the obligation to disclose all material information.[263] In addition, the disclosure document must be prepared in accordance with the Securities Act and Company Act or the exemptions from the registration requirements of those Acts on which the pool relies.[264] If the CPO of a 4.12(b) Pool chooses to provide performance data to prospective investors, that performance disclosure must comply with the applicable CEA regulations.

The CPO of a 4.12(b) Pool may solicit, accept and receive funds and other property from prospective investors (even investors that are not accredited investors under Securities Act Regulation D) immediately after filing the pool's disclosure document with the NFA and providing it to the prospective investors.[265] The utility of this exemption may be limited, however, if the NFA requires changes to the disclosure document, because the CPO may be required to provide the revised document to all prospective investors who received the original version and to offer rescission of any investment made on the basis of the original version.

The NFA generally does not review even the initial disclosure document of a fund-of-funds that is a 4.12(b) Pool and that invests in commodity interests only through other 4.12(b) Pools.[266]

CPOs of 4.12(b) Pools also are relieved from some of the CEA's reporting and recordkeeping requirements. For example, CPOs are required to send reports only quarterly, rather than monthly, to participants in their 4.12(b) Pools, and the reports need not be as detailed as reports to participants in other commodity pools.[267]

ii. Offshore Pools

A registered CPO that operates an offshore pool is exempt from all disclosure and reporting and some recordkeeping requirements of the CEA regulations with respect to that pool, if:

- the pool is organized and will remain and be operated outside the United States;
- the pool does not hold pool owner meetings or conduct administrative activities within the United States;
- no pool owner is a U.S. person (as described below);

---

261.   CEA Rules 4.12(b)(3) and 4.12(b)(5), 17 C.F.R. §§ 4.12(b)(3) and 4.12(b)(5).

262.   CEA Rule 4.12(b)(2), 17 C.F.R. § 4.12(b)(2).

263.   CEA Rules 4.12(b)(2)(i)(c) and 4.24(w), 17 C.F.R. §§ 4.12(b)(2)(i)(c) and 4.24(w).

264.   *See* §§ 6.2 and 6.3, *supra.*

265.   CEA Rule 4.8(b), 17 C.F.R. § 4.8(b).

266.   CFTC Advisory 95-44, 1999 CFTC Ltr. LEXIS 41 (Apr. 20, 1995).

267.   CEA Rule 4.12(b)(2)(ii), 17 C.F.R. § 4.12(b)(2)(ii).

- the pool does not contain any capital directly or indirectly contributed from sources within the United States; and
- the CPO, the pool and persons affiliated with them will not solicit participation in the pool by U.S. persons.[268]

For purposes of this exemption, the following persons are not considered to be U.S. persons:

- a natural person who is not a resident of the United States;
- a partnership, corporation or other entity (other than an entity organized principally for passive investment) organized under the laws of a non-U.S. jurisdiction and which has its principal place of business in a non-U.S. jurisdiction;
- an estate or trust, the income of which is not subject to U.S. income tax, regardless of source;
- any entity organized principally for passive investment, such as a pool, investment company or similar entity, if units of participation in the entity held by U.S. persons represent in the aggregate less than ten percent of the beneficial interest in the entity, and if the entity was not formed principally for the purpose of facilitating investment by U.S. persons in a pool with respect to which the operator is exempt from specified requirements of Part 4 of the CFTC's regulations by virtue of its participants being non-U.S. persons; and
- a pension plan for the employees, officers or principals of an entity organized and with its principal place of business outside the United States.[269]

To claim this exemption, a CPO must file a notice with the NFA before beginning to operate the offshore pool.[270]

iii. QEP Pools

Under CEA Rule 4.7, a CPO that is registered with the NFA is not required to provide any disclosure document and is granted significant relief from periodic reporting and recordkeeping requirements with respect to a pool (a "QEP Pool"), the interests of which are offered and sold only to "qualified eligible persons" in an offering that is exempt from registration under the Securities Act pursuant to Securities Act section 4(2) or Regulation S.[271] As discussed in sections 6.6.4.iii.a and 6.6.4.iii.b, below, there are two categories of qualified eligible persons: those who are required to meet certain portfolio holdings requirements, and those who are not.

To claim the relief available to a QEP Pool, the CPO must file a notice with the NFA.[272] Although the CEA and CEA regulations do not require the

---

268. CFTC Advisory 18-96, Comm. Fut. L. Rep (CCH) ¶ 26,659, 1996 CFTC Ltr. LEXIS 24 (Apr. 11, 1996).
269. *Id.*, n. 7.
270. *Id.*
271. CEA Rule 4.7(b), 17 C.F.R. § 4.7(b).
272. CEA Rule 4.7(d), 17 C.F.R. § 4.7(d).

CPO of a QEP Pool to provide a disclosure document to prospective investors, compliance with the requirements of the Securities Act, the Company Act and SEC rules thereunder necessitates complete and adequate disclosure.[273] The disclosure document, however, is not subject to review by the NFA and need not include any CFTC-mandated disclosure, except for a legend required by the CEA regulations.[274]

a. Qualified Eligible Persons Not Required to Meet Portfolio Requirements

A qualified eligible person is any person that the CPO reasonably believes, at the time the person purchases a pool participation or opens an account, is:

- a futures commission merchant registered under the CEA;
- a securities broker or dealer registered under the Exchange Act;
- a CPO or CTA that has been registered and active as such for two years or advises pools or accounts, as the case may be, that have total assets in excess of $5,000,000, or a principal of such a CPO or CTA;
- an investment adviser registered under the Advisers Act, or any state law, that has been so registered and active for two years or provides securities investment advice to accounts having total assets in excess of $5,000,000;
- a qualified purchaser, as defined in Company Act section 2(a)(51);[275]
- a knowledgeable employee, as defined in Company Act Rule 3c-5;[276]
- the CPO, CTA or investment adviser of the pool, any of their affiliates, any principal of the pool or any of the foregoing, certain employees of the pool or any of the foregoing, certain family members of any such principal or employee (provided the investment is made at the direction of such principal or employee), persons acquiring an interest in the pool through gift, bequest or divorce from such principal or employee and any company established by any of the foregoing;
- a trust not formed for the specific purpose of investing in the QEP Pool, if the trustee or other person authorized to make the investment decisions for the trust and each settlor of the trust are qualified eligible persons;
- certain charitable organizations if the trustee or other person authorized to make the investment decisions for the trust and the persons who established the organization are qualified eligible persons;
- any non-U.S. person (as defined above);[277] and
- any entity in which all of the owners or participants are qualified eligible persons, QEP Pools or accounts described in CEA Rule 4.5 in which all owners or participants are qualified eligible persons.[278]

---

273.   *See* § 6.2, *supra*.
274.   CEA Rule 4.7(b), 17 C.F.R. § 4.7(b).
275.   *See* § 3.3.2.i, *supra*.
276.   *See* § 3.2.2.iv, *supra*.
277.   CEA Rule 4.7(a)(1)(iv), 17 C.F.R. § 4.7(a)(1)(iv). *See* § 6.6.4.ii, *supra*.
278.   CEA Rule 4.7(a)(2), 17 C.F.R. § 4.7(a)(2).

b. Qualified Eligible Persons Required to Meet Portfolio Requirements

A person may also be a qualified eligible person if the CPO of the QEP Pool reasonably believes, at the time that such person invests in the QEP Pool, that the person is:

- an investment company registered under the Company Act or a business development company as defined in Company Act section 2(a)(48)[279] not formed for the specific purpose of investing in the QEP Pool;
- a bank as defined in Securities Act section 3(a)(2)[280] or a savings and loan association or other institution as defined in Securities Act section 3(a)(5)(A),[281] whether acting for its own account or the account of a qualified eligible person;
- an insurance company as defined in Securities Act section 2(13)[282] acting for its own account or the account of a qualified eligible person;
- a plan established and maintained by a state, its political subdivisions, or any agency or instrumentality of a state or its political subdivisions, for the benefit of its employees, if such plan has total assets in excess of $5,000,000;
- an employee benefit plan within the meaning of ERISA (a) if the investment decision is made by a plan fiduciary, as defined in ERISA section 3(21),[283] which is a bank, a savings and loan association, an insurance company, or a registered investment adviser, or (b) if the employee benefit plan has total assets in excess of $5,000,000, or (c) if the employee benefit plan is a self-directed plan and the investment decisions are made solely by persons that are qualified eligible persons;
- a private business development company as defined in Advisers Act section 202(a)(22);[284]
- an organization described in Tax Code section 501(c)(3),[285] with total assets in excess of $5,000,000;
- a corporation, Massachusetts or similar business trust, or partnership, limited liability company or similar business venture, other than a commodity pool, not formed for the specific purpose of acquiring the securities offered, with total assets in excess of $5,000,000;
- any natural person whose individual net worth, or joint net worth with that person's spouse, at the time of purchase exceeds $1,000,000;
- any natural person who had an individual income in excess of $200,000 in each of the two most recent years or joint income with that person's spouse in excess of $300,000 in each of those years and has a reasonable expectation of reaching the same income level in the current year;

---

279. 15 U.S.C. § 80a-2(a)(48).
280. 15 U.S.C. § 77c(a)(2)(C)(iii).
281. 15 U.S.C. § 77c(a)(5)(A).
282. 15 U.S.C. § 77b(a)(13).
283. 29 U.S.C. § 1002(21).
284. 15 U.S.C. § 80b-2(a)(22).
285. 26 U.S.C. § 501(c)(3).

- a pool, trust, insurance company separate account or bank collective trust, with total assets in excess of $5,000,000, not formed for the specific purpose of acquiring the securities offered, whose purchase is directed by a qualified eligible person; and
- except as provided for the governmental entities described above, if otherwise authorized by law to engage in such transactions, a governmental entity (including the United States, a state, or a non-U.S. government) or political subdivision thereof, or a multinational or supranational entity or an instrumentality, agency or department of any of the foregoing.[286]

The CPO of the QEP Pools must also, however, reasonably believe, at the time that the person invests in the QEP pool, that the person:

- owns securities of issuers not affiliated with the person (including pool participations) and other investments with an aggregate market value of at least $2,000,000;
- has had on deposit with a futures commission merchant, for the person's own account at any time during the six-month period preceding the date of sale to the person of a participation in a QEP Pool, at least $200,000 in commodity exchange-specified initial margin and option premiums for commodity interest transactions; or
- owns a portfolio comprising a combination of the funds or properties described in the two preceding clauses in which the sum of the funds or property includable under the first clause, expressed as percentage of the minimum amount required thereunder, and the amount of futures margin and option premiums includable under the second clause, expressed as a percentage of the minimum amount required thereunder, equals at least 100 percent (for example, a composite portfolio consisting of $1,000,000 in securities and other investments and $100,000 in exchange-specified initial margin and option premiums on commodity interests would satisfy this requirement).[287]

5. Anti-Fraud Provisions

CTAs and CPOs are subject to broad anti-fraud provisions under the CEA. Under CEA section 4o(1), it is unlawful for any CTA, CPO or associated person of a CPO or CTA: (A) to employ any device, scheme, or artifice to defraud any client or participant or prospective client or participant; or (B) to engage in any transaction, practice, or course of business which operates as a fraud or deceit upon any client or participant or prospective client or participant.[288] These provisions are similar to subsections (1) and (3) of Rule 10b-5.[289] At least one court has held

---

286.   CEA Rule 4.7(a)(3), 17 C.F.R. § 4.7(a)(3).
287.   CEA Rule 4.7(a)(1)(v), 17 C.F.R. § 4.7(a)(1)(v).
288.   CEA § 4o(1), 7 U.S.C. § 6o(1).
289.   *See* § 6.4.1, *supra*.

that section 4o(1)(A) includes the same scienter requirement as Rule 10b-5, while 4o(1)(B) does not.[290]

Unlike Exchange Act section 10(b) and Rule 10b-5, however, no private right of action is implied under CEA section 4o.[291] Instead, CEA section 22(a)(1) provides that a plaintiff has an express right of action in several circumstances, not all of which are applicable in the hedge fund context. Among other things, section 22(a)(1) provides that:

> Any person (other than a contract market, clearing organization of a contract market, licensed board of trade, or registered futures association) who violates this chapter or who willfully aids, abets, counsels, induces, or procures the commission of a violation of this chapter shall be liable for actual damages resulting from one or more of the transactions referred to in subparagraphs (A) through (D) of this paragraph and caused by such violation to any other person—
>
> (A) who received trading advice from such person for a fee;...
> (C) who purchased from or sold to such person or placed through such person an order for the purchase or sale of –...
>   (iii) an interest or participation in a commodity pool....[292]

In addition, the CEA includes a mechanism for a person to file a private claim with the CFTC to recover any damages that the person suffered as a result of a violation of any provision of the CEA by any person registered under the CEA, including any person registered as a CPO or CTA.[293]

§ 6.7 Privacy Regulations

Pursuant to the GLBA,[294] the FTC and SEC adopted regulations concerning the disclosure of non-public personal information by financial institutions. For this purpose, "financial institutions" include hedge funds and investment advisers. The SEC regulation, Regulation S-P,[295] applies to SEC-registered investment advisers; the FTC regulation[296] applies to SEC-Exempt Advisers. The two sets of regulations impose substantially similar disclosure obligations on investment advisers and hedge funds.

---

290. *Messer v. E.F. Hutton & Co.*, 847 F.2d 673, 677 (11th Cir. 1988). *But see Commodities Futures Trading Commission v. Savage*, 611 F.2d 270 (9th Cir. 1979), holding that neither subsection of § 4o(1) requires a showing of scienter, if the defendant's action was intentional.
291. CEA § 22(a)(2), 7 U.S.C. § 25(a)(2).
292. 7 U.S.C. § 25(a)(1).
293. CEA § 14, 7 U.S.C. § 18.
294. 15 U.S.C. §§ 6801 *et seq.*
295. 17 C.F.R. pt. 248.
296. 16 C.F.R. pt. 313.

These FTC and SEC regulations require each investment adviser or hedge fund to deliver to each new customer[297] an initial notice describing in detail:

- the categories of non-public personal information that the investment adviser or hedge fund collects;
- the categories of such information that the investment adviser or hedge fund may disclose to affiliates and non-affiliated third parties;
- the categories of affiliates and third parties to whom the investment adviser or hedge fund might disclose the information;
- the policies and practices of the investment adviser or hedge fund with respect to protecting confidential information;
- if the investment adviser or hedge fund discloses non-public personal information about former customers, the categories of such information that the investment adviser or hedge fund discloses and the categories of affiliates and third parties to whom the investment adviser or hedge fund might disclose that information; and
- if the investment adviser or hedge fund discloses non-public personal information about its customers to nonaffiliated third parties, with certain exceptions, additional information about the disclosures and an election for the consumer to "opt-out" of the disclosure.[298]

A "customer" of an investment adviser or a hedge fund is a consumer with whom the investment adviser or hedge fund enters into a relationship or agreement to provide financial services, including investment advisory services.[299] A "consumer" is an individual who applies for financial services, including investment advisory services, from an investment adviser or a hedge fund.[300]

Thereafter, the investment adviser or hedge fund must deliver a notice containing the same disclosure items to each existing customer at least once during each twelve-month period.[301] The investment adviser or hedge fund may define the twelve-month period, but must apply it consistently.[302] After providing a notice to a customer, the investment adviser or hedge fund may not disclose any non-public personal information of that customer to an affiliate or a third party other than as described in the notice, unless a new notice describing the proposed disclosure is given to the customer.[303] The notice thus establishes the boundaries of disclosure by the investment adviser or hedge fund and the persons to whom the investment adviser or hedge fund may disclose it.

An investment adviser or hedge fund that does not disclose non-public personal information to affiliates or third parties (except as discussed in the following

---

297.   Regulation S-P Rule 248.4, 17 C.F.R. § 248.4; FTC Privacy Rule 313.4, 16 C.F.R. § 313.4.
298.   Regulation S-P Rule 248.6, 17 C.F.R. § 248.6; FTC Privacy Rule 313.6, 16 C.F.R. § 313.6.
299.   Regulation S-P Rule 248.3(g), (j) and (k), 17 C.F.R. §§ 248.3(g), (j) and (k); FTC Privacy Rules 313.3(e), (h) and (i), 16 C.F.R. §§ 313(e), (h) and (i).
300.   Regulation S-P Rule 248.3(g), 17 C.F.R. § 248.3(g); FTC Privacy Rule 313(e), 16 C.F.R. § 313(e).
301.   Regulation S-P Rule 248.5, 17 C.F.R. § 248.5; FTC Privacy Rule 313.5, 16 C.F.R. § 313.5.
302.   *Id.*
303.   Regulation S-P Rule 248.10(a)(1)(i), 17 C.F.R. § 248.10(a)(1)(i); FTC Privacy Rule 313.10(a)(1)(i), 16 C.F.R. § 313.10(a)(1)(i).

paragraph) may use a fairly simple form of notice to comply with the privacy regulations. The SEC and the FTC have published examples of acceptable notices.[304]

The privacy regulations identify disclosures that do not need to be described in the notices. First, providing information that is necessary to effect, administer or enforce a transaction that a consumer requests or authorizes is not considered disclosing the information.[305] Second, releasing information to various parties involved in the business of the investment adviser or hedge fund is specifically permitted and is not subject to the notice requirements.[306] This includes disclosures to the attorneys, accountants and auditors of the investment adviser or hedge fund. In addition, disclosures required by law, such as disclosures to regulatory agencies, are permitted.[307] Finally, disclosures expressly requested by the customer (such as to a mortgage banker in connection with a loan application) are not subject to the notice requirements.[308] An investment adviser or hedge fund that releases non-public personal information about its customers only within the foregoing exceptions may state in its initial and annual notices to customers that it does not release non-public personal information except as permitted by law.[309]

If an investment adviser or hedge fund wants to disclose to non-affiliated third parties non-public personal information about customers outside of the above exceptions, the investment adviser or hedge fund must deliver more complicated disclosure notices to its customers and provide a reasonable means for the customer to opt out of having personal information disclosed.[310]

Notices must also be provided to consumers who have given the investment adviser or hedge fund non-public personal information but have not established a customer relationship with the investment adviser or hedge fund, if the investment adviser or hedge fund will disclose to non-affiliated third parties non-public personal information about those consumers, other than the excepted disclosures described above.[311] These notices must be provided before the non-public personal information is disclosed to the third party and must permit the consumer to opt out.[312]

The opt-out requirements do not apply when an investment adviser or hedge fund shares non-public personal information about customers or consumers with

---

304. Appendix A to Regulation S-P, 17 C.F.R. pt. 248, Appendix A; Appendix A to FTC Privacy Rule, 16 C.F.R. pt. 313, Appendix A.

305. Regulation S-P Rule 248.14, 17 C.F.R. § 248.14; FTC Privacy Rule 313.14, 16 C.F.R. § 313.14.

306. Regulation S-P Rule 248.15(a)(3), 17 C.F.R. § 248.15(a)(3); FTC Privacy Rule 313.15(a)(3), 16 C.F.R. § 313.15(a)(3).

307. Regulation S-P Rule 248.15(a)(7), 17 C.F.R. § 248.15(a)(7); FTC Privacy Rule 313.15(a)(7), 16 C.F.R. § 313.15(a)(7).

308. Regulation S-P Rule 248.15(a)(1), 17 C.F.R. § 248.15(a)(1); FTC Privacy Rule 313.15(a)(1), 16 C.F.R. § 313.15(a)(1).

309. Regulation S-P Rule 248.6(c)(5), 17 C.F.R. § 248.6(c)(5); FTC Privacy Rule 313.6(c)(5), 16 C.F.R. § 313.6(c)(5).

310. Regulation S-P Rules 248.7 and 248.10(a), 17 C.F.R. §§ 248.7 and 248.10(a); FTC Privacy Rules 313.7 and 313.10(a), 16 C.F.R. §§ 313.7 and 313.10(a).

311. Regulation S-P Rule 248.4, 17 C.F.R. § 248.4; FTC Privacy Rule 313.4, 16 C.F.R. § 313.4.

312. Regulation S-P Rules 248.4(a)(2) and 248.10(a)(1), 17 C.F.R. §§ 248.4(a)(2) and 248.10(a)(1); FTC Privacy Rules 313.4(a)(2) and 313.10(a)(1), 16 C.F.R. §§ 313.4(a)(2) and 313.10(a)(1).

a non–affiliated third party who performs services for the investment adviser or hedge fund or functions on its behalf, such as an outside consultant, solicitor or marketer, if (a) the investment adviser or hedge fund discloses in its initial and annual notices that it makes such disclosures (detailing categories of personal information disclosed as well as the types of third parties that receive the information), and (b) the agreement with the third party prohibits the third party from disclosing the information.[313]

If an investment adviser is affiliated with another entity or has associated persons who are affiliated with another entity, such as a broker that is a member of the NASD, the investment adviser may share information with that affiliate, pursuant to either legal requirements or business arrangements. For example, if a person associated with the investment adviser is a registered representative of a broker, NASD rules require the broker to supervise the activities of that person.[314] The notices provided by an investment adviser that is affiliated with another entity may need to include additional disclosure about the sharing of information with the affiliate.

---

313.   Regulation S-P Rule 248.13, 17 C.F.R. § 248.13; FTC Privacy Rule 313.13, 16 C.F.R. § 313.13.
314.   NASD Conduct Rule 3010.

CHAPTER 7

State Blue Sky Regulation

§ 7.1 Introduction

Sales of securities, including limited partner or member interests in a hedge fund, are regulated by state securities laws, often called "Blue Sky" laws, in addition to the Securities Act and the SEC rules thereunder.[1] A state's securities laws apply to offers and sales of securities within the state, and may require the registration of the persons who make those offers and sales, such as brokers and agents.

Before the National Securities Markets Improvement Act of 1996 ("NSMIA")[2] was enacted, state securities laws typically required a hedge fund to register or qualify its securities with a state securities regulatory authority before the securities could be offered or sold in that state. Most states provided exemptions from registration or qualification similar to those available under the Securities Act and Exchange Act.[3] If a hedge fund failed to comply with the requirements of such an exemption in a state, however, every purchaser of interests in that state could have a right of rescission against the hedge fund and its general partner and other controlling persons.

In enacting NSMIA, Congress intended to create uniformity among the various state Blue Sky laws and the Securities Act.[4] NSMIA, among other things, preempts state law in connection with the offer and sale of certain types of securities and securities sold in certain types of transactions. Most importantly for hedge funds, NSMIA prohibits states from requiring the registration or qualification of securities that are exempt from registration under the Securities Act pursuant to any rule or regulation issued by the SEC under Securities Act section 4(2), including Rule 506 of Regulation D.[5] States may, however, require issuers to make

---

1. *See* Chapter 5, *supra.*
2. Pub. L. 104–290, Oct. 11, 1996, 110 Stat. 3416 (codified in scattered sections of 15 U.S.C.).
3. *See* Chapter 5, *supra,* and Chapter 10, *infra.*
4. Conference Report on the National Securities Markets Improvement Act of 1996, House Report No. 104–864 at 39 (Sep. 28, 1996).
5. Securities Act § 18(b)(4)(D), 15 U.S.C. § 77r(b)(4)(D). *See* § 5.3.2, *supra*, regarding Rule 506 of Regulation D.

filings concerning the securities they sell.[6] In addition, NSMIA does not preempt state registration of brokers and other persons who sell securities. Accordingly, hedge funds still must comply with Blue Sky laws that require registration of those persons.

On August 25, 1956, the National Conference of Commissioners on Uniform State Laws adopted the Uniform Securities Act (the "1956 Uniform Securities Act") "to promote, insofar as may be practicable, uniformity in legislation having for its purpose the regulation of commerce of securities or the suppression of fraud therein, and the procedure thereunder."[7] The 1956 Uniform Securities Act has been adopted or substantially adopted (with modifications) in the following jurisdictions:[8]

Alabama	Alaska	Arkansas	Colorado
Connecticut	Delaware	District of Columbia	Guam
Hawaii	Indiana	Kentucky	Maryland
Massachusetts	Michigan	Minnesota	Mississippi
Nebraska	Nevada	New Hampshire	New Jersey
New Mexico	North Carolina	Oregon	Pennsylvania
Puerto Rico	Rhode Island	South Carolina	Utah
Virginia	Washington	West Virginia	Wisconsin
Wyoming			

In 2002, the National Conference of Commissioners on Uniform State Laws adopted a new uniform securities act, the Uniform Securities Act (2002) (the "2002 Uniform Securities Act").[9] The 2002 Uniform Securities Act is intended principally to reconcile federal and state securities laws in view of NSMIA.[10] The 2002 Uniform Securities Act has been adopted in six states and the U.S. Virgin Islands and has been proposed in five states.[11]

Several states, including California, Florida, Illinois, New York, Ohio and Texas, have not adopted either version of the Uniform Securities Act, but instead rely on their own securities laws.[12] This chapter does not review the laws of all states. Instead, it discusses the 1956 Uniform Securities Act, which is or approximates the law of thirty-six states, the 2002 Uniform Securities Act and the securities laws of California and New York.[13]

---

6. Securities Act § 18(c)(2), 15 U.S.C. § 77r(c)(2).
7. Official Comment to the 1956 Uniform Securities Act, 1 Blue Sky Law Rptr. (CCH) ¶5501.01.
8. Prefatory Note to the 1956 Uniform Securities Act, 1 Blue Sky Law Rptr. (CCH) ¶5500.
9. 1 Blue Sky Law Rptr. (CCH) ¶6431.
10. 1 Blue Sky Law Rptr. (CCH) ¶5600.
11. *See* "A Few Facts About the Uniform Securities Act (2002)," available at the website of the National Conference of Commissioners on Uniform State Laws, www.nccusl.org/Update/uniformact_factsheets/uniformacts-fs-usa.asp. *See* § 7.4, *infra.*
12. 1 Blue Sky Law Rptr. (CCH) ¶6431.
13. Cal. Corp. Code §§ 25000 *et seq.*; N.Y. Gen. Bus. Law §§ 352 *et seq.*

§ 7.2 Pre-NSMIA State Blue Sky Regulation

1. 1956 Uniform Securities Act

The 1956 Uniform Securities Act requires securities offered and sold in a state to be registered with that state's securities regulatory authority.[14] It also requires registration of persons that offer and sell such securities within that state.[15]

i. Offers and Sales of Securities within a State

The 1956 Uniform Securities Act registration requirements, both for securities and for brokers, apply only if there is an offer or sale of a security within the state.[16] An "offer" includes every attempt to offer to dispose of, or solicitation of an offer to buy, a security or an interest in a security for value.[17] A "sale" includes every contract of sale of, contract to sell, or disposition of a security or interest in a security for value.[18] These definitions are substantially the same as the definitions of offer and sale in the Securities Act.[19] The 1956 Uniform Securities Act definition of "security" is also substantially the same as the definition of that term in the Securities Act.[20]

The securities and broker registration requirements of the 1956 Uniform Securities Act apply when an offer to sell is made in the state or an offer to buy is made and accepted in the state.[21] An offer to sell a security is made in a state, whether or not either party is present in the state at the time of the offer, if the offer originates from that state or is directed by the offeror to that state and is received at the place to which it is directed (or at any post office in that state if the offer is made by mail).[22] An offer to sell is accepted in a state if acceptance is communicated to the offeror in that state and has not previously been communicated to the offeror, orally or in writing, outside that state.[23] In addition, acceptance is communicated to an offeror in a state, whether or not either party is present in that state at the time of the communication, if the offeree directs it to the offeror in that state reasonably believing that the offeror is in that state and it is received at the place to which it is directed (or at any post office in that state in the case of a mailed acceptance).[24] The state in which an individual is a resident or the state in which an entity is formed

---

14.   1956 Uniform Securities Act § 301, 1 Blue Sky Law Rptr. (CCH) ¶ 5531.
15.   1956 Uniform Securities Act § 201(a), 1 Blue Sky Law Rptr. (CCH) ¶ 5521.
16.   1956 Uniform Securities Act §§ 301 and 401(c), 1 Blue Sky Law Rptr. (CCH) ¶¶ 5531 and 5541.
17.   1956 Uniform Securities Act § 401(j)(2), 1 Blue Sky Law Rptr. ¶ 5541.
18.   1956 Uniform Securities Act § 401(j)(1), 1 Blue Sky Law Rptr. ¶ 5541.
19.   *See* Securities Act § 2(a)(3), 15 U.S.C. § 77b(2)(a)(3).
20.   *See* § 5.1, note 2, *supra*. *Compare* 1956 Uniform Securities Act § 401(i), 1 Blue Sky Law Rptr. (CCH) ¶ 5541, *with* Securities Act § 2(a)(1), 15 U.S.C. § 77b(2)(a)(1).
21.   1956 Uniform Securities Act § 414(a), 1 Blue Sky Law Rptr. (CCH) ¶ 5554.
22.   1956 Uniform Securities Act § 414(c), 1 Blue Sky Law Rptr. (CCH) ¶ 5554.
23.   1956 Uniform Securities Act § 414(d), 1 Blue Sky Law Rptr. (CCH) ¶ 5554.
24.   *Id.*

or organized is not relevant under these definitions for determining which state securities laws apply.[25]

ii. Securities Registration under the 1956 Uniform Securities Act

a. Securities Registration Requirements

The 1956 Uniform Securities Act requires the registration in a state of any security offered or sold within that state.[26] Under the 1956 Uniform Securities Act, registration may be accomplished in one of three ways: by coordination, by filing or by qualification.[27] Registration by coordination is available only if the issuer has filed a registration statement with the SEC in connection with the same offering.[28] Registration by filing is only available for issuers that have securities registered under the Securities Act and meet other specified requirements.[29] Neither of these forms of registration is available for use by a hedge fund, because of the prohibition on public offerings by hedge funds.[30]

Registration by qualification is available for any issuer to register any security.[31] Accordingly, if a hedge fund is required to register with a state securities regulatory authority, it ordinarily would register by qualification. To register by qualification, the issuer must file a registration statement.[32] The registration statement must include detailed disclosure similar to that required in a Form S–1 registration statement filed with the SEC,[33] including:[34]

- identifying information about the issuer and its subsidiaries, including name, form and jurisdiction of organization, address, general character and organization of its business, a description of its physical properties and equipment, and a statement of the general competitive conditions in the industry in which it is or will be engaged;
- information about every director and officer of the issuer (or person occupying a similar status or performing similar duties), any person who beneficially owns ten percent or more of the outstanding shares of any class of the issuer's securities and any promoter of the issuer (if the issuer was organized in the past three years), including name, address, principal occupation for the prior five years, the amount of securities of the issuer held by him or her as of a date within thirty days of filing the registration statement, the amount

---

25.   1956 Uniform Securities Act § 414, 1 Blue Sky Law Rptr. (CCH) ¶ 5554.

26.   1956 Uniform Securities Act § 301, 1 Blue Sky Law Rptr. (CCH) ¶ 5531.

27.   1956 Uniform Securities Act §§ 302, 303 and 304, 1 Blue Sky Law Rptr. (CCH) ¶¶ 5532, 5533 and 5534.

28.   1956 Uniform Securities Act § 303(a), 1 Blue Sky Law Rptr. (CCH) ¶ 5533.

29.   1956 Uniform Securities Act § 302(a), 1 Blue Sky Law Rptr. (CCH) ¶ 5532.

30.   *See* §§ 3.2.5 and 3.3.1, *supra.*

31.   1956 Uniform Securities Act § 304(a), 1 Blue Sky Law Rptr. (CCH) ¶ 5534.

32.   1956 Uniform Securities Act § 304(b), 1 Blue Sky Law Rptr. (CCH) ¶ 5534.

33.   *See* § 6.2.1.iii, *supra*, regarding the information required by Form S–1.

34.   1956 Uniform Securities Act § 304(b), 1 Blue Sky Law Rptr. (CCH) ¶ 5534.

of the securities covered by the registration statement for which he or she has indicated he or she intends to subscribe, a description of any material interest in any material transaction with the issuer or any of its significant subsidiaries effected within the past three years or proposed to be effected, and the remuneration paid during the prior twelve months and estimated to be paid during the next twelve months to all such persons in the aggregate;

- the capitalization and long term debt (on both a current and a pro forma basis) of the issuer and any significant subsidiary, including a description of each security outstanding or being registered or otherwise offered, and a statement of the amount and kind of consideration for which the issuer or any subsidiary has issued any of its securities within the past two years or is obligated to issue any of its securities;

- the kind and amount of securities to be offered, the proposed offering price or the method by which it is to be computed, any variation therefrom at which any proportion of the offering is to be made to any person or class of persons other than the underwriters (specifying any such person or class), the basis on which the offering is to be made if other than for cash, the estimated aggregate underwriting and selling discounts or commissions and finders' fees (including securities, contracts or anything else of value to accrue to the underwriters or finders in connection with the offering), the estimated amounts of other selling expenses, including legal and accounting charges, the name and address of every underwriter and every recipient of a finder's fees, a copy of any underwriting or selling group agreement pursuant to which the distribution is to be made (or the proposed form of any such agreement whose terms have not been determined), and a description of the plan of distribution of any securities that are to be offered otherwise than through an underwriter;

- the estimated cash proceeds to be received by the issuer from the offering, the purposes for which the proceeds are to be used by the issuer, the amount to be used for each purpose, the order or priority in which the proceeds will be used for the purposes stated, the sources of any such funds, and if any part of the proceeds is to be used to acquire any property other than in the ordinary course of business, the names and addresses of the vendors, the purchase price, the names of any persons who have received commissions, and any other expense in connection with the acquisition (including the cost of borrowing money to finance the acquisition);

- a description of any stock options or other security options outstanding or to be created in connection with the offering;

- the dates of, parties to and general effect of every management or other material contract made or to be made other than in the ordinary course of business if it is to be performed as a whole or in part at or after the filing of the registration statement or if it was made within the past two years, together with a copy of every such contract;

- a description of any pending litigation or proceeding to which the issuer is a party and that materially affects its business or assets (including any such litigation or proceeding known to be contemplated by governmental authorities);

- a copy of any prospectus, pamphlet, circular, form letter, advertisement or other sales literature intended as of the effective date to be used in connection with the offering;
- a specimen or copy of the security being registered, a copy of the issuer's articles of incorporation and by-laws or their substantial equivalents, and a copy of any indenture or other instrument covering the security to be registered;
- a signed or conformed copy of an opinion of counsel as to the legality of the security being registered, stating whether the security when sold will be legally issued, fully paid and non-assessable and, if it is a debt security, whether it will be a binding obligation of the issuer;
- the written consent of any accountant, appraiser or other person whose profession gives authority to a statement made by him or her, if any such person is named as having prepared or certified a report or valuation (other than a public and official document or statement) that is used in connection with the registration statement;
- a balance sheet of the issuer as of a date within four months before the filing of the registration statement, a profit and loss statement and analysis of surplus for each of the three fiscal years preceding the date of the balance sheet and for any period between the close of the last fiscal year and the date of the balance sheet, or for the period of the issuer's and any predecessor's existence if less than three years, and if any part of the proceeds of the offering is to be applied to the purchase of any business, the same financial statements as would be required if that business were the registrant; and
- such additional information as the relevant state regulatory authority requires by rule or order.

b. Limited Offering Exemption from Securities Registration Requirements

Similarly to the Securities Act, the 1956 Uniform Securities Act includes several exemptions from its securities registration requirements.[35] Before NSMIA was adopted, the exemption under the 1956 Uniform Securities Act on which a hedge fund typically would rely is the exemption provided by 1956 Uniform Securities Act section 402(b)(9), which exempts

> any transaction pursuant to an offer directed by the offeror to not more than ten persons (other than those designated in paragraph 8) in this state during any period of twelve consecutive months, whether or not the offeror or any of the offerees is then present in this state, if (A) the seller reasonably believes that all the buyers in this state (other than those designated in paragraph 8) are purchasing for investment, and (B) no commission or other remuneration is paid or given directly or indirectly for soliciting any prospective buyer in this

---

35. *See* 1956 Uniform Securities Act § 402, 1 Blue Sky Law Rptr. (CCH) ¶ 5542.

state (other than those designated in paragraph 8); but the [applicable state regulatory authority] may by rule or order, as to any security or transaction or any type of security or transaction, withdraw or further condition this exemption, or increase or decrease the number of offerees permitted, or waive the conditions in Clauses (A) and (B) with or without the substitution of a limitation on remuneration.[36]

Paragraph 8 of 1956 Uniform Securities Act section 402(b) exempts any offer or sale of securities to "a bank, savings institution, trust company, insurance company, investment company as defined in the [Company Act], pension or profit sharing trust, or other financial institution or institutional buyer, or to a broker–dealer, whether the purchaser is acting for itself or in some fiduciary capacity."[37] Accordingly, a U.S. or offshore hedge fund offering its securities under the exemption provided by 1956 Uniform Securities Act section 402(b)(9) is not required to include such entities when determining the number of investors to which it has offered securities in a particular state.

The Official Code Comments on the 1956 Uniform Securities Act state that, although a written representation concerning an investor's investment intent is not required, "it would be prudent on the part of the seller to obtain something in writing."[38] An investor who acquires an interest in a U.S. or offshore hedge fund can later change his mind and resell the interest without violating section 402(b)(9).[39] The shorter the interval between purchase and sale, however, the more difficult it will be for the investor to prove a bona fide intent to invest at the time of investment.[40]

Some states have modified section 402(b)(9) to include an express prohibition on advertising and general solicitation, similar to that in Regulation D under the Securities Act.[41] In addition, some states have increased the number of offerees to which an issuer may offer securities in an exempt offering.[42]

iii. Broker-Dealer and Agent Registration under the 1956 Uniform Securities Act

The 1956 Uniform Securities Act prohibits a person from transacting business in a state as a broker–dealer or an agent unless the person is registered as such under the 1956 Uniform Securities Act.[43] In addition, the 1956 Uniform Securities Act

---

36. 1956 Uniform Securities Act § 402(b)(9), 1 Blue Sky Law Rptr. (CCH) ¶ 5542.

37. 1956 Uniform Securities Act § 402(b)(8), 1 Blue Sky Law Rptr. (CCH) ¶ 5542.

38. Official Comment to 1956 Uniform Securities Act § 402(b)(9), 1 Blue Sky Law Rptr. (CCH) ¶ 5542.01.

39. *Id.*

40. *Id.*

41. *See, e.g.*, Ala. Code § 8-6-11(9)(c); Ga. Code Ann. § 10-5-9(13)(B); Haw. Rev. Stat. § 485-6(9)(D); Neb. Rev. Stat. § 8-1111(9)(d); Nev. Rev. Stat. § 90.530(11)(b).

42. *See, e.g.*, Ark. Code Ann. § 23-42-504(a)(9)(A) (thirty-five offerees); Fla. Stat. § 517.061(11)(a)(1) (thirty-five offerees); Ga. Code Ann. § 10-5-9(13)(A) (fifteen offerees); Haw. Rev. Stat. § 485-6(9)(A) (twenty-five offerees); Neb. Rev. Stat. § 8-1111(9) (fifteen offerees); Nev. Rev. Stat. § 90.530(11)(a) (twenty-five offerees); N.C. Gen. Stat. § 78A-17(9) (twenty-five offerees).

43. 1956 Uniform Securities Act § 201(a), 1 Blue Sky Law Rptr. (CCH) ¶ 5521.

prohibits an issuer or a broker-dealer from employing an agent unless the agent is registered.[44]

a. Definitions of Broker-Dealer, Issuer and Agent

A "broker-dealer" under the 1956 Uniform Securities Act is "any person engaged in the business of effecting transactions in securities for the account of others or for his own account."[45] The definition of "broker-dealer" excludes:

> (1) an agent, (2) an issuer, (3) a bank, savings institution, or trust company, or (4) a person who has no place of business in this state if (A) he effects transactions in this state exclusively with or through (i) the issuers of the securities involved in the transactions, (ii) other broker-dealers, or (iii) banks, savings institutions, trust companies, insurance companies, investment companies as defined in the [Company Act], pension or profit-sharing trusts, or other financial institutions or institutional buyers, whether acting for themselves or as trustees, or (B) during any period of twelve consecutive months he does not direct more than fifteen offers to sell or buy into this state in any manner to persons other than those specified in clause (A), whether or not the offeror or any of the offerees is then present in this state.[46]

An "issuer" is "any person who issues or proposes to issue any security...."[47] U.S. and offshore hedge funds are "issuers" because they issue limited partner interests and shares, respectively. A few exceptions from the definition of "issuer" are included in 1956 Uniform Securities Act section 401(g), but none applies to a U.S. or offshore hedge fund.[48] A U.S. or offshore hedge fund is thus an issuer and as such is excluded from the definition of "broker-dealer."

An "agent" under the 1956 Uniform Securities Act is "any individual other than a broker-dealer who represents a broker-dealer or issuer in effecting or attempting to effect purchases or sales of securities."[49] The definition of "agent" excludes an individual representing an issuer effecting a transaction exempted under 1956 Uniform Securities Act section 402(b), which includes the limited offering exemption described above,[50] but not all states have adopted this exemption. In addition, "a partner, officer, or director of a broker-dealer or issuer, or a person occupying a similar status or performing similar functions, is an agent only if he otherwise comes within the definition."[51] Such persons are not required to register as agents, and information about them is included in a broker-dealer's application for registration.[52] Accordingly, the officers of a general partner of a hedge fund

---

44.   1956 Uniform Securities Act § 201(b), 1 Blue Sky Law Rptr. (CCH) ¶ 5521.
45.   1956 Uniform Securities Act § 401(c), 1 Blue Sky Law Rptr. (CCH) ¶ 5541.
46.   *Id.*
47.   1956 Uniform Securities Act § 401(g), 1 Blue Sky Law Rptr. (CCH) ¶ 5541.
48.   *Id.*
49.   1956 Uniform Securities Act § 401(b), 1 Blue Sky Law Rptr. (CCH) ¶ 5541.
50.   *Id. See* § 7.2.1.ii.b, *supra.*
51.   1956 Uniform Securities Act § 401(b), 1 Blue Sky Law Rptr. (CCH) ¶ 5541.
52.   *See* § 7.2.1.iii.b, *infra.*

typically are exempt from agent registration, unless they receive compensation directly tied to their solicitation activities.

b. Broker-Dealer and Agent Registration Process

Under the 1956 Uniform Securities Act, a broker-dealer or an agent must register by filing an application and consent to service of process with the appropriate state regulatory authority.[53] The application must contain any information that the state regulatory authority requires by rule concerning such matters as:

- The applicant's form and place of organization;
- The applicant's proposed method of doing business;
- The qualifications and business history of the applicant and any of its partners, officers or directors, any person occupying a similar status or performing similar functions, or any person directly or indirectly controlling the broker-dealer;
- Any injunction or administrative order or conviction of a misdemeanor involving a security or any aspect of the securities business and any conviction of a felony; and
- The applicant's financial condition and history.[54]

The appropriate state regulatory authority also may require the broker-dealer to publish an announcement of its application for registration in one or more specified newspapers.[55] The registration typically becomes effective thirty days after filing of an application, unless a denial order is in effect or a proceeding for a denial order has commenced.[56] The applicant also must pay a filing fee specified by the state.[57]

The 1956 Uniform Securities Act gives the appropriate state regulatory authority the authority to establish minimum capital requirements for broker-dealers or to require registered broker-dealers (other than broker-dealers whose net capital exceeds $25,000) to post surety bonds of up to $10,000.[58]

Because a broker-dealer's registration application must include information about its partners, officers, directors and similarly situated persons, such persons need not register as agents.[59] Instead, the broker-dealer's registration "automatically constitutes registration of any agent who is a partner, officer or director."[60] Consequently, the state regulatory authority may "institute a proceeding to deny or revoke the registration of a particular partner, officer or director without disturbing the status of the firm. At the same time, the disqualification of a director, officer or partner, as distinct from an ordinary agent, is also a basis for proceeding against the

---

53.   1956 Uniform Securities Act § 202(a), 1 Blue Sky Law Rptr. (CCH) ¶ 5522.

54.   *Id.*

55.   *Id.*

56.   *Id.*

57.   1956 Uniform Securities Act § 202(b), 1 Blue Sky Law Rptr. (CCH) ¶ 5522.

58.   1956 Uniform Securities Act § 202(c) and (d), 1 Blue Sky Law Rptr. (CCH) ¶ 5522.

59.   *See* § 7.2.1.iii.a, *supra.*

60.   Official Code Comment to 1956 Uniform Securities Act § 202(a), 1 Blue Sky Law Rptr. (CCH) ¶ 5522.01.

firm's registration if the [state securities administrator] finds it in the public interest to do so."[61]

c. Post-Registration Requirements

Under the 1956 Uniform Securities Act, a registered broker–dealer must make and keep "such accounts, correspondence, memoranda, papers, books, and other records as the [Administrator] by rule prescribes" for at least three years, unless the state regulatory authority otherwise prescribes.[62] The model rules proposed under the 1956 Uniform Securities Act require that a broker–dealer registered or required to be registered under the 1956 Uniform Securities Act make, maintain and preserve books and records in compliance with SEC rules 17a-3, 17a-4, 15c2-6 and 15c2-11.[63] In addition, a registered broker–dealer must file such financial reports as the state regulatory authority may require by rule.[64] A registered broker–dealer also must amend any document filed with the state regulatory authority promptly after it becomes inaccurate or incomplete in any material respect.[65] The state regulatory authority has the right to conduct periodic, special or other examinations of the books and records required to be maintained by a registered broker–dealer.[66]

d. Denial, Revocation or Suspension of Registration

Under the 1956 Uniform Securities Act, a state regulatory authority may deny a broker–dealer's application for registration or suspend or revoke such a registration on finding that doing so is in the public interest and that the applicant or registrant, any partner, officer, director or person occupying a similar position or performing a similar function for the applicant or registrant, or any person directly or indirectly controlling the applicant or registrant:

- Has filed a registration application that, as of its effective date, was incomplete in any material respect or contained any statement that was, in light of the circumstances under which it was made, false or misleading with respect to any material fact;
- Has willfully violated or willfully failed to comply with any provision of the 1956 Uniform Securities Act or a predecessor act or any order under the 1956 Uniform Securities Act or a predecessor act;
- Has been convicted, within the past ten years, of any misdemeanor involving a security or any aspect of the securities business or any felony;
- Is permanently or temporarily enjoined by any court of competent jurisdiction from engaging in or continuing any conduct or practice involving any aspect of the securities business;

---

61.   *Id.*
62.   1956 Uniform Securities Act § 203(a), 1 Blue Sky Law Rptr. (CCH) ¶ 5523.
63.   1998 NASAA Amended Rules under the Uniform Securities Act, rule 203(a)-1(a), 1 Blue Sky Law Rptr. (CCH) ¶ 5523.60, referring to 17 C.F.R. §§ 240.17a-3, 240.17a-4, 240.15c2-6 and 240.15c2-11.
64.   1956 Uniform Securities Act § 203(b), 1 Blue Sky Law Rptr. (CCH) ¶ 5523.
65.   1956 Uniform Securities Act § 203(c), 1 Blue Sky Law Rptr. (CCH) ¶ 5523.
66.   1956 Uniform Securities Act § 203(d), 1 Blue Sky Law Rptr. (CCH) ¶ 5523.

- Is the subject of an order of the state regulatory authority denying, suspending or revoking registration as a broker-dealer, agent or investment adviser;
- Was within the past five years determined by a securities or commodities agency or administrator of another state or a court to have violated the Securities Act, the Exchange Act, the Company Act, the Advisers Act, the CEA, or the securities or commodities law of any other state;
- Has engaged in dishonest or unethical practices in the securities business;
- Is insolvent, either in the sense that liabilities exceed assets or in the sense that obligations cannot be met as they mature;
- Is not qualified on the basis of such factors as training, experience and knowledge of the securities business, except that the state regulatory authority may not enter an order on the basis of the lack of qualification of any person other than the applicant or registrant if the applicant or registrant is a natural person, may not enter an order solely on the basis of lack of experience if the applicant or registrant is qualified by training or knowledge or both, must consider that an agent who will work under the supervision of a registered broker-dealer need not have the same qualifications as a broker-dealer, and may require that an applicant pass an examination;[67]
- Has failed reasonably to supervise its agents; or
- Has failed to pay the proper filing fee, but the state regulatory authority must vacate any such order when the deficiency is corrected.[68]

iv. Consequences of Failure to Register under the 1956 Uniform Securities Act

a. Regulatory Action

Under the 1956 Uniform Securities Act, the applicable state regulatory agency may issue a cease and desist order (with or without a prior hearing) or bring an action in an applicable state court for an injunction or to enforce compliance with the Act, if it appears that a person has engaged or is about to engage in any act or practice that violates the Act.[69] On a proper showing by such regulatory agency, a court may also enter an order of rescission, restitution or disgorgement directed to any person who has violated any provision of the 1956 Uniform Securities Act or any rule or order under that Act.[70]

b. Criminal Actions

Any person who violates any provision of the 1956 Uniform Securities Act or any rule or order under the Act is subject to a fine of up to $5,000 or imprisonment

---

67. 1956 Uniform Securities Act § 204(b), 1 Blue Sky Law Rptr. (CCH) ¶ 5524.
68. 1956 Uniform Securities Act § 204(a), 1 Blue Sky Law Rptr. (CCH) ¶ 5524.
69. 1956 Uniform Securities Act § 408, 1 Blue Sky Law Rptr. (CCH) ¶¶ 5548 and 5548.05.
70. *Id.*

for up to three years or both.[71] A person who proves he or she had no knowledge of a rule or order may not, however, be imprisoned for violating it.[72]

c. Private Actions

A person who offers or sells a security in violation of the broker–dealer or agent registration requirements of the 1956 Uniform Securities Act is liable to the person buying the security for damages or for the consideration paid for the security, plus interest, costs and reasonable attorneys' fees, less the amount of any income received on the security.[73] A purchaser of securities may also recover from the seller of the securities under the 1956 Uniform Securities Act if the seller offered or sold the security "by means of any untrue statement of a material fact or any omission to state a material fact necessary in order to make the statements made, in light of the circumstances under which they are made, not misleading (the buyer not knowing of the untruth or omission)" and if the seller does not sustain the burden of proof that he did not know and in the exercise of reasonable care could not have known the untruth or omission.[74] In addition,

> every person who directly or indirectly controls a seller liable [for such a violation], every partner, officer, or director of such a seller, every person occupying a similar status or performing similar functions, every employee of such a seller who materially aids in the sale, and every broker–dealer or agent who materially aids in the sale are also liable jointly and severally with and to the same extent as the seller, unless the non-seller who is so liable sustains the burden of proof that he did not know, and in the exercise of reasonable care could not have known, of the existence of the facts by reason of which the liability is alleged to exist.[75]

Under these provisions, not only a hedge fund, but also its investment adviser or general partner and their officers, may be liable to the hedge fund's limited partners for failure to comply with the requirements of the 1956 Uniform Securities Act.

Any private action brought under the 1956 Uniform Securities Act must be brought no more than two years after the contract of sale.[76] In addition, a buyer may not bring a private action under the 1956 Uniform Securities Act,

> (1) if the buyer received a written offer, before suit and at a time when he owned the security, to refund the consideration paid together with interest at six percent per year from the date of payment, less the amount of any income received on the security, and he failed to

---

71.   1956 Uniform Securities Act § 409, 1 Blue Sky Law Rptr. (CCH) ¶ 5549.

72.   *Id.*

73.   1956 Uniform Securities Act § 410(a)(1), 1 Blue Sky Law Rptr. (CCH) ¶ 5550.

74.   1956 Uniform Securities Act § 410(a)(2), 1 Blue Sky Law Rptr. (CCH) ¶ 5550. *See also* § 6.4, *supra,* regarding the anti-fraud provisions of the Securities Act and the Exchange Act.

75.   1956 Uniform Securities Act § 410(b), 1 Blue Sky Law Rptr. (CCH) ¶ 5550.

76.   1956 Uniform Securities Act § 410(e), 1 Blue Sky Law Rptr. (CCH) ¶ 5550.

accept the offer within thirty days of its receipt, or (2) if the buyer received such an offer before suit and at a time when he did not own the security, unless he rejected the offer in writing within thirty days of its receipt.[77]

Any provision in a contract for sale of securities purporting to waive the buyer's right to bring any such action is void.[78]

2. Other State Securities Laws

As noted, not all states have adopted the 1956 Uniform Securities Act. The laws of two of those states, California and New York, are reviewed below.

i. California

a. Registration of Securities

Under the California Corporate Securities Law of 1968, it is unlawful to offer or sell in California any security in an issuer transaction unless the sale has been qualified or unless the security or transaction is exempted or not subject to qualification.[79] "Offer" and "sell" have the same meaning under the California Securities Law as under the 1956 Uniform Securities Act.[80] "Security" has generally the same definition under the California Securities Law as under the 1956 Uniform Securities Act, except that under the California Securities Law, "security" expressly includes a non-management interest in a limited liability company.[81] "Issuer transaction" is not defined under the California Securities Law, but a "nonissuer transaction" means any transaction not directly or indirectly for the benefit of the issuer,[82]

---

77. *Id.*

78. 1956 Uniform Securities Act § 410(g), 1 Blue Sky Law Rptr. (CCH) ¶ 5550.

79. Cal. Corp. Code § 25110.

80. *Compare* Cal. Corp. Code § 25017 *with* 1956 Uniform Securities Act § 401(j), 1 Blue Sky Law Rptr. (CCH) ¶ 5541. *See* § 7.2.1.i, *supra.*

81. Cal. Corp. Code § 25019. Under this section, "security means any note; stock; treasury stock; membership in an incorporated or unincorporated association; bond; debenture; evidence of indebtedness; certificate of interest or participation in any profit-sharing agreement; collateral trust certificate; preorganization certificate or subscription; transferable share; investment contract; viatical settlement contract or a fractionalized or pooled interest therein; voting trust certificate; certificate of deposit for a security; interest in a limited liability company and any class or series of such interest (including any fractional interest), except a membership interest in a limited liability company in which the person claiming this exception can prove that all of the members are actively engaged in the management of the limited liability company; provided that evidence that members vote or have the right to vote, or the right to information concerning the business and affairs of the limited liability company, or the right to participate in management, shall not establish, without more, that all members are actively engaged in the management of the limited liability company; certificate of interest or participation in an oil, gas or mining title or lease or in payments out of production under such a title or lease; put, call, straddle, option or privilege on any security, certificate of deposit, or group or index of securities (including any interest therein or based on the value thereof); or any put, call, straddle, option or privilege entered into on a national securities exchange relating to foreign currency; any beneficial interest or other security issued in connection with a funded employees' pension, profit sharing, stock bonus, or similar benefit plan; or, in general, any interest or instrument commonly known as a 'security'; or any certificate of interest or participation in, temporary or interim certificate for, receipt for, guarantee of, or warrant or right to subscribe to or purchase, any of the foregoing."

82. Cal. Corp. Code § 25011.

which implies that an issuer transaction is a transaction directly or indirectly for the benefit of the issuer. A transaction is indirectly for the benefit of the issuer if "any portion of the purchase price of any securities involved in the transaction will be received indirectly by the issuer."[83] This section addresses the qualification requirements only for issuer transactions, including securities issuances issued by a U.S. or offshore hedge fund.

As under the 1956 Uniform Securities Act, the California Securities Law provides for qualification by coordination with respect to securities for which a registration statement has been filed under the Securities Act in connection with the same offering.[84] In addition, the California Securities Law permits an issuer that has any class of shares registered under Exchange Act section 12 or that is registered as an investment company under the Company Act to qualify additional securities by notification.[85] Neither of these methods of qualification generally is available for a U.S. or offshore hedge fund engaged in a private offering of securities.[86]

The qualification method for securities issued by a hedge fund is by permit.[87] To qualify by permit, an issuer must file an application in the form specified by the California Commissioner of Corporations.[88] As with the 1956 Uniform Securities Act, this application requires extensive disclosure somewhat similar to that required by Form S-1 under the Securities Act.[89]

b. Exemptions from Securities Registration Requirements

The California Securities Law provides several exemptions from its qualification requirements.[90] As under the 1956 Uniform Securities Act, the exemption that most often applies to a U.S. or offshore hedge fund is a form of limited offering exemption.[91] The California Securities Law limited offering exemption is similar to Rule 506 of Regulation D[92] and is available if:

- Sales of securities are not made to more than thirty-five persons, including persons not in California;[93]
- All purchasers either have a preexisting personal or business relationship with the offeror or any of its partners, officers, directors, controlling persons or managers, or by reason of their business or financial experience or the business or financial experience of their professional advisers who are unaffiliated with and are not compensated by the issuer or any affiliate or selling agent of the

---

83.   *Id.*
84.   Cal. Corp. Code § 25111(a).
85.   Cal. Corp. Code § 25112(a).
86.   *See* § 7.2.1.ii.a, *supra.*
87.   Cal. Corp. Code § 25113.
88.   10 Cal. Code Reg. §§ 260.110 and 260.113.
89.   *Id. See* § 6.2.1.iii, *supra.*
90.   *See* Cal. Corp. Code §§ 25101 and 25102.
91.   Cal. Corp. Code § 25102(f).
92.   *Compare* Cal. Corp. Code § 25102(f) and 10 Cal. Code Reg. §§ 260.102.12–260.102.14 *with* 17 C.F.R. §§ 230.501-230.503 and 230.506-230.508. *See also* § 5.3.2, *supra.*
93.   Cal. Corp. Code § 25102(f)(1).

issuer, directly or indirectly, could be reasonably assumed to have the capacity to protect their own interests in connection with the transaction;[94]

- Each purchaser represents that the purchaser is purchasing for the purchaser's own account (or a trust account if the purchaser is a trustee) and not with a view to or for sale in connection with any distribution of the security;[95]
- The offering and sale of the security is not accomplished by the publication of any advertisement;[96] and
- A notice of transaction is filed with the California Commissioner of Corporations on a form prescribed by the Commissioner.[97]

In determining the number of purchasers, an issuer may exclude purchasers that are accredited investors under Rule 501(a) of Regulation D.[98] An issuer may also count a husband and wife, or a custodian or trustee acting for the accounts of his or her minor children, as one purchaser.[99] In addition, the issuer is not required to count any of its officers, directors, affiliates, managers, trustees, general partners (or officers, directors or general partners of a general partner) or any person who occupies a position with the issuer or a general partner of the issuer with duties similar to those of an executive officer of a corporation.[100] The California Securities Law also excludes from the number of purchasers any bank, savings and loan association, trust company, insurance company, investment company registered under the Company Act, pension or profit-sharing trust (other than a pension or profit sharing trust of the issuer, a self-employed individual retirement plan or an individual retirement account) or other institutional investor designated by rule, whether the purchaser is acting for itself or as trustee.[101] The California Commissioner of Corporations also has excluded the following categories of persons from the thirty-five person limit:

- Any relative, spouse or relative of the spouse of a purchaser who has the same principal residence as the purchaser;[102]
- Any trust or estate in which a purchaser and any of the persons related to such purchaser as specified in the preceding clause or the following clause collectively have more than fifty percent of the beneficial interest (excluding contingent interest);[103]
- Any corporation or other organization of which a purchaser and any of the persons related to the purchaser as specified in the two preceding clauses beneficially own more than fifty percent of the equity securities (excluding directors' qualifying shares) or equity interests;[104]

94.   Cal. Corp. Code § 25102(f)(2).
95.   Cal. Corp. Code § 25102(f)(3).
96.   Cal. Corp. Code § 25102(f)(4).
97.   Cal. Corp. Code § 25102(f) and Cal. Code Reg. § 260.102.14.
98.   10 Cal. Code Reg. § 260.102.13(g); 17 C.F.R. § 230.501(a). *See* § 5.3.2.ii, *supra*.
99.   Cal. Corp. Code § 25102(f).
100. Cal. Corp. Code § 25102(f); Cal. Code Reg. §§ 260.102.13(a) and (b).
101. Cal. Corp. Code §§ 25102(f) and (i); Cal. Code Reg. § 260.102.10.
102. 10 Cal. Code Reg. § 260.102.13(c)(1).
103. 10 Cal. Code Reg. § 260.102.13(c)(2).
104. 10 Cal. Code Reg. § 260.102.13(c)(3).

- Any individual who is a promoter of the issuer (that is, a person who, acting alone or in conjunction with others, takes the initiative in founding and organizing the business or enterprise of the issuer);[105]
- Any person who purchases $150,000 or more of the securities offered in the transaction, provided that the issuer reasonably believes that either such purchaser has the capacity to protect such person's own interest in connection with the transaction or the investment (including mandatory assessments) does not exceed ten percent of such person's net worth or joint net worth with his or her spouse;[106] and
- Any entity in which all of the equity owners are accredited investors or persons described above.[107]

c. Registration of Broker-Dealers and Agents

The California Securities Law provides that "no broker-dealer shall effect any transaction in, or induce or attempt to induce the purchase or sale of, any security in this state unless the broker-dealer has first applied for and secured from the commissioner a certificate, then in effect, authorizing that person to act in that capacity."[108] In addition, "no person shall, on behalf of a broker-dealer licensed pursuant to section 25211, or on behalf of an issuer, effect any transaction in or induce or attempt to induce the purchase or sale of, any security in this state unless that broker-dealer and agent have complied with any rule as the commissioner may adopt for the qualification and employment of those agents."[109]

Under the California Securities Law, a "broker-dealer" is "any person engaged in the business of effecting transactions in securities in this state for the account of others or for his own account."[110] The definition of "broker-dealer" expressly excludes an issuer (other than a person engaged in the regular business of issuing or guaranteeing options with regard to securities not of his own issue) and an agent, when an employee of a broker-dealer or issuer.[111] Accordingly, in issuing its own securities, a U.S. or offshore hedge fund is excluded from the definition of "broker-dealer."

An "agent" is "any individual, other than a broker-dealer or a partner of a licensed broker-dealer, who represents a broker-dealer or who for compensation represents an issuer in effecting or attempting to effect purchases or sales of securities in this state."[112] An officer or director of a broker-dealer or issuer, or an individual occupying a similar status or performing similar functions, is an agent only if he or she otherwise comes within the definition of an agent and receives compensation specifically related to purchases or sales of securities.[113] Accordingly, the general

---

105.   10 Cal. Code. Reg. §§ 260.102.13(d) and 260.102.12(f).
106.   10 Cal. Code Reg. § 260.102.13(e).
107.   10 Cal. Code Reg. § 260.102.13(h).
108.   Cal. Corp. Code § 25210(a).
109.   Cal. Corp. Code § 25210(b).
110.   Cal. Corp. Code § 25004.
111.   Cal. Corp. Code §§ 25004(a) and (b).
112.   Cal. Corp. Code § 25003(a).
113.   Cal. Corp. Code § 25003(d).

partner of a U.S. hedge fund and its officers, and the directors of an offshore hedge fund, are only agents if they receive compensation specifically related to their sales of securities.

An application for a certificate as a broker-dealer must be accompanied by a consent to service of process and include such information as the California Commissioner of Corporations may by rule require.[114] The Commissioner may deny, suspend or revoke a broker-dealer certificate for reasons similar to those under the 1956 Uniform Securities Act.[115]

d. Consequences of Failure to Register under the California Securities Law

(1) Administrative Actions

If the California Commissioner of Corporations determines that any person has engaged or is about to engage in any act or practice that violates the California Securities Law or any rule or order under the California Securities Law, the Commissioner may bring an action to enjoin such act or practice or to enforce compliance with the California Securities Law.[116] The Commissioner also may include an action for ancillary relief, including a claim for restitution or disgorgement or damages on behalf of the persons injured by the act or practice.[117]

If in the opinion of the California Commissioner of Corporations the sale of a security is subject to qualification or a notice filing under the California Securities Law and the security is being offered or sold without being qualified, the Commissioner may order the issuer to desist and refrain from further offers or sales of the security until the security is qualified or the notice filing is made.[118] Similarly, if in the opinion of the Commissioner a person has been or is acting as a broker-dealer in violation of the registration requirements under the California Securities Law, the Commissioner may order that person to desist and refrain from such activity until the person is appropriately licensed or has filed the appropriate notices.[119] A person subject to such an order may request a hearing. Failure to request a hearing within one year after being served with the order will result in the order being deemed final.[120]

(2) Criminal and Civil Penalties

Any person who willfully violates any provision of the California Securities Law or any rule or order under it is subject to a fine of up to $1,000,000, up to one year in prison or both.[121] Any person who violates the California Securities Law or any rule or order under it also may be liable for a civil penalty of up to $25,000

---

114. Cal. Corp. Code § 25211(a).
115. Cal. Corp. Code § 25212. *See* § 7.2.1.iii.d, *supra*.
116. Cal. Corp. Code § 25530(a).
117. Cal. Corp. Code § 25530(b).
118. Cal. Corp. Code § 25532(a).
119. Cal. Corp. Code § 25532(b).
120. Cal. Corp. Code § 25532(d).
121. Cal. Corp. Code § 25540(a).

for each violation.[122] Any action to enforce such a civil penalty must be brought within four years after the act or transaction constituting the violation.[123]

(3) Private Actions

Any person who violates the securities qualification requirements of the California Securities Law is liable to any person who aquired the securities from the violator for the consideration paid for the securities, with interest at the legal rate, less the amount of any income the purchaser received therefrom, on tender of the securities to the issuer.[124] If the purchaser no longer owns the securities or if the consideration for the securities is not capable of being returned, the purchaser may sue for damages equal to the difference between the purchaser's purchase price plus interest at the legal rate from the date of purchase less the total value of the securities when sold by the plaintiff and any income received by the purchaser from the securities.[125] In addition, every person who directly or indirectly controls a person liable under these provisions, every partner in a firm so liable, every principal executive officer or director of a corporation so liable, every person occupying a similar status or performing similar functions, and every employee of a person so liable who materially aids in the act or transaction constituting the violation, is also liable jointly and severally with and to the same extent as such person, unless the latter person had no knowledge of or reasonable grounds to believe the existence of the facts by reason of which the liability is alleged to exist.[126] Any person who materially assists in any such violation also is jointly and severally liable with any other person so liable.[127]

Such a private action must be brought within two years after the violation on which it is based or one year after the purchaser discovers the facts constituting the violation, whichever period ends earlier.[128] No purchaser can commence any such action if, before the suit is commenced, the purchaser received a written offer approved in form by the California Commissioner of Corporations stating the respect in which such liability may have arisen, offering to repurchase the security for a cash price payable on delivery of the security, offering to pay the purchaser an amount in cash equal to the amount recoverable by the purchaser or offering to rescind the transaction by putting the parties back in the same position as before the transaction, providing that such offer may be accepted by the purchaser at any time within a specified period of at least thirty days after receipt of the offer, setting forth the provisions of California Corporate Securities Law section 25507(b) and containing such other information as the California Commissioner of Corporations may require, and the purchaser fails to accept such offer in writing within the specified period.[129]

---

122.   Cal. Corp. Code § 25535(a).
123.   Cal. Corp. Code § 25535(c).
124.   Cal. Corp. Code § 25503.
125.   *Id.*
126.   Cal. Corp. Code § 25504.
127.   Cal. Corp. Code § 25504.1.
128.   Cal. Corp. Code § 25507(a).
129.   Cal. Corp. Code § 25507(b).

ii. New York

The issuance of securities and registration of brokers in New York is governed by the New York Fraudulent Practices Act, or "Martin Act."[130] The securities and broker registration requirements of the Martin Act are closely intertwined[131] and are addressed together in this section.

a. Definitions

A "dealer" under the Martin Act is

> any person, firm, association or corporation engaged in the business of buying and selling securities from or to the public within or from this state for his or its own account, through a broker or otherwise ...,but does not include any person, firm, association or corporation in so far as he or it buys or sells securities for his or its bona fide investment account, either individually or in some fiduciary capacity.[132]

"Dealer" also includes "a person, firm, association or corporation selling or offering for sale from or to the public within or from this state securities issued by it."[133] The definition of "dealer" excludes a person selling or offering for sale any security or securities as part of a private placement of securities, if the sales and offers are made only to banks, corporations, savings institutions, trust companies, insurance companies, investment companies (as defined under the Company Act), pension or profit-sharing trusts or other financial institutions or institutional buyers.[134] Most hedge funds offer interests to individual investors, as well as institutional investors, and therefore cannot rely on this exemption. As a result, a hedge fund generally is a "dealer" under the Martin Act.

A "broker" is a "person, firm, association or corporation, other than a dealer, engaged in the business of effecting transactions in securities for the account of others within or from this state."[135] Hedge funds ordinarily are not "brokers" under this definition because, in general, they are dealers and also because they effect transactions in securities for their own accounts, not the accounts of others.

A "salesman" is a person employed by a broker or dealer "for the purpose of representing such broker or dealer in the sale or purchase of securities to or form the public within or from this state."[136] A "principal" is "every person or firm directly or indirectly controlling any broker or dealer."[137] Under these definitions, the general partner of a U.S. hedge fund, and its officers, directors, managers and other controlling persons, and the directors of an offshore hedge fund, are all "principals" of the hedge fund. They generally are not, however, salesmen of the

---

130. *See* N.Y. Gen. Bus. Law §§ 352 *et seq.*
131. *See* N.Y. Gen. Bus. Law § 359-e.
132. N.Y. Gen. Bus. Law § 359-e(1)(a).
133. *Id.*
134. *Id.*
135. N.Y. Gen. Bus. Law § 359-e(1)(b).
136. N.Y. Gen. Bus. Law § 359-e(1)(c).
137. N.Y. Gen. Bus. Law § 359-e(1)(d).

hedge fund, unless they are employed for the purpose of representing the hedge fund in the purchase or sale of securities.

b. Registration Requirements

Before an issuer may offer its securities in New York, the Martin Act requires it to file a registration statement for each broker, dealer or salesman engaged in the offering, a state notice and a further state notice.[138]

(1) Registration Statement for Brokers and Dealers

No dealer or broker may sell, purchase or offer to sell or purchase any security to or from the public within or from New York unless the dealer, broker or salesman has filed a registration statement.[139] The registration statement for brokers and dealers is called the "broker-dealer statement" and must include "such information pertaining to the business history for the last preceding five years, criminal record, and educational background of the applicant and his or its partners, officers, directors or other principals thereof deemed pertinent by the attorney-general."[140] Registration as a broker or dealer must be renewed every four years.[141]

Generally, an issuer of securities must file a Form M-11 under this section.[142] After NSMIA was adopted, however, the New York Department of Law, Bureau of Investor Protection and Securities, adopted the Form 99 Notification Filing Pursuant to NSMIA.[143] An issuer relying on Rule 506 of Regulation D may file a Form 99 instead of a Form M-11.[144] Accordingly, a hedge fund may satisfy the requirement to file a broker-dealer statement by filing a Form 99. An issuer filing a Form 99 also must file:

- a consent to services of process;
- copies of its offering documents;
- a copy of its Form D, as filed with the SEC; and
- filing fees that range from $1,050 to $1,950, depending on the size of the offering in New York.[145]

(2) Registration Statement for Salesmen

No salesman may sell, purchase or offer to sell or purchase any security to or from the public within or from New York unless the salesman has filed a registration statement.[146] Furthermore, no broker or dealer may employ a salesman unless the salesman is registered.[147] The registration statement for a salesman is called

---

138.   N.Y. Gen. Bus. Law §§ 359-e(2), (3) and (8).
139.   N.Y. Gen. Bus. Law § 359-e(3).
140.   N.Y. Gen. Bus. Law § 359-e(3)(a).
141.   N.Y. Gen. Bus. Law § 359-e(3)(c).
142.   N.Y. Comp. Codes R. & Regs. tit. 13, § 10.1.
143.   Form 99 – Notification Filing Pursuant to National Securities Market Improvement Act of 1996, 2A Blue Sky Law Rptr. ¶ 42,587.
144.   *Id.*
145.   *Id.*
146.   N.Y. Gen. Bus. Law § 359-e(3).
147.   N.Y. Gen. Bus. Law § 359-e(11).

the "salesman's statement" and requires the same information as is required by the broker–dealer statement described above.[148] A salesman also must pass the NASD's Series 63 or Series 66 examination before applying for registration as a salesman.[149]

A partner, officer, director or principal of a broker or dealer who is named as such in the broker's or dealer's registration statement is not required to register as a salesman of the broker or dealer.[150] As discussed above, neither the general partner of a U.S. hedge fund, nor its officers, directors, managers and other controlling persons, nor the directors of an offshore hedge fund, are likely to be considered salesmen of the hedge fund. Even if they were, however, as long as they are identified in the Form 99, they are not required to register as salesmen under the foregoing exception.

The Martin Act also generally requires all persons regularly employed in New York by a broker or dealer required to register under the Martin Act to file their fingerprints with the New York Attorney General.[151] This requirement does not apply, however, to employees of dealers required to register under the Martin Act solely because the dealers are "engaged in selling or offering securities issued by themselves."[152] Accordingly, the fingerprinting requirements ordinarily do not apply to principals or employees of a hedge fund.

(3) State Notice

No dealer or broker may sell, purchase or offer to sell or purchase to or from the public within or from New York, as a principal or a broker, any securities until it files a "state notice" with the New York Department of State.[153] As a dealer, a hedge fund must file a state notice. The state notice must include:

- the name and business or post office address of the dealer or broker;
- if the dealer or broker is a corporation, the state or country of incorporation; and
- if the dealer or broker is a partnership, the names of its partners.[154]

State notices are published in the New York state bulletin.[155]

(4) Further State Notice

A dealer may not sell or offer for sale to the public in New York, as a principal or an agent, any securities unless the dealer files a "further state notice."[156] The further state notice must contain the same information as the state notice described above, except that the names of partners of a dealer organized as a partnership do not need to be included.[157] The further state notice also must include the name of

---

148. N.Y. Gen. Bus. Law § 359-e(3)(b).
149. *Id.*
150. N.Y. Gen. Bus. Law § 359-e(5).
151. N.Y. Gen. Bus. Law § 359-e(12).
152. *Id.*
153. N.Y. Gen. Bus. Law § 359-e(3).
154. *Id.*
155. N.Y. Gen. Bus. Law § 359-c.
156. N.Y. Gen. Bus. Law § 359-e(8).
157. *Id.*

the security or securities and the name, post office address and state or country of incorporation or organization of the corporation, association, common law trust or similar organization issuing the securities.[158] If two or more dealers are engaged in the offering, they may file a joint further state notice and must identify the syndicate manager or managers.[159]

Several categories of securities are exempt from the requirement to file a further state notice, but none of these exclusions applies to a hedge fund.[160] Accordingly, a hedge fund ordinarily must file a further state notice.

§ 7.3 NSMIA

1. State Securities Registration under NSMIA

In 1996, Congress enacted NSMIA "to eliminate duplicative and unnecessary regulatory burdens while preserving important investor protections by reallocating responsibility over the regulation of the nation's securities markets in a more logical fashion between the Federal government and the states."[161] NSMIA provides, among other things, that

> no law, rule, regulation, or order, or other administrative action of any State or any political subdivision thereof (1) requiring, or with respect to, registration or qualification of securities, or registration or qualification of securities transactions, shall directly or indirectly apply to a security that (A) is a covered security; or (B) will be a covered security upon completion of the transaction.[162]

Several categories of securities are included in the definition of "covered security" under NSMIA.[163] Only one of these categories is relevant to U.S. and offshore hedge funds.[164] Securities Act section 18(b)(4)(D) provides that

> a security is a covered security with respect to a transaction that is exempt from registration under [the Securities Act] pursuant to commission rules or regulations issued under [Securities Act] section 4(2), except that this subparagraph does not prohibit a State from

---

158.   *Id.*

159.   *Id.*

160.   *See* N.Y. Gen. Bus. Law § 359-f.

161.   Conference Report on the National Securities Markets Improvement Act of 1996, House Report No. 104–864 at 39 (Sep. 28, 1996).

162.   Securities Act § 18(a)(1), 15 U.S.C. § 77r(a).

163.   *See* Securities Act § 18(b), 15 U.S.C. § 77r(b).

164.   *See* §§ 3.2.5 and 3.3.1, *supra.*

imposing notice filing requirements that are substantially similar to those required by rule or regulation under section 4(2) that are in effect on September 1, 1996.[165]

Rule 506 of Regulation D was promulgated by the SEC under Securities Act section 4(2).[166] Accordingly, securities sold by a U.S. or offshore hedge fund in a transaction that is exempt under Rule 506 of Regulation D are "covered securities" under NSMIA. NSMIA preempts the states from requiring registration of such securities. As a result, states can no longer pursue civil or criminal remedies against, or grant rescission rights to investors in, a U.S. or offshore hedge fund that fails to register its securities with the state, if the hedge fund complies with the requirements of Rule 506 of Regulation D.

NSMIA expressly provides, however, that the states retain jurisdiction "to investigate and bring enforcement actions with respect to fraud or deceit, or unlawful conduct by a broker or dealer, in connection with securities or securities transactions."[167] In addition, NSMIA permits the states to continue to collect filing or registration fees with respect to securities or securities transactions.[168] NSMIA also permits the states to require issuers of "covered securities" to file notices with the cognizant state regulatory authority.[169] If an issuer fails to make a notice filing with a state or pay to a state a fee permitted under NSMIA, the state may suspend the offer or sale of securities within the state.[170]

Accordingly, although a U.S. or offshore hedge fund issuing securities in a state pursuant to Rule 506 of Regulation D is not required to register such securities under that state's securities laws, the hedge fund may be required to file a notice and pay a fee with the applicable state regulatory authority. A 1997 amendment to the 1956 Uniform Securities Act permits the state regulatory authority to require an issuer to file a notice no later than fifteen days after the first sale of a federally covered security in the state.[171] Most states require an issuer relying on Rule 506 of Regulation D to file a notice within fifteen days after the first sale of securities in that state.[172] The required filing consists of a copy of the Form D filed with the SEC under Regulation D, a consent to service of process and a fee established by state law or regulation.[173] A notable exception is New

165. Securities Act § 18(b)(4)(D), 15 U.S.C. § 77r(b)(4)(D).

166. *See* § 5.3.2, *supra*.

167. Securities Act § 18(c)(1), 15 U.S.C. § 77r(c)(1).

168. Securities Act § 18(c)(2)(B)(i), 15 U.S.C. § 77r(c)(2)(B)(i).

169. Securities Act § 18(b)(4)(D) and 18(c)(2)(A), 15 U.S.C. § 77r(b)(4)(D) and (c)(2)(A).

170. Securities Act § 18(c)(3), 15 U.S.C. § 77r(c)(3).

171. 1956 Uniform Securities Act § 307 and Rule 307(b)-1, 1 Blue Sky Law Rptr. (CCH) ¶¶ 5536.10 and 5536.15.

172. The following states require filing of SEC documents no later than fifteen days after the first sale in the state: Alabama, Alaska, Arizona, Arkansas, California, Colorado, Connecticut, Delaware, the District of Columbia, Hawaii, Idaho, Indiana, Iowa, Kansas, Kentucky, Louisiana, Maine, Maryland, Massachusetts, Michigan, Minnesota, Mississippi, Missouri, Montana, Nebraska, Nevada, New Hampshire, New Jersey, New Mexico, North Carolina, North Dakota, Ohio, Oklahoma, Oregon, Pennsylvania, South Carolina, South Dakota, Tennessee, Texas, Utah, Vermont, Virginia, Washington, West Virginia, Wisconsin and Wyoming. *See* 1 Blue Sky Law Rptr. (CCH) ¶ 6251 (listing state filing requirements).

173. *Id.* and 1956 Uniform Securities Act § 307(b) and Rule 307(b)-1, 1 Blue Sky Law Rptr. (CCH) ¶¶ 5536.10 and 5536.15.

York, which, as discussed above, in addition to requiring the filing of a Form D, consent to service of process and a filing fee, requires the filing of a Form 99, Notification Filing Pursuant to National Securities Markets Improvement Act of 1996, a State Notice and a Further State Notice.[174]

New Hampshire, New York and Rhode Island require a filing before the first sale of securities in the state.[175] Rhode Island requires that the filing be made at least ten days before the first sale of securities in that state.[176]

Some states require the filing only with the first sale of securities. A few states require filings periodically. For example, Illinois law provides that a filing is only good for one year and must be renewed if securities will be sold in Illinois more than one year after the last filing in Illinois.[177] Similarly, the notice filing in New York must be renewed every four years.[178]

2. NSMIA and Broker-Dealer and Agent Registration

Although NSMIA preempts state securities registration requirements that otherwise would apply to sales of limited partner interests in U.S. hedge funds and shares of offshore hedge funds, it does not preempt the broker–dealer registration requirements under state securities laws.[179] Accordingly, even after the adoption of NSMIA, investment advisers that serve as the general partners of hedge funds or as the investment advisers to offshore hedge funds may be required to comply with such registration requirements.[180]

3. Amendments to the 1956 Uniform Securities Act Following NSMIA

After NSMIA was adopted, NASAA proposed amendments to the 1956 Uniform Securities Act that expressly exclude "federal covered securities" from the registration requirements of 1956 Uniform Securities Act section 301.[181] "Federal covered security" means

> any security that is a covered security under section 18(b) of the [Securities Act] or rules or regulations promulgated thereunder, except, up through October 10, 1999, or such other date as may be legally permissible, a federal covered security for which a fee has not been paid and promptly remedied following written notification from

---

174. *See,* N.Y. Gen. Law § 359-e; New York Form 99, Notification Filing Pursuant to National Securities Markets Improvement Act of 1996, 2A Blue Sky Law Rptr. (CCH) ¶ 42,587. *See* § 7.2.2.ii.b, *supra.*

175. *See,* N.H. Stat. Ann. § 421-B:11.I-a(a); New York Form 99, Notification Filing Pursuant to National Securities Markets Improvement Act of 1996, 2A Blue Sky Law Rptr. (CCH) ¶ 42,587; R.I. Gen. Laws § 7-11-402(18)(ii).

176. R.I. Gen. Laws § 7-11-402(18)(ii).

177. Ill. Stat. Ann. § 5/2a.

178. N.Y. Gen. Law § 359-e(3)(c).

179. *See* Conference Report on the National Securities Markets Improvement Act of 1996, House Report No. 104-864 at 39 (Sep. 28, 1996).

180. *See* § 7.2.1.iii, *supra.*

181. 1 Blue Sky Law Rptr. (CCH) ¶ 5531.05.

the [state securities administrator] to the issuer of the nonpayment or underpayment of such fees, as required by this Act, shall not be a federal covered security.[182]

The amendment also gives the state regulatory authority the authority to require the issuer of a federal covered security described in Securities Act section 18(b)(4)(D), such as a security issued pursuant to Rule 506 of Regulation D, to file a Form D, a consent to service of process and a filing fee with the state regulatory authority within fifteen days of the date on which the first sale of securities occurs in the state.[183]

The NASAA amendments exclude from the definition of "agent" an individual who represents an issuer in "effecting transactions in a covered security as described in section 18(b)(3) and 18(b)(4)(D) of the [Securities Act]."[184] An individual representing a U.S. or offshore hedge fund in selling its securities in a transaction under Rule 506 of Regulation D is therefore not an agent and is not required to register as such.

§ 7.4 2002 Uniform Securities Act

In 2002, the National Conference of Commissioners on Uniform State Laws proposed the 2002 Uniform Securities Act. The stated goals of the 2002 Uniform Securities Act are to achieve greater uniformity among state securities laws, to achieve consistency with NSMIA and to facilitate electronic records, signatures and filings.[185] The 2002 Uniform Securities Act has been adopted in Idaho, Iowa, Kansas, Missouri, Oklahoma, South Dakota and the U.S. Virgin Islands[186] and has been introduced in the Alabama, Alaska, Nebraska, Vermont and Virginia legislatures.[187]

1. Offers and Sales of Securities within a State

As with the 1956 Uniform Securities Act, the 2002 Uniform Securities Act registration requirements, both for securities and for brokers, apply only if there is an offer or sale of a security within the state.[188] "Offer" and "sale" have

---

182.   1956 Uniform Securities Act § 401(c2), 1 Blue Sky Law Rptr. (CCH) ¶ 5541.30.

183.   1956 Uniform Securities Act § 307, 1 Blue Sky Law Rptr. (CCH) ¶ 5536.10. *See also* the NASAA proposed rule that implements this section, Rule 307(b)-1, at 1 Blue Sky Law Rptr. (CCH) ¶ 5536.15.

184.   1956 Uniform Securities Act § 401(b)(1)(C), 1 Blue Sky Law Rptr. (CCH) ¶ 5541.30.

185.   1 Blue Sky Law Rptr. (CCH) ¶ 5600.

186.   *See* "A Few Facts About the Uniform Securities Act (2002)," available at the website of the National Conference of Commissioners on Uniform State Laws, www.nccusl.org/Update/uniformact_factsheets/uniformacts-fs-usa.asp.

187.   *Id.*

188.   2002 Uniform Securities Act §§ 301 and 401(a), 1 Blue Sky Law Rptr. (CCH) ¶¶ 5610 and 5617.

substantially the same definitions under the 1956 Uniform Securities Act and the 2002 Uniform Securities Act.[189] The 2002 Uniform Securities Act definition of "security" has been updated to reflect, among other things, amendments to the Securities Act definition and "to amplify the definition of investment contract so that it can expressly reach interests in limited partnerships, limited liability companies, or viatical settlement agreements, among other contracts, when they satisfy the definition of investment contract."[190] To this end, "security" under the 2002 Uniform Securities Act:

> (D) includes as an "investment contract," among other contracts, an investment in a common enterprise with the expectation of profits to be derived primarily from the efforts of a person other than the investor and a "common enterprise" means an enterprise in which the fortunes of the investor are interwoven with those of either the person offering the investment, a third party, or other investors, and (E) includes as an "investment contract," among other contracts, an interest in a limited partnership and a limited liability company and an investment in a viatical settlement or similar agreement.[191]

2. Securities Registration under the 2002 Uniform Securities Act

Under the 2002 Uniform Securities Act, no person may offer or sell a security in a state unless the security is a federal covered security, the security, transaction or offer is exempt from registration, or the security is registered under the 2002 Uniform Securities Act.[192] A "federal covered security" is "a security that is, or upon completion of a transaction will be, a covered security under Section 18(B) of the [Securities Act] or rules or regulations adopted pursuant to that provision."[193] Under the 2002 Uniform Securities Act, the appropriate state regulatory authority may require by rule that an issuer of a federal covered security under Securities Act section 18(b)(4)(D),[194] which includes a security issued pursuant to Rule 506 of Regulation D,[195] file a Form D, file a consent to service of process and pay a filing fee.[196] A hedge fund that complies with Rule 506 of Regulation D generally is required only to make such notice filings under the 2002 Uniform Securities Act and is not required to register its securities with a state.

---

189.   *Compare* 2002 Uniform Securities Act § 102(26), 1 Blue Sky Law Rptr. ¶ 5602, *with* 1956 Uniform Securities Act § 401(j), 1 Blue Sky Law Rptr. ¶ 5541.

190.   Prefatory Note to the 2002 Uniform Securities Act, 1 Blue Sky Law Rptr. ¶ 5600.

191.   2002 Uniform Securities Act § 102(28), 1 Blue Sky Law Rptr. (CCH) ¶ 5602.

192.   2002 Uniform Securities Act § 301, 1 Blue Sky Law Rptr. (CCH) ¶ 5610.

193.   2002 Uniform Securities Act § 102(6), 1 Blue Sky Law Rptr. (CCH) ¶ 5602.

194.   15 U.S.C. § 77r(b)(4)(D).

195.   *See* §§ 5.3.2 and 7.3.1, *supra.*

196.   2002 Uniform Securities Act § 302(c), 1 Blue Sky Law Rptr. (CCH) ¶ 5611.

If a hedge fund is required to register its securities with a state, the 2002 Uniform Securities Act registration requirements are substantially the same as the registration requirements of the 1956 Uniform Securities Act.[197]

3. Broker-Dealer and Agent Registration under 2002 Uniform Securities Act

Like the 1956 Uniform Securities Act, the 2002 Uniform Securities Act provides that a person may not transact business in a state as a broker–dealer or as an agent, unless the person is registered as such under the 2002 Uniform Securities Act.[198] The 2002 Uniform Securities Act also forbids an issuer or a broker–dealer to employ an agent, unless the agent is registered.[199]

i. Definitions of Broker-Dealer, Issuer and Agent

Under the 2002 Uniform Securities Act, a "broker–dealer" is "any person engaged in the business of effecting transactions in securities for the account of others or for his own account."[200] The definition of "broker–dealer" excludes, among others, agents and issuers.[201]

An "issuer" is "any person who issues or proposes to issue any security."[202] U.S. and offshore hedge funds are "issuers" of their limited partner interests or shares. As an issuer, a U.S. or offshore hedge fund is thus excluded from the definition of "broker–dealer."

An "agent" is "any individual other than a broker–dealer who represents a broker–dealer or issuer in effecting or attempting to effect purchases or sales of securities."[203] The definition of "agent" includes a "partner, officer, or director of a broker–dealer or issuer, or an individual having a similar status or performing similar functions only if the individual otherwise comes within the term."[204] An individual is exempt from the agent registration requirements of the 2002 Uniform Securities Act if the individual represents an issuer in transactions solely in federal covered securities and, for federal covered securities that are described in Securities Act section 18(b)(4)(D), if the individual is not compensated by the payment of commissions or other remuneration based, directly or indirectly, on transactions in those securities.[205]

---

197. *See* §§ 7.2.1.ii.a and 7.2.1.ii.b, *supra*.
198. 2002 Uniform Securities Act §§ 401(a) (broker-dealer registration) and 402(a) (agent registration), 1 Blue Sky Law Rptr. (CCH) ¶¶ 5617 and 5618.
199. 2002 Uniform Securities Act § 402(b), 1 Blue Sky Law Rptr. (CCH) ¶ 5618.
200. 2002 Uniform Securities Act § 401(c), 1 Blue Sky Law Rptr. (CCH) ¶ 5617.
201. 2002 Uniform Securities Act § 102(4), 1 Blue Sky Law Rptr. (CCH) ¶ 5602.
202. 2002 Uniform Securities Act § 102(17), 1 Blue Sky Law Rptr. (CCH) ¶ 5602.
203. 2002 Uniform Securities Act § 102(2), 1 Blue Sky Law Rptr. (CCH) ¶ 5602.
204. *Id.*
205. 2002 Uniform Securities Act § 402(b)(5), 1 Blue Sky Law Rptr. (CCH) ¶ 5618.

ii. Broker-Dealer and Agent Registration Process

Under the 2002 Uniform Securities Act, a broker-dealer or an agent must register by filing an application and a consent to service of process with the cognizant state regulatory authority and paying the appropriate filing fee.[206] The application must contain the information required for filing of a uniform application and any other financial or other information or records that the state regulatory authority may request.[207] Registration as a broker-dealer or agent remains effective until December 31 of the year of the application and then may be automatically renewed each year by filing such records as are required by rule or order of the state regulatory authority.[208]

The 2002 Uniform Securities Act authorizes the appropriate state regulatory authority to establish minimum capital requirements for broker-dealers, to require broker-dealers to file financial reports and to require broker-dealers to maintain books and records specified by the regulatory authority.[209]

iii. Denial, Revocation or Suspension of Registration

Under the 2002 Uniform Securities Act, a state regulatory authority may deny a broker-dealer's application for registration or suspend or revoke such a registration on substantially the same grounds as those identified in the 1956 Uniform Securities Act.[210]

4. Consequences of Failure to Register under 2002 Uniform Securities Act

i. Regulatory Action

The 2002 Uniform Securities Act provides that the applicable state regulatory agency may issue a cease and desist order (with or without a prior hearing) or bring an action in an appropriate state court for an injunction or to enforce compliance with that Act if it appears to that agency that a person has engaged or is about to engage in any act or practice constituting a violation of that Act.[211] On a proper showing by such regulatory agency, a court may also enter an order of rescission, restitution or disgorgement directed to any person who has violated any provision of the 2002 Uniform Securities Act or any rule or order under it.[212]

---

206. 2002 Uniform Securities Act § 406(a), 1 Blue Sky Law Rptr. (CCH) ¶ 5622.
207. *Id.*
208. 2002 Uniform Securities Act § 406(d), 1 Blue Sky Law Rptr. (CCH) ¶ 5622.
209. 2002 Uniform Securities Act § 411, 1 Blue Sky Law Rptr. (CCH) ¶ 5627.
210. 2002 Uniform Securities Act § 412, 1 Blue Sky Law Rptr. (CCH) ¶ 5628; *see* § 7.2.1.iii.d, *supra.*
211. 2002 Uniform Securities Act § 603(a), 1 Blue Sky Law Rptr. (CCH) ¶ 5641.
212. 2002 Uniform Securities Act § 603(b), 1 Blue Sky Law Rptr. (CCH) ¶ 5641.

ii. Criminal Actions

Any person who willfully violates any provision of the 2002 Uniform Securities Act or any rule or order under that Act, except for the notice filing requirement for federal covered securities, is subject to a fine or imprisonment or both.[213] An individual so convicted of violating a rule or order may be fined but not imprisoned, if the individual did not know of the rule or order.[214]

iii. Private Actions

A person who offers or sells a security in violation of the broker-dealer, agent or securities registration requirements of the 2002 Uniform Securities Act is liable for damages to the person buying the security.[215] Similarly, a person is liable for damages to the purchaser of a security if the person offered or sold the security

> by means of any untrue statement of a material fact or any omission to state a material fact necessary in order to make the statements made, in light of the circumstances under which they are made, not misleading, the purchaser not knowing of the untruth or omission and the seller not sustaining the burden of proof that the seller did not know and, in the exercise of reasonable, care could not have known the untruth or omission.[216]

Any such private action must be brought within one year after the violation occurred.[217] Any provision in a contract for sale of securities that purports to waive the purchaser's right to bring such an action is void under the 2002 Uniform Securities Act.[218] Like the 1956 Uniform Securities Act, the 2002 Uniform Securities Act prohibits a purchaser from recovering if the issuer or broker-dealer makes a rescission offer that complies with that Act.[219]

---

213.   2002 Uniform Securities Act § 508(a), 1 Blue Sky Law Rptr. (CCH) ¶ 5636.
214.   *Id.*
215.   2002 Uniform Securities Act § 509(b) and (d), 1 Blue Sky Law Rptr. (CCH) ¶ 5637.
216.   2002 Uniform Securities Act § 509(b), 1 Blue Sky Law Rptr. (CCH) ¶ 5637.
217.   2002 Uniform Securities Act § 509(j)(1), 1 Blue Sky Law Rptr. (CCH) ¶ 5637.
218.   2002 Uniform Securities Act § 509(l), 1 Blue Sky Law Rptr. (CCH) ¶ 5637.
219.   2002 Uniform Securities Act § 510, 1 Blue Sky Law Rptr. (CCH) ¶ 5638.

CHAPTER **8**

Marketing Activities

§ 8.1 Introduction

As discussed in Chapter 5, in offering and selling its interests to investors in the United States, a hedge fund (whether domestic or offshore) relies on the private offering exemption from registration under the Securities Act. Hedge funds that offer and sell interests outside of the United States generally rely on the exemption provided by Regulation S under the Securities Act. The Advisers Act regulates "advertising" by investment advisers. These rules narrowly circumscribe how a hedge fund manager may market interests in a hedge fund.

§ 8.2 Private Offering Exemption

1. Limitation on Manner of Offering and Qualification of Persons Solicited

Securities Act section 4(2)[1] and its progeny, including Rule 502(c) of Regulation D, proscribe the offer or sale of securities in a private offering by any form of general solicitation or general advertising,[2] which includes (a) any advertisement, article, notice or other communication published in any newspaper, magazine or similar medium or broadcast over television or radio and (b) any seminar or meeting whose attendees have been invited by any general solicitation or general advertising.[3] This rule implicates the medium, the message and the audience. The issuer may not communicate anything about its offering using any of the proscribed media. As discussed in Chapter 6, regardless of the medium, the message must satisfy the issuer's obligation to make complete and accurate

---

1.   15 U.S.C. § 77d(2).

2.   17 C.F.R. § 230.502(c). *See, generally*, III Loss, L. and Seligman, J., *Securities Regulation*, Aspen Law & Business (3d Ed. 1999), at 1361-1399; Schneider, The Statutory Law of Private Placements, 14 Rev. Sec. Reg. 869 (1981).

3.   Regulation D Rule 502(c), 17 C.F.R. § 230.502(c).

disclosure. And, as discussed in Chapter 5, the audience should include only persons who the issuer reasonably believes are sufficiently sophisticated in business and financial matters to be able to understand the merits and risks of the investment and are able to bear the financial risk of the investment.[4] Such a belief may be based on a pre-existing substantive relationship between the issuer or its promoters and the offeree or may be formed by other means, and such relationships can help show the absence of a general solicitation.

Whether a general solicitation occurs depends on the facts and circumstances of the particular case.[5] The SEC staff has stated that the Rule 502(c) analysis can be divided into two separate inquiries:

> First, is the communication in question a general solicitation or general advertisement? Second, if it is, is it being used by the issuer or by someone on the issuer's behalf to offer or sell the securities? If either question can be answered in the negative, then the issuer will not be in violation of Rule 502(c). Questions under Rule 502(c) typically present issues of fact and circumstances that the staff is not in a position to resolve.[6]

Without being particularly helpful, SEC staff interpretations of Rule 502(c) (discussed below) suggest that the following factors should be considered in determining whether a solicitation or advertisement violates Rule 502(c):

- The relationship, if any, between the issuer and the person making the communication;
- The relationship, if any, between the issuer and the person receiving the communication;
- The timing of the communication; and
- The subject matter of the communication.

Determining whether or not a solicitation is general often involves subjective judgment. In the hedge fund context, the stakes are considerable, because miscalculation could be the basis for claims that the hedge fund and its manager have violated not only the registration requirement of the Securities Act,[7] but also the requirement for registration as a mutual fund under the Company Act[8] and, possibly, the requirement that the hedge fund manager register as an investment adviser under the Advisers Act.[9]

---

4.   *See, e.g., In re Mineral Lands Research and Marketing Corp.*, SEC No-Action Letter (Nov. 4, 1985).

5.   Securities Act Release No. 6825, 54 F.R. 11,369 (Mar. 20, 1989).

6.   Securities Act Release No. 6455, 48 F.R. 10,045 (Mar. 10, 1983).

7.   *See* §§ 5.2 and 5.3, *supra.*

8.   *See* Chapter 3, *supra.* The SEC staff has observed that, if an offer is public for purposes of the Securities Act, it would also ordinarily be public for purposes of the Company Act. *See, e.g., Lamp Technologies, Inc.*, SEC No-Action Letter (May 29, 1998).

9.   *See* § 2.1.2 *supra.*

2. Relationship between Hedge Fund and Person Making Communication

When a hedge fund or its representative arranges or is otherwise responsible for a general solicitation or general advertisement about the hedge fund or its offering, the private offering exemption is not available. If, however, an unrelated third party makes a general solicitation or advertisement without involving the hedge fund or its representatives, the Rule 502(c) prohibition should not be violated.

i. Advertisements by Affiliates

Press releases or other communications by a person that is an affiliate of a hedge fund may be deemed to be general advertisements or solicitations on behalf of the hedge fund for purposes of Rule 502(c) if that person "expect[s] to exercise direct and active management control over any substantial part of the activities, business dealings or administration" of the hedge fund.[10] In *In re Robert Testa,* an affiliate of a corporation that had formed a limited partnership to raise funds to develop the corporation's intellectual property rights assisted a selling agent by drafting a solicitation letter and obtaining a large mailing list. The SEC found that the affiliate had participated in a proscribed general solicitation on behalf of the issuer.[11]

ii. Advertisements by Nonaffiliates

When a hedge fund or its affiliate arranges for a third party to publish an advertisement or a solicitation, the third party will be deemed to be acting on the hedge fund's behalf, even though the third party may have independently decided to communicate information regarding the hedge fund or may have been solely responsible for the decision to publish a particular newsletter, trade journal or other publication containing the hedge fund's solicitation. In *J.D. Manning, Inc.,* the SEC staff determined that a publisher's proposed newsletter containing a list and description of closely held businesses that were expected to raise capital in future private placements would constitute a general solicitation on behalf of the participating businesses.[12]

A hedge fund should not, however, be viewed as conducting a general solicitation by virtue of a communication by a person who is not an affiliate of the hedge fund, is otherwise independent from any offering of the hedge fund's interests and does not look to the hedge fund or its affiliates for assistance or compensation with respect to the materials communicated, even if that communication might constitute a general advertisement or solicitation if it were made by the hedge fund

---

10. American Bar Association proposal to the SEC Division of Corporation Finance on behalf of the Subcommittees on Partnerships, Trusts and Unincorporated Associations and Registration Statements – Securities Act (June 1984).

11. *In re Robert Testa,* Securities Act Release No. 7018 (Sep. 29, 1993). *See also In re EMX Corp. & EMF Assocs., L.P.,* Securities Act Release No. 7019 (Sep. 29, 1993).

12. *J.D. Manning, Inc.,* SEC No-Action Letter (Jan. 27, 1986).

or its affiliate.[13] In such circumstances, the hedge fund would be allowed to retain any benefits flowing from the communication. If, however, a publication were to contain analyses and recommendations or feature forward-looking information from persons likely to participate in a future hedge fund offering, the SEC staff has stated that it would likely withhold no-action relief,[14] presumably on the grounds that the publication could be deemed a general solicitation or advertisement by the hedge fund.

iii. Matching Services

The SEC staff has allowed computer matching services to link issuers with potential investors in limited circumstances. In *Texas Capital Network, Inc.,* the SEC staff allowed a non-profit corporation ("TCN") to develop a computer database of subscribers consisting of investors and entrepreneurs to be matched, each of whom paid an annual membership fee. In deciding that the activities did not involve a general solicitation, the SEC focused on the following facts as evidence that TCN was not acting on any issuer's behalf:

- TCN had no affiliation or association with any participating entrepreneur;
- In soliciting investors to participate in its network, TCN used generic advertisements and never mentioned specific entrepreneurs;
- TCN undertook no investigation of the information entrepreneurs provided to it;
- TCN's service was limited to matching, and TCN did not assist in developing the terms of any investment opportunity;
- TCN did not receive compensation from any participant except for nominal administrative expenses; and
- Persons associated with TCN were prohibited from participating in the matching network.[15]

3. Relationship between Person Making Communication and Offeree

The SEC and its staff have repeatedly underscored the importance of the existence and substance of a pre-existing relationship between an issuer and those being solicited in determining what would not constitute a general solicitation.[16] The relationship should be extensive enough to enable the hedge fund or someone acting on its behalf to be aware of the financial circumstances and investment sophistication of the person solicited. Alternatively, the relationship should be one of significant substance or duration. An offer should generally be personally

---

13. *Richard Daniels,* SEC No-Action Letter (Dec. 19, 1984); *Nancy H. Blasberg,* SEC No-Action Letter (June 12, 1986).

14. Securities Act Release No. 6455, at 2637-13, 48 F.R. 10,045 (Mar. 10, 1983).

15. *Texas Capital Network, Inc.,* SEC No-Action Letter (Feb. 23, 1994). *See also* Chapter 9, *infra.*

16. *In the Matter of Kenman Corp. and Kenman Securities Corp.,* Admin. Proc. File No. 3-6505 (Apr. 19, 1985). *See also Woodtrails-Seattle, Ltd.,* SEC No-Action Letter (July 8, 1992).

directed to the offeree; the SEC staff has consistently viewed impersonal communications as general solicitations.[17]

i. Pre-existing Relationship

A substantive relationship is established when an issuer or its agent has sufficient information to evaluate the prospective offeree's sophistication and financial circumstances. Substantive relationships can also be established through business dealings or questionnaires. Even when a hedge fund solicits previous investors, however, it must believe that "each of the proposed offerees currently has such knowledge and experience in financial and business matters that he or she is capable of evaluating the merits and risks of the proposed investments."[18]

In *Royce Exchange Fund, Quest Advisory Corp.*,[19] the SEC staff permitted a registered investment adviser setting up a new fund to solicit the past and present directors and officers of portfolio companies, the immediate family members of such directors and officers, clients of various investment advisers that were significantly involved in the fund adviser's financial network and parties related to the portfolio companies who were referred by a placement agent who believed that the parties met the fund's suitability criteria.[20] The SEC staff noted the nature and extent of pre-existing relationships between the investment adviser and portfolio companies whose officers and directors were to be solicited, between the investment adviser and other registered investment advisers whose clients were to be solicited and between such clients and their investment advisers.

ii. Questionnaires

A substantive relationship may also be established through the use of an investor questionnaire, if sufficient time passes between receipt of the completed questionnaire and the time when an offering is first contemplated.[21] How much time is "sufficient" is unclear. Such a questionnaire must provide sufficient information for the hedge fund to evaluate a prospective offeree's sophistication and financial circumstances.[22]

---

17. *See, e.g., In the Matter of EMX Corporation and EMF Assocs., L.P.,* Admin. Proc. File No. 3-8185 (Sept. 29, 1993); *In the Matter of Kenman Corp. and Kenman Securities Corp.,* Admin. Proc. File No. 3-6505; *Pennsylvania Securities Commission,* SEC No-Action Letter (Jan. 16, 1990); *Webster Management Assured Return Equity Management. Group Trust,* SEC No-Action Letter (Feb. 7, 1987); *Aspen Grove,* SEC No-Action Letter (Dec. 8, 1982); *Trust Mortgage and Loan Svcs., Inc.,* SEC No-Action Letter (Dec. 27, 1979); *A.A. Ajax Co., Inc.,* SEC No-Action Letter (Jan. 15, 1979); and *Thoroughbred Racing Stable,* SEC No-Action Letter (Jan. 5, 1976).

18. *Woodtrails-Seattle, Ltd.,* SEC No-Action Letter (July 8, 1982).

19. *Royce Exchange Fund, Quest Advisory Corp.,* SEC No-Action Letter (Aug. 28, 1996).

20. *Royce Exchange Fund, Quest Advisory Corp.,* SEC No-Action Letter (Aug. 28, 1996).

21. *E.F. Hutton,* SEC No-Action Letter (Nov. 3, 1985); *H.B. Shaine & Co.,* SEC No-Action Letter (Mar. 31, 1987).

22. *E.F. Hutton,* SEC No-Action Letter (Nov. 3, 1985); *H.B. Shaine & Co.,* SEC No-Action Letter (Mar. 31, 1987).

iii. Brokers

The SEC staff has generally taken the view that traditional relationships between brokers and their customers, which require brokers to deal fairly with and make suitable recommendations to the customers, are "substantive" in the private offering context.[23] Accordingly, the SEC staff has held that a broker's program of contacting prospective investors will not constitute a general solicitation or advertisement, if the proposed solicitation is generic and does not refer to any specific investment that the broker is then offering or contemplating offering, and the broker implements procedures to ensure that persons solicited are not offered any securities that were offered or contemplated for offering at the time of the solicitation.[24]

A broker's generic recruitment of prospective investors must be followed, however, by the development of a more substantive relationship before any offer is made. The SEC staff has stated that a subsequent offer to a person who responds to a broker's generic recruitment efforts will be deemed made by general solicitation as a result of the initial contact, unless the broker or the issuer establishes a substantive relationship with the offeree between the initial solicitation and the later offer. Again, the broker or the issuer must obtain sufficient information to evaluate the prospective offeree's sophistication and financial circumstances.[25]

4. Timing

When a general solicitation or general advertisement coincides with the timing of an offer and sale of hedge fund interests, the advertisement or other communication will likely be deemed to have been used in connection with the offer or sale of hedge fund interests.[26] Even a public relations or marketing campaign that promotes a hedge fund but that does not invite prospective investors to contact the hedge fund directly may be deemed a general solicitation if it "conditions the market." The SEC staff has noted:

> Rule 502(c) does not specifically prohibit advertising or other activities intended to promote or market an issuer's products or services. Rather, it prohibits the use of general solicitation or general advertising in connection with the offer or sale of the issuer's securities in reliance on Regulation D. Whether or not an issuer's product promotion can also be deemed general solicitation or general advertising for the offer or sale of its securities under Regulation D is a question of fact that the Division [of Corporation Finance] generally will not be in a position to resolve. The question requires an evaluation not only of the content of the specific advertising but also of the actual use of each advertisement in relation to the offering of securities.[27]

---

23.   Securities Act Release Nos. 33-7856 ("Use of Electronic Media") (Apr. 28, 2000), 65 F.R. 25,843 (May 4, 2000).

24.   *Bateman, Eichler, Hill Richards, Inc.*, SEC No-Action Letter (Dec. 3, 1985).

25.   *Id.*

26.   *J.D. Manning, Inc.*, SEC No-Action Letter (Jan. 29, 1986).

27.   *Printing Enterprise Management Science, Inc.*, SEC No-Action Letter (Mar. 23, 1983).

5. Subject Matter

If a broker is assisting in placing a hedge fund's interests, it may solicit only those investors with whom it had a pre-existing substantive relationship before it offers particular investments.[28] The offeror must ensure that each offeree understands that the hedge fund offers interests only by way of its disclosure documents and only to persons that the hedge fund's general partner believes are qualified for purposes of the private offering exemption.[29]

6. Number of Persons Solicited

The number of persons solicited is not necessarily a critical factor in determining whether or not a solicitation is general. In interpretations of Rule 502(c), for example, the SEC focuses primarily on the nature of persons solicited. When the SEC staff has found the nature of the persons solicited acceptable, it has not objected to solicitations to hundreds of persons. In *Woodtrails-Seattle, Ltd.*, a solicitation of more than 300 former investors was acceptable.[30] In *Mineral-Lands Research and Marketing Corporation,* the acceptable class of offerees included 600 persons who were existing clients of an officer who was also an insurance broker.[31] The focus on a pre-existing relationship between an offeror and offeree requires that the offeror be in a position to evaluate all of the prospective offerees, no matter how few or how numerous they are, to determine whether each of them is sophisticated in business and financial matters.[32] If the issuer cannot demonstrate pre-existing relationships with its offerees, it may not be able to bear its burden of proof that its solicitation was private and not general.

7. Sophistication of Offerees

That an offeree is financially sophisticated or wealthy does not by itself enable a hedge fund to solicit that offeree without having any prior contact or relationship. In *Kenman Corporation and Kenman Securities Corporation,* the SEC sued an SEC-registered broker and its associated person for mailing information relating to interests in a land development limited partnership to an unknown number of persons identified on lists of executive officers of Fortune 500 companies, persons who had previously invested $10,000 or more in real estate offerings by other issuers, physicians in California, managerial engineers employed by aircraft companies and presidents of companies listed in the Morris County, New Jersey, Industrial Directory.[33] In *EMX Corporation and EMF Associates, L.P,* the SEC sued a company that had mailed solicitation materials to between 80,000 and 90,000 physicians throughout the United States.[34] There, the SEC noted, "[a]lthough the

---

28.   *Bateman, Eichler, Hill Richards, Inc.*, SEC No-Action Letter (Dec. 3, 1985).

29.   *E. F. Hutton & Co.*, SEC No-Action Letter (Nov. 3, 1985); *see also* Chapter 6, *supra.*

30.   *Woodtrails-Seattle, Ltd.*, SEC No-Action Letter (July 8, 1982).

31.   *Mineral Lands Research & Marketing Corp.*, SEC No-Action (Dec. 4, 1985).

32.   *Woodtrails-Seattle, Ltd.*, SEC No-Action Letter (July 8, 1982); *E.F. Hutton & Co.*, SEC No-Action Letter (Dec. 5, 1985).

33.   *In the Matter of Kenman Corp. and Kenman Securities Corp.*, Admin. Proc. File No. 3-6505 (Apr. 19, 1985).

34.   *In the Matter of EMX Corp. and EMF Associates, L.P,* Admin. Proc. File No. 3-8185 (Sep. 29, 1993).

make-up of the lists may indicate that the persons themselves have some degree of sophistication or financial well being, utilization of lists of thousands of persons with no pre-existing relationship to the offeror clearly does not comply with the limitations of Rule 502(c) on the manner of solicitation."[35]

8. Disclosure Requirements

Regulation D does not require that any particular information be furnished to purchasers if a hedge fund sells interests only to accredited investors. The SEC staff directs an unregistered hedge fund to use Form N-1A as a guide for the preparation of its Regulation D disclosure documents.[36] If, however, a sale is made to any non-accredited investor, the hedge fund must furnish the more extensive information specified in Rule 502(b)(2) a "reasonable time before the sale."[37] A hedge fund may choose to furnish to potential investors a short-form offering memorandum in anticipation of actual selling activities, so long as it follows with delivery of an expanded disclosure document such that "all the information is delivered prior to sale."[38]

§ 8.3 Marketing Activities Outside of the United States

1. Regulation S; Directed Selling

The SEC adopted Regulation S[39] in 1990 to clarify its position that securities offered and sold outside of the United States do not need to be registered under the Securities Act, if specified conditions are met. Regulation S provides a safe harbor exemption from the registration requirements of the Securities Act. Under Regulation S, no "directed selling efforts" may be made in the United States in connection with an offer, sale or resale.[40] "Directed selling efforts" include mailing printed materials to U.S. investors; conducting promotional seminars in the United States; placing advertisements in publications with general circulation in, or with radio or television stations broadcasting into, the United States; and making offers directed at identifiable groups of U.S. citizens in another country.[41]

---

35. *Id.*

36. Regulation D Rule 502(b)(2)(i)(A), 17 C.F.R. § 230.502(b)(2)(i)(A); *Robert T. Willis, Jr., P.C.*, SEC No-Action Letter (Jan. 18, 1988). *But see* Chapter 6, *supra.*

37. *Robert T. Willis, Jr., P.C.*, SEC No-Action Letter (Jan. 18, 1988). *See* § 5.3.2.vii and Chapter 6, *supra.*

38. Securities Act Release No. 6455, Question (4), at 2637-8, 48 F.R. 10,045, Question 4 (Mar. 10, 1983); *see* Chapter 6, *supra.*

39. Regulation S Rules 901 through 904, 17 C.F.R. §§ 230.901-904.

40. Regulation S Adopting Release, Release No. 6863, Fed. Sec. L. Rep. (CCH) 84,524, at 80,666 (Apr. 24, 1990), 55 F.R. 18,306 (May 2, 1990).

41. Regulation S Rule 902(c)(2), 17 C.F.R. § 230.902(c)(2).

The following activities are specifically excluded from the definition of "directed selling efforts":

- advertising that is required under law or regulations;
- communicating with persons excluded from the definition of "United States person";
- advertising in the form of tombstones in publications with less than twenty percent of their circulation in the United States;
- prospective investors making bona fide visits to real estate facilities;
- distributing quotations of a non-U.S. broker using a third-party system in non-U.S. countries, as long as the system does not allow any security transaction to be executed between the non-U.S. broker and any person in the United States and no contact with U.S. persons is initiated;
- giving proper notice under Rule 135 under the Securities Act that an issuer intends to make a registered public offering of its securities;
- providing journalists with access to issuer meetings held outside of the United States;
- having isolated and limited contact;
- placing routine advertisements unrelated to selling efforts; and
- conducting customary and legal activities outside of the United States.[42]

2. Private Offering; Marketing to Non-U.S. Investors

A hedge fund may make offers and sales in the United States without registration in reliance on the private offering exemption, including Rule 506 of Regulation D, while simultaneously making an offering to non-U.S. investors without registration in reliance on either or both of the private offering exemption and Regulation S. Alternatively, a hedge fund may rely solely on the private offering exemption for an offering of hedge fund interests to both U.S. and non-U.S. persons, as long as all of the requirements of Regulation D are met.[43]

In *Jack B. Straus*,[44] a non-U.S. investment adviser sought to conduct a public solicitation through non-U.S. media to attract non-U.S. investors while offering and selling the same securities in the United States pursuant to Rule 505 of Regulation D. He proposed to solicit investors in his country through advertisements in non-U.S. magazines and newspapers that were published and distributed in his country and then follow up leads from those advertisements. The SEC staff noted that since the investment adviser was considering advertising the offering in French newspapers of general circulation, there could be no assurance that such newspapers would not ultimately be distributed in the United States. Accordingly, the SEC staff concluded that, although the investment adviser's intent may have been to solicit investors outside of the United States, the effect may have been a solicitation of U.S. citizens or residents in violation of Rule 502(c).

---

42.   Rule 902(c)(3); 17 C.F.R. § 230.902(c)(3).
43.   *Intron, Ltd.*, SEC No-Action Letter (Sep. 14, 1984).
44.   *Jack B. Straus*, SEC No-Action Letter (Aug. 20, 1985).

3. Non-U.S. Exchange Listing

Offshore hedge funds sometimes list their interests on recognized non-U.S. exchanges, often because some non-U.S. investors may be restricted or prohibited from investing, or reluctant to invest, in unregistered securities that are not listed on a recognized or regulated exchange. An offshore hedge fund seeking to expand its marketing reach may list its shares on the Irish Stock Exchange, the Hong Kong Stock Exchange, the Bermuda Stock Exchange, the Cayman Islands Stock Exchange, or another appropriate exchange—various jurisdictions recognize different exchanges for these purposes. These stock exchanges typically impose requirements such as an application with a prospectus, investment guidelines and limitations, periodic audited financial statements and ongoing duties to update disclosures. These requirements are usually less onerous than the listing requirements of U.S. exchanges. Local counsel may be engaged to coordinate the listing process and oversee maintenance procedures.

§ 8.4 Advisers Act Regulation of Content

Advertisements relating to hedge funds are subject to the prohibitions of false and misleading advertisements in Advisers Act section 206(4)[45] and Rule 206(4)-1[46] under the Advisers Act and to the general anti-fraud prohibitions of Advisers Act sections 206(1) and (2).[47] The Advisers Act imposes these requirements on all investment advisers, whether or not registered with the SEC as investment advisers. Rule 206(4)-1(b) provides, in part, that:

> For purposes of this rule the term "advertisement" shall include any notice, circular, letter or other written communication addressed to more than one person, or any notice or other announcement in any publication or by radio or television, which offers (1) any analysis, report, or publication concerning securities, or which is to be used in making any determination as to when to buy or sell any security, or which security to buy or sell, or (2) any graph, chart, formula or other device to be used in making any determination as to when to buy or sell any security, or which security to buy or sell, or (3) any other investment advisory service with regard to securities.

Accordingly, most hedge fund confidential offering circulars would be or contain "advertisements" for this purpose, notwithstanding their narrowly controlled distribution for purposes of the private offering exemption.

---

45.   15 U.S.C. § 80b-6(4).
46.   17 C.F.R. § 275.206(4)-1.
47.   15 U.S.C. §§ 80b-6(1) and 80b-6(2).

1. Fraudulent, Deceptive or Manipulative Advertising

Rule 206(4)-1 defines the following practices in any advertisement as fraudulent, deceptive or manipulative:

- publishing or distributing testimonials of any kind concerning the investment adviser or concerning any advice, analysis, report or other services rendered by that investment adviser (see below);
- referring to past specific recommendations of the investment adviser that were or would have been profitable to any persons, unless such advertisement sets out or offers to furnish a list of all recommendations made by the investment adviser within the preceding year and contains a legend that states: "It should not be assumed that recommendations made in the future will be profitable or will equal the performance of the securities in this list";[48]
- representing that any graph, chart, formula or other device offered in the advertisement (1) can, in and of itself, be used to determine which securities to buy or sell or when to buy and sell securities or (2) will assist any person in making investment decisions, without prominently disclosing the limitations of such graph, chart, formula or other device used;
- falsely promising to furnish reports or analyses free of charge to investors; and
- containing any untrue statement of a material fact or otherwise being false or misleading.[49]

i. Testimonials

The prohibition of Rule 206(4)-1 on testimonials reflects the SEC's view that statements of a customer's experience or endorsement are likely to give rise to a fraudulent or deceptive implication or mistaken inference that the positive experience of the person providing the testimonial is typical of the experience of all of the investment adviser's clients. The SEC has stated that advertisements containing testimonials are inherently misleading, as they inevitably emphasize favorable reactions while ignoring unfavorable ones.[50]

The SEC staff has interpreted the term "testimonial" to include "any statement of a client's experience with, or endorsement of, an adviser,"[51] including statements about an investment adviser's character, religious affiliation, diligence, attention to detail, prudence or knowledge of investing.[52] The SEC staff has stated that even a statement that a mutual acquaintance would be willing to act as a reference and discuss with an investment adviser's potential client his investment experience with

---

48. *See* §§ 17.2 and 17.3, *infra.*
49. Advisers Act Rule 206(4)-1(a), 17 C.F.R. § 275.206(4)-1.
50. Advisers Act Release No. 121 (Nov. 2, 1961); 26 F.R. 10,549 (Nov. 9, 1961).
51. *Cambiar Investors, Inc.,* SEC No-Action Letter (Aug. 28, 1997).
52. *Journal of Financial Planning,* SEC No-Action Letter (Feb. 2, 1996).

that investment adviser would be a testimonial.[53] In *Investor Intelligence,* the SEC staff viewed a proposed statement that an investment adviser was a "recognized powerful psychic medium" as a prohibited indirect testimonial to that person's capabilities.[54] The SEC staff has stated, however, that an article by an unbiased third party concerning an investment adviser's performance is not a testimonial, unless it includes a statement of a client's experience with, or endorsement of, the investment adviser.[55]

ii. Favorable Press

The SEC staff has stated that the reprint of an article or publication by an unbiased third party that refers to an investment adviser's performance is not a testimonial, unless the article includes a quote from a client. An article that contains favorable quotes only from non-clients is not considered to be a testimonial.[56] Even if a reprint is not a testimonial, however, its distribution is subject to the anti-fraud provisions of the Advisers Act. If the reprint implies something about, or is likely to cause an unwarranted inference to be drawn about, the experience of advisory clients, the possibility of other clients enjoying an investment experience similar to that of prior clients or the investment adviser's competence, it could be a fraudulent, deceptive or manipulative practice prohibited by Rule 206(4)-1.[57]

iii. Use of Client Lists

An investment adviser may use an advertisement that includes a list of representative clients if (a) the investment adviser uses objective criteria (such as account size, geographic location or client classification) to determine which clients to include in the list, and the criteria do not include the performance of clients' accounts; (b) each client list includes a statement disclosing the objective criteria used to determine which clients to include in the list; and (c) each client list includes a disclaimer stating that "it is not known whether the listed clients approve or disapprove of [name of investment adviser] or the advisory service provided."[58] In addition, state rules sometimes require that an investment adviser obtain the consent of a client before it discloses the identity, affairs or investments of that client to any third party (unless such disclosure is required by law).[59]

---

53. *Analytic Inv. Mgmt., Inc.,* SEC No-Action Letter (Mar. 22, 1971).

54. *Investor Intelligence (John Anthony),* SEC No-Action Letter (Apr. 18, 1975).

55. *Richard Silverman,* SEC No-Action Letter (Feb. 25, 1985).

56. *Stalker Advisory Services,* SEC No-Action Letter (Jan. 18, 1994).

57. *Id.*; *Kurtz Capital Mgmt.,* SEC No-Action Letter (Jan. 18, 1988).

58. *Denver Investment Advisors, Inc.,* SEC No-Action Letter (July 30, 1993); and *Cambiar Investors, Inc.,* SEC No-Action Letter (Aug. 28, 1997).

59. *See e.g.,* 10 Cal. Code of Reg., § 260.238(m).

iv. Ratings

The SEC staff will likely allow the dissemination of numerical ratings of a hedge fund prepared by an independent company based on client surveys when the following conditions are met:

- All participating investment advisers have had to meet specified eligibility criteria;
- The rating firm is not affiliated with any participating investment adviser or representative;
- The rating firm surveys all or a statistically valid sample of the investment adviser's clients;
- All participating investment advisers are charged a fee by the rating firm;
- The rating firm issues ratings only when statistically valid; and
- Any survey results published identify the percentage of participants that received each rating.[60]

Such use of ratings information in advertisements is always subject, however, to the prohibition of false or misleading advertising in Advisers Act section 206(4).[61]

v. Misleading Implications

All advertisements must disclose any material facts concerning the information conveyed that are necessary to avoid any misleading implications. If the overall impression conveyed by an advertisement is misleading or deceptive, the advertisement will be prohibited, even if no individual statement in it is untrue and it does not violate any of the other specific prohibitions discussed above.[62] Whether an advertisement is false or misleading depends on the facts and circumstances, including the form and content of the advertisement; the investment adviser's ability to perform what it has advertised; the implications arising out of the advertisement in its total context; and the sophistication of the prospective client,[63] although the SEC staff on some occasions has stated that advertisements must be evaluated "from the viewpoint of a person unskilled and unsophisticated in investment matters."[64] The SEC may also deem an advertisement to be misleading, and take enforcement action against the investment adviser, if it involves even a single particular statement that is specifically prohibited.[65]

---

60. *Dalbar, Inc.*, SEC No-Action Letter (Mar. 24, 1998).

61. 15 U.S.C. § 80b-6(4).

62. *SEC v. C.R. Richmond & Co.*, 565 F.2d 1101, 1106–07 (9th Cir. 1977).

63. *Triad Asset Mgmt., Inc.*, SEC No-Action Letter (April 22, 1993); *Anametrics Inv. Mgmt.*, SEC No-Action Letter (May 5, 1977).

64. *SEC v. C.R. Richmond & Co.*, 565 F.2d 1101, 1104 (9th Cir. 1977); *Marketlines, Inc. v. SEC*, 384 F.2d 264, 266 (2d Cir. 1967).

65. James E. Anderson et al., *Investment Advisers: Law & Compliance* (2003), § 7.04.

vi. Information Relating to Third Parties

If an investment adviser to a hedge fund advises investors in the hedge fund about the services of third parties, the investment adviser should not distribute misleading marketing materials regarding those third parties.[66]

vii. Information Provided to Consultants or Publications

The SEC also applies its standards for investment adviser advertisements to a variety of communications from an investment adviser to an intermediary who may be expected to relay that information to investors who may invest in a hedge fund managed by the investment adviser. Accordingly, the anti-fraud rules apply to information that an investment adviser distributes to consultants and reporting services,[67] press releases,[68] interviews with advisory publications,[69] and other materials provided by investment advisers to newspapers and other periodicals.[70]

viii. Communications Not Deemed "Advertisements"

To constitute an advertisement, a communication must "offer" advisory services. Periodic reports to existing clients (such as monthly or quarterly statements or narrative reports) are not considered advertisements, if all material disclosures are included.[71] Communications intended to induce existing clients to renew advisory services, however, are "advertisements."[72]

2. General Anti-Fraud Provisions

Even if a communication is not an "advertisement" under Rule 206(4)-1, it may nevertheless be subject to the anti-fraud provisions of Advisers Act sections 206(1) and (2).[73] Section 206(1) prohibits investment advisers from using the mails or any means or instrumentality of interstate commerce to employ any device, scheme or artifice to defraud any current or prospective client. In an enforcement action under this provision, the SEC must prove that an investment adviser acted with scienter (that is, a knowing or reckless disregard for the truth).[74] Advisers Act section 206(2) prohibits an investment adviser from engaging in any transaction, practice or course of business that operates as a fraud or deceit on any current or prospective client. In an enforcement action under this provision, the SEC must prove only negligence.[75]

---

66.   *In re Performance Analytics, Inc.*, Advisers Act Release No. 1978 (Sep. 27, 2001).

67.   *In re Oxford Capital Mgmt., Inc.*, Advisers Act Release No. 2061 (Sep. 23, 2002); *In re Engebretson Capital Mgmt., Inc.*, Advisers Act Release No. 1825 (Sep. 13, 1999); *In re Boston Inv. Counsel. Inc.*, Advisers Act Release No. 1801 (June 10, 1999); *In re Profitek, Inc.*, Advisers Act Release No. 1764 (Sep. 29, 1998); *Investment Company Institute*, SEC No-Action Letter (Sep. 23, 1988).

68.   *In re Finarc, LLC*, Advisers Act Release No. 1763 (Sep. 29, 1998).

69.   *In re C&G Asset Mgmt., Inc.*, Advisers Act Release No. 1536 (Nov. 9, 1995).

70.   *In re Profitek, Inc.*, Advisers Act Release No. 1764 (Sep. 29, 1998).

71.   *Askin Capital Mgmt., L.P.*, Advisers Act Release No. 1492 (May 23, 1995).

72.   *In re Spear & Staff*, Advisers Act Release No. 188 (Mar. 25, 1965).

73.   15 U.S.C. §§ 80b-6(1) and 80b-6(2).

74.   *SEC v. Steadman*, 967 F.2d 636 (D.C. Cir. 1992).

75.   *Id.*

3. Holding Out to the Public

Advisers Act section 203(b)(3) exempts from registration certain investment advisers that do not hold themselves out generally to the public as investment advisers.[76] Although no bright-line rules establish when one is holding oneself out to the public as an investment adviser, the SEC staff has interpreted the concept broadly to include: advertising related to investment advisory activities; maintaining a listing as an investment adviser in a telephone or building directory;[77] letting it be known through word of mouth or other channels that the investment adviser is accepting new clients;[78] participating in a "mini-account" or similar investment advisory program;[79] using the label "investment adviser" on business cards or stationery;[80] and using an Internet website to provide information about its services.[81]

The SEC staff does not view the manager of a hedge fund that participates in a non-public offering of interests in the hedge fund as "holding itself out publicly" for purposes of Advisers Act section 203(b)(3).[82] Moreover, the SEC staff has deemed certain password protected online services that offer targeted groups biographical and contact information about hedge fund managers (such as names, phone numbers, biographical information about the managers, data about the firms and their assets under management and the like) not to violate the "holding out" prohibition.[83] In *Thomson Financial Inc.*, Thomson proposed to provide investment professionals with data, analyses and information tools on the equity and bond holdings of mutual funds, pension plans, insurance companies and variable annuity products, as well as biographical information about these companies' investment managers that had been derived from non-public sources (the fund managers themselves). The SEC staff granted no action relief, based particularly on Thomson's representations (a) that it would make its services available exclusively to institutional sales and trading desks of registered brokers to streamline their communications with institutional investors and to fund managers to allow them to monitor the portfolio holdings of competing funds with similar investment strategies and (b) that it had implemented procedures to prevent persons seeking investment advisory services from gaining access to its services.[84]

When dealing with the media to discuss analyses, current holdings or past recommendations, an investment adviser to a hedge fund that is relying on the

---

76. Advisers Act § 203(b)(3); 15 U.S.C. § 806-3(b)(8). *See* §§ 2.1.2.iii and 2.1.2.iv, *supra*.

77. *Dale M. Muller*, SEC No-Action Letter (Feb. 20, 1984).

78. *Peter H. Jacobs*, SEC No-Action Letter (Feb. 7, 1979).

79. Company Act Release No. 21260 n. 8 (July 27, 1995), 60 F.R. 39,574 (Aug. 2, 1995); *Resource Bank and Trust*, SEC No-Action Letter (Mar. 29, 1991).

80. *Richard W. Blanz*, SEC No-Action Letter (Jan. 28, 1985).

81. Securities Act Release No. 7288 (May 9, 1996), 61 F. R. 24,644 (May 15, 1996). If sufficient procedures exist to limit access to selected accredited investors, the SEC staff has permitted a website provider to post hedge fund information on an Internet website, without causing the investment advisers to such hedge funds to be deemed to be holding themselves out to the public within the meaning of Advisers Act § 203(b)(3). *See Lamp Technologies, Inc.*, SEC No-Action Letter (May 29, 1997). *See* Chapter 9, *infra*.

82. *Resource Bank and Trust*, SEC No-Action Letter (Mar. 29, 1991); *Weiss, Barton Asset Management*, SEC No-Action Letter (Mar. 12, 1981).

83. *Thomson Financial Inc.*, SEC No-Action Letter (July 10, 2002).

84. *Id. See* § 9.2.1, *infra*.

exemption from registration in Advisers Act section 203(b)(3) should not describe its advisory services in ways that could be construed as advertising those services.[85]

4. "Brochure Rule"

Advisers Act Rule 204-3 (the "brochure rule")[86] requires an SEC-registered investment adviser to provide Part II of its Form ADV, or a comparable document providing at least the information elicited by Part II, to prospective investors in hedge funds that the investment adviser manages. The investment adviser must provide the brochure at least forty-eight hours before an investor enters into a written or oral advisory contract, unless the investor has the right to terminate the contract without penalty for five business days after entering the contract, in which case the required information must be delivered when the advisory contract is formed.[87]

5. Solicitation Disclosures

Advisers Act Rule 206(4)-3 (the "solicitors rule") establishes conditions under which an SEC-registered investment adviser may pay a cash fee to an independent contractor who solicits hedge fund investors.[88] To comply with the safe harbor established by the solicitors rule, the investment adviser and the solicitor must enter into a written agreement governing the arrangement, the solicitor must provide to each person solicited, among other things, the investment adviser's brochure and written disclosure about the investment adviser's relationship with the solicitor (including the compensation paid), and the investor must acknowledge in writing receipt of the disclosure. The investment adviser must retain copies of this disclosure and acknowledgement.[89] A solicitor for impersonal advisory services (such as an advisory newsletter) is not required to provide such written disclosure.[90] A partner, officer, director or employee of an investment adviser is subject to the solicitors rule and must disclose his or her status as a partner, officer, director or employee of the investment adviser, but is not required to disclose his or her compensation for solicitation activities or to receive a written acknowledgment from the investor.[91]

An investment adviser may not pay fees to a solicitor (whether or not an employee of the investment adviser and whether or not the solicitation is for impersonal advisory services) who has been convicted within the past ten years of certain felonies or misdemeanors, has violated the federal securities laws, is subject to an SEC order or decree, or is permanently or temporarily enjoined by order, judgment or decree of any court of competent jurisdiction from acting as, or as

---

85. *See* §§ 2.1.2.iii and 2.1.2.iv, *supra.*
86. *See* § 6.5, *supra.*
87. Advisers Act Rule 204-3, 17 C.F.R. § 275.204-3. *See* § 6.5.1, *supra.*
88. Advisers Act Rule 206(4)-3, 17 C.F.R. §§ 275.206(4)-3.
89. Advisers Act Rule 206(4)-3(b), 17 C.F.R. 275.2 206(4)-3(b).
90. Advisers Act Rule 206(4)-3(a)(2)(i), 17 C.F.R. § 275.206(4)-3(a)(2)(i).
91. Advisers Act Rule 206(4)-3(a)(2)(ii), 17 C.F.R. § 275.206(4)-3(a)(2)(ii).

an affiliated person or employee of, an investment adviser, underwriter, broker, dealer, transfer agent or certain other occupations relating to the purchase or sale of securities.[92] The solicitors rule prohibits an investment adviser from hiring as a solicitor a person whom the investment adviser is not permitted to hire as an employee, and thus from doing indirectly what it cannot do directly.[93] If an independent contractor is assisting an investment adviser in marketing hedge fund interests, the independent contractor ordinarily will be required to register as a broker, as well as comply with the solicitors rule.[94]

The SEC has stated that an investment adviser that is not registered with the SEC in reliance on the Private Adviser Exemption (discussed above in section 2.1.2) may not rely on the solicitors rule, because an investment adviser that engages a solicitor is holding itself out to the public as an investment adviser.[95] In addition, the solicitors rule only authorizes the payment of cash referral fees to solicitors. Although no formal SEC statement prohibits the payment of non-cash referral fees to solicitors, the SEC might question the propriety of such payments, particularly absent full disclosure about the arrangement. All investment advisers should make at least the disclosures required by the solicitors rule to any potential investor solicited by a paid solicitor. In recent years, the SEC has instituted an increasing number of enforcement actions alleging violations of the solicitors rule by investment advisers and solicitors.[96]

6. Broker Requirements

Exchange Act section 15[97] makes it unlawful for a person to sell securities unless that person is registered with the SEC as a broker.[98] A general partner of a hedge fund or any employee, officer, director or partner of the general partner of the hedge fund, however, may be exempt from registration under Rule 3a4-1[99] under the Exchange Act. Rule 3a4-1 provides a safe harbor exemption from the broker registration requirements for any person who is considered to be an "associated person of an issuer" if such person meets certain conditions.[100]

7. Record Retention

Under the Advisers Act, an SEC-registered investment adviser to a hedge fund must keep the following marketing records:[101]

- each notice, circular, advertisement, newspaper article, investment letter, bulletin or other communication that the adviser circulates or distributes,

---

92.   Advisers Act Rule 206(4)-3(a)(1)(ii), 17 C.F.R. § 275.206(4)-3(a)(i)(ii).
93.   Advisers Act Release No. 688 (July 12, 1979), 44 F.R. 42,130 (July 18, 1979).
94.   Advisers Act Rule 206(4)-3, 17 C.F.R. § 275.206(4)-3. *See* § 8.4.6 and Chapter 10, *infra*.
95.   Advisers Act Release No. 688 (July 12, 1979), 44 F.R. 42,130 (July 18, 1979).
96.   Advisers Act Release No. 1409 (Apr. 6, 1994); Advisers Act Release No. 1500 (June 16, 1995).
97.   15 U.S.C. § 78o.
98.   *See* Chapter 10, *infra*.
99.   17 C.F.R. § 240.3a4-1.
100.   *Id.*
101.   *See also* § 2.8, *supra*.

directly or indirectly, to ten or more persons (other than persons connected with the adviser), and if the communication recommends the purchase or sale of a specific security, but the communication does not state the reasons for a recommendation, a memorandum by the adviser indicating the adviser's reasons for the recommendation;[102]

- a copy of each Part II of Form ADV and amendment or revision given to any person and a record of the dates and persons to whom such statements were given or offered to be given;[103]

- all written acknowledgments of receipt obtained from advisory clients relating to disclosure of solicitor fees paid by the adviser and copies of all disclosure statements delivered to the adviser's clients by such solicitors;[104]

- all accounts, books, internal working papers and any other records or documents that are necessary to form the basis for or demonstrate the calculation of the performance or rate of return of any or all managed accounts or securities recommendations in any marketing material, except that, with respect to the performance of managed accounts, this requirement is satisfied by the retention of all account statements, if they reflect all debits, credits and other transactions in a client's account for the period of the statement, and the retention of all worksheets necessary to demonstrate the calculation of the performance or rate of return of all managed accounts;[105] and

- originals of all written communications received and copies of all written communications sent by the investment adviser relating to recommendations or advice given or proposed; receipt, disbursement or delivery of funds or securities; or the placing or execution of securities transaction orders. When sending correspondence to a client, the investment adviser should either retain a copy of the correspondence or retain a form of the correspondence sent to all or a group of clients with a list of the clients to whom such correspondence is sent.[106]

An investment adviser must also maintain complete records relating to its compliance with the private offering exemption,[107] so that it will be able to demonstrate the availability of the exemption should the need arise. Those records include, among other things, copies of the hedge fund's offering circular and other

---

102.   Advisers Act Rule 204-2(a)(11), 17 C.F.R. § 275.204-2(a)(11). 10 Cal. Code of Reg., § 260.241.3(a)(11).

103.   Advisers Act Rule 204-2(a)(14), 17 C.F.R. § 275.204-2(a)(14). *See* § 6.5, *supra*.

104.   Advisers Act Rule 204-2(a)(15), 17 C.F.R. § 275.204-2(a)(15).

105.   Advisers Act Rule 204-2(a)(16), 17 C.F.R. § 275.204-2(a)(16). *See Jennison Associates LLC,* SEC No-Action Letter (July 6, 2000).

106.   Advisers Act Rule 204-2(a)(7), 17 C.F.R. § 275.204-2(a)(7); *see* § 2.8, *supra*. Under the Advisers Act, an investment adviser is not required to keep any unsolicited market letters and other similar communications of general public distribution not prepared by or for the investment adviser, and if the investment adviser sends any notice, circular or other advertisement offering any report, analysis, publication or other investment advisory service to more than ten persons, the investment adviser is not required to keep a record of the names and addresses of the persons to whom it was sent, except that, if such notice, circular or advertisement is distributed to persons named on any list, the investment adviser must retain with the copy of such notice, circular or advertisement a memorandum describing the list and its source.

107.   *See* §§ 5.3 and 8.2, *supra*.

offering documents, the names of all offerees and a log showing that offering circulars were sent to them, records evidencing the investment sophistication and financial capacity of the offerees, and records showing the investment adviser's pre-existing relationships with them. If the investment adviser uses a broker or finder, it should obtain and keep copies of all similar records collected by the broker or finder, as well as its written agreement with the broker or finder.

CHAPTER **9**

Websites

§ 9.1 Introduction

Websites are increasingly important tools for hedge funds and investment advisers in building and maintaining relationships with investors, gauging investor suitability and marketing hedge funds. The prohibition of general solicitation and advertising in private offerings[1] applies equally to online communications. The anti-fraud rules of the Securities Act and the Exchange Act, discussed above in section 6.4, apply to anything on or linked to the investment adviser's or the hedge fund's website that is (or might be deemed to be) part of the hedge fund's offering materials. The general partner of a hedge fund must exercise great care in using the Internet, both to preserve the hedge fund's private offering exemption under the Securities Act and its exception from definition of "investment company" under the Company Act[2] and, if the investment adviser is an SEC-Exempt Adviser relying on the Private Adviser Exemption, to avoid holding itself out to the public as an investment adviser.[3] Interpretive issues also arise when a hedge fund's or investment adviser's website hyperlinks to third-party information. Websites must also comply with state and other regulatory regimes, and websites that offer interests in hedge funds to non-U.S. investors must comply with the additional requirements of Regulation S.[4]

§ 9.2 Preserving Private Offering Exemption

In general, the general partner of a hedge fund should not offer or sell interests in the hedge fund by using the Internet. When the SEC first considered whether a private offering could be conducted over the Internet, it concluded that an offering made through an unrestricted and publicly available website would violate the

---

1.   *See* Chapters 5 and 8, *supra.*
2.   *See* Chapter 3, *supra.*
3.   *See* §§ 2.1.2.iii and 8.4.3, *supra.*
4.   *See* §§ 5.4 and 8.3, *supra.*

prohibition of general solicitation or advertising.[5] Accordingly, access to a hedge fund's website should be strictly controlled to ensure that neither unsophisticated nor non-accredited investors can gain access.[6]

The SEC interpretations discussed below for the most part address private offerings made in reliance on Regulation D. It is an open question whether those interpretations would be applied to a private offering made in reliance on Securities Act section 4(2) apart from Regulation D, but the tenor of the pre-Regulation D case law suggests that they would not.

1. Online Marketing by Affiliated Brokers

In *IPONET*,[7] the SEC staff gave no-action relief to a registered broker and its affiliate ("IPONET") that planned to invite prospective investors who had previously registered as members of IPONET to complete a questionnaire posted on IPONET's Internet website "as a means of building a customer base and database of accredited and sophisticated investors." A password-protected web page that permitted access to private offerings would become available to prospective investors only after they had been qualified by the affiliated broker as accredited or sophisticated, had opened an account with the broker and had been qualified by IPONET. The affiliated broker would determine whether each prospective investor was "accredited" or "sophisticated" within the meaning of Rule 506 of Regulation D based on a questionnaire that the investor completed. The SEC staff allowed such use of the website, in part because the questionnaire would be generic in nature and would not refer to any specific transactions posted or to be posted on the password-protected page of IPONET.[8] The SEC staff concluded that a general solicitation would not occur when a preexisting, substantive relationship exists between an issuer or its broker, and offerees.[9]

2. Third Party Websites

In the *Lamp Technologies, Inc.* no action letters,[10] the SEC staff allowed Lamp Technologies, Inc. ("Lamp") to establish and administer a website containing hedge funds' offering memoranda, performance information and other information. The hedge funds were excepted from Company Act registration under section 3(c)(1) or 3(c)(7) and privately offered their securities under Regulation D. The SEC staff agreed that posting such information on the website would not (a) involve any form of general solicitation or general advertising within the meaning of Rule 502(c) of Regulation D, (b) constitute a public offering

---

5. Securities Act Release No. 7233 (Oct. 6, 1995), 60 F.R. 53,458 (Oct. 6, 1995). *See* Chapters 5 and 8, *supra.* If an offer is public for purposes of the Securities Act, it would also be public for purposes of Company Act §§ 3(c)(1) and 3(c)(7). *See, e.g., Gerard Rizzuti,* SEC No-Action Letter (June 7, 1983). *See* Chapter 3, *supra.*

6. *See* § 5.3 and Chapter 8, *supra. In re PriorityAccess, Inc., Endpoint Technologies, Inc. and Roger Shearer,* SEC Administrative Proceeding File 3-10621 (Oct. 3, 2001); *In re CGI Capital, Inc.,* SEC Administrative Proceeding File No. 3-10331 (Sep. 29, 2000).

7. *IPONET,* SEC No-Action Letter (July 26, 1996).

8. *Id.*

9. *See* §§ 5.3.1.iii and 8.2, *supra.*

10. *Lamp Technologies, Inc.,* SEC No-Action Letters (May 29, 1997, and May 29, 1998).

of securities for purposes of Company Act sections 3(c)(1) and 3(c)(7), or (c) cause any investment adviser to a participating hedge fund to be deemed holding itself out generally to the public as an investment adviser within the meaning of Advisers Act section 203(b)(3).[11] The SEC staff emphasized that placing private offering materials on an Internet website requires procedures that limit access to accredited investors and impose a waiting period.[12]

Lamp represented in its request for no-action relief that it would use procedures designed to limit access to website information to a select group of accredited investors and require that managers of the private hedge funds listed on the website post only information related to those hedge funds and not offer other services or products on the website. Neither Lamp nor any of its affiliates would operate or provide investment advisory services to any of the hedge funds listed on the website. Lamp was not a broker or affiliated with a broker; no employee of Lamp was a registered representative of a broker; and Lamp, its affiliates and their employees would not be involved in effecting transactions in securities or assisting participants by negotiating transactions in securities in connection with the website. To gain access to the hedge fund information, a subscriber would be required to complete a questionnaire designed to allow Lamp to "form a reasonable basis for determining" that the subscriber was an "accredited investor" within the meaning of Rule 501(a) of Regulation D. Such subscribers would then receive passwords giving them access to the hedge fund information posted on the website. Lamp would require subscribers to agree not to invest in any posted hedge fund (other than a hedge fund in which the subscriber was then already invested or considering investment or for which the subscriber had already been solicited) for thirty days following qualification.[13] Lamp maintained that this waiting period and the fact that most hedge funds were available for subscription on a quarterly or annual basis would ensure that subscribers would not join the website specifically to invest in any particular hedge fund and that Lamp's qualification of a subscriber would not be deemed a solicitation for any particular hedge fund.

3. Self-Qualification

Third-party service providers that are neither registered brokers nor affiliates of registered brokers and that establish websites inviting prospective investors to qualify themselves as accredited or sophisticated raise significant concerns that such services involve general solicitation. The SEC staff has stated that these third-party service providers that act as brokers in connection with securities

---

11.   *Id.*

12.   *Lamp Technologies, Inc.,* SEC No-Action Letter (May 29, 1997).

13.   Lamp also required subscribers to agree not to deliver hedge fund information posted on the website to anyone other than their authorized personnel and professional advisers. For SEC staff treatment of other matching or listing services, *see Venture Listing Services,* SEC No-Action Letter (June 15, 1994); *Investex Investment Exchange Inc.,* SEC No-Action Letter (Apr. 9, 1990); *Petroleum Information Corporation,* SEC No-Action Letter (Nov. 28, 1989); *Tri-State Livestock Credit Corp.,* SEC No-Action Letter (Oct. 18, 1989); *CNB Corp.,* SEC No-Action Letter (June 9, 1989); *Real Estate Financing Partnership,* SEC No-Action Letter (Apr. 4, 1989); *Venture Capital Network, Inc.* SEC No-Action Letter (May 7, 1984); *Venture Capital Exchange, Inc.* SEC No-Action Letter (Apr. 23, 1986); *Venture Capital Network of New York, Inc.,* SEC No-Action Letter (Nov. 10, 1986).

offerings must register as brokers under the Exchange Act, even when the securities are exempt from registration under the Securities Act. The SEC staff has also indicated that these websites may not give an issuer the ability to form a reasonable belief before a sale as to the qualifications of the purchasers, which belief may be necessary depending on the Securities Act exemption on which the issuer is relying.[14]

§ 9.3 Advisers Act Rules

1. Access Rules

If an investment adviser does not strictly control access to its website, it may not be eligible for the Private Adviser Exemption from SEC registration, because the website may hold the investment adviser out to the public as an investment adviser.[15] Accordingly, a splash page for the website of an investment adviser that is not SEC-registered should bear only the investment adviser's name and no other contact information, and entry to the website should be password-protected. A disclosure and use agreement may help to prove that access is limited and that users meet qualification and sophistication standards. SEC-registered investment advisers have more latitude with respect to their websites, because they may hold themselves out to the public as investment advisers.

2. Advertising Rules

The SEC advertising rules[16] apply to websites of registered investment advisers. As investment advisers increasingly use customized websites as marketing tools and as vehicles for providing client services, the SEC staff is focusing more scrutiny on the access to and content of those websites.

Hedge funds should limit the use of charts and graphs on their websites. Rule 206(4)-1(3)[17] under the Advisers Act proscribes representing that investors can use charts, graphs, formulae or other devices included in marketing materials to determine which securities they should buy, sell or hold. This rule may be implicated when an investment adviser's website offers tools (such as interactive questionnaires) designed to assist an investor in making portfolio decisions. These pages should include appropriate disclaimers and explanations about the limitations of the tools (such as imputed rates of return). Hedge fund websites are subject to the general anti-fraud rules of the Advisers Act, and any description on a website

---

14.   Securities Act Release No. 33-7856 ("Use of Electronic Media") (Apr. 28, 2000), 17 C.F.R. Parts 231, 241 and 271.

15.   *See* §§ 2.1.2.iii, 2.1.2.iv and 8.4.3, *supra*.

16.   *See* § 8.4, *supra*.

17.   17 C.F.R. § 275.206(4)-1(3).

of a hedge fund's investment strategy and other characteristics must be consistent with information in the hedge fund's offering circular.

§ 9.4 Hyperlinks

Hyperlinked information on an investment adviser's website may give rise to liability under the securities laws for fraud, misrepresentation, unregistered public offerings, or other violations. According to the SEC, liability for hyperlinked information may arise if a hedge fund or investment adviser has adopted the hyperlinked content, which may occur if it has "involved itself in the preparation of the information, or explicitly or implicitly endorsed or approved" the information.[18] Investment advisers that use hyperlinks on their websites should follow the principles that govern the use of reprints in advertising materials; for example, hyperlinks may not be testimonial in nature and their use may not be false or misleading.[19]

1. Adoption of Another's Content

The SEC considers the following factors in determining whether a hedge fund or investment adviser has adopted the hyperlinked information, for purposes of attributing liability:

- Context—A reference on the hedge fund's or the investment adviser's website to linked information on a different website as "authoritative" may imply that the hedge fund or investment adviser has adopted it.
- Risk of Confusion—A "jump page" that indicates that the viewer is leaving the hedge fund's or investment adviser's website to move to another website may reduce the likelihood that an investor would be confused about the source of linked information. The SEC has indicated that the presence of a disclaimer alone will not shield against liability.
- Presentation—Hyperlinking selectively to specific information, rather than to a third party's website generally, may indicate that the hedge fund or investment adviser has adopted that particular material. An investment adviser may violate the anti-fraud rules of the Advisers Act by singling out, in analyses or other communications, hyperlinks that advantage it or are otherwise misleading.[20]

---

18.   Securities Act Release No. 33-7856 (Apr. 28, 2000), 65 F.R. 25,843 (May 4, 2000).

19.   *See* § 8.3.1, *supra*, and "Web Compliance Revisited," *IA Week,* May 22, 2000.

20.   Securities Act Release No. 33-7856 (Apr. 28, 2000), 65 F.R. 25,843 (May 4, 2000). *See also* "Web Compliance Revisited," IA Week, May 22, 2000.

2. Guidelines

If an investment adviser or a hedge fund hyperlinks to third-party information from its website, it should follow the following guidelines:

- Hyperlinks should only go to the home pages of non-affiliated websites, rather than to specific pages in those websites.
- Investment advisers and hedge funds should not download content from other websites to their own without express written consent. "Deep linking" (that is, connecting directly to the desired feature in a third party's website while skipping the home page and other pages where solicitations and advertisements are placed) may infringe copyrights.
- Investment advisers and hedge funds should not use the logos or trademark designs of any other business without the approval of the business that owns them.
- Investment advisers should carefully review hyperlinked third-party websites to ensure that nothing in those websites might be misleading.
- If any information about a hedge fund is hosted by a solicitor's website, the hedge fund should make clear that the host website is not recommending or endorsing the hedge fund, ensure that the presentation looks like a conventional marketing document in print media, and avoid using any "framing" technology to ensure that a potential investor that follows a link will properly leave the host website to go to the controlled hedge fund website before being offered any interest in the hedge fund.[21]

§ 9.5 Other Regulations

1. NASD Guidance

Concerned about the correlation between sharp increases in the volume of electronic messages relating to low-priced securities and dramatic increases in the price, volatility and volume of such securities, the NASD issued a Notice to Members in 1996, which emphasized that members should exercise their supervisory and regulatory responsibilities and duties to customers with respect to the use of electronic media by themselves or associated persons.[22]

---

21.   *See* "Web Compliance Revisited," *IA Week*, May 22, 2000.
22.   NASD Notice to Members 96-50 (July 1996).

2. State Laws

Laws of some states require investment advisers with websites to make specified disclosures to avoid state licensure or certification requirements. For example, an investment adviser located outside of California will not be deemed to be "transacting business" in California if the investment adviser's website includes a legend prescribed by the California Commissioner of Corporations and meets certain other requirements.[23]

§ 9.6 Offshore Offerings via the Internet

The SEC has outlined procedures that a hedge fund must use in soliciting non-U.S. investors over the Internet to ensure that the hedge fund complies with the restrictions of Regulation S:[24]

- The website should contain a prominent, meaningful disclaimer to the effect that the offer is directed only to countries other than the United States. If applicable, the disclaimer should make clear that the offering is not open to U.S. investors.
- The hedge fund should implement procedures reasonably designed to prevent actual sales of hedge fund interests in the United States or, where applicable, to U.S. investors.
- The hedge fund should confirm that that there are no indirect indications (such as payments drawn on U.S. banks) that investors are in the United States or are U.S. persons.
- The hedge fund should take precautions to ensure that the content of the solicitation does not appear to be targeted to persons in the United States or, where applicable, to U.S. persons.[25]
- The hedge fund should limit access to the posted materials to persons or entities that provide residence information to confirm their non-U.S. address and, where applicable, their status as non-U.S. persons.[26]

---

23. *See* California Corporate Securities Release No. 107-C.
24. Securities Act Release No. 7516 (Mar. 23, 1998), 63 F.R. 14,806 (Mar. 27, 1998). *See also* § 8.3, *supra.*
25. *Id.*
26. 1933 Act Release No. 7856, n.68 (Apr. 28, 2000), 65 F.R. 25,843 (May 4, 2000).

CHAPTER 10

Avoiding Broker Registration

§ 10.1 Exchange Act

The Exchange Act generally defines a "broker" as a person engaged in the business of effecting transactions in securities for the accounts of others[1] and generally defines a "dealer" as a person engaged in the business of buying and selling securities for that person's own account, through a broker or otherwise.[2] The general partner of a hedge fund must consider whether it is required to register as a broker or dealer by virtue of the role it plays in offering and selling interests in and buying and selling securities on behalf of the hedge fund.

1. Rule 3a4-1 Safe Harbor Exemption from Broker Registration

Exchange Act section 15[3] provides generally that it is unlawful for any broker to use the mails or any means or instrumentality of interstate commerce to effect any transactions in, or to induce or attempt to induce the purchase or sale of, any security, unless that broker is registered as such with the SEC. Rule 3a4-1[4] under the Exchange Act provides a safe harbor exemption from the broker registration requirements for any "associated person of an issuer" if that person meets conditions specified in the rule. "Associated person of an issuer" includes any general partner of an issuer and any natural person who is an employee, officer, director or partner of a corporate general partner of a limited partnership that is the issuer. Presumably, although no definitive authority has been published, natural persons who are managers of a limited liability company that is the general partner of an issuer are also associated persons of the issuer.

An investment adviser, as the general partner of a hedge fund, and its managers and employees who solicit investors for the hedge fund, may qualify for the Rule 3a4-1 exemption from broker registration if they (a) are not subject to a statutory disqualification, as that term is defined in Exchange Act section 3(a)(39),[5] (b) do not receive any compensation related to the amount of hedge fund interests sold

---

1. Exchange Act § 3(a)(4), 15 U.S.C. § 78c(a)(4).
2. Exchange Act § 3(a)(5), 15 U.S.C. § 78c(a)(5).
3. 15 U.S.C. § 78o.
4. 17 C.F.R. § 240.3a4-1.
5. 15 U.S.C. § 78c(a)(39).

(whether by commission or otherwise), (c) primarily perform or intend primarily to perform at the end of the offering substantial duties (other than in connection with the offering) for or on behalf of the hedge fund, (d) are not associated with a broker or dealer, (e) were not employed by a broker or dealer within the preceding twelve months, and (f) do not participate in an offering of securities (other than in certain limited circumstances) more than once every twelve months. A person is subject to a "statutory disqualification" if such person:

(a) has been and is expelled or suspended from membership or participation in, or barred or suspended from being associated with a member of, any self-regulatory organization, non-U.S. equivalent of a self-regulatory organization, non-U.S. or international securities exchange, contract market designated pursuant to CEA section 5,[6] or any substantially equivalent non-U.S. statute or regulation or futures association registered under CEA section 17,[7] or any substantially non-U.S. statute or regulation, or has been and is denied trading privileges on any such contract market or non-U.S. equivalent;

(b) is subject to

(1) an order of the SEC, other appropriate regulatory agency, or non-U.S. financial regulatory authority

(i) denying, suspending for a period not exceeding twelve months, or revoking his registration as a broker, dealer, municipal securities dealer, government securities broker, or government securities dealer or limiting his activities as a non-U.S. person performing a function substantially equivalent to any of the above; or

(ii) barring or suspending for a period not exceeding twelve months his being associated with a broker, dealer, municipal securities dealer, government securities broker, or government securities dealer, or non-U.S. person performing a function substantially equivalent to any of the above;

(2) an order of the CFTC denying, suspending, or revoking his registration under the CEA;[8] or

(3) an order by a non-U.S. financial regulatory authority denying, suspending, or revoking the person's authority to engage in transactions in contracts of sale of a commodity for future delivery or other instruments traded on or subject to the rules of a contract market, board of trade, or non-U.S. equivalent thereof;

(c) by his conduct while associated with a broker, dealer, municipal securities dealer, government securities broker, or government securities dealer, or while associated with an entity or person required to be registered under the CEA,[9] has been found to be a cause of any effective suspension, expulsion, or order of the character described in clause (a) or (b) above, and in entering such a suspension, expulsion, or order, the SEC, an appropriate regulatory

---

6. 7 U.S.C. § 7.
7. 7 U.S.C. § 21.
8. 7 U.S.C. §§ 1 *et seq.*
9. *Id.*

agency, or self-regulatory organization has jurisdiction to find whether or not any person was a cause thereof;

(d) by his conduct while associated with any broker, dealer, municipal securities dealer, government securities broker, government securities dealer, or any other entity engaged in transactions in securities, or while associated with an entity engaged in transactions in contracts of sale of a commodity for future delivery or other instruments traded on or subject to the rules of a contract market, board of trade, or non-U.S. equivalent thereof, has been found to be a cause of any effective suspension, expulsion, or order by a non-U.S. or international securities exchange or non-U.S. financial regulatory authority empowered by a non-U.S. government to administer or enforce its laws relating to financial transactions as described in clause (a) or (b) above;

(e) has associated with him any person whom he knows, or in the exercise of reasonable care should know, to be a person described by clause (a), (b), (c) or (d) above; or

(f) (1) has committed or omitted any act, or is subject to an order or finding, enumerated in subparagraph (D), (E), (H), or (G) of paragraph (4) of Exchange Act section 15(b),[10] (2) has been convicted of any offense specified in subparagraph (B) of such paragraph (4) or any other felony within ten years of the date of filing an application for membership or participation in, or to become associated with a member of, such self-regulatory organization, (3) is enjoined from any action, conduct, or practice specified in subparagraph (C) of such paragraph (4), (4) has willfully made or caused to be made in any application for membership or participation in, or to become associated with a member of, a self-regulatory organization, report required to be filed with a self-regulatory organization, or proceeding before a self-regulatory organization, any statement which was at the time, and in the light of circumstances under which it was made, false or misleading with respect to any material fact, or (5) has omitted to state in any such application, report, or proceeding any material fact required to be stated therein.

2. Non-Safe Harbor Cases

Even if the general partner of a hedge fund or its managers or employees fail to satisfy the safe harbor conditions, they might not be required to register as brokers on the grounds that they are not in the business of selling securities. Whether they are in the business of selling securities depends on the extent of their securities activities.[11] The SEC examines a number of factors in assessing whether securities activities are extensive: the type of and basis for any compensation received, the extent to which the general partner holds funds or securities for others, the extent of contact with the public, and whether the general partner is "engaged in the

---

10. 15 U.S.C. § 78o(b)(4).
11. See, e.g., *Boston Advisory Group*, SEC No-Action Letter (Aug. 7, 1984); *In Touch Global*, SEC No-Action Letter (Nov. 14, 1995).

business" of effecting transactions in securities.[12] If a person engages in securities activities often enough to support the inference that those activities are part of the person's business, he or she will be deemed to be "engaged in the business."[13]

The SEC views receipt of compensation related to sales of securities as an important factor in determining whether a person is acting as a broker. The SEC staff has declined to take a no-action position where a registered investment adviser proposed to assist a broker or dealer with solicitation and to receive transaction-related compensation.[14] In one no-action letter, an investment adviser proposed to assist a brokerage firm in presenting and explaining section 8 housing limited partnerships and other real estate partnerships or oil and gas partnerships to interested persons. For the investment adviser's services, the brokerage firm was to pay the investment adviser a consulting fee based on sales of partnership units to customers. The SEC staff concluded that the proposed activities would require the investment adviser to register as a broker or dealer, or as an associated person of a registered broker or dealer.

Even a person that is not paid any commissions or other transaction-related fees may be required to register as a broker if the person proposes to locate issuers, solicit new clients and act as a customers' agent in structuring or negotiating transactions. In one SEC no-action letter,[15] an investment adviser requested relief from registering as a broker where it proposed to locate prospective real estate investment trust (REIT) issuers and negotiate the terms of private placements by the REITs. The investment adviser would then attempt to interest its clients in purchasing those REIT securities. No registered broker or dealer would be involved in effecting these transactions. Even though the investment adviser was to be compensated by an annual fee based on the percentage of its assets under management, rather than on a transaction-specific basis, the SEC staff declined to provide no-action relief.

In another no-action letter,[16] an investment adviser proposed to engage in three activities: (a) advising both U.S. and non-U.S. clients as to the value of U.S. securities, U.S. mutual funds and American Depositary Receipts; (b) publishing a newsletter, available for a flat subscription fee, containing business and economic information on India, including closing stock prices for Indian stocks and buy/sell/hold recommendations for Indian stocks; and (c) acting as a "purchaser's representative" by buying and selling securities on behalf of clients. The SEC warned the investment adviser that it might be required to register as a broker or dealer under the Exchange Act.

The SEC staff generally views with suspicion an arrangement under which a person claims to be soliciting investors as no more than a finder. In rare cases,[17] however, the SEC staff has not objected to a finder's participation in private

---

12. *In Touch Global*, SEC No-Action Letter (Nov. 14, 1995).

13. *Id.*

14. *Boston Advisory Group*, SEC No-Action Letter (Aug. 7, 1984)

15. *PRA Securities, L.P.*, SEC No-Action Letter (Mar. 3, 1993).

16. *In Touch Global*, SEC No-Action Letter (Nov. 14, 1995).

17. *See, e.g., Paul Anka*, SEC No-Action Letter (July 24, 1991) (Paul Anka will provide names of potential investors but will not contact them, solicit them, make any recommendations to them, participate in any negotiations with them or contact them concerning the issuer).

offerings, if the putative finder does no more than introduce investors to the issuers or their promoters. The SEC staff would not agree that a solicitor is a finder, rather than a broker, if the solicitor assists in any other way in selling securities or negotiating or documenting the securities transactions.

Except for that limited exception for finders, a person that is not employed by the general partner or that is a corporation or other entity and that assists in offering interests in a hedge fund must be registered with the SEC as a broker. The general partner should enter into a written agreement with any finder or broker it engages to assist it in the offering. The agreement should reflect the applicable requirements of the private offering exemption, the Exchange Act, the Advisers Act and state law. The hedge fund's offering circular should disclose the nature and terms of any such relationship or arrangement.[18]

3. Solicitors

The Advisers Act generally prohibits an investment adviser required to be registered under the Advisers Act from paying cash fees directly or indirectly with respect to solicitation of clients, except under arrangements that comply with Advisers Act Rule 206(4)-3 (the "solicitors rule").[19] To comply with the solicitors rule, the investment adviser's agreement with the solicitor must be in writing. The agreement must require the solicitor to provide to each client written disclosure about the solicitor's relationship with the investment adviser (including the compensation arrangement). The client must acknowledge in writing receipt of the written disclosure, and the investment adviser must retain copies of this disclosure and acknowledgement.[20] The investment adviser must make a bona fide effort to ascertain whether the solicitor has complied with the agreement and have a reasonable basis for believing that the solicitor has complied. No such disclosure, however, is required if the solicitor solicits only clients for impersonal advisory services (such as an advisory newsletter).[21] Although a partner, officer, director or employee of an investment adviser is subject to the solicitors rule and must be compensated pursuant to a written agreement and disclose his or her affiliation with the investment adviser, he or she need not disclose his or her compensation for solicitation activities or obtain an acknowledgment from each client solicited.[22]

The written disclosure document provided to each prospective client must include the names of the solicitor and the investment adviser, the nature of the relationship (including any affiliation) between the solicitor and the investment adviser, and a statement that the investment adviser will compensate the solicitor for his services. The terms of the compensation arrangement, including a description of the compensation paid or to be paid to the solicitor, must also be disclosed, as well as the amount, if any, that the client will be charged in addition to the advisory fee because of the solicitor's involvement, and any differences among

18.   *See* §§ 6.2.1.ii and 6.2.1.iii, *supra.*
19.   17 C.F.R. § 275.206(4)-3.
20.   Advisers Act Rule 206(4)-3(b), 17 C.F.R. § 275.206(4)-3(6). *See also* § 8.4.5, *supra.*
21.   Advisers Act Rule 206(4)-3(a)(2)(i), 17 C.F.R. § 275.206(4)-3(a)(2)(i).
22.   Advisers Act Rule 206(4)-3(a)(2)(ii), 17 C.F.R. § 275.206(4)-3(a)(2)(i).

clients in the amount or level of advisory fees charged by the investment adviser that are attributable to any arrangement pursuant to which the investment adviser compensates the solicitor for soliciting clients for, or referring clients to, the investment adviser.

The solicitors rule prohibits an SEC–registered investment adviser from paying fees to a solicitor (whether or not an employee and whether or not the solicitation is for impersonal advisory services) who has been convicted within the past ten years of certain felonies or misdemeanors, has violated the federal securities laws, is subject to an SEC order or decree, or is permanently or temporarily enjoined by order, judgment or decree of any court of competent jurisdiction from acting as, or as an affiliated person or employee of, an investment adviser, underwriter, broker, dealer, transfer agent or certain other occupations relating to the purchase or sale of securities.[23] This part of the solicitors rule effectively prevents an SEC–registered investment adviser from hiring as a solicitor a person whom the investment adviser would not be permitted to hire as an employee because of other provisions in the Advisers Act, and thus it prevents the investment adviser from doing indirectly what it cannot do directly.[24]

The solicitors rule is primarily a disclosure rule that reflects the SEC's concern about the potential for clients to be misled or unduly influenced by a solicitor whose arrangement with the investment adviser is not fully disclosed. It is not a safe harbor from any broker registration requirements. Thus, a solicitor who assists an investment adviser in marketing interests in a hedge fund in full compliance with the solicitors rule is nevertheless likely required to register as a broker.

The SEC has stated that an investment adviser that is not registered with the SEC may not rely on the solicitors rule.[25] In addition, the solicitors rule only authorizes the payment of cash referral fees to solicitors. Although no formal SEC statement prohibits the payment of non–cash referral fees to solicitors, the SEC might question the propriety of such payments, particularly absent full disclosure about the arrangement.[26] Any investment adviser, whether or not registered with the SEC, should make at least the disclosures required by the solicitors rule to any potential client that a paid solicitor solicits for the investment adviser. In recent years, the SEC has instituted an increasing number of enforcement actions alleging violations of the solicitors rule and the broker registration requirements by investment advisers and solicitors.[27]

4. Dealer Registration

Because a hedge fund buys and sells securities for its own account, it might arguably be comprehended by the definition of "dealer." The SEC staff has, however, provided no-action relief from dealer registration where the partnership in question did not (1) act as an underwriter or participate in a selling group in

---

23. Advisers Act Rule 206(4)-3(a)(1)(ii), 17 C.F.R. § 275.206(4)-3(a)(1)(ii).
24. Advisers Act Release No. 688 (Jul. 12, 1979), 44 F.R. 42126 (Jul. 18, 1979).
25. *Id.*
26. *See* § 14.2, *infra.*
27. Advisers Act Release No. 1409 (Apr. 6, 1994); Advisers Act Release No. 1500 (June 16, 1995).

any distribution of securities, (2) carry a dealer inventory in securities, (3) quote a market in any security, (4) advertise or otherwise hold itself out to the public as a dealer, or as being willing to buy or sell any security on a continuous basis, (5) render any investment advice, or (6) extend or arrange for the extension of credit on securities or lend any securities.[28] On other occasions, the SEC has also considered whether the person purchases or sells securities as principal to or from customers, runs a book of repurchase and reverse repurchase agreements, uses an interdealer broker for securities transactions, issues or originates any securities, or guarantees contract performance or indemnifies the parties for any loss or liability from the failure of the transaction to be successfully consummated.[29]

Other than issuing or originating securities (the interests in the hedge fund), the typical hedge fund does not engage in any of the above activities. Even the fifth factor listed above (rendering investment advice) is not present, because the investment adviser to the hedge fund, not the hedge fund itself, provides investment advice to the partnership. As a result, a hedge fund should not be considered a dealer.

No authority provides guidance on whether the general partner of a hedge fund should be considered a dealer. The lack of reported judicial opinions and SEC staff no-action letters, in the face of such a common practice, suggests that the general partner should not be regarded as a dealer. If that is so, it may be because the general partner engages in securities transactions for the account of the hedge fund, not for its own account (disregarding that it may have itself invested in the hedge fund), or because the general partner does not provide investment advice about investing in the hedge fund and is not in any of the other categories described above.

§ 10.2 Avoiding State Registration

1. Generally

Definitions of broker and dealer in many state laws are similar to those in the Exchange Act, and many state laws provide similar exemptions from those definitions.[30] A general partner that offers and sells hedge fund interests in a particular

---

28.   *Davenport Management, Inc.*, SEC No-Action Letter (Apr. 13, 1993). The SEC staff also provided relief from broker registration for the investment partnership's general partner, based on the requester's assertion that all investments and other decisions of the partnership were controlled by the general partner and the general partner's activities making decisions on behalf the partnership to buy or sell securities were not the activities of a broker, but rather activities necessary to carry out the business of the partnership. *See also International Investment Group, Inc.*, SEC No-Action Letter (July 23, 1987); *Acqua Wellington North American Equities Fund, Ltd.*, SEC No-Action Letter (July 11, 2001).

29.   *Acqua Wellington North American Equities Fund, Ltd.*, SEC No-Action Letter (July 11, 2001).

30.   *See, e.g.*, Cal. Corp. Code § 25004. *See* §§ 7.2.1.iii, 7.2.2.i.c, 7.2.2.ii, 7.3.2 and 7.4.3, *supra*.

state and does not qualify for an exemption from broker or dealer registration under that state's laws would be required either to register as a broker or dealer, or to rely on the position that it is not "in the business" of selling securities, notwithstanding its activities in offering and selling hedge fund interests. As noted above, although managers of private investment funds frequently maintain this position, it is subject to challenge by securities regulatory authorities or a private plaintiff. For example, California defines "broker-dealer" as any person engaged "in the business" of effecting transactions in securities for the accounts of others or his own account[31] and explicitly excludes an issuer and its agents from the registration requirements. Nevertheless, the California Commissioner of Corporations has indicated that an investment adviser and the hedge fund that it manages, if located in California, might be required to register as broker-dealers because they may be deemed to be in the business of effecting transactions in securities.[32]

2. Employees as "Agents"

Employees of a hedge fund's general partner may be required to register as agents or salespersons under state law. Many states, however, exclude from their definitions of agent any individual who represents the issuer in selling federally covered securities if no remuneration is paid specifically for selling the securities.[33]

3. New York

Unlike most states' laws, New York law does not exclude issuers from the definition of broker or dealer. Accordingly, before offering or selling interests in a hedge fund in New York, the general partner must file, among other things, a "broker-dealer statement."[34] This statement generally requires information regarding business history for the last five years, criminal record and educational background of the general partner and its partners, officers, directors or other principals. The broker-dealer statement is effective for four years from the date of filing. A general partner that fails to file the broker-dealer statement before offering hedge fund interests in New York could be subject to penalties and other disciplinary action assessed or prosecuted by the New York attorney general.

---

31. *Id.*
32. Cal. Blue Sky Letter (9/21/98).
33. *See, e.g.,* Cal. Corp. Code § 25003(d); Utah Uniform Securities Act § 61-1-13(2). *See* §§ 7.2.1.iii, 7.2.2.i.c, 7.2.2.ii, 7.3.2 and 7.4.3, *supra.*
34. N.Y. GBL § 359-e. *See* § 7.2.1.ii, *supra.*

CHAPTER 11

ERISA Considerations

§ 11.1 Introduction

If an employee benefit plan invests in a hedge fund, the hedge fund makes collective investments of assets that include funds of the employee benefit plan. Employee benefit plans are generally subject to the Employee Retirement Income Security Act of 1974, as amended ("ERISA"), to some parallel requirements in the Tax Code, and to oversight by the U.S. Department of Labor (the "DOL") and the Internal Revenue Service (the "IRS"). ERISA applies to most employee benefit arrangements established by private employers for their employees or by unions for their members (including, for example, employer pension plans and health plans, disability and life insurance plans and severance pay plans). If ERISA-covered or other employee benefit plans own twenty-five percent or more of the total interests of a hedge fund (excluding interests held by the general partner), the manager and the hedge fund will generally become subject to ERISA's requirements and prohibitions, including fiduciary conduct standards, prohibitions against engaging in certain transactions, bonding requirements, special requirements as to investment in foreign securities, indemnification and reporting. The penalties for noncompliance can be severe. Many hedge funds implement policies to prevent employee benefit plans from reaching the twenty-five percent level. Depending on how their hedge funds are structured and the instruments traded, however, some hedge fund managers find the advantages of being able to admit more investors outweigh the burdens and risks of ERISA and the Tax Code, and of DOL and IRS oversight. Moreover, employee benefit plan trustees have become increasingly interested in adding non-traditional investments, such as hedge funds, to their portfolios; thus the number of plan assets hedge funds has been increasing and that trend is likely to continue.

§ 11.2 Plan Asset Regulations—Look-Through Rule

The DOL's Final Regulation Relating to the Definition of Plan Assets (the "Plan Asset Regulations")[1] generally provides that when an ERISA-regulated employee

---

1. DOL Regulation § 2510.3-101, 29 C.F.R. § 2510.3-101.

benefit plan or another "benefit plan investor" (as defined below) acquires an equity interest in a fund, such as a hedge fund, that is neither a publicly offered security nor a security issued by an investment company registered under the Company Act, the plan's assets will include both the equity interest and an undivided interest in each of the underlying assets of the fund, unless (a) equity participation in the fund by benefit plan investors is not significant, (b) the fund is an "operating company," or (c) the fund satisfies the special "grandfather" rule.[2] If the plan is deemed to have an interest in the underlying assets of a hedge fund, the hedge fund's assets will then be deemed "plan assets." In that case, the hedge fund's investment adviser will be treated as managing plan assets and be subject to various requirements and prohibitions imposed by ERISA and the Tax Code. In addition, assets of an employee benefit plan generally must be held in trust;[3] the trust requirement is satisfied with respect to the hedge fund if the indicia of ownership of the benefit plan's interest in the hedge fund are held in trust.[4]

The Plan Asset Regulations apply not only to plans subject to ERISA, but also to plans that cover only the owners of the businesses that sponsor them ("owner–only plans"), SEPs, Keogh plans, individual retirement accounts ("IRAs"), governmental plans, non–U.S. plans, aggregations in which twenty-five percent or more of the value of any class of equity interests is held by any of the foregoing investors, and any other persons deemed to hold plan assets, such as bank collective trust funds or insurance company separate accounts.[5] All of these plans and other entities are "benefit plan investors."

1. Definition of Equity Interest

The Plan Asset Regulations define an "equity interest" as "any interest in any entity other than an instrument that is treated as indebtedness under applicable local law and which has no substantial equity feature." Under the Plan Asset Regulations, a "profit interest in a partnership, an undivided interest in property, and a beneficial interest in a trust" are all equity interests.[6] Thus, an investor's interest in a hedge fund is an "equity interest."

2. Twenty-Five-Percent Test

Benefit plan investors are considered to hold a "significant" amount of a hedge fund's equity interests if they hold, in the aggregate, twenty-five percent or more of the value of any class of the hedge fund's equity interests. Classes treated as distinct for these purposes should have different substantive rights. For purposes of determining the percentage, the value of equity interests held by certain parties related to the hedge fund, such as the general partner, is disregarded. Benefit plan investors include, however, any entity (for example, a fund of funds) whose

---

2. DOL Regulation § 2510.3-101(k), 29 C.F.R. § 2510.3-101(k).
3. ERISA § 403(a), 29 U.S.C. § 1103(a).
4. DOL Regulation § 2550.403a-1(b)(3), 29 C.F.R. § 2550.403a-1(b)(3).
5. DOL Regulation § 2510.3-101, 29 C.F.R. § 2510.3-101.
6. DOL Regulation § 2510.3-101(b)(1), 29 C.F.R. § 2510.3-101(b)(1).

underlying assets include plan assets by reason of plans' investment in such entity.[7] The twenty-five-percent test is applied each time an investor acquires (or redeems) any equity interest in the hedge fund.[8] Accordingly, determining the percentage of a hedge fund's equity interests held by benefit plan investors under the Plan Asset Regulations requires continuous monitoring, careful attention to hedge fund contributions and withdrawals, and restrictions on resales.

3. "Operating Company" Exception

A plan will not be deemed to have an interest in the underlying assets of a fund if the fund is an "operating company" (including a "venture capital operating company" or a "real estate operating company"). The Plan Asset Regulations define "operating company" as an "entity that is primarily engaged, directly or through a majority-owned subsidiary, in the production or sale of a product or service other than the investment of capital."[9] Hedge funds rarely satisfy the conditions for the operating company exemptions.

4. Grandfather Rule

Generally, a hedge fund qualifies for the "grandfather" exception from the Plan Asset Regulations if it existed on March 13, 1987, and no plan has acquired any equity interests in the hedge fund since that date.[10]

§ 11.3 Fiduciary Duty

If benefit plan investors hold twenty-five percent or more of any class of equity interests in a hedge fund and one or more of those benefit plan investors is subject to ERISA, the hedge fund's investment adviser becomes an ERISA "fiduciary" with respect to all of the plan assets invested in the hedge fund. The fiduciary must comply with the fiduciary responsibility provisions of ERISA[11] in addition to the fiduciary principles to which investment advisers are otherwise subject. Under ERISA, fiduciary status is determined with reference to a person's activities with respect to a plan; it does not depend on any formal undertaking or agreement.[12] A "fiduciary" is any person who (a) exercises discretionary authority or control in the management of a plan, or authority or control in the management or

---

7. DOL Regulation § 2510.3-101(f)(2)(iii), 29 C.F.R. § 2510.3-101(f)(2)(iii).

8. *Id.* DOL Advisory Opinion 89-05A (Apr. 5, 1989) indicated that a redemption of an equity interest in the hedge fund should also be treated as an acquisition for this purpose, because such redemption results in an increase in the interests of the remaining partners.

9. DOL Regulation § 2510.3-101(d), 29 C.F.R. § 2510.3-101(d).

10. DOL Regulation § 2510.3-101(k), 29 C.F.R. § 2510.3-101(k).

11. *See* ERISA § 3(21), 29 U.S.C. § 1002(21).

12. *See* H.R. Rep. No. 1280 94d Cong., 2d Sess., 323 (1974).

disposition of its assets, (b) provides investment advice to a plan for a fee or other compensation, direct or indirect, with respect to any moneys or other property of such plan, or (c) has discretionary authority or responsibility in the administration of such plan.[13]

In general, the trustee of a benefit plan has exclusive authority and discretion to manage and control the assets of the plan. Under ERISA section 402(c)(3),[14] however, the trustee may appoint an "investment manager" to manage, acquire or dispose of assets of the plan, if the plan so provides. When a plan trustee invests plan assets in a hedge fund in which benefit plan investors hold at least twenty-five percent of any class of equity interests, the trustee effectively appoints the fund's investment adviser as an "investment manager" for the plan. ERISA provides that if the plan trustee chooses and retains the investment manager prudently, the investment manager is registered under the Advisers Act or under a state securities law,[15] and the investment manager acknowledges in writing that he or she is acting as a fiduciary,[16] the trustee will not be liable for the acts or omissions of the investment manager. The trustee remains responsible, however, for monitoring the investment manager's performance.[17]

1. Exclusive Purpose; Plan Documents

An ERISA fiduciary must act for the exclusive purpose of providing benefits to plan participants and their beneficiaries and defraying the reasonable expenses of administering the plan.[18] The fiduciary must also act in accordance with the documents and instruments governing the ERISA plan, insofar as those documents and instruments are consistent with ERISA.[19] A fiduciary with investment responsibility should review a benefit plan's governing documents to make sure that investments in or by a particular hedge fund are not prohibited by the plan and should satisfy itself that the plan provisions comply with ERISA. In addition, such a fiduciary must not favor any other accounts over a plan assets fund when it allocates trades among that fund and other accounts that it manages.

2. Standard of Prudence

An ERISA fiduciary must act with the care, skill, prudence and diligence that a prudent person acting in a like capacity and familiar with such matters would use under the circumstances in the conduct of an enterprise of a like character with

---

13. ERISA § 3(21)(A), 29 U.S.C. § 1002(21)(A).

14. 29 U.S.C. § 1102(c)(3).

15. *See* §§ 2.2 and 2.3, *supra*.

16. ERISA §§ 3(38) and 405(d), 29 U.S.C. §§ 1002(38) and 1105(d). DOL Regulation 2510.3–38, 29 C.F.R. § 2510.3–38, also requires state-registered investment advisers seeking this investment manager-adviser status to register electronically through the Investment Advisers Registration Depository ("IARD"). *See* § 2.4, *supra*.

17. ERISA §§ 405(c)(2) and 405(d)(1), 29 U.S.C. §§ 1105(c)(2) and (d)(1); DOL Regulation § 2509.75-9, Q&A FR-17, 29 C.F.R. § 2509.75-9, Q&A FR-17.

18. ERISA § 404(a)(1)(A), 29 U.S.C. § 1104(a)(1)(A).

19. ERISA § 404(a)(1)(D), 29 U.S.C. § 1104(a)(1)(D).

like aims.[20] The prudence standard can also apply to a fiduciary's appointment of another fiduciary with investment discretion. Under the prudence standard, fiduciaries must take into account the "special nature and purpose" of employee benefit plans.[21] The prudence rule applies to the total performance of a plan's entire portfolio, rather than the actual performance of any particular investment. Accordingly, in determining whether any investment is imprudent, the investment must be analyzed in the context of the overall portfolio. Evidence of due diligence and analysis performed by the fiduciary is useful to show that the fiduciary has met this standard of care.[22]

A plan's trustee should determine whether an investment in a particular hedge fund is appropriate and prudent by comparing that plan's risk tolerance and objectives to the hedge fund's investment strategy. A hedge fund's investment adviser generally manages plan assets that are invested in the hedge fund on an aggregate basis with other invested funds and thus does not examine each investing plan's objectives, risk tolerance, diversification strategies and other individualized needs. Accordingly, subscription documents for a hedge fund that accepts benefit plan investors should expressly allocate responsibility for diversification, market risk testing, liquidity, consistency with the plan documents and with ERISA and other considerations to the plan trustee or named fiduciary that has chosen to invest in the hedge fund, rather than to the hedge fund's general partner or investment adviser.

3. Diversification

A plan fiduciary must diversify the investments of the ERISA plan to minimize the risk of large losses, unless under the circumstances it is clearly prudent not to do so.[23] Diversification analysis may entail examining and monitoring the plan's entire portfolio. The DOL has concluded that derivatives sometimes used by hedge funds (such as futures, options, options on futures, forward contracts, swaps, structured notes and collateralized mortgage obligations) may be useful tools for managing risks and for broadening a plan's portfolio investments. The DOL has also taken the position, however, that investments in certain derivatives characterized by high price volatility or leverage or illiquidity (such as structured notes and collateralized mortgage obligations) may require the hedge fund's investment adviser to have a higher degree of sophistication and understanding than for other investments.[24]

4. Proxy Voting

The fiduciary act of managing plan assets that are shares of corporate stock includes the voting of proxies appurtenant to those shares of stock. As a result,

---

20. ERISA § 404(a)(1)(B), 29 U.S.C. § 1104(a)(1)(B).

21. H.R. Conf. Rep. No. 93-1280, p. 302 (1974).

22. *See., e.g., In re Unisys Sav. Plan Litigation*, 74 F.3d 420, 19 Employee Benefits Cas. (BNA) 2392 (3rd Cir. 1996); *Glennie V. Abitibi-Price Corp.,* 912 F. Supp. 993 (W.D. Mich. 1996).

23. ERISA § 404(a)(1)(C), 29 U.S.C. § 1104(a)(1)(C).

24. Letter from Olena Berg, Assistant Secretary, Pension and Welfare Benefits Administration, DOL, to Eugene A. Ludwig, Comptroller of the Currency (Mar. 21, 1996).

the responsibility for voting proxies lies exclusively with a benefit plan's trustee except to the extent that either (a) the trustee is subject to the directions of a named fiduciary pursuant to ERISA section 403(a)(1),[25] or (b) pursuant to ERISA section 403(a)(2),[26] a named fiduciary has delegated the power to manage, acquire or dispose of the relevant assets to one or more investment managers pursuant to ERISA section 402(c)(3)[27] as discussed above (for example, by investing plan assets in a hedge fund in which benefit plan investors hold at least twenty-five percent of a class of equity interest). If the authority to manage plan assets has been delegated, no person other than the investment manager has authority to vote proxies appurtenant to such plan assets except to the extent that the named fiduciary has reserved to itself (or to another named fiduciary so authorized by the plan document) the right to direct a plan trustee regarding the voting of proxies. A named fiduciary, in delegating investment management authority to an investment manager, could reserve to itself the right to direct a trustee with respect to the voting of all proxies or reserve to itself the right to direct a trustee as to the voting of only those proxies relating to specified assets or issues.[28]

If a hedge fund's investment adviser has responsibility for voting proxies, it must act prudently, solely in the interests of ERISA plan participants and beneficiaries, and for the exclusive purpose of providing benefits to them. Such a hedge fund's investment adviser is not relieved of fiduciary responsibility in proxy voting by following the directions of some other person or by delegating its proxy voting duty to another person.[29] A hedge fund's investment adviser that has the authority to vote proxies has an obligation under ERISA to take reasonable steps under the particular circumstances to ensure that the proxies for which it is responsible are received and to keep accurate records of its voting of proxies. According to the DOL, ERISA plan fiduciaries must treat proxy-voting rights essentially as ERISA plan assets.

ERISA does not require a hedge fund's investment adviser that has responsibility for voting plan proxies automatically to tender shares to capture any premium over the market price in takeover situations. Rather, the investment adviser must weigh the terms of any offer against the underlying intrinsic value of the company and the likelihood that such value will be realized by current management or by another offer.[30]

5. Penalties and Co-Fiduciary Liability

ERISA provides that any fiduciary that breaches its responsibilities, obligations or duties is personally liable to the plan for any losses that result, as well as any profits that the fiduciary has obtained through use of the plan's assets. Courts may also

---

25.   29 U.S.C. § 1103(a)(1).

26.   29 U.S.C. § 1103(a)(2).

27.   29 U.S.C. § 1102(c)(3).

28.   DOL Interpretive Bulletin Relating to Written Statements of Investment Policy, Including Proxy Voting Policy or Guidelines, 59 F.R. 38,863 (July 29, 1994), codified as DOL Regulation § 2509.94-2, 29 C.F.R. § 2509.94-2.

29.   *Avon Products, Inc.*, DOL Letter (Feb. 23, 1988).

30.   Joint Department of Labor/Department of Treasury Statement on Pension Investments (Jan. 31, 1989).

fashion equitable relief, such as removal of the plan fiduciary.[31] A hedge fund's investment adviser may also be liable for another fiduciary's breach by knowingly participating in or concealing such breach, if the hedge fund's investment adviser's failure to comply with fiduciary obligations enables the second fiduciary's breach, or if the hedge fund's investment adviser knows of the other fiduciary's breach and does not take reasonable actions to remedy it.[32]

§ 11.4 Prohibited Transactions

The fiduciary responsibility provisions of ERISA also include prohibited transaction rules that restrict the manner in which fiduciaries may deal with the assets of a plan.[33] In general, an ERISA fiduciary may not use the assets of a plan to engage in transactions with "parties in interest" to the plan or plans (including ERISA plans, IRAs and owner-only plans) for which the fiduciary is acting.[34] The Tax Code complements the prohibited transaction provisions of ERISA by imposing an excise tax on "disqualified persons" who engage in prohibited transactions.[35] A "party in interest" of an employee benefit plan includes a fiduciary; a service provider; a contributing employer; an employee organization whose members are covered by that plan; an owner of fifty percent or more of such employer or employee organization; a spouse, ancestor, lineal descendant or spouse of a lineal descendent of any such person; a corporation, partnership, trust or estate fifty percent or more of which is owned directly or indirectly by such persons; an employee, officer, director or ten percent or more shareholder of any such person (except a fiduciary or relative); and a ten percent or more partner of any such person (except a fiduciary or relative).[36] "Disqualified person," as defined in the Tax Code, has essentially the same meaning as "party in interest" as defined in ERISA. Accordingly, we use the term "party in interest" in the remainder of this section 11.4.

1. Specific Transactions Prohibited

ERISA and the Tax Code specifically enumerate, as prohibited transactions, any direct or indirect:

- selling, exchanging or leasing of property, including securities or swap contracts, between the plan and a party in interest;

---

31.   ERISA § 409, 29 U.S.C. § 1109.
32.   ERISA § 405(a), 29 U.S.C. § 1105(a).
33.   *See* ERISA § 406, 29 U.S.C. § 1106.
34.   DOL Regulation § 2510.3-101, 29 C.F.R. § 2510.3-101.
35.   *See* Tax Code § 4975, 26 U.S.C. § 4975.
36.   ERISA § 3(14), 29 U.S.C. § 1002(14); Tax Code § 4975(e)(2), 26 U.S.C. § 4975(e)(2).

- lending of money or other extension of credit between the plan and a party in interest;
- furnishing of goods, services or facilities (other than the specific services for which the party in interest is engaged) between the plan and a party in interest;
- transfer to, or use by or for the benefit of, a party in interest of any assets of the plan (other than reasonable compensation for the services rendered to the plan); or
- acquiring or holding by the plan of any employer security or employer real property, in violation of limits specified in ERISA.[37]

2. Fiduciary Self-Dealing

In addition, an ERISA fiduciary is prohibited from:

- dealing with the assets of the plan in the fiduciary's own interest or for the fiduciary's own account;
- acting in the fiduciary's individual capacity or in any other capacity, in any transaction involving the plan, on behalf of a party whose interests are adverse to the interests of the plan or its participants; and
- receiving any consideration for the fiduciary's personal account from any party dealing with the plan, in connection with a transaction involving the plan.[38]

The DOL has also taken the position that a fiduciary's receipt of soft dollars, in a form other than brokerage and research services falling within the safe harbor of Exchange Act section 28(e), is a prohibited transaction.[39]

3. Prohibited Transaction Exemptions

ERISA provides statutory exemptions for certain transactions deemed necessary for the operation of plans and authorizes the DOL to grant individual or class exemptions.[40] Some prohibited transaction exemptions that may apply to hedge fund structures or transactions are discussed below.

i. "Services" Exemption

ERISA allows a plan to make reasonable arrangements with a party in interest for office space or legal, accounting or other services necessary for the establishment or operation of the plan, if no more than reasonable compensation is paid.[41] A

---

37.   ERISA §§ 406(a)(1)(A)-(E) and 406(a)(2), 29 U.S.C. §§ 1106(a)(1)(A)-(E) and 1106(a)(2); Tax Code § 4795(c)(1)(A)-(D), 26 U.S.C. § 4975(c)(1)(A)-(D).

38.   ERISA § 406(b), 29 U.S.C. § 1106(b); Tax Code §§ 4975(c)(1)(E)-(F), 26 U.S.C. §§ 4975(c)(1)(E)-(F).

39.   ERISA Technical Release 86-1, Statement on Policies Concerning Soft Dollar and Directed Commission Arrangements (May 22, 1986). *See* § 14.2.5.ii, *infra*.

40.   ERISA § 408, 29 U.S.C. § 1108.

41.   ERISA § 408(b)(2), 29 U.S.C. § 1108(b)(2).

fiduciary may receive reasonable compensation (such as reasonable investment management fees) for services rendered or for reimbursement of expenses incurred in the performance of the fiduciary's duties to the plan, unless the fiduciary is receiving full-time pay from an employer or employer association whose members are participants in the plan, in which case the fiduciary may only receive reimbursement for expenses.[42] The exemption for necessary services does not apply to the fiduciary self-dealing prohibitions.[43]

ii. "Securities" Exemption

An early DOL administrative exemption allows plans, subject to certain conditions, to engage in some commonplace securities transactions that would otherwise be prohibited transactions, including:

- principal transactions when the party in interest is a registered broker or reporting dealer in government securities that customarily trades for its own account;
- purchases of securities from a member of an underwriting syndicate of which the fiduciary is a member, if the purchase is not from the fiduciary;
- purchases or sales of securities from a fiduciary that is a market-maker for those securities; and
- extensions of credit to a plan by a broker in connection with settlements, short sales and option contracts, if no interest is received by a broker that is a fiduciary or an affiliate of a fiduciary.[44]

iii. Affiliated Broker Exemption

An investment adviser that is an ERISA fiduciary would be engaging in a prohibited transaction if the investment adviser-fiduciary were to direct the hedge fund's brokerage business to an affiliated broker. Such transactions, however, are common. In recognition of this industry practice, the DOL issued ERISA Prohibited Transaction Class Exemption ("PTE") 86–128. This exemption permits a hedge fund's investment adviser to direct the hedge fund's brokerage transactions to an affiliated broker, as long as the following general conditions are met:

- The investment adviser must not be an administrator or a trustee (except for a non-discretionary trustee) of the plan or an employer of any employees covered by the plan;
- The brokerage services must be provided under a written authorization executed in advance by a plan fiduciary (typically the plan's trustee) that is independent of the investment adviser and the broker;
- The independent fiduciary's authorization must be terminable at will by the plan on the investment adviser's receipt of written notice of termination, and

---

42.   ERISA § 408(c)(2), 29 U.S.C. § 1108(c)(2).
43.   DOL Regulation § 2550.408b-2, 29 C.F.R. § 2550.408b-2.
44.   DOL Prohibited Transaction Exemption 75-1. 40 F.R. 50,845 (Oct. 31, 1975).

the broker must annually provide this termination form to the independent fiduciary; and

- The investment adviser must furnish the independent fiduciary with various reports described in PTE 86-128 relating to the brokerage services rendered to the plan, such as the total of all transaction-related charges during the period, the amount of such charges retained by the fiduciary and paid to others, and the portfolio turnover rate.[45]

iv. Performance-Based Fees

A fee or a special profit allocation calculated on the basis of portfolio performance may constitute a prohibited transaction for an investment adviser that is an ERISA fiduciary if the investment adviser can manipulate the formula or mechanism for calculating it. The plan (or a participant) might assert that the investment adviser is "using the assets" for the investment adviser's benefit or that the investment adviser (who is a fiduciary) is "dealing with the assets" of the plan in the investment adviser's own interest, either of which would be a prohibited transaction.

The DOL has issued limited guidance, in a few Advisory Opinions, permitting ERISA fiduciaries to receive performance fees in some circumstances. *BDN Investment Advisers, Inc.* involved a fee consisting of a base fee and an incentive fee based on a percentage of net capital appreciation in the plan's account.[46] *Batterymarch Financial Management* involved a fulcrum fee, under which the investment adviser's fee varied in accordance with the account's performance relative to a recognized index.[47] *Alliance Capital Management Corporation* involved three different fee structures, with each client plan selecting one of the fee structures: (1) a percentage of appreciation fee (similar to the fee structure in *BDN*); (2) a "base plus" fee; and (3) a fulcrum fee (similar to the fee structure in *Batterymarch*).[48] *Mount Lucas Management Corporation* involved the investment of plan assets in commodity futures and forward contracts, and in options on commodities and commodity future contracts.[49] Under *Mount Lucas*, for certain plans, permitted fees included an annual performance fee equal to a specified percentage (established through arms-length negotiations) of the amount by which the cumulative profits of a plan client's account at the end of a performance period exceeded the highest level of cumulative profits for that account as of the end of any prior performance period, and in some cases exceeded a pre-established hurdle rate.[50]

Although the DOL did not articulate the specific factors on which it based its decisions allowing performance fees, the following features were common to all four arrangements:

---

45. DOL Prohibited Transaction Exemption 86-128, 51 F.R. 41,686 (Nov. 5, 1986).

46. DOL Advisory Opinion 86-20A, *BDN Investment Advisers, Inc.* (Aug. 29, 1986), hereinafter *BDN*.

47. DOL Advisory Opinion 86-21A, *Batterymarch Financial Management* (Aug. 29, 1986), hereinafter *Batterymarch*.

48. DOL Advisory Opinion 89-28A, *Alliance Capital Management Corporation* (Oct. 11, 1989), hereinafter *Alliance*.

49. DOL Advisory Opinion 99-16A, *Mount Lucas Management Corporation* (Dec. 9, 1999), hereinafter *Mount Lucas*.

50. *Id.*

- Investments generally were limited to securities with readily available market quotations, and the small number of investments in securities without readily available market quotations were valued by third parties independent of the investment advisers;
- The compensation formula took into account both realized and unrealized gains and losses and income during pre-established valuation periods and the measurement period generally exceeded twelve months;
- The investment advisers were registered under the Advisers Act;
- The arrangements complied with Advisers Act Rule 205-3 (the "performance fee rule");
- The plans were substantial in size (each had aggregate assets of at least $50,000,000); and
- Not more than ten percent of any plan's assets were managed by the investment adviser.

The DOL has indicated that performance-based compensation arrangements can nevertheless give rise to prohibited transactions, that preformance fees should be structured to avoid conflicts of interest and that each arrangement must be evaluated on its own facts and circumstances.[51] The $50,000,000 in assets standard probably suggests financial sophistication to the DOL and the ten-percent limit probably indicates diversification. The DOL has not indicated, however, whether or not these amounts are absolute thresholds or bright-line tests.

v. Dual Fees

A hedge fund that includes plan assets may not impose a dual fee—that is, an investment management fee payable to the fund's investment adviser in addition to another such fee charged by that investment adviser, for example, for managing a mutual fund or other hedge fund in which the first hedge fund invests.[52] ERISA Prohibited Transaction Class Exemption 77-4, however, permits a pension plan adviser or fiduciary to cause plan assets to be invested in a mutual fund it advises under the following conditions:

- The plan does not pay a mutual fund advisory fee (this condition would be satisfied if the plan pays an investment advisory fee based on total plan assets, from which a credit is subtracted representing the plan's pro rata share of the mutual fund advisory fee);
- The plan does not pay a sales commission when purchasing or selling mutual fund shares;
- The plan does not pay any redemption fee, unless (1) the fee is paid only to the mutual fund and (2) the fee is disclosed in the mutual fund's prospectus that is effective at the time of both the purchase and the redemption of the mutual fund shares;

---

51   *See, e.g., BDN, Alliance* and *Mount Lucas..*
52.   DOL Prohibited Transaction Exemption 77-4, 42 F.R. 18,732 (Mar. 31, 1977).

- A second plan fiduciary that is independent of the investment adviser receives a current mutual fund prospectus and written disclosure of the fees to be paid by the plan, the reasons why the investment adviser may consider a purchase of mutual fund shares appropriate for the plan and any limitation on the investment adviser regarding which plan assets may be invested in mutual fund shares;
- The second fiduciary approves the mutual fund share purchases as consistent with the ERISA fiduciary obligations; and
- The second fiduciary approves in writing any change in the fees to be paid by the plan.

The DOL has not extended ERISA Prohibited Transaction Exemption 77-4 to hedge funds. Thus, a fund-of-funds in which benefit plan investors equal or exceed the twenty-five percent level may not rely on Prohibited Transaction Exemption 77-4 with respect to fees charged by hedge funds in which it invests that are managed by the fund-of-funds' investment adviser.

vi. Agency Cross Transactions

ERISA Prohibited Transaction Class Exemption 86-128 allows an authorized person to effect or execute certain agency cross transactions on behalf of a plan asset hedge fund as long as the plan fiduciary does not have discretion for or provide investment advice to both the buyer and the seller in the transaction.[53] The exemption requires that a person engaging in a covered transaction receive written authorization, executed in advance, from an independent fiduciary. Thereafter, the authorized person must notify the plan at least annually that the plan may terminate the authorization at will and without penalty. Such notice must include both a statement that failure to terminate the authorization will result in its continuation and a form on which to effect such a termination. The exemption applies only if the person engaging in the covered transaction is not a trustee or an administrator of the plan, or an employer whose employees are covered by the plan,[54] and the following conditions are satisfied:

- The investment adviser must disclose the potential for conflicts of interest in connection with agency cross transactions;
- The annual summary must include a statement identifying the total number of agency cross transactions and the total amount of all commissions or other remuneration received by the broker (or any of its affiliates) in connection with the transactions;
- Each transaction must be a purchase or sale for no consideration other than a cash payment against prompt delivery of a security, and the security must be one for which market quotations are readily available; and

---

53. DOL Prohibited Transaction Exemption 86-128, 51 F.R. 41,686 (Nov. 18, 1986). An agency cross transaction is a transaction in which securities are transferred by the seller to the buyer, both using the same broker. *See* §§ 13.5.3, 13.5.4 and 13.5.5, *infra*.

54. *Id.*

- Each agency cross transaction must be effected at a price that is at or between the independent bid price and independent asked price for the security prevailing at the time of the transaction.[55]

The DOL determined that a hedge fund's investment adviser may not exercise discretion on both sides of a cross transaction:[56]

> ERISA's fiduciary responsibility and prohibited transaction provisions are designed to help assure that the fiduciary's decisions are made in the best interest of the plan and not colored by self-interest. These provisions require that a plan fiduciary act with an "eye single" to the interests of the plan involved in the transaction. Therefore, the Department is not convinced that reliance upon an objective fair price alone will ameliorate the conflicts . . . [inherent in cross trades where the fiduciary has discretion on both sides], such as the potential for "cherry picking" or dumping of securities or allocating investment opportunities among client accounts in a manner designed to favor one account over the other.[57]

vii. Qualified Professional Asset Manager Exemption

The DOL has granted a class exemption[58] for certain prohibited transactions where the decision to engage in a particular transaction is made by a qualified professional asset manager ("QPAM") who is unrelated to the party in interest involved in the transaction. In general, the QPAM exemption permits a plan assets fund to acquire securities or borrow money from or engage in a swap transaction with a service provider (or other party in interest). The party in interest cannot be the party that has the power to appoint or terminate the QPAM. The QPAM exemption dose not, however, generally permit principal transactions between the QPAM (or its related person) and the plan assets fund and does not exempt securities lending transactions, although the DOL permits some such transactions if specified requirments are satisfied.[59] The QPAM Exemption does not apply to cross trades or allow an investment adviser to engage in conflict of interest transactions.

A QPAM includes, among other institutions, an SEC-registered investment adviser that has total non-proprietary client assets under its management in excess of $50,000,000 and shareholders' or partners' equity in excess of $750,000 (although the DOL has proposed increasing these requirements to $85,000,000 and $1,000,000, respectively). The equity requirement may be met by a guaranty of payment of all liabilities of the investment adviser by certain affiliates, (such as a registered broker), shareholders or partners of that investment adviser, as long as such affiliates, shareholders or partners, together with the investment adviser,

---

55. *Id.*

56. DOL Notice, Cross-Trades of Securities by Investment Managers, 63 F.R. 13,696 (Mar. 20, 1998).

57. *Id.*

58. DOL Prohibited Transaction Exemption 84-14, 49 F.R. 9,494 (Mar. 13, 1984), amended by 50 F.R. 41,430 (Oct. 10, 1985).

59. DOL Prohibited Transaction Exemption 81-6, 46 F.R.7, 527 (Jan. 23, 1981).

meet the $750,000 equity requirement. A QPAM must acknowledge in the advisory contract that it is a fiduciary with respect to the employee benefit plan that retains it. An investment adviser cannot be a QPAM with respect to a plan if the assets of the plan managed by the investment adviser (together with the assets of other plans of the same plan sponsor managed by the investment adviser) are more than twenty percent of all the assets managed by the investment adviser or if the investment adviser or any owner of five percent or more of the investment adviser has been convicted of specified felonies within ten years.[60]

4. Directed Brokerage in Exchange for Referrals

As noted above, the DOL has opined that an ERISA fiduciary's receipt of soft dollars in the form of goods or services falling outside the safe harbor of Exchange Act section 28(e) is a prohibited transaction. The safe harbor of Exchange Act section 28(e) is not available for directed brokerage transactions.[61] Accordingly, a hedge fund investment adviser's decision to direct brokerage transactions with respect to plan assets must be made prudently and solely in the best interest of the plan participants and beneficiaries.[62] The investment adviser is not permitted to consider other factors, such as relationships with the broker or its employees outside of the plan context, in directing brokerage.[63] An investment adviser that refers a plan's brokerage business to a broker in exchange for the broker's referring advisory business to the investment adviser would be engaging in a prohibited transaction, because the investment adviser would be using the plan's assets for the investment adviser's own benefit and receiving consideration from a party dealing with the plan.

5. Participant-Controlled Accounts

ERISA provides that, if ERISA plan participants or beneficiaries exercise investment control over the assets in individual plan accounts, the participants or beneficiaries are not treated as fiduciaries; even so, persons who are otherwise fiduciaries are not liable for any losses or any breaches resulting from the participants' or beneficiaries' exercise of investment control.[64] An investment adviser engaged by an individual participant or beneficiary to manage the account may be liable, however, for losses resulting from the investment adviser's breaches.

6. Caution

The prohibited transaction rules may appear straightforward on their face, but can be extraordinarily complex in their application. Prohibited transactions can

---

60. *Id.*

61. DOL Prohibited Transaction Exemption 77-4, 42 F.R. 18,732 (Mar. 31, 1977).

62. *Id.* A failure to fulfill this requirement would violate the prudence requirements of ERISA § 404(a)(1)(B), 29 U.S.C. § 1104(a)(1)(B).

63. *Id.*

64. ERISA § 404(c), 29 U.S.C. § 1104(c); DOL Regulation § 2550.404c-1(b)(2), 29 C.F.R. § 2550.404c-1(b)(2).

arise when an investment adviser inadvertently and unknowingly engages in a transaction with a plan, such as in a transaction with a company or partnership or involving an asset (such as real estate) that is partially or wholly owned by a plan. For example, if an investment adviser to a plan rents an office in a building that is partly owned by the plan, the plan and the investment adviser may, depending on the circumstances, be engaging in a prohibited transaction. Prohibited transactions may also arise when an investment adviser causes an employee benefit plan to engage in a transaction with an affiliate of the investment adviser, another service provider of the plan (such as another investment adviser or the hedge fund's administrator) or an affiliate of such other service provider. In addition, it may be a prohibited transaction for an investment adviser fiduciary to exercise discretion to cause idle cash balances to be invested in a manner that allows the fiduciary to control the amount of fees it receives from a benefit plan. For these reasons, potential derivative counterparties or service providers may be hesitant or unwilling to deal with a plan assets hedge fund. An investment adviser to a plan assets hedge fund should keep records of the parties in interest and monitor any cicumstances that might be or cause a prohibited transaction.

7. Penalties

The penalty for a prohibited transaction is an excise tax of fifteen percent of the "amount involved" in the prohibited transaction for each year that such transaction exists. The tax must by paid by any "disqualified person" who participates in the transaction, which generally includes any party in interest to the transaction (such as an investment adviser fiduciary).[65] If the transaction is not corrected within the taxable period, a tax may be assessed equal to the full amount involved in the prohibited transaction.[66] In addition to the excise tax, the DOL has authority to impose a civil penalty for a breach of fiduciary responsibility. The penalty is generally twenty percent of the "applicable recovery amount" and is payable by the fiduciary or any other person who knowingly participates in the breach.[67] The amount of this penalty is reduced by the amount of the excise tax imposed with respect to the same transaction under Tax Code Section 4975. Plaintiffs also typically seek rescission damages in the case of prohibited transactions to put the plan back in the position it would have occupied had the transaction not occurred. This relief can require restoration of losses to a plan whether or not those losses were causally related to the prohibited transaction.

---

65. Tax Code § 4975(a), 26 U.S.C. § 4975(a).
66. Tax Code § 4975(b), 26 U.S.C. § 4975(b).
67. ERISA § 502(l), 29 U.S.C. § 1132(l).

§ 11.5 Other ERISA Rules Applicable to Hedge Funds

1. Bonding Requirements

ERISA imposes bonding requirements on certain fiduciaries and other persons (including the investment advisers or general partners of hedge funds) who "handle" funds or other property of employee benefit plans.[68] "Handle" means have physical contact with, have power to transfer or disburse, or have or exercise discretionary control over the investment of plan assets. Thus, the ERISA bonding requirements apply to the investment adviser and general partner of a hedge fund if at least twenty-five percent of any class of its equity interests is owned by benefit plan investors. Generally, the amount of the bond is determined on a per-plan basis (rather than a per-hedge-fund basis), at ten percent of the plan assets handled by the investment adviser, with a minimum of $1,000 and a maximum of $500,000 per plan.[69] No bonding is required for an investment adviser that renders investment advice for a fee but does not "handle" plan assets.

2. Foreign Security Custody Rules

Except in limited circumstances, the fiduciary of an ERISA plan may not maintain indicia of ownership of any assets of the plan outside the jurisdiction of the U.S. District Courts (including foreign securities maintained by a non-U.S. custodian).[70] The requirement to maintain the indicia of ownership of a hedge fund's assets within U.S. jurisdiction does not, however, strictly prohibit or restrict non-U.S. investments. Rather, "indicia of ownership" refers to the evidence of ownership of the hedge fund's assets (such as stock certificates). If the hedge fund has a U.S. custodian, assets maintained by that custodian are within the jurisdiction of U.S. District Courts.

The DOL has promulgated custody regulations that provide exceptions to permit a "foreign security" (such as a security issued by a corporation that is not organized under U.S. law and that does not have its principal place of business in the United States) to be held outside U.S. jurisdiction under the "asset manager alternative." This alternative requires that the custodian be a hedge fund investment adviser (that is, a fiduciary) that is a substantial U.S. bank, an insurance company or an SEC-registered investment adviser.[71]

---

68.   ERISA § 412(a), 29 U.S.C. § 1112(a).
69.   *Id.*
70.   ERISA § 404(b), 29 U.S.C § 1104(b); DOL Regulation § 2550.404b-1, 29 C.F.R. § 2550.404b-1.
71.   *See* DOL Regulation § 2550.404b-1, 29 C.F.R. § 2550.404b-1.

3. Indemnification

Under ERISA, any agreement that purports to relieve a fiduciary from liability for an ERISA fiduciary breach is void as against public policy. An agreement under which a plan is obligated to indemnify the fiduciary for such a breach is also void. The use of plan assets to indemnify a fiduciary, whether or not on account of a breach of an ERISA fiduciary duty, may constitute a prohibited transaction. Thus, a hedge fund partnership agreement provision that obligates the hedge fund to indemnify the general partner or investment adviser of the hedge fund could not be enforced if the hedge fund assets are plan assets and the general partner or investment adviser is an ERISA fiduciary of a plan investor.[72] ERISA does not, however, prohibit third parties from indemnifying fiduciaries or prohibit fiduciaries from obtaining insurance to protect themselves against losses. Insurance and proper indemnification can be important tools for investment advisers to limit some of the risks related to ERISA-covered plans.

4. Reporting Requirements

When a hedge fund holds plan assets, the plans that hold interests in the hedge fund also hold an interest in the underlying assets of the hedge fund. Consequently, when the plans make their annual reports to the DOL and IRS on Form 5500, they must report their interests in both the hedge fund and its underlying assets. The hedge fund is obligated to provide this information to the plans. As an alternative, the hedge fund itself may report its underlying assets directly to the government, and each partner plan could then report only its interest in the hedge fund.[73] This alternative filing may be made only if the hedge fund and the plan investors have agreed that the hedge fund will provide the information directly to the government.[74]

---

72.   ERISA § 410, 29 U.S.C. § 1110.
73.   DOL Regulation § 2520.103-12, 29 C.F.R. § 2520.103-12.
74.   *Id.*

CHAPTER 12

Custody

---

§ 12.1 SEC-Registered Investment Advisers

---

1. Definition of Custody

An SEC-registered investment adviser that holds, directly or indirectly, client funds or securities, or has any authority to obtain possession of client funds or securities, is deemed to have "custody" of those funds or securities under the SEC's custody rule.[1] An SEC-registered investment adviser that is authorized to deduct fees from its clients' accounts has custody of the assets of those accounts.[2] The rule also specifically provides that an SEC-registered investment adviser that serves as the general partner of an investment limited partnership has custody of the partnership's assets. An SEC-registered investment adviser can avoid being deemed to have custody of client assets that it receives inadvertently if it returns the assets to the sender (rather than forwarding them to the intended recipient) within three business days.[3]

Before the current SEC custody rule was adopted, an SEC-registered investment adviser with custody of client assets was required to undergo an annual surprise examination and file an audited balance sheet with Part II of its Form ADV. Many such investment advisers that otherwise would have had custody of the assets of hedge funds instead chose to follow the series of SEC no-action letters commonly called the *PIMs/Bennett* letters.[4] Under those letters, the investment adviser was not deemed to have custody if it entered into an arrangement with the hedge fund's prime broker that required an "independent representative" to authorize all payments by the hedge fund to the investment adviser or its affiliates.

The 2003 amendments to the custody rule eliminated for most purposes the annual surprise examination and audited balance sheet requirement. The SEC also stated in the adopting release that SEC-registered investment advisers could no longer rely on the *PIMs/Bennett* letters.[5] Accordingly, a hedge fund general partner that is an SEC-registered investment adviser can no longer avoid custody by

---

1. Advisers Act Rule 206(4)-2, 17 C.F.R. § 275.206(4)-2.
2. Advisers Act Rules 206(4)-2(c)(1)(ii) and (iii), 17 C.F.R. §§ 275.206(4)-2(c)(1)(ii) and (iii).
3. Advisers Act Rule 206(4)-2(c)(1), 16 C.F.R. § 275.206(4)-2(c)(1).
4. *Bennett Management Co.*, SEC No-Action Letter (Feb. 26, 1990); *PIMS, Inc.*, SEC No-Action Letter (Oct. 21, 1991).
5. Advisers Act Release No. 2176, 68 F.R. 56,692 (Oct. 1, 2003).

submitting to an independent representative all requests for payment of management fees, special profit allocations or performance fees, and reimbursement of expenses. Instead, such a general partner is deemed to have custody by virtue of its status as a general partner, and must comply with the rules summarized below.

2. Qualified Custodian

An SEC-registered investment adviser with custody of client assets must maintain those assets with one or more "qualified custodians."[6] Qualified custodians are banks, registered broker-dealers, futures commission merchants and certain non-U.S. financial accounts that customarily hold assets for their clients and segregate those assets from their proprietary assets.[7] An SEC-registered investment adviser that trades mutual fund shares may use the mutual fund transfer agents as qualified custodians for the limited purpose of holding those shares.[8] Privately offered uncertificated securities also need not be held by a qualified custodian under certain conditions.[9]

3. Notice to Clients

When an SEC-registered investment adviser with custody opens an account in the custodial client's name or in the investment adviser's name as agent, it must promptly notify the client in writing of the qualified custodian's name and address and the manner in which the funds or securities are held. Thereafter, it must promptly notify the client if any of that information changes.[10]

4. Account Statement Delivery Requirement

An SEC-registered investment adviser with custody must arrange for the qualified custodian to deliver account statements at least quarterly directly to the custodial client (and not through the investment adviser).[11] The statements must show the amount of funds and each security in the account at the end of the quarter and each transaction in the account during the quarter.[12] For this purpose, each investor in a hedge fund managed by the investment adviser is considered a "client."[13] Alternatively, the investment adviser may send the statements directly to clients if the investment adviser arranges for an annual surprise examination by an independent public accountant to verify the funds and assets in the custodial client's account.[14] Clients (or investors in a hedge fund) who do not want to receive quarterly statements may appoint an independent representative to receive the account statements on their behalf.[15]

---

6.   Advisers Act Rule 206(4)-2(a)(1), 17 C.F.R. § 275.206(4)-2(a)(1).
7.   Advisers Act Rule 206(4)-2(c)(3), 17 C.F.R. § 275.206(4)-2(c)(3).
8.   Adviser's Act Rule 206(4)-2(b)(1), 17 C.F.R. § 275.206(4)-2(b)(1).
9.   Adviser's Act Rule 206(4)-2(b)(2), 17 C.F.R. § 275.206(4)-2(b)(2).
10.   Adviser's Act Rule 206(4)-2(a)(2), 17 C.F.R. § 275.206(4)-2(a)(2).
11.   Adviser's Act Rule 206(4)-2(a)(3)(i), 17 C.F.R. § 275.206(4)-2(a)(3)(i).
12.   *Id.*
13.   Adviser's Act Rule 206(4)-2(a)(3)(iii), 17 C.F.R. § 275.206(4)-2(a)(3)(iii).
14.   Adviser's Act Rule 206(4)-2(a)(3)(ii), 17 C.F.R. § 275.206(4)-2(a)(3)(ii).
15.   Adviser's Act Rule 206(4)-2(a)(4), 17 C.F.R. § 275.206(4)-2(a)(4).

Providing a hedge fund's quarterly account statements to investors in the fund or their independent representative is intended to help prevent improper payments to the hedge fund's general partner and its affiliates.[16]

5. Alternative Procedure for Hedge Funds

An SEC-registered investment adviser that is the general partner of a hedge fund need not deliver the quarterly account statements to each investor as described above, if the investment adviser sends the hedge fund's audited annual financial statements to each investor within 120 days after the end of the hedge fund's fiscal year.[17] The financial statements must be prepared in accordance with generally accepted accounting principles (GAAP). Most hedge funds have their annual financial statements audited, but some common hedge fund practices might not comply with GAAP. For example, a hedge fund may amortize organizational costs over several years or may decline to attach to the audited financial statements a list of certain of the hedge fund's holdings, either of which may not accord with GAAP. A hedge fund that has financial statements that span a period longer than one year (for example, from the hedge fund's inception on October 1 of a year to the end of the following calendar year) may not take advantage of this alternative procedure, even if its financial statements accord with GAAP and are audited.

§ 12.2 State-Registered Investment Advisers

The above custody rule applies only to SEC-registered investment advisers. Many states, such as California, have rules that specify procedures an investment adviser registered in those states must follow if it has custody of client assets.[18] The SEC's custody rule does not affect those states' custody rules. Many states allow investment advisers to hedge funds to follow the *PIMs/Bennett* disbursement procedures to avoid being deemed to have custody. Under the *PIMs/Bennett* interpretations, if an investment adviser that is the general partner of a hedge fund wants to avoid having custody, it must adopt and implement the following procedures restricting its access to the hedge fund's assets, including its own capital and its fees and expense reimbursements:

- One or more independent banks or brokerage firms must hold the hedge fund's funds and securities in the name of the hedge fund;
- Investors in the hedge fund must deposit subscription funds directly with the custodian;

---

16. Advisers Act Release No. 2176, 68 F.R. 56,692 (Oct. 1, 2003).
17. Adviser's Act Rule 206(4)-2(b)(3), 17 C.F.R. § 275.206(4)-2(b)(3).
18. *See, e.g.*, California Code of Reg. § 260.237.

- The hedge fund must retain an independent representative (a lawyer or certified public accountant) to review and authorize transfers to the general partner or manager;
- Each time the general partner or manager requests a payment, withdrawal or distribution, it must send simultaneously to the independent representative and the custodian a statement showing (a) the amount of the payment or withdrawal, (b) if a fee payment, the value of the hedge fund's assets on which the fee is based, (c) if a fee payment, the manner in which the payment is calculated, (d) if the withdrawal is by the general partner or manager, the amount in the general partner's or manager's capital account before and after the withdrawal and (e) the aggregate amount in all partners' or members' capital accounts before and after the withdrawal;
- The custodian may transfer funds from the hedge fund's account to the general partner or manager only with the written authorization of the independent representative, and only if the custodian receives a copy of the written request from the general partner or manager; and
- The custodian must provide quarterly statements to the hedge fund and the independent representative.[19]

These procedures should be set forth in an appropriate written agreement between the investment adviser and the custodian. If the general partner intends to follow these procedures, it should direct all other brokers and dealers that hold any of the hedge fund's assets to remit such assets only to the hedge fund's custodian for the hedge fund's account.

The North American Securities Administrators Association (NASAA) has adopted a model rule for consideration by states that combines certain aspects of the SEC's custody rule with the *PIMs/Bennett* disbursement procedures.[20] Under the model rule, it is unlawful for an investment adviser that is registered or required to be registered to have custody of client funds or securities unless:

- The investment adviser notifies the state regulatory authority promptly via its Form ADV that the investment adviser has or may have custody;
- A qualified custodian maintains the funds and securities in a separate account under the client's name or in accounts that contain only the investment adviser's clients' funds and securities under the investment adviser's name as agent or trustee for the clients;
- The investment adviser notifies its clients of the qualified custodian's name and address and the manner in which the funds or securities are maintained promptly when the account is opened and when that information changes;

---

19.   *Bennett Management Co.*, SEC No-Action Letter (Feb. 26, 1990); and *PIMS, Inc.*, SEC No-Action Letter (Oct. 21, 1991).

20.   NASAA Custody Requirements for Investment Advisers, Model Rule 102(e)(1)-1, adopted Apr. 3, 2000, amended Apr. 18, 2004, *available at* http://www.nasaa.org/nasaa/scripts/fu_display_list.asp?ptid=142 (June 10, 2004).

- Either (1) a qualified custodian sends account statements at least quarterly to each client (if the client is a hedge fund, each investor) for which the investment adviser maintains funds or securities, identifying the amount of funds and securities in the account at the end of the period and setting forth all transactions in the account during that period; or (2) the investment adviser sends such account statements and (a) an independent certified public accountant verifies all client funds and securities by surprise examination at least once a year and files a copy of the auditor's report and financial statements with the state regulatory authority within thirty days after completion of the examination along with a letter stating that it examined the funds and securities and describing the nature and extent of the examination, and (b) the accountant notifies the state regulatory authority within one day of finding any material discrepancy;
- If the investment adviser has fees directly deducted from client accounts, the investment adviser obtains written authorization from the client, provides notice of the fee deduction to the client and provides notice of the safeguards described above to clients through its Form ADV; and
- If the investment adviser has custody because it is the general partner or manager of a hedge fund and it is not subject to an annual audit, the investment adviser engages an independent party to review all fees, expenses and capital withdrawals from the hedge fund.

As with the SEC custody rule, an investment adviser may use a mutual fund's transfer agent in lieu of a qualified custodian. In addition, investment advisers are not required to comply with the above requirements with respect to certain privately offered securities. A hedge fund subject to an annual audit is not required to comply with the quarterly account statement requirement if it distributes its financial statements to each beneficial owner within 120 days of the end of its fiscal year and notifies the state regulatory authority, via its Form ADV, that it intends to use the safeguards described above. Registered investment companies and certain beneficial trusts are also not required to comply with the above requirements. An investment adviser that intends to have custody but is not able to use a qualified custodian must first obtain approval from the state regulatory authority and comply with all applicable safekeeping provisions of the rule.

§ 12.3 Unregistered Investment Advisers

An investment adviser that is not registered with the SEC or any state is generally not subject to the custody rules described above. Nevertheless, such an investment adviser would be well advised to adopt and implement custody procedures that comply with the laws of its state.

CHAPTER 13

Trading Activities and Reporting

---

§ 13.1 Consequences of Large Shareholdings

---

1. Exchange Act Section 13(d) Filing Requirements

Exchange Act section 13(d)[1] requires any person or group that acquires beneficial ownership of more than five percent of any class of equity securities registered under the Exchange Act (a "Five Percent Owner") to report that person's or group's beneficial ownership in filings with the SEC.

i. Persons Subject to Filing Requirement

a. Beneficial Ownership

One who has all of the economic rights in a security may not beneficially own it; one who has none of the economic rights in a security may be its only beneficial owner. A person "beneficially owns" a security if the person has or shares the power to vote or dispose of the security.[2] The investment adviser to a hedge fund typically has discretionary authority to purchase, sell and vote the securities held by the hedge fund and, therefore, the investment adviser and its control persons beneficially own the securities held by the hedge fund. A person also beneficially owns any securities that the person has the right to acquire (such as on exercise of an option), if the right is exercisable within sixty days or was acquired with the purpose or effect of changing or influencing control of the issuer.[3] Thus, a hedge fund that retains the right to terminate its investment management agreement with an investment adviser within sixty days also beneficially owns the securities

---

1. 15 U.S.C. § 78m(d).
2. Exchange Act Rule 13d-3(a), 17 C.F.R. § 240.13d-3(a).
3. Exchange Act Rule 13d-3(d)(1), 17 C.F.R. § 240.13d-3(d)(1).

in its account.[4] A hedge fund for which the investment adviser also is the general partner or manager, however, usually does not have the ability to terminate the advisory relationship within sixty days. Thus most hedge funds organized as partnerships or limited liability companies usually do not beneficially own the securities they hold.[5] An investor in a hedge fund does not beneficially own the securities held by the hedge fund unless that investor has the power to require the distribution to the investor of specific securities (as opposed to securities selected by the general partner or cash) within sixty days. The governing documents of hedge funds ordinarily do not include such a term.

b. *"Group" Status*

When two or more persons act in concert "for the purpose of acquiring, holding, voting or disposing of equity securities," the group formed thereby is considered to beneficially own all the equity securities owned by each member of the group.[6] Persons can be members of a group for this purpose without any formal agreement among them. The SEC or a court may infer from circumstantial evidence that two or more persons have a formal or informal understanding and are acting in furtherance of a common objective and thus constitute a group.[7] A mere relationship among persons or entities, however, whether family, personal or business, is insufficient to create a group under Exchange Act section 13(d).[8] Thus, although an investment adviser to hedge funds and separate accounts may cause those hedge funds and accounts to trade *pari passu*, those hedge funds and accounts generally are not considered to form a "group" for purposes of filings under Exchange Act section 13(d).[9] The investment adviser to those hedge funds

---

4. Exchange Act Rule 13d-3(d)(1), 17 C.F.R. § 240.13d-3(d)(1).

5. *See also Washington Bancorporation v. Washington*, CCH Fed. Sec. L. Rep. ¶ 94,893 (D.D.C. 1989) (a partnership that has ceded all voting and investment power to its general partner is not a beneficial owner under Exchange Act § 13(d) of the securities held by the partnership and therefore may not be a member of a § 13(d) group).

6. Exchange Act Rule 13d-5(b)(1), 17 C.F.R. § 240.13d-5(b)(1).

7. *Wellman v. Dickinson*, 682 F.2d 355, 362-64 (2nd Cir. 1982).

8. *Transcon Lines v. A. G. Becker, Inc.*, 470 F. Supp. 356, 375 (S.D.N.Y. 1979), quoting *Texasgulf, Inc. v. Canada Development Corp.*, 366 F. Supp. 374, 403 (S.D. Tex. 1973). *See also, Management Assistance, Inc. v. Edelman*, 584 F. Supp. 1016, 1019 (S.D.N.Y. 1984) (principal of corporation who was a limited partner in a limited partnership that was a member of § 13(d) group was deemed not to be a member of that group); *Polaroid Corp. v. Disney*, 698 F. Supp. 1169, 1180 (D. Del. 1988) (limited partners in a partnership that hold shares directly and indirectly, through the partnership, do not necessarily form a group with the partnership).

9. *Wellman v. Dickinson, supra* (mutual fund clients of an investment adviser that was a member of a § 13(d) group were not named as defendants or as members of the § 13(d) group); *Bath Industries, Inc. v. Blot*, 427 F.2d 97, 103, 112 (7th Cir. 1970) (investment firm that exercised continuous voting control over its clients' securities deemed to possess beneficial ownership of the securities and to be a member of § 13(d) group, but no indication that clients of that firm were members of the group); *Champion Parts Rebuilders, Inc. v. Cormier Corp.*, 661 F. Supp. 825, 834 (N.D. Ill. 1987) (investment adviser and several stockholders deemed to be members of § 13(d) group, but clients of adviser not listed as defendants or referred to in court's opinion); *Jacobs v. Pabst Brewing Co.*, 549 F. Supp. 1050, 1065-1066 (D. Del. 1982) (§ 13(d) group does not exist where investment adviser and its clients have not agreed to act together); and *National Home Products, Inc. v. Gray*, 416 F. Supp. 1293, 1323-24 (D. Del. 1976) (stockholder who sought investment advice from member of § 13(d) group not a member of the group in absence of evidence of agreement to act in concert). *But see Schaffer v. Soros*, 1994 WL 381442 (S.D.N.Y. July 20, 1994) (an investment adviser, investment advisory firm under the investment adviser's control, the director of the firm and two investment companies whose investments were under the control of the investment advisers deemed to be members of a § 13(d) group).

and separate accounts is required, however, to file reports under Exchange Act section 13(d) for itself if the discretionary accounts it manages collectively exceed the five percent threshold, even if some or all of its clients are not considered part of a group.

ii. Filing Requirements and Deadlines

Reports under Exchange Act section 13(d) are made on Schedule 13D or 13G. Schedule 13G requires less information and must be amended less frequently than Schedule 13D.[10]

a. Form 13D

A Five Percent Owner must report its holdings on a Form 13D within ten days after the date on which its beneficial ownership exceeds five percent, unless it is eligible to file the shorter-form Schedule 13G.[11] A report on Schedule 13D must be amended "promptly" (which can mean "immediately" in some circumstances) if the information disclosed in the Schedule changes materially. Any acquisition or disposition of one percent or more of the class of securities is deemed material for this purpose. Acquisitions and dispositions of less than one percent may or may not be material, depending on the circumstances.[12]

b. Form 13G Exceptions for Certain Filers

A Five Percent Owner may file a Schedule 13G instead of a Schedule 13D to report the Five Percent Owner's holdings if the Five Percent Owner acquired the securities in the ordinary course of business and without the purpose or effect of changing or influencing the control of the issuer. A Schedule 13G may be filed under either of two different Exchange Act rules, and the two types of Schedule 13G have slightly different filing and amedment requirements. If the Five Percent Owner is one of the listed types of persons, including a registered investment adviser (state or federal), it may file a Schedule 13G under Exchange Act Rule 13d–1(b) (the "Investment Adviser Rule").[13] A Five Percent Owner that does not qualify to file a Schedule 13G under Exchange Act Rule 13d–1(c), because it is not a type of person on such list, may nevertheless file on Schedule 13G under Exchange Act Rule 13d–1(c), if it is a passive holder as described above and owns, directly or indirectly, less than twenty percent of the outstanding securities of the applicable class (the "Passive Owner Rule").[14] If a Five Percent Owner initially files on Schedule 13G in reliance on the Investment Adviser Rule or the Passive Owner Rule and subsequently develops the purpose or effect of changing or influencing the control of the issuer (in the case of a Five Percent Owner relying on the Investment Adviser Rule or the Passive Owner Rule) or exceeds

---

10. Exchange Act Rules 13d-1(b) and 13d-1(c), 17 C.F.R. §§ 240.13d-1(b) and 240.13d-1(c).
11. Exchange Act Rule 13d-1(a), 17 C.F.R. § 240.13d-1(a).
12. Exchange Act Rule 13d-2(a), 17 C.F.R. § 240.13d-2(a).
13. Exchange Act Rule 13d-1(b), 17 C.F.R. § 240.13d-1(b).
14. Exchange Act Rule 13d-1(c), 17 C.F.R. § 240.13d-1(c).

the twenty percent threshold (in the case of a Five Percent Owner relying on the Passive Owner Rule), it must file a Schedule 13D within ten days after that change occurs.[15] From the date of the triggering event until ten days after it files a Schedule 13D, the Five Percent Owner may not vote the securities or acquire any additional equity securities of the issuer.[16]

A Five Percent Owner relying on the Investment Adviser Rule is generally not required to file its initial Schedule 13G until forty-five days after the end of the year in which it becomes a Five Percent Owner. If, however, such Five Percent Owner's beneficial ownership exceeds ten percent on the last day of any month before the end of that year, it must file its initial Schedule 13G within ten days after the end of that month. A Five Percent Owner relying on the Passive Owner Rule must file an initial Schedule 13G within ten days after becoming a Five Percent Owner, and is subject to more stringent amendment requirements than a filer relying on the Investment Adviser Rule.[17]

An investment adviser is not eligible for the relaxed filing requirements associated with reliance on the Investment Adviser Rule if any hedge fund it manages beneficially owns more than five percent of a security, because a hedge fund is not one of the types of persons described in the Investment Adviser Rule. To take advantage of the Investment Adviser Rule, an investment adviser could disclaim ownership in a group with the hedge fund and cause the hedge fund to file its own separate Schedule 13G (assuming the hedge fund is eligible to rely on the Passive Owner Rule). In many cases, however, this approach will not reduce the investment adviser's administrative burden and filing costs, because the investment adviser, as the general partner or manager of the hedge fund, is responsible for filing the Form 13G on behalf of the hedge fund.

A Five Percent Owner may not rely on the Investment Adviser Rule if a parent holding company or control person of the Five Percent Owner (such as the manager of the investment adviser) holds more than one percent of the class of securities.[18] To determine a parent holding company's or control person's interest, that person's direct ownership of the securities must be aggregated with that person's indirect ownership interests. For example, a person who has invested in a hedge fund is deemed to own indirectly that portion of securities held by a hedge fund equal to the person's proportionate interest in the hedge fund. The control person of an investment adviser seeking to rely on the Investment Adviser Rule should aggregate all of his or her indirect holdings—for example, indirect holdings through the investment adviser's ownership interest in hedge funds as a result of that person's ownership interest in the investment adviser—in calculating whether he or she exceeds the one-percent limit.

All Five Percent Owners must amend their reports on Schedule 13G within forty-five days after the end of each calendar year to reflect any changes in the

---

15.   Exchange Act Rules 13d-1(e)(1) and 13d-1(f)(1), 17 C.F.R. §§ 240.13d-1(e)(1) and 240.13d-1(f)(1).

16.   Exchange Act Rules 13d-1(e)(2) and 13d-1(f)(2), 17 C.F.R. §§ 240.13d-1(e)(2) and 240.13d-1(f)(2).

17.   Exchange Act Rules 13d-1(b), 13d-1(f)(1) and 13d-2(c), 17 C.F.R. §§ 240.13d-1(b), 240.13d-1(f)(1) and 240.13d-2(c).

18.   Exchange Act Rule 13d-1(b)(1)(ii)(G), 17 C.F.R. § 240.13d-1(b)(1)(ii)(G).

information in the preceding report.[19] A Five Percent Owner relying on the Investment Adviser Rule must also amend its Schedule 13G within ten days after the end of the first month in which its beneficial ownership as of the last day of that month exceeds ten percent, and thereafter, within ten days of the end of the first month in which its beneficial ownership as of the last day of that month changes by more than five percent. A Five Percent Owner relying on the Passive Owner Rule must amend its Schedule 13G promptly when its beneficial ownership exceeds ten percent and, thereafter, promptly when its beneficial ownership changes by more than five percent.

iii. Delivery Requirements

Each Schedule 13D or 13G and each amendment to it must be filed with the SEC through its EDGAR System. A copy of a Schedule 13D and each amendment to it must be sent to the issuer of the securities and to each national securities exchange on which the securities are traded. If the securities are traded on the Nasdaq Stock Market, the Schedule 13D does not need to be sent to the NASD.[20] A copy of each Schedule 13G and its amendments must be sent to the issuer of the securities.[21] Schedules 13G do not need to be filed with any stock exchange.

iv. Non-Compliance

a. SEC Penalties

The SEC may require an investment adviser and hedge funds to file the reports required under section 13(d), if they do not do so of their own accord. The SEC may also levy fines or recommend criminal prosecution for violations of section 13(d).[22]

b. Private Right of Action

Neither section 13(d) nor the rules thereunder expressly provide for private enforcement of the filing requirements. Courts have implied private causes of action for issuers to require necessary filings, but no reported federal decision has allowed an issuer a cause of action for damages.[23]

---

19.   Exchange Act Rule 13d-2(b), 17 C.F.R. § 240.13d-2(b).

20.   Exchange Act Rule 13d-7, 17 C.F.R. § 240.13d-7.

21.   *Id.*

22.   Exchange Act §21(d)(1), 15 U.S.C. § 78u(d)(1).

23.   *Hallwood Realty Partners, L.P. v. Gotham Partners, L.P.*, 286 F.3d 613, 620 (2d Cir. 2001) (holding, in a case of first impression for that circuit, that there is no private right of action for damages to issuers under § 13(d)). *Also see Dan River, Inc. v. Unitex Ltd.*, 624 F.2d 1216, 1224 (4th Cir. 1980) (issuer can require filer of an incorrect Schedule 13D to amend such filing until it is accurate); *Ind. Nat'l Corp. v. Rich*, 712 F.2d 1180, 1184, 1186 (7th Cir. 1983) (issuer has right to injunctive relief); *Gearhart Indus., Inc. v. Smith Int'l. Inc.*, 741 F.2d 707, 714, 717 (5th Cir. 1984) (issuer must demonstrate likelihood of irreparable harm to apply for injunctive relief); and *Chevron Corp. v. Pennzoil Co.*, 974 F.2d 1156, 1158 (9th Cir. 1992).

2. Exchange Act Section 16(a) Filing Requirements

Exchange Act section 16[24] requires any person who directly or indirectly beneficially owns (discussed below) more than ten percent of any class of equity securities registered under the Exchange Act, or who is an officer or director of an issuer with a class so registered (each, an "insider"), to report that person's beneficial ownership of and transactions in such securities.

Investment advisers and hedge funds usually are more concerned about the ten percent beneficial ownership test than the "officer" or "director" definitions, because most do not involve themselves in managing portfolio companies as officers or directors. "Beneficial ownership" under Exchange Act section 16 is determined using a two-part test. The first beneficial ownership test is applied to determine if a person owns more than ten percent of any class of equity securities registered under the Exchange Act (a "ten percent holder"). This test is intended to identify persons that, due to their stock holdings, have the potential to gain nonpublic information about an issuer. This first test is used only to identify who is a ten percent holder subject to the filing and short-swing profit recapture requirements of section 16. The second beneficial ownership test, the "pecuniary interest" test, is applied to a ten percent holder to identify the profit potential of that holder's securities holdings, which holdings and transactions that holder must report, and which such transactions give rise to short-swing profit liability.

i. "Beneficial Ownership"

The first beneficial ownership test under section 16 generally applies the same analysis, relating to the possession of voting or dispositive power, used under Exchange Act section 13(d).[25] In addition, however, a federal or state registered investment adviser may exclude from its beneficial ownership any shares held in a customer or fiduciary account in the ordinary course of business, if and so long as the securities were acquired and are held without the purpose or effect of changing or influencing control of the issuer. A control person and parent holding company of such an investment adviser may also rely on this exclusion from beneficial ownership if such person or company owns, directly and indirectly, no more than one percent of that class of securities.[26]

ii. "Pecuniary Interest"

Under the "pecuniary interest" test, a beneficial owner is "any person who, directly or indirectly, through any contract, arrangement, understanding, relationship or otherwise, has or shares a direct or indirect pecuniary interest in the equity securities."[27] A direct pecuniary interest is defined as "the opportunity, directly or indirectly, to profit or share in any profit derived from a transaction in the subject

---

24. 15 U.S.C. § 78p(a).
25. *See* § 13.1.1.i.a, *supra*.
26. Exchange Act Rule 16a-1(a)(1)(vii), 17 C.F.R. § 240.16a-1(a)(1)(vii).
27. Exchange Act Rule 16a-1(a)(2), 17 C.F.R. § 240.16a-1(a)(2).

securities."[28] The investment adviser to a hedge fund may be deemed to have an "indirect pecuniary interest" with respect to, among other things:

- if the investment adviser is also the general partner of the hedge fund, its proportionate interest in the portfolio securities held by the hedge fund, which is the greater of its share of the hedge fund's profits or its capital account in the hedge fund;[29] some commentators have suggested that if a partnership agreement specifies different profits participations for different types of income, the appropriate percentage would be that related to capital gains;[30]
- securities held by immediate family members of the adviser sharing the same household; and
- all of the securities in a hedge fund, if the adviser receives a performance fee or performance allocation and either (1) the performance fee or allocation is calculated over a period of less than one year or (2) equity securities of the issuer in question account for more than ten percent of the hedge fund's market value.[31] Thus, an adviser that receives quarterly performance allocations must include all of the hedge fund's securities in computing its own pecuniary interest. An investment adviser also will need to be especially vigilant with respect to this test if the hedge fund's investment strategy involves taking large positions in a few issuers, or if the hedge fund also has significant other assets managed by other investment advisers that use the same strategy.

A ten percent holder is also deemed to have an indirect pecuniary interest in securities that it has a right to acquire through the exercise of any derivative security (such as a put or call), whether or not that security is presently exercisable.[32]

A typical investor in a hedge fund does not need to make any section 16 filings and does not have short-swing profit liability for securities held by the hedge fund. An investor in a hedge fund is not deemed to have a pecuniary interest in the hedge fund's portfolio securities if the investor is not a "controlling shareholder" of the hedge fund and does not have or share investment control over the hedge fund's portfolio.[33] A "controlling shareholder" is an investor that has the power to exercise control over the hedge fund by virtue of its interest in the hedge fund.[34] Most hedge funds grant plenary management authority to the hedge fund's general partner or manager. The investors in the hedge fund typically have no authority to remove the general partner or manager, and thus have no ability to exercise control over the hedge fund.

---

28. Exchange Act Rule 16a–1(a)(2)(i), 17 C.F.R. § 240.16a–1(a)(2)(i).
29. Exchange Act Rule 16a–1(a)(2)(ii)(B), 17 C.F.R. § 240.16a–1(a)(2)(ii)(B).
30. *See, e.g.,* Jacobs, Arnold S., *Section 16 of the Securities Exchange Act,* § 2:9, West (2003).
31. Exchange Act Rule 16a–1(a)(2)(ii)(C), 17 C.F.R. § 240.16a–1(a)(2)(ii)(C).
32. Exchange Act Rule 16a–1(a)(2)(ii)(F), 17 C.F.R. § 240.16a–1(a)(2)(ii)(F).
33. Exchange Act Rule 16a–1(a)(2)(iii), 17 C.F.R. § 240.16a–1(a)(2)(iii); *Widett, Slater & Goldman, P.C.,* SEC No-Action Letter (Mar. 25, 1992).
34. Exchange Act Rule 16a–1(a)(2)(iii), 17 C.F.R. § 240.16a–1(a)(2)(iii).

Because of the two prongs of the test for beneficial ownership under section 16, a hedge fund manager may be considered a ten percent holder under the first test but not have any pecuniary interest in securities that are subject to the reporting or short-swing profit recapture provisions of section 16 under the second test. For example, a hedge fund manager ordinarily has the power to vote and dispose of securities acquired by the hedge fund (and may be unable to exclude them from the ten percent calculation because it fails to meet the conditions described above), thereby satisfying the first test; but it may not have a pecuniary interest in such securities if it only receives an asset-based fee or a conforming performance allocation or both (thereby failing the second test). In such case, the investment adviser must file a beneficial ownership report on Form 3, because all insiders must file a Form 3, but the report may either state that no securities are beneficially owned, or report the securities but disclaim beneficial ownership of them. Such an adviser would not be required to file Forms 4 or 5 to report changes in its beneficial ownership if it has no pecuniary interest in the securities, because only changes to beneficial ownership that reflect changes in the insider's pecuniary interest are required to be reported on Forms 4 and 5.

iii. Filing Requirements and Deadlines

a. Initial Report: Form 3

A person who becomes an insider must file an initial ownership report on Form 3 within ten days after becoming an insider.[35] The report must disclose all equity securities of the issuer in which the insider has a pecuniary interest, whether or not those securities are of a class that is registered under the Exchange Act.[36]

b. Subsequent Reports: Form 4

When an insider's pecuniary interest in the securities changes, the insider must file a report on Form 4 with the SEC before the end of the second business day following the day on which the transaction is executed.[37]

c. Annual Report: Form 5

An annual report on Form 5 must be filed within forty-five days after the end of the issuer's fiscal year by every person who was an insider of the issuer at any time during the fiscal year, to report (a) previously unreported transactions for the fiscal year that were required to have been reported but were not, (b) transactions exempt from short-swing profit recapture under Exchange Act section 16(b) (other than, among other things, exempt exercises and conversions of derivative securities) and not reported voluntarily on Form 4, and (c) any small acquisitions or series

---

35.   Exchange Act Rule 16a-3, 17 C.F.R. § 240.16a-3; Securities Act Release No. 8230 (May 7, 2003), 68 F.R. 25,788 (May 13, 2003).

36.   Exchange Act § 16(a)(3)(A), 15 U.S.C. § 78p(a)(3)(A); Exchange Act Rule 16a-2, 17 C.F.R. § 240.16a-2.

37.   Exchange Act Rule 16a-3(g)(1), 17 C.F.R. § 240.16a-3(g)(1); Securities Act Release No. 8230 (May 7, 2003), 68 F.R. 25,788 (May 13, 2003).

of acquisitions in a six-month period during the issuer's fiscal year that in the aggregate do not exceed $10,000 market value.[38] An insider with no transactions reportable on Form 5 for a fiscal year is not required to file a report on Form 5 for that year.[39]

iv. Delivery Requirements

Forms 3, 4 and 5 must be filed with the SEC through its EDGAR system.[40] Copies of the reports filed with the SEC must also be sent to the issuer and, if the security is registered on a national securities exchange, including the Nasdaq Stock Market, to the stock exchange on which the securities are traded.[41]

v. Non-Compliance

a. SEC Penalties

The SEC may require the investment adviser and hedge fund to file the reports required under section 16(a), if they do not do so of their own accord. The SEC may also levy fines or recommend criminal prosecution for violations of section 16(a).[42]

b. No Private Right of Action

The courts have not sustained any claim of a private right of action, whether for injunction relief or damages, for an investment adviser's or hedge fund's failure to file the required reports under section 16(a).[43]

3. Exchange Act Section 16(b) Short-Swing Profits

Insiders are subject to liability for "short-swing" trades that produce profits. Under Exchange Act section 16(b), an insider may be required to disgorge to the issuer any profits received from the insider's purchases and sales or sales and purchases of securities of the issuer within any six-month period. Each ten percent holder[44] is subject to the short-swing profit rule to the extent of that person's pecuniary interest in the securities.[45]

Insiders (including ten percent holders) may be required to disgorge profits received from purchases and sales or sales and purchases of securities within a six-month period.[46] The transaction that results in a person becoming a ten

---

38. Exchange Act Rule 16a-3(f)(1), 17 C.F.R. § 240.16a-3(f)(1); Securities Act Release No. 8230 (May 7, 2003), 68 F.R. 25,788 (May 13, 2003).

39. Exchange Act Rule 16a-3(f)(2), 17 C.F.R. § 240.16a-3(f)(2).

40. Regulation S-T, Rule 101(a)(iii), 17 C.F.R. § 232.101(a)(iii).

41. Exchange Act § 16(a)(1), 15 U.S.C. § 78p(a)(1).

42. Exchange Act §21(d)(1), 15 U.S.C. § 78u(d)(1).

43. Jacobs, Arnold S., *§ 16 of the Securities Exchange Act*, § 2:1, West (2003).

44. *See* § 13.1.2, *supra*.

45. *CBI Industries, Inc. v. Horton*, 682 F.2d 643, 646 (7th Cir. 1982).

46. Exchange Act § 16(b), 15 U.S.C. § 78p(b).

percent beneficial owner is not subject to the short-swing profit recapture rules, unless that person is already otherwise subject to Exchange Act section 16 with respect to the same issuer (for example, if the person is an officer or director of the issuer).[47] Complex and technical issues are involved in computing profits received, matching purchases and sales of securities within a six-month period, determining which types of transactions constitute purchases and sales, and determining which transactions are exempt from Exchange Act sections 16(a) and 16(b). Those issues are not addressed in this book.[48]

Issuers and shareholders (derivatively, if the issuer fails to bring a suit) are the only persons authorized to bring actions pursuant to section 16(b). The SEC has no authority to sue for disgorgement, to impose a penalty or to seek a penalty from any court.[49]

4. Exchange Act Section 13(f) Filing Requirements

Any investment adviser, including a hedge fund manager, or a hedge fund that, on the last trading day of any month of a calendar year, exercises investment discretion over or owns $100,000,000 or more invested in equity securities traded on stock exchanges and the Nasdaq Stock Market must report to the SEC on Form 13F[50] its holdings as of December 31 of that year.[51] The initial report is due by February 14 of the following year. Thereafter, a Form 13F filing is required within forty-five days after the end of each calendar quarter. The last Form 13F filing required is with respect to the last quarter of the calendar year after the calendar year in which the investment adviser does not have investment discretion over, or the hedge fund does not own, at least $100,000,000 invested in equity securities on the last trading day of any month. In calculating its assets under management, an investment adviser should include all personal securities portfolios over which persons under its control exercise investment discretion (which may include portfolios held by such persons' family members). Filed Forms 13F are publicly available unless the investment adviser applies to the SEC for and is granted confidential treatment. Confidential treatment is rarely granted.

5. State Anti-Takeover Statutes

State anti-takeover laws may affect a hedge fund's rights as a large shareholder. For example, some state statutes require approval of an issuer's board of directors or shareholders before a shareholder can acquire stock representing more than a specified percentage interest in the issuer. The statutes apply to issuers that are incorporated in those states. If an investment adviser exceeds the prescribed percentage, any hedge fund that it manages may lose its right to vote its shares, or the transaction that caused the hedge fund to exceed the percentage may be

---

47. Exchange Act Rule 16a-2(c), 17 C.F.R. § 240.16a-2(c).
48. *See generally*, Jacobs, Arnold S., *Section 16 of the Securities Exchange Act*, West (2003); and Romeo, Peter J. & Alan L. Dye, *Peter Romeo's and Alan Dye's Comprehensive § 16 Outline*, E.P. Executive Press, Inc. (Oct., 2003).
49. Exchange Act § 16(b), 15 U.S.C. § 78p(b).
50. Exchange Act Release No. 40934 (Jan. 12, 1999), 64 F.R. 2,843 (Jan. 19, 1999).
51. Exchange Act Rule 13f-1(b), 17 C.F.R. § 240.13f-1(b).

voided.[52] Some states empower the issuer in such cases to redeem the controlling shareholder's shares at the shareholder's average purchase price.[53]

Statutes of other states, such as Delaware and New York, target tender offers instead of merely large shareholdings.[54] Those statutes generally prohibit specified business combinations between large shareholders and issuers. For many hedge fund managers, these statutes are less worrisome because, as passive investors, the managers do not plan to acquire or engage in other transactions with the companies in which they invest. The definitions of the business combinations that are subject to these statutes, however, typically are written broadly, so investment advisers should review them carefully before assuming that their passive investments will not cause complications under these statutes.

Some of these state statutes allow an issuer to opt out of the anti-takeover provisions by amending its charter documents. An investment adviser should review the issuer's charter documents in considering whether those state statutes apply.

6. Issuer's Takeover Defenses

Before taking a substantial position in an issuer's securities, an investment adviser should investigate whether the issuer has adopted takeover defenses that may affect any large shareholding, even if the investment adviser does not intend to attempt a takeover or to influence management. Some such mechanisms may be in the issuer's charter documents or a contract, but all should be available from the SEC.

§ 13.2 Trading Restricted Securities and Control Securities

A hedge fund that has purchased unregistered securities in a private offering ("Restricted Securities") directly from an issuer or an affiliate of the issuer, or that holds securities that constitute a controlling interest in an issuer, whether or not those securities are registered ("Control Securities"), may not resell those securities unless either the resale is registered under Securities Act section 5[55] or an exemption from the registration requirements of section 5 is available.

Securities Act section 4(1)[56] exempts from the registration requirements of Securities Act section 5 transactions by any person other than an issuer, underwriter or dealer. An issuer is any "person who issues or proposes to issue

---

52. *See, e.g.,* Ohio Gen. Corp. L. § 31701.831.
53. *See, e.g.,* Nevada Gen. Corp. L. § 78-3792.
54. *See, e.g.,* Delaware Gen. Corp. L. § 203; N.Y.L. 1985 Ch. 915 Bus. Corp. L. § 513(e).
55. 15 U.S.C. § 77(e).
56. 15 U.S.C. § 77(d)(1).

any security."[57] A dealer is any "person who engages either for all or part of his time, directly or indirectly, as agent, broker, or principal, in the business of offering, buying, selling, or otherwise dealing or trading in securities issued by another person."[58] Hedge funds generally rely on the common law "trader" exception from the definition of "dealer."[59] Except in unusual circumstances, a hedge fund that desires to resell securities under Securities Act section 4(1) is neither an issuer nor a dealer.

The definition of "underwriter" is framed in terms of the purchaser's mental state and therefore is subjectively applied. An underwriter is "any person who has purchased from an issuer with a view to, or offers or sells for an issuer in connection with, the distribution of any security, or participates or has a direct or indirect participation in any such undertaking...."[60] The SEC has adopted Securities Act Rule 144[61] and has acquiesced in an informal exemption commonly called "Section 4(1 1/2)" that exempts certain resales of Restricted Securities and Control Securities by deeming the resellers of those securities not to be "underwriters" within the meaning of Securities Act section 4(1). Rule 144 applies to public resales of Restricted Securities and Control Securities by brokers through securities exchanges or in over-the-counter markets (unless the securities have been held for two years and Rule 144(k) applies). "Section 4(1 1/2)" applies to private resales of Restricted Securities and Control Securities.

1. Securities Act Rule 144

Rule 144[62] allows a holder of Restricted Securities or Control Securities to resell those shares publicly without being deemed to be an underwriter and, therefore, without registering those shares pursuant to Securities Act section 5, if the reseller and the resale satisfy the conditions of Rule 144. Those conditions are summarized below.

i. "Control Securities"

If a hedge fund is an "affiliate" of the issuer, the securities of the issuer that it owns are Control Securities (whether or not they are also Restricted Securities). Rule 144(a) defines an "affiliate" of an issuer as a person that directly, or indirectly through one or more intermediaries, controls, or is controlled by, or is under common control with, an issuer.[63] "Control" means "the possession, direct or indirect, of the power to direct or cause the direction of the management and policies of a person, whether through the ownership of voting securities, by contract, or otherwise."[64] Percentage ownership does not determine control, but

---

57. Securities Act § 2(a)(4), 15 U.S.C. § 77b(a)(4).
58. Securities Act § 2(a)(12), 15 U.S.C. § 77b(a)(12).
59. Poser, Norman S., *Broker-Dealer Law and Regulation*, §14.01[A], at 14-8.1 (3rd ed. Supp. 2004).
60. Securities Act § 2(a)(11), 15 U.S.C. § 77b(a)(11).
61. 17 C.F.R. § 230.144.
62. *Id.*
63. 17 C.F.R. § 230.144(a).
64. Securities Act Regulation C, Rule 405, 17 C.F.R. § 230.405.

the SEC has attempted to establish rules of thumb. To avoid controversy, a hedge fund may assume that it is an affiliate of the issuer if it owns ten percent or more of the voting power of the issuer.[65] "Control," however, is ultimately a question of fact and a more aggressive position may be justified in some circumstances.

ii. Current Public Information

For Restricted Securities or Control Securities to be sold under Rule 144, adequate current public information about the issuer must be available.[66] This condition is satisfied if the issuer (a) has securities registered pursuant to Exchange Act section 12;[67] (b) has been subject to the reporting requirements of Exchange Act section 13[68] for at least ninety days preceding the sale of securities in question; and (c) has filed all reports required to be filed under Exchange Act section 13 during the twelve months preceding such sale. Alternatively, this condition is satisfied if the issuer (a) has securities registered pursuant to the Securities Act; (b) has been subject to the reporting requirements of Exchange Act section 15(d)[69] for at least ninety days preceding the sale of the securities; and (c) has filed all reports required by Exchange Act section 15(d) during the twelve months preceding such sale.

iii. Holding Period

Control Securities that were purchased in the public market are not subject to any holding period requirement under Rule 144. Before Restricted Securities are sold in reliance on Rule 144, however, a holding period of at least one year must elapse between the date the seller acquires the Restricted Securities from the issuer or an affiliate of the issuer and the date it sells them.[70] The holding period begins when the hedge fund pays the full purchase price or other consideration.

In 1990, the SEC amended Rule 144 to eliminate the tolling of holding periods under Rule 144 for short positions.[71] Thus, a holder of Restricted Securities can sell securities of the same class short to hedge its position without tolling the holding period under Rule 144.[72]

Under paragraph (k) of Rule 144, if a holding period of two years has elapsed from the date the hedge fund acquired the Restricted Securities, and the hedge fund is not an affiliate and has not been an affiliate of the issuer during the three months preceding the sale, the hedge fund need not comply with the requirement

---

65. *See, e.g., Servo Sys., Inc.*, SEC No-Action Letter (Sep. 10, 1979) (owner of a fourteen percent interest in the issuer deemed an affiliate); *Torr Laboratories, Inc.*, SEC No-Action Letter (May 16, 1975) (owner of approximately ten percent interest in the issuer deemed an affiliate); and *Dataproducts Corp.*, SEC No-Action Letter (June 30, 1976) (owner of two percent of the common stock of issuer that was also represented on the issuer's board of directors deemed an affiliate).

66. Securities Act Rule 144(c), 17 C.F.R. § 230.144(c).

67. 15 U.S.C. § 78l.

68. 15 U.S.C. § 78m.

69. 15 U.S.C. § 78o(d).

70. Securities Act Rule 144(d)(1), 17 C.F.R. § 230.144(d)(1).

71. Securities Act Release No. 6862 (Apr. 30, 1990).

72. *Jesse M. Brill*, SEC No-Action Letter (June 8, 1990).

that adequate public information be available reqarding the Restricted Securities or any of the other conditions of Rule 144 described below.

a. Tacking (Non-Affiliates)

In calculating the holding period, a hedge fund may add or "tack" to its own holding period the holding period of prior holders of Restricted Securities, provided in general that the prior holders were not affiliates of the issuer (see exception below).[73] If the shares are re-acquired by an affiliate of the issuer within the one-year holding period (thus converting the Restricted Securities into Control Securities), however, the affiliate may not tack the holding period of any prior holder, and any subsequent resale of those Control Securities by the affiliate to a non-affiliate purchaser will begin a new holding period for that non-affiliate.[74]

b. Tacking (Affiliates)

A subsequent holder may tack the holding period of an affiliate of the issuer if there is an identity of interest between the transferor and transferee.[75] For example, if a donee acquires Control Securities from an affiliate of the issuer as a gift, the donee is deemed to have acquired them when the donor-affiliate acquired them.[76]

iv. Volume Limits

The number of Restricted Securities or Control Securities that a holder may sell in any three-month period may generally not exceed the greatest of:

- One percent of the shares or other units of the class outstanding;
- The average weekly reported volume of trading in such securities on all national securities exchanges or reported through the automated quotation system of a registered securities association during the four calendar weeks preceding the filing of the notice of sale on Form 144, or if no such notice is required, the receipt of the order to execute the transaction by the broker or the date of execution of the transaction directly with a market maker; and
- The average weekly volume of trading in such securities reported through the consolidated transaction reporting system.

The volume limits apply to all Control Securities held by a hedge fund (that is, all securities, whether registered or unregistered, of an issuer held by a hedge fund that is an affiliate of the issuer). If the hedge fund is not an affiliate of the issuer, the volume limits apply only to the Restricted Securities held by the hedge fund.

In some circumstances, a hedge fund's sales must be aggregated with those of another person for purposes of the volume limits. For example, when two or

---

73. Securities Act Rule 144(d)(1), 17 C.F.R. § 230.144(d)(1).
74. *Id.*
75. Securities Act Rule 144(d)(3), 17 C.F.R. § 230.144(d)(3).
76. Securities Act Rule 144(d)(3)(v), 17 C.F.R. § 230.144(d)(3)(v).

more affiliates or other persons agree to act in concert for the purposes of selling securities of an issuer, all securities of the same class sold for the account of all such persons must be aggregated for the purpose of determining compliance with the volume limitation.[77] If an investment adviser manages two hedge funds *pari passu,* the hedge funds may be subject to this aggregation rule.[78]

v. Manner of Sale

Under Rule 144, Restricted Securities and Control Securities must be sold in "brokers" transactions or in transactions directly with "market makers." The seller may not (a) solicit or arrange for the solicitation of orders to buy the shares in anticipation of or in connection with the Rule 144 transaction, or (b) make any payment in connection with the offer or sale of the shares to any person other than the broker who executes the order to sell the shares.[79]

vi. Notice of Proposed Sale

If the amount of Restricted Securities or Control Securities to be sold during any three-month period exceeds 500 shares or other units or if the aggregate sale price is greater than $10,000, three copies of a Form 144 notice must be filed with the SEC. The notice must be signed by the stockholder and sent to the SEC not later than the time that the sell order is placed with a broker or executed by a market maker. If the shares are admitted to trading on any national securities exchange, one copy of the notice must also be submitted to the principal exchange on which the shares are admitted.

2. "Section 4(1-1/2)"

Rule 144 is available only for public resales on securities exchanges or in the over-the-counter market (unless the securities have been held for two years and Rule 144(k) applies).[80] In contrast, the informal "Section 4(1-1/2)" exemption exempts private resales of Restricted Securities that meet the requirements described below, whether or not the seller is an affiliate of the issuer. "Section 4(1-1/2)" is an exemption from the registration requirements of Securities Act section 5 under Securities Act section 4(1) for transactions by any person other than an issuer, underwriter or dealer. "Section 4(1-1/2)" derives its nickname from the importation into section 4(1) of the private offering standards of Securities Act section 4(2).[81] Whether the reseller of Restricted Securities is an "underwriter" for purposes of section 4(1) depends on whether the resale "in all

---

77.   Securities Act Rule 144(e)(3)(vi), 17 C.F.R. § 230.144(e)(3)(vi).

78.   Securities Act Release No. 6099, at 2819-6 n.7 (Aug. 2, 1979), 44 F.R. 46,752 (Aug. 8, 1979) (if a fiduciary administers various trusts and estates in a manner that results in their acting in concert, they would be treated as one person).

79.   Securities Act Rule 144(f), 17 C.F.R. § 230.144(f).

80.   *See The Section "4(1-1/2)" Phenomenon: Private Resales of "Restricted" Securities,* A Report to the ABA Comm. on Fed. Reg. of Sec. from the Study Group on Section 4(1-1/2) of the Subcomm. on the 1933 Act, 34 Bus. Law 1961 (1979).

81.   *See* § 5.2.1, *supra.*

other respects comport[s] fully with the requirements of bona fide [Securities Act section] 4(2) transactions."[82] The Supreme Court described these criteria in, among other cases, *SEC v. Ralston Purina Co.*[83]

To avoid being deemed an "underwriter," a non–affiliate that desires to resell Restricted Securities acquired from an issuer must be able to prove that it did not purchase the Restricted Securities with a view to distributing those securities. The following criteria may be used to determine whether a reseller purchased Restricted Securities from an issuer with no view to distributing those securities and is not reselling them for the issuer, and thus, is not an "underwriter" for purposes of section 4(1).[84]

i. Investment Intent

The reseller should have purchased the Restricted Securities with the intent to hold those securities for an indefinite time, and not with a view to selling or distributing any of those securities in any public or private sale or other disposition. The reseller must conduct some due diligence to satisfy itself that the buyer intends to hold the securities for an indefinite period of time and does not intend to distribute the shares to others; relying on representations made by the buyer in a purchase agreement may not be sufficient.[85] The reseller should inquire into the buyer's record with respect to holding Restricted Securities for long–term investment.[86] The certificates evidencing the shares should bear a legend stating that the shares have not been registered and are subject to restrictions on disposition.[87]

The SEC and courts have also stated that a stop–transfer order that requires an opinion of counsel as to the legality of the resale is an effective device to avoid illegal resales.[88] Thus, resellers taking advantage of "Section 4(1-1/2)" typically obtain an opinion of counsel that the transaction is exempt from registration based on representations of the seller and the buyer designed to assure that neither party is an underwriter or an affiliate of the issuer.[89]

ii. Offeree Qualification

The reseller should inquire into the buyer's financial condition to assess whether the buyer can reasonably assume the financial risk of the investment and hold the securities for an indefinite time. The reseller should ascertain that the buyer:

---

82.   H.R. Rep. No. 96-1341, 96th Cong., 2d Sess. 40 n.7 (1980).

83.   346 U.S. 119, 125 (1953).

84.   *SEC v. Cavanaugh*, 1 F. Supp. 2d 337, 368 (S.D.N.Y. 1998); *see also The Section "4(1-1/2)" Phenomenon: Private Resales of "Restricted" Securities*, A Report to the ABA Comm. on Fed. Reg. of Sec. from the Study Group on Section 4(1-1/2) of the Subcomm. on the 1933 Act, 34 Bus. Law 1961 (1979).

85.   *SEC v. Cavanaugh, id.* at 369.

86.   *SEC v. Cavanaugh, id.,* at 370; Loss, Louis & Joel Seligman, *Securities Regulation*, Ch. 3, pp. 1502-1504, Aspen Law & Business (3rd ed. 1989).

87.   *SEC v. Cavanaugh, id.* at 369; *see also* Securities Act Rule 502(d)(3), 17 C.F.R. § 230.502(d)(3).

88.   *See Use of Legends and Stop-Transfer Instructions as Evidence of Non-Public Offerings*, Securities Act Release No. 5121; *see also SEC v. Cavanaugh*, 1 F.Supp. 2d 237 (S.D.N.Y. 1998).

89.   Loss, Louis & Joel Seligman, *Securities Regulation*, Ch. 3, pp. 1502-1504, Aspen Law & Business (3rd ed. 1989).

- is able to bear the economic risk of the purchase;
- has sufficient knowledge and experience in financial and business matters to be capable of evaluating the risks and merits of the investment; and
- has the capacity to protect the buyer's own interests in connection with the transaction.[90]

iii. Information

The buyer should be furnished with, or at least have access to, all financial and other information about the investment and the business and proposed business of the issuer that the buyer considers necessary in connection with the investment.[91]

iv. Manner of Offering

The seller should communicate the offer directly to the buyer. No form of general advertising or general solicitation may be used. The number of offerees should also be limited.[92]

§ 13.3 Purchasing Shares in Public Offerings

1. NASD New Issue Rule

i. Purpose

NASD Conduct Rule 2790, entitled "Restrictions on the Purchase and Sale of Initial Equity Public Offerings" (the "New Issue Rule"),[93] purportedly is designed to protect the integrity of the public offering process by ensuring that (a) NASD members make *bona fide* initial public offerings of equity securities ("New Issues") at the offering price; (b) NASD members do not withhold New Issues for their own benefit or use such securities to reward persons (such as hedge funds and their advisers) who are in a position to direct future business to members; and (c) industry insiders, including NASD members and their associated persons, do not take advantage of their "insider" position to purchase New Issues for their own benefit at the expense of the public.[94]

---

90. Loss, Louis & Joel Seligman, *Securities Regulation*, Ch. 3, pp. 1502–1504, Aspen Law & Business (3rd ed. 1989). *See also* § 5.2.1, *supra*.
91. *Id.*
92. *Id.*
93. NASD Manual – Conduct Rule 2790.
94. NASD Notice to Members 03–79 (Dec. 2003), p. 832.

In furtherance of these objectives, the New Issue Rule prohibits an NASD member from selling a New Issue to any account in which a "restricted person" has a beneficial interest.[95] The New Issue Rule provides certain exceptions from this general prohibition.[96] The NASD member also must meet specified "preconditions for sale" before selling a New Issue to any account.[97]

ii. New Issues

The New Issue Rule applies only to initial public offerings of equity securities. It does not apply to subsequent offerings, private placements, offerings of securities in commodity pools, rights offerings, exchange offers, offerings in mergers or acquisitions, offerings of investment grade asset-backed securities, offerings of convertible securities, offerings of preferred securities, offerings of registered investment companies and offerings of securities with pre-existing markets outside the United States.[98] The New Issue Rule applies to all New Issues, whether or not they would have been "hot" under the prior NASD rule in effect until March 23, 2004.

The New Issue Rule prohibits hedge funds from allocating their profits (and losses) from New Issues to restricted persons (except to the *de minimis* extent described below).[99] The New Issue Rule does not, however, require a hedge fund to sell the New Issue before restricted persons can be allocated subsequent profits and losses from the New Issue. Thus, a hedge fund may begin to allocate profits and losses from a New Issue to restricted persons when the New Issue no longer is traded at the initial public offering price and instead is traded at secondary market prices.[100]

iii. Restricted Persons

Restricted persons include:

- Brokers or dealers and their personnel,[101] other than limited business brokers or dealers (defined as brokers or dealers whose authorization to engage in the securities business is limited solely to the purchase and sale of investment company/variable contracts securities and direct participation program securities);[102]
- Finders and any person acting in a fiduciary capacity to the managing underwriter, including, but not limited to, attorneys, accountants and financial consultants;[103]

---

95.   NASD Manual – Conduct Rule 2790(a)(1).
96.   *See* §§ 13.3.1.v and 13.3.1.vi, *infra*.
97.   NASD Manual – Conduct Rule 2790(b).
98.   NASD Manual – Conduct Rule 2790(i)(9).
99.   *See* § 13.3.1.v, *infra*.
100. NASD Notice to Members 03-79 (Dec. 2003), p. 842.
101. NASD Manual – Conduct Rule 2790(i)(10)(A) and (i)(10)(B).
102. NASD Manual – Conduct Rule 2790(i)(10)(B) and (i)(7).
103. NASD Manual – Conduct Rule 2790(i)(10)(C).

- Portfolio managers, defined to include any person who has the authority to buy or sell securities for a bank, savings and loan institution, insurance company, investment company, investment adviser or collective investment account (which includes a hedge fund, investment partnership, investment corporation or other collective investment vehicle), but a person with authority to buy or sell securities for an investment club or family investment vehicle is not a portfolio manager for this purpose;[104]
- Owners of brokers or dealers;[105]
- Affiliates of brokers or dealers;[106] and
- Immediate family members of restricted persons. "Immediate family" means a person's parents, parents-in-law, spouse, siblings, brothers-in-law, sisters-in-law, sons-in-law, daughters-in-law, children, and any individuals to whom the person provides material support. "Material support" means the direct or indirect provision of more than twenty-five percent of a person's income in the preceding calendar year. Members of an immediate family living in the same household are deemed to provide material support to each other.[107]

iv. Beneficial Interest

The New Issue Rule defines "beneficial interest" as any economic interest.[108] The New Issue Rule excludes from the definition of beneficial interest, however, the receipt of a management fee or performance-based fee for operating a hedge fund.[109] Members of the NASD staff have indicated informally that the receipt of management or performance-based fees by persons other than the investment adviser would cause such persons to have a "beneficial interest" in a hedge fund's profits and losses from New Issues, but any such payment or allocation by a hedge fund to affiliated parties of the investment adviser who are involved in the investment adviser's portfolio management for that hedge fund would not cause such persons to have a "beneficial interest" in the New Issue profits and losses of that hedge fund.[110] Thus, a restricted person other than a hedge fund's investment adviser and its affiliates who are involved in portfolio management (such as a broker or finder who receives referral fees) who receives a portion of a management or performance-based fee based in part on proceeds from New Issues may only receive that portion to the extent that it is within the *de minimis* exemption, which reduces the amount available to investors in the hedge fund who are restricted.

In addition, if fees are deferred, the accumulation of such amounts, if subsequently invested in the hedge fund (as a deferred fee arrangement or otherwise), constitutes

---

104.   NASD Manual – Conduct Rule 2790(i)(10)(D).

105.   NASD Manual – Conduct Rule 2790(i)(10)(E).

106.   *Id.*

107.   NASD Manual – Conduct Rule 2790(i)(10)(B)(iii), 2790(i)(10)(C)(ii), 2790(i)(10)(D)(ii) and 2790(i)(10)(E)(vi).

108.   NASD Manual – Conduct Rule 2790(i)(1).

109.   *Id.*

110.   Telephone conversation with Gary Goldsholle, Esq. and Afshin Atabaki, Esq., NASD, Feb. 10, 2004.

a beneficial ownership interest in the hedge fund's account under the New Issue Rule.[111]

v. De Minimis *Exemption*

An account (such as a hedge fund) in which restricted persons are allocated no more than ten percent of the New Issue profits and losses is exempt from the New Issue Rule's prohibition.[112] To comply with the *de minimis* exemption, some hedge funds may establish separate brokerage accounts that purchase only New Issues and allocate to restricted persons ten percent or less of the profits or losses from purchases and sales of New Issues through those accounts. A hedge fund may also purchase New Issues through a general brokerage account, but adjust the profit and loss allocations to remove or reduce allocations to Restricted Persons of gains (or losses) attributable to New Issues as needed to comply with the New Issue Rule.[113]

vi. *Other Exemptions*

The New Issue Rule provides that the following are not "restricted persons," even if they might otherwise be within the definition:

- A person with authority to buy or sell securities for a family investment vehicle, defined as a legal entity beneficially owned solely by immediate family members;
- A registered investment company (mutual fund);
- A common trust fund or similar fund, as described in Securities Act section 3(a)(12)(A),[114] that has investments from 1,000 or more accounts and that does not limit beneficial interests principally to trust accounts of restricted persons;
- An insurance company general, separate or investment account funded by premiums from 1,000 or more policyholders, or an insurance company general account, if the insurance company has 1,000 or more policyholders and does not limit participation principally to restricted persons;
- A publicly traded entity (other than a broker or dealer or an affiliate of a broker or dealer where such broker or dealer is authorized to engage in the public offering of New Issues either as a selling group member or underwriter) that is listed on an exchange or the Nasdaq Stock Market, or that is a foreign issuer who meets the criteria for listing on an exchange or the Nasdaq Stock Market;
- A non-U.S. investment company listed on a non-U.S. exchange or authorized for sale to the public by a non-U.S. regulatory authority in which no person owning more than five percent is a restricted person;
- An ERISA plan that is not sponsored solely by a broker or dealer;

---

111.   NASD Notice to Members 03-79 (Dec. 2003), p. 841.
112.   NASD Manual – Conduct Rule 2790(c)(4).
113.   NASD Notice to Members 03-79 (Dec. 2003), p. 836.
114.   15 U.S.C. § 78c(a)(12)(A).

- A state or municipal government benefits plan subject to state or municipal regulation;
- A tax-exempt charitable organization under Tax Code section 501(c)(3);[115]
- A church plan under Tax Code section 414(e);[116] and
- Specified issuer-directed securities.[117]

vii. Application to Hedge Funds

Before selling a New Issue to a hedge fund, an NASD member must, in good faith, obtain a representation from the hedge fund or its investment adviser that the hedge fund's purchases of New Issues comply with the New Issue Rule. The NASD member must receive the representation during the twelve months before the sale.[118] The initial representation must positively affirm the hedge fund's non-restricted status. Thereafter, the NASD member must annually verify the hedge fund's status. Annual verification may be effected by negative confirmation, such as a letter to the hedge fund that recites the hedge fund's non-restricted status and asks the hedge fund to respond only if that status has changed.[119]

To enable the hedge fund to make an accurate representation, the hedge fund's subscription documents should require each investor to make an initial representation as to its status. Thereafter, the hedge fund manager annually may follow the negative confirmation procedure described above by sending a letter to each investor confirming the investor's non-restricted status and asking the investor to respond only if the investor's status has changed. Following these procedures will enable the hedge fund manager to respond appropriately to requests from brokers concerning the hedge fund's ability to purchase New Issues.

To make an accurate representation to a broker regarding its restricted status, a hedge fund in which other funds ("funds-of-funds") have invested must ascertain the restricted status of the investors in those funds-of-funds. If a hedge fund is unable to ascertain the status of investors in a fund-of-funds, the hedge fund should deem that entire fund-of-funds to be restricted. A hedge fund may rely on information that is no more than twelve months old from a fund-of-funds. To determine the ownership level of restricted persons in a hedge fund, the interests of restricted persons in each fund-of-funds should be attributed to the hedge fund in an amount equal to restricted persons' beneficial interests in the fund-of-funds multiplied by the fund-of-funds' interest in the hedge fund. For example, if restricted persons beneficially own fifty percent of a fund-of-funds and that fund-of-funds beneficially owns ten percent of the hedge fund, the resulting ownership level of restricted persons in the hedge fund attributable to that fund-of-funds would be five percent.

A hedge fund must "look through" to the investors in any fund-of-funds investor in this manner to determine whether the hedge fund complies with the *de minimis*

---

115.   26 U.S.C. § 501(c)(3).
116.   26 U.S.C. § 414(e); NASD Manual – Conduct Rule 2790(c).
117.   NASD Manual – Conduct Rule 2790(d).
118.   NASD Manual – Conduct Rule 2790(b).
119.   NASD Notice to Members 03-79 (Dec. 2003), pp. 834–835.

exemption. A hedge fund cannot treat a fund-of-funds that itself meets the *de minimis* exemption as wholly unrestricted for purposes of determining whether the hedge fund meets the *de minimis* exemption. Instead, the hedge fund must count the percentage of restricted investors in the fund-of-funds (multiplied by the fund-of-funds' percentage interest in the hedge fund) toward the hedge fund's own percentage of restricted investors.[120]

viii. Provision in Hedge Fund Agreement

To assure that Restricted Persons are allocated only the appropriate portion of profits and losses from New Issues, a hedge fund's governing agreement should provide that the hedge fund will allocate profits and losses from New Issues in accordance with the New Issue Rule, but otherwise consistently with the general allocation provisions in the agreement.

ix. Fiduciary Duty to Allocate New Issues

An investment adviser that manages more than one hedge fund or other client accounts has a fiduciary duty to consider the appropriateness of each New Issue for each eligible hedge fund or other client account, and adequately to disclose its policy for allocating New Issues among its eligible clients. The SEC staff has recently begun to insist that investment advisers have written policies and procedures for allocating shares of initial public offerings among their accounts.[121]

2. Regulation M

The SEC rules that apply to short sellers of securities immediately prior to a public offering are discussed below in section 13.4.9.

§ 13.4 Short Selling Rules

Hedge funds often sell securities short. A "short sale" is a sale of securities that the seller does not own (whether or not the seller owns other securities of the same class). The seller borrows the securities sold short, usually from a broker, for delivery to the buyer, posting cash or securities as collateral for the loan. The short seller typically buys a like number of the securities in the market at a later time for delivery to the lending broker to discharge the debt. Short selling is subject to extensive regulation, mostly under the Exchange Act.[122]

---

120.   Telephone call with Gary Goldsholle, Esq. and Afshin Atabaki, Esq., NASD, Feb. 10, 2004.

121.   *See* § 13.9, *infra.*

122.   15 U.S.C. § 77j(a)(1). Short selling also implicates the margin rules of the Federal Reserve Board, Regulations T, U and X, 12 C.F.R. §§ 220 through 224, which are not addressed in this book.

1. Short Sale Rule

A "short sale" is any sale of a security (a) that the seller does not own, or (b) where the seller intends to complete a transaction by delivering borrowed shares.[123] Under Exchange Act Rule 10a-1[124] (the "Short Sale Rule"), short sales of securities that are registered, or admitted to unlisted trading privileges, on a national securities exchange ("listed securities") may only be effected, except for certain limited exceptions,[125] (a) at a price above the price at which the preceding sale was effected (uptick) or (b) at the last sale price if that was higher than the last different price (zero-plus tick). If a security is a listed security, the short sale rule applies whether the trade is made on an exchange or in an over-the-counter market. The SEC has permitted most stock exchanges to adopt their own short sale rules that mirror, to a large extent, Exchange Act Rule 10a-1.[126]

During the regular trading day, the Short Sale Rule operates relative to the last reported price on the Consolidated Tape[127] or, if an exchange has expressly provided in its rules, the last sale price reported on that exchange. At the beginning of the trading day, the benchmark is the last reported sales price shown on the Consolidated Tape or reported on an exchange's internal system at the previous trading day's regular close.

2. "Net Long" or "Net Short" Determination

A seller is generally deemed to "own" securities (and thus cannot be deemed to be engaged in short selling with respect to those securities) to the extent that the

---

123.   Exchange Act Rule 3b-3, 17 C.F.R. § 240.3b-3.

124.   17 C.F.R. § 240.10a-1.

125.   Sales made through the Portfolio System for Institutional Trading ("POSIT") are exempt from the tick provisions of Exchange Act Rule 10(a)-1(a) if (a) persons relying on the exemption are not represented in the primary market offer and do not influence the primary market bid or offer at the time of the transactions and (b) transactions effected on POSIT are not made for the purpose of creating actual or apparent active trading in, or depressing or otherwise manipulating the price of, any security. See *Portfolio System for Institutional Trading*, SEC No-Action Letter (Dec. 9, 1994).

126.   Exchange Act Rules 10a-1(a)(2) and 10a-1(a)(1)(ii), 17 C.F.R. §§ 240.10a-1(a)(2) and 10a-1(a)(i)(ii). *See, e.g.,* NYSE Rule 440B; Amex Rule 7; PSE Rule 5.18; and NASD Conduct Rule 3350. The exchanges and the NASD also have rules requiring member firms to report, as of the 15th of each month, aggregate short positions in all customer and proprietary accounts in securities listed on such exchanges or traded in the Nasdaq Stock Market. This information is published toward the end of the month in *The Wall Street Journal* and *Barrons*, among other publications. The published information is set forth in tabular form and includes the current and prior month's aggregate short interest for those securities where either the current or prior month's short interest exceeded 50,000 shares, the percentage change in short interest from the prior month and the average daily trading volume. Some market technicians believe the relationship between the short interest and the daily trading volume is informative because it gives an indication of the likely effect if the short positions were to be covered. *See* NYSE Rule 421; AMEX Rules 30 and 590; and Article III, § 41, of the NASD Rules of Fair Practice.

127.   Exchange Act Rule 10a-1(a), 17 C.F.R. § 240.10a-1(a), covers transactions in any security registered on a national securities exchange, if trades in such security are reported in the "consolidated transaction reporting system," also known as the Consolidated Tape. These terms refer to "the consolidated transaction reporting system" for which a plan originally was submitted to the Commission pursuant to Exchange Act Rule 17a-15 (subsequently amended and redesignated as Rule 11Aa3-1, 17 C.F.R. § 240.11Aa3-1). The Consolidated Tape Association ("CTA"), comprising various national securities exchanges and the NASD, collects and disseminates reports for transactions on those markets on the Consolidated Tape.

seller is "net long" in those securities.[128] Conversely, a person who is not "net long" the stock is short the stock and the Short Sale Rule applies. All sales of securities must be designated "long" or "short" or "short-exempt" so that the specialists and floor brokers on the exchanges will know to execute a short sale only on an uptick or zero-plus tick.[129] A broker may mark a Sell order "long" only if the hedge fund's account with the broker owns or is deemed to own the security involved and the security either is in the physical possession or control of the broker or is reasonably expected to be so by the time the transaction settles. A broker may mark a Sell order "short-exempt" if it qualifies for an exception from the Short Sale Rule or a corresponding rule of any exchange or national securities association.[130] The broker must generally aggregate the number of those securities that the seller "owns" in all accounts held by the broker to determine whether and the extent to which the seller is "net long" in that security. If, however, the broker qualifies for "independent trading unit aggregation," each independent trading unit, rather than the entire brokerage firm, may aggregate its positions in a security to determine its net position. "Independent trading unit aggregation" is available if the brokerage firm's written organizational plan identifies and describes each independent trading unit and its trading objective and supports its independent identity, and traders in that unit pursue only that unit's trading objective without coordinating with other units.[131]

Regulation SHO Rule 200(b)[132] provides generally that a seller is deemed to "own" a security if the seller or its agent has title to it. A person also "owns" a security for these purposes if such person (a) owns a security convertible into or exchangeable for the security and has tendered such security for conversion or exchange, (b) has an option, warrant or right to purchase or acquire the security and has exercised the option, warrant or right, (c) has purchased the security or entered into an unconditional contract, binding on both parties, to purchase the security, but has not yet received it, or (d) holds a security futures contract to purchase the security, has received notice that the position will be physically settled, and is bound to receive the underlying security.[133] Long positions in convertible securities, rights, warrants or call options are not considered long positions in the underlying securities, unless they have been converted or exercised.

A broker does not count Restricted Securities in determining whether a customer is net long in a stock, because Restricted Securities are not "in good deliverable form." Thus, a person placing an order to sell a security will not be deemed to be net long (and the sale will be a short sale and the Short Sale Rule will apply) even if the person owns an equal or greater number of shares of the same class that are Restricted Securities. Moreover, because shares underlying a

---

128.   *Id.* Regulation SHO provides limited exceptions to this rule by deeming a seller to own securities even if it is not "net long" if it acquired them while acting as a block positioner and has entered into offsetting arbitrage or hedge transactions, and in connection with unwinding certain index arbitrage positions. Regulation SHO Rules 200(d) and 200(e), 17 C.F.R. §§ 242.200(d) and 200(e).

129.   Regulation SHO Rule 200(g), 17 C.F.R. § 242-200(g).

130.   *Id.*

131.   Regulation SHO Rule 200(f), 17 C.F.R. § 242.200(f).

132.   17 C.F.R. § 242.200(b).

133.   *Id.*

short sale are deemed to be sold at the time of the short sale, covering a short sale with those Restricted Securities could violate Securities Act section 5, because the cover of the short sale would be deemed a sale of unregistered securities.[134]

3. Prohibition of Naked Short Sales

A naked short sale is a sale of securities to a buyer without owning or borrowing the necessary securities to make delivery to that buyer. Because of naked short sales' perceived negative effects on the market, Regulation SHO Rule 203 establishes a uniform standard specifying procedures for all short sellers to locate securities for borrowing. Regulation SHO Rule 203 prohibits a broker-dealer from accepting a short sale order from another person or executing a short sale order for its own account unless the broker-dealer has (a) borrowed the securities or entered into a *bona fide* arrangement to borrow the securities, or (b) reasonable grounds to believe that the securities could be borrowed so that they could be delivered on the date delivery is due. Rule 203 provides certain exceptions from this "locate requirement" relating to orders received from introducing brokers, orders executed by market makers, and certain sales where delivery of the security is delayed.[135]

4. NASD Short Sale Rule

Short sales of securities traded on the Nasdaq National Market are subject to the NASD short sale rule.[136] The NASD short sale rule prohibits NASD member firms from effecting short sales in securities traded on the Nasdaq National Market at or below the current national best (inside) bid whenever that bid is lower than the previous national best (inside) bid in the security.[137] When the current best bid is lower than the preceding best bid, a short sale must be executed at a price at least $0.01 above the current inside bid when the current inside spread is $0.01 or greater. The last sale report for such a trade would, therefore, be above the inside bid by at least $0.01.[138]

Similar to the "tick" test under the Short Sale Rule, the calculation of "up bids" and "down bids" under the NASD short sale rule does not start with the opening bid of the trading day. Rather, the calculation at the beginning of the trading day incorporates bids from the previous day's best close. The benchmark at the beginning of the trading day is the previous day's closing inside bid. Thus, if the opening inside bid is the same as the previous day's closing inside bid, and the closing bid was a down bid, the opening bid is a down bid and short sales are prohibited. Similarly, if the opening inside bid is below the previous day's closing inside bid, the opening inside bid is a down bid and short sales are prohibited.

---

134. *See* § 13.4.10, *infra*.

135. Regulation SHO Rule 203, 17 C.F.R. § 242.203.

136. NASD Manual – Conduct Rule 3350. The NASD short sale rule does not apply to other OTC securities such as those traded on the Nasdaq Small Cap Market or quoted on the NASD's OTC Bulletin Board or in the pink sheets, or to listed securities. The NASD short sale rule does not apply to odd lots or to non-U.S. securities.

137. NASD Manual-Conduct Rule 3350(a)(2).

138. NASD Manual Interpretive Material IM-3350(b)(2). *See also* Exchange Act Release No. 48701 (Oct. 24, 2003), 68 F.R. 62,126 (Oct 31, 2003).

The NASD short sale rule is commonly called a "bid test" because it is activated based on movements in the inside bid on Nasdaq. A bid test is used instead of a "tick" test, because last sale reports for Nasdaq stocks are received from numerous sources (all market makers in the security) and are not necessarily reported in exact order, so that it is difficult to know which sale was last.

The NASD short sale rule permits a short sale at a price below the current inside bid when the current inside bid is an "up" bid. Thus, a person can short on a down bid if the down bid is above the benchmark. The NASD short sale rule only prohibits short sales when there is a "down" bid relative to the benchmark. During the trading day, Nasdaq calculates the inside or best bid from all market makers in a security (including bids from stock exchanges trading Nasdaq securities on an unlisted trading basis), and disseminates symbols to denote whether the current inside bid is an "up bid" or a "down bid," so that NASD members will have that information quickly available when asked to effect short sales. An "up bid" is denoted by a green "up" arrow symbol next to the security's symbol on the broker's screen, and a "down bid" is denoted by a red "down" arrow. If there is a red down arrow on the screen, an NASD member cannot execute a short sale at or below the inside bid in that security.

i. Definition of "Short Sale" under NASD Short Sale Rule

The NASD short sale rule incorporates the definition of "short sale" under the Short Sale Rule.[139]

ii. "Net Long" or "Net Short" Determination under NASD Short Sale Rule

The "net long" or "net short" determination is made using the same procedure used under the Short Sale Rule.[140]

5. After-Hours Trading

i. Short Sale Rule

The Short Sale Rule and the corresponding rules of the exchanges apply in after-hours trading of listed securities. The benchmark used depends on the facility through which the trade is executed. If trades are placed through an alternative trading system (such as Archipelago Exchange, Market XT and The Island ECN) rather than on an exchange, short sales must be based on the last sale price reported to the Consolidated Tape at the end of the trading day. This may change in the future, as alternative trading systems have asked the SEC to

---

139.   NASD Manual-Conduct Rule 3350(k)(1). *See* § 13.4.1, *supra.*
140.   NASD Manual-Conduct Rule 3350(k)(1). *See* § 13.4.2, *supra.*

permit them to establish their own internal "last sale prices" for purposes of the tick test, just as many exchanges have done.[141]

ii. NASD Short Sale Rule

The NASD short sale rule does not apply to after-hours trading. Therefore, in after-hours trading, traders can short all Nasdaq and OTC securities without regard to whether the current inside bid is an up bid or a down bid.

6. Exemptions from Short Sale Rule

Rules 10a-1(e)(1) through (12) and no-action letters provide several exemptions from the Short Sale Rule.[142] As Charles Schwab & Co., Inc. pointed out in a comment letter dated December 23, 1999, in response to the SEC's request for comments about proposed amendments to the short sale rule: "The short sale rule unfairly favors market professionals over retail investors. Most of these exceptions permit short selling by institutional and professional traders, while leaving in place prohibitions for retail investors."

7. Regulation SHO Pilot Program[143]

Regulation SHO, some provisions of which are described above in sections 13.4.2 and 13.4.3, was adopted in July 2004 and amended or replaced various provisions of the Short Sale Rule. As proposed, Regulation SHO would have replaced the current "tick" test with a requirement that short sales be effected at a price above the consolidated best bid. The SEC did not include this provision in Regulation SHO as adopted, but instead initiated a pilot program to evaluate the effectiveness of price tests for short sales.[144]

8. Exchange Act Section 16(c) Short Sale Prohibition

Exchange Act section 16(c) prohibits an insider of an issuer from selling any equity security of the issuer if the insider (a) does not own the security sold or (b) if owning the security, does not deliver it within twenty days after selling it or does not, within five days after such sale, deposit the security in the mail.[145] Although section 16(c) thus permits insiders to engage in short sales against the box, an insider cannot borrow shares to meet its delivery obligation.[146]

---

141.   Comment letters from Orrick, Herrington & Sutcliffe, counsel for Market XT (Dec. 10, 1999) and The Island ECN, Inc. (Jan. 21, 2000) regarding Securities Exchange Act Concept Release No. 42037 (Oct. 20, 1999), 64 F.R. 57,996 (Oct. 28, 1999).

142.   Exchange Act Rule 10a-1(e)(10), 17 C.F.R. § 240.10a-1(e)(10) (sales by underwriters in distribution of over-allotments); Exchange Act Rule 10a-1(e)(7), 17 C.F.R. § 240.10a-1(e)(7) (sales for a "special arbitrage account"); and Exchange Act Rule 10a-1(e)(8), 17 C.F.R. § 240.10a-1(e)(8) (sales for a "special international arbitrage account").

143.   Exchange Act Release No. 50103 (July 28, 2004), 69 F.R. 48,008 (Aug. 6, 2004).

144.   Regulation SHO Rule 202T, 17 C.F.R. § 242.202T.

145.   Exchange Act § 16(c), 15 U.S.C. § 78p(c).

146.   *See Willkie Farr & Gallagher*, SEC No-Action Letter (Mar. 26, 1980).

9. Covering Short Sales from Publicly Offered Stock

A hedge fund (or any other person) cannot purchase securities in a public offering from a participating underwriter or broker-dealer (other than an offering not conducted on a firm commitment basis) to cover any short position if it made short sales of the security during the five business days before the offering was priced. For example, a purchase of shares in a public offering to cover a short sale made ten days before the pricing would be illegal if the hedge fund had put on another short position within five days of the pricing. The five-day prohibition may be shortened to the period beginning with the initial filing of the registration statement or notification on Form 1-A and ending with the pricing.

The purpose of this rule is to limit short sellers' ability to put pressure on the price of a public offering, lowering the offering price and yielding reduced proceeds for the issuer. A hedge fund that puts on a short position cannot have a pre-arrangement to purchase shares to cover the short position from someone who buys in the public offering, but it may purchase shares in the public market to cover the short position. If the hedge fund buys shares in the public market to cover the short position, and sells shares it was allocated in the public offering, it should wait a substantial period between these trades. This rule does not apply to derivatives, such as options. Thus, a hedge fund may close out an options position with stock allocated to it in a public offering. In the release adopting Regulation M,[147] the SEC said that an extension of the prohibitions of this rule to derivative securities would be inconsistent with the approach of Regulation M, which is to focus on those securities having the greatest manipulative potential.[148] Manipulative short sales involving derivatives are nevertheless addressed by the general anti-manipulation provisions, including Exchange Act section 9(a)(2)[149] and Exchange Act Rule 10b-5.[150]

10. Prohibition on Covering Short Sales with Restricted Securities

A short sale is deemed to occur when the short sale is executed and not when it is covered.[151] A holder of Restricted Securities under Securities Act Rule 144[152] may not cover a short sale of equity securities with the Restricted Securities, because the Restricted Securities are unregistered and therefore cannot be legally sold to the public when the short sale is executed without complying with the registration requirements of Securities Act section 5.[153] For the same reasons, the person cannot wait two years to cover a short sale with Restricted Securities and claim that he or she was allowed to sell without restriction under Securities Act Rule 144(k).[154]

---

147. 17 C.F.R. § 242.105.
148. Exchange Act Release No. 38067 (Dec. 20, 1996), 62 F.R. 520 (Jan. 3, 1997).
149. 15 U.S.C. § 78i(a)(2).
150. 17 C.F.R. § 240.10b-5.
151. Securities Act Release No. 6099, question 80 (Aug. 2, 1979), 44 F.R. 46,752, question 80 (Aug. 8, 1979).
152. 17 C.F.R. § 230.144.
153. 15 U.S.C. § 77e; Securities Act Release No. 7391 (Feb. 20, 1997), 62 F.R. 9,246 (Feb. 28, 1997).
154. 17 C.F.R. § 230.144(k).

One technique to hedge a restricted position is for the person (a) to sell other stock short to hedge the risk of owning the Restricted Securities for a year, (b) after the Rule 144 holding period is satisfied, to sell the Restricted Securities under Rule 144, and (c) use the sale proceeds to buy shares in the marketplace to close out the short position. This three-step approach involves the following costs: two extra brokerage commissions for the three transactions; the spread in closing out the position resulting from selling the Restricted Securities at the bid price and buying (to cover the short) at the asked price; and the margin costs involved in keeping a short position open for one year.[155]

§ 13.5 Related Party Trades Involving Investment Adviser and Its Other Clients or Its Affiliated Broker

An investment adviser's duty to its clients includes the duty to put its clients' interests ahead of its own. An investment adviser or any of its affiliates may not act as principal or broker in buying securities from or selling securities to a client of the investment adviser (such as a hedge fund), unless the investment adviser provides written disclosure to the hedge fund of the investment adviser's capacity in the transaction and obtains the client's consent.[156] For this purpose, each investor in the hedge fund should be regarded as a client, even if for other purposes the hedge fund is considered the investment adviser's client. Otherwise, an investment adviser that is also the general partner or manager of a hedge fund could approve such transactions itself on behalf of the hedge fund, without notice to or the consent of the investors.[157] Advisers Act section 206(3)[158] requires that this disclosure be provided "before the completion of the transaction." The exact timing and content of the disclosure depend on the circumstances, including the nature and extent of the investment adviser's position in the securities sold and the availability of information about the transaction before and after execution.

1. Broker Transactions

An investment adviser may also be registered as a broker-dealer or affiliated with a broker-dealer (for example, as its parent, subsidiary or sister corporation), or a

---

155. *See The Corporate Counsel*, Vol. XXV, No. 3 (May-June 2000). *See also The Corporate Counsel*, Vol. XVII, No. 2, at p. 5 (Mar.-Apr. 1992); *The Corporate Counsel*, Vol. XXII, No. 1, at p. 1 (Jan.-Feb. 1997); and *The Corporate Counsel*, Vol. XXIII, No. 5, at p. 2 (Sep.-Oct. 1998).

156. Advisers Act § 206(3), 15 U.S.C. § 80b-6(3); *see also* California Corporations Code § 25235(c); *see In the Matter of Credit Suisse Asset Management Inc.*, Advisers Act Release No. 1452 (Nov. 16, 1994).

157. *But see Merrill Lynch Asset Mgmt.*, SEC No-Action Letter (Apr. 28, 1997) (allowing mutual fund's portfolio manager who is also an officer or authorized signatory of a mutual fund to execute such transactions without providing such notice to itself or to mutual fund's investors).

158. 15 U.S.C. § 80b-6(3).

registered representative of a broker-dealer may be a principal or employee of an investment adviser or registered as an investment adviser ("RR/IA") (in all three situations, we refer to the affiliated broker-dealer as an "IA/BD"). If an IA/BD executes client transactions as a broker-dealer, the IA/BD must inform its clients (a) that they may request that their transactions be executed through broker-dealers other than the IA/BD, (b) that the clients may be able to obtain a better price elsewhere if the brokerage commissions plus advisory fees are higher than otherwise obtainable and (c) of the nature and extent of the investment adviser's interest in the transaction, including the compensation the IA/BD will receive.[159]

2. Principal Transactions

If an IA/BD effects any principal transaction with a client (for example, out of the inventory of the broker-dealer or in an over-the-counter transaction), the investment adviser typically must disclose in writing to the client the IA/BD's capacity in the transaction and obtain the client's consent before the transaction is completed.[160]

An investment adviser to a separate account client that causes that client to invest in a hedge fund affiliated with the investment adviser could be deemed to be engaging in an "indirect" principal transaction because the hedge fund, as an entity controlled by the investment adviser, sold the securities to the client. An investment adviser might be able to avoid the need to make the disclosures otherwise required under Advisers Act section 206(3) in this case by (a) waiving duplicative fees or providing value to the client separately from the value that the investment adviser provides to the hedge fund (for example, if the investment in the hedge fund is made in connection with asset allocation services), (b) fully disclosing any conflicts and obtaining the informed consent of its separate account client prior to any such transaction with the client, (c) selling or redeeming interests of the hedge fund only at their net asset value, and (d) forgoing any transaction-based compensation for the investment adviser or its affiliates.[161]

3. Agency Cross Transactions

An "agency cross transaction" is a transaction in which an IA/BD acts as a broker both for its advisory client and for its brokerage client on the other side of the transaction. An open market transaction through an IA/BD is not an agency cross transaction. An investment adviser to a hedge fund must receive the prior written consent of each investor in the hedge fund to execute agency cross

---

159. *United Missouri Bank of Kansas City*, SEC No-Action Letter (May 11, 1990); Title 10, California Code of Regulations, § 260.238(k).

160. Advisers Act Release No. 1560 (Apr. 9, 1996) (IA/BD violated Advisers Act § 206(3) by failing to get client consent to principal transactions prior to each such transaction); *In re Feldman Inv. Group, Inc.*, Advisers Act Release No. 1538 (Nov. 27, 1995) (IA/BD failed to obtain client consent prior to execution of riskless principal transaction); *In re Concord Inv. Co.*, Advisers Act Release No. 1585 (Sep. 27, 1996); *In re Calamos Asset Mgmt.*, Advisers Act Release No. 1594 (Oct. 16, 1996); *In re Rothschild Inv. Corp.*, Advisers Act Release No. 1714 (Apr. 13, 1998) (IA/BD failed to obtain client consent prior to execution of a riskless principal transaction).

161. *Q&A: Principal Trades for Hedge Fund IAs*, Compliance Reporter, Jan. 26, 2004, relying in part on *Merrill Lynch Trust Co.*, SEC No-Action Letter (July 6, 2000) (allowing an investment adviser to place clients in affiliated mutual funds without making the disclosure and client consent required by Advisers Act § 206(3)).

transactions involving the hedge fund. Unlike principal transactions, however, the investors may provide advance blanket written consents authorizing all agency cross transactions, if the IA/BD has fully disclosed the capacities in which it will act and the potentially conflicting division of loyalties and responsibilities regarding both parties to such transactions. The IA/BD must also provide to each investor a confirmation of each agency cross transaction and an annual summary of all agency cross transactions (including the number of agency cross-transactions, the commissions generated for the IA/BD and the commissions generated for the RR/IA). A blanket consent is insufficient, however, if the IA/BD recommends the transaction to both the seller and the purchaser or acts as the placement agent for the issuer or seller.[162] All statements to investors must disclose that the investor may terminate the agency cross transaction authority at any time by written notice to the IA/BD.[163] The governing documents of a hedge fund may allow the hedge fund to expel any investor that terminates such authority.

4. Cross Transactions

An investment adviser to a hedge fund may cross trade between or among accounts that it manages to maintain a *pari passu* investment strategy. An investment adviser that arranges a cross trade between client accounts is not subject to the disclosure and consent requirements of Advisers Act section 206(3)[164] if it does not "act as a broker" by receiving compensation for effecting the cross trade. The investment adviser's management fee is not deemed "compensation" for this purpose. The relatively lenient treatment accorded to cross trades is based on the SEC's reasoning that the primary conflict of interest involved with agency cross transactions (that is, the IA/BD's incentive to earn additional commissions) is not present in cross trades.[165]

Cross trading, however, can implicate an investment adviser's fiduciary duties under Advisers Act sections 206(1) and (2).[166] For example, SEC enforcement actions have focused on the quality of the execution of those transactions.[167] An investment adviser may accomplish a cross trade simply by journaling a position from one hedge fund or client to another, which could provide an opportunity for pricing irregularities. The basis for the price in such a journal cross trade should be the market price at that time and should be well-documented. To

162. Additional procedures are required if the IA/BD acts as the placement agent.

163. Advisers Act Rule 206(3)-2, 17 C.F.R. § 275.206(3)-2; *see also* applicable state laws, *e.g.*, Title 10, California Code of Regulations, § 260.235.3.

164. 15 U.S.C. § 80b-6.

165. Advisers Act Release No. 1732 (July 17, 1998), 63 F.R. 39,505 (July 23, 1998).

166. 15 U.S.C. §§ 80b-6(1) and 80b-6(2).

167. *In re Michael L. Smirlock*, Advisers Act Release No. 1393 (Nov. 29, 1993) (officer of investment adviser aided and abetted violations of Advisers Act § 206(2) by setting price of agency cross transactions without asking broker for an independent evaluation of price and failing to follow adviser's procedure of obtaining price information from more than one broker); *In re Renberg Capital Management Inc.*, Advisers Act Release No. 2064 (Oct. 1, 2002) (adviser violated Advisers Act § 206(2) by cross trading between two sets of client accounts at slightly higher prices than the prices at which the first set of accounts purchased the shares when slightly lower price was available in the market).

satisfy the anti-fraud rules of Advisers Act sections 206(1) and (2), an investment adviser should disclose to its clients and hedge fund investors that it engages in cross trades, and should consider providing specific information regarding those trades.[168]

5. Cross Transactions under ERISA

An investment adviser that is an ERISA plan fiduciary because the hedge fund it manages has at least twenty-five percent "plan assets" may be prohibited from effecting cross trades involving ERISA plans.[169]

6. NASD Rules on Registered Representative/ Investment Adviser

NASD Conduct Rule 3040 requires that any associated person of an NASD member who participates in a private securities transaction, beyond the mere provision of recommendations, must, prior to such participation, provide written notice to the NASD member describing the proposed transaction, the associated person's role[170] and any selling compensation that the associated person will receive. "Selling compensation" is broadly defined as any compensation paid directly or indirectly, from whatever source, in connection with or as a result of the purchase or sale of a security, including, but not limited to, commissions, finder's fees, securities or rights to acquire securities, profit participation rights, tax benefits, dissolution proceeds, asset-based advisory fees, and expense reimbursements. Thus, if an investment adviser manages a hedge fund and is affiliated with (or is) an NASD member, it or its principals and employees may be subject to Rule 3040.

In a transaction in which an associated person has received or may receive selling compensation, the NASD member must advise the associated person in writing whether the NASD member approves or disapproves of the associated person's participation in the proposed transaction. If the NASD member approves the associated person's participation, the NASD member must record the transaction on its books and records and supervise the associated person's participation in the transaction, as if the transaction were executed on behalf of the NASD member. To comply with Rule 3040, an RR/IA must report to the affiliated brokerage firm all securities transactions in the RR/IA's hedge fund and other discretionary advisory accounts. The brokerage firm must supervise the RR/IA in these transactions and record them on its books and records. The record keeping and supervisory system must be adequate to ensure that full and complete transaction information is captured and to detect and prevent misconduct that could violate the federal securities laws or NASD Rules.

If the NASD member disapproves of an associated person's participation, the associated person may not participate in the transaction in any manner, directly or indirectly. In a transaction or a series of related transactions in which an associated

---

168.   Advisers Act Release No. 1732 (July 17, 1998), 63 F.R. 39,505 (July 23, 1998).

169.   *See* § 11.4.3.vi, *supra*.

170.   NASD Notice to Members 96-33 (May 1996), pp. 237-241.

person has not and will not receive any selling compensation, the NASD member must promptly acknowledge in writing the associated person's notice describing his or her participation, and the NASD member may, in its discretion, require the associated person to adhere to specified conditions in connection with the associated person's participation.

7. Other Considerations

Exchange Act section 11(a)[171] may restrict an IA/BD from effecting transactions of hedge funds and other discretionary accounts on a securities exchange of which the IA/BD is a member, unless an exception applies.[172]

§ 13.6 Personal Trading

The personal trading of investment advisers, portfolio managers and other investment professionals has provided a fertile source of cases for the SEC's Division of Enforcement.[173] As interpreted by courts, Advisers Act sections 206(1) and 206(2) impose on an investment adviser, as a fiduciary, an affirmative duty of utmost good faith, and full disclosure of material facts, including conflicts of interest, to its advisory clients.[174] When questionable trading practices are not adequately disclosed to clients, suits and enforcement actions are also brought under the anti-fraud provisions of Exchange Act section 10(b)[175] and Rule 10b-5[176] thereunder.

---

171.   15 U.S.C. § 78k(a).

172.   Markham, Jerry W. & Thomas Lee Hazen, *Broker Dealer Operations under Securities and Commodities Law*, § 9:3 (West 2003).

173.   *See, e.g., In re Embry*, Advisers Act Release No. 1382 (Sep. 16, 1993) and *SEC v. Embry*, Lit. Release No. 13777 (Sep. 9, 1993) (investment adviser and portfolio manager violated Advisers Act §§ 206(1) and 206(2), Exchange Act § 10(b) and Exchange Act Rule 10b-5 by, in part, failing to disclose availability and by purchasing common stock that functioned as an equity "kicker" to help sell high-yield securities purchased on behalf of clients); *In re Strong/Corneliuson Cap. Mgmt., Inc.*, Advisers Act Release No. 1425 (July 12, 1994) (adviser violated Advisers Act §§ 206(1) and 206(2) by failing to disclose that it invested in securities recommended to clients and that it recommended securities of an investment fund to clients in which the adviser had an interest); *In re Conan*, Advisers Act Release No. 1446 (Sep. 30, 1994) (portfolio manager violated Advisers Act §§ 206(1) and 206(2) by purchasing stock warrants from an issuer for her personal account when, if she had allowed her clients to purchase such warrants, they would have enhanced the value of notes of the same issuer that were held by those advisory clients; the portfolio manager failed to (a) preclear the purchase with the adviser, (b) report the purchase to the adviser or the advisory clients and (c) purchase the warrants for the advisory clients); *In re Chancellor Cap. Mgmt., Inc.*, Advisers Act Release No. 1447 (Oct. 18, 1994) (citing the need for disclosure of conflicts when a portfolio manager directs client purchases of securities issued in two public offerings while personally holding securities of the same companies that he had purchased privately more than a year earlier at nominal prices); and *In re Honour*, Advisers Act Release No. 1527 (Sep. 29, 1995) (finding violations by a portfolio manager who bought and sold securities for his personal account at about the same time as purchases and sales made for client accounts without getting advance approval from the investment adviser, without reporting the trades as required by Advisers Act Rule 204-2(a)(12) and without disclosing the conflicts of interest to the advisory clients).

174.   15 U.S.C. §§ 80b-6(1) and (2); *SEC v. Capital Gains Research Bureau, Inc.*, 375 U.S. 180, 194 (1963)

175.   15 U.S.C. § 78j(b).

176.   17 C.F.R. § 240.10b-5.

These enforcement actions may be brought for failing to report personal trades as required by the Advisers Act,[177] failing to avoid conflicts of interest, failing to disclose potential conflicts of interest to the clients,[178] failing to disclose conflicts of interest on the Form ADV,[179] or failing to establish or consistently enforce adequate procedures to prevent the misuse of material nonpublic information[180] and to detect unauthorized trading.[181]

To avoid violations of the Advisers Act and SEC rules regarding personal trading, investment advisers and their employees should (a) establish procedures to bring to light and to avoid situations in which the investment adviser's or its employees' investing conflicts with the interests of its advisory clients; (b) if such a conflict cannot be avoided, provide notice to clients and obtain written client consent to the transaction before the transaction; (c) adopt a written policy for reporting personal securities transactions and take reasonable measures to assure that employees read, understand and comply with the policy; (d) disclose all potential conflicts of interest in the investment adviser's Form ADV; and (e) implement procedures to prevent the misuse of material nonpublic information.[182]

1.   Report Personal Trades

An investment adviser must maintain records of all personal securities transactions by its advisory representatives.[183] Advisory representatives are generally all persons in a position to have advance information about the investment adviser's recommendations on behalf of the hedge fund and its other accounts.[184] An advisory representative must disclose any trades involving securities in which he or she has beneficial ownership.[185] For this purpose, the test for beneficial ownership is the same as in the rules under Exchange Act section 16.[186] For example, trades by an advisory representative's spouse and other immediate family members must be reported. Disclosure of employees' trades can highlight insider trading and front-running (trading ahead of the investment adviser's recommendations to its clients) and facilitate preventive or remedial action.

---

177.   Advisers Act Rule 204-2(a)(12), 17 C.F.R. § 275.204-2(a)(12); *In re Honour*, Advisers Act Release No. 1527 (Sep. 29, 1995).

178.   Advisers Act §§ 206(1) and (2), 15 U.S.C. §§ 80b-6(1) and (2); *In re Conan*, Advisers Act Release No. 1446 (Sep. 30, 1994).

179.   *In re Chancellor Cap. Mgmt., Inc.*, Advisers Act Release No. 1447 (Oct. 18, 1996); Advisers Act § 207, 15 U.S.C. § 80b-7.

180.   *In re Gabelli & Co., Inc.*, Advisers Act Release No. 1457 (Dec. 8, 1994); *In re Alliance Cap. Mgmt., L.P.*, Advisers Act Release No. 1630 (Apr. 28, 1997); Advisers Act § 204(A), 15 U.S.C. § 80b-4(a).

181.   *In re First Capital Strategists*, Advisers Act Release No. 1648 (Aug. 13, 1997); *In re Nicholas Applegate Cap. Mgmt.*, Advisers Act Release No. 1741 (Aug. 12, 1998); *In re Rhumbline Advisers*, Advisers Act Release No. 1765 (Sep. 29, 1998); *In re Scudder Kemper Inv., Inc.*, Advisers Act Release No. 1848 (Dec. 22, 1999).

182.   *See also, Report of the Advisory Group on Personal Investing*, Investment Company Institute, May 9, 1994. *See* § 2.7.5, *supra*.

183.   Advisers Act Rules 204-2(a)(12)(i) and 204-2(a)(13)(i), 17 C.F.R. §§ 275.204-2(a)(12)(i) and 275.204-2(a)(13)(i).

184.   Advisers Act Rule 204-2(a)(12)(ii)(A), 17 C.F.R. § 275.204-2(a)(12)(ii)(A).

185.   Advisers Act Rule 204-2(a)(12)(iii)(B), 17 C.F.R. § 275.204-2(a)(12)(iii)(B).

186.   *See* § 13.1.2, *supra*.

2. Written Policy

Advisers Act Rule 206(4)-7, compliance with which became mandatory on October 5, 2004, requires an SEC-registered investment adviser to adopt and implement written policies and procedures reasonbably designed to prevent violation by the investment adviser and its supervised persons of the Advisers Act and the rules thereunder. Advisers Act Rule 204A–1 requires an SEC-registration investment adviser to adopt, maintain and enforce a written code of ethics, which must include (among other things) provisions requiring all "access persons" to report, and the investment adviser to review, their personal securities transactions and holdings. Compliance with Rule 204A–1 was required beginning January 7, 2005.[187]

3. Investment Company Act Section 17(j)

A hedge fund investment adviser that is also affiliated with an investment company regulated by the Company Act must also comply with Company Act section 17(j)[188] and Rule 17j-1[189] thereunder. Rule 17j-1 requires that an investment adviser affiliated with an investment company (a) adopt a code of ethics and procedures to detect and prevent improper personal trading; (b) file quarterly reports concerning personal securities transactions and initial and annual reports concerning personal securities holdings; and (c) maintain records regarding personal trading, including a copy of the code of ethics and a list of violations thereof, copies of all reports made by all persons required to submit such reports and a list of all such persons.[190]

§ 13.7 Policies and Procedures Regarding Insider Trading

An investment adviser may receive material, nonpublic information from its industry sources or in connection with serving on the boards of directors of issuers or other relationships. To ensure that investment advisers do not tip or trade on material, nonpublic information, Advisers Act section 204A[191] requires investment advisers to establish, maintain and enforce written policies and procedures designed to prevent insider trading.

---

187. Advisers Act Rules 206(4)–7 and 204A–1, 17 C.F.R. § 270.206(4)–7 and 270.204A–1; *see also* § 2.7, *supra*.

188. 15 U.S.C. § 80a–17(j).

189. 17 C.F.R. § 270.17j-1.

190. Lemke, Thomas P., Gerald T. Lins & A. Thomas Smith III, *Regulation of Investment Companies*, § 8.05, Matthew Bender & Co., Inc. (2003).

191. 15 U.S. § 80b-4a.

1. Insider Trading

Exchange Act section 10(b)[192] and Exchange Act Rule 10b-5[193] are frequently the bases for SEC investigations and prosecutions. Section 10(b) prohibits any "manipulative or deceptive device in connection with the purchase or sale of any security." Among other things, Rule 10b-5, as interpreted by courts, prohibits insider trading, which has been given high priority in SEC enforcement efforts. While the law concerning insider trading is evolving, it is generally understood that the law prohibits:

- Trading in securities by an "insider" while in possession of material, nonpublic information.[194] This includes "temporary insiders", such as attorneys, accountants, consultants and others who temporarily become fiduciaries of the corporation.[195] Trading on such information by any such "insider" is a "deceptive" device under Exchange Act section 10(b) and a device to defraud under Exchange Act Rule 10b-5, because the insider breaches his or her relationship of trust and confidence with the shareholders of a corporation by using for his or her own benefit information obtained by reason of his or her position with the corporation.

- Trading in securities by a non-insider while in possession of material, nonpublic information, where the information either was disclosed to the non-insider in violation of an insider's duty to keep it confidential, or was misappropriated.[196] Instead of basing liability on a fiduciary relationship between the company insider and the purchaser or seller of the company's stock, the misappropriation theory bases liability on a fiduciary-turned-trader's deception of those who entrusted him or her with confidential information.[197]

- Communicating material, nonpublic information to others, or recommending a securities transaction to others while in possession of material, nonpublic information about the security or the company in question (commonly called "tipping").

i. Material Nonpublic Information

Trading while in possession of nonpublic information may be illegal if the information is "material." "Material" information is information about a company or its securities of such importance that it has a substantial likelihood of altering the "total mix of information" regarding the company.[198] It is information that,

---

192.   15 U.S.C. § 78j(b).

193.   17 C.F.R. § 240.10b-5.

194.   *Dirks v. SEC*, 463 U.S. 646, 655, n.14 (1983).

195.   *Chiarella v. U.S.*, 445 U.S. 222, 228 (1980); *Dirks v. U.S.*, 463 U.S. 646, 655, n.14 (1983).

196.   *U.S. v O'Hagan*, 521 U.S. 642 (1997) (partner in law firm misappropriated information from his law firm and law firm's clients by trading in securities of company regarding which law firm's client was preparing a tender offer, in breach of his fiduciary duty owed to the law firm and the client).

197.   *Id.* at 652.

198.   *TSC Industries v. Northway, Inc.*, 426 U.S. 438, 449 (1976); *Harkavy v. Apparel Industries, Inc.*, 571 F.2d 737, 741 (2d Cir. 1978) (applying *TSC Industries* to insider trading cases).

if generally known, would affect the market price of the security.[199] Material information can relate to current events or to possible future events. When information relates to a possible future event, materiality is determined by balancing the probability that the event will occur and the anticipated magnitude of the event in light of the totality of the company's activities.[200] The more likely it is that an event will occur, the less significant the event needs to be for the information to be deemed material; the more significant the event, the less likely the probability of its occurrence needs to be for the information to be deemed material. Whether a particular item of information is material may depend on how specific it is, the extent to which it differs from public information, and its reliability in light of its source, its nature, and the circumstances under which it is received.

Information that an investment adviser's personnel should consider material includes, among other things, information about earnings estimates; changes in previously released earnings estimates; manufacturing problems; changes in control or management; mergers; acquisitions; tender offers; joint ventures; changes in assets; major litigation; liquidity problems; significant new products, discoveries, services or contracts; cancellation or loss of significant orders, products, services or contracts; change in auditors or auditor notification that the issuer may no longer rely on an auditor's audit report; events regarding the issuer's securities; defaults on senior securities; calls of securities for redemption; repurchase plans; stock splits or changes in dividends; changes to rights of security holders; public or private sales of additional securities; and bankruptcies or receiverships.[201]

Material information can also relate to events or circumstances affecting the market for a company's securities. For example, a reporter for *The Wall Street Journal* was criminally liable for disclosing to others the dates that articles about various companies would be published in *The Wall Street Journal* and whether those reports would or would not be favorable.[202]

"Nonpublic" information is information that has not been disseminated in a manner that makes it available to public investors generally. If brokers and institutional analysts are generally disseminating information to traders, it would be considered public unless there is a reasonable basis to believe that such information is confidential and came from an insider.[203] Information that has been selectively disclosed to a few analysts or investors is not public. Public information is information that has been effectively disclosed in a manner sufficient to ensure that it is available to the investing public, such as by disclosure in a report filed with the SEC or publication in the Dow Jones broad tape, Reuters Economic Services, the Associated Press or United Press International wire services, newspapers of general circulation in New York City, or, if the subject company's operations or stockholders are geographically localized, in local news media, or the electronic

---

199.   *Elkind v. Liggett & Myers, Inc.*, F.2d 156, 166 (2d Cir. 1980).

200.   *SEC v. Texas Gulf Sulphur Co.*, 401 F.2d 833, 849 (2d Cir. 1968).

201.   *See, e.g., SEC v. Howard*, SEC Litigation Release No. 13965 (Feb. 10, 1994) (new product); *Elkind v. Ligget & Myers, Inc.*, 635 F.2d 156 (2d Cir. 1980) (change in earnings estimates); and Securities Act Release No. 7881 (Aug. 15, 2000), 65 F.R. 51,716 (Aug. 24, 2000) (SEC's list of various matters that may be considered material).

202.   *Carpenter v. U.S.*, 484 U.S. 19 (1987).

203.   *Elkind v. Liggett & Myers, Inc.*, 635 F.2d 156, 168 (2d Cir. 1980).

media. Even after information becomes public, persons who were aware of the information when it was nonpublic must wait to trade until the market absorbs the information.[204]

ii. Insiders

"Insiders" of a company are generally its officers, directors, employees and controlling shareholders. Thus, an investment adviser that has a large position in an issuer and has frequent conversations with management may be deemed an insider, as would an investment adviser whose personnel serve on the board of an issuer. In addition, persons outside a company who gain inside information in the course of dealings with that company may be considered "temporary insiders" of the company and thus be bound by the same legal restrictions as traditional insiders. For example, investment advisers, investment bankers, lawyers or accountants retained to represent or assist the company on an ongoing basis or in major corporate transactions may be insiders for purposes of insider trading laws. Under this analysis, an investment adviser and its employees could be deemed temporary insiders of a company if the investment adviser advises or performs other services for the company. Thus, an investment adviser's policies and procedures should warn its personnel that if they receive material, nonpublic information regarding a company that might have originated directly or indirectly from any insider (temporary or traditional), they should not trade in that company's securities for a hedge fund or other client, and should not discuss the information with any other person, without first consulting the appropriate persons.

iii. Misappropriation

"Misappropriation" is a basis for insider trading liability that is established when trading occurs based on material, nonpublic information that was misappropriated from another person. This theory has been used to reach a variety of individuals who are not traditional or temporary insiders. *The Wall Street Journal* reporter mentioned above was found by the U.S. Supreme Court to have defrauded the newspaper when he misappropriated information about upcoming articles from the newspaper and used the information for trading in the securities markets.[205] Similarly, a partner in a law firm was held to have used a "deceptive device" in violation of Exchange Act section 10(b) by misappropriating information from his law firm and the law firm's client, in breach of his fiduciary duty owed to this law firm and the client, and using it in trading in securities of a company regarding which the client was preparing a tender offer.[206]

---

204.   *U.S. v. Libera*, 989 F.2d 596, 601 (2d Cir. 1993).

205.   *Carpenter v. U.S.*, 484 U.S. 19 (1987).

206.   *U.S. v O'Hagan*, 521 U.S. 642 (1997)

iv. Tipping

"Tipping" is the disclosure of material, nonpublic information about a company or its securities to a third party, when such disclosure is not made strictly for corporate purposes. The disclosure may be made by an insider of the company, by one who has misappropriated the information from the company in question or from another person or company, or by anyone who received information traceable to an insider or one who has misappropriated the information.[207] Those who disclose the information are called "tippers"; those who receive the information are called "tippees." Criminal and civil liability for trading on the basis of tipped information may attach even where the information is received second- or third-hand, or more remotely, if the other requirements for finding liability are present.[208] The same legal standards apply to remote tippees. In addition, the tipper may be liable for any profits gained or losses avoided by a tippee, even if the tipper did not trade.[209] Thus, an investment adviser's policies and procedures should forbid its personnel from disclosing to anyone any information someone has tipped to him or her. The individual and the investment adviser may be liable if anyone trades on material, nonpublic information received from or through that person.

2. Penalties for Insider Trading

Penalties for trading on or tipping material, nonpublic information are severe. They may include a civil injunction, disgorgement of the profit gained or the loss avoided, a civil penalty of up to three times the profit gained or the loss avoided, a criminal fine of up to $5,000,000 for an individual or $25,000,000 for an entity (in addition to civil penalties based on the profit gained or the loss avoided) and jail time of up to twenty years.[210]

Even if an investment adviser and any managerial and supervisory personnel or other controlling persons (collectively, "Controlling Persons") do not engage in insider trading, a Controlling Person may be civilly liable in the amount of the greater of $1,000,000 or up to three times the profit realized or loss avoided by the person who made the illegal trades, if (a) the Controlling Person knew or recklessly disregarded the fact that the person was likely to engage in insider trading and failed to take appropriate steps to prevent the violation, or (b) such Controlling Person knowingly or recklessly failed to establish, maintain or enforce the policies and procedures required by Advisers Act section 204A.[211] In addition, contemporaneous traders in the market may bring private suits for damages against insider trading violators and their Controlling Persons.[212]

---

207.   *Dirks v. SEC*, 463 U.S. 646 (1983). In *Dirks*, an investment analyst received information from a former insider regarding massive fraud at a company. The analyst discussed his findings with the contacts and investors, some of whom traded on the information. The court held that the analyst was not a "tippee" and thus had no duty to refrain from communicating the information to others because the insiders had not acted for profit and had not breached a duty to the company.

208.   *U.S. v. Chestman*, 903 F.2d 75 (2d. Cir.1990).

209.   *SEC v. Texas Gulf Sulphur Co.*, 446 F.2d 1301, 1308 (2d Cir. 1971).

210.   Exchange Act §§ 21A (civil penalties) and 32(a) (criminal penalties), 15 U.S.C. §§ 78u-1 and 78ff(a).

211.   Exchange Act § 21A(b)(1), 15 U.S.C. § 78u-1(b)(1).

212.   Exchange Act § 20A(a), 15 U.S.C. § 78t-1(a).

§ 13.8 Order Aggregation

1. In General

An investment adviser to multiple hedge funds or other clients has a fiduciary duty not to prefer one account over another and to treat each account fairly.[213] For example, an investment adviser that manages a hedge fund and separate accounts should treat those accounts fairly when it aggregates those clients' trades.

2. Aggregation of Trades for Clients and Investment Adviser Personnel

In a 1995 no-action letter,[214] the SEC staff stated that it would not recommend enforcement action under Company Act section 17(d),[215] Company Act Rule 17d-1[216] or Advisers Act section 206,[217] if an SEC-registered investment adviser aggregates trades of non-affiliated clients and clients in which persons associated with the investment adviser have invested, as long as the investment adviser implements the following policies:

- Aggregation of transactions is fully disclosed in the investment adviser's Form ADV and separately to the investment adviser's existing clients and the brokers through which such orders are placed, and the policies for aggregation are submitted to and approved by the board of directors of any registered investment company for which transactions are aggregated;
- The investment adviser does not aggregate transactions unless it believes that aggregation is consistent with its duty to seek best execution for its clients and is consistent with the investment adviser's investment advisory agreement with each client for which trades are aggregated;
- No advisory client is favored over any other client, and each client that participates in an aggregated order participates at the average share price for all of the investment adviser's transactions in that security on a given business day, with transaction costs shared pro rata based on each client's participation;
- The investment adviser prepares, before entering an aggregated order, a written allocation statement specifying the participating client accounts and how it intends to allocate the order among those clients, and such statements, as well as any record of deviation therefrom, are maintained in the investment adviser's records for at least five years (the first two years in the investment adviser's office) and are easily accessible;[218]

---

213. *In re Acct. Mgmt. Corp.*, Advisers Act Release No. 1529 (Sep. 29, 1995) (adviser breached its fiduciary duty by consistently allocating short-term trading opportunities in "hot IPOs" to a limited group of accounts); Advisers Act Release No. 1702 (Feb. 28, 1998).

214. *SMC Capital, Inc.*, SEC No-Action Letter (Sep. 5, 1995).

215. 15 U.S.C. § 80b-17(d).

216. 17 C.F.R. § 270.17d-1.

217. 15 U.S.C. § 80b-6.

218. *See* § 2.8.1, *supra*.

- If the aggregated order is filled in its entirety, it is allocated among clients in accordance with the allocation statement, and if the order is partially filled, it is allocated pro rata based on the allocation statement;
- The order may be allocated on a basis different from that specified in the allocation statement, if all client accounts receive fair and equitable treatment and if the reason for the different allocation is explained in writing and is approved in writing by the investment adviser's compliance officer no later than one hour after the opening of the markets on the trading day following the day the order is executed;
- The investment adviser's books and records separately reflect, for each client account the orders of which are aggregated, the securities held by or bought or sold for that account;
- Funds and securities of clients whose orders are aggregated are deposited with one or more banks or broker-dealers, and neither the clients' cash nor their securities are held collectively any longer than is necessary to settle the purchase or sale in question on a delivery versus payment basis; and cash or securities held collectively for clients are delivered to the custodian bank or broker as soon as practicable following settlement;
- The investment adviser receives no additional compensation or remuneration of any kind as a result of the proposed aggregation;
- Individual investment advice and treatment are accorded to each advisory client;
- The investment adviser annually reviews its aggregation procedures to ensure that they are adequate to prevent any account from being systematically disadvantaged as a result of the aggregation of orders; and
- No separate employee accounts are included in the aggregation (unless those employee accounts are also client accounts).

§ 13.9 Other Trade Allocation Issues

An investment adviser may breach its fiduciary duty to its clients in violation of Advisers Act sections 206(1) and 206(2)[219] and, in some cases, state law, by unfairly favoring one account over another or not allocating securities and advisory recommendations among its clients on an equitable basis.[220] The SEC staff typically demands that an investment adviser adopt and implement a formula or program for allocating securities and recommendations among its clients (for example, a pro rata allocation based on the amount of assets each client has

---

219.   15 U.S.C. §§ 80b–6(1) and (2).
220.   SEC Inspection Manual (1980), p. 29; *In re Acct. Mgmt. Corp.*, Advisers Act Release No. 1529 (Sep. 29, 1995) (adviser breached fiduciary duty by consistently allocating short-term trading opportunities in "hot IPOs" to a limited group of accounts); Advisers Act Release No. 1702 (Feb. 28, 1998).

under the investment adviser's management or the suitability of each client for an investment). The SEC has sanctioned investment advisers under both the Advisers Act[221] and the Company Act[222] for failing to allocate trades promptly or fairly among client accounts. Investment advisers should be particularly careful when allocating securities that are difficult to obtain or in short supply, such as hot initial public offerings, and when allocating profitable securities to hedge funds for which they receive performance allocations and other accounts for which they charge performance fees. The SEC has brought several enforcement actions involving delayed allocations,[223] discrimination among clients[224] and misappropriation of client opportunities.[225] Other forms of favoritism that an investment adviser should avoid are allocating profitable trades to accounts for which it receives a higher management fee and making a disproportionate number of trades on behalf of a hedge fund that has authorized the investment adviser to use soft dollars for its own benefit.

§ 13.10 Trading Errors

An investment adviser has an obligation to place orders correctly for its advisory accounts. If an investment adviser makes an error while placing a trade for an

---

221.   *In re Smirlock,* Advisers Act Release No. 1393 (Nov. 29, 1993) (adviser sanctioned for executing purchase transactions in securities in which it failed to allocate to particular client accounts for periods of two to nine days).

222.   *In re Kemper Fin. Servs., Inc.,* Advisers Act Release No. 1387 (Oct. 20, 1993) (adviser sanctioned for delaying the designation of futures trades and later allocating such trades to mutual funds).

223.   *Id.* (involving portfolio manager of funds who time-stamped securities transactions after the time of order entry); *In re Smirlock,* Advisers Act Release No. 1393 (Nov. 29, 1993) (involving failure to allocate to particular client accounts for periods of two to nine days); *In re Richards,* Advisers Act Release No. 1495 (June 6, 1995) (involving portfolio manager who delayed designation of the account for which securities trades were being placed until after the trades were effected); *In re Burstein,* Advisers Act Release No. 1511 (July 28, 1995) (involving intra-day pre-arranged purchases in which an investment manager did not identify purchaser at the time of such transactions and subsequently allocated any profits therefrom to a bank with which he was affiliated).

224.   *In re Acct. Mgmt. Corp.,* Advisers Act Release No. 1529 (Sep. 29, 1995) (investment adviser consistently allocated short-term trading opportunities in hot IPOs to a limited group of accounts); *In re McKenzie Walker Inv. Mgmt., Inc.,* Advisers Act Release No. 1571 (July 16, 1996) (discrimination between performance-based fee accounts and asset-based fee accounts in the allocation of equity trades and hot IPOs); *In re The Dreyfus Corp.,* Advisers Act Release No. 1870 (May 10, 2000) (allocation of securities purchased in IPOs favored one fund over three other of investment adviser's funds); *In re F.W. Thompson Co., Inc.,* Advisers Act Release No. 1895 (Sep. 7, 2000) (allocations of securities purchased in IPOs were made solely to fifteen of investment adviser's twenty-nine accounts eligible to purchase such securities).

225.   *In re Conan,* Advisers Act Release No. 1446 (Sep. 30, 1994) (portfolio manager misappropriated client opportunity by purchasing for her personal account profitable warrants without first offering to her clients eligible to purchase such warrants the opportunity to purchase them); Advisers Act Release No. 1476 (Mar. 2, 1995); *In re Speaker,* Advisers Act Release No. 1605 (Jan. 13, 1997) (portfolio manager breached his fiduciary duty to a mutual fund by personally purchasing debentures without disclosing such opportunity to and first obtaining prior consent of the mutual fund).

account, the investment adviser must bear any costs of correcting the error.[226] The SEC staff has recently taken an increased interest in the manner in which investment advisers resolve trading errors. Investment advisers should have trading error policies and procedures in place, and consistently implement them. The SEC has not dictated any particular policies or procedures and has not published guidance on what constitutes an error. The following examples are typically cited as investment adviser errors:

- buying or selling a stock that results in the account being managed outside of its written investment guidelines or contrary to client instructions (for example, buying a stock that is on the client's restricted list, or buying or selling a stock that causes the account to be improperly concentrated in a particular industry or asset class);[227]
- executing a discretionary trade in a non-discretionary account;
- entering an order as a sell rather than a buy or vice versa;[228]
- buying or selling the incorrect amount of shares (for example, 1,000 instead of 10,000 shares);
- buying or selling the wrong stock (for example, buying ticker symbol ZYX instead of XYZ);
- buying or selling the right stock in the right amount, but for the wrong account;
- allocating a transaction incorrectly among accounts;
- incorrectly noting the price executed; and
- sending the trade to the wrong broker.

A clerical error may not always rise to the level of a trading error. For example, a trade may be properly executed and entered into a client's account, but an incorrect notation entered on the order ticket. In that case, the proper action may be to correct the order ticket and add a notation explaining why the correction was made. An investment adviser should be careful, however, when excluding categories of errors from its error correction policies. Several of the most typical trading errors, such as over- and under-purchases, or purchases of the wrong stock are, in essence, "clerical" errors.

Trading errors should be corrected as quickly as possible after detection. By promptly resolving errors, investment advisers can limit their potential market exposure and liability to clients. Moreover, the Advisers Act and rules thereunder

---

226. *See Charles Lerner*, SEC No-Action Letter (Oct. 25, 1988) (investment adviser that makes trade error for an account must bear costs of correcting).

227. *In re Pirrie*, Advisers Act Release No. 1284 (July 29, 1991) (investment adviser made trading error by purchasing stock in contravention of the client's investment guideline prohibiting purchases and sales of securities of companies doing business in South Africa); *In re Balatsos*, Advisers Act Release No. 1324 (Aug. 18, 1992) (investment adviser's portfolio summaries erroneously reported that client acquired bonds in a single transaction when such bonds were actually acquired in two transactions).

228. *In re M & I Inv. Mgmt. Corp.*, Advisers Act Release No. 1318 (June 30, 1992) (investment adviser's trader erroneously directed broker to sell certain stock with respect to which investment adviser had placed a buy order).

require that certain records be kept accurate and current.[229] An undetected or uncorrected error may result in a firm's records not being accurate and current and therefore lead to a recordkeeping violation.[230] An investment adviser should not delay correction in the hope that a favorable market or offsetting transaction will allow the error to be corrected with no loss to the client or cost to the investment adviser.

The cost of errors includes both direct costs, such as market losses and commission charges to reverse the error, as well as indirect costs, such as the opportunity costs of not being able to invest the erroneously invested assets. An investment adviser may compensate a client for missed investment opportunities due to an error by paying a fixed rate of interest or a rate based on the performance of the remainder of the account. In general, the longer an erroneous trade remains undetected and uncorrected, the greater the difficulty of determining the cost of the error.

The SEC staff has stated that an investment adviser's use of client assets to correct trading errors without disclosing the corrective action to the client and obtaining the consent of the client is a breach of the investment adviser's fiduciary duty and a violation of the anti-fraud provisions of the Advisers Act.[231] In addition, an investment adviser violates its fiduciary duties to treat each client fairly if it disadvantages one client to make another client whole. Soft dollars should not be used to cover an investment adviser's errors. Error correction through the use of a soft-dollar arrangement with a broker is not within the safe harbor of Exchange Act section 28(e),[232] because error correction is not a brokerage or research service.[233] This issue may arise when a broker with whom an investment adviser has a long-standing relationship offers to bear all or part of the loss involved in error correction. If an investment adviser accepts such an offer, it should make clear that such acceptance does not create any express or implied commitment to direct brokerage, or any other benefit, to that broker.

---

229.   *See* Advisers Act Rule 204-2(a), 17 C.F.R. § 275.204-2(a); *see also* § 2.8, *supra.*

230.   *In re Smirlock,* Advisers Act Release No. 1393 (Nov. 29, 1993) (failure to write trade tickets promptly after trades caused investment adviser's records to fail to reflect accurate date of entry, resulting in violation of record keeping provisions of Advisers Act Rule 204(c)(1)-(2)).

231.   *In re M & I Inv. Mgmt. Corp.,* Advisers Act Release No. 1318 (June 30, 1992) (by failing to have a procedure for disclosing trading errors, investment adviser violated Advisers Act § 206(1)-(3)); *In re Balatsos,* Advisers Act Release No. 1324 (Aug. 18, 1992) (failure to disclose erroneous portfolio summaries was a factor in SEC finding that investment adviser violated Advisers Act § 206(3)); Company Act Release No. 1270 (Jan. 31, 1991) (alleging that investment adviser violated Advisers Act §§ 206(1) and (2) because its president did not disclose to client the investment adviser's conflict of interest in not realizing the loss created by investment adviser's error).

232.   15 U.S.C. § 78bb(e); *see* § 14.2.5.i, *infra.*

233.   *In re Pirrie,* Advisers Act Release 1284 (July 29, 1991) (investment adviser violated Advisers Act §§ 206(1) and (2) by failing to disclose that investment adviser used soft-dollar arrangements to offset loss that resulted from investment adviser's trading error); *Charles Lerner,* SEC No-Action Letter (Oct. 25, 1988) (investment management firm and broker using soft-dollar arrangements to correct orders would not be able to rely on the safe-harbor of Exchange Act § 28(e)).

CHAPTER 14

Brokerage Allocation Practices

The fiduciary duties regarding brokerage allocation practices apply to every investment adviser, whether or not registered with the SEC. In recent years, the SEC, and especially the SEC inspection staff, have increased their focus on brokerage allocation issues, such as best execution and soft dollar transactions.

§ 14.1 Best Execution

The SEC has indicated repeatedly that all investment advisers (whether or not registered or required to be registered with the SEC) have a fiduciary duty to clients to obtain "best execution," that is, to execute securities transactions for their clients so that the clients' total costs or proceeds in each transaction are the most favorable under the circumstances.[1] Best execution is not merely a matter of paying the lowest possible commissions. The brokerage transaction must represent the best qualitative execution for the client, taking into account a variety of factors, such as the efficiency of execution, the timing of the transaction, the price of the security purchased or sold, the commission rate, the financial responsibility of the broker and the broker's responsiveness to the investment adviser.

The SEC inspection staff requires investment advisers periodically and systematically to evaluate the quality and cost of services received from brokers with whom they place client orders. Although until 2004[2] neither the Advisers Act nor any rule under it required investment advisers to adopt written policies and procedures to evaluate execution, the SEC inspection staff has over several years become increasingly aggressive in wanting every investment adviser to

---

1. Exchange Act Release No. 23170 (Apr. 23, 1986), 51 F.R. 16,004 (Apr. 30, 1986); *In the Matter of Synovus Securities,* Advisers Act Release No. 1423 (July 5, 1994) (willful failure to obtain best execution and non-disclosure of brokerage practices violates Exchange Act § 10(b), Exchange Act Rule 10b–5, and Advisers Act §§ 206(1) and 206(2)); *In the Matter of Portfolio Management Consultants,* Advisers Act Release No. 1568 (June 27, 1996) (willful failure to obtain best execution violates Advisers Act § 206(2)); *In the Matter of Fleet Investment Advisors,* Advisers Act Release No. 1821 (Sep. 9, 1999) (failure to seek best available price violates Advisers Act §§ 206(1) and 206(2)).

2. Advisers Act Rule 206(4)-7, 17 C.F.R. 275-206(4)-7.

conduct formal periodic evaluations of execution and the brokerage and research services provided by brokers, to determine whether the investment adviser is achieving best execution in client transactions. The SEC inspection staff has indicated that, as part of those evaluations, the investment adviser should consider possible execution alternatives such as ECNs, alternative brokers, market makers and market centers.[3] The investment adviser should also analyze conflicts of interest resulting from receiving services from brokers, such as client referrals and soft dollar payments for research and other services, in exchange for directing transactions to brokers.[4] The SEC inspection staff has recently expressed concern about how investment advisers manage and control those conflicts of interest. The staff wants investment advisers to document their evaluations of best execution and make them available to the SEC for inspection on request. The SEC inspection staff has indicated that appropriate documentation might include minutes of meetings, including the conclusions reached and decisions made, copies of information received and evaluated, and a determination that execution practices are consistent with disclosures in the investment adviser's Form ADV. Under new Advisers Act Rule 206(4)-7, such policies and procedures must be formalized in writing and made available to the SEC on request.[5] The execution practices should also be consistent with the disclosures in the offering materials of hedge funds the investment adviser manages.

§ 14.2 Soft Dollar Arrangements

1. Definition

A soft dollar arrangement generally involves an investment adviser's receipt from a broker of goods or services other than client trade executions in exchange for the investment adviser's directing client brokerage transactions to the broker.[6]

2. Disclosure Duty in General

An investment adviser has a fiduciary duty to disclose all soft dollar arrangements and describe all associated potential and actual conflicts of interest to its clients.[7]

---

3. Exchange Act Release No. 23170 (Apr. 23, 1986), 51 F.R. 16,004 (Apr. 30, 1986).

4. *Valuation, Trading and Disclosure: Three Compliance Imperatives*, Lori A. Richards, Director, Office of Compliance Inspections and Examinations, SEC, 2001 Mutual Fund Compliance Conference of the Investment Company Institute, June 14, 2001.

5. *Id.*

6. Inspection Report on the Soft Dollar Practices of Broker-Dealers, Investment Advisers and Mutual Funds, Office of Compliance, Inspections and Examinations, SEC (Sep. 22, 1988) (www.sec.gov/news/studies/softdlr. htm).

7. *SEC v. Capital Gains Research*, 375 U.S. 180, 191-192 (1963).

If an SEC-registered or state-registered investment adviser has the discretion to select, or even to suggest, a broker to a client and the value of products, research or services that the broker provides to the investment adviser is a factor in the investment adviser's choice or suggestion, the investment adviser must describe in writing, in Part II of its Form ADV, to each client or prospective client, the products, research and services obtained, whether clients may pay commissions higher than those obtainable from other brokers in return for those products and services, whether the research so obtained is used to service all of the investment adviser's accounts or only those accounts paying for it, and any procedures the investment adviser used during the last fiscal year to direct client transactions to a particular broker in return for products and research services.[8]

3. Section 28(e) Safe Harbor

As a fiduciary to its clients, an investment adviser has a duty to deal fairly with them in all respects.[9] In response to investment advisers' concerns that an investment adviser that receives anything from brokers other than the lowest possible commissions for its clients would be subject to a claim of breach of its fiduciary duty, Congress enacted Exchange Act section 28(e).[10] Section 28(e) provides a safe harbor from a breach of fiduciary duty claim under state or federal law if the investment adviser causes a client to pay to a broker a commission for effecting a securities transaction in excess of the commission that another broker would have charged for effecting that transaction, if the investment adviser determines in good faith that the amount of the commission is reasonable in relation to the value of the brokerage and research services provided.[11] Brokerage and research services are defined in Exchange Act section 28(e)(3), but the SEC deems the phrase generally to include products and services that provide "lawful and appropriate assistance to the money manager in the performance of his investment decision-making responsibilities."[12] Section 28(e) assumes that the lowest commission rate would not necessarily be in clients' best interest.[13]

Section 28(e) does not, however, provide any exception or exemption from an investment adviser's fiduciary duty to obtain best execution for its clients. Thus, an investment adviser that determines in good faith that the value of the research and brokerage services it generates is reasonable in relation to the commissions charged could nevertheless violate its duty of best execution if those commissions are in fact higher than the most favorable under the circumstances.[14]

---

8.   Form ADV, Part II, Item 12.B, 68 C.F.R. 42247. *See* § 14.2.4, *infra*, regarding disclosure required for soft dollar arrangements outside the safe harbor.

9.   *SEC v. Capital Gains Research*, 375 U.S. 180, 191-192 (1963); Exchange Act Release No. 23170 (Apr. 23, 1986), 51 F.R. 16,004 (Apr. 30, 1986); *In the Matter of Kidder, Peabody*, Advisers Act Release No. 232 (Oct. 16, 1968).

10.   15 U.S.C. 78bb(e).

11.   *Id.*

12.   Exchange Act Release No. 23170 (Apr. 23, 1986), 51 F.R. 16,004 (Apr. 30, 1986).

13.   Inspection Report on the Soft Dollar Practices of Broker-Dealers, Investment Advisers and Mutual Funds, Office of Compliance, Inspections and Examinations, SEC (Sep. 22, 1988) (www.sec.gov/news/studies/softdlr.htm).

14.   Exchange Act Release No. 23170 (Apr. 23, 1986), fn. 30., 51 F.R. 16,004, fn.30 (Apr. 30, 1986).

i. Third Party Research

Under appropriate circumstances, an investment adviser relying on the section 28(e) safe harbor may receive from a broker research services that the broker does not produce internally. The SEC distinguishes between a broker that arranges to have research materials or services produced by a third party and provided to an investment adviser, and a broker that merely pays obligations of the investment adviser directly to the third party. In the former case, the investment adviser can select the research services or products to be provided and still rely on section 28(e), as long as the broker is aware of the specific services that the investment adviser will receive, and the broker is the party that actually purchases the services. This level of communication is intended to ensure that the broker is not simply paying bills at the request of the investment adviser.[15] If a broker pays an investment adviser's expenses without being aware of the specific research services provided, the broker is merely paying the investment adviser's bills, rather than "providing" such research services, and such payments are not sheltered by section 28(e).

ii. Principal Transactions

The section 28(e) safe harbor is only available for soft dollars paid out of "commissions." For this purpose, the SEC interprets commissions as being paid in transactions in which the broker acts as agent and in eligible riskless principal transactions. Eligible riskless principal transactions are transactions in which a broker purchases and sells a security in a principal capacity at the same price and the investment adviser receives full disclosure of the mark-up, mark-down, fee or commission-equivalent paid to the broker and the transaction price.[16] Underlying this extension of the section 28(e) safe harbor to certain principal transactions is the assumption that the investment adviser has sufficient price transparency to determine whether the transaction costs are in fact reasonable in relation to the brokerage and research services that the broker provides.[17]

Section 28(e) is not available for mark-ups or mark-downs on principal transactions other than eligible riskless principal transactions. Thus, soft dollars generated in transactions in the over-the-counter market executed on a principal basis are not protected by the safe harbor of section 28(e). In addition, a broker that fills a customer order using securities from its own inventory is acting as a principal, and the safe harbor is unavailable.[18]

4. Soft Dollar Arrangements outside Section 28(e)

An investment adviser does not necessarily breach its fiduciary duty by engaging in soft dollar practices outside the section 28(e) safe harbor. Such transactions

---

15.   Exchange Act Release No. 23170 (Apr. 23, 1986), 51 F.R. 16,004 (Apr. 30, 1986).

16.   Exchange Act Release No. 45194 (Dec. 27, 2001), 67 F.R. 6 (Jan. 2, 2002).

17.   *Id.*

18.   Letter to Charles Lerner, Director of Enforcement, Pension and Welfare Benefit Administration, from Richard Ketchum, Director, SEC Division of Market Regulation (July 25, 1990); *Ronald H. Hoenig*, SEC No-Action Letter (Oct. 15, 1990).

are risky, however, even if the commission rates the clients pay are not higher than those charged by other brokers. The SEC insists on specific and extensive disclosure of any soft-dollar arrangement outside the safe harbor, including the conflicts of interest inherent in such a relationship.[19] The SEC has typically focused on the lack of adequate disclosure by the investment adviser and not on the soft-dollar arrangement itself as the basis for enforcement under the Advisers Act.[20]

In 1996 and 1997, the SEC staff examined the soft dollar practices and disclosures of 280 investment advisers and investment companies. The SEC staff's report the following year noted, among other things, that many investment advisers failed to provide sufficient disclosure to their clients or potential clients to enable the clients to understand the investment advisers' soft dollar practices and the conflicts of interest those practices present. The SEC staff characterized most investment advisers' descriptions of their soft dollar practices as simply "boilerplate," even while acknowledging that similarly situated investment advisers with similar soft dollar practices might be expected to make similar disclosures. The SEC staff also observed that many investment advisers used soft dollars to pay for products and services not used in the investment advisers' investment decision-making processes (that is, not protected by the section 28(e) safe harbor) and did so without providing detailed disclosures of these products and services. The SEC continues to focus on investment advisers' soft dollar practices and related breaches of fiduciary duty.

An investment adviser that uses soft dollars generated by a hedge fund's trades to pay expenses that are not within the section 28(e) safe harbor and that are typically paid by the investment adviser rather than the hedge fund (such as office rent, employee salaries, employee benefits, office equipment, telephone charges and other overhead expenses) should disclose those soft dollar arrangements to clients in specific detail. The disclosure should include the name of the broker to whom the hedge fund's brokerage transactions are directed, the brokerage commissions charged, the transaction volume, the amount that would be paid to an ECN for the same transactions, and the nature, provider and value of the goods and services provided.

i. Payment of Expenses of the Hedge Fund

Soft dollar arrangements are those by which the investment adviser uses soft dollar credits to pay expenses for which the investment adviser is responsible. Brokerage

---

19.　See Exchange Act Release No. 23170 (Apr. 23, 1986), 51 F.R. 16,004 (Apr. 30, 1986); *SEC v. Capital Gains Research*, 375 U.S. 180, 190-92 (1963); *In the Matter of Kingsley, Jennison, McNulty & Morse*, SEC Administrative Proceeding 3-7446 (Nov. 14, 1991); *SEC v. Galleon Capital Management*, Litigation Release No. 14315 (Nov. 1, 1994); *In the Matter of Sheer Asset Management*, Advisers Act Release No. 1459 (Jan. 3, 1995); *In the Matter of Acevedo*, Advisers Act Release No. 1496 (June 6, 1995); *SEC v. Tandem Management*, Litigation Release No. 14670 (Oct. 2, 1995); *In the Matter of S Squared Technology*, Advisers Act Release No. 1575 (Aug. 7, 1996); *In the Matter of Oakwood Counselors*, Advisers Act Release No. 1614 (Feb. 11, 1997); *In the Matter of Parnassus Investments*, Advisers Act Release No. 1634 (May 28, 1997); *In the Matter of Fleet Investment Advisors*, Advisers Act Release No. 1821 (Sep. 9, 1999); *In the Matter of Marvin & Palmer Associates*, Advisers Act Release No. 1841 (Sep. 30, 1999).

20.　*In the Matter of Kingsley, Jennison, McNulty & Morse*, SEC Administrative Proceeding 3-7446, note 8 (Nov. 14, 1991) (investment adviser violated Advisers Act by not adequately disclosing use of soft dollars for its own marketing and training purposes, even though the investment adviser paid no more in brokerage commissions than it would otherwise have paid and the soft dollars used for non-research purposes represented a miniscule fraction of the total commissions).

credits generated by hedge fund trades are not "soft dollars" if they are used to pay expenses for which the hedge fund is responsible under the terms of the hedge fund's governing documents. Using a hedge fund's brokerage credits to pay the hedge fund's own expenses may nevertheless violate the hedge fund manager's fiduciary duty to the hedge fund, even if only the amount by which the hedge fund arguably "pays up" is used to pay the hedge fund's expenses. This practice could artificially lower the hedge fund's expense ratio if the hedge fund only includes in the expense ratio expenses that it pays with hard dollars and effectively hides the additional expenses as brokerage commissions. Again, however, such a potential breach of fiduciary duty can be avoided by complete and adequate disclosure.

Investment advisers to one or more hedge funds and other clients sometimes use soft dollar credits generated by one hedge fund or client to benefit another hedge fund or client or pay for another hedge fund's or client's expenses. For example, the investment adviser may use research that is paid for by brokerage generated by one hedge fund to benefit another hedge fund's portfolio. Such arrangements should be permissible if they are disclosed in advance to each hedge fund's investors. This type of arrangement, however, is subject to abuse, if, for example, a hedge fund uses all of the soft dollar credits it generates to pay for its own non-research expenses, and receives its research at no cost from the brokerage credits generated by the investment adviser's other hedge funds and clients.

ii. Mixed-Use Products

If a product or service has more than one use, only some of which are research-related, an investment adviser relying on the section 28(e) safe harbor must make a reasonable allocation of the cost of the product or service according to its use. The percentage used to assist the investment adviser in investment decision-making may be paid in commission, or "soft," dollars and the remaining percentage must be paid from the investment adviser's own funds or "hard" dollars. Mixed-use products may include information management systems that integrate trading and execution, on the one hand, and accounting, recordkeeping and other administrative matters, on the other hand; computer hardware that runs software used for research for a client's benefit and also assists the investment adviser in non-research capacities, such as bookkeeping, recordkeeping or other administrative functions; and quotation equipment that serves a research function in pricing securities and keeping the investment adviser informed of market developments, but also performs non-research functions, such as client reporting. If an investment adviser attends a research seminar or similar program, the SEC interprets section 28(e) as covering the cost of the seminar, but not the non-research aspects of the trip, such as travel costs, hotel charges and meals and entertainment expenses.[21]

iii. Client Referrals

Directing brokerage transactions to brokers that refer hedge fund investors to an investment adviser is not sheltered by the section 28(e) safe harbor, because

---

21.   1934 Act Release No. 23170 (Apr. 23, 1986), 51 F.R. 16,004 (Apr. 30, 1986).

referring clients is not providing research or brokerage services. Depending on the circumstances, this practice may violate the anti-fraud provisions of the Advisers Act if the investment adviser fails adequately to disclose to its clients that it directs brokerage commissions to brokers in exchange for client referrals.[22] As in all situations when the investment adviser determines how to allocate brokerage, the investment adviser has a fiduciary duty to achieve best execution for its client. Thus, an investment adviser that agrees to direct brokerage to a particular broker in exchange for client referrals or other solicitation services should provide in any agreement with such solicitor or broker that any commitment to direct client trades to that person is subject to the investment adviser's fiduciary duty of best execution and other fiduciary duties to its clients. The investment adviser must in all events fully disclose any such arrangement to its clients that may be affected by it.

iv. Futures Transactions

Section 28(e) is not available for transactions with futures commission merchants. Section 28(e) applies only to "securities" transactions, and futures and other commodity interests are not "securities" under Exchange Act section 3(a)(10).[23] For this purpose, financial futures and single-stock futures are also deemed not to be "securities," and thus commissions generated by transactions in single-stock futures are not within the section 28(e) safe harbor.[24] Soft dollars generated by securities transactions may, however, be used to obtain research regarding futures and other commodity interests.[25]

5. Prohibited Soft Dollar Arrangements

i. Trade Error Correction

A hedge fund's investment adviser should not use soft dollars to pay any expense related to correcting a trading error if it has not disclosed such potential use to the hedge fund's investors. Even if the investment adviser does disclose that possibility, it is unclear whether such disclosure would be sufficient to insulate the investment adviser from liability.[26] Some commentators have suggested, however, that a hedge

---

22. *In the Matter of Fleet Investment Advisors,* Advisers Act Release No. 1821 (Sep. 9, 1999); *In the Matter of Michalski,* Advisers Act Release No. 1822 (Sep. 9, 1999); *In the Matter of Capital Markets Research,* Advisers Act Release No. 1834 (Sep. 27, 1999); *In the Matter of Lieberman,* Advisers Act Release No. 1835 (Sep. 27, 1999); *In the Matter of Marvin & Palmer Associates,* Advisers Act Release No. 1841 (Sep. 30, 1999).

23. 51 U.S.C. 78e(a)(10).

24. Exchange Act § 28(e)(4), 15 U.S.C. 78bb(e)(4).

25. *Department of Labor,* SEC No-Action Letter (Nov. 25, 1990), note 4.

26. *In the Matter of Pirrie,* Advisers Act Release No. 1284 (July 29, 1991) (investment adviser used soft dollar credits to pay for trade errors without disclosing such use to clients); *Charles Lerner, Esq.,* SEC No-Action Letter (Oct. 25, 1988). *See also Uhlenhop and Sammares,* "Best Execution and Soft Dollar Arrangements," National Association of Compliance Professionals, 258, 269 (Oct. 6-9, 1993), quoted in Lemke and Lins (*see* note 27, *infra*) (stating that the only safe course of conduct for an investment adviser is to obtain specific consent to using future brokerage to settle an error or, alternatively, be certain that the future business given to the broker-dealer will be executed at best price and commission).

fund's investment adviser may use soft dollars to pay expenses relating to trading errors if the hedge fund's governing documents specify that trade errors are the hedge fund's responsibility or liability.[27] If a broker offers to bear some of the financial loss resulting from a trading error, the investment adviser should make clear that the broker cannot use the investment adviser's soft dollars to offset any portion of that loss and that the investment adviser will not direct future transactions to that broker because the broker does so.[28]

ii. ERISA Considerations

An investment adviser may not engage in soft dollar practices outside the section 28(e) safe harbor with respect to any hedge fund whose assets are twenty-five percent or more "plan assets."[29] An investment adviser that manages such a "plan assets" hedge fund, as well as accounts that are not subject to ERISA (whether other hedge funds or separate accounts), may violate its fiduciary duties if it causes the "plan assets" hedge fund to pay more than its share of research expenses, for example, by using soft dollar credits generated by the other accounts to pay those accounts' non-research expenses and using a disproportionate amount of soft dollar credits generated by the "plan assets" hedge fund to pay research expenses that benefit all of the accounts.

§ 14.3 Reciprocal Brokerage

Reciprocal brokerage is the direction of a hedge fund's trades to a broker in exchange for the broker's assistance in selling interests in the hedge fund. Such assistance may include inviting the investment adviser to speak at conferences organized by the broker, and the broker's conducting its own solicitation activities on behalf of the hedge fund. In the context of investment companies, the SEC has acknowledged and seems grudgingly to permit reciprocal brokerage practices.[30] The practice must be disclosed in the investment company's prospectus and approved by its board of directors. The SEC has censured an investment company's investment adviser that engaged in reciprocal brokerage allocation practices on an undisclosed basis.[31] In permitting reciprocal brokerage allocation practices by investment companies, the SEC reasoned that an open-end investment company was permitted to bear the distribution expenses of selling its shares and that reciprocal brokerage was another form of distribution expense. The SEC has not extended this principle to hedge

---

27.   Lemke, Thomas P., and Gerald T. Lins, *Soft Dollars and other Brokerage Arrangements,* §4.04, 2003 Ed.

28.   *Charles Lerner, Esq.*, SEC No-Action Letter (Oct. 25, 1988); *see also* § 13.10, *supra.*

29.   *See* § 11.4.2, *supra.*

30.   NASD Manual - Conduct Rule 2830(k)(7)(B); *In the Matter of NASD,* Exchange Act Release No. 17599 (Mar. 4, 1981).

31.   *In the Matter of Stein, Roe & Farnham,* Advisers Act Release No. 1217 (Jan. 22, 1990).

funds, but by analogy, the SEC might permit reciprocal brokerage by a hedge fund that is obligated to pay the distribution expenses for offering and selling hedge fund interests, if the practice is fully disclosed to investors.[32]

---

32.   The SEC has broadened the scope of Company Act § 17(e)(1), 15 U.S.C. 80a-17(e)(1), by maintaining that disclosure of soft dollar practices outside the safe harbor of Exchange Act § 28(e) does not cure a Company Act § 17(e)(1) violation. An SEC administrative law judge has held that § 17(e)(1) is violated even if the investment company actually benefits from the investment adviser's receipt of such soft dollar services and even if such soft dollar practices are fully disclosed. In finding that the investment adviser and its founder/president violated § 17(e)(1), the judge reasoned that an investment adviser's receipt of non-research soft dollar services constituted "compensation in connection with the purchase or sale of property to or from the investment company," the "essence of a violation of [s]ection 17(e)(1)." The judge further reasoned that prior disclosures, if made with specificity and accuracy, would have been an ineffectual defense, consistent with Congress's determination that "disclosure alone is not adequate protection in the investment company field." *See In the Matter of Parnassus Investments, Jerome L. Dodson, Marilyn M. Chou and David L. Gibson*, Administrative Proceeding 3-9317 (Sep. 3, 1998); Exchange Act Release No. 23170 (Apr. 23, 1986), 51 F.R. 16,004 (Apr. 30, 1986); *In the Matter of Portfolio Management Consultants*, Advisers Act Release No. 1821 (Sep. 9, 1999).

CHAPTER 15

Fees and Special Profit Allocations

Except for performance fees or allocations and excessive fees discussed below, the Advisers Act does not specifically address the types or amounts of advisory fees an investment adviser may charge a hedge fund. The Advisers Act requires, however, that the investment adviser, as a fiduciary, make full and fair disclosure to its clients about the fees it charges. An investment adviser to a hedge fund should disclose those fees and special profit allocations to hedge fund investors in the hedge fund's offering materials and (if the investment adviser is registered) in Item 1.D of Part II of the investment adviser's Form ADV.

§ 15.1 Management Fee

Investment advisers to hedge funds typically charge management fees at annual rates of one to two percent of managed assets, although a few investment advisers charge up to four percent. Management fees typically are paid quarterly or monthly. For U.S. hedge funds, the expense of the management fee is typically charged to the investors' capital accounts (except for the investment adviser's own capital account, and, if the investment adviser elects, the capital accounts of its affiliates, employees and family members). For an offshore hedge fund that is structured as a corporation, the fee is typically charged to the hedge fund itself, and the hedge fund's governing documents allocate the fee as appropriate among the classes and series of its shares. A few investment advisers charge management fees on a decreasing scale, with different investors being charged different amounts based on the amount each has invested in the hedge fund.

Management fees may be charged in advance or arrears. Typically, an investment adviser that charges fees in advance does not return the unearned portion of the fee to an investor that withdraws from a hedge fund before the end of the period for which the management fee is charged. In the SEC staff's view, an investment adviser should refund prepaid but unearned advisory fees to a client when the client terminates the investment advisory relationship.[1]

---

1. *Robert D. Brown Investment Counsel, Inc.*, SEC No Action Letter (July 19, 1984).

Otherwise, in the staff's view, the investment adviser would be requiring its client to forfeit the entire prepayment as a penalty for termination, which would violate the investment adviser's fiduciary duty to its clients.[2] This staff position may not apply to an investment adviser to a hedge fund, if the hedge fund, rather than the withdrawing investor, may be regarded as the client, but the SEC has not ruled definitively.[3] The refund issue does not arise, of course, if withdrawals or redemptions are permitted only at the end of the monthly or quarterly fee period or if the fees are charged in arrears.

§ 15.2 Performance Fees and Allocations

Performance-based compensation is a defining characteristic of a hedge fund. An investment adviser to a hedge fund typically receives a performance fee, if the hedge fund is organized as a corporation (as are many offshore hedge funds), or a performance allocation, if the hedge fund is organized as a limited liability company or a limited partnership (as are most domestic hedge funds) and the investment adviser is a member or partner of the hedge fund (as is also typical). The performance fee or allocation is most commonly twenty percent of the profits generated during each given measurement period, subject to a "high water mark" as described below. A few investment advisers charge higher performance fees or allocations, ranging up to fifty percent; higher fees are more common in hedge funds managed by investment advisers with extensive and highly successful track records. For regulatory reasons described below, investment advisers to other investment funds, such as mutual funds and registered hedge funds, are generally unable to charge similar performance fees or allocations.

1. Implications of Performance Fee versus Allocation

i. Implications for Investment Adviser

If the investment adviser is a partner or member of the hedge fund and the hedge fund is a partnership or limited liability company,[4] the investment adviser may be compensated by a special, disproportionate allocation of periodic profits of the hedge fund. This special profit allocation is made directly to the investment adviser's capital account and thus reduces the amount of profit that would otherwise be allocated to the investors in the hedge fund. As an allocation,

---

2. *Id.*

3. Advisers Act Rule 203(b)(3)-1, 17 C.F.R. § 275.203(b)(3)-1; *but see* Advisers Act Release No. 2333, Part II.J (Dec. 2, 2004), 69 F.R. 72,054 (Dec. 10, 2004) (until February 2006, a partnership or LLC will continue to be considered a single client for purposes of the Private Adviser Exemption); *see also* §§ 2.1.2.iii and 2.1.2.iv, *supra.*

4. *See* § 4.2, *supra.*

rather than a fee, the special profit allocation retains the tax characteristics of the underlying profits on which it is based. This provides two advantages to the investment adviser: depending on the tax character of the hedge fund's profits, all or part of the income may be characterized as long-term capital gain, rather than ordinary income; and tax on the special profit allocation is deferred until the gains are realized. For example, if twenty-five percent of the hedge fund's profits are unrealized and fifteen percent are realized gains subject to long-term capital gain tax rates, twenty-five percent of the investment adviser's special profit allocation will not be taxed currently and fifteen percent will be taxed as long-term capital gain.[5]

ii. Implications for Investors in the Hedge Fund

A performance fee is treated as a miscellaneous itemized deduction for income tax purposes. Thus it is charged as an expense to the investor but often is not deductible. A special profit allocation, by comparison, has more favorable tax consequences for a hedge fund's investors because, by reducing the amount of profits that would otherwise be allocated to their capital accounts, it creates a corresponding reduction in their taxable income from the hedge fund.[6]

2. Features

i. High-Water Mark

Traditionally, an investment adviser's performance fee or allocation is charged only against profits above the previous highest value of each account. This is colloquially called a "high-water mark" provision. Because investors may invest at different times, each investor typically begins with a unique high-water mark. A standard high-water mark provides that a hedge fund investor's capital account or shares will not be charged a performance allocation or fee until losses previously allocated to the capital account or shares are fully recouped, after adjusting for additions to and withdrawals from the investment account. Thus, for example, if an investor contributes $500,000 on January 1, which depreciates to $400,000 on December 31, but appreciates to $505,000 on the following December 31, the investment adviser's performance fee or allocation would be payable only for the second year and would be based on only the $5,000 of overall profits above the high-water mark. The high-water mark almost never looks forward, however, and the investor in this example that was charged a performance fee or allocation for the second year would not receive a refund if the hedge fund loses money in its third year.

The high-water mark ordinarily is adjusted for partial withdrawals. The high-water mark is reduced in the proportion that the capital account balance immediately after the withdrawal bears to the capital account balance immediately before the withdrawal.

---

5. *See* § 16.8, *infra.*
6. *See* §§ 4.2.2, *supra,* and 16.3.2, *infra.*

Multiple investments in a hedge fund by a single investor may or may not be tracked separately with their own high-water marks. For example, assume that an investor contributes $500,000 on January 1, which depreciates to $400,000 the following December 31, and the investor contributes another $500,000 on the second January 1. Assume further that the hedge fund appreciates by ten percent in the second year, so that the first investment is worth $440,000 and the second is worth $550,000. If the high-water marks for both investments are aggregated, the investment adviser will not be entitled to a performance fee or allocation for the second year, because only $90,000 of the total $100,000 loss will have been recouped. If, however, the high-water marks are not aggregated and the two contributions are viewed as separate investments, the investment adviser will not be entitled to a performance fee or allocation for the first investment, because it will have appreciated in the second year only from $400,000 to $440,000 (still $60,000 below its high-water mark), but will be entitled to a performance fee or allocation for the second investment, based on the $50,000 gain (from $500,000 to $550,000).[7]

With the decline of the stock markets from 2000 to 2003, some hedge funds experienced unprecedented depreciation in value, rendering it unlikely that losses would be recouped any time soon and vividly illustrating for some investment advisers a weakness in the traditional high-water mark provision. As a result, a few investment advisers restructured their high-water mark provisions to mitigate the consequences to them of extraordinary market declines. For example, some limited their high-water marks to look back only a year or two, establishing a new high-water mark every year or two and disregarding prior losses. The asserted rationale for such changes was the need to provide incentive to the investment adviser and its most skilled portfolio managers (in the form of a realistic possibility of earning a performance fee or allocation), without which the investment adviser could liquidate and dissolve its hedge fund and form a new hedge fund with new investors (and any investors from the old hedge fund willing to forego their high-water marks in the old hedge fund). A limited look back also decreases an investment adviser's incentive to take greater risk to recoup prior losses. Other investment advisers diluted the high-water mark concept and began charging a reduced performance fee or allocation on profits that recoup prior losses. To make such arrangements palatable to investors, such an investment adviser typically continues to charge a reduced performance fee or allocation on some specified amount of profits in excess of the high-water mark, thus giving investors an added incentive to remain in the hedge fund when the prior losses are recouped. High-water mark provisions will likely continue to evolve in response to market conditions and investor expectations.

ii. Hurdle rates

Some hedge funds employ a hurdle, limiting the investment adviser's performance fee or allocation to an amount by which the hedge fund's performance exceeds a specified index, benchmark or rate of return. Some other hedge funds pay a

---

7. This discussion relates primarily to U.S. hedge funds. *See* § 15.3, *infra*, for more on performance fee computation methods for offshore hedge funds.

full performance fee or allocation, on the entire return, but only if it exceeds the hurdle. Thus, for example, an investment adviser to a hedge fund with a $1,000,000 gain on a $10,000,000 account that is subject to a twenty percent performance allocation with a five percent hurdle rate would receive $100,000 under the former provision and $200,000 under the latter. The latter can produce anomalous results if the appreciation is only slightly above the hurdle rate, because it can result in a performance allocation for the investment adviser and a return below the hurdle for the investor.

3. Rules

i. The Performance Fee Rule

An SEC-registered investment adviser that receives a performance fee or allocation from a hedge fund must comply with the Performance Fee Rule, Advisers Act Rule 205-3,[8] to avoid the general prohibition in Advisers Act section 205(a)(1)[9] of compensation based on the capital appreciation of a client's account. The Performance Fee Rule reflects the SEC's belief that fees and allocations of profits calculated as a portion of an account's performance are potentially abusive, but that wealthy investors can fend for themselves against such abuses.[10]

The Performance Fee Rule provides that an investment adviser may charge an investor in a hedge fund that relies on Company Act section 3(c)(1)[11] a performance-based fee only if, at the time the investor invests in the hedge fund, one of the following conditions is met: (a) the investor has at least $750,000 under the management of the investment adviser, (b) the investment adviser reasonably believes that the investor has a net worth in excess of $1,500,000 or (c) the investment adviser reasonably believes that the investor is a "qualified purchaser," as defined in Company Act section 2(a)(51)(A).[12] Most hedge funds limit participation to accredited investors, each of whom has a net worth of at least $1,500,000,[13] and as a result, most investment advisers rely on the $1,500,000–net-worth standard and not on the $750,000–under-management standard. If the hedge fund relies on Company Act section 3(c)(7)[14] rather than section 3(c)(1), the test need only be met by the hedge fund itself, rather than each investor.[15]

The Performance Fee Rule does not apply to advisory contracts with non-U.S. persons.[16] An investment adviser may not, however, charge a performance fee to

---

8. 17 C.F.R. § 275.205-3.

9. 15 U.S.C. § 80b-5(a)(1).

10. Advisers Act Release No. 996 (Nov. 14, 1985), 50 F.R. 48,556 (Nov. 26, 1985).

11. 15 U.S.C. § 80a-3(c)(1); *see also* § 3.2, *supra*.

12. 15 U.S.C. § 80a-2(a)(51)(A); *see also* Advisers Act Rule 205-3(d), 17 C.F.R. § 275.205-3(d); and Advisers Act Release No. 1731 (July 15, 1998), 63 F.R. 39,027 (July 28, 1998). *See* § 3.3.2, *supra*, regarding qualified purchasers. *See* § 2.1.2.iv, *supra*, regarding amendment of the Performance Fee Rule.

13. Securities Act § 4(2), 15 U.S.C. § 77d(2); Securities Act rules 506 and 501(a), 17 C.F.R. §§ 230.506 and 230.501(a); *see also* § 5.3, *supra*.

14. 15 U.S.C. § 80a-3(c)(7); *see also* § 3.3, *supra*.

15. Advisers Act § 205(b)(4), 15 U.S.C. § 80b-5(b)(4). *See* Chapter 3, *supra*.

16. Non-U.S. persons are persons who are not residents of the United States. *See* Advisers Act § 205(b)(5), 15 U.S.C. § 80b-5(b)(5).

the U.S. investors in an offshore hedge fund that relies on Company Act section 3(c)(1),[17] except in compliance with the Performance Fee Rule. If another hedge fund or a registered investment company (such as a mutual fund or registered hedge fund) invests in a hedge fund, each investor in the investing fund must meet the test of the Performance Fee Rule if the investing fund is charged a performance fee or allocation with respect to its investment in the hedge fund.

Some states have similar rules that apply to state-registered investment advisers. For example, California follows the Performance Fee Rule, but, as discussed below, also expressly requires that the investment adviser fully disclose all material information about the proposed compensation arrangement.[18] Some other states have not amended their performance fee rules to reflect amendments to the Performance Fee Rule that took effect in 1998. Thus, those states require the investment adviser to calculate the performance fee or special profit allocation over a one-year period and impose other obligations that were previously part of the Performance Fee Rule.[19]

The Performance Fee Rule does not apply to specified knowledgeable persons. Thus, an executive officer, director, general partner or person serving in a similar capacity with the investment adviser who invests in the investment adviser's hedge fund may be charged a performance fee or special profit allocation even if he or she does not meet the Performance Fee Rule's net worth or minimum investment test.[20] Employees of the investment adviser who participate in the investment adviser's investment activities and have performed those functions and duties for the investment adviser or substantially similar duties for or on behalf of another company for at least twelve months also need not meet any of the other tests to be charged a performance fee or allocation.[21]

An investment adviser may admit to its hedge fund investors that do not meet any of the tests of the Performance Fee Rule. In such a case, the investment adviser may not charge performance fees or allocations to such investors. If the hedge fund's charter documents so provide, the investment adviser may instead charge a higher asset-based management fee to investors that do not meet any of the tests. All such waivers and alternative fee arrangements should be disclosed to all prospective investors in the hedge fund.[22]

Although the Performance Fee Rule does not explicitly require any particular disclosure, an investment adviser has an obligation as a fiduciary to deal fairly with its clients and make full and fair disclosure of its compensation arrangements.[23] The investment adviser must fully disclose all material information about a performance fee or allocation arrangement and any material conflicts posed by

---

17.   *See Rosenberg Institutional Equity Management*, SEC No Action Letter (Mar. 14, 1990); Advisers Act § 205(b)(5), 15 U.S.C. § 80b-5(b)(5).

18.   Title 10, California Code of Regulations, § 260.234(b)(3); California Corporate Securities Law of 1968 § 25234(a)(1).

19.   *See, e.g.,* Code of Vermont Rules, Regulation § S-95-3.10.d, and Utah Administrative Code, Rule R164-2-1-E.

20.   Advisers Act Rule 205-3(d)(1)(iii)(A), 17 C.F.R. § 275.205-3(d)(1)(iii)(A).

21.   Advisers Act Rule 205-3(d)(1)(iii)(B), 17 C.F.R. § 275.205-3(d)(1)(iii)(B).

22.   *See* Chapter 6, *supra.*

23.   Advisers Act Release No. 1731 (July 15, 1998), 63 F.R. 39,022 (July 21, 1998); *see also* Chapter 6, *supra.*

that arrangement.[24] Accordingly, any investment adviser that charges performance-based compensation should disclose, among other things:

- that the fee or allocation arrangement may create an incentive for the investment adviser to make investments that are riskier or more speculative than it would make absent performance-based compensation;
- if relevant, that the investment adviser may receive increased compensation with regard to unrealized appreciation as well as realized gains in the client's account;
- the periods that will be used to measure investment performance throughout the contract and their significance in computing the fee or allocation;
- the nature of any index that will be used as a comparative measure of investment performance, the significance of the index and the reason the investment adviser believes the index is appropriate; and
- if the compensation is based in part on the unrealized appreciation of securities for which market quotations are not readily available, how the securities will be valued and the extent to which the valuation will be independently determined.

ii. When the Performance Fee Rule Does Not Apply

The prohibition of performance fees in Advisers Act section 205(a) does not apply to an SEC-Exempt Adviser, which usually is an investment adviser that has $30,000,000 or more under its management and relies on the Private Adviser Exemption in Advisers Act Section 203(b). The Private Adviser Exemption, however, will not be available to most investment advisers to hedge funds after January 2006.[25] Under Advisers Act section 203A,[26] enacted as part of the National Securities Markets Improvement Act of 1996, an investment adviser with less than $25,000,000 under its management is (with some exceptions) prohibited from registering under the Advisers Act, so that the exemption in Advisers Act section 203(b) is not needed, although its conditions may be met. Such an investment adviser could refrain from SEC registration in reliance on both section 203A and section 203(b). If that investment adviser were to fail to meet the conditions of section 203(b), however, it would not be an SEC-Exempt Adviser and, by its terms, the prohibition in Advisers Act section 205(a) would apply. In that case, the investment adviser would need to comply with the Performance Fee Rule, even if the investment adviser were also subject to a different (even inconsistent) state law performance fee rule.

Whether either or both of the Performance Fee Rule and a similar state rule apply, an investment adviser must comply with its fiduciary duties under federal and state law to the hedge fund's investors. In addition to making complete and accurate disclosure, even an unregistered investment adviser should conform its

---

24. Advisers Act Release No. 1731 (July 15, 1998), 63 F.R. 39,022 (July 21, 1998); *see also* Advisers Act § 206, 15 U.S.C. § 80b-6.

25. Advisers Act § 205(a), 15 U.S.C. § 80b-5(a); *see* §§ 2.1.2.iii and 2.1.2.iv, *supra*.

26. 15 U.S.C. § 80b-3A.

performance-based fees or allocations to otherwise applicable state and federal standards.[27]

iii. ERISA Limits

Investment advisers that are deemed plan fiduciaries may be prohibited from charging performance fees or allocations to certain ERISA plan investors in the hedge fund.[28] Investment advisers to U.S.-based hedge funds can usually waive performance fees or allocations that would otherwise be due from ERISA plan investors, because such fees and allocations are typically calculated and charged separately for each investor. An investment adviser to an offshore hedge fund, however, should consider providing a separate class of shares to be held by any investors for whom performance fees will be waived, so that the hedge fund can maintain a single net asset value for each series and class of its shares.[29]

§ 15.3 Performance Fee Computation Methods for Offshore Hedge Funds

Performance fee computations are often more complicated for offshore hedge funds than for U.S. hedge funds, because offshore hedge funds are typically structured as corporations. The corporate structure requires a single net asset value for each class and series of shares, unlike a partnership or limited liability company with a separate capital account for each investor. A performance fee charged to a corporation is an expense that affects the net asset value of each share in the same way. Without some adjustment, an investor that purchases shares in an offshore hedge fund on a date other than the first day of the period over which the performance fee is calculated would suffer the same per-share decrease in net asset value on payment of the performance fee at the end of the period as investors that held shares from the beginning of the period, even if the new investor's shares enjoyed less appreciation. Similarly, an investor that purchases shares on other than the first day of the performance fee calculation period at a time when the net asset value of the shares is less than its value at the beginning of the period will not be charged a performance fee at the end of the period if the net asset value has then increased back to its value at the beginning of the period, even though that investor's shares will have appreciated. Thus, equitable problems arise in charging performance fees to an offshore hedge fund, because investors may invest at different times during the year, when the offshore hedge fund has accrued differing performance fees or high-water marks.[30] Several ways of addressing these problems are described below.

---

27. *See* § 15.5, *infra.*
28. *See* § 11.4.3.iv, *supra.*
29. *See* § 15.3, *infra.*
30. *See* § 4.4.4, *supra.*

1. Equalization of Shares

The "equalization of shares" method equalizes the investment of an investor admitted at a time when the other shareholders are already subject to an accrued performance fee (because the hedge fund has appreciated) or when the other shareholders have an unrecouped loss and are below their high-water mark (because the hedge fund has depreciated). Without an adjustment, a shareholder who invests during a year in which the offshore hedge fund has appreciated would immediately suffer a reduction in net asset value per share due to the accrued performance fee, even though the shareholder would not have been in the offshore hedge fund to enjoy the appreciation. To "equalize" such a shareholder's interest in the offshore hedge fund, the shareholder is granted an equalization credit with respect to each of its shares equal to the performance fee percentage multiplied by the difference between the net asset value per share at the time the investor invests and the last net asset value per share at which a performance fee was charged. The equalization credit appreciates or depreciates based on the offshore hedge fund's performance and ensures that all investors in the offshore hedge fund bear the same degree of risk.

If, on the other hand, a shareholder purchases shares during a year at a time when shares have decreased in value, the shareholder should equitably pay a performance fee on any appreciation of those shares even though the other investors are charged a lesser fee or no fee. This is accomplished by redeeming, for no consideration, a number of the investor's shares with a value equal to the performance fee that should equitably be due from that investor. This procedure is followed until the net asset value of the shares match the previous net asset value at which a performance fee was charged to the other shareholders.

2. Classes and Series

A less complicated alternative is the "classes and series" approach, which creates a new "series" of each class of shares on each date that investors purchase that class of shares of the offshore hedge fund. The performance fee is calculated and charged separately for each series of each class, in essence imposing partnership accounting on the corporation.

This method potentially creates different net asset values for the various series of shares of the offshore hedge fund. Some investors may be troubled by the different net asset values, but this method is simpler to administer. To reduce the proliferation of series, at the end of each year, all shares in a series that are charged a performance fee are generally converted into the original "benchmark series" of the same class. Shares of a series that have unrecouped loss and are below their high-water mark remain in that series until the net asset value of that series appreciates to the high-water mark for that series. At that time, the shares of that series are converted into the "benchmark series."

3. Monthly Accrual

Under this method, the performance fee is computed and paid monthly. Monthly payment of the performance fee eliminates the performance fee computation problems as long as the offshore hedge fund appreciates, because (assuming monthly openings) each new investor purchases shares at a net asset value that reflects the performance fee accrued to date. Adjustments are appropriate, however, if an investor purchases shares when other shareholders are below their high-water mark. Given the advanced accounting software in use today, this method is rarely used, because administrators and accountants can readily calculate a monthly net asset value for an offshore hedge fund using either the equalization method or the classes and series method. Sophisticated offshore hedge fund investors might not accept the difficulty of calculation as a rationale for being required to pay the performance fee monthly, and an offshore hedge fund might find that charging a performance fee monthly creates a competitive disadvantage in attracting investors.

4. Rough Justice

As noted above, shareholders that invest when the offshore hedge fund has unrecouped losses and is below the high-water mark receive a windfall because their shares are not assessed a performance fee until the offshore hedge fund makes up those losses, even though they did not suffer the loss. Conversely, shareholders that invest when the offshore hedge fund has appreciated and accrued a performance fee that is not yet payable are penalized, because when the performance fee is paid, the net asset value of their shares will be reduced, even though they did not participate in the appreciation. As the name "rough justice" suggests, some offshore hedge funds choose simply to accept these inequities on the theory that investors should perceive that, over time, they are likely to receive both the benefits and the burdens of the structure. For example, assume that Investor A's shares originally bore their pro rata portion of the offshore hedge fund's performance fee even though they did not appreciate. If a subsequent Investor B also purchases shares when the offshore hedge fund has accrued a performance fee, Investor A benefits because Investor B's shares will absorb part of the performance fee that otherwise would be charged to Investor A.

§ 15.4 Other Fees Charged by Hedge Funds

1. Soft Lock-Up Fees

Some hedge funds charge a withdrawal fee, typically ranging from one to three percent of the withdrawal, for withdrawals during a given period, such as six months or one year, following the investor's investment in the hedge fund. Such a fee replaces or is offered as an alternative to a strict lock-up period during which withdrawals are prohibited. This soft lock-up may be rationalized as compensation for the hedge fund's costs in setting up the new account and unexpectedly liquidating positions to fund the withdrawal.

2. Fees on Special Withdrawals

Hedge funds often charge a fee, typically ranging from one to three percent of the withdrawal, to an investor that is allowed to withdraw funds at a time other than a prescribed withdrawal date. The fee may be rationalized as compensation for the hedge fund's accounting costs resulting from an extra break point date, when the hedge fund must value its assets and calculate its liabilities for the purpose of allocating profits and losses. Accordingly, some hedge funds limit the total fee for a special withdrawal to the estimated accounting and other administrative costs associated with a special break point date.

§ 15.5 Excessive Fees

The SEC has stated that charging an excessive fee may breach an investment adviser's fiduciary duty to a client and violate Advisers Act section 206(2).[31] Many state securities laws include similar provisions.[32] The fiduciary duty rules apply to all investment advisers, whether or not they are registered or required to be registered with the SEC. In certain circumstances, a high fee (whether asset-based or performance-based) may not breach an investment adviser's fiduciary duty if the investment adviser discloses fully to its clients that the fee exceeds fees customarily charged to accounts of similar size and objectives and that the same or similar services may be available at a lower fee from another investment adviser.[33] In other instances, however, the SEC has found an advisory fee to be so excessive that disclosure could not cure the breach of fiduciary duty.[34] The SEC and some state regulatory authorities have indicated that, depending on the services provided, they may consider an annual asset-based fee in excess of three percent of assets under management to be excessive,[35] but they have not provided definitive guidance. State securities law administrators have also stated informally that performance-based fees in excess of twenty percent may be scrutinized more closely than the customary twenty percent performance fee or allocation.[36]

---

31. Advisers Act § 206(2), 15 U.S.C. § 80b-6(2), makes it unlawful for an investment adviser "to engage in any transaction, practice, or course of business which operates as a fraud or deceit upon any client or prospective client."

32. *See, e.g.*, Cal. Corp. Code § 25238; 10 Cal. Code of Reg. § 260.238(j); Mass. Reg. § 950, CMR 12.205(9)(b)10; Colorado Rules under the Col. Sec. Act § 51-4.8(1A).J.

33. *Shareholder Services Corp.*, SEC No Action Letter (Feb. 3, 1989); *see also* Title 10, California Code of Regulations, § 260.238(j).

34. *H & H Investments*, SEC No Action Letter (Sep. 17, 1981).

35. *SEC Inspection Manual* (1980) page 15; telephone conversation with Meryl Wilson, California Department of Corporations.

36. Telephone conversation with Colorado Division of Securities.

§ 15.6 Rescission Remedy

Advisers Act section 215[37] provides that a contract for investment advisory services is void if its formation or performance would violate the Advisers Act. An advisory client has a private right of action under this section for restitution of advisory fees paid.[38] Restitution does not include compensation for any diminution in value of the client's account managed by the investment adviser, but such remedies may be available under other federal or state laws.[39]

---

37.   15 U.S.C. § 80b-15.

38.   Advisers Act § 215(b), 15 U.S.C. § 80b-15(b).

39.   *See, e.g., Transamerica Mortgage Advisors, Inc. v. Lewis*, 444 U.S. 11 (1979) (limited private right of action exists under Advisers Act only for restitution of fees paid); *Stokes v. Henson*, 217 Cal. App. 3d 187 (1990) (granting investors damages equal to rescission for investment adviser's breach of fiduciary duty and constructive fraud); *Scalp & Blade, Inc. v. Franger*, 2003 N.Y. App. Div. LEXIS 10031 (Oct. 2, 2003) (claim for lost profits is appropriate when alleging investment adviser's breach of fiduciary duty, negligence, breach of contract and fraud, among other claims).

CHAPTER 16

Tax Considerations

§ 16.1 Federal Income Tax Treatment as a Partnership

This chapter discusses U.S. Federal tax treatment of a U.S. hedge fund in sections 16.1 through 16.6, some U.S. Federal tax considerations relevant to offshore hedge funds in section 16.7, and some U.S. Federal tax considerations for the investment adviser to U.S. and offshore hedge funds in section 16.8.

1. Election to Be Taxed as Partnership

For income tax purposes, U.S. hedge funds generally prefer to be treated as partnerships to obtain "pass-through" tax treatment. Accordingly, most U.S. hedge funds are established as limited partnerships, or occasionally as limited liability companies, under state law. Treasury Regulations provide that a domestic business entity with two or more members that is not a corporation or one of certain other specified entities under state law may elect for federal income tax purposes to be taxed as either a partnership or an association taxable as a corporation.[1] Thus, a hedge fund with two or more investors established under state law as a limited partnership or limited liability company will be classified as a partnership unless it files with the IRS an election to be taxed as an association. If it does not file such an election, it will automatically, under the default classification rules, be taxed as a partnership, unless it is deemed to be a publicly traded partnership as discussed in the next section.[2]

2. Publicly Traded Partnerships

Tax Code section 7704[3] treats certain publicly traded partnerships that engage in active business activities as corporations for income tax purposes. A publicly traded

---

1. Treas. Reg. § 301.7701-3(a), 26 C.F.R. § 301.7701-3(a).
2. Treas. Reg. § 301.7701-3(b), 26 C.F.R. § 301.7701-3(b).
3. 26 U.S.C. § 7704.

partnership is a partnership whose interests (a) are traded on an established securities market (including the over-the-counter market), or (b) are readily tradeable on a secondary market or the substantial equivalent thereof. Interests in hedge funds generally are not traded on established securities markets. Under Treasury Regulations, however, interests in a hedge fund could be treated as being readily tradeable on the substantial equivalent of a secondary market if the hedge fund allows such frequent withdrawals and contributions that its liquidity is comparable to that of a security traded on a secondary market.[4] For example, a hedge fund that allows monthly withdrawals and contributions risks being deemed to be tradeable on the equivalent of a secondary market.

Tax Code section 7704(c)[5] provides an exception from treatment as a publicly traded partnership for a partnership ninety percent or more of the income of which is certain passive-type income, including interest, dividends and capital gains from disposition of property held to produce dividend or interest income. Treasury Regulations provide that income from notional principal contracts is passive income for this purpose if the property, income or cash flow that measures the amount to which the hedge fund is entitled would give rise to such passive type income.[6] While most hedge funds would meet this test, some hedge funds might engage in investments whose income tax characterization is uncertain, and the IRS may maintain that such investments do not produce qualifying passive-type income.

Even if ten percent or more of a hedge fund's income in a year does not qualify as passive-type income, the hedge fund may avoid being treated as a publicly traded partnership under Tax Code section 7704 if it qualifies for one or more safe harbors from such treatment provided in the Treasury Regulations. The safe harbor on which hedge funds commonly rely provides that interests in a hedge fund will not be considered readily tradeable on a secondary market or the substantial equivalent thereof if (a) all interests in the partnership were issued in one or more transactions that were not required to be registered under the Securities Act and (b) the partnership does not have more than 100 partners at any time during the taxable year of the partnership.[7] Offerings of interests in hedge funds generally are not required to be registered under the Securities Act. Generally, an entity that owns a hedge fund interest is treated as only one partner in determining whether the hedge fund has 100 or more partners. If, however, an entity that is a pass-through vehicle for tax purposes invests in a hedge fund, if substantially all of the entity's value is attributable to its interest in the hedge fund, and if a principal purpose of the tiered structure is to avoid the 100-partner limitation, all of the entity's owners are counted as partners in the hedge fund. A hedge fund will not comply with this safe harbor if it relies on Company Act section 3(c)(7)[8] and admits more than 100 partners. A hedge fund that fails to meet one of the safe-harbor requirements is not, however, necessarily classified as a publicly traded partnership, if its liquidity is sufficiently limited.

---

4. Treas. Reg. § 1.7704-1(c)(2), 26 C.F.R. § 1.7704-1(c)(2).
5. 26 U.S.C. § 7704(c).
6. Treas. Reg. § 1.7704-3(a)(1), 26 C.F.R. § 1.7704-3(a)(1).
7. Treas. Reg. § 1.7704-1(h), 26 C.F.R. § 1.7704-1(h).
8. *See* § 3.3, *supra*.

§ 16.2 Issues on Formation of Hedge Fund—Capital Contributions

1. Tax Basis

An investor in a hedge fund has a tax "basis" in the investor's interest in the hedge fund. This basis determines whether the investor has taxable gain or loss on a transfer of the investor's interest in the hedge fund, or on receipt of a distribution from the hedge fund. This is commonly called the investor's "outside" basis in the hedge fund. The hedge fund itself also has a tax basis for each asset it holds, which is commonly called the hedge fund's "inside" basis in such asset.

Generally, the initial basis of an investor's interest in a hedge fund equals the amount of money the investor contributed to the hedge fund, plus the adjusted tax basis of any property the investor contributed to the hedge fund, plus the investor's share of the hedge fund's liabilities. If an investor transfers property in kind to a hedge fund, and that transaction is taxable to the investor, the investor's tax basis in the hedge fund increases by the amount of any gain the investor recognizes on the transfer. If any investors are personally liable for any hedge fund liability, only those investors that are personally liable may include their proportionate shares of that liability in their adjusted tax bases. For this purpose short sales are treated as liabilities.[9]

An investor's basis is increased by the investor's share of hedge fund income and the investor's additional investments in the hedge fund. The investor's basis is reduced (but not below zero) by the investor's share of hedge fund distributions and losses. The initial basis is also decreased by any liabilities of the investor that the hedge fund assumes at the time of investment, although this adjustment typically is not relevant in the hedge fund context.

2. Special Issues on Contribution of Securities

i. Transfer to an "Investment Company"

Generally, a transferor does not recognize taxable gain or loss on the transfer of appreciated or depreciated property to the capital of a partnership. This general rule does not apply, however, and consequently gain will be recognized, if the transfer is to an "investment company" and results in diversification of the transferor's interests.[10] An entity is an investment company for this purpose if: (a) it is a registered investment company (a "mutual fund"); (b) it is a real estate investment trust (a "REIT"); or (c) more than eighty percent of the value of

---

9. Rev. Rul. 95-26, 1995-1 C.B. 131.
10. Tax Code § 721(b), 26 U.S.C. § 721(b); Treas. Reg. § 1.351-1(c)(1), 26 C.F.R. § 1.351-1(c)(1).

its assets consist of certain types of property,[11] including money, stocks or other equity interests in a corporation, evidences of indebtedness, options, forward or futures contracts, notional principal contracts and derivatives, foreign currency, interests in precious metals, interests in registered investment companies or REITS, or interests in other non-corporate entities that are convertible into any of such assets.[12] Most hedge funds are treated as "investment companies" under this eighty percent test.

A transfer will not result in diversification if each transferor transfers identical assets, or only an insignificant amount of the assets transferred by all transferors, in the aggregate, is nonidentical.[13] It is uncertain what percentage of the transferred assets can be nonidentical without causing the transfer to be taxable. Treasury Regulations provide an example in which only one percent of the transferred assets are nonidentical and state that such amount is deemed insignificant.[14] The IRS has ruled that five percent of the assets being nonidentical is insignificant but that eleven percent is significant.[15] For this purpose, cash is deemed to be nonidentical to a security.

A transfer also will not result in diversification if each transferor contributes a "diversified portfolio of assets" to the hedge fund.[16] A diversified portfolio of assets for this purpose generally is one in which not more than twenty-five percent of the value of the assets is invested in the stock or securities of one issuer and not more than fifty percent is invested in the stock or securities of five or fewer issuers. Cash transferred is generally not included in the numerator or the denominator of this formula. Government securities are included in the denominator but not in the numerator of the formula. It is not clear if short sales should be treated in this formula as liabilities or as security positions. Each transferor must transfer a diversified portfolio; if one transferor transfers a non-diversified portfolio when other transferors transfer diversified portfolios as part of the same transaction, all such transferors will be taxed on the transfer.

Whether a transfer results in diversification is generally determined by reference to the facts existing immediately after the transfer.[17] Treasury Regulations provide, however, that if a plan exists at the time of the transfer to contribute assets at a later date, those transactions can be treated as one transaction.[18]

Because most hedge funds qualify as investment companies for this purpose, and investors rarely contribute identical assets, an investor who contributes securities to a hedge fund will likely recognize taxable gain, unless that investor, and all other investors who contribute at the same time, contribute diversified portfolios of assets.

---

11. Tax Code § 351(e)(1), 26 U.S.C. § 351(e)(1); Treas. Reg. § 1.351-1(c)(1), 26 C.F.R. § 351-1(c)(1).
12. Tax Code § 351(e)(1), 26 U.S.C. § 351(e)(1).
13. Treas. Reg. § 1.351-1(c)(5), 26 C.F.R. § 1.351-1(c)(5).
14. Treas. Reg. § 1.351-1(c)(7) (Example 1), 26 C.F.R. § 1.351-1(c)(7).
15. Priv. Ltr. Rul. 200006008 (Sep. 30, 1999), 1999 PRL LEXIS 1774; Rev. Rul. 87-9, 1987-1 C.B. 133.
16. Treas. Reg. § 1.351-1(c)(6), 26 C.F.R. § 1.351-1(c)(6).
17. Treas. Reg. § 1.351-1(c)(2), 26 C.F.R. § 1.351-1(c)(2).
18. Treas. Reg. §§ 1.351-1(c)(2) and 1.351-1(c)(5), 26 C.F.R. §§ 1.351-1(c)(2) and 1.351-1(c)(5).

ii. Allocation of Gain/Loss to Contributing Partner

If an investor who contributes appreciated or depreciated securities to a hedge fund does not recognize taxable gain at the time of transfer as discussed above in section 16.2.2.i, the hedge fund generally will be required, when it eventually disposes of those contributed securities, to allocate the resulting taxable gain or loss first to the contributing investor to take into account the variation between the adjusted tax basis to the hedge fund of such securities and their fair market value when they were contributed.[19]

iii. Special Rules Regarding Contributed Securities

If a hedge fund distributes a contributed security (which was not taxed at the time of contribution) to an investor other than the contributing investor at any time within seven years after such contribution, the contributing investor generally will be required to recognize gain or loss at that time based on the unrealized appreciation or depreciation in the security when the contributing investor contributed it to the hedge fund.[20] Moreover, if the hedge fund distributes other property to that contributing investor within seven years after that investor contributed securities, the contributing investor may be required to recognize gain at the time of the distribution to reflect the unrealized appreciation in the contributed securities at the time of the contribution.[21]

If an investor who contributed a security to a hedge fund in a nontaxable transaction simultaneously or subsequently receives a distribution of cash, the contribution may be treated as if the investor sold the securities to the hedge fund for fair market value, causing the investor to recognize gain on the transfer. Treasury Regulations establish a rebuttable presumption that if an investor receives a distribution within two years after contributing securities, the distribution will be deemed to have been part of a disguised sale; the investor must disclose the transaction to the IRS, if it treats the distribution as other than a sale.[22] If, when the investor made the contribution, it did not intend to receive a distribution of cash in exchange for such contribution, and if the investor's investment in the hedge fund was subject to the appreciation or depreciation of the assets of the hedge fund while invested, the investor should be able to rebut this presumption. Similarly, if an investor receives a security in kind in a distribution within two years after contributing cash to the hedge fund, that transaction will be rebuttably presumed to have been a sale of the security by the hedge fund to the investor.[23]

---

19. Tax Code § 704(c), 26 U.S.C. § 704(c).
20. Tax Code § 704(c)(1)(B), 26 U.S.C. § 704(c)(1)(B).
21. Tax Code § 737, 26 U.S.C. § 737.
22. Treas. Reg. § 1.707-3(c), 26 C.F.R. § 1.707-3(c).
23. Treas. Reg. § 1.707-6(a), 26 C.F.R. § 1.707-6(a).

§ 16.3 Allocations of Profits and Losses for Tax Purposes

1. Pass-Through Tax Treatment

A hedge fund usually receives pass-through tax treatment as a partnership.[24] Thus, the investors in a hedge fund, and not the hedge fund itself, are taxed on the hedge fund's realized income and gains (to the extent that the investors are subject to income tax). This tax liability exists even absent cash distributions. Accordingly, an investor may have taxable income and tax liability from the hedge fund in a fiscal year when the hedge fund distributes no cash to the investor, or even in a fiscal year when such investor's capital account balance is reduced (for example, when the investor's share of net unrealized losses exceeds the investor's share of net realized income and gain for the fiscal year). Most hedge funds do not make annual distributions, even to allow investors to pay their taxes, but instead reinvest all income. Investors are expected to use other assets to pay taxes that arise from their investment in the hedge fund. Most hedge funds have, however, relatively frequent withdrawal rights, such as quarterly or semi-annually, so investors can withdraw funds to pay taxes, but many hedge funds also specify a minimum amount that an investor can withdraw. A hedge fund may grant investors a special withdrawal right to pay taxes in years when the hedge fund's taxable income allocated to investors causes a tax liability that they could not pay without liquidating other investments.

An investor may deduct its share of hedge fund losses only up to the amount of the investor's basis.[25] Losses in excess of adjusted tax basis may be carried over until the investor's outside basis is increased above zero.

The various tax items that pass through to an investor's tax return on a Form 1040, Schedule K-1 (and comparable state tax form) retain their tax character for the investor. Discussed below in this section are some of the typical tax items that pass through to a hedge fund's investors.

2. Special Incentive Profit Allocation

The general partner of most hedge funds receives a share of the profits that is disproportionate to the general partner's capital contributions. Typically, the general partner is allocated twenty percent of the profits otherwise allocable to each limited partner in excess of that limited partner's previous losses that have not yet been recouped. The hedge fund usually treats this special incentive profit allocation as an allocation of partnership profits to the general partner rather than as a guaranteed payment under Tax Code section 707(c).[26] Accordingly, such profits allocated to the general partner retain the tax character of the underlying income of the hedge fund (that is, interest, dividends, long-term or short-term

---

24. *See* § 16.1, *supra.*
25. *See* § 16.2.1, *supra,* regarding calculation of basis.
26. 26 U.S.C. § 707(c); *see* § 15.2.1, *supra.*

capital gains and unrealized gains). A limited partner's allocable share of profits is correspondingly reduced.

Hedge funds treat this special incentive profit allocation as a partnership allocation rather than as a fee, because the allocation is contingent on the partnership having profits, and is not guaranteed.[27] The IRS has indicated, however, in its Market Segment Specialization Program Guide for Partnerships, designed to assist examiners in examining partnership tax returns, that it believes that such an arrangement could be an improper shifting of the nature of the income for the general partner, and suggests that examiners consider treating it as a payment to a partner in a non-partner capacity under Tax Code section 707(a),[28] especially if the general partner does not have any of its own capital at risk in the hedge fund.[29]

3. Ordinary Income

Hedge funds generate ordinary income on interest and dividends (other than qualifying dividends) from their investments. The current maximum tax rate for individuals and corporations on ordinary income is thirty-five percent.

4. Qualifying Dividends

Hedge funds may generate qualifying dividend income that is taxed to individual partners at a maximum rate of fifteen percent.[30] Qualifying dividend income generally includes dividends received from U.S. corporations and from certain "qualified foreign corporations," subject to a holding period requirement. To be eligible for the lower tax rate, a hedge fund must hold the stock for more than sixty days during the 120-day period beginning sixty days before the ex-dividend date.[31] With respect to certain preferred stock, the hedge fund must have held the shares more than ninety days during the 180-day period beginning ninety days before the ex-dividend date. The holding period must be satisfied for each dividend payment. Days on which the stock is hedged are generally not included in the holding period.[32] Moreover, the hedge fund must not be obligated to make related payments with respect to positions in substantially similar or related property.[33]

5. Capital Gains and Losses

Hedge funds may generate capital gains on the sale or other disposition of capital assets. The current maximum rate of tax for individuals on capital gains from assets held more than a year generally is fifteen percent and on capital gains on assets held for a year or less is thirty five percent. Individuals are allowed to use

---

27.   *See* Rev. Rul. 67-158, 1967-1 C.B. 188.

28.   26 U.S.C. § 707(a).

29.   Internal Revenue Service, Market Segment Specialization Program: Partnerships (Sep. 2002) at http://www.irs.gov/pub/irs-mssp/partnershipsatg12-16.pdf (last visited Apr. 21, 2004).

30.   Tax Code § 1(h)(11), 26 U.S.C. § 1(h)(11).

31.   Tax Code § 1(h)(11)(B)(iii), 26 U.S.C. § 1(h)(11)(B)(iii).

32.   Tax Code § 246(c)(4), 26 U.S.C. § 246(c)(4).

33.   Tax Code § 246(c)(1)(B), 26 U.S.C. § 246(c)(1(B).

capital losses to offset in full capital gains. To the extent that capital losses exceed capital gains in a taxable year, such excess capital losses are also allowed against a maximum of $3,000 of ordinary income. Any capital losses not used in a taxable year may be carried forward.

The current maximum tax rate for corporations on long-term or short-term capital gains is thirty-five percent. Corporations are allowed to use capital losses to offset in full capital gains but are not allowed to offset ordinary income. Corporations generally may carry capital losses back three years and forward five years.

Rules relating to "straddle" transactions may affect a hedge fund's holding period for a security or may otherwise affect whether gain or loss is characterized as short-term or long-term, as well as when gains and losses are recognized.[34] A "straddle" for tax purposes generally arises when a hedge fund holds two or more offsetting positions in stocks, securities, option contracts, futures contracts or forward contracts, which positions, when considered together, have the effect of reducing the hedge fund's risk of loss. Adverse tax consequences may arise from these transactions, such as the deferral of losses on a straddle position and the deferral of interest deductions related to a straddle position. In addition, in determining whether any two or more positions are offsetting, an investor is treated as holding any position held by the hedge fund.[35] Consequently, an investor may be required to treat a position held individually as offsetting a position held by the hedge fund. In such a case, the straddle rules could affect the investor's holding period for the securities involved and may defer the investor's recognition of losses.

6. Gain or Loss from Short Sales

Gain or loss from a short sale of securities is generally considered a capital gain or loss to the extent that the asset used to close the short sale is a capital asset in the hedge fund's hands.[36] Except when the hedge fund has held the securities used to close a short sale for more than a year before entering into the short position, gains on short sales generally are short-term capital gains, subject to less favorable tax rates.[37] A loss on a short sale generally is treated as a long-term capital loss if, on the date of the short sale, the hedge fund has held "substantially identical property" for more than a year.[38] Special rules may also shorten the holding period of any assets held by the hedge fund that are "substantially identical" to those used to close the short sale.

7. Constructive Sale Transactions

Under Tax Code section 1259,[39] if a hedge fund engages in a constructive sale of an appreciated financial position, the transaction results in recognition of gain. A constructive sale for this purpose includes: (a) a short sale of the same or

---

34.   Tax Code § 1092, 26 U.S.C. § 1092.
35.   Tax Code § 1092(d)(4), 26 U.S.C. § 1092(d)(4).
36.   Tax Code § 1233(a), 26 U.S.C. § 1233(a).
37.   Tax Code § 1233(b), 26 U.S.C. § 1233(b).
38.   Tax Code § 1233(d), 26 U.S.C. § 1233(d).
39.   26 U.S.C. § 1259.

substantially identical property (short sales "against the box"); (b) an offsetting notional principal contract of the same or substantially identical property; (c) a futures or forward contract to deliver the same or substantially identical property; (d) with respect to an appreciated financial position that is one of the above, acquiring the same or substantially identical property; or (e) other transactions provided in Treasury Regulations.[40] A constructive sale does not result in recognition of gain during a taxable year if the offsetting position is closed within thirty days after the end of the taxable year, and the appreciated position is held unhedged for at least sixty days after the closing of the offsetting position.[41] The Treasury has yet to promulgate Treasury Regulations under Tax Code section 1259. In drafting the statute, Congress indicated, however, that it expected that Treasury Regulations would cause transactions such as collars to be treated in some instances as constructive sales.[42]

8. Wash Sales

If a hedge fund sells or disposes of a security for a loss and within the period beginning thirty days before and ending thirty days after such sale or disposition, acquires, or enters into an option or contract to acquire, substantially identical securities, the loss will be disallowed.[43] The tax basis of the acquired securities is adjusted generally to reflect the amount of the disallowed loss.

9. Section 1256 Contracts

Tax Code section 1256[44] generally requires that "section 1256 contracts" held by a partnership at the end of each taxable year be treated as if the partnership sold them for their fair market value on the last business day of such taxable year. A hedge fund must include in its income for the year the net gain or loss from such deemed sales (called "marking to market"), together with any gain or loss from actual sales of section 1256 contracts (adjusted to reflect prior deemed sales). Section 1256 contracts include certain regulated futures contracts, foreign currency forward contracts and options contracts. Forty percent of the capital gains and losses from deemed and actual sales of section 1256 contracts generally is short-term capital gains and losses and the other sixty percent is long-term capital gains and losses.[45] Gains and losses with respect to certain options purchased by options dealers or futures contracts purchased by futures dealers are short-term capital gains and losses to limited partners.[46]

---

40. Tax Code § 1259(c)(1), 26 U.S.C. § 1259(c)(1). No such Treasury Regulations have yet been issued.
41. Tax Code § 1259(c)(3), 26 U.S.C. § 1259(c)(3).
42. Committee Reports on P.L. 105-34.
43. Tax Code § 1091, 26 U.S.C. § 1091.
44. 26 U.S.C. § 1256.
45. Tax Code § 1256(a)(3), 26 U.S.C. § 1256(a)(3).
46. Tax Code § 1256(f)(4), 26 U.S.C. § 1256(f)(4).

10. Deduction Items

i. Trader vs. Investor

Whether a hedge fund is characterized as an "investor" or as a "trade or business" determines how the investors in the hedge fund may treat the hedge fund's expenses (including the management fee) on their tax returns. A trader for this purpose generally seeks profits from short-term swings in the market. Thus, a trader usually generates little interest, dividends or long-term capital gain income.[47] An investor, on the other hand, purchases and sells securities with the principal purpose of realizing income in the form of interest, dividends and long-term appreciation of securities.[48] The Tax Court has set forth three factors to consider in determining whether a taxpayer trading for its own account is a trader or investor: (a) the taxpayer's investment intent; (b) the nature of the income derived from the activity (long-term capital gains, interest and dividends as opposed to mainly short-term capital gains); and (c) the frequency, extent and regularity of the taxpayer's securities transactions.[49] Under this last factor, a hedge fund may be deemed to be a trader based on the frequency of its trading, if the portfolio is large enough that it is making daily trades, even if most of its income is derived from long-term capital gains.

A trader's expenses relating to its trade or business are fully deductible in determining adjusted gross income. The deductibility of an investor's expenses is limited. Under Tax Code section 67(c),[50] temporary Treasury Regulations[51] prevent a taxpayer from deducting indirectly, through a pass-through entity such as a partnership, expenses that would not be deductible if paid or incurred directly by such taxpayer. The Tax Code limits a number of deductions characterized as "miscellaneous itemized deductions," including those for expenditures related to investment income or property, which are deductible under Tax Code section 212.[52] Miscellaneous itemized deductions, including those related to investment income or property, are deductible only to the extent that in total they exceed two percent of the taxpayer's adjusted gross income.[53] The deductible portion, if any, of such expenditures is further reduced if a partner's adjusted gross income exceeds a specified threshold amount.[54] If the hedge fund is an investor, management fees payable to the hedge fund's investment adviser and other expenses of the hedge fund constitute expenditures related to investment income or property and thus are deductible by a limited partner only to the extent that those expenditures plus the limited partner's other miscellaneous itemized deductions exceed two percent of the limited partner's adjusted gross income in any taxable year. The

---

47.   *Chang Hsiao Liang v. Commissioner*, 23 T.C. 1040, 1955 Tax Ct. LEXIS 223 (1955).

48.   *Yaeger Estate v. Commissioner*, 55 (CCH) TCM 1101 (1988), aff'd 889 F.2d 29, 89-2 U.S. Tax Cas. (CCH) ¶ 9633 (1989).

49.   *Hart v. Commissioner*, 73 (CCH) TCM 1684 (1997).

50.   26 U.S.C. § 67(c).

51.   Treas. Reg. § 1.67-2T, 26 C.F.R. § 1.67-2T.

52.   26 U.S.C. § 212.

53.   Tax Code § 67(a), 26 U.S.C. § 67(a).

54.   Tax Code § 68, 26 U.S.C. § 68.

IRS might also argue that the special incentive profit allocation[55] to the general partner of a hedge fund is an expense, rather than a partnership profit allocation, in which case its deductibility would also be subject to these limits.

If the hedge fund is instead deemed to be engaged in a trade or business, management fees and other expenses are not deemed to be investment expenditures, and their deductibility is not limited as described above.

ii. Interest Expense

Under Tax Code section 163(d),[56] a taxpayer generally may deduct investment interest only to the extent of the taxpayer's "net investment income." Interest expense on indebtedness incurred to invest in or hold interests in a hedge fund is subject to the investment interest limitation. Any deduction for investment interest that is disallowed may be carried over to subsequent years to offset net investment income. An investor's share of interest expense incurred by a hedge fund in carrying on its business also might be subject to the investment interest expense limitation, depending on whether the hedge fund is a trader or investor.

Tax Code section 265(a)(2)[57] disallows any deduction for interest paid by a taxpayer on indebtedness incurred or continued for the purpose of purchasing or holding tax-exempt obligations. The IRS has announced that such purpose will be deemed to exist with respect to indebtedness incurred to finance a "portfolio investment," and that while a partnership's purpose in incurring indebtedness will be attributed to its general partners, an investment in a hedge fund will be regarded as a "portfolio investment." Therefore, if a hedge fund investor owns tax-exempt obligations outside of the hedge fund, the IRS might take the position that any interest the investor pays in connection with the investment in the hedge fund should be viewed as incurred to enable the investor to continue holding those tax-exempt obligations, and that the investor should not be allowed to deduct the investor's full allocable share of such interest.

iii. Organization and Syndication Expenses

No deduction is allowed for expenses paid or incurred to organize a partnership or to promote the sale of, or sell interests in, a partnership.[58] A partnership may, however, elect to deduct $5,000 of organizational expenses (reduced, but not below zero, by organizational expenses in excess of $50,000) in the first year of operation and amortize the remainder over fifteen years.[59] Under Treasury Regulations, organizational expenses include filing fees and legal costs of negotiating and preparing the partnership agreement, whereas syndication expenses include brokerage fees related to sales of interests, legal costs of preparing the private placement memorandum, and costs of securities law counseling.[60]

---

55. *See* § 16.3.2, *supra.*
56. 26 U.S.C. § 163(d).
57. 26 U.S.C. § 265(a)(2).
58. Tax Code § 709, 26 U.S.C. § 709.
59. Tax Code § 709(b), 26 U.S.C. § 709(b).
60. Treas. Reg. § 1.709-2, 26 C.F.R. § 1.709-2.

A general partner of a hedge fund may pay a finder a share of the general partner's asset-based management fees or incentive profit allocations for introducing investors to the hedge fund. Such expenses are arguably syndication expenses under these rules and thus may be nondeductible by the hedge fund or its general partner.

11. Hedge Funds Are Not Engaged in Passive Activities

A hedge fund generally is not considered to be engaged in a passive activity, and the investors' distributive shares of income, gain or loss are not considered passive income, gain or loss. Temporary Treasury Regulations section 1.469-1T(e)(6)[61] provides that trading personal property, including stocks, bonds and other securities, for the account of owners of the trading entity is not a passive activity, whether or not such trading is a trade or business. Accordingly, an investor's ability to deduct losses of the hedge fund is not limited by the passive loss rule (other limitations may apply, however, as discussed above in sections 16.3.1, 16.3.5, 16.3.8 and 16.3.10). An investor's passive losses from other investment activities are not deductible against the investor's distributive share of the hedge fund's income or gain.

12. Aggregate Allocations versus Layering

Hedge funds maintain capital accounts for book purposes, taking into account unrealized gains and losses as provided in Treasury Regulations.[62] Taking unrealized gains and losses into account is necessary both to reflect gain and loss equitably when partners withdraw or contribute funds and to calculate the general partner's special incentive profit allocation. Income tax allocations are, however, calculated by taking into account only realized gains and losses. Accordingly, book allocations of gain or loss may (and typically do) differ each period from tax allocations of gain or loss. A partnership that revalues its capital accounts to reflect unrealized gains and losses must use a reasonable method to take into account any variation between the adjusted tax basis of the property and its revalued value for book purposes.[63] A partnership is not required to use the same method for allocating gain or loss to partners who have contributed property in kind (704(c) allocations) as it does to make allocations with respect to revalued property (reverse 704(c) allocations).

A hedge fund that qualifies as a "security partnership" under Treasury Regulations can make reverse 704(c) allocations by aggregating gains and losses related to qualified financial assets. To qualify as a securities partnership, a hedge fund must: (a) make its book allocations in proportion to capital account balances (except for reasonable incentive profit allocations to the general partner or

---

61.   26 C.F.R. § 1.469–1T(e)(6).

62.   Treas. Reg. § 1.704–1(b)(2)(iv)(f), 26 C.F.R. § 1.704–1(b)(2)(iv)(f).

63.   Treas. Reg. §§ 1.704–3(a) and 1.704–3(a)(6), 26 C.F.R. §§ 1.704–3(a) and 1.704–3(a)(6).

investment adviser); (b) on the date of each capital account revaluation, have at least ninety percent of its non–cash assets qualify as qualified financial assets; and (c) expect to make revaluations at least annually.[64] Qualified financial assets are generally assets that are traded on an established financial market.[65] Accordingly, a hedge fund generally cannot hold more than ten percent of its assets as private securities as of any revaluation date (generally the end of each fiscal quarter) if it wants to use the aggregate method of tax allocations. The Treasury Regulations provide examples of permissible aggregate allocation methods, including full netting and partial netting approaches.[66]

A hedge fund that is not permitted to use an aggregate allocation method must allocate taxable gains and losses on a security by security basis whenever a particular security is sold or otherwise disposed of and taxable gain or loss is realized, by taking into account which partners' capital accounts were credited or debited for book purposes with appreciation or depreciation of that security (called "layering"). Layering is generally more costly for a hedge fund and more difficult to administer than using an aggregate allocation method.

13. Unrelated Business Taxable Income

Tax-exempt investors are taxed on their pro-rata shares of any unrelated business taxable income ("UBTI") of a hedge fund.[67] UBTI is generally defined as the gross income from any trade or business unrelated to the tax-exempt business of the entity.[68] To the extent that UBTI, from all sources, of a tax-exempt entity, less its allocable share of deductions directly connected with carrying on any such trade or business, exceeds $1,000 in any year, the tax-exempt entity is liable for taxes with respect to the excess at tax rates that would apply if the organization were not exempt from taxation.

Generally, hedge funds do not invest in other entities that are themselves engaged in a trade or business and that are structured as pass-through entities for tax purposes. A hedge fund that invests in private securities may, however, occasionally invest in a start-up company that is engaged in a trade or business and structured as a pass-through entity, such as a limited liability company, which might generate UBTI.

UBTI does not include interest and dividend income, or gains on the sale, exchange or other disposition of assets held for investment.[69] Income from "debt-financed property" (such as gain from the sale of stock purchased on margin) will, however, constitute UBTI to tax-exempt entities, in the percentage that such property is subject to "acquisition indebtedness" (the percentage that acquisition indebtedness respecting such property bears to the hedge fund's adjusted tax

---

64.   Treas. Reg. § 1.704-3(e)(3), 26 C.F.R. § 1.704-3(e)(3).
65.   Treas. Reg. § 1.1092(d)-1, 26 C.F.R. § 1.1092(d)-1.
66.   Treas. Reg. §§ 1.704-3(e)(iv) and 1.704-3(e)(v), 26 C.F.R. §§ 1.704-3(e)(iv) and 1.704-3(e)(v).
67.   Tax Code § 511, 26 U.S.C. § 511.
68.   Tax Code § 512(a)(1), 26 U.S.C. § 512(a)(1).
69.   Tax Code §§ 512(b)(1) and 512(b)(5), 26 U.S.C. §§ 512(b)(1) and 512(b)(5).

basis for such property).[70] Generally, "acquisition indebtedness" is indebtedness incurred directly or indirectly in connection with the acquisition or improvement of property. Indebtedness incurred after the acquisition or improvement of any debt-financed property also constitutes "acquisition indebtedness," if the indebtedness would not have been incurred but for such acquisition or improvement and the incurrence of such indebtedness is reasonably foreseeable at the time of such acquisition or improvement.[71] Many hedge funds purchase securities through margin accounts and other debt-financed means, and under other circumstances that may be treated as involving acquisition indebtedness. The IRS has ruled, however, that short sales generally are not treated as liabilities for purposes of determining UBTI.[72] If a tax-exempt entity borrows to invest in a hedge fund, the acquisition financing of the investment may result in the realization of UBTI.

The receipt of UBTI by a tax-exempt entity generally does not affect that entity's tax-exempt status or the exemption of its other income. If a charitable remainder trust, however, receives any UBTI during a taxable year, all of its income from all sources for that year will be taxable.[73] Accordingly, charitable remainder trusts ordinarily do not invest in hedge funds that invest on margin. In addition, in some circumstances the continued receipt of UBTI over time may cause some other types of tax-exempt entities to lose their tax exemptions. Tax-exempt entities that want to avoid incurring UBTI with respect to an investment in a hedge fund that trades on margin may consider investing in an offshore hedge fund that is structured as a corporation for U.S. income tax purposes.[74]

14. Marking to Market

A hedge fund that is treated as a "trade or business"[75] may elect to mark to market its portfolio under Tax Code section 475(f).[76] If it makes this election, the hedge fund's securities or commodities on the last business day of each year are treated as though they are sold for tax purposes and the resulting gain or loss is ordinary in character. A hedge fund that is treated as an "investor," as opposed to a "trade or business," is not permitted to make this election. The election may accelerate recognition of income or loss and convert long-term capital gains to ordinary income. The mark-to-market election simplifies tax accounting, however, and eliminates the need to make many tax adjustments described above (such as wash sales, straddles and constructive sales) because income and character adjustments are done in the aggregate with respect to all securities. A hedge fund that trades frequently and generates little or no long-term capital gain income may benefit from making the election, because it obviates the tracking of those adjustments. A hedge fund that trades in both commodities and securities can make a separate

---

70. Tax Code § 512(b)(4), 26 U.S.C. § 512(b)(4).
71. Tax Code § 514(c), 26 U.S.C. § 514(c).
72. Rev. Rul. 95-8, 1995-1 C.B. 107.
73. Tax Code § 664(c), 26 U.S.C. § 664(c).
74. *See* § 16.7.6, *infra*.
75. *See* § 16.3.10.i, *supra*.
76. 26 U.S.C. § 475(f).

election to mark to market either its securities trading activities or its commodities trading activities.[77] Once made, the election remains in effect for all succeeding years (including with respect to securities or commodities purchased in succeeding years) and cannot be revoked without the permission of the IRS.[78]

§ 16.4 Withdrawals

1. Distribution of Cash

An investor is taxed on the taxable income of the hedge fund, whether or not the hedge fund distributes any income or capital to the investor.[79] A partner's adjusted tax basis increases by the amount of any taxable income allocated to it. A cash distribution of the hedge fund's income normally does not result in further taxable income to the investor, except to the extent that the distribution exceeds the investor's adjusted tax basis, in which case, it generally is treated as gain from the sale or exchange of an interest in the hedge fund. The taxation of such gain is subject to the same kinds of considerations as are discussed below in section 16.4.3.

2. Distribution of Securities in Kind

Hedge funds sometimes distribute securities in kind. A distribution of marketable securities is treated under Tax Code section 731(c)[80] as a distribution of cash subject to the consequences discussed above in section 16.4.1, unless the distributing partnership qualifies as an "investment partnership" and the other requirements of Tax Code section 731(c) are met. An "investment partnership" for this purpose is any partnership that has never been engaged in a trade or business (other than as a trader of securities) and substantially all of the assets of which have always consisted of money, stock, notes, bonds and other evidences of indebtedness, interest rate, currency or equity notional principal contracts, foreign currencies and derivatives (including options and forward contracts). Marketable securities for this purpose generally means financial instruments and foreign currencies that are treated as actively traded under Tax Code section 1092(d)(1),[81] and certain other assets listed in Tax Code section 731(c)(2)(B).[82] Most hedge funds qualify as investment partnerships and thus their distributions of securities in kind, whether or not marketable, generally should not be treated as distributions of cash, but instead are nontaxable.

77.   Tax Code § 475(f)(3), 26 U.S.C. § 475(f)(3).
78.   *Id.*
79.   *See* § 16.3.1, *supra.*
80.   26 U.S.C. § 731(c).
81.   26 U.S.C. § 1092(d)(1).
82.   26 U.S.C. § 731(c)(2)(B).

When a hedge fund distributes a security in kind in a nontaxable transaction, other than on withdrawal of all of an investor's capital account, the investor's adjusted tax basis in the security distributed is the lesser of the hedge fund's adjusted tax basis in that security and the investor's adjusted tax basis in the investor's interest in the partnership.[83] If a hedge fund distributes a security in kind in a nontaxable transaction on withdrawal of all of an investor's capital account, the investor's adjusted tax basis in the security distributed is the same as the investor's adjusted tax basis in the investor's interest in the hedge fund, reduced by any cash received in the distribution.[84] The investor's gain or loss on a later sale of such asset is the difference between the amount realized on the sale and the investor's adjusted tax basis in the asset. The character of such gain (capital gain or ordinary income) depends on the character of the asset in the hands of the investor. The investor normally may add the hedge fund's holding period to the investor's holding period to determine whether the gain is long-term or short-term.[85]

When a partner withdraws, therefore, a hedge fund can distribute to that investor securities with an aggregate fair market value equal to the investor's capital account, but with a tax basis to the hedge fund less than the investor's adjusted tax basis in its interest in the hedge fund, and effectively reduce the unrealized gains in the hedge fund for the remaining investors. The remaining partners would realize those gains ultimately when they withdraw from the hedge fund or the hedge fund dissolves. On the other hand, if the hedge fund distributes to a withdrawing partner securities with an aggregate tax basis higher than the withdrawing investor's adjusted tax basis, the hedge fund increases unrealized gains for the remaining investors, and those remaining investors are more likely to realize a capital loss when they withdraw from the hedge fund or the hedge fund dissolves.

A distribution of securities to a partner who initially contributed securities to the hedge fund, or who has invested in the hedge fund within the last two years, and a distribution of securities originally contributed to the hedge fund by an investor, are subject to additional tax considerations.[86]

If a hedge fund distributes short positions in kind to an investor, the IRS might contend that the transaction is a disguised sale, because the investor assumed a liability of the hedge fund.

3. Sale of Interests

In general, when an investor sells or disposes of its interest in a hedge fund, in a taxable transaction, the investor realizes gain or loss equal to the difference between the amount realized on the disposition and the adjusted tax basis of the investor's interest in the hedge fund. If the investor's interest in the hedge fund is a capital asset (as ordinarily is the case), the gain or loss from the sale or other taxable disposition is generally treated as capital gain or loss, and will be short-term or long-term depending on whether the investor held that interest for more than a year.

---

83. Tax Code § 732(a), 26 U.S.C. § 732(a).
84. Tax Code § 732(b), 26 U.S.C. § 732(b).
85. Tax Code § 1223, 26 U.S.C. § 1223.
86. *See* § 16.2.2.iii, *supra*.

4. Section 754 Election

When an investor transfers an interest in a hedge fund to another investor, including on the transferor's death, the transferee investor's outside tax basis in the interest in the hedge fund may not match the transferee's share of the hedge fund's inside basis in its assets, because the transferee's basis in the interest reflects the hedge fund's unrealized gains or losses. In such case, when those gains or losses are realized, the transferee would be required to pay tax on gains or be allocated losses that effectively occurred before the transferee's investment, even though those gains or losses presumably were reflected in the price paid for the interest. To avoid these discrepancies, the hedge fund can make an election under Tax Code section 754[87] pursuant to which the basis of the hedge fund's securities is adjusted on a transfer, but only with respect to the new investor. If the hedge fund had unrealized gains at the time of the transfer, and thus the transferee's outside basis is higher than the hedge fund's inside basis in its assets, the election results in an increase in the hedge fund's basis in its assets. On the other hand, if the hedge fund had unrealized losses at the time of the transfer, the election will ordinarily decrease the hedge fund's inside basis in its assets. Accordingly, if a hedge fund's assets have appreciated, the failure to make such an election generally causes a transferee to recognize more taxable income on the disposition of the hedge fund's assets than if such election had been made (although the transferee would then ordinarily receive an offsetting loss when it withdraws from the hedge fund or the hedge fund dissolves). Hence, a transferee may not be willing to pay as much for interests in the hedge fund as the transferee would pay if an election under Tax Code section 754 had been made.

A similar adjustment may be made under Tax Code section 754 when an investor withdraws from a hedge fund and receives a distribution that is more or less than its adjusted tax basis, which also can result in a discrepancy between the hedge fund's aggregate inside basis in its assets and the partners' aggregate outside basis in the hedge fund interest.

As a practical matter, hedge funds rarely make elections under Tax Code section 754, because of the administrative and accounting difficulties that arise in tracking those adjustments with frequent contributions and withdrawals. Once made, a Tax Code section 754 election is irrevocable without the consent of the IRS.[88] As noted above, such an election results in both increases and decreases in the hedge fund's inside basis in its assets, and thus can have both positive and negative results.

Tax Code section 743 requires a section 754 adjustment on a transfer of a partnership interest with a "substantial" built-in loss (loss of more than $250,000 in the value of partnership property) and on a distribution resulting in a substantial basis reduction (more than $250,000).

Most hedge funds do not permit frequent transfers of interests between parties, so the adjustment required under Tax Code section 743 will probably have limited effect. Tax Code section 743 also provides that an "investment partnership" can elect not to make the basis adjustment, and instead may disallow losses for the

---

87. 26 U.S.C. § 754.
88. *Id.*

transferee partner from the sale of partnership property, except to the extent that such losses exceed the loss recognized by the transferor. Most hedge funds will not, however, qualify as investment partnerships under this provision and thus will not be able to make this election. To qualify as an investment partnership for purposes of Tax Code section 743, a hedge fund must, among other things, (a) have substantive restrictions on each partner's ability to redeem its interests, (b) never have been a "trader," as opposed to an "investor,"[89] (c) have a life of no more than fifteen years (twenty years for partnerships in existence prior to June 4, 2004), and (d) have issued all partnership interests pursuant to a private offering within twenty-four months of the first capital contribution to the hedge fund.

A hedge fund may be able to avoid the mandatory adjustment on distributions under Tax Code section 734 when there would be a downward adjustment by using a fill-up provision (discussed below).

5. "Fill-Up" or "Stuffing" Provisions

Instead of making an election under Tax Code section 754, some hedge funds use what is commonly called a "fill-up" or "stuffing" provision to attempt to keep the hedge fund's inside basis in its assets approximately equal to the partners' aggregate outside bases and avoid the discrepancies that occur when an investor withdraws some or all of an investment from the hedge fund when there are unrealized gains or losses. Under a "stuffing" provision in the hedge fund's partnership agreement, the hedge fund allocates taxable gain and income first to a partner who has withdrawn an amount in excess of the partner's adjusted tax basis in the hedge fund to the extent of such difference. Similarly, a partner who withdraws from a hedge fund when the partner's outside basis exceeds the partner's capital account is allocated taxable losses to the extent of such difference. While such an allocation generally does not increase or decrease the amount of gain or loss the partner incurs due to withdrawal, it can change the character of the gain for the withdrawing partner. For example, if a partner has held an interest in the hedge fund for more than a year, gain on a withdrawal in excess of the partner's basis would generally be long-term capital gain, but the hedge fund might allocate short-term capital gain and ordinary income to the partner under the stuffing provision, thus changing the character and resulting in a higher tax rate. Additionally, the stuffing provision could cause a withdrawing partner to recognize gain in the year of withdrawal, rather than the year payment is received, with respect to a partner who withdraws near the end of a taxable year.

Absent an election under Tax Code section 754 or a stuffing provision, when a partner withdraws an amount in excess of the partner's adjusted tax basis, the remaining partners could be allocated the taxable gains or income incurred in disposing of assets to fund the withdrawal. Although a stuffing provision arguably should be treated as a reasonable aggregate allocation method for making reverse 704(c) allocations,[90] the IRS has not specifically ruled that such a provision will be respected. The IRS might argue that such a provision is an inappropriate

---

89.   *See* § 16.3.10.i, *supra.*
90.   *See* § 16.3.12, *supra.*

means of avoiding making an election under Tax Code section 754. In addition, the IRS might well challenge such a provision if it were not applied consistently to all withdrawing partners.

§ 16.5 Divisions and Combinations of Hedge Funds

Investment advisers occasionally restructure their hedge funds, for example, by dividing one hedge fund into two or by merging two hedge funds into one. An investment adviser with one hedge fund that relies on the exception from the definition of "investment company" provided by Company Act section 3(c)(1) might want to establish a second hedge fund that will rely on the exception in Company Act section 3(c)(7), and move those investors who qualify as "qualified purchasers" into the new section 3(c)(7) hedge fund. Similarly, an investment adviser with a section 3(c)(1) hedge fund and a section 3(c)(7) hedge fund may decide that having two hedge funds is unnecessary and combine them.[91]

1. Division of Hedge Funds

At least two alternative structures are available for moving investors into a new hedge fund. First, the hedge fund can distribute assets in kind to the investors who are being moved, and then those investors can contribute those assets to the new hedge fund in exchange for partnership interests. The distribution of securities in kind to the investors generally should not be a taxable event as long as the transaction qualifies under Tax Code section 731[92] as a distribution by an investment partnership, and none of the special circumstances discussed above in section 16.2.2.iii apply (such as a disguised sale of a security to a partner who recently contributed cash, or a distribution of a security that itself was recently contributed to the hedge fund). The subsequent contribution of the securities to the new hedge fund will also not be taxable if the transfer does not result in a diversification of the transferors' interests,[93] either because all of the transferors transfer identical securities and no other transferors transfer nonidentical assets at the same time, or because all transferors transfer diversified portfolios of assets.

Alternatively, the hedge fund could contribute the assets in kind first to the new hedge fund and then distribute interests in the new hedge fund in kind to the investors who are being moved. That transaction will also generally be nontaxable if no diversification occurs on the contribution and the requirements of Tax Code section 731 and other special provisions are met with respect to the subsequent distribution.

---

91. *See generally* Chapter 3, *supra.*
92. *See* § 16.4.2, *supra.*
93. *See* § 16.2.2.i, *supra.*

The new hedge fund's tax basis in its assets may differ after the transfer under these two approaches. Generally, if the existing hedge fund ("hedge fund 1") fully redeems an investor's interest in hedge fund 1 by distributing to the investor a proportionate share of hedge fund 1's assets, and the investor subsequently recontributes those assets to the new hedge fund ("hedge fund 2") in a nontaxable transaction, hedge fund 2 will receive a basis in the contributed assets equal to the investor's former outside basis in hedge fund 1. In contrast, if hedge fund 1 contributes its assets to hedge fund 2 in exchange for interests in hedge fund 2 and then distributes those interests in kind to investors in hedge fund 1, hedge fund 2 will receive a basis in the contributed assets equal to hedge fund 1's former inside basis in its assets. Whether one of these options is preferable depends on the difference between the aggregate outside bases of the investors being moved and the inside basis of the hedge fund in the assets being transferred. Absent clear evidence of which approach is being used, the IRS will deem the assets to have first been contributed to the new hedge fund and then interests in that hedge fund to have been distributed in kind to the investors.[94] In addition, the IRS may not respect a transaction that is structured as a distribution of assets followed by a contribution if the investors never formally take title to the assets before transferring them to the new hedge fund.[95]

When a partnership divides into two or more partnerships, and a new partnership is more than fifty percent owned after the transaction by the former partners of the prior partnership, the new partnership is deemed to be a continuation of the prior partnership. Even if the transaction is structured as a formation of a new partnership and the transfer of some partners to that new partnership, the new partnership may be treated for tax purposes as the continuing partnership, and the old partnership as a new entity.[96] The new partnership would thus keep the taxpayer identification number and retain the elections made by the old partnership.

A hedge fund could distribute cash to an investor and then have that investor contribute that cash to the new hedge fund. This would be a taxable event, but may not materially increase the tax liability if the investor is a tax–exempt entity or has little or no gain (or has a loss) in the interest. If an investor with an unrealized loss in a hedge fund interest is distributed cash and contributes that cash to the new hedge fund, which holds the same securities as held by the old hedge fund, the wash sale rules[97] would likely disallow deduction of the loss.

2. Combination of Hedge Funds

Two hedge funds can be combined by having one hedge fund either (a) contribute all of its assets to the other hedge fund and then distribute interests of the other hedge fund in kind, or (b) distribute all of its assets to its partners in kind and then have them contribute such assets in kind to the other hedge fund. These transfers

---

94.   Treas. Reg. § 1.708–1(d)(3), 26 C.F.R. § 1.708–1(d)(3).

95.   *Id.*

96.   Treas. Reg. § 1.708–1(d), 26 C.F.R. § 1.708–1(d).

97.   *See* § 16.3.8, *supra.*

would generally have the same consequences as discussed above in section 16.5.1 with respect to divisions of hedge funds, and could result in a different tax basis in the transferred securities for the continuing hedge fund, depending on which form is used.

When two hedge funds are merged or otherwise combined, the combined hedge fund is deemed the continuation of the hedge fund in which the former partners own more than fifty percent of the capital and profits of the combined hedge fund. If the combined hedge fund can be considered to be a continuation of both hedge funds (due to overlap of partners) the hedge fund that contributes the greater amount of assets to the combined hedge fund is deemed to be the continuing hedge fund.[98] Accordingly, even if the transaction is structured for state law purposes as the merger or other combination of hedge fund 1 into hedge fund 2, the IRS may deem the transaction to have been the combination of hedge fund 2 into hedge fund 1. If it is not clear which form of transaction is being used, the IRS will deem the hedge fund that is going out of existence for tax purposes to have contributed its assets to the continuing hedge fund, and then to have distributed the interests in the continuing hedge fund to its partners in dissolution.[99]

§ 16.6 Dissolution

When a hedge fund dissolves, any of its remaining assets normally would be sold, which would cause the investors to realize taxable gain or loss. Distributions of cash in complete liquidation of a hedge fund are generally treated first as a return of capital to the extent of an investor's tax basis in the hedge fund and thereafter as a capital gain, to the extent of the amount of cash distributed. Generally, when a hedge fund liquidates or terminates, an investor recognizes income only to the extent that cash distributed exceeds the investor's adjusted tax basis in the investment at the time of distribution. A distribution of assets on liquidation generally has the results discussed in section 16.4.2.

---

98. Treas. Reg. § 1.708-1(c)(1), 26 C.F.R. § 1.708-1(c)(1).
99. Treas. Reg. § 1.708-1(c)(3), 26 C.F.R. § 1.708-1(c)(3).

§ 16.7 Offshore Hedge Funds

1. General

Except with respect to certain withholding taxes,[100] a hedge fund established under the laws of a jurisdiction outside the United States generally is subject to U.S. income taxation only if it is deemed to be engaged in the conduct of a trade or business within the United States. If the offshore hedge fund is treated as a corporation for U.S. tax purposes, the investors generally are not subject to U.S. tax on their proportionate shares of the income of the entity (subject to special rules discussed below).[101] Most offshore hedge funds are therefore structured to be treated as corporations for U.S. income tax purposes.

Offshore hedge funds are generally marketed to non-U.S. investors and U.S. investors that are exempt from income tax. Non-U.S. investors often prefer to invest in the U.S. securities market through offshore hedge funds, rather than investing directly in U.S. securities or in U.S.-based hedge funds, primarily to limit their exposure to the IRS and other U.S. regulatory authorities, and in some cases to avoid U.S. estate taxes. U.S. tax-exempt entities invest in offshore hedge funds to be able to invest in leveraged portfolios without recognizing unrelated business taxable income (UBTI).[102]

2. Classification of Entity

Under Treasury Regulations, a business entity established under the laws of a jurisdiction outside the United States can elect to be treated as a corporation or a partnership for U.S. income tax purposes, unless it is one of certain entities listed by the IRS as "Per Se" corporations that are automatically treated as corporations.[103]

A non-U.S. entity that is not treated as a Per Se corporation is classified: (a) as a partnership if it has two or more members and at least one member has unlimited liability; (b) as a corporation if all members have limited liability; or (c) disregarded as an entity separate from its owner if it has only one owner and that owner has unlimited liability.[104] If an entity that is not treated as a Per Se corporation wants to be classified differently from its treatment under these default rules, the entity must file an election on Form 8832. The election must be filed no earlier than twelve months before and no later than seventy-five days after the desired effective date.[105]

---

100. *See* § 16.7.5, *infra.*

101. *See* § 16.7.4, *infra.*

102. If the offshore hedge fund is treated as a partnership for U.S. tax purposes, any income, gain, loss or credit of the offshore hedge fund will pass through to the investors, and will be taxable or not to the investors based on their status as non-resident aliens, non-U.S. entities, U.S. taxpayers or U.S. tax-exempt entities. *See also* § 16.7.6, *infra.*

103. Treas. Reg. § 301.7701-2(b)(8), 26 C.F.R. § 301.7701-2(b)(8).

104. Treas. Reg. § 301.7701-3(b)(2), 26 C.F.R. § 301.7701-3(b)(2).

105. Treas. Reg. § 301.7701-3(c), 26 C.F.R. § 301.7701-3(c).

Most offshore hedge funds are entities in which all members have limited liability under the laws of the local jurisdiction, such as exempted limited companies under the laws of the Cayman Islands. These entities are treated as corporations under the default classification rule. Offshore hedge funds that desire to be treated for tax purposes as partnerships, such as master funds,[106] often are structured as limited partnerships under the laws of the offshore jurisdiction, and thus are classified as partnerships under the default rule. An offshore hedge fund that is uncertain as to the default classification may file a protective Form 8832 on its formation to assure the desired treatment.

3. U.S. Trade or Business

As noted above, an offshore hedge fund is generally not subject to U.S. income taxation (except with respect to certain withholding taxes),[107] if it is not engaged in a U.S. trade or business. Tax Code section 864(b)(2)(A) and Treasury Regulations section 1.864-2(c)(2)(ii) provide that "trade or business within the United States" does not include trading in securities for a taxpayer's own account. "Securities" for this purpose means any note, bond, debenture or other evidence of indebtedness or any evidence of an interest in or right to purchase any of the above.[108] The volume or frequency of stock transactions in which the offshore hedge fund engages is irrelevant for this determination. It does not matter whether the hedge fund is deemed to be a "trader," rather than an "investor," as described above.[109]

This exception does not apply, however, if the taxpayer is a dealer in stocks or securities.[110] A "dealer" for this purpose is defined as a merchant of stocks or securities with an established place of business regularly engaged in purchasing stocks or securities and selling them to customers with a view to the gains and profits to be derived therefrom.[111] An offshore hedge fund that trades only for its own account and does not purchase and sell securities to customers should not be considered to be a dealer in stocks or securities.

Tax Code section 864(b)(2)(B) provides a similar exclusion from treatment as a U.S. trade or business for an offshore hedge fund that only trades in commodities for its own account and is not a dealer in commodities.

Before 1997, to avoid being deemed to be engaged in a U.S. trade or business, an offshore hedge fund was required to have its principal place of business outside the United States.[112]

An offshore hedge fund will also be deemed to be engaged in a U.S. trade or business if it invests in U.S. real property interests as defined in Tax Code section

---

106. *See* § 16.7.7, *infra.*

107. *See* § 16.7.5, *infra.*

108. Treas. Reg. § 1.864-2(c)(2), 26 C.F.R. § 1.864-2(c)(2).

109. Treas. Reg. § 1.864-2(c)(1), 26 C.F.R. § 1.864-2(c)(1). *See* § 16.3.10.i, *supra.*

110. In some contexts, the Tax Code and Treasury Regulations distinguish "stocks" from "securities," the latter sometimes being confined to various types of debt instruments. The discussion in this § 16.7 generally conforms to the terminology of the Tax Code and the Treasury Regulations.

111. Treas. Reg. § 1.864-2(c)(2)(iv), 26 C.F.R. § 1.864-2(c)(2)(iv).

112. *See* § 4.4.1, *supra*, regarding the so-called "ten commandments" that were relevant to the taxation of offshore hedge funds.

897. U.S. real property investments include fee ownership and co-ownership of land and improvements thereon, leaseholds of land or improvements thereon, options to acquire land or improvements thereon, and options to acquire leaseholds of land and improvements thereon.[113] A U.S. real property interest also includes stock in a corporation, a significant portion of the assets of which are U.S. real property interests.[114] An offshore hedge fund that owns an interest in a real estate investment trust (a "REIT") must treat distributions by the REIT as gain recognized from the sale or exchange of U.S. real property interests to the extent that the distribution is attributable to gains from the sale or exchange by the REIT of U.S. real property interests. This rule does not apply, however, to a distribution by a REIT with a class of stock that is regularly traded on an established securities market in the United States, if the offshore hedge fund does not own more than five percent of that class of stock at any time during the taxable year.[115]

If an offshore hedge fund has any U.S. trade or business income, it may fail to satisfy the requirement that it trade solely for its own account, and in that case all of its income might be taxed in the United States. An offshore hedge fund could have U.S. trade or business income in connection with an investment in a privately held company, for example if it invests in a U.S. start-up company structured as a pass-through vehicle for U.S. tax purposes, or if the offshore hedge fund receives some fee income (for example directors' fees) with respect to its investment in such company. An offshore hedge fund could encounter a similar result if any of its investments do not qualify as stocks, securities or commodities.

4. U.S. Ownership

As noted above, offshore hedge funds that are structured as corporations for U.S. tax purposes are ordinarily marketed to non-U.S. investors and U.S. tax-exempt entities. The passive foreign investment company rules[116] generally make investment in offshore hedge funds structured as corporations for U.S. tax purposes inappropriate for U.S. taxable investors. Offshore hedge funds that have significant U.S. ownership may also be treated as controlled foreign corporations and as such subject to special rules.[117]

i. Controlled Foreign Corporations

If U.S. investors own a significant percentage of the shares of an offshore hedge fund structured as a corporation for U.S. tax purposes, the offshore hedge fund may be treated as a "controlled foreign corporation" (a "CFC") for U.S. income tax purposes. A CFC is generally any non-U.S. corporation of which more than fifty percent of the vote or value of the stock is directly or indirectly owned by "U.S. Shareholders."[118] A U.S. Shareholder is generally a U.S. person who

---

113.   Tax Code § 897(c)(6)(A), 26 U.S.C. § 897(c)(6)(A).
114.   Tax Code § 897(c)(2), 26 U.S.C. § 897(c)(2).
115.   Tax Code § 897(h)(1), 26 U.S.C. § 897(h)(1).
116.   *See* § 16.7.4.ii, *infra*.
117.   *See* § 16.7.4.i, *infra*.
118.   Tax Code § 957, 26 U.S.C. § 957.

owns directly or indirectly ten percent or more of the voting power of the corporation.[119] For example, an offshore hedge fund owned entirely by unrelated U.S. investors, each of whom owns less than nine percent of the stock, is not a CFC. In addition, an offshore hedge fund held forty-nine percent by one U.S. investor, two percent by another unrelated U.S. investor and forty-nine percent by non-U.S. persons is not a CFC. On the other hand, an offshore hedge fund held eleven percent by one U.S. investor, ten percent each by four other U.S. investors and forty-nine percent by non-U.S. persons, would be a CFC. With non-U.S. corporations that have classes of stock with different voting rights, it is often not clear how to measure voting power. Treasury Regulations provide special rules that can result in deemed control when U.S. investors can elect, appoint or replace persons who have power over the corporation similar to that of a U.S. board of directors or who can effectively control such persons.[120]

A U.S. Shareholder of a CFC must include in its income each year its proportionate share of certain types of "tainted" income of the CFC, including "foreign personal holding company income." Foreign personal holding company income includes dividends, interest and gains from sales of securities. Thus, most income of an offshore hedge fund is foreign personal holding company income. The included amount is treated as a dividend distributed from the CFC and is taxed as ordinary income to the extent of the CFC's earnings and profits, then as a return of basis, and then as gain from the sale of stock. These rules generally should not result, however, in taxable income for U.S. tax-exempt entities, which typically are the only U.S. investors in an offshore hedge fund, even if that offshore hedge fund trades on margin.[121] Nevertheless, the U.S. Shareholders of a CFC must file U.S. information returns and must obtain information from the CFC to complete such forms.[122] To avoid CFC status, an offshore hedge fund generally should assure that U.S. Shareholders never own fifty percent or more of its stock.

ii. Passive Foreign Investment Companies

A U.S. taxpayer who invests in a non-U.S. corporation generally is taxed on dividends received from that corporation at ordinary income rates and is taxed on gain from the sale of the stock of that corporation at capital gain rates. This result is altered, however, if the corporation is a "passive foreign investment company" (a "PFIC"). A PFIC is generally any non-U.S. corporation if (a) at least seventy-five percent of the corporation's income is certain passive income (including dividends, interest and gains on the sale of securities) or (b) at least fifty percent of its assets produce such passive income.[123] An offshore hedge fund

119. Tax Code § 951(b), 26 U.S.C. § 951(b).
120. Treas. Reg. § 1.957-1(b); 26 C.F.R. § 1.957-1(b).
121. PLR 9407007 (Nov. 12, 1993); PLR 9024086 (Mar. 22, 1990). While private letter rulings are not binding on the IRS, they are indicative of the IRS's views. *See also* H.R. Rep. No. 586, 104th Cong. 2d. Sess. F2 (1996), where the House Ways and Means Committee stated in connection with H.R. 3448 that the Committee believed there should be no look-through rule in determining whether dividends from a CFC should be treated as UBTI.
122. Tax Code § 6038(a)(4), 26 U.S.C. § 6038(a)(4).
123. Tax Code § 1297, 26 U.S.C. § 1297.

established to trade stocks and securities for its own account typically is treated as a PFIC, because all of its income is passive and all of its assets generate such income. A U.S. taxpayer who invests in a PFIC is subject to certain adverse tax consequences under a method of taxation known as the "interest charge" method. These rules apply to any taxable U.S. investor who owns an interest in the PFIC, regardless of the amount of that investor's ownership of the PFIC. A U.S. taxpayer may elect, however, not to be subject to the interest charge rules if the taxpayer elects to treat the PFIC as a Qualified Electing Fund ("QEF") under Tax Code section 1295, or makes a mark-to-market election under Tax Code section 1296.

a. Interest Charge Method

As stated above, a U.S. investor in a PFIC is subject to the interest charge method unless he or she makes the mark-to-market or QEF election. Under the interest charge method, the U.S. taxpayer does not report any income with respect to an investment in the PFIC until it receives distributions from the offshore hedge fund or sells shares of the offshore hedge fund. If a taxpayer receives an "excess distribution," the taxpayer must treat that excess distribution as being earned ratably over the time the taxpayer held the stock and pay an interest charge as if the taxpayer had reported that income in the previous years but had not paid the tax. These rules are designed to approximate the tax that would have been recognized if the PFIC had distributed all of its income annually, and thus prevent taxpayers from deferring income by investing in offshore corporations.

Whether a distribution is an excess distribution depends on the amount of the distribution in comparison to prior years' distributions. A distribution from the offshore hedge fund is generally an excess distribution only to the extent that the total distributions in a year exceed 125 percent of the average of the distributions received in the prior three years.[124] All gain recognized on disposition of PFIC stock (that is, sale of the stock or redemption of stock by the U.S. person) is treated as an excess distribution.[125]

The aggregate excess distributions for a year are allocated ratably to all of the days the investor held the PFIC stock. Any amounts attributable to a prior year in which the company was a PFIC are treated as taxed at the highest rate (that is, the ordinary income rate) for the year in which earned and then interest is calculated as if such tax had not been paid in that year.[126] The sum of that tax and interest is then taxable to the investor for the current year, even if the taxpayer has a net operating loss carry forward or other offsetting amounts for the current year.[127] The taxpayer need not, however, file amended tax returns for prior years.

A U.S. taxpayer may invest in a PFIC because of a belief that the PFIC will be able to out-perform the IRS interest rate over the course of the investment, so that the tax deferral results in an overall benefit. For this benefit to be realized, the

---

124. Tax Code § 1291(b), 26 U.S.C. § 1291(b).
125. Tax Code § 1291(a)(2), 26 U.S.C. § 1291(a)(2).
126. Tax Code § 1291(a), 26 U.S.C. § 1291(a).
127. Tax Code § 1291(a)(1)(C), 26 U.S.C. § 1291(a)(1)(C).

projected out-performance should be analyzed in view of the calculation rules, including that (a) the interest charge is determined as if the gains were earned ratably over the period, whereas ordinarily a larger percentage of the gains would be earned in the later years due to compounding, and (b) all of the gains are taxed as ordinary income rates, whereas if the taxpayer held the securities directly or invested in a pass-through tax vehicle, a portion of the gains may have been taxed at the lower long-term capital gain rate.

b. Qualified Electing Fund

A U.S. taxpayer can avoid being subject to the interest charge method by electing to treat the PFIC as a QEF.[128] The offshore hedge fund must consent to the election and be willing to supply certain information to the U.S. investor, if the IRS audits the investor.[129] An offshore hedge fund may not consent to a QEF election, because it involves additional accounting and administrative costs, opens the offshore hedge fund's records to IRS scrutiny and risks revealing the identities of its other investors.

Under a QEF election, the taxpayer includes in income each year the taxpayer's proportionate share of the QEF's earnings and profits, based on share ownership. This income retains its character as ordinary income or capital gain income.[130] Thus, investment in a QEF is similar to investment in a U.S. pass-through vehicle, such as a U.S. partnership. One significant difference is that, if the PFIC has a deficit in earnings and profits for a taxable year, that deficit does not pass through to the investor to offset income from other investments. In addition, if the QEF has net losses in one year followed by profits in the next year, the profits are not offset by the prior year's deficit.[131] Those losses may be offset only on ultimate disposition of the PFIC stock.

One advantage of investing in a PFIC for which a QEF election has been made is that the U.S. taxpayer can elect to defer payment of taxes on the income passed through to the taxpayer until actual distributions are made from the offshore hedge fund, at which time the taxpayer must pay the tax and interest on the deferred amounts.[132] An advantage of this approach over being subject to the "interest charge" method[133] is that the interest is attributed to the year in which the earnings were actually earned rather than ratably over the period.

c. Mark-to-Market Election

Tax Code Section 1296 allows a U.S. taxpayer to avoid the interest charge method by electing to mark-to-market marketable stock in a PFIC each year and include the resulting gain or loss in taxable income as ordinary gain or loss. The amount of loss deduction a taxpayer can take each year, however, is limited to the amount of gains previously reported under this election with respect to

---

128. Tax Code § 1291(d), 26 U.S.C. § 1291(d).
129. Tax Code § 1295(a), 26 U.S.C. § 1295(a).
130. Tax Code § 1293(a), 26 U.S.C. § 1293(a).
131. Tax Code § 1293(a), 26 U.S.C. § 1293(a).
132. Tax Code § 1294, 26 U.S.C. § 1294.
133. *See* § 16.7.4.ii, *supra*.

that stock that have not already been offset.[134] "Marketable stock" is generally stock that (a) is regularly traded on a qualified securities exchange or (b) stock in a PFIC that is similar to a U.S. mutual fund.[135] Treasury Regulations provide that for a PFIC to be similar to a U.S. mutual fund, among other things: (a) its stock must be redeemable at net asset value; (b) its stock must be available to the general public at its net asset value; (c) its stock must be purchasable by new investors in initial amounts not greater than $10,000; (d) quotations for its shares must be determined and published weekly in a widely available medium; (e) the corporation must be supervised as an investment company by a foreign government or instrumentality; and (f) at all times during the year the corporation must have one hundred or more shareholders with respect to the class of shares at issue.[136] This election is thus not available for investors in most offshore hedge funds, because the stock is not deemed "marketable stock."

5. Withholding Taxes on Certain U.S. Income

i. Income Subject to Withholding

Offshore hedge funds generally are subject to U.S. withholding at the rate of thirty percent on the following types of income:

- Dividends from any U.S. corporation that receives less than eighty percent of its income from an active non-U.S. business;
- Interest from bonds or other securities of any U.S. corporation that receives less than eighty percent of its income from an active non-U.S. business, except as set forth below;
- Interest from other U.S. obligors, except as set forth below; and
- Rents and royalties.[137]

The broker or other payor who has control of the funds generally withholds. An offshore hedge fund structured as a corporation for U.S. tax purposes is required to provide the withholding agent with a Form W-8BEN certifying that it is a non-U.S. entity and is not a pass-through entity for U.S. tax purposes. The thirty percent withholding rate can be reduced under tax treaties, but most offshore hedge funds are established in tax haven jurisdictions with which the United States does not have tax treaties.

For non-U.S. investors investing in U.S. securities through an offshore hedge fund, withholding generally does not reduce their returns, because those investors would generally be subject to the same withholding if they had made the investments in U.S. securities directly. In contrast, a U.S. tax-exempt entity that invests in an offshore hedge fund structured as a corporation for U.S. tax

---

134. Tax Code § 1296(a), 26 U.S.C. § 1296(a).
135. Tax Code § 1296(e)(i), 26 U.S.C. § 1296(e)(i).
136. Treas. Reg. § 1.1296-2(d), 26 C.F.R. § 1.1296-2(d).
137. Tax Code § 1442, 26 U.S.C. § 1442.

purposes will have its return reduced by the withholding taxes. This disadvantage may be offset by the benefit of avoiding UBTI,[138] if the offshore hedge fund purchases securities on margin.

ii. Exempt Income

The following types of income generally are exempt from withholding:

- Interest on deposits in a bank, including savings accounts, checking accounts and certificates of deposits;
- Interest on deposits in certain qualified savings and loans;
- Distributions from a regulated investment company that constitute "capital gains dividends" under Tax Code section 852(b)(3)(C);[139]
- Exempt interest dividends (as defined in Tax Code section 852(b)(5)(A))[140] from a regulated investment company;
- Interest-related dividends and short-term capital gain dividends (as defined in Tax Code section 871(k)) from a regulated investment company;[141]
- Original issue discount on an obligation payable 183 days or less from the date of original issue; and
- Interest from "portfolio debt investments," defined as (a) certain unregistered debt instruments (bearer bonds) that meet specific tests to ensure that they are sold only to non–U.S. investors, that state on their face that any U.S. investor that holds that instrument is subject to limitations under U.S. income tax laws, and the interest on which is payable only outside the United States, and (b) certain obligations in registered form, if the person required to withhold obtains certification (IRS Form W-8 or equivalent) that the beneficial owner (in this case the offshore hedge fund) is not a U.S. investor; an obligation is in "registered form" (i) if it can be transferred only by surrender of the old instrument to the new holder or issuance of a new instrument to the new holder, (ii) if it can be transferred only by a book entry system maintained by the issuer or its agent or (iii) a combination of (i) and (ii).

Many of the U.S. debt instruments in which an offshore hedge fund typically invests qualify as portfolio debt investments. Portfolio debt does not include, however, debt when the holder also owns stock having ten percent or more of the total combined voting power of the corporate issuer.[142] In addition, portfolio debt does not include certain debt instruments with contingent interest, including debt if the amount of interest due on such debt is contingent on the receipts, sales, cash flow, profits or income of the issuer or a related person, any change in value of the issuer or a related person, or the amount of dividends or other distributions

138.   *See* § 16.7.6, *infra*.
139.   26 U.S.C. § 852(b)(3)(C).
140.   26 U.S.C. § 852(b)(5)(A).
141.   Tax Code § 871(k); 26 U.S.C. § 871(k).
142.   Tax Code § 871(h)(3), 26 U.S.C. § 871(h)(3).

made by the issuer or a related person[143] (provided that the amount and timing of interest can be contingent on factors other than the profits or performance of the issuer, such as other interest rates or indices).[144] Certain types of debt in which an offshore hedge fund might invest, such as distressed securities and bankruptcy claims, also might not qualify as either bearer bonds or registered debt and thus not be considered portfolio debt.

6. Unrelated Business Taxable Income

As noted above, to avoid recognition of unrelated business taxable income ("UBTI") U.S. tax-exempt entities may invest in offshore hedge funds structured as corporations for U.S. tax purposes. UBTI is generally defined as the gross income from any trade or business unrelated to the tax-exempt business of the entity.[145] To the extent that UBTI, from all sources, of a tax-exempt entity, less its allocable share of deductions directly connected with carrying on any such trade or business, exceeds $1,000 in any year, the tax-exempt entity will incur tax liability with respect to the excess at tax rates that would apply if the organization were not otherwise exempt from taxation. UBTI does not include interest and dividend income, or gains on the sale, exchange or other disposition of assets held for investment.[146] Income from "debt-financed property" (such as gain from the sale of stock purchased on margin) will, however, constitute UBTI to tax-exempt entities, in the percentage that such property is subject to "acquisition indebtedness" (the percentage that acquisition indebtedness respecting such property bears to the acquiror's adjusted tax basis for such property).[147]

If a U.S. tax-exempt entity invests in a U.S. hedge fund structured as a partnership that invests on margin, the tax-exempt entity will be required to treat a portion of the income of the hedge fund as debt-financed income giving rise to UBTI, because the character of the income of the hedge fund passes through to the investor.[148] No rules require, however, that a tax-exempt investor in a corporation treat itself as having received an allocable share of the income of the corporation.[149] Accordingly, unless the tax-exempt investor borrows funds to purchase stock of an offshore hedge fund, the investor should not recognize any UBTI from its investment in the offshore hedge fund, even if the offshore hedge fund trades on margin.

Even if a U.S. tax-exempt entity invests in an offshore corporation that is treated as a CFC and trades on margin, it nevertheless should not recognize UBTI. The IRS has ruled that income from the offshore hedge fund retains its character as dividend income and is not treated as a pass through of debt-financed income.[150]

---

143. Tax Code § 871(h)(4), 26 U.S.C. § 871(h)(4).

144. Tax Code § 871(h)(4)(c), 26 U.S.C. § 871(h)(4)(c).

145. Tax Code § 512(a)(1), 26 U.S.C. § 512(a)(1).

146. Tax Code §§ 512(b)(1) and 512(b)(5), 26 U.S.C. §§ 512(b)(1) and 512(b)(5).

147. Tax Code § 512(b)(4), 26 U.S.C. § 512(b)(4).

148. *See* § 16.3.13, *supra*.

149. Tax Code § 512(b)(1), 26 U.S.C. § 512(b)(1).

150. *See* note 121, *supra*.

7. Master Fund Structure

As noted above, offshore hedge funds are usually structured as corporations for U.S. tax purposes. Sometimes the offshore corporation invests all of its assets in another hedge fund established (generally offshore) as a limited partnership under local law and treated as a partnership for U.S. tax purposes (a "Master Fund"). Typically, the investment adviser is the general partner of the Master Fund, and the offshore hedge fund and a U.S. hedge fund are the limited partners (feeders) in the Master Fund. This structure allows a manager to combine all of the assets of the offshore hedge fund and the U.S. hedge fund into one pool, which can reduce administrative costs and may be helpful for marketing because the two hedge funds should have identical performance.

Typically, non–U.S. investors and U.S. tax-exempt investors invest through the offshore feeder and U.S. taxable investors invest through the U.S. feeder. With respect to the non–U.S. investors and U.S. tax-exempt investors, the tax results are as discussed above with a typical offshore hedge fund. Thus, U.S. tax-exempt entities retain their protection from UBTI, which usually is their primary motivation for investing in offshore hedge funds.

Under a Master Fund structure, the manager frequently receives its compensation at the level of the two limited partner entities: as performance fees and asset-based fees from the offshore hedge fund, and as performance allocations and asset-based fees (treated as guaranteed payments) from the U.S. hedge fund. Alternatively, the manager may receive performance allocations and asset-based fees from the Master Fund, in which case the feeders do not charge any fees or allocations. If the investment adviser is paid a performance fee from the offshore feeder, it may be able to defer that compensation. If, however, the Master Fund generates significant long–term capital gains or qualifying dividend income or has substantial unrealized gains, the investment adviser may prefer for tax reasons to receive performance–based compensation in the form of allocations from the Master Fund.[151]

The Master Fund is typically established under the laws of a jurisdiction outside the United States. If the Master Fund is organized in an offshore jurisdiction, withholding will apply on payments to the Master Fund.[152] The Master Fund will need to provide the withholding agent with an IRS form W-8IMY, which must include information regarding what percentage of the Master Fund is held by non–U.S. investors that should be subject to withholding. For this purpose, the offshore feeder would provide the Master Fund a Form W-8BEN and would be treated entirely as a non–U.S. investor, even if that feeder has some U.S. tax-exempt investors. If the Master Fund is established under the laws of a U.S. jurisdiction, payments to the Master Fund will not be subject to withholding, but the Master Fund will be required to withhold on the offshore feeder's allocable share of U.S. source dividend and interest income.

---

151. *See* § 16.8.6, *infra.*
152. *See* § 16.7.5, *supra.*

8. U.S. Estate Taxes on Non-U.S. Individuals

Non-U.S. individuals may prefer investing in offshore hedge funds to avoid U.S. estate taxes. Tax Code section 2103[153] subjects a non-U.S. individual's gross estate that is situated in the United States to U.S. estate tax. Stock of a corporation incorporated in the United States is deemed to be situated in the United States.[154] Thus, if a non-resident alien dies while holding stock in U.S. corporations directly, the non-resident alien's gross estate for U.S. purposes includes the value of such stock. An investment in a hedge fund structured as a partnership for tax purposes would most likely also be treated as being situated in the United States if the manager or general partner is located in the United States and the hedge fund holds U.S. securities. The IRS generally takes the position that an interest in a partnership is situated where the partnership does business.[155] Stock in a non-U.S. corporation is generally not included in a non-resident alien's estate, however, even if that corporation itself holds U.S. securities. As a result, non-U.S. taxpayers may prefer investing in offshore hedge funds structured as corporations to avoid U.S. estate tax.

§ 16.8 U.S. Taxation of General Partner/Investment Adviser

1. In General

For non-tax reasons, the investment adviser is usually established as an entity with limited liability. Typically, the investment adviser entity is organized as a limited liability company, a limited partnership or a corporation that elects to be treated as a Subchapter S corporation. Those entities, unlike Subchapter C corporations, all have the advantage of being subject to a single level of tax. Some investment advisers have two entities: one that receives fee income, such as asset-based fees from hedge funds or separate accounts (including offshore hedge funds), and a second entity that receives performance-based allocations from hedge funds structured as partnerships for tax purposes.

2. Types of Income

An investment adviser typically receives the following types of income: (a) asset-based fees from hedge funds, which are treated as guaranteed payments under

---

153.   26 U.S.C. § 2103.
154.   Tax Code § 2104, 26 U.S.C. § 2104.
155.   Rev. Rul. 55-701, 1955-2 C.B. 836.

Tax Code section 707(c)[156] and taxed as ordinary income; (b) asset-based or performance-based fees from separate accounts (including offshore hedge funds), which are also taxed as ordinary income; (c) performance-based allocations from hedge funds, which retain the tax character of the hedge funds' income;[157] and (d) return on investment of the investment adviser's own proprietary capital, which is taxed as long-term or short-term capital gain, interest or dividend income.

Because the investment adviser is structured as a pass through entity for income tax purposes, each individual owner of the investment adviser receives a Schedule K-1 from that entity reporting its pro rata share of the income, which retains its tax character as it passes through to such individual. One of the principal tax advantages for the individual owners of the investment adviser is the pass-through of the character of performance-based allocations, based on the activities of the underlying hedge fund. For example, if a manager receives a twenty percent performance-based allocation as general partner of a hedge fund and the hedge fund has $1,000,000 of gains for the year, comprising $400,000 of realized long-term capital gains, $400,000 of realized short-term capital gains and $200,000 of gains that have not been realized for tax purposes, the general partner receives a book allocation of profits from the hedge fund of $200,000, which for tax purposes would consist of $80,000 of realized long-term capital gains, $80,000 of realized short-term gains and $40,000 of unrealized gains. An individual who owns a fifty percent interest in the investment adviser thus would have his or her capital account credited for book purposes with $100,000 and would receive a Schedule K-1 from the investment adviser reporting $40,000 of long-term capital gain (taxable at rates up to fifteen percent) and $40,000 of short-term gains (taxable at rates up to thirty-five percent). In contrast, if the investment adviser were paid a performance-based fee, that individual would have reported $100,000 of ordinary income.

3. Limited Partnerships and Limited Liability Companies

If the investment adviser is a limited partnership or a limited liability company, it is treated as a partnership for income tax purposes, unless it elects to be taxed as a corporation. Partnerships offer significantly more flexibility than S corporations, because Subchapter S limits the number of shareholders in S corporations, limits the types of shareholders and restricts an S corporation to one class of stock.[158] Partnerships also can make distributions in kind without triggering gain on any appreciation in the assets, and allow the owners to increase their tax bases by their shares of the entity's liabilities. Partnerships also allow more flexibility for admitting new owners without the owners being required either to purchase their interests or to pay tax on receipt of their interests.

---

156.   26 U.S.C. § 707(c).

157.   *See* § 16.3.2, *supra,* regarding the risk that the IRS might maintain that the performance-based allocation is actually a fee that should be taxed to the investment adviser or its owners as ordinary income.

158.   Tax Code § 1361, 26 U.S.C. § 1361.

i. Flexibility in Allocating Profits

As discussed below in section 16.8.4, an S corporation can only have one class of stock. Accordingly, income and loss must be allocated, and all distributions must be made, in proportion to share ownership. Partnerships (including limited liability companies) are not similarly restricted. Partnerships can allocate profits in different proportions from capital contributions. Partnerships can divide their income into sources, or baskets, and allocate each source in different proportions, and specially allocate items of income, gain, loss and deduction, as long as the allocations have substantial economic effect.[159]

For example, an investment adviser organized as a limited liability company may provide in its limited liability company agreement that income will be divided into four sources: first, return on investment of the investment adviser's own capital (for example when a member invests capital through the investment adviser into the hedge fund) (the "Investment Source"); second, asset-based management fees from U.S. and offshore hedge funds and performance-based fees from offshore hedge funds and other separate accounts (reduced by the expenses of operating the business) (the "Fee Source"); third, performance-based profit allocations from U.S. hedge funds (the "Performance Source"); and fourth, gain or loss from sale of the business (the "Sale Source"). Profits and losses from the Investment Source are generally allocated among the owners of the investment entity in proportion to the amount of capital each invests. The Fee Source, Performance Source and Sale Source may be divided in varying proportions, according to the members' agreement. For example, the principals of the investment adviser may allocate all of the Fee Source to themselves, but allocate shares of the Performance Source and the Sale Source to analysts and others. An individual may benefit from receiving a share of the Performance Source through an allocation from the investment adviser, rather than as a bonus taxable as ordinary income, because allocations of profits from the Performance Source may include long-term capital gains and unrealized gains, depending on the character of the income of the hedge fund.[160] Similarly, if the business is sold, a member who shares in the Sale Source would recognize some capital gain income if a portion of the purchase price is allocated to good will, but if he or she receives a share of the proceeds as a bonus, it would all be ordinary income.

ii. Admission of Partners or Members

When an investment adviser that is structured as a partnership for tax purposes (including a limited liability company) admits a partner, the tax consequences to the partner depend on whether the partner receives a "capital" or "profits" interest. A capital interest is generally an interest under which the partner receives a capital account balance in excess of the partner's capital contribution, or an interest that would cause the partner to receive proceeds greater than its capital contribution if the partnership were liquidated immediately after the partner is

---

159. Tax Code § 704, 26 U.S.C. § 704.
160. *See* § 16.8.2, *supra.*

admitted. A profits interest, on the other hand, affords the partner only the right to share in future profits earned, and if the partnership were to be liquidated immediately after the partner receives the interest, the partner would not receive any amounts in excess of capital contributed.

A partner's receipt of a capital interest in exchange for services performed or to be performed results in compensation income for the partner, and presumably a corresponding compensation deduction for the entity. A profits interest generally is not taxable to the partner on receipt; instead, the partner pays income tax on allocations of subsequent profits.[161]

An investment adviser entity typically would not grant a partner an interest with a capital account balance in excess of the amount contributed. A partner might, however, receive a disguised capital interest through the right to share in one of the sources of profits. As noted in section 16.8.3.i above, an investment adviser may divide its income into separate baskets to be allocated separately. A partner would generally be entitled to share in the Investment Source only to the extent of any capital actually contributed. The partner's share of the Fee Source or the Performance Source should generally be treated as a profit's interest (unless the IRS were to maintain that the right to the asset-based fee constitutes a substantially certain stream of income) and thus not be taxable on receipt. If a partner is admitted in the middle of a fiscal period when the assets of the hedge fund have appreciated, however, so that the investment adviser would be entitled to a performance allocation or fee as of that date if the fiscal period were to end, the IRS might maintain that such partner has received a capital interest. Arguably, the partner should not recognize compensation income in that case, because the assets in the hedge fund could depreciate by the end of the measurement period, leaving no amount to be allocated to the new partner. On the other hand, under the definition of "capital interest," if the hedge fund and the investment adviser were both to liquidate as of the admission date, an allocation would typically be due under the partnership agreement for the hedge fund, and the new partner would be allocated some amount in excess of capital contributed.[162]

If a partner is admitted to the investment adviser and is granted a share of the Sale Source at a time when the investment adviser has established good will, the partner would likely be deemed to have received a taxable capital interest. The investment adviser could avoid this result by adjusting its capital accounts before admitting the new partner, to reflect the unrealized appreciation in the investment adviser's assets, so that the new partner only shares in appreciation that occurs after the new partner's admission. Arguably, however, little or no good will attaches to the typical investment adviser that advises only hedge funds, because the business could not be sold without the principals' agreement to enter into employment

---

161. Revenue Procedure 93-27, 1993-2 C.B. 343. Exceptions to this rule apply if the profits interest relates to a substantially certain stream of income (such as from a long-term net lease) or the partner sells the interest within two years of receipt.

162. An election to defer performance-based compensation based on a period of at least twelve months must be made no later than six months into the period. Tax Code § 409A, 26 U.S.C. § 409A. By analogy, one could argue that a member admitted to an investment adviser less than six months into an annual measurement period for a performance-based allocation should not be deemed to have earned any income on admission.

agreements and covenants not to compete, and thus any good will attaches to the individuals and not the business.[163]

iii. Distributions

The distribution of an asset by a partnership generally does not result in recognition of unrealized appreciation on the asset, in contrast to a distribution by an S corporation, which results in a deemed sale of the asset for its fair market value.[164] A distribution of marketable securities by a partnership is treated under Tax Code section 731(c)[165] as a distribution of cash unless the distributing partnership qualifies as an "investment partnership"[166] and the other requirements of Tax Code section 731(c) are met. An investment adviser that only acts as the general partner of hedge funds likely would qualify as an investment partnership. A partnership is not treated as engaged in a trade of business that would disqualify it as an investment partnership by reason of performing reasonable and customary services to an investment partnership, in which the former partnership holds an interest, in exchange for reasonable and customary fees.[167] If the investment adviser also manages separate accounts, however, such as an offshore hedge fund structured as a corporation, the investment adviser may be deemed to be engaged in a trade or business activity that disqualifies it as an investment partnership. The investment adviser may also be disqualified if it receives other types of fee income, such as director's fees, if they are not incidental to the investment activities.[168]

iv. Departure of Partner or Member

An investment adviser may determine that a departing partner in the investment adviser entity is entitled to receive only his or her capital account on departure, because the entity has little or no good will or going concern value.[169] The result may differ if the investment adviser entity agrees to pay a departing partner an amount in excess of his or her capital account, depending on how the transaction is structured.

First, the remaining partners can buy the departing partner's interest directly, in which case the departing partner will generally have capital gain income on the excess of the proceeds over his or her adjusted tax basis (except for the portion of the purchase price allocable to unrealized receivables or inventory under Tax Code section 751).[170]

Second, the investment adviser can pay the departing partner fixed payments for a period of time not based on the income of the partnership, which should be treated as guaranteed payments under Tax Code section 736(a),[171] and which

---

163. *See* § 16.2.2, *supra*, regarding contributions in kind.
164. *See* § 16.4.2, *supra*.
165. 26 U.S.C. § 731(c).
166. *See* § 16.4.2, *supra*.
167. Treas. Reg. § 1.731-2(e); 26 C.F.R. § 1.731-2(e).
168. Id.
169. *See* §§ 16.4 and 16.8.3.iii, *supra*.
170. 26 U.S.C. § 751.
171. 26 U.S.C. § 736(a).

would generally be ordinary income to the withdrawing partner and deductible (subject to other limitations) by the partnership.

Third, the departing partner can remain a partner for a period of time with a declining share of the investment adviser's profits. This should generally result under Tax Code section 736(a)(1)[172] in that partner being allocated income in his or her capacity as a partner, effectively causing the payments to be deductible by reducing the remaining partners' allocable shares of the income. An individual who remains a partner or member for income tax purposes might, however, also retain rights as a partner or member under state law, such as the right to inspect books and records.

Finally, the investment adviser could make a distribution to the partner and treat it as a payment under Tax Code section 736(b).[173] This would generally result in the departing partner receiving capital gain income and the distribution not being deductible for the remaining partners.

v. Tax Basis

A partner's outside tax basis in a partnership interest increases by his or her share of the partnership's liabilities.[174] Short sales are treated as liabilities for this purpose.[175] In contrast, a shareholder's tax basis in shares of an S corporation is not increased by a share of the corporation's liabilities (except that an S corporation shareholder can use the basis of any indebtedness of the corporation to the shareholder to determine the amount of losses or distributions that can be passed through to the shareholder).[176] Distributions from partnerships and S corporations are generally not taxed unless they exceed tax basis, and items of loss and deduction can only be used to the extent of tax basis. For an investment adviser, an increased tax basis can be useful, if an individual member's capital account includes unrealized appreciation in assets invested indirectly in the hedge fund, and if withdrawal of such amounts would otherwise trigger capital gain income.

4. S Corporation Structure

Some investment advisers are structured as S corporations. S corporations are subject to several limitations that do not apply to partnerships. First, an S corporation can only have one class of stock, and distributions and allocations of taxable income must be made in proportion to share ownership.[177] An S corporation cannot divide its income into separate sources and cannot specially allocate specific items of income and loss. An S corporation can effectively divide income into separate baskets only by paying increased salaries and bonuses. If the income used to pay the bonus is long-term capital gain from the performance-based allocation from the hedge fund, the recipient pays tax at the higher ordinary income rates, and

---

172. 26 U.S.C. § 736(a)(1).
173. 26 U.S.C. § 736(b).
174. Tax Code § 752, 26 U.S.C. § 752.
175. *See* § 16.2.1, *supra.*
176. Tax Code § 1366(d)(i), 26 U.S.C. § 1366(d)(i).
177. Tax Code § 1361(b)(1)(D), 26 U.S.C. § 1361(b)(1)(D).

the income is subject to self-employment taxes (dividends from S corporations generally are not subject to self-employment taxes).[178]

An S corporation cannot have more than 100 shareholders or have any nonresident alien shareholders.[179] With limited exceptions, an S corporation cannot have any entities as owners. This might prohibit an investment adviser from accepting seed capital from an institutional investor.

A person who acquires shares in an S corporation either must pay fair market value for the shares or incur tax liability on the excess of fair market value over the amount paid. An S corporation cannot issue "profits interests" apart from "capital interests."[180] S corporations do offer the advantage, however, of being able to grant incentive stock options as provided in Tax Code section 422.[181] A distribution of an asset in kind by an S corporation, unlike a partnership, results in recognition of any unrealized gain on that asset.[182]

5. Self-Employment Taxes

Self-employment tax is imposed on the self-employment income of each individual. The social security tax rate is 12.4 percent of self-employment income up to the amount provided in Tax Code section 1402(b).[183] The Medicare tax rate is 2.9 percent of all self-employment income.[184] A general partner generally pays self-employment tax on the portion of the partnership's income that passes through to that partner and that constitutes income from a trade or business. Capital gains and dividends are generally excluded from self-employment income, so the performance-based allocation that passes through to owners of an investment adviser structured as a partnership should not be subject to self-employment tax.[185] In addition, income allocable to limited partners (other than guaranteed payments), is generally exempt from self-employment tax.[186] It is unclear whether passive owners of limited liability companies constitute general or limited partners for this purpose.[187] Accordingly, owners of an investment adviser structured as a limited partnership might avoid self-employment taxes on the income from asset-based fees, if it is allocated to them as limited partners. The IRS might challenge this result, however, for limited partners who actively participate in the business and are not paid a reasonable salary.

Shareholders generally are not subject to the self-employment tax on dividends that they receive from an S corporation. Thus, an S corporation might reduce self-employment taxes on fee income by paying such amounts to its shareholders as dividends. If, however, the shareholders are receiving little or no compensation

---

178.   Tax Code § 1402(a)(2), 26 U.S.C. § 1402(a)(2). *See* § 16.8.5, *infra.*
179.   Tax Code § 1361(b)(1), 26 U.S.C. § 1361(b)(1).
180.   *See* § 16.8.3.ii, *supra.*
181.   26 U.S.C. § 422.
182.   Tax Code § 1371, 26 U.S.C. § 1371.
183.   26 U.S.C. § 1402(b)(1).
184.   Tax Code § 1401, 26 U.S.C. § 1401.
185.   Tax Code §§ 1402(a)(2) and 1402(a)(3), 26 U.S.C. §§ 1402(a)(2) and 1402(a)(3).
186.   Tax Code § 1402(a)(13), 26 U.S.C. § 1402(a)(13).
187.   The IRS has proposed regulations on when an individual is a limited partner. Prop. Regs. § 1.1402(a)-2(h).

from the S corporation, the IRS might assert that all or part of the dividends should be subject to self-employment tax.

6. Fee Deferral by Investment Adviser

An investment adviser to an offshore hedge fund may defer receipt of the asset-based fees or performance-based fees otherwise payable by the offshore hedge fund. Typically, the investment adviser and the offshore hedge fund would agree to defer some or all of such fees by treating the fee that would otherwise be due as an unsecured account payable owed by the offshore hedge fund to the investment adviser with a specified maturity date (usually not exceeding ten years). This account payable is typically adjusted during the deferral period to reflect the subsequent profits and losses of the offshore hedge fund (as if the deferred amount were invested in the offshore hedge fund, except that the offshore hedge fund does not pay fees to the investment adviser on the amount deferred). At the end of the deferral period, the offshore hedge fund pays the fees as adjusted to the investment adviser and the fees are taxable at ordinary income rates. If the assets of the offshore hedge fund appreciate during the deferral period, the investment adviser benefits from not paying tax on the appreciation of the deferred fees during the deferral period.

Complex and detailed rules govern how fee deferrals must be structured to avoid being taxable until they are paid. The investment adviser must use the cash method of accounting and must not be deemed to have "constructive receipt" of the funds, which generally means that the assets cannot be set apart for the investment adviser and the investment adviser cannot gain access to the funds. The investment adviser must enter into a binding agreement not to receive the fees until the end of the deferral period. Under Tax Code section 409A,[188] the election to defer must be made before the beginning of the tax year (which presumably refers to the tax year of the investment adviser rather than that of the offshore hedge fund). For performance-based compensation based on services over a period of at least twelve months, however, the election may be made no later than six months before the end of the service period, which apparently allows investment advisers to wait to elect to defer annual performance-based fees for up to six months into the performance period. Since most offshore hedge funds offer frequent withdrawals that can cause performance-based fees to be charged for stub periods of less than twelve months, it would be risky for investment advisers to rely on this rule absent further guidance from the IRS.[189]

The agreement must provide that the fees will not be paid earlier than (a) separation from service, (b) the date the participant becomes disabled, (c) death of the participant, (d) a specified time, (e) to the extent provided in Regulations, a change of ownership or control of the corporation or its assets, or (f) the occurrence of an unforeseeable emergency.[190] These rules on their face address an individual payee. It is unclear how they will be interpreted when the payee is an entity, such as

---

188.   26 U.S.C. § 409A.
189.   *Id.*
190.   *Id.*

an investment adviser entity. For example, could an entity payee accelerate receipt of deferred fees on the death of an individual owner of the entity who is entitled to share in the fees? Tax Code section 409A also generally allows deferred fees to be further deferred for a subsequent period, if the election to do so is made more than a year before the first payment is otherwise due and the added deferral period is at least five years.

The investment adviser also must not receive any "economic benefit" or cash equivalent for the fees to be deferred for tax purposes. The fees may not be secured or guaranteed, and must be available to the creditors of the payor. Tax Code section 409A provides that if the fees are set aside in an offshore trust or similar arrangement (to be determined under Regulations) then the fees will be deemed paid for tax purposes.

Tax Code section 409A provides for an interest charge and a penalty of twenty percent of the amount deferred with respect to a deferral that does not comply with the rules.

§ 16.9 State Taxation Issues

Each state has its own system of taxation that could subject all or part of the income of a hedge fund, its investors, or the investment adviser to state tax or obligate them to file information returns or other documents with state tax authorities. Those topics are not addressed in this book.

CHAPTER 17

Performance Advertising

§ 17.1 Introduction

If the past performance information of a hedge fund or its investment adviser is material to a decision whether to invest in the hedge fund, that information must be disclosed in the hedge fund's offering circular or private placement memorandum.[1] If it is not material, the hedge fund may, but is not required to, disclose past performance information. Investors, however, generally consider past performance information relevant. The SEC focuses considerable attention on investment adviser advertising and conducts vigorous enforcement actions when it perceives misleading or inappropriate advertising practices.[2]

§ 17.2 Disclosure of Past Performance

SEC staff no-action letters relating to performance advertising are promulgated under the anti-fraud provisions of the Advisers Act and apply to all investment advisers, whether or not registered with the SEC. The SEC imposes the following limitations on the use of actual or model performance results:[3]

- The effect of material market or economic conditions on the results portrayed must be disclosed (that is, results must be compared to market performance for the same period);
- The results must reflect the deduction of advisory fees, brokerage or other commissions and other expenses that a client paid or, in the case of a model portfolio, would have paid, with limited exceptions;[4]

---

1. *See* Chapter 6, *supra.*

2. *See, e.g., In re Van Kampen Investment Advisory Corp., et al.,* Advisers Act Release No. 1819 (Sep. 8, 1999); *In re Leeb Investment Advisors;* Advisers Act Release No. 1545 (Jan. 16, 1996); *In re Wall Street Money Management Group, Inc.,* Advisers Act Release No. 1464 (Jan. 30, 1995); *In re Seaboard Investment Advisers, Inc.,* Advisers Act Release No. 1431 (Aug. 3, 1994). *See also* Chapters 6, 8 and 9, *supra.*

3. *Clover Capital Management, Inc.,* SEC No-Action Letter (Oct. 28, 1986) (hereinafter, *Clover*). *See also* CFA Institute, formerly Association for Investment Management and Research, AIMR Performance Presentation Standards, as amended and restated February 12, 1999, available at www.cfainstitute.org/standards/pps/pps_outlines/pps_outline.html.

4. *See* § 17.2.1, *infra.*

- The advertisement must state whether and to what extent the results portrayed include the reinvestment of dividends and other earnings;
- An advertisement that suggests or makes claims about the potential for profit must also disclose the possibility for loss;
- Any comparison of model or actual results to an index must be to a closely comparable index and must disclose all material facts relevant to the comparison (such as differences in security selection, volatility and diversification); and
- Material conditions, objectives or investment strategies used to obtain the performance advertised must be disclosed.

These disclosures must be made clearly and prominently; disclaimers in small type or obscure font are not sufficient to dispel an advertisement's potential to mislead investors. If past performance is shown only for a selected group of clients, the investment adviser must also disclose the basis on which the selection was made and the effect of this practice on the results portrayed, if material.[5] If including the performance of other accounts managed by the investment adviser would materially affect the performance data shown, the investment adviser should explain why those accounts were excluded (for example, because they use different investment strategies).

1. Inclusion of Advisory Fees

In some instances, the SEC has relaxed the general requirement that performance results be portrayed net of all actual fees and expenses. For example, the SEC staff stated that it would not recommend enforcement action against an investment adviser that proposed to advertise the composite performance of all accounts for which the investment adviser would employ a particular investment strategy, deducting only a model fee equal to the highest fee charged to any account employing that strategy during the period of the performance.[6] In addition the SEC staff has taken the position that performance data need not deduct custodian fees paid to a bank or other orgnization for safekeeping client funds and securities.[7]

The SEC staff has also permitted written performance material that shows performance on a gross basis, if it is used only in one-on-one presentations made to sophisticated persons[8] in a private and confidential manner and not made available to the public. The SEC staff based this position on a belief that an investment adviser's fees are frequently negotiable in one-on-one meetings with sophisticated clients.[9] The SEC staff requires in such circumstances that investment advisers provide the following in writing:[10]

---

5.   *Clover.*

6.   *J.P. Morgan Investment Management, Inc.,* SEC No-Action Letter (May 7, 1996).

7.   *Investment Company Institute,* SEC No-Action Letter (Aug. 24, 1987).

8.   In this context, wealthy individuals, pension funds, universities and other institutions may be sophisticated. *Investment Company Institute,* SEC No-Action Letter (Sep. 23, 1988).

9.   *Id. See also J.P. Morgan Investment Management, Inc.,* SEC No-Action Letter (May 7, 1996).

10.   *Clover. See also* § 17.4.2, *infra.*

- disclosure that the performance figures do not reflect the deduction of advisory fees;
- disclosure that the client's return will be reduced by the advisory fees and other expenses that it may incur as a client;
- a statement that the investment adviser's fees are described in Part II of the investment adviser's Form ADV or an equivalent disclosure document; and
- a representative example showing the effect the advisory fees would have on the total value of the client's portfolio, compounded over a period of years.

If the presentation is made to a consultant who will use it in presentations to potential clients, the investment adviser must instruct the consultant to provide the gross performance data and the additional information described above only to similarly sophisticated prospective advisory clients, and only in one-on-one presentations.[11]

2. Model Results

Model results are results for hypothetical or model portfolios that do not reflect the performance of actual accounts. Managers of new hedge funds that have not yet generated actual performance over a significant period sometimes include in marketing materials model results that reflect the performance of their investment model, particularly if the model is based on a software program or objective, technical system, rather than fundamental analysis, and the program or system, when fed the relevant factual data for a given period, can be applied to generate hypothetical portfolios for that period. The SEC staff has warned that the use of hypothetical portfolios in marketing materials can raise various fraud problems and requires the following additional disclosures when an investment adviser advertises model results:[12]

- the limitations inherent in model results, particularly that such results do not represent actual trading and may not reflect the effect of material economic and market factors on the investment adviser's decision-making if the investment adviser were actually managing clients' assets;
- if applicable, material changes in the conditions, objectives or investment strategies of the model portfolio during the period portrayed and the effect thereof;
- if applicable, that some of the securities or strategies reflected in the model portfolio do not relate, or relate only partially, to the services currently offered by the investment adviser; and
- if applicable, that the investment adviser's clients actually had investment results that were materially different from those portrayed in the model.

If the results are generated by the retroactive application of a model (such as back testing), the investment adviser should consider including additional disclosures,

---

11. *Investment Company Institute*, SEC No-Action Letter (Sep. 23, 1988).
12. *See Scientific Market Analysis*, SEC No-Action Letter (March 21, 1976); *Clover*.

such as disclosure about the methodology used to create the model and the statistical validity of the results.

The SEC has sanctioned a number of investment advisers that advertised misleading model performance results, finding that they violated Advisers Act section 206(4)[13] and Rule 206(4)-1[14] under the Advisers Act by failing to disclose in advertisements that the advertised performance was developed by retroactive or inappropriate application of a model,[15] lack of actual trading,[16] deduction of various fees that would have been incurred,[17] market conditions that may have affected client accounts,[18] and the potential for losses.[19] The above list of limitations on model performance advertising is not necessarily exhaustive and does not define a safe harbor. Whether model performance results are misleading depends on the facts and circumstances and may depend in part on the nature and sophistication of the intended recipients.[20]

§ 17.3 Specific Recommendations

Advisers Act Rule 206(4)-1 applies to advertisements by an investment adviser that is required to be registered with the SEC. It prohibits any advertisement that refers, directly or indirectly, to any past specific recommendations of the investment adviser, unless the advertisement contains or offers to furnish information about all recommendations the investment adviser made during at least the past year.[21] This rule is grounded in a concern that investment advisers could publish selective lists of only their most successful investment recommendations. The SEC has stated that

> material of this nature, which may refer only to recommendations which were or would have been profitable and ignore those which were or would have been unprofitable, is inherently misleading and

---

13. 15 U.S.C. § 80b-6(4).

14. 17 C.F.R. § 275.206(4)-1.

15. *In re Patricia Owen-Michel*, Advisers Act Release No. 1584 (Sep. 27, 1996); *In re Profitek, Inc. and Edward G. Smith*, SEC Administrative Proceeding, File No. 3-9743 (Sep. 29, 1998); *In re LBS Capital Management, Inc.*, Advisers Act Release No. 1644 (July 18, 1997).

16. *In re Engebretson Capital Management, Inc. and Lester W. Engebretson*, SEC Administrative Proceeding File No. 3-10010 (Sep. 13, 1999); *In re Profitek, Inc. and Edward G. Smith*, SEC Administrative Proceeding, File No. 3-9743 (Sep. 29, 1998).

17. *In re Engebretson Capital Management, Inc. and Lester W. Engebretson*, SEC Administrative Proceeding File No. 3-10010 (Sep. 13, 1999); *In re Meridian Investment Management Corp.*, SEC Administrative Proceeding File No. 3-9796 (Dec. 28, 1998); *In re Patricia Owen-Michel*, Advisers Act Release No. 1584 (Sep. 27, 1996)

18. *In re Patricia Owen-Michel*, Advisers Act Release No. 1584 (Sep. 27, 1996).

19. *Id.*

20. *In re LBS Capital Management, Inc.*, Advisers Act Release No. 1644 (July 18, 1997).

21. Advisers Act Rule 206(4)-1(a)(2), 17 C.F.R. 275.206(4)-1. *See also Sutro & Co., Inc.*, SEC No-Action Letter (June 22, 1977); *E.F. Hutton, & Co., Inc.*, SEC No-Action Letter (Feb. 2, 1979); and Chapter 8, *supra*.

deceptive, and consequently the rule prohibits this type of advertising unless all recommendations for a minimum specified period are included.[22]

1. Selected Past Specific Recommendations

Notwithstanding the general prohibition in Rule 206(4)-1, an investment adviser to a hedge fund may in limited circumstances prepare and distribute a periodic report that contains a list of selected past specific recommendations. The following conditions must be met:[23]

- The investment adviser uses objective, nonperformance-based criteria to select the specific securities that it lists;
- The investment adviser uses the same selection criteria for each report of each particular investment category;
- The report does not discuss, directly or indirectly, the amount of profits or losses, realized or unrealized, of any of the specific securities; and
- The investment adviser maintains, and makes available to the SEC for inspection on request, records that show (a) the complete list of all securities that the investment adviser recommended in the last year for the specific category covered by each report, (b) the information regarding each recommendation described above and (c) the criteria used to select the specific securities listed in each report.

In a recent no action letter,[24] the SEC staff concluded that a written communication by an investment adviser that does no more than respond to an "unsolicited" request by a client, prospective client or consultant for specific information about the investment adviser's past specific recommendations is not an "advertisement" for purposes of Advisers Act Rule 206(4)-1(b).[25] A "solicited" request would be the result of, for example, an affirmative effort by the investment adviser that is intended or designed to induce a client, prospective client or consultant to request the investment adviser to provide past specific recommendations, or an advertisement that the investment adviser is willing to provide past specific recommendations on request. Moreover, the SEC staff continued, the same conclusion would apply to an investment adviser's provision of the same information to (a) one consultant who requests the information for several clients or (b) several consultants as long as the investment adviser provides the information in response to a specific, unsolicited request for information about the investment adviser's past specific recommendations. The SEC staff added that a written communication by an investment adviser to its existing clients generally would not be an "advertisement" merely because it discusses the

---

22. All investment advisers, whether or not registered, are subject to the Advisers Act anti-fraud provisions. Advisers Act Release No. 121 (Nov. 2, 1961), 26 F.R. 10,549 (Nov. 9, 1961).

23. *Franklin Management, Inc.*, SEC No-Action Letter (Dec. 10, 1998).

24. *Investment Counsel Association of America, Inc.*, SEC No-Action Letter (Mar. 1, 2004).

25. 17 C.F.R. § 275.206(4)-1(b).

investment adviser's past specific recommendations concerning securities held or recently held in those clients' accounts, because such communications are generally part of the investment adviser's services, unless the context suggests that the purpose of the communication is to offer advisory services.

2. Required Disclosures

Each advertisement or report showing past recommendations must include the following information:[26]

- the name of each security recommended;
- the date and nature of each recommendation (that is, whether to buy or sell);
- the market price at that time;
- the price at which the recommendation was to be acted on; and
- the market price of each security as of the most recent practicable date.

The advertisement and any separately provided list must also contain the following legend in type at least as large as the largest print used in the text: "It should not be assumed that recommendations made in the future will be profitable or will equal the performance of the securities on this list."[27] Any list proffered pursuant to the rule must be provided free of charge.[28]

3. Portfolio Holdings and Other Current Recommendations

The investment adviser to a hedge fund may want to include lists of representative current portfolio holdings—as opposed to past recommendations—in its marketing materials. The SEC staff has indicated informally that it would not view such lists as involving past recommendations, as long as the list is truly representative of current holdings and is a non-manipulated sample (such as a list of top ten holdings or all holdings above a *de minimis* level) rather than a cherry-picked sample. Similarly, the SEC staff has indicated that a list of current recommendations is not subject to Rule 206(4)-1(a)(2).[29] Whether a list consists of current or past recommendations, however, depends on exactly what information is presented and how it is presented. For example, a list would involve past recommendations and thus be subject to the rule if it includes some securities that the investment adviser no longer recommends or if it indicates that any of the securities listed were recommended in the past.[30] In any event, all such advertisements are subject to the general prohibition of false or misleading advertising of Rule 206(4)-1(a)(5).[31] An investment adviser may also breach its fiduciary duty by making this information available only to selected investors in its hedge fund.

---

26. Advisers Act Rule 206(4)-1(a)(2)(A), 17 C.F.R. § 275.206(4)-1(a)(2)(A).
27. Advisers Act Rule 206(4)-1(a)(2)(B), 17 C.F.R. § 275.206(4)-1(a)(2)(B).
28. *Scientific Market Analysis*, SEC No-Action Letter (Mar. 24, 1976).
29. 17 C.F.R. § 275.206(4)-1(a)(2). *Franklin Management, Inc.*, SEC No-Action Letter (Dec. 10, 1998).
30. *Id.*
31. 17 C.F.R. § 275.206(4)-1(a)(5). *See* Chapter 8, *supra*.

The SEC staff has allowed an investment adviser to send to clients with separately managed accounts quarterly reports containing information about some, but not all, specific portfolio management decisions made during the preceding quarter. In *Franklin Management, Inc.*, an investment adviser proposed to use a report that would identify some securities that were bought, sold or held for accounts that the investment adviser managed using a particular investment strategy, some of the reasons for the portfolio management decisions, and a brief analysis of each issuer. The report would not discuss any transactions in accounts that the investment adviser managed using other strategies. In issuing no-action relief, the SEC staff also noted that the investment adviser would use objective, nonperformance-based criteria to select the securities discussed in the report and that the report would not discuss the amount of profit or loss on any particular recommendation discussed.[32]

§ 17.4 Other Issues

1. Recordkeeping Requirements

An SEC-registered investment adviser that advertises its performance must maintain all records necessary to substantiate the performance information. The investment adviser must retain for five years from the end of the fiscal year in which the advertisement is last published or otherwise disseminated all worksheets and account statements necessary to demonstrate the accuracy of the advertisement.[33] The investment adviser must keep records that cover the entire period for which performance is advertised. These record retention requirements also apply to performance achieved at a predecessor or prior investment adviser (discussed below), if the investment adviser continues to use it in its own marketing materials.[34] If an investment adviser does not retain the required records, it may be precluded from advertising the unsubstantiated historical performance. Independent audit or review of performance information, however, is not required by law.

2. CFA Institute Standards

The CFA Institute (CFAI), formerly the Association for Investment Management and Research, an industry trade group, has published Performance Presentation Standards, which differ from the SEC guidelines described above. For example, CFAI requires presentation of performance data gross of fees.[35] To satisfy both

---

32. *Franklin Management, Inc.*, SEC No-Action Letter (Dec. 10, 1998). *See also* § 17.3.1, *supra*.

33. Advisers Act Rules 204-2(a)(16) and 204-2(e)(3), 17 C.F.R. §§ 275.204-2(a)(16) and 275.204-2(e)(3). *See also* § 2.8, *supra*.

34. *Horizon Asset Management, LLC*, SEC No-Action Letter (Sep. 13, 1996); *Great Lakes Advisors, Inc.*, SEC No-Action Letter (Apr. 3, 1992).

35. AIMR Performance Presentation Standards 77 (2d Ed. 1997).

SEC guidelines and CFAI standards, an investment adviser may present two sets of performance data, one gross and one net of fees, as long as they are presented with equal prominence and in a format designed to facilitate ease of comparison, and as long as the accompanying disclosure is sufficient to ensure that the material presented is not misleading.[36] In addition, CFAI requires all performance data to be supplemented with substantial additional information, such as the number of accounts, their net asset value and the percentage of total assets managed by the investment adviser that the accounts represent.[37] Although an investment adviser is not required to comply with CFAI standards unless it is a member of CFAI, some investors may expect that their investment advisers will comply. It would be a violation of the anti-fraud provisions of the Advisers Act discussed in Chapter 8 for an investment adviser to represent that its performance presentations comply with CFAI standards if that is not true, and the SEC staff has noted this violation in inspections of investment advisers who claim that their data comply with CFAI standards when they do not.

3. NASD Rules Governing Hedge Fund Sales Literature

The NASD issued two interpretive letters to the Securities Industry Association under NASD Rule 2210 that together state that a broker-dealer may not publish or distribute sales materials for a Company Act section 3(c)(1) hedge fund that present "related performance information," even if the sales materials (other than offering circulars per the NASD's informal comments) were prepared by the hedge fund or its investment adviser rather than the broker-dealer.[38] "Related performance information" includes information about performance of predecessor funds, clone funds and comparable managed accounts, extracts, hypothetical and composite records and the like. Recently the NASD also sanctioned a member firm for using marketing materials regarding hedge funds and funds of funds that "listed a targeted rate of return without providing a sound basis for evaluating the target, improperly used hypothetical returns in charts or graphs and/or [sic] failed to include inadequate risk dislcosure."[39]

4. Commodity Funds

As discussed in section 6.6 above, a manager of hedge funds that trade commodities or futures may be subject to CFTC and NFA rules regarding performance advertising.

---

36. *The Association for Investment Management and Research*, SEC No-Action Letter (Dec. 18, 1996).

37. AIMR Performance Presentation Standards 77 (2d Ed. 1997).

38. NASD Interpretive Letter (Oct. 2, 2003) as revised in part by NASD Interpretive Letter (Dec. 30, 2003).

39. "NASD Fines Citigroup Global Markets, Inc. $250,000 in Largest Hedge Fund Sales Sanction to Date," NASD Notice to Members, Disciplinary Actions, November 2004, at D15-D16.

§ 17.5 Portability of Performance

An investment adviser who was previously employed by another firm may want to advertise the performance he or she achieved in the prior position. The investment adviser may not advertise such prior performance unless the investment adviser was solely responsible[40] for achieving the results represented and the prior account was sufficiently similar to the hedge fund to make comparison meaningful and relevant to a potential investor.[41]

1. Performance Results from Previous Advisory Firms

The SEC staff will generally allow an investment adviser to advertise the performance of accounts the investment adviser managed at a previous firm, if the following conditions are met:

- The person or persons who manage the accounts currently were also responsible for achieving the prior performance results;
- The accounts managed at the old firm were so similar to those currently managed that their performance would be relevant to prospective clients of the new firm;
- The advertisements are consistent with all other relevant rules and SEC staff interpretations relating to performance advertising in all other respects; and
- The advertisements include disclosure that the performance results shown were of accounts managed at another firm.[42] All other material factors should also be disclosed.[43]

A successor investment adviser, portfolio manager or hedge fund seeking to use a predecessor's performance data must also keep all records necessary to form the basis for or calculate the performance data.

In the context of a mutual fund, the SEC staff has stated that when a portfolio manager joins a new investment adviser, the prospectus for the fund managed by the portfolio manager may include the performance of the fund previously managed by the individual if the following conditions are met:[44]

- Both the current and previously managed funds have substantially similar investment objectives, policies and strategies;

---

40. Where an investment adviser selects portfolio securities by committee, a "substantial identity" of personnel is needed for a successor fund to use the predecessor's performance. *Great Lakes Advisors, Inc.,* SEC No-Action Letter (Apr. 3, 1992). If an investment adviser leaves one hedge fund to start another, he may advertise the performance of the first hedge fund in marketing materials for the second hedge fund only if he was actually responsible for making the investment decisions at the first hedge fund and will also be so responsible for the second hedge fund. *Horizon Asset Management, LLC,* SEC No-Action Letter (Sep. 13, 1996).

41. *Growth Stock Outlook,* SEC No-Action Letter (Apr. 7, 1988).

42. *Horizon Asset Management, LLC,* SEC No-Action Letter (Sep. 13, 1996).

43. *Great Lakes Advisors, Inc.,* SEC No-Action Letter (Apr. 3, 1992).

44. *Bramwell Growth Fund,* SEC No-Action Letter (Aug. 7, 1996).

- The portfolio manager managed no other comparable registered funds or private accounts while managing the prior fund;
- No other person played a significant part in achieving the prior fund's performance; and
- The performance of the prior fund is not presented in a misleading way.

The performance of the prior fund should be presented separately from and given no greater prominence than the current fund's performance.

2. CFA Institute Standards

CFAI takes the position that performance is generally the record of the firm, not of an individual. CFAI permits an investment adviser to present performance data from a prior fund or affiliation, however, if the past record is clearly identified as such, is not linked to the results of the new fund or investment adviser, and is not used to represent the historical record of the new fund or investment adviser.[45]

---

45.   AIMR Performance Presentation Standards 77 (2d Ed. 1997).

Index

About the Authors

The authors are present or former partners and associates of Shartsis Friese LLP in San Francisco, California. Shartsis Friese LLP is nationally recognized as a leader in representing hedge fund managers in all aspects of their businesses, including initial organization, capitalization, employee incentive arrangements, initial licensing and ongoing regulatory compliance (both federal and state), contract negotiation and forms for retail and institutional investors, custodians and broker-dealers, and organization and operation of hedge funds and other investment pools. This practice has developed expertise in the complex and evolving requirements of the Advisers Act, the Company Act, the Exchange Act, the Securities Act, the CEA, the Tax Code, ERISA and other relevant federal laws, and the volumes of rules and regulations of the SEC, CFTC, NASD, IRS and DOL, as well as myriad comparable (but differing) requirements of state law and regulations. The Firm's private investment fund/investment adviser group represents more than 500 private investment fund managers and other investment advisers around the United States.

Shartsis Friese LLP also has an extensive securities enforcement defense and litigation practice, including four former SEC lawyers, and has expertise in the representation of investment advisers, broker-dealers and other financial services professionals.

Douglas L. Hammer, Carolyn R. Reiser, Geoffrey W. Haynes and Neil J. Koren are partners, and Anthony J. Caldwell, James J. Frolik and Christina E. Mickelson are associates of Shartsis Friese LLP. Barry H. Sacks and John F. Milani formerly were partners and Hannah E. Dunn is a former associate. More information about the Firm appears at www.sflaw.com.